GW00503102

ARGUMENTS FOR A BETTER WORLD

ESSAYS IN HONOR OF
AMARTYA SEN

ARGUMENTS FOR A BETTER WORLD

ESSAYS IN HONOR OF AMARTYA SEN

Volume I: Ethics, Welfare, and Measurement

Edited by

KAUSHIK BASU

and

RAVI KANBUR

OXFORD

UNIVERSITY PRESS

OXFORD
UNIVERSITY PRESS

Great Clarendon Street, Oxford OX2 6DP

Oxford University Press is a department of the University of Oxford.
It furthers the University's objective of excellence in research, scholarship,
and education by publishing worldwide in

Oxford New York

Auckland Cape Town Dar es Salaam Hong Kong Karachi
Kuala Lumpur Madrid Melbourne Mexico City Nairobi
New Delhi Shanghai Taipei Toronto

With offices in

Argentina Austria Brazil Chile Czech Republic France Greece
Guatemala Hungary Italy Japan Poland Portugal Singapore
South Korea Switzerland Thailand Turkey Ukraine Vietnam

Oxford is a registered trade mark of Oxford University Press
in the UK and in certain other countries

Published in the United States
by Oxford University Press Inc., New York

© Oxford University Press 2009

British Library Cataloguing in Publication Data

Data available

Library of Congress Cataloging in Publication Data

Arguments for a better world : essays in honor of Amartya Sen /
edited by Kaushik Basu Ravi Kanbur.
p. cm.
ISBN 978–0–19–923911–5 (hbk. : v. 1) – ISBN 978–0–19–923997–9 (hbk. : v.2)
1. Welfare economics.   2. Institutional economics.   3. Economics–Moral and
ethical aspects.   I. Basu, Kaushik.   II. Kanbur, S. M. Ravi   III. Sen, Amartya Kumar.
IV. Title:
Essays in honor of Amartya Sen.
HB846.094   2008
330–dc22   2008036360

Typeset by SPI Publisher Services, Pondicherry, India
Printed in Italy by
Rotolito Lombarda S.p.A.

ISBN 978–0–19–923911–5 (Volume 1)
ISBN 978–0–19–923997–9 (Volume 2)
ISBN 978–0–19–923999–3 (Set)

1 3 5 7 9 10 8 6 4 2

Contents

PART I ETHICS, NORMATIVE ECONOMICS AND WELFARE

PART II AGENCY, AGGREGATION AND SOCIAL CHOICE

PART III   POVERTY, CAPABILITIES AND MEASUREMENT

PART IV   IDENTITY, COLLECTIVE ACTION AND PUBLIC ECONOMICS

LIST OF FIGURES

LIST OF TABLES

List of Contributors

Sabina Alkire, University of Oxford

Paul Anand, Open University

Sudhir Anand, University of Oxford

Kwame Anthony Appiah, Princeton University

A. B. Atkinson, University of Oxford

Kaushik Basu, Cornell University

Walter Bossert, Université de Montréal

François Bourguignon, Paris School of Economics

John Broome, University of Oxford

Satya R. Chakravarty, Indian Statistical Institute

Rajat Deb, Southern Methodist University

Bhaskar Dutta, University of Warwick

James E. Foster, Vanderbilt University

Wulf Gaertner, University of Osnabrück

Indranil K. Ghosh, Winston-Salem State University

Peter Hammond, University of Warwick

Christopher Handy, Cornell University

Christopher Harris, University of Cambridge

Satish K. Jain, Jawaharlal Nehru University

Ravi Kanbur, Cornell University

Isaac Levi, Columbia University

Oliver Linton, London School of Economics and Political Science

S. R. Osmani, University of Ulster

Prasanta K. Pattanaik, University of California, Riverside

Edmund S. Phelps, Columbia University

Mozaffar Qizilbash, University of York

Martin Ravallion, World Bank

Kevin Roberts, University of Oxford

Ingrid Robeyns, Erasmus University

Maurice Salles, Université de Caen

Cristina Santos, University College London

Thomas M. Scanlon, Harvard University

Arjun Sengupta, Indian Parliament

Tae Kun Seo, Southern Methodist University

Anthony Shorrocks, UNU-WIDER

Ronald Smith, Birkbeck College

Joseph E. Stiglitz, Columbia University

S. Subramanian, Madras Institute of Development Studies

Kotaro Suzumura, Waseda University

Alain Trannoy, École des hautes études en sciences sociales and GREQAM-IDEP

Guanghua Wan, UNU-WIDER

John A. Weymark, Vanderbilt University

Yongsheng Xu, Georgia State University

INTRODUCTION

KAUSHIK BASU

RAVI KANBUR

WHEN Amartya Sen received the Nobel Prize in Economics in 1998, there was much confusion in popular reportage about which of his contributions were being honored by the prize. Some wrote that he got the prize for his large contributions to development economics, some claimed this was recognition for his pioneering work on the history and causes of famines, and yet others suggested that he got it for the moral causes he espoused.

Sen got the prize for welfare economics. Part of the blame for the confusion in people's minds has to be directed at him, for it is caused by the truly remarkable range of his writings. He has indeed contributed to all the fields people thought he had got the prize for and he has been a relentless campaigner for moral causes, such as human rights, basic freedoms and capabilities and the guarantee of minimum living standards. What is even more remarkable is that he has continued to broaden the areas of his attention and inquiry since 1998. He has worked on Indian history and the politics of identity and violence, and has recently chaired the Commonwealth Commission on "Civil Paths to Peace". He can lay claim to being a social scientist in a way that few others can.

On 3 November 2008, Amartya Sen will turn 75; and we, as his one-time students and, subsequently, colleagues in the broader sense of the term, felt that it was a fitting occasion to celebrate his remarkable achievements. We wanted to do this by presenting him with a book that tries to push the frontiers further on the full range of academic themes and activist causes that Sen has been associated with. One thing was immediately evident—this would not be a small project. We decided to invite prominent economists, philosophers, historians, policy-makers and social scientists in general who have had some association with Sen—as student, colleague, editor, co-author or co-activist—to contribute to what would be a major multi-volume work. Yet so many people have been associated with Amartya Sen in one way or the other and so many have been profoundly influenced by him that there was no way we could accommodate them all. We are aware that this is an idiosyncratic collection of authors, and the list of those who could legitimately make claims to being a part of this project, but had to be left out for reasons of space, is long.

Amartya Sen did not start out in welfare economics. As an undergraduate student at Trinity College, Cambridge University (where he later returned as Master), Sen wrote a dissertation on the choice of technology. That dissertation gained him a Ph.D. and in 1960 was published as a book. *Choice of Techniques* became a celebrated text, which students of development, planning and growth read, did research on and modified. This work had many spin-offs for Sen himself. He contributed to growth theory, cost–benefit analysis and development; he became full professor at the Delhi School of Economics in 1963.

During this time his interests were, however, beginning to shift as he became intrigued by the problems of welfare and the conundrums of voting and social choice. There was a small literature on the latter at that time. It had all begun in the early fifties with the publication of Kenneth Arrow's path-breaking "impossibility theorem". Amartya began working on this seriously after he moved to the Delhi School of Economics and this resulted in his seminal book *Collective Choice and Social Welfare*. With a diverse set of ideas, from mathematical logic, through welfare economics to ethics, crowding its pages, the book quickly became a classic. It drew the attention of not just economists, but also professional philosophers.

In the 1970s Amartya Sen moved to England, first as Professor of Economics at the London School of Economics (LSE) and later to Oxford, where he became Drummond Professor. It is at this stage that we, the editors of this book, got to know him. Kaushik Basu did his Ph.D. with him from 1974 to 1976 at the LSE. Ravi Kanbur had him as his D.Phil. adviser at Oxford from 1978 to 1980.

During his stay at the LSE, Amartya Sen's interest moved on to something which had always been there, though somewhat subliminally—the subject of poverty and inequality. He published his celebrated book, *The Economics of Inequality*, and later the seminal paper on poverty measurement in *Econometrica*. After seven years at the LSE, he moved to Oxford in 1977. And his interest in philosophy flourished. The first evidence of Amartya's interest in philosophy was a paper he wrote in 1959 in *Enquiry*. This little-known paper consisted of a lucid elaboration of the conflict between determinism and free will. Sen's philosophical interest continued to grow in Oxford, where he interacted with the philosophers, and his papers appeared in *Philosophical Quarterly*, *Mind*, *Philosophy and Public Affairs*, *Theory and Decision* and the *Journal of Philosophy*. When he moved to Harvard in 1987 his appointment would be in the economics and philosophy departments and he offered a course jointly with Robert Nozick.

His work on poverty and basic needs, coupled with his interest in moral philosophy, led Sen to question the pervasive use of income to measure and compare human welfare. Up until then, the most popular way of ranking the economic performance of countries had been in terms of the per capita incomes of the people. Sen argued repeatedly for the need to bring in other indicators of the standard of living in order to evaluate the overall well-being of societies. This work has had enormous practical implications, ever since the United Nations Development Programme, openly acknowledging Sen's influence, began computing the Human Development Index (HDI) to evaluate societies.

Since moving to Harvard in the 1980s, and during his term as Master of Trinity College Cambridge in the 1990s before returning to Harvard, Sen's academic reach and popular engagement has continued to broaden. He has written on identity, on history and on culture. He has engaged vigorously in policy debates, advancing an egalitarian, tolerant and pluralistic perspective on the issues of the day. Sen's later work has come under criticism from academic writers for being populist but that is more a reflection on his critics than on him. A large part of his recent work is that of a person with a cause, and he has devoted his considerable analytical powers to a relentless campaign to win over the hearts of the common person, journalists and policy-makers and not simply engaging in debates with other academics. This argumentative Indian, to use the title of one of his recent books, has joined and enriched the arguments for a better world.

It is this full range of Sen that we try to engage with in this rather mammoth project. Our two volumes mirror Amartya Sen's own two-volume collected works—*Choice, Welfare and Measurement* and *Resources, Values and Development*—and, in addition, we try to stretch the contours further to accommodate his expanding range of interests since these collected works were published in 1982 and 1984 respectively. We have called our two volumes, respectively, *Ethics, Welfare and Measurement* and *Society, Institutions and Development*.

The first volume begins with matters of ethics and moral philosophy—appropriately we feel, given the foundational status of philosophy and given that so much of modern social choice and welfare draws on principles of moral philosophy and the philosophy of human rights. Several essays in this collection then go into matters of social choice theory and evaluative measurement, matters that were close to Amartya Sen's heart through the seventies and eighties. His influential papers and books on the "capabilities approach" to social evaluation appeared mostly after the publication of his collected works, and this has been enormously influential in the social sciences, perhaps even more outside of economics than within. We felt that this deserves a full subsection and so there is a cluster of eight papers on the subject. The first volume ends with some more applied essays on collective action and also some on Sen's recent interest and an urgent subject of our times—identity.

Volume II is on the subject of development, on which Amartya Sen has contributed extensively throughout his life, and which was, we have noted, widely (and wrongly) believed to be the work for which he was awarded the Nobel Prize. But we decided to place this subject within a much larger social science context than usual. Thus this second volume has contributions from political scientists, sociologists, philosophers and historians, and of course there is the ubiquitous presence of economists. In its first part the second volume picks up from where the first volume left off—the subject of capabilities in actual developmental settings. The second part turns to the topic of gender and the household. Sen is a prominent figure in the field of feminist economics and his contributions on differences in the treatment of the girl child and boy child have been of great influence for both academic research and policy-making. His writing on the millions of "missing girls" in India and China stirred consciences and drew the attention of bureaucrats and politicians. He has also worked, in more academic ways, on the problem of decision-making within the household by applying ideas of Nash bargaining to the nature of "cooperative conflict" among householders. These interests are reflected in the second part of that volume.

Interestingly, among Amartya Sen's earliest research were several papers on growth theory and a famous edited volume on the subject of growth. The third part of Volume II consists of papers on growth but with special attention to the urgent problems of poverty, climate change and labor standards. The final part of the volume deals with the role of sociology, politics and history in the context of development and economics. While one may debate the end *of* history as intellectuals have done in recent times, we for our part wanted to emphasize the importance of this subject for economics by ending *with* history. Scholars have argued that we need to embed economics in the related social sciences to enrich our understanding of not just the social sciences, but economics itself. The last eight essays try to carry this agenda forward, however slowly.

This sizeable project would not have been possible but for the supportive atmosphere of Cornell University. Our faculty colleagues have been a source of discussion and stimulus, so important for this kind of work. Kiran Gajwani helped greatly with research assistance. Sue Snyder provided excellent administrative support throughout in keeping the volumes on track. Sarah Caro of Oxford University Press has been an enthusiastic backer at each of the many long stages of this project, from inception to production. We thank them all.

Ithaca, New York
4 March 2008

PART I

ETHICS, NORMATIVE ECONOMICS AND WELFARE

CHAPTER 1

WHY ECONOMICS NEEDS ETHICAL THEORY

JOHN BROOME

I

ECONOMICS is a branch of ethics. At least, much of it is. Part of economics is pure science; it aims to account for the behavior of people and institutions in the economic arena. But more than most scientists, economists have their eye on practical applications. Most of them are interested in economic science because they are interested in finding better ways of running the economy, or of structuring the economic system, or of intervening or not intervening in the economy. All of that practical part of economics is a branch of ethics.

Why? First, it is about how things ought to be done, which means it is normative. (By "normative" I mean concerned with what ought to be done.) But merely being normative is not necessarily being ethical. You ought to clean your car occasionally. That is a normative requirement on you, but it is not an ethical requirement. It is not universally agreed just how the ethical is to be distinguished from the rest of the normative. But in contexts that involve conflicts between the interests of different people, normative claims are certainly ethical, and this includes virtually all normative claims that are made in economics. For example, to claim that the interest rate ought to go up raises a conflict of interest between lenders, who stand to gain by an increase, and borrowers, who stand to lose.

All his life, Amartya Sen has worked to establish the importance of ethics in economics. He has argued for it, formalized it in economic theory, applied it constantly, and exhibited it in his own life. Yet despite his work, many economists still believe their discipline is independent of ethics. This brief chapter adds a little support to Sen's own arguments.

It is well known that economists are self-effacing people, who do not like to throw their weight about. They hate the idea of imposing their ethical views on other people. So they sometimes pretend to themselves and other people that economics is an ethics-free zone. Macroeconomists can do this to some extent by dealing with broad national aggregates that elide conflicts of interest; if you concentrate on national income, you may not notice some people's income going down as other people's goes up. Microeconomists sometimes do it by concentrating on "economic efficiency", which is supposed to be an ethically neutral notion. Surely there could not be any conflict of interest over making the economy more efficient. For example, no one could reasonably be opposed to liberalizing international trade, which makes the world economy more efficient. That is the idea. But actually, there are *always* conflicts of interest. Some people are benefited by free international trade; others are harmed. No practicable economic change is good for everyone; there are always some losers.

Another strategy for evasion is to recognize that economic questions may raise ethical issues, but try to keep the ethics separate from the economics. Faced with a question, economists should work out the answer from the point of view of economics alone. What ethics says about it is another matter. The ethics may be important—it may even override the answer from economics—but nevertheless the answer from economics is independent of the ethics.

For instance, take the value of human life: the question of what sacrifices it is worthwhile for us to make in order to save some people's lives. It is sometimes said that, from the point of view of economics, the value of life should be determined by people's willingness to pay to avoid exposing their lives to danger. Willingness to pay is the standard measure of value in economics, and it should apply to life as to other goods. One implication of this measure is that the lives of poor people, such as people who live in India, are less valuable than the lives of rich people, such as those who live in Britain, because poor people are willing to pay less. (They are inevitably willing to pay less, because they have less money to pay.) That is the conclusion of economics, it is sometimes said. It may be that this conclusion is ethically unacceptable, so that we may want to override the economic conclusion on ethical grounds. Nevertheless, that is the economic, ethics-free conclusion. This seems to be the argument of Pearce *et al.* (1996: 196–7), for example.

But actually the ethical and the economic are far too intimately entangled to be separated in this way. When it comes to making normative claims, economics has no separate source of normativity apart from ethics. It is not like aesthetics. Aesthetics is perhaps normative in its own right, independently of ethics. Perhaps aesthetics independently justifies the claim that you ought to clean your car occasionally, so this claim is genuinely ethics-free. But when economics makes a normative claim, it cannot be anything other than an ethical claim. There is no other basis for it. That goes for evaluative claims in economics too, such as claims about the value of life, because evaluative claims are implicitly normative. Normative and evaluative economics cannot help being ethical from the start. The ethical cannot just be wheeled in when the economics is done.

Many economists have recognized this, and they make their ethical assumptions and arguments explicit. By tradition, the branch of economics where ethical issues are made explicit has been called "welfare economics". Nowadays, it is badly neglected within economics as a whole. It is little taught, and many economists know almost nothing of it. The name "welfare economics" is a poor one in the first place. For one thing, welfare is not the only thing within economics that matters ethically. Many people think the ethical issue of national autonomy is at stake in the economic question of whether Britain should adopt the Euro, and national autonomy may have nothing to do with welfare. For another thing, the name "welfare economics" does not make the ethical dimension explicit. The subject is ethics in its application to economics. Ethics applied to medicine is called medical ethics. Ethics applied to business is called business ethics. So we should speak of "economic ethics". (Not, following the precedent of medical ethics, "economical ethics", which would give the wrong impression.)

So far, I have said that economics requires ethics. But why should it need ethical *theory*? Why, too, should *economists* need ethical theory? After all, businesspeople probably do not need much ethical theory to conduct their business in the way they ought, and nor do doctors. Chiefly, these people need moral awareness and sensitivity. Training in medical ethics for doctors does not include much theory. Instead, it aims to give them sensitivity to ethical issues. Also—to use the old-fashioned, high-flown language of moral philosophy—it aims to make them virtuous; it aims to instill in them ways of thinking that make them naturally inclined to behave in a moral way. For much of medicine that may be enough.

On the other hand, moral sensitivity and virtue need not play much part in the professional life of economists. Their business is mostly the complex interactions of lots of people. Here, the natural responses of a sensitive person would not be enough to carry them through to the right answer. They need to do complex, quantitative calculations, and those must be guided by a theory. So in economics, ethical theory is inescapable.

II

Welfare economics is the branch of economics where the ethical issues are made explicit. But the natural reticence of economists shows itself even in welfare economics. Economists do not like to take ethical positions of their own, and one way they try to avoid doing so is to leave the ethics to the public. They try to leave ethical judgements to the individual preferences of the people who make up the society. The rest of this chapter is concerned with that idea.

In economic ethics, people's preferences can be called on in two places, because the concern of economic ethics can be roughly separated into two parts. First of all, we need to know what is good for people individually: what determines people's well-being, in other words. Second, having worked that out, we need in some way to put together the good or well-being of all the different individuals, to arrive at an overall assessment of the goodness of the society. Both of these problems come within the domain of ethics. Only the second is concerned with conflicts between different people's interests, but ethics itself is not exclusively concerned with conflicts. It is also very concerned with what is good for individuals; since ancient times that has been one of its main topics. So both problems are the concern of ethics, but in economics, both are frequently referred back to people's preferences.

I have just described the concern of economic ethics in terms of goodness. But this is already to set aside a major ethical question. It is a matter of dispute within ethics whether we should be concerned with goodness. Many philosophers and economists think that the idea of the overall goodness of a society is mistaken anyway; there is no such thing. Those people will evidently not like my formulation of the problem of economic ethics. For them, the need for ethical theory in economics will appear in a very different guise. But I cannot take up this major issue here. I shall continue on the assumption that the good of society does indeed exist, and has at least some ethical importance.

III

First, then, there is the question of what is good for individuals. In welfare economics, the good of individuals is almost invariably judged by their preferences. In practice, people's preferences are garnered from the data available, from markets, from focus groups, from questionnaires or in some other way, and then those preferences are taken as the basic data for judgements about what ought to be done. To some extent this allows an economist to avoid taking a stance on what, actually, is good for a person. We do not have to worry whether, say, a person's good consists in experiencing pleasure, or in living virtuously, or in achieving various excellences, or in whatever else some philosopher might think is good for us. Instead we leave it to people themselves to determine what is good for them through their preferences.

However, theory can only partly be avoided. It takes an ethical theory to justify the use of preferences in the first place for the purpose of assessing people's well-being. One possible justification is the theory that a person's well-being actually consists in the satisfaction of her preferences. If you prefer A to B, this prefer-ence makes it the case that A is better for you than B. Call this the "preference-satisfaction" theory of well-being. It is an ethical theory, like any other theory of well-being. However, it is not a very good one. It seems plausible in some contexts, but it is not plausible when a person's preference is itself derived from her own belief about what is better for her. If it is your preference for A over B that makes A better for you than B, and if this preference of yours is derived from your belief that A is better for you than B, then your belief would ensure its own truth. That is not credible. Some beliefs ensure their own truth, such as a belief that you have a belief, but it is not credible that a belief of this sort does.

Furthermore, many of your preferences are indeed derived from beliefs of this sort. Your preferences about anything at all complex, such as a career or a car, involve some computation. They involve the balancing, comparing and aggregating of benefits and disadvantages. That means they have to depend on beliefs. For instance, your preferences about avoiding danger to your life, which determine your willingness to pay for avoiding danger, should depend on how long you believe you still have to live if you survive now, how well you believe your life will go, what responsibilities you believe you have to other people, and so on. These beliefs should combine together to determine your beliefs about how much money it would be better to pay rather than bear a particular risk of dying. That belief in turn should determine your willingness to pay.

I say "should" because I suspect most of us find this problem too difficult to cope with properly. For most of us, our preferences about risks to life are not formed in the rational way I described but in some less commendable way. If so, our preferences do not depend on our beliefs about goodness, at least not in the proper way. These preferences are irrational, and they plainly do not satisfy the preference-satisfaction theory of well-being. Being irrational, they cannot determine what is actually better for us. On the other hand, preferences that are rationally derived from beliefs about goodness also cannot determine what is better for us, as I have just explained. They do not satisfy the preference-satisfaction theory either. So the preference-satisfaction theory fails, at least for preferences over complex matters such as the value of life.

An alternative argument for using preferences comes from the idea that a person is the best judge of her own well-being. The argument is not the preference-satisfaction theory that a person's preferences *determine* what is good for her, but that a person's preferences *indicate* what she judges to be good for her, and hers is the best judgement we have. This is very plausible in many contexts; in many contexts preferences are surely a good indicator of well-being. But there are also contexts where we may be able to make better judgements about people's well-being than the people can themselves. Clearly people are not *always* the best judges of their own well-being, as they themselves recognize. People often take advice from doctors or financial advisers because they think these experts are better judges of what is good for them than they are themselves. The value of life is a context of this sort. The value of your life is difficult to judge. Your life extends over time, and its value depends on aggregating together in some way the goodness of all the different times within it, but it is not easy to know how the aggregation should be done. For example, should you give more weight to earlier times compared with later ones, by applying a discount factor? Questions of aggregation are a place where ethical theory can improve on people's naive preferences. The fact that people are often the best judges of their own well-being is not an excuse for an economist never to try and do better.

If a person's well-being is judged from her preferences, things will go particularly badly wrong when her preferences are not self-interested but based on her ethical beliefs. Take the way environmental economists sometimes assess the "existence value" of some feature of the environment, say an unpolluted lake. "Existence value" is the name for the value the lake has apart from the benefit people get from drinking its water, swimming in it, looking at it, and so on. To calculate this value, people are asked how much money they would be willing to pay to preserve the lake, setting aside whatever benefit they themselves get from using it. These amounts are added up to get the lake's total existence value (for instance, see Bishop and Woodward 1995: 562–4).

Evidently, this is to interpret each person's willingness to pay as a measure of the benefit the person herself receives from the existence of the lake. Otherwise it would not be appropriate to add it up across people. It is to assume implicitly that the lake makes a contribution to a person's well-being through its mere existence, and that preferences in the form of willingness to pay measure this contribution. But that is plainly wrong. People may be prepared to contribute to saving a lake even if they do not benefit from it at all, in any way. I was faced with a question much like this when Greenpeace asked me to contribute to saving the Atlantic from oil exploration. When I decided my willingness to contribute, I thought a bit about the true value of the clean Atlantic, and also about what my responsibilities were to contribute, given my financial and other circumstances. Greenpeace helped me with the first consideration by telling me about the purity of the area and the whales that live there. They never tried to persuade me that the existence of the unpolluted Atlantic is good for *me*, and it never occurred to me to think in those terms when I determined my willingness to contribute. Indeed, it simply is not good for me, so far as I can tell, and even if it is, my willingness to contribute had nothing to do with the benefit to me.

IV

That is a case where preferences based on ethical beliefs are badly abused. But ethical preferences are also used by economists in a less abusive manner. Let us come to the second place I mentioned where preferences can be called on to replace an ethical commitment on the part of economists. This is where different people's well-being has somehow to be put together to arrive at an overall judgement of the goodness of the society. Let us suppose we have managed to judge the well-being of people individually, by their preferences or in some other way. Now we have to aggregate their well-beings together. How?

Some ethical theory is inescapable at this point. It takes theory even to justify the idea that the goodness of society is an aggregate of people's well-being. But here too, some economists have tried to reduce their ethical commitment by calling on people's preferences. To take one example, so-called "empirical ethics" has become an important influence in health economics (Nord 1999). Health economics often raises ethical questions conspicuously. For instance, there is the question of what relative priority to give to treating the young compared with treating the old. Another instance is the question of what priority to give to saving people's lives compared with improving people's lives. Empirical ethics starts by investigating empirically people's preferences about these priorities. Then it aims to use these preferences to determine what the priorities actually should be.

What grounds are there for proceeding this way? The obvious grounds are democratic. Economists are servants of their society, and surely they should do things the way that society wants. In matters such as priority in medicine, they should follow the preferences of the people. It would be undemocratic if economists were to insist on their own judgements of priority, and impose them in their work.

I think that argument mistakes the nature of democracy and the economist's role in it. Democracy has at least two departments. One department is decision-making, and here democracy requires that the people's preferences should prevail. (Actually, not even this is true in a representative democracy, in which the representatives are supposed to exercise their judgement and sometimes override the people's preferences. But I shall set aside that complication. We can safely ignore it because economists obviously do not play the role of representatives.) Another department of the democratic political process is the forming of people's preferences. A democratic society cannot just let these preferences be whatever they happen to be. Our preferences about complex matters depend on our beliefs, and democracy requires a process of discussion, debate and education, aimed at informing and improving people's beliefs, and moving them nearer the truth. This is why we have election campaigns as well as elections.

The role of economists in a democracy is in the second department, not the first. Economists rarely make decisions directly, in their role as economists. They advise rather than decide. They advise politicians, businesspeople, brokers or other participants in the economy, or else they publish academic papers and newspaper articles, with the aim of influencing the beliefs of influential people and ordinary voters. So their role is within the process of discussion, debate and education, and not much in the decision-making department of democracy.

This means their job is not to garner people's preferences and act on them in a democratic fashion. It is to contribute to the public debate, in order to influence people's preferences for the better. Economists should aim to influence preferences, not take preferences for granted. In forming their preferences about complex matters, people naturally need advice, and an important job for economics is to give it to them. Economists should not see themselves as advisers to the high and mighty only, but also as advisers to the rest of us.

Economists do not like to impose their ethical opinions on people, but there is no question of that. Very few economists are in a position to impose their opinions on anyone. Like almost everyone else, all they can do is present their opinions to the rest of us, and argue for them as well as they can. They should not be diffident about this. True, economists can offer only their own opinions. But in ethics, or in economics, or in physics, or geography, or anywhere else, no one can do more than offer their own opinions.

More exactly, they can do one more thing: they can also defend their opinions. Some opinions are better founded than others, and those can be more convincingly defended. Economists are right to be diffident about their own ethical opinions if they are not founded on good arguments and well-worked-out ethical theory. In that case, their opinions will not prosper in the market place of ideas. The solution is for them to get themselves good arguments, and work out the theory. It is not to hide behind the preferences of other people, when those preferences may not be well founded, and when the people themselves may be looking for help from economists in forming better preferences.

REFERENCES

BISHOP, R. C., and WOODWARD, R. T. (1995), "Environmental Quality under Certainty", in Daniel Bromley (ed.), *The Handbook of Environmental Economics* (Oxford: Blackwell), 543–67.

NORD, ERIK (1999), *Cost–Value Analysis in Health Care: Making Sense of QALYs* (Cambridge: Cambridge University Press).

PEARCE, D. W., CLINE, W. R., ACHANTA, A. N., FANKHAUSER, S., PACHAURI, P. K., TOL, R. S. J., and VELLINGA, P. (1996), "The Social Costs of Climate Change: Greenhouse Damage and the Benefits of Control", in Intergovernmental Panel on Climate Change, *Climate Change 1995. Volume III: Economic and Social Dimensions of Climate Change* (Cambridge: Cambridge University Press), 179–224.

CHAPTER 2

THE SEN SYSTEM OF SOCIAL EVALUATION

S. R. OSMANI

I. INTRODUCTION

How does one evaluate the quality of life of an individual or a society? How can one judge the goodness of a social arrangement, or of public policies, rules and institutions, or norms and conventions that affect the lives of the people? A large part of Amartya Sen's writings—spanning the three disciplines of development economics, social choice theory and moral philosophy—is concerned with seeking answers to these foundational questions. Answers to these questions are of interest not only in themselves but also as guides to enlightened actions by individuals as well as societies as a whole; and Sen's writings have been inspired by both these motivations. Although Sen has written extensively on this and related subjects, it is arguable that neither he nor anyone else has put together his diverse contributions as an integrated system of social evaluation. Of course, whether the panoply of his ideas, rich as they are, amounts to a coherent system of social evaluation is a prior question that itself demands inquiry. I shall argue in this chapter that it does constitute a coherent system, and try to provide a brief outline of the elements of this system and indicate how they cohere.

Many an element of what I call the Sen system of social evaluation has been developed by him through a dialectical process of engagement with other great thinkers of past and present—most notably Aristotle, Adam Smith, Karl Marx, John Stuart Mill and Immanuel Kant of the past and John Rawls, Kenneth Arrow, Isaiah Berlin and Bernard Williams of the modern era. While drawing inspiration from each of them, he also found reasons to deviate from their respective systems and build a system of his own that has indelible marks of all these great thinkers and yet can be seen as a distinctive creation of his own. Without a clear understanding of this dialectic, it is impossible to grasp fully the deep subtleties and richness of his contributions. To provide a complete exposition of this dialectic is of course a daunting task; but fortunately I have the convenient excuse of limitation of space not to attempt it here. I do sometimes point to some of the antecedents of his ideas, but not with the degree of completeness or rigor that a proper inquiry into the history of thought would demand.[1]

The Sen system of social evaluation is best motivated by comparing and contrasting it with utilitarianism—that great idea of the nineteenth century which provided the moral underpinnings of a great many subsequent developments in philosophy, political theory and the social sciences. A useful starting point is the familiar factorization of utilitarianism into its three components:[2]

- Consequentialism
- Welfarism
- Sum-ranking

These three components can be seen as raising three general questions regarding the contents of an evaluative system and then providing specific answers to them that together constitute the system of utilitarianism (Sen 1979). The first question is: what matters most in the context of evaluation—the rightness or goodness of an act (or a rule, or an institution) in itself, or the goodness of the consequences that follow from it? The answer utilitarianism gives is: the only thing that matters is the consequences. On this view, the importance of actions and rules is purely instrumental—they are neither good nor bad in themselves. Hence the characterization of utilitarianism as consequentialist. The second question asks: if the focus of evaluation is to be on the consequences, which particular features of the consequent states of affairs should count towards valuation? The utilitarian answer is: the only aspect of the consequent state of affairs that matters for moral or social evaluation is the well-being of individuals as measured by the level of utility they enjoy. This exclusive focus on utility as the object of evaluation is known as

---

[1] Space also does not permit a full-fledged critical evaluation of Sen's system of social evaluation by judging it against competing perspectives. My modest aim in this paper is merely to lay out the structure of Sen's system as I understand it (without implying that Sen would necessarily endorse it).

[2] The usefulness of this starting point derives not just from the fact that these three components, or rather the questions they purport to answer, provide a convenient organizing framework for weaving together the questions Sen poses and the answers he offers, but also from the historical fact that many of his ideas actually took shape in the process of grappling with the questions underlying these components of utilitarianism.

welfarism. The third question raises the issue of aggregation across individuals: in judging the goodness of a social state, how should one aggregate the advantages and disadvantages of different members of the society? The utilitarian answer is: take the simple arithmetic sum of the utilities enjoyed by all members of the society; the higher the sum of utilities the better the state of affairs (and by implication the better the action or rule that brings about that state of affairs). This is the principle of sum-ranking.

While a large segment of modern philosophy has long been uncomfortable with one or more of these components of utilitarianism, modern economics, and in particular modern welfare economics, has by and large accepted the first two components without any serious questioning. It is only the sum-ranking principle that came to be rejected when the "new welfare economics", inspired by Lionel Robbins in the 1930s, replaced the traditional conception of cardinally measurable and interpersonally comparable utility with an alternative conception of utility that was ordinal and did not permit interpersonal comparison. This so-called ordinal revolution rang the death knell of sum-ranking because, bereft of cardinality and comparability, utilities could not in any meaningful sense be summed across individuals. Alternative principles of aggregation had to be explored, and much of social choice theory, inspired by Kenneth Arrow, has been engaged in this enterprise. In his initial forays into social choice theory, Sen remained mainly within this framework. Although he had some quarrels with the purely ordinal view of utility and the alleged impossibility of interpersonal comparison, he was firm in his rejection of sum-ranking and keen on examining alternative principles of aggregation, and on this he has offered many distinctive insights that constitute an integral part of his system of evaluation.

His main departures with tradition, however, came with the rejection of welfarism while retaining consequentialism to begin with. He maintained that in any moral account of actions or social arrangements, consequences for individuals mattered, but the aspect of consequences that really mattered was not adequately captured by the notion of utility. The issue involved was how to conceptualize the "appropriate" space of outcomes. While welfarism focused exclusively on the space of utilities, Sen argued for an alternative space that retained some concern for a particular conception of utility but went much beyond it. However, in the process of building an alternative to welfarism he was soon led to consider important modifications of consequentialism as well. While strongly defending the principle of taking consequences seriously, he accepted the arguments of many opponents of utilitarianism that an exclusive focus on outcomes, even if defined much more broadly than utility, was not enough for the purposes of moral evaluation. He argued, however, that the moral imperative of taking non-consequence-related issues into consideration did not justify jettisoning the concern for consequences altogether, as some critics of utilitarianism tended to maintain. What was needed, in his view, was an appropriate method of blending non-consequence considerations into the evaluation of consequences. The resulting Sen system of social evaluation can thus be defined as consisting of his distinctive views on three inter-related sets of issues: (1) what should count as an appropriate space of outcomes in the evaluation of consequences?, (2) how can we take adequate note of both consequences and relevant non-consequence concerns in the process of evaluation?, and (3) what principles of aggregation should be employed?

II. The Space of Outcome: Welfarism versus Freedom

Sen articulated two main reasons for the inadequacy of utility as the space of outcome in the context of social evaluation: (1) the metric of utility is likely to give a "distorted" account of an individual's advantages in many circumstances, and (2) there are aspects of outcome other than utility that people might value, and yet welfarism must exclude those considerations because respect for them is inconsistent with exclusive focus on utilities. These two arguments can be described respectively as the "distortion argument" and the "exclusion argument".

Sen's initial rejection of welfarism was motivated by the exclusion argument, as embodied in his famous demonstration of the impossibility of the Paretian liberal (Sen 1970b). He showed that the welfarist framework does not permit respect for even "minimal liberty"—defined as the liberty of a person to make decisions within a small personal domain involving matters that directly affect no one but herself. In particular, respect for minimal liberty was found to be inconsistent with the Pareto principle—the most uncontroversial postulate of welfarism, which states that a social state B is superior to state A if the move from A to B gives more utility to at least one person without diminishing the utility of anyone else. If as undemanding a condition as the Pareto principle cannot live alongside respect for minimal liberty, then obviously respect for rights and liberties has no place in the welfarist system, which makes it a very inadequate system indeed for the purposes of moral evaluation.

Subsequently Sen found in the distortion argument an additional reason for rejecting welfarism. To see the point of this argument, it is necessary to begin by noting that there is more than one interpretation of utility (Sen 1985a). Utility has been variously conceived as (1) a numerical representation of an individual's choice among feasible alternatives—e.g., if x is chosen when y is also available, x should be represented by a higher utility value than y, or (2) a measure of desire fulfillment, representing the extent to which a state of affairs fulfills the desires of an individual, or (3) a measure of a person's happiness—the sum total of pain and pleasure that an individual derives from different aspects of a state of affairs. The pure choice interpretation (as in the theory of revealed preferences) is vacuous for the purposes of moral evaluation until it is known why an individual chooses one alternative rather than another. If choice is deemed to be guided by the degree of happiness or desire fulfillment embodied in different alternatives, then it merges with the other two interpretations of utility.[3] The perspective of desire fulfillment, however, involves an inherent ambiguity. Do we desire something because we value it for some reason, or does the very act of desiring something impart value to it? If the former, the concept is morally vacuous, just like the "choice interpretation", until we know the reason for desiring.[4] If the latter, it does provide a plausible basis for valuation, just as the happiness interpretation does. But the problem with both desire and happiness is that they can give a distorted view of people's advantages (Sen 1985b).

The possibility of distortion arises from such phenomena as "false consciousness" and "adaptive preferences". Social conditioning may distort the reflective powers of a person in such a way that she may feel happy even in a state of utter deprivation because she is not aware that a better alternative exists even in principle— that is a case of false consciousness. Adaptive expectation refers to the idea that people often adapt their expectations in the face of persistent adversities so as to learn to be happy at little mercies. In Sen's writings, the long-suffering women of the Indian sub-continent repeatedly appear as the archetypal case of these distortions driving a wedge between a person's well-being and her perception of happiness (or desire fulfillment). More generally, he has observed that tyrannical social structures often tend to perpetuate gross inequalities by making an ally of the victims, because thanks to false consciousness and adaptive expectations the latter's happiness may not be seriously compromised. Persistence of gender discrimination in patriarchal societies is a case in point, but it is not the only one. Perceived happiness, in such situations, is a poor guide to how a person would rate her own well-being if she had the opportunity to reflect on her conditions in a rational manner in full knowledge of the possibilities that are open in principle.

The manifest limitations of the utility perspective led Sen eventually to adopt a broader view of what should constitute the space of outcome in the context of evaluating alternative social states. This broadening happened in stages. The

[3] Choice of course need not always be driven by the consideration of one's own happiness or desire; instead it may be guided by values and commitments that may sometimes run counter to one's self-interest. Yet in the standard neo-classical model of economics, the three interpretations of utility are often merged together, thereby projecting the picture of a *homo economicus* that cannot distinguish between different motivations behind choices made under different circumstances a picture Sen has caricatured as the "rational fool" (Sen 1977).

[4] For instance, no value can be sensibly attached to the desire for acquiring nuclear power until we know whether it is desired for peaceful applications or for making an atomic bomb.

first proposition to emerge was that well-being should be deemed to consist not in utility but in the opportunities people have to live the kind of life they have reason to value. What matters is whether people can do and be the things they value and have reason to value—for example, whether they can live a life free from hunger, or be adequately nourished, or be able to take part in the affairs of the community, and so on. Sen uses the term "functioning" to denote a person's actual achievement of these valuable "doings" and "beings". Well-being, in the first instance, is judged by the levels of these functionings. The concept of well-being thus becomes multi-dimensional—no longer measured by a single entity called utility, but by a combination (vector) of measures, each representing the level of achievement of some aspect of life that a person values (Sen 1985a, 1985b). The level of happiness is one element of this combination, because "to be happy" is surely one of the "beings" (a functioning) that normal people would have reason to value, but unlike in the utilitarian system it is no longer the sole criterion by which well-being is to be judged.

This reconceptualization of well-being has a profound impact on how one views the goodness of social arrangements. For instance, persistent gender inequalities can no longer be glossed over on the utilitarian grounds that women themselves might feel reasonably happy with the status quo. The manifest inequalities in the levels of functionings that women experience vis-à-vis men in many different spheres of life—e.g., in being adequately nourished or being educated or being able to take part in the affairs of society—should suffice for the status quo to be treated with moral opprobrium. More generally, the fact that oppressive social systems thrive by making an ally of the victims, who might willingly acquiesce in the perpetuation of the system under the influence of false consciousness and adaptive preferences, no longer gives ground for according moral approval to such systems in a way that the calculus of happiness might otherwise do.

The next step in the broadening of the concept of well-being is to recognize that even the concept of functioning may not always be adequate to capture the real extent of a person's well-being. Given the resources at her command, a person could in principle choose many different combinations of functionings, trading off some functioning in order to have more of another. The particular combination of functionings she actually achieves is one of many possible combinations she could have achieved. All the possible combinations she could have achieved together constitute the extent of opportunities that was really open to her. Sen calls this opportunity set the "capability" of a person, and argues that in many instances one may have to look at capability (the overall opportunity) rather than the particular combination of functionings achieved by a person in order to gauge the level of her well-being (Sen 1985b).

The classic example is that of a fasting saint, who chooses to starve even though he has the opportunity not to, as contrasted with the case of a poor man who has to starve because he cannot avoid it.[5] In terms of being free from hunger, the two starving men may have the same level of functioning, but the saint is clearly better off insofar as he has better opportunities—he enjoys a higher level of capability. To put it differently, the saint enjoys a higher level of freedom, in the sense that he has the freedom to choose a life without hunger, which the other person does not have. Generally speaking, a higher level of capability implies a higher degree of freedom to lead the kind of life one values. Insofar as people value this freedom to choose, and not just the actual level of achievement, well-being can be said to reside in one's capability and not in functioning. The concept of capability thus emerges as the relevant space for the purpose of evaluating the well-being of people under alternative states of affairs.

Sen argues, however, that in many contexts the space of outcome may have to be broadened even further to include what he calls "agency considerations" in addition to considerations of well-being. This perspective emerges from seeing human beings as socially conscious citizens, who may have many goals in life other than pursuing their own well-being—for example, to uphold the cause of oppressed people, or to help protect the environment. The totality of a social being's goals—i.e., the valuable ends he or she wants to pursue in life—is called "agency goals". One's own well-being is one of those goals, but by no means the only one. Indeed, quite often one's commitments to agency goals may even conflict with one's own well-being—for example, when someone forgoes the comfort of traveling by car in order to make a contribution towards protecting the environment. It is arguable that the goodness of a state of affairs should be judged on the basis of the extent to which people are able to achieve their agency goals—including, but not confined to, the goal of their well-being (Sen, 1985a).

It should be noted that just as in the case of well-being there is a contrast between actual achievement (functioning) and the opportunity or the freedom to achieve (capability), so in the case of agency goals there is a contrast between achievement and the freedom to achieve. Accordingly, it is possible to identify four possible spaces for social evaluation: (1) well-being achievement (functioning), (2) well-being freedom (capability), (3) agency achievement and (4) agency freedom. Each of these spaces marks an improvement over the narrow conception of utility, with agency freedom being the broadest concept of them all, because agency goals include well-being goals (but not vice versa) and the focus is on the opportunity to achieve and not just on actual achievement.

The broadness of the concept of agency freedom does not entail, however, that the other three spaces are redundant for the purpose of social evaluation. The relevance of a particular space would depend on the context of evaluation. For

---

[5] In the language of Sen's entitlement analysis, one would say that the entitlement set of the poor man—as determined by his endowments and exchange opportunities—does not contain any consumption bundle that would give him enough food to avoid hunger.

instance, the narrower focus on capabilities might be justified in matters of public policy or in dealing with the demands of equality and justice, where the perspective of well-being may be deemed more relevant than that of non-well-being agency goals. For the same reason, Sen defines poverty in the space of capabilities— a person is said to be poor when the resources available to her do not permit her to achieve minimally acceptable levels of some basic capabilities (Sen 1992). And more generally, when Sen defines development as expansion of freedoms, he focuses mainly on capabilities or well-being freedom rather than on agency freedom (Sen 1999).[6]

In developing this focus on freedom as the relevant space for social evaluation, Sen was profoundly inspired by Rawls's theory of justice as fairness (Rawls 1971). But the inspiration took the form of building upon Rawls's insight rather than subscribing to it in its entirety. In his famous Difference Principle, Rawls advocated social arrangements that gave primacy to the need of the least-advantaged members of society, with advantage being measured in terms of possession of what he called the "primary goods". Primary goods are "things that every rational man" is "presumed to want", and include "income and wealth", "the basic liberties", "freedom of movement and choice of occupation", "powers and prerogatives of offices of positions and responsibility", and "social bases of self-respect". It is noteworthy that Rawls did not define an individual's advantage in terms of what he or she could actually achieve with the help of primary goods, but only in terms of the possession of such goods. In other words, he focused on the "means" rather than the "ends". This was deliberate. Rawls was concerned with principles of fairness in a "liberal" society that respected plurality of values. In such a society, different individuals will be expected to pursue different ends in keeping with their respective value systems, or what Rawls called their "comprehensive doctrine of the good". Since their achievements will be shaped as much by their respective values as by their possession of primary goods, respect for plural values demands that we should not pass judgement on the relative goodness of their achievements. In other words, the justness of a social arrangement cannot be judged with reference to individuals' achievements. According to Rawls, the only way we can evaluate social arrangements in a manner that is consistent with respect for plural values is by looking at the distribution of primary goods. Given their possession of primary goods, individuals are free to decide what goals to pursue in accordance with their

---

[6] This does not mean that agency considerations are altogether irrelevant in these contexts, for agency may actually play a very important instrumental role in affecting well-being. For instance, whether people have the agency freedom to participate effectively in the affairs of the state may influence the quality of governance, which in turn may influence the quality of policies (and their implementation) that have a bearing on the well-being of the people. The point is simply that if well-being is judged to be the appropriate space for evaluation in a particular context, agency considerations of course lose their intrinsic relevance but they may still be instrumentally relevant.

respective value systems. The more primary goods a person possesses, the greater is the extent of freedom she has to achieve the goals she values. Thus Rawls's scheme to evaluate social arrangements in the space of primary goods amounts to focusing on the space of freedom, in a manner that is consistent with respect for plural values.

Sen fully endorses the idea of focusing on freedom for the purposes of social evaluation, but differs from Rawls on the issue of choosing primary goods as the relevant space for evaluation. He argues that possession of primary goods may not properly reflect the extent of freedom a person has, because people differ in their ability to convert goods into freedoms (Sen 1980).[7] To take a simple example, people with different metabolic rates will convert the same amount of food into different nutritional outcomes and hence into different levels of freedom to live a healthy life. Given these differences in the efficiency of converting goods into freedoms, it is proper to deal with the space of freedom itself rather than with the means to freedom, which is what primary goods are. Of course, we still have to ensure respect for plural values, which was Rawls's rationale for dealing with the means rather than the ends. But Sen argues, cogently, that the respect for plural values can be maintained in his framework by focusing on freedom instead of achievements—in particular, by dealing with capability instead of functioning. The level of functionings a person achieves may be shaped by her values, but her capability is independent of her value system, because capability refers to the opportunity or the freedom a person has to live the kind of life she values—in terms of whatever value system she has. The focus on capability or freedom is thus fully consistent with Rawls's concern for plural values. One way of looking at the contrast between Rawls and Sen is to note the existence of two kinds of pluralities—plural values on the one hand and plural efficiency of converting goods into freedoms on the other. Rawls's focus on primary goods solves the problem of plural values, but ignores the problem of plural efficiency, whereas Sen's focus on capability or freedom deals successfully with both kinds of plurality at the same time.

With this insistence on freedom as the relevant space for social evaluation, Sen's two lines of departure from welfarism finally converged. The perspective of freedom is not subject to the kind of distortions that utility suffers from, and it can also accommodate the kind of concern for rights and liberties that motivated the "liberal paradox". However, the incorporation of rights and liberties in his conception of freedom called for a re-examination of the methodology of consequentialism, to which we now turn.

---

[7] The root of this idea can be traced to an argument Sen had previously made against utilitarianism, embodied in what he had called the Weak Equity Axiom (Sen 1973). The Axiom was motivated by the concern that people may differ in their ability to convert goods into utility—for example, a bicycle given to a cripple will not yield the same level of happiness (utility) as when it is given to an able-bodied man. A similar argument applies to the conversion of goods into freedom.

III. THE MODIFICATION OF CONSEQUENTIALISM

The perspective of freedom has greatly enriched the basis of social evaluation by breaking away from the narrow confines of utilitarianism, which attaches moral significance to nothing else but utility. In one respect, however, the focus on freedom continues to maintain an umbilical tie with utilitarianism—it judges the goodness of actions, rules, institutions, etc. in terms of their consequences. The content of consequences has changed—from utility to freedoms enjoyed by the people—but the basic methodology of judging actions, rules, etc. by their consequences still remains. As a result, the perspective of freedom has to contend with the criticisms that have been made of consequentialism, mainly as part of the critique of utilitarianism. Sen has tried to meet these criticisms, without, however, compromising on the fundamental importance of freedom. The methodological and conceptual innovations he has made to meet these criticisms are an essential part of his system of social evaluation.

Of the many criticisms that have been made of consequentialism in the philosophical literature, three are of special significance in the present context:

1 Exclusion of deontological considerations
2 Disregard for autonomy
3 Disregard for agent-relativity of evaluation

The objection to consequentialism based on deontological considerations takes the following form. Certain actions, rules or institutions can be considered to be good in themselves, and not because of their consequences, whatever they might be. To take a simple example from daily life, telling the truth may be held to be morally the right thing to do regardless of consequences. It has been argued that respect for such deontological considerations makes any consequence-based system of moral evaluation either inadequate or irrelevant.

Sen's defense of his freedom-based consequentialist approach against this deontological onslaught consists of two steps: first, he argues that respect for deontological considerations cannot justify disregarding consequences altogether, and then he shows that his freedom-based approach can adequately allow respect for deontological values without abandoning concern for consequences.

Sen has developed his arguments mainly in the course of engaging with the deontology-based notions of rights and liberties advanced by Nozick (1974) and Rawls (1971). Nozick proposed a set of "just procedures" for acquiring property such that anyone acquiring property in accordance with those procedures would have an inalienable right or entitlement to it. The legitimacy of this right derives from conformity with "just procedures", and not from its consequences. Indeed, in his scheme this right must be respected regardless of consequences. If this scheme is accepted, then the goodness of a state of affairs or of social institutions will have to be judged solely on the basis of whether the Nozickian rights are being respected or not—no other information will be relevant for this purpose. Nozick thus imposes a severe deontological constraint on what information could be used for the purposes of moral evaluation and on what public action could be undertaken for the benefit of the people. For instance, if poor peasants are found to be starving while rich landlords are wallowing in luxury but both the peasant and the landlord are known to have acquired their land through "just procedures", the consequent state of affairs could not be judged morally repugnant nor could redistributive land reform be justified. The respect for Nozickian rights trumps all other considerations, including the consideration of consequences.

To see exactly how the Nozickian scheme poses a challenge to Sen's freedom-based evaluation, it is useful to begin by noting the distinction between negative and positive freedoms.[8] Negative freedom is related to the idea of freedom from interference. In the Nozickian system a person has the (negative) right to enjoy without let or hindrance any property he has "justly acquired", and respect for his negative freedom demands that no one must violate this right. Positive freedom, by contrast, refers to the ability of a person to do and be the things he values; this is the notion of freedom underlying Sen's concept of capability. In the preceding example, the starving peasant does not have the positive freedom to avoid hunger, and in Sen's system of evaluation this would be seen as a pretty bad state of affairs. The Nozickian system, however, would be quite unconcerned about it, so long as nobody has violated the peasant's negative freedom to own and use whatever land he has. By contrast, if redistributive land reforms were undertaken to transfer some land from rich landlords to the poor peasants and as a result the positive freedom of the peasants to avoid hunger was ensured (without drastically reducing the positive freedoms of rich landlords), the consequent state of affairs might be deemed an improvement according to Sen's freedom-based system of evaluation. But Nozick's system would disapprove of it on the grounds that the landlords' negative freedom was violated. The fact that the peasant's positive freedom—and perhaps the overall positive freedom of the society as a whole—may have improved in the consequent state of affairs would not justify the violation of the landlords' negative freedom. The deontological importance of negative freedom has absolute priority over the consequent improvement in positive freedom.

Clearly, if we were to attach overriding priority to negative freedom, a là Nozick, the Sen system of freedom-based consequential evaluation could not be justified. Sen argues, however, that the idea of according overriding priority to negative freedom is itself unjustified. To him, it is unacceptable to treat negative freedom as

---

[8] This distinction has been explored most systematically by Berlin (1969). Sen's own interpretation of the distinction is slightly different, however, from that of Berlin. In particular, his definition of negative freedom is narrower and that of positive freedom is broader than Berlin's. On these differences, see the discussion in Sen (1993a) and Sen (2002b).

the sole object of moral significance even when non-violation of negative freedoms goes hand in hand with terrible consequences for human lives. In his famous study of contemporary famines, Sen has shown that millions have died in famines not because they were denied the negative freedom to acquire food in a legitimate manner, but because the amount of food acquired through legitimate means was simply not enough to ensure the positive freedom to survive (Sen 1981). Because of this lack of a necessary correspondence between negative and positive freedoms, any system of evaluation that attaches moral significance to negative freedoms alone must be inadequate.[9]

Sen recognizes, however, that the moral significance of negative freedoms cannot be denied altogether. His solution is to incorporate the respect for negative freedoms—and generally, for rights and liberties—within the framework of consequential evaluation. This is done by evaluating rights through a "goal rights system", in which rights and liberties are treated not merely as constraints that ought to be obeyed but as goals to be actively promoted (Sen 1982, 1985c). The rights corresponding to negative freedoms become valued goals in this system, just as positive freedoms are. The evaluation of a state of affairs will then have to take note of the extent to which both positive and negative freedoms are fulfilled. If the two types of freedom are found to be in conflict with each other in any particular instance, the evaluator will have to consider the trade-off—i.e. weigh up the loss of one against the gain of another—so as to arrive at a comprehensive evaluation of freedoms.

In doing this evaluation, it may even be possible to attach an additional weight to negative freedom on the ground that its violation involves a moral failure on the part of some agent in a way that the failure of positive freedom might not (see Sen 1985a). For example, a state of affairs in which poor peasants are starving because their tyrannical landlord has unfairly evicted them from the land may be judged worse than an alternative situation in which the peasants are starving to the same extent but because they have lost their land through river erosion. The loss of the peasants' positive freedom to avoid hunger is similar in the two situations, but the former scenario has the additional feature of the loss of negative freedom as well, and for that reason it would rank lower in the scale of moral evaluation.

The methodological innovation involved here is to employ a richer description of the state of affairs for the purposes of consequential innovation. Traditionally,

---

[9] Unlike the Nozickian system, Rawls's system of justice as fairness attaches moral significance to positive freedom through the Difference Principle, but negative freedom (liberties) is given lexicographic priority over it (Rawls 1971). The positive freedom of the least-advantaged members of the society is to be promoted, but only in a manner that respects the liberties of every member of the society. This priority of liberty is also inconsistent with Sen's system of social evaluation, and Sen rejects it for the same reason that he rejects Nozick's exclusive focus on negative freedom—that respect for liberties cannot be made independent of the consequences for positive freedoms.

in consequence-based evaluations a state of affairs is defined as "x happened" (e.g. the peasant lost his land). Sen calls this the "culmination outcome" and contrasts it with the notion of "comprehensive outcome", which would also specify the process through which x happened (Sen 1997). By using this concept, it is possible to evaluate the following two cases differently—(1) the peasant lost his land because the landlord evicted him, and (2) the peasant lost his land through river erosion. Thus, by defining the state of affairs in terms of comprehensive outcomes instead of culmination outcomes, it becomes possible not only to incorporate negative freedom—and more generally, deontological considerations—but also to attach an additional weight to it in the consequential evaluation of freedom.

The second line of objection to consequentialism—its alleged disregard for autonomy—runs along the following lines. People may attach value not just to the properties of a state of affairs but also to their role in the process of bringing it about. For example, people may value their active participation in the process of decision-making at local and national levels of governance in addition to valuing whatever outcome results from those decisions. Underlying the value attached to participation is the value people attach to their autonomy. The consequentialist approach allegedly disregards this value of autonomy by focusing exclusively on the outcome and ignoring the process through which the outcome is achieved.

Sen's defense of his approach against this criticism employs a two-pronged strategy. The first prong is the claim that freedom-based evaluation can readily embrace the value of autonomy by employing a broad concept of freedom. On this view, freedom can be seen to have two aspects—the opportunity aspect and the process aspect (Sen 2002c). The opportunity aspect is captured by the concept of capability—namely, the opportunity or freedom people have to live the kind of life they value. The process aspect of freedom relates to whether people have the freedom to participate in decision-making processes. Once the latter aspect of freedom is recognized, it can be seen that a freedom-based system of evaluation has no difficulty in valuing autonomy.

The second prong consists in invoking the distinction mentioned above between culmination outcome and comprehensive outcome. A comprehensive outcome will specify not only what happened as a result of the decisions taken but also the process through which they were taken. Thus by defining the state of affairs in terms of comprehensive outcomes, it should be possible to distinguish situations in which people actively participated in decision-making processes from those in which they did not, and attach different values to them.

The final objection to consequentialism—the one based on agent-relativity of moral evaluation—is also related to the issue of process, but the nature of the argument is somewhat different. The argument begins by noting that moral intuition demands that moral evaluation of an action should sometimes vary depending on who is doing the evaluation. In particular, the evaluation may need to be different from the perspective of a person who actually committed the act compared to another evaluator who had no direct involvement in it. To go back to our earlier example, if a poor peasant is suffering because he was evicted unfairly by a tyrannical landlord, the evaluation of the act of eviction should be different from the perspective of the landlord himself (he should view the act more negatively) compared to other people in the village who witnessed the eviction but did nothing to stop it. However, by judging an action solely in terms of its consequences the methodology of consequentialism fails to allow for this distinction, because the consequence—namely, the suffering of the peasant—is the same no matter who is doing the evaluation. Consequentialism thus makes the evaluation agent-neutral whereas moral intuition suggests that evaluation of an action should be agent-relative. This is seen as an inadequacy of consequential evaluation.[10]

Sen recognizes the importance of agent-relativity and indeed broadens it to the concept of "evaluator relativity" to signify that evaluation of a state of affairs may well depend on the particular vantage point of an evaluator, whether or not she happens to be the agent that helped bring about the state of affairs in question (Sen 1982, 1983).[11] But he argues that his approach is perfectly capable of allowing for agent-relativity of evaluation. If actions can be judged differently by the agent and the non-agent, there is no reason why the consequences of an action cannot be judged differently by them. Traditionally, the agent-relativity of evaluation has been seen as incompatible with consequentialism only because of the latter's historical association with welfarism, in which no information other than utility is allowed in the description of consequences. Obviously, if consequences are defined solely in terms of utility, there can be no room for agent-relativity (since, in the example above, the utility loss is the same for the peasant no matter who is doing the evaluation). But the problem no longer exists when consequentialism is liberated from the monolithic hegemony of utility, as in Sen's freedom-based approach. Agent-relativity can now be accommodated by using the concept of "comprehensive outcome". By defining the consequence as "the peasant lost his land because of unfair eviction by the landlord" (comprehensive outcome), instead of simply as "the peasant lost his land" (culmination outcome), it is possible to allow that the evaluation of the state of affairs should be different from the perspective of the landlord compared to others.

Thus Sen is able to meet each of the objections to consequentialism by taking advantage of the fact that the rejection of utility as the sole basis of evaluation allows

[10] Illuminating discussions of the issues involving agent-relativity, and its implications for consequentialism in general and utilitarianism in particular, may be found in Williams (1973), Nagel (1980) and Parfit (1981), among others.

[11] This notion has a close affinity with the concept of "positional objectivity", which was developed by Sen to argue the point, among others, that allowing the same state of affairs to be evaluated differently by different people does not necessarily involve subjectivism (Sen 1993b).

his freedom-based approach to incorporate relevant non-consequence information (such as deontological respect for rights and liberties, regard for decision-making autonomy, and the agent-relativity of evaluation). Because of this broadening of scope, he describes his approach by using such phrases as "consequence-based" or "consequence-sensitive" evaluation, as distinct from consequentialist evaluation (e.g. Sen 1982).[12] He needed to make one methodological innovation for this broadening to be possible: defining the state of affairs to be evaluated as the comprehensive outcome, as distinct from the culmination outcome. The comprehensive outcome describes not only what happened, but also how it happened and who made it happen. With this innovation, Sen's freedom-based consequential evaluation can proceed without being encumbered by the inadequacies of consequentialism that philosophers have identified in their critiques of utilitarianism.

IV. THE PRINCIPLES OF AGGREGATION

Aggregation is involved at several levels in Sen's evaluative framework. In the first place, the need for aggregation arises from the fact that freedom is a multi-dimensional concept. It has two broad components—well-being freedom (capability) and agency freedom—and each of these components is also multi-dimensional. Capability, it may be recalled, is defined as the set of all possible functioning vectors open to an individual, where each functioning vector has several dimensions corresponding to the various "doings" and "beings" a person has reason to value. Aggregation will thus be required over many aspects of well-being. Secondly, different individuals may have different systems of valuation, or what Rawls calls "comprehensive doctrines of the good". In that case, if we are to arrive at a social as distinct from an individual evaluation of a state of affairs, and if that evaluation has to respect plurality of values, then aggregation will be required across individual valuations as well. Thirdly, even a single individual may have multiple value-systems, and ways must be found to deal with this plurality. Sen has drawn on social choice theory, as developed by himself as well as others, to deal with these issues of aggregation. Many others have also been involved in this enterprise, following the lead of Sen, but this is not yet a finished exercise. However, Sen insists on several guiding principles, which must be regarded as integral parts of this evaluative framework. These principles can be grouped into two broad themes.

---

[12] More recently, he has simply used the term "consequential evaluation" to denote the same methodology (Sen 2000), indicating a certain degree of assertiveness in favour of consequences, as opposed to the hint of defensiveness that the earlier terminology seemed to convey.

The first broad theme states that in evaluating any social state of affairs, individual preferences must count, but with several qualifications (Sen 2002b).

First, preferences should be broadly defined, to include values (including agency values) and not just self-centered interests of individuals. It is this broad sense in which Arrow had originally conceived the term "preference" (as reflected in the title of his book, *Social Choice and Individual Values*), but subsequent elaboration of social choice theory has not always stuck to this.

Second, not just any values should count in defining an individual's preferences, but only those that can be "rationally" derived through critical scrutiny. Rationality is here defined very broadly to mean reasoned and informed scrutiny of one's values and prejudices, not just in the narrow sense of maximizing some composite index of well-being or as mere internal consistency of choice.

Third, it must be recognized that an individual may have multiple preferences both at a point in time and over time. At any point in time, an individual may have multiple values which may conflict with each other, generating different preference orderings over the same state of affairs. The values may also change over time— either because of external influences or because of continued introspection, or even because people may choose to cultivate new preferences.

The second broad theme states that incompleteness of preference orderings (both at individual and societal levels) must be accepted, not as an unfortunate consequence of irreconcilable values but as a positive attribute of a valuation system that celebrates the existence of diversity (Sen 1970a, 1997, 2004b). Incompleteness does not mean, however, that alternative social states cannot be ranked at all in terms of the extent of freedom achieved. The dominance relationship may yield a partial order, allowing ranking of some of the alternative states, and this may be extended by using a weighting system that employs a range of values (which may be acceptable to all) rather than specific values (on which agreement may be hard to achieve). But even after these extensions, one will have to accept the fact that it may not be possible to rank all possible alternatives—the idea of completeness may have to be abandoned as a general rule.

Incompleteness of ranking, however, should not be taken as a reason for paralysis or inaction. For practical purposes, decisions can be taken on the basis of the "maximality" criterion (choosing a state of affairs that is no worse than any other) instead of insisting on the "optimality" criterion (trying to choose a state of affairs that is at least as good as any other). For dealing with situations in which the available alternatives cannot be ranked *vis-à-vis* each other, Sen offers the following dictum: don't be a Buridan's ass![13]

---

[13] Buridan's ass, immortalized through numerous writings of Sen, starved to death because when faced with a choice between two haystacks it chose neither, as it could not decide which one was better.

V. Concluding Remarks

The essence of Sen's system of social evaluation may be captured in the following three propositions. First, the evaluation of any social state or the actions leading to it must take note of the consequences for individuals in terms of their advantages and disadvantages, as measured by the opportunity or the freedom they have to lead the kinds of life they have reason to value rather than in terms of some mental metric, such as happiness and desire fulfillment, or some metric of opulence, such as the extent of material possession. Second, while the system is essentially consequentialist in nature, in that actions and institutions are to be evaluated in terms of their consequences for the freedoms enjoyed by individuals, morally significant non-consequential features such as deontological values, autonomy, and the agent-relativity of evaluation are also to be given due weight in the process of evaluation by defining the consequent state of affairs broadly as comprehensive outcomes rather than as culmination outcomes. Third, the aggregation of different individuals' freedoms along the many different dimensions of life that will necessarily be involved in any exercise in social evaluation must take as its starting point the values and preferences of individuals themselves, with the proviso that only values arrived at through reasoned scrutiny should count.

Three meta-principles lie at the foundation of Sen's system of social evaluation: (1) emphasis on the need for incorporating informational diversity in the structure of analysis, (2) advocacy of the notion that no moral system may be capable of yielding a complete evaluation in a world characterized by irreducible plurality of values and attributes of both individuals and of the social state they inhabit, and (3) a deep commitment to democratic values.

The quest to broaden the informational basis of social analysis has been one of the defining features of Sen's life-long intellectual journey. It is this quest that has moved him to take a broad view of people's motivations, going beyond the simple idea of being happy, to define well-being as multi-dimensional freedom, to recognize that people differ greatly in their ability to convert commodities into freedoms, to view development as the expansion of freedom in many dimensions, to demand that both consequences of action and relevant non-consequential information (such as deontological rights, autonomy and the agent-relativity of evaluation) be taken into account while evaluating social states, to define consequences as comprehensive rather than culmination outcomes, to accord due importance to both positive and negative freedoms, to allow for multiplicity of values in a single individual as well as across individuals, and so on.

Sen's acceptance of incompleteness as an essential feature of moral evaluation stems mainly from this recognition of diversity. The idea was first formulated in the welfarist context in his landmark paper on "Interpersonal Aggregation and Partial

Comparability" (Sen 1970c). As his focus gradually widened to encompass the perspective of freedom, the idea of incompleteness was not only retained, but also became elevated to the status of a fundamental philosophical principle. According to this principle, the incompleteness of evaluative exercise is not just a fate that has to be reluctantly accepted but a virtue that has to be positively advocated because the search for completeness when none can possibly exist can only lead to tortured logic and contrived solutions.[14]

Sen's commitment to democratic values also derives partly from the recognition of diversity—in particular, diversity in people's values and preferences. Respect for this diversity demands that social choice among alternative policies, institutions and rules be determined through a democratic process. Partly, the demand for democracy also emerges from his commitment to freedom, because the democratic practice of taking part in decision-making processes is an essential part of the process aspect of freedom. To a significant extent, democracy is also needed in Sen's system of evaluation because of the demands of rationality. Recall that Sen conceives of rationality as reasoned scrutiny of one's values and preferences, and he insists that in using people's values as the basis of social choice only those should be counted that have been subjected to reasoned scrutiny. The same demand for reasoned scrutiny is also explicit in his concept of capability, which he defines as the freedom to live the kind of lives that people have "reason to value". But reasoned scrutiny is only possible in an environment in which alternative views of the world can be freely discussed and debated—to wit, in a democratic environment (Sen 2004b). Finally, democracy is integral to Sen's system because of its instrumental role in advancing the cause of freedom, as embodied in his famous observation that famine has never occurred in an independent democratic society.

The three overarching principles of respecting diversity, incompleteness and democratic values inform the whole philosophical outlook of Sen, not just his system of social evaluation, and find expression in many different contexts. The respect for diversity thus leads him to emphasize the multiple identities of human beings, noting that disregard for this multiplicity of identity lies at the root at many a conflict in the world (Sen 2006). His advocacy of incompleteness as an essential feature of moral evaluation in a diverse world lies behind his famous witticism that "it is better to be vaguely right than to be precisely wrong". And his celebration of democratic debates allows him to look upon the "Argumentative Indian" (Sen 2005) as someone to be proud of rather than as a national embarrassment.

---

[14] This is indeed a central theme of Sen's forthcoming book on theories of justice, where he argues that many of the differences between views in this field arise from the hopeless search for completeness (personal communication).

REFERENCES

BERLIN, I. (1969), *Four Essays on Liberty* (Oxford: Oxford University Press).

NAGEL, T. (1980), "The Limits of Objectivity", in S. McMurrin (ed.), *Tanner Lectures on Human Values*, vol. 1 (Cambridge: Cambridge University Press).

NOZICK, R. (1974), *Anarchy, State and Utopia* (New York: Basic Books).

PARFIT, D. (1981), "Prudence, Morality and the Prisoner's Dilemma", in *Proceedings of the British Academy for 1979* (London: Oxford University Press).

RAWLS, J. (1971), *A Theory of Justice* (Cambridge, Mass.: Harvard University Press).

SEN, A. (1970a), *Collective Choice and Social Welfare* (San Francisco: Holden-Day).

—— (1970b), "The Impossibility of a Paretian Liberal", *Journal of Political Economy*, 72: 152 7.

—— (1970c), "Interpersonal Aggregation and Partial Comparability", *Econometrica*, 38: 393–409.

—— (1973), *On Economic Inequality* (Oxford: Clarendon Press; expanded edn 1996).

—— (1977), "Rational Fools: A Critique of the Behavioural Foundations of Economic Theory", *Philosophy and Public Affairs*, 6: 317–44.

—— (1979), "Utilitarianism and Welfarism", *Journal of Philosophy*, 76: 463–89.

—— (1980), "Equality of What?", in S. McMurrin (ed.), *Tanner Lectures on Human Values*, vol. 1 (Cambridge: Cambridge University Press), repr. in Sen (1982).

—— (1981), *Poverty and Famines: An Essay on Entitlement and Deprivation* (Oxford: Clarendon Press).

—— (1982), "Rights and Agency", *Philosophy and Public Affairs*, 11: 3–19.

—— (1983), "Evaluator Relativity and Consequential Evaluation", *Philosophy and Public Affairs*, 12: 113–32.

—— (1985a), "Well-Being, Agency and Freedom: The Dewey Lectures 1984", *Journal of Philosophy*, 82: 169–221.

—— (1985b), *Commodities and Capabilities* (Amsterdam: North-Holland).

—— (1985c), "Rights as Goals", in S. Guest and A. Milne (eds), *Equality and Discrimination: Essays in Freedom and Justice* (Stuttgart: Franz Steiner).

—— (1992), *Inequality Reexamined* (Oxford: Clarendon Press).

—— (1993a), "Markets and Freedoms", *Oxford Economic Papers*, 45: 519–41.

—— (1993b), "Positional Objectivity", *Philosophy and Public Affairs*, 22: 126–45.

—— (1997), "Maximization and the Act of Choice", *Econometrica*, 65: 745–79.

—— (1999), *Development as Freedom* (New York: Alfred A. Knopf; Oxford and New Delhi: Oxford University Press).

—— (2000), "Consequential Evaluation and Practical Reason", *Journal of Philosophy*, 97: 477–502.

—— (2002a), *Rationality and Freedom* (Cambridge, Mass.: Belknap Press).

—— (2002b), "Opportunities and Freedom", in Sen (2002a).

—— (2002c), "Processes, Liberty and Rights", in Sen (2002a).

—— (2004a), "Elements of a Theory of Human Rights", *Philosophy and Public Affairs*, 32: 315–56.

SEN, A. (2004b), "Incompleteness and Reasoned Choice", *Synthese*, 140: 43–60.

SEN, A. (2005), *The Argumentative Indian: Writings on Indian History, Culture and Identity* (London: Allen Lane).

—— (2006), *Identity and Violence: The Illusion of Destiny* (New York: W. W. Norton).

WILLIAMS, B. (1973), "A Critique of Utilitarianism", in J. J. C. Smart and B. Williams, *Utilitarianism: For and Against* (Cambridge: Cambridge University Press).

CHAPTER 3

....

THE GOOD LIFE AND THE GOOD ECONOMY

THE HUMANIST PERSPECTIVE OF ARISTOTLE, THE PRAGMATISTS AND THE VITALISTS, AND THE ECONOMIC JUSTICE OF JOHN RAWLS

....

EDMUND S. PHELPS

I begin by discussing the *humanist* perspective on the good life. The humanists asked what sort of life gives people the deepest, most lasting satisfaction and they arrived at arresting insights. I survey the conception of the good life in Aristotle; the

This paper was read at the public lecture "Aristotle and the Moderns", Columbia University, October 2007.

variant of that conception represented by John Dewey and our own Amartya Sen, for example; and the variant that can be seen, for instance, in William James and Henri Bergson. Then I argue that the humanist insights into the good life help us to understand how and why an enterprising and innovative kind of economy began to sprout up once countries could afford it; merely to point to the falling away of restraints—the "unfreedoms"—does not by itself get us there. Furthermore, I suggest, the humanist conception of the good life takes us a long way toward a justification for society's support of an entrepreneurial, innovative economy. This leads finally to viewing the good economy more broadly; and here I try to weave in the strands of economic inclusion and Rawlsian justice.

I. Aristotle's Perspective on the Good Life

Perhaps we owe to Aristotle the very *concept* of the good life. It means the sort of life that people prefer—that they would always choose if feasible after meeting prior needs such as food and shelter. In a book put together from his lectures, the *Nicomachean Ethics*, which looks as if it will be around as long as people read, he contrasts ways of life that are just *means* to some end with the *good life*, which is not a means to some end but rather an end in itself—lived for its own sake.[1] To paraphrase him: a society needs food (by producing it or trading domestic products to get foreign food) in order to get energy, needs energy in order to get roofs over their heads, needs roofs in order to get clothing to avoid being cold or sunburned, and so forth. Any *final good*—gourmet food, *haute couture*, and so forth—is the end of a hierarchy. He is interested in the *ranking* of the corresponding "activities"— being a gourmet, a clothes horse, etc. This may sound like economics, with the sole difference that most economists (*classical* ones anyway) do not like to override or even pass judgement on the preferences of the consumer: they like to stay "neutral". However, Aristotle too credits people with a sense of what the "highest good" is— the life we should and do admire. He aims to explain the ranking, not to be a guru for those who have lost their way.

Aristotle recognizes that a certain amount of "moneymaking" is "forced" on society (1096a). That might suggest that he conceives of the good life as affordable only to an elite. However, he does not say that those who can afford the good life are going at it "24/7" while everyone else takes no part in it. Furthermore, it is

---

[1] Quotations are from the helpful edition prepared by Terence Irwin (see References). Following convention, page numbers refer to Immanuel Bekker's classic edition of Aristotle (1831).

implausible to imagine that he would have made an effort spanning many years to develop his thesis if he didn't believe that the good life was already—or would eventually be—affordable to people of normal (or maybe above-average) ability and education. However, the question of whether the good life would ever be accessible to people on the bottom rungs of society is one I want to come back to later on.

One other comment here. Aristotle implies that pursuit of the "good" by a person making his entire life on a deserted island, even a rich island, would not compare, generally speaking, to pursuit of the good "in cities"—in a society, in other words. Thus he recognizes the many interactions and complementarities *at the level of ideas* among people in a society. As a consequence, in choosing the economic institutions to support and the culture to transmit in school, a society needs to decide what the good life consists of. Thus, "we should try to grasp, in outline at any rate, what the good is" (1094b).

So what is the substance of the good life? For me, some of Aristotle's finest passages are about what the good life is *not*. It is not doing the correct thing. That may be the objective of politicians, he says, but "it appears to be too superficial to be what we are seeking, for it seems to depend more on those who honor than on the one honored, whereas we intuitively believe that the good is something of our own and [it is] hard to take from us" (1095b). Next he argues that the good does not consist of virtues either. We require some virtues to pursue the good life successfully but virtue is not sufficient. You could be miserable being virtuous if you had no sense of the right track to be on—the track toward happiness (1095b). When referring to the conception of the good that people seek and tend to reach, he often uses *eudaimonia*—the Greek word for happiness—as a synonym for the good (see e.g. 1095b). I think these positions of Aristotle convey very well his humanist spirit. Aristotle is sharply differentiating his thinking from those religious conceptions of the good in which men and women dutifully perform the function of utilizing resources to survive and reproduce themselves in order that another generation might survive and reproduce themselves, and so on over an indefinite future.

Aristotle hastens to explain that happiness does *not* derive from "amusement": "It would be absurd if [our] end were amusement and our lifelong efforts and sufferings aimed at amusing ourselves ... We amuse ourselves to relax ... so that we can go back to do something serious" (1176b).[2] It could be that Aristotle is having a bit of fun with his student-age listeners. Yes, a night at the opera or the movie house is an input that increases or improves my scholarly output; but there is *some* consumption value in it—on a good night, anyway.

I have to add that Aristotle did not foresee the political philosophers and political economists (notably Hayek and Friedman) who asserted that the good life means simply "freedom"—no matter what people choose to do with that freedom. These

---

[2] So having the occasional gourmet meal or watching the occasional soccer match is a purely instrumental, not a final, good. But for one whose life revolves around, say, soccer, that would be a final good.

social thinkers do not want to *specify* the life that people would prefer to lead upon having sufficient grasp of the choices, at any rate. I am not sure what Aristotle would have said about that conception of the good life. But I believe that they have boxed themselves into a position from which they cannot offer any arguments for one system or another as long as individuals have individual freedom in both. The weakness of their position is that in an economic system the individual freedom of everyone to take some actions may have adverse consequences for everyone or, if not, may none the less be adverse in some decisive way.

So what *is* Aristotle's conception of the good life? It is the *pursuit of knowledge*. In his words, "The best [thing] is understanding...This activity is supreme, since understanding is the supreme element in us" (1177a). "Happiness [derives] from some sort of study" (*Politics*, 1324a). Study is the "highest good", he argues, largely because it requires "reason" and reason is the main faculty that separates human beings from the other animals. He adds that this fits with his observation that happiness is not felt by the other animals (1100a).

I would not dare appraise Aristotle's *argument* for this proposition as a *philosopher* would. But I would say this. Suppose that dogs, dolphins or others *did* possess reason and a capability for happiness. (My wife and I always thought that our dog Shaggy led a happy life, even an exuberant life.) That would not refute the proposition that knowledge is the "best [good]" and pursuit of it the "supreme activity". I think that Aristotle's basic argument is that as our knowledge increases or productivity of the entire society increases, people use the increase in their opportunities to pursue more and more elevated kinds of satisfactions rather than just enjoying more and more of the good old ones; and satisfaction from knowledge and its pursuit are at the top of the hierarchy. A day devoted to this *last* activity of study rather than other activities must have the highest value, since it is chosen over the others in spite of the sacrifice of the (less elevated) goods that alternative activities would have yielded.

What bothers me as an *economist* about Aristotle's thesis—I imagine it bothers you too—is the *narrowness* of the knowledge he regards as the "highest good" and whose pursuit is the "supreme activity". For Aristotle the pursuit of knowledge appears to be a highly ascetic activity, practiced in a cloistered setting, perhaps stimulated by the occasional study group or conversation with a friend—the sort of activity carried on by mathematicians, theoretical physicists and scholars, such as philosophers and historians. It's fair to say, I should think, that Aristotle's experience and observation was confined to the classical world, so his thinking was naturally oriented around classical knowledge and the classical way of acquiring it—by study.

This is bothersome not so much because it would be nice to have a more general theory but because, if I'm not mistaken, there is a problem with the thesis in its original form. If Aristotle is right that the highest good is exclusively knowledge that is not used for anything, a society, as it becomes more and more productive or rich, will devote more and more time to the leisure activity of pursuing such knowledge, which has no commercial value in the market place. So the theory predicts that as hourly productivity increases in a country, we should observe at some point little or no further increase in the production and sale of goods—only steady further increases in leisure activity in the pursuit of knowledge. This is precisely the prediction made in an essay by John Maynard Keynes, "Economic Possibilities for our Grandchildren" (Keynes 1931: 358–73)—an essay admirable to some and appalling to others. But we do not observe that outcome.[3] I believe, however, that this puzzle is obviously resolved once we take a broader view of knowledge.

II. Further Visions from the Aristotelian Perspective

Succeeding philosophers and writers have focused on *other kinds* of knowledge and *other kinds* of activities in pursuit of such knowledge while bearing in mind Aristotle's fundamental insights: the hierarchy of desires, the desire for knowledge, and the place of knowledge as the most desirable, yet the last to be affordable.

Humanist writers and philosophers after Aristotle have introduced *practical* knowledge, a good that is definitely *not* valued just for itself—much of it *informal* knowledge, which does not make its way into documents. These humanists have also introduced the quite different kinds of activities that are carried on in gaining such knowledge—the worldly contexts in which much knowledge is pursued, the formal and particularly the informal. I have selected several of these humanists for a brief review and placed them into two groups.

II.1 The "pragmatists"

In one group (will call them the "pragmatists"), knowledge is seen as acquired and used for the *purpose* of producing or acting in some way. An early figure here is the poet Virgil, who was born of peasant stock in the Po Valley in 70 BC (some 300 years after Aristotle's birth) and who settled in Rome during the age of emperor Augustus. Virgil's well-known *Georgics* somehow came to be viewed as a primer on agriculture until fairly recently, but at a deeper level it is an ode to humanity

---

[3] Aristotle could not have been pleased with the finding of recent happiness researchers that, *after a point*, further increases in productivity do not add to reported happiness. See, for example, Layard (2007). I have discussed this paradox elsewhere.

and Roman culture.[4] It speaks at great length and admiringly of the vast knowledge the farmer acquires and draws upon in plowing, planting trees, tending cattle, and keeping bees. It expresses the farmer's engagement in this work and his satisfaction at a successful harvest. This poem contains one of Virgil's immortal lines: *Felix qui potuit rerum cognoscere causas* (Happy is he who knows the causes of things).

I would like to put Voltaire into this same group. He manifests appreciation of the satisfaction that can come from a life of action—of work. As he dramatizes in his book *Candide*, the action need not be in social causes or to right wrongs; Voltaire advises us to forget all that. Instead, he suggests that seemingly unromantic careers in the commercial sphere could be deeply meaningful and amply rewarding—after all, Voltaire was writing in the late eighteenth century, when the feudal manor was at an end and the flux and growth of commerce had begun. I love the stirring finale for sextet and chorus of the musical *Candide* composed by Leonard Bernstein, with words taken from Voltaire by Stephen Sondheim:

> We're neither pure nor wise nor good.
> We'll do the best we know.
> We'll build our house, and chop our wood.
> And make our garden grow.

I suppose it is implicit in Voltaire's conclusion that making a business grow is a challenge requiring a lot of one's knowledge of things and the acquisition of much more knowledge along the way; and that such a life is interesting and rewarding. (Incidentally, the French economists were the first to see any kind of role at all for the *entrepreneur*.)

In the middle decades of the twentieth century closer attention was paid to the *nature* of the satisfactions deriving from the workplace and to the part played by the individual's *acquisition* and *use* of *private knowledge* in those satisfactions. A pioneer is John Dewey, the American pragmatist philosopher. Dewey, anticipating Hayek, understands that ordinary workers do, or at any rate could, possess considerable private knowledge—specialized knowledge of use in the course of their work. He emphasizes the *human need* for problem-solving activity.[5] Even the worker with an ordinary education can be engaged in and can gain intellectual development from the formation of the skills—a type of knowledge—arising from problems that are put to him or her in the workplace—or that could be put to him or her if the workplace were properly organized.[6]

---

[4] This change of interpretation is credited to Roger Mynors (1990).

[5] As nearly as I can tell, Dewey's discussions range from *Human Nature and Conduct* (Dewey 1922) to *Experience and Education* (Dewey 1938).

[6] Dewey was upset by the arrival of Fordian mass production and hoped the workplace would be reformed again to provide the intellectual satisfactions of which it was capable. Of course, market forces have by now pretty much eliminated the assembly line—or, in many cases, moved it to Guangdong Peninsula.

The psychologist Abraham Maslow, in a much-read paper (Maslow 1943), drew up a hierarchy of human needs, starting with the most basic. In this hierarchy he gives a place to the need to acquire "mastery" of a trade or skill—typically after some apprenticeship. This need comes immediately after the physiological needs at the base and, next up the ladder, security needs. (Incidentally, Maslow accords the need for an ongoing *process* of problem-solving a loftier place in the hierarchy; but more of that below.)

John Rawls, toward the end of his magisterial work on economic justice, sets out with great clarity the main theme of this literature—the "Aristotelian perspective" (Rawls 1970: 424–33). One's acquisition of knowledge, he says, constitutes the development of one's "talents", or "capacities", which is the essence of one's "self-realization". And this self-realization, or as much of it as we obtain, is the central drive that every one of us has. All this is attributed to Aristotle.[7]

A relatively recent contribution to this topic is that by Amartya Sen (1992, 1999). There is something fundamentally missing, Sen suggests, in present-day thinking about the generation of happiness. Neoclassical theory takes happiness to be a function of the bundle of consumer goods and leisure chosen; and this happiness could be seen as *indirectly* a function of the resources possessed. It is as if the actors in an economy all participate in a comprehensive once-and-for-all auction in which they contract their entire future. For whatever reason, Rawls tacitly uses that theory in treating a person's "self-realization" as a function of his or her "primary goods". Sen objects:

[Besides the *indirect* one there is a] connection between capability and well-being … making … well-being … depend [*directly*] on the *capability* to function. *Choosing* may itself be a valuable part of living, and a genuine choice with serious options may be seen to be—for that reason—richer. … [A]t least some types of capabilities contribute *directly* to well-being, making one's life richer with the opportunity of reflective choice.[8]

(Sen 1992: 41; italics added)

Possibly Sen had in mind not only some joy of choosing but also that a person wants to acquire *backup* capabilities because life is subject to probabilistic *risks*. Anyone

---

[7] His argument can be condensed as follows: "[H]uman beings enjoy the exercise of their realized capacities (their innate or trained abilities) and this enjoyment increases the more the capacity is realized or the greater its complexity … [It] is a principle of motivation. It accounts for many of our major desires … Moreover, it expresses a psychological law governing changes in the pattern of our desires. [It] implies that as a person's capacities increase over time … and as he trains these capacities and learns how to exercise them, he will in due course come to prefer the more complex activities he can now engage in which call upon his newly realized abilities. The simpler things he enjoyed before are no longer sufficiently interesting or attractive. … Now accepting the Aristotelian Principle, it will generally be rational, in view of the other assumptions, to realize and train mature capacities … A rational plan … allows a person to flourish, so far as circumstances permit, and to exercise his realized abilities as much as he can" (Rawls 1970: 428–9).

[8] Sen cites Marx and Hayek among several precursors who placed a value on freedom independently of outcomes.

intending to become an oboist might fear a car accident doing irreparable damage to his or her embouchure; so as a precaution the person would see the *option value* of developing some capability to function as an economist, say, alongside the capability to function as an oboist.

One might reply that an oboist can buy insurance against such an accident. But another point made by Sen in the exposition of his "capabilities approach" shows at once how unacceptable such a reply would be. He emphasizes with exceptional force that in order to achieve any sort of fulfillment, people need to *do* things. (Since almost any career we might choose will require problem-solving, there is a derived need for capabilities.) If so, the insurance award paid on loss of the oboist's embouchure would hardly compensate for the loss of a career. Thus the need for backup capabilities.

Of course, another kind of "risk" (in Knight's terminology) is *uncertainty*. There is Knightian uncertainty in business owing to people's limited knowledge of the directions the economy will take. (The intended oboist has little idea of what the demand and the supply will be.) But that takes us to a whole different world— the world of Hayek.

The post-Aristotelian literature of the "pragmatists" stops short of saying some of the most important things that must be said about knowledge. This literature is strikingly dry in portraying life at its best as one long series of pragmatic exercises in problem-solving which serve to keep us engaged and yield other valued results more times than not. In the *modern* age, business life—and life outside business— is unquestionably more than just drawing on past "knowledge" and then applying "reason" in order to derive new implications, thus adding new knowledge to past knowledge. Modern business life involves—is largely driven by—another kind of knowledge, typically so-called *personal* knowledge, which involves originality, in- spiration, intuition, animal spirits. (It is called "personal" because it cannot easily be imparted to others. But, in principle, it can be acted upon.) As some participants act on such imperfect knowledge, they create uncertainty for themselves and every- one else. But not everything remains uncertain for ever. There are discoveries and other outcomes, so some uncertainties are being resolved as new ones arise. This is a world of creativity and adventure, first perceived by Hayek.

II.2 The "vitalists"

Happily, there is a significant literature about life in that world and its value. This literature expressed what Jacques Barzun (1943) and Harold Bloom (1994) call *vitalism*.

I was introduced to it at Amherst College, though I am not sure that I was aware at the time that I was being indoctrinated in "vitalism". My first exposure to it was the *Autobiography* by the sculptor Benvenuto Cellini. There Cellini, a larger-than-life figure of the Renaissance (and the protagonist of the Berlioz opera named after him), conveyed the joys of *creativity* and of *making it*. I have to say that I was taken aback by his raw ambition, which was beyond anything I had seen or heard of.

In the Baroque era, Cervantes and Shakespeare dramatize the individual's quest. The message of Cervantes' *Don Quixote*, it seems to me, is that a life of challenge and adventure is necessary for human fulfillment; and if the barren economy of the Spanish desert does not supply such challenges one must somehow create them by one's self—*imagining* them, if necessary.

In the eighteenth-century Enlightenment, such a view is reflected by some, though not all, of the key figures. David Hume, disputing the *rationalism* of the French, gives a crucial place to the "passions" in decision-making and to "imagination" in the growth of society's knowledge. (Hume must be the first modern philosopher.) As already mentioned, Voltaire urged people to look for satisfaction in individual pursuits, to "cultivate your own garden". Jefferson wrote of the "pursuit of happiness" and commented that people came to America "to make their fortune". The term "pursue" conveys the point that seeking a fortune is more valuable than *having* one: "The journey is the end."

Needless to say, the Romantic Age was wild about exploration and celebrated discovery as well as the determination and perseverance it often takes. We all recall the line of Keats about the time when Cortés "stared at the Pacific...silent upon a peak in Darien". And that fierce stanza in William Ernest Henley's *Invictus*:

> It matters not how strait the gate,
> How charged with punishments the scroll,
> I am the master of my fate:
> I am the captain of my soul.

Finally, there is the Age of Modernism. No American philosopher wrote of vitalism more than William James. He saw great vitality with his own eyes. Born in New York City in 1842, he was witness throughout his life to the transformation of the American economy from relatively slow-paced to explosively innovative. In his ethics, so to speak, the excitement of fresh problems and new experiences are at the heart of the good life.[9] If Walt Whitman is the poet of the American ethos, James is its philosopher.

The great French thinker Henri Bergson, a friend of James and likewise a witness to the dawning decades of the modern era, was in his day (and is still) the main interpreter, or philosopher, of vitalism.[10] His book *Creative Evolution* advocates a

---

[9] William James wrote somewhere, "My *flux*-philosophy may well have to do with my extremely impatient temperament. I am a motor, need change, and get very quickly bored" (quoted in Barzun 1983: 265). By "motor" he did not mean anything like a mechanical device, as Barzun remarks.

[10] Bergson rose to fame with *Creative Evolution*, published in Paris in 1907 and attaining wider renown in its first English edition (Bergson 1911). He was appointed to the Collège de France and won the Nobel Peace Prize in 1925. (Incidentally, Henrik Ibsen's dramatic poem *Peer Gynt* (1867)

life of incessant "becoming" over mere "being" and urges us to find in ourselves the required *élan vital*. Bergson also grasps that the very idea of creativity would not make sense if we lived in a world of *determinism* rather than "free will". (Nietzsche was a precursor in this regard.)[11]

Is all this vitalism and pragmatism—in short, the Aristotelian perspective—the prevailing ethos in the present age? We don't have to make our own estimates based on people we know. The path-breaking World Values Survey created by Ronald Inglehardt and colleagues at the University of Michigan surveyed household attitudes and compiled the results in many countries over the years 1991–3. "When you look for a job," they asked, "do you look for opportunities for initiative?" The percentage who said yes was 52 in the United States, 54 in Canada. "Opportunities for interesting work?" Sixty-nine per cent in the US, 72 per cent in Canada. "Opportunities for taking responsibility?" Sixty-one per cent in the US, 65 per cent in Canada. (In France 38 per cent said yes to the initiative question, 59 per cent to the interesting work question, and 58 per cent to the responsibility question.)

In Iceland a month ago I asked a native resident there what the Icelanders think about the spectacular fortunes of many of Iceland's new entrepreneurs. He said, "They don't feel bad about it. They are thinking only about how to achieve their own success."

No doubt the Aristotelian ethic has never been unanimously embraced in North America and has been embraced less in continental Europe. Yet it may be widespread enough that, given the opportunity, it could set the tone of the economy—at least until some countervailing force or forces turn the tide in one or another country.

III. The Rise of Capitalism: the Protestant Ethic v. the Aristotelian Ethic

I want to argue that the Aristotelian ethic—Aristotle on happiness, the pragmatists on problem-solving and capabilities, and the vitalists on adventure and exploration—played an *essential* part in a huge development in our economic history.

anticipates Bergson's theme when the Button Moulder says, "To be yourself is to slay yourself. | But on you, that answer's sure to fail; | So let's say: To make your life evolve | From the Master's meaning to the last detail.")

[11] The latest item in the vitalist literature may be Jamison (2004).

Every schoolchild seems to know the provocative hypothesis of Max Weber that capitalism took root over the 1600s in the northern European countries, from Germany, Switzerland and Scandinavia to England and Scotland, owing to the fertile soil created by the "Protestant ethic" of hard work and high saving.[12] Subsequent scholarship has not found favor with that hypothesis. Aminitore Fanfani showed that a similar rise of capitalism occurred in northern Italy. Some scholars have found that while Protestantism expanded in the years following Luther's Ninety-Five Theses, the proportion of Catholics in the population returned to its previous high levels by the end of the century in most of those countries. Some demographers point to threshold effects as population in one area after another reached levels that made it economic to develop the area.

Another weakness of Weber's hypothesis arises from the point that capitalism is not well measured by the size of the GDP; the growth rate of productivity would be a better indicator, though that too could rise or fall for reasons that do not reflect any change in the dynamism of the economy in generating successful innovations. It is a problem for Weber's hypothesis, therefore, that even if populations increased and employment and output levels increased even more (in proportionate terms) over that century, there was no shifting of gears that put *labor productivity*—that is, output per hour worked—onto a steeper growth path. (In contrast, there is evidence of somewhat faster growth over the 1700s in some countries.) As implied in the paragraph above, the *marked* acceleration of *productivity* in several cutting-edge economies occurred at various times in the last half of the nineteenth century. So it is hard to argue that the rise of Protestantism, however brief or long-lasting, caused the later breakout of *dynamism*.

The hypothesis which still survives is that the institutions of capitalism began to evolve and led ultimately to waves of innovation (and faster growth) thanks to the gradual removal of institutions restricting economic freedoms—including the freedom to exercise various property rights, to form (and to close) companies, to file for bankruptcy protection and so forth—all this under a reliable and impartial rule of law. That hypothesis was boldly stated by the late Milton Friedman in his *Capitalism and Freedom*: new economic freedoms begat capitalism and capitalism bolstered liberties in other dimensions.[13]

A fault, or at least a lacuna, in this theory of the rise of capitalism is that it takes the preconditions it quite plausibly argues are *necessary* for a well-functioning capitalism—the key economic freedoms—to be *sufficient*: when an economic system of key freedoms protected by the rule of law is open for business, some

---

[12] Weber (1930). The book is based on a two-part article for a German journal in 1921/2.

[13] Friedman (1962). Also relevant here, of course, is Hayek (1944). To be sure, Hayek argues that departures from capitalism toward socialism or corporatism are a threat to personal and political freedom (and certain economic freedoms almost by definition), but I do not recall an argument by him that capitalism sprung up naturally, automatically, with the establishment of various economic freedoms.

participants in the economy will, after some experience with the operation of the new system, step forward with the entrepreneurial proposals; others will, amid vast uncertainty, step into roles as lenders or investors to finance some of these projects; and managers of enterprises will bravely evaluate and sometimes make pioneering applications of the new products and methods in spite of the uncertainties.

It is necessary to add that some sort of ethos, or culture, must be present to drive the economy toward the entrepreneurial, financial and managerial behavior that will generate the innovative activities that are the defining characteristic of finance capitalism. If the prevailing ethos, or value system, is not specified, we cannot be sure that the economic freedoms will not lead to some sort of monastic economy, or perhaps an economy populated entirely by worker cooperatives and banking cooperatives, in which very possibly there is little incentive to innovate for fear of causing damages of unknown probability to some employees or some savers.

The hypothesis to which I am led, then, is that capitalism is the product of a marriage between key economic freedoms and key cultural values. It is compelling (to me at any rate) that the prevalence of the Aristotelian ethic played a critical part, particularly in the nineteenth century, in the spectacular rise of *finance capitalism* and the ensuing explosion of innovation from the mid-nineteenth century well into the twentieth century (and erupting once or twice later in the century). The impulse to exploration and innovation, born of a desire for self-expression, and the desire of workers and financiers to engage in meeting the ensuing problems and bearing the ensuing risks, must be fundamental to the choice of capitalism over other systems.

IV. The Aristotelian Ethic and the "Good Economy"

I want to close by discussing briefly the *good economy*. As my colleague Joseph Stiglitz commented the other day, economics has not possessed a clear foundation for the economic system called capitalism. What *passes* for such a theory among libertarians is a *neoclassical justification* of a *free-market economy* in the sense of one with minimal government—one based on a model in which there is little for the government to do! The economy in the model is already perfect without a government! In my estimate, there is no greater economist in the twentieth century than Friedrich Hayek. But Hayek's vision of the good economy is filled with arbitrary exceptions, to which you and I would add our own; and he fails to see that capitalism is a creative system with much *disorder* alongside some elements of order, so the government has to stand nearby to be ready to *step in* when things go awry.

A theme of my book *Rewarding Work* (Phelps 1997) and of my introduction to the conference volume *Designing Inclusion* (Phelps 2003) is that economic dynamism has valuable effects on the workplace experience—benefits consisting of the personal or intellectual development of employees and entrepreneurs. In advanced economies at any rate, the mechanisms of innovation and of discovery largely shape that experience, such as the degree to which employees feel engaged in their jobs, and the rewards, such as job satisfaction, of participating in the workplace. Without such dynamism jobs would not offer much in the way of non-pecuniary rewards.

The generation of dynamism, I came to see, involves three actors:

1. the *creativity* and *abundance* of the new ideas conceived and available for development;
2. the *diversity* of views among the canny financiers who select which entrepreneurs to back and to support through the development stages; and
3. the *vibrancy* of managers and consumers in grasping and acting on the new ideas made available in the market place.

A country's economic institutions and its economic culture—not just the rule of law and private property rights—have an impact on the actors in the innovation process and thus add to or detract from an economy's dynamism.

In the theoretical framework that Friedrich Hayek started, capitalism is the premier economic system for *dynamism*—theoretically. Capitalism is all about innovation in *commercial ideas*—their birth, development and, finally, their "discovery", or adoption, in the market place. Empirically, it is clear that where a well-functioning capitalism is feasible, or supportable, a well-functioning capitalism is better for the stimulation, development and evaluation of innovative ideas than either eastern European socialism or western continental European corporatism. (We mustn't repeat that debate for another century.)

The live question is whether capitalism is *just*—or less unjust, as Rawls would put it. Among the so-called advanced economies, the relatively capitalist ones look better than the other systems in some respects and worse in some others—whether that is inherently so is a question. To say which system would be acceptable—provided it will be able to function well in the country in question—we need some ordering device, such as might be provided by a conception of the *good economy*.

I suppose that the *good economy* depends upon what the *good life* is. Calvin endorsed hard work within a vocation as an expression of devotion to God. For

Hayek and Friedman it was a life of freedom. The appeal of work and of freedom are that they are necessary for a good life.[14] But what is the *substance* of a good life, its essence?

The Aristotelian perspective gives an answer. Man seeks knowledge, as Aristotle says. People need the engagement and satisfaction that comes from problem-solving, as the pragmatists say. And there is the vitalist need for exploration and for the self-expression that lies in originality.

If this is *good life* and if the good *economy* must promote a good *life* for its participants, it follows that an economy cannot be good that does not produce the stimulation, challenge, engagement, mastery, discovery and intellectual develop-ment that constitute the good life. Socialism and corporatism are unjust in creating stultifying economies that are inimical to the good life.

What about the least advantaged workers, though? They have a legitimate claim to some satisfactory level of *inclusion*. (In Rawls, of course, justice requires that the terms of their employment are as favorable as possible, thus providing them with the greatest incentive to take work and the greatest self-realization that society can manage.)

A country can simultaneously promote both the good life and inclusion by harnessing two sets of institutions to their best employment. A higher level of problem-solving and exploration in the business sector can be sought by aiming for greater dynamism through institutions fostering the originality of entrepreneurs, the diversity of financiers and sophistication among managers. A higher level of inclusion can be sought by fiscal incentives—a system of low-wage employment subsidies as well as classical education subsidies in order to attract marginalized workers to the business sector, shrink their unemployment rates and boost their pay.

Are the good life and inclusion competing goods, so that gains in the one undo gains in the other? There are two fallacies here. One is the belief, with no foundation I know of, that a fiscal policy aimed at broad economic inclusion would substantially preclude ample dynamism and thus the good life for all. I have argued in *Rewarding Work* that, on the contrary, well-designed employment subsidies actually bolster the bourgeois culture, revive the ethic of self-support and increase prosperity in low-wage communities. That boosts a country's dynamism, and builds popular support for capitalist institutions.

The other fallacy is that the dynamism of capitalism harms disadvantaged work-ers. I argue that economic dynamism works to increase inclusion. Heightened

---

[14] In any case, these conceptions of the good economy are not rich enough to provide a political economy for our times. Calvinism appears consistent with property-owning market socialism. Aside from Friedman's negative income tax and middle-Hayek's several exceptions, both of them appeared more enthusiastic about a free market economy—small government and atomistic competition—than the speculative swings and gleeful commercialism of today's capitalism (in those places where it thrives).

entrepreneurial activity indirectly lifts up *both* those already enjoying much of the good life *and*—up to a point, at any rate—disadvantaged workers too, taken as a group. The reason is that increased dynamism—that is, a faster rate of successful innovation—creates jobs in product development, marketing and managing, and in so doing it ultimately pulls the disadvantaged into better work and higher pay. (My reasoning is structuralist, not Keynesian.) The record of the present decade suggests that the disadvantaged suffer an acute failure of inclusion in economies resistant to innovation. Heightened innovation also serves the disadvantaged directly by making their jobs less burdensome and dangerous—and perhaps also more engaging. Innovation is not unjust if it tends to heighten the life prospects of the disadvantaged (alongside those of the advantaged).

My conclusion is that a morally acceptable economy must have enough well-directed interventions to make sure it possesses a satisfactory level of dynamism and enough interventions to ensure a satisfactory degree of inclusion.

REFERENCES

ARISTOTLE, *Nicomachean Ethics,* ed. T. Irwin, revd edn (Indianapolis: Hackett Publishing Co., 1999).

BARZUN, J. (1943) *Romanticism and the Modern Ego* (Boston: Little, Brown).

—— (1983), *A Stroll with William James* (New York: Harper).

BERGSON, H. (1911), *Creative Evolution* (New York: Henry Holt).

BLOOM, H. (1994), *The Western Canon* (New York: Harcourt Brace).

DEWEY, J. (1922), *Human Nature and Conduct* (New York: Holt).

—— (1938), *Experience and Education* (New York: Simon and Schuster).

FRIEDMAN, M. (1962), *Capitalism and Freedom* (Chicago: University of Chicago Press).

HAYEK, F. (1944), *The Road to Serfdom* (London: Routledge).

JAMISON, K. R. (2004), *Exuberance: The Passion for Life* (New York: Alfred Knopf).

KEYNES, J. M. (1931), *Essays in Persuasion* (London: Macmillan).

LAYARD, R. (2007), *Happiness: Lessons from a New Science* (London: Penguin).

MASLOW, A. (1943), "A Theory of Motivation", *Psychological Review*, 50: 370–96.

MYNORS, R. A. B. (ed.) (1990), *Georgics by Virgil* (Oxford: Clarendon Press).

PHELPS, E. (1997), *Rewarding Work: How to Build Participation and Self-Support to Free Enterprise* (Cambridge, Mass.: Harvard University Press).

—— (ed.) (2003), *Designing Inclusion* (Cambridge, Mass.: Harvard University Press).

RAWLS, J. (1971), *A Theory of Justice* (Cambridge, Mass.: Harvard University Press).

SEN, A. (1992), *Inequality Reexamined* (New York: Norton).

—— (1999), *Commodities and Capabilities* (New York: Oxford University Press).

WEBER, M. (1930), *The Protestant Ethic and the Spirit of Capitalism* (London: Unwin).

CHAPTER 4

THE ADAPTATION PROBLEM, EVOLUTION AND NORMATIVE ECONOMICS

MOZAFFAR QIZILBASH

I. INTRODUCTION

ONE of Amartya Sen's arguments against utilitarianism, and "utility"-based views more generally, involves the idea that certain underdogs may "adapt" to, or learn to live with, their living conditions in a variety of ways—such as by suppressing suffering, cutting back their desires or finding pleasure in small mercies. If they do so, the calculus of "utility" might be a misleading guide to a person's quality of life or advantage in the evaluation of normative claims. This argument goes by a variety of names. In earlier work (Qizilbash 2006b: 83), I referred to the difficulty it

A very preliminary version of this paper was prepared for the workshop on 'Naturalistic Perspectives on Human Behavior—Are there any Normative Correlates?', Jena, October 2006. I am very grateful to all those who commented on the paper at that workshop, especially to Ken Binmore, Wulf Gaertner, Christian Schubert, Ulrich Witt, and also to Martin Binder for his written comments. I have also benefited from discussions and exchanges on this topic with Abigail Barr, David Clark, James Foster, James Griffin, Daniel Neff, Amartya Sen and Robert Sugden.

poses for some accounts of well-being as the "adaptation problem". I use this term in this paper in a slightly modified form to refer to the problem posed, not just for accounts of well-being, but for normative evaluation and for claims more broadly, including claims of justice. Elsewhere Roger Crisp and Andrew Moore (1996) refer to it (following Crocker 1992) as the "small mercies argument" and indeed it is also often referred to under the somewhat imprecise heading of "adaptive preferences". The use of the term "adaptive preferences" to refer to Sen's claims about adaptation is misleading, because he usually makes no claim about preferences in the relevant discussions. In contrast, Jon Elster (1981, 1983) argues—in closely related work—that "adaptive preferences" pose significant difficulties for utilitarianism. Differences between Elster's and Sen's arguments have been discussed elsewhere (Nussbaum 2000: 136–8 and Qizilbash 2006b: 93 *inter alia*), and a variety of responses to the adaptation problem can be found in modern forms of utilitarianism (Griffin 1986; Sumner 1996; Qizilbash 2006b)—and arguably an early response can also be found in the writings of John Stuart Mill (Qizilbash 2006a).

In this paper, I argue that one difference between Elster's and Sen's discussions—which has received little or no attention—is that Sen is often concerned that underdogs adapt with a view to *survival*. His related work on the Darwinian view of progress and evolution helps to make more sense of some of his concerns about adaptation and survival. This chapter goes on to address the following questions: is the adaptation problem relevant to recent contributions in normative economics—notably on happiness and justice?—and do these contributions provide any plausible response to the adaptation problem? I take Richard Layard's writings to be an example of recent work on happiness which has been influential at the policy level, and Ken Binmore's writings as a contemporary account of justice. Both Layard and Binmore are influenced by evolutionary biology. The scope and claims of this chapter are thus limited to examining whether the adaptation problem arises for these authors, rather than for all those working on happiness and accounts of justice which build on evolutionary biology in economics. Examining these specific authors nonetheless provides some insight into the enduring relevance of Sen's writings on adaptation to contemporary economics. The paper is structured as follows: in section II, I explain and discuss Elster's account; in section III, I explain Sen's views and show how they differ from Elster's; in section IV, I focus on Layard's recent discussion of happiness; in section V, I discuss aspects of Binmore's account of justice; and section VI concludes the chapter.

II. ELSTER ON ADAPTIVE PREFERENCES

Jon Elster's discussion of adaptive preferences dedicates considerable space to distinguishing adaptive preferences from those formed in other ways. Indeed, for

Elster, adaptive preferences are closely identified with a specific phenomenon: "sour grapes". To illustrate it he uses La Fontaine's tale of the fox ("*un certain Renard Gascon*") who, dying of hunger, thinks he sees some apparently ripe grapes, but on realizing that they are unattainable decides that they are too green and only fit for "boors" (*goujats*) (Elster 1983: 109). Elster refers to the phenomenon of sour grapes as "adaptive preference formation" and to preferences shaped by this process of preference formation as "adaptive preferences" (Elster 1983: 110). The fox-and-grapes example highlights the way in which preferences may not be independent of the set of feasible options. Indeed, while Elster's discussion is aimed primarily at utilitarianism, it is relevant more generally for preference-based accounts of rational choice, including social choice (see Elster 1989 and Qizilbash 2007a). So he asks: "why should the choice between feasible options only take account of individual preference, if people tend to adjust their aspirations to their possibilities?" (Elster 1983: 109). As regards many modern forms of utilitarianism—which rank outcomes, rules or dispositions in terms of the average or sum of welfare they produce, and which conceptualize welfare in terms of the satisfaction of desires or preferences—the implication is also clear. As Elster puts it: "there would be no welfare loss if the fox were excluded from the consumption of the grapes, since he thought them sour anyway" (109). Put another way, if the fox preferred starving to eating the grapes, preference-based utilitarianism would have no basis for claiming that the fox was worse off starving.

Elster discusses a wide range of related phenomena, which include: "counteradaptive preferences"; manipulation; "character planning"; addiction; and preference change through learning. By distinguishing these phenomena from that of adaptive preference formation, he hopes to explain why adaptive preferences are problematic. His ultimate charge against utilitarianism is that it does not distinguish between adaptive preferences and preferences formed in other ways and thus does not begin to address the problem he isolates. To clarify this point, I explain these different phenomena. In his conceptual map, "counteradaptive preferences" refers to the "opposite" phenomenon to sour grapes, i.e. that "forbidden fruit is sweet". Here, as in the case of adaptive preferences, preferences are shaped by the feasible set. However, in counteradaptive preferences, the preference is for unattainable, rather than attainable, options. As regards preference formation through learning, Elster notes that choices depend on tastes, which in turn depend on past choices (112). Someone reared in the country may prefer a country lifestyle to an urban one, while someone with experience of only an urban lifestyle might then prefer that to country life. On the other hand, someone who has experience of both lifestyles may be better informed—and have learnt from experience. The informed person's preferences are then not simply reversed by changing the set of feasible options, as is the case if the preferences are adaptive (114).

Elster also distinguishes sour grapes from the case of addiction, where "people get hooked on certain goods, which they then consume compulsively" (121). He thinks that adaptive and addictive preferences have a certain amount in common because both preferences are "induced by the choice situation rather than given independently of it" (120). However, he suggests that these phenomena differ both in the consequences of withdrawal and because in the case of addiction the object of addiction plays an important role, whereas in adaptation it is the feasible set which is crucial.

Elster also crucially distinguishes adaptive preferences from "character planning". In the phenomenon of "sour grapes", the process of adaptation occurs—on Elster's account—"behind the back" of the person and is not the outcome of deliberation. If it is a person's choice to alter her preferences in the light of the actual possibilities she faces, for Elster that makes her *free*, in a way that she is not free in the case of adaptive preferences. In the case of adaptive preferences, the process of preference formation is purely causal and to some degree undermines the person's *autonomy*.

Adaptive preferences are also distinct from "manipulation" on Elster's view. In the case of manipulation, the process of preference formation is driven by the fact that it benefits people *other than* those whose preferences are being shaped. In the case of sour grapes, however, the process is driven by the fact that it is (apparently) good for—and presumably can be seen as improving the *welfare* of—those who adapt (117) while undermining their freedom or autonomy. Elster's discussion of sour grapes thus focuses on the potential conflict between autonomy and welfare in evaluating the effects of adaptation. This is especially clear when he discusses the possibility of *release from adaptive preferences*, which occurs when people raise their (previously dampened) hopes or expectations when new possibilities open up (124). His own further analysis of such release—which continues in his discussion of the evaluation of the effects of the Industrial Revolution—focuses on the fact that social changes which lead to such a release can involve both "inducement of frustration and creation of autonomous persons" (135). This point is clearly important for the evaluation of progress or development, which is a central theme in Sen's writings.

III. Sen on Adaptation, Capability and Evolution

While there is significant overlap between Sen's and Elster's discussions of adaptation, there are also significant differences. In Sen's writings, claims about adaptation are put to (at least) two distinct uses. The argument is used: (1) to undermine

confidence in "utility"—understood as desire satisfaction, pleasure or happiness—
as a reliable measure of well-being or the quality of life; and (2) to signal significant worries about any view of justice which focuses on "utility" as a metric for
interpersonal comparisons of advantage. Indeed, this argument motivates in part
Sen's own well-known views of the quality of life and justice, constituted in part
by his "capability approach", which is concerned with what a person *can* do or be
(Sen 1982, 1987, 1992, 1993a and 1999 *inter alia*). In more precise terms, the relevant
things a person can do or be, her "doings" and "beings", are called "functionings"
and her *capability* refers to "the alternative combinations of functionings the person
can achieve, and from which he or she can choose one collection" (Sen 1993a:
31). A person's capability thus "reflects her freedom to lead different types of life"
(Sen 1993a: 33) and, in this sense, the opportunities open to her. On the capability
approach, the quality of life, egalitarian claims, and development can be evaluated
in terms of what people are able to do or be, not just in terms of what their "utility"
is or in terms of their income or resources.

There are a number of ways in which Elster's and Sen's discussions of adaptation
differ. One is simply that Elster's discussion is much more systematic than Sen's.
Sen typically invokes cases of adaptation to make a point, but does not develop
a more fully articulated account of the sort that Elster provides, distinguishing
adaptation from other, related phenomena.[1] As regards the actual substance of their
discussions, Sen's writings on adaptation differ from Elster's in that Elster focuses
on sour grapes, whereas Sen is concerned specifically with various "underdogs" in
society. Another respect in which the discussions differ is that in Sen's discussions
the notion of *survival* tends to feature. When underdogs adapt to their situations, it
is sometimes—in Sen's examples—with a view to survival.

To pursue this claim, I use one of a number of passages where Sen invokes the
phenomenon of adaptation. In *On Ethics and Economics* he writes that:

> A person who has had a life of misfortune, with very limited opportunities, and rather little
> hope, may be more easily reconciled to deprivations than others reared in more fortunate
> and affluent circumstances. The metric of happiness may, therefore, distort the extent of de-
> privation, in a specific and biased way. The hopeless beggar, the precarious landless labourer,
> the dominated housewife, the hardened unemployed or the overexhausted coolie may all
> take pleasures in small mercies, and manage to suppress intense suffering for the necessity
> of continued survival, but it would be ethically deeply mistaken to attach a correspondingly
> small value to the loss of their well-being because of this survival strategy.   (Sen 1987: 45–6)

The related notions of adaptation with a view to survival, and of a strategy undertaken in the face of adversity with a view merely to continuing to live, can be
found in many of Sen's texts from his earlier to his later statements of the capability
approach (see, for example, Sen 1984: 309, 512; 1992: 6–7, and 1999: 63). The cases

---

[1] The nearest Sen comes to expressing the argument in a systematic way as one of three limitations
of the utilitarian perspective can be found in Sen (1999: 62).

Sen cites in the quotation above to exemplify the phenomenon of adaptation—the hopeless beggar, the precarious landless labourer, etc.—are very specific and are, as we will see, both in one sense broader, and in another narrower, than those which exemplify Elster's notion of "adaptive preferences". On the one hand, if an affluent but rejected lover who faces many opportunities in life decides that the object of his affection is not as beautiful as he earlier thought she was, and that someone he previously thought less attractive but who is more likely to respond positively to his overtures is to be preferred, this is no doubt a case of adaptive preferences in Elster's terms, since it is a form of sour grapes—the affluent lover's preferences are reversed in the light of a contraction in the feasible set. It is clearly not, however, the sort of phenomenon Sen has in mind. The affluent but fickle lover has a wide range of opportunities in life while the underdogs in Sen's examples typically do not. In this sense, Sen's examples are narrower than Elster's cases of adaptive preferences, since Sen focuses on cases of significant deprivation or inequality. However, Sen's examples are less restrictive than Elster's in another way. Consider the case of the dominated housewife who learns to live with her situation by accepting ideological claims put forward with a view to advancing the interests of men at the expense of women. In this context, Sen tells us that Simone de Beauvoir's work illuminated for him how "women readily accept the pro-inequality apologia as a true description of reality" (Sen 2003: 322). Gender inequality is one of a range of cases where Sen invokes how people might adjust to the inequitable conditions in which they find themselves. While he mentions such cases primarily in questioning the use of "utility"-based views in the context of justice rather than well-being, they fall squarely within the category of examples he mentions in discussing adaptation, though in Elster's terms they would not be cases of adaptive preferences if those who gain because of adaptation are men rather than women. In Elster's terms these are rather cases of manipulation.[2]

It is worth mentioning here another phenomenon which Elster distinguishes from adaptive preferences: "rationalization". Here the situation a person finds herself in shapes—indeed distorts—her *perception* rather than her *evaluations*. Elster (1983: 123) readily accepts that this situation is often hard to disentangle from one of adaptive preferences. In the case of the spurned lover, for example, both phenomena are arguably at work. The lover both changes his beliefs about the beauty of the woman who rejects him and alters his evaluation of the merits of different women. By contrast, Sen's discussion of adaptation (notably Sen 1993b and 2002: 473–4) often invokes what he terms "objective illusion"—which relates, roughly speaking,

---

[2] It may, of course, be claimed that even in these cases, women who adapt to their situations are doing so primarily, or in part, out of self-interest. So there may be some blurring of the distinction between the phenomena that Elster terms "adaptive preference formation" and "manipulation". The point I am making is that *if* there were a case of "pure" manipulation, that would not count as an instance of adaptive preference formation on Elster's account but would be a standard case of adaptation in the face of injustice for Sen. I am grateful to James Foster for raising this point.

to distortions in perception—and the Marxian notion of "false consciousness" in relation to such illusion. In spite of these differences between Elster and Sen, there are numerous overlaps between their discussions which sometimes obscure the differences. Just as in Sen's examples, where the underdog often reconciles herself to, or reduces her hopes or aspirations in the light of, her situation, so also in Elster's writings the phenomenon of adaptive preferences is usually described in terms of resignation or adjusted aspirations (Elster 1983: 113). In both discussions, also, people adjust to limited freedom in the range of choice open to them. Furthermore, both Elster and Sen clearly see adaptation as a problem for utilitarianism.

Sen's reference to a "survival strategy" in the quotation from *On Ethics and Economics* above can be seen as related to what he regards as the limits of Darwinian analysis in the social sciences. Sen has no worries about Darwinian analysis as an approach to how evolution takes place (2002: 485). Rather, his concerns have to do with what he calls the "Darwinian view of progress"—which relates to what constitutes progress and to the way in which evolution brings about progress.[3] Sen sees the Darwinian criterion of progress as involving two steps, one of which is more direct than the other. The first judges progress directly in terms of the quality of the species produced (488). Sen himself distinguishes this "quality-of-species" approach from a "quality-of-life" approach, which focuses on *individual* lives rather than species, and he sees his own capability approach as an instance of the latter type of approach to the evaluation of progress (486). The second step involves judging the excellence of the species in terms of reproductive success—"the power to survive and multiply and thus, collectively, to outnumber and outlive competing groups" (489).

It is in the context of this second step in the evaluation of progress that Sen returns to the notion of adaptation. He writes:

We recognize many virtues and achievements that do not help survival but that we do have reason to value; and on the other side there are many correlates of successful survival that we find deeply objectionable. For example, if a species of vassals—some variant of homo sapiens—is kept in inhuman conditions by some tribe and that species adapts and evolves into being super-rapid reproducers, must we accept that development as a sign of progress? An exact analogue of this is, of course, imposed on those animals on which we feed. But such an arrangement would hardly seem acceptable for human beings, and it is not at all clear ... that it should be acceptable in the case of animals either.   (494)

Here adaptation is explicitly linked to survival and evolution and Sen finds the inhuman conditions which lead to it objectionable even if it promotes reproductive success. There are at least two points that are central to Sen's argument: (1) survival is not the only thing we have reason to value; and (2) if evolutionary pressures lead

---

[3] It may be argued that Sen's account of the Darwinian view of progress is inaccurate. My purpose here is not to defend that account, but only to elucidate Sen's views of adaptation in the light of that account.

us to adapt to inhuman conditions and be "super-rapid" reproducers, the "quality of species" judged in terms of reproductive success is *completely* unconnected to the quality of life of individual members of the species. The first point suggests that we should be concerned with a multiplicity of things we have reason to value—and that is entirely compatible with Sen's capability approach, which is "inescapably pluralist" at a number of levels (Sen 1999: 76), and allows for a variety of different valuable functionings of which merely surviving can be seen as the most basic. The second point underlines what Sen sees as the limitations of the quality-of-species as compared to the quality-of-life view.

Sen also expresses a worry that "the Darwinian perspective, seen as a general view of progress, suggests concentration on adapting the species rather than adjusting the environment in which the species lead their lives" (Sen 2002: 496). Adapting the species could involve either lending a "helping hand to nature" through genetic improvement or "trusting to nature" to weed out unfit genes. Neither approach, Sen thinks, suggests that we should adjust or reform the environment with a view to improving the quality of life. While Sen's claims here do not distinguish between different views of the quality of life, his claim that we should not in general see adaptation of the species as a solution without seriously considering the possibility of adapting the environment to improve people's lives and make progress is relevant to modern views, especially views of happiness.

IV. LAYARD ON HAPPINESS, ADAPTATION AND EVOLUTION

Richard Layard's recent book *Happiness: Lessons from a New Science* reports on, and draws out lessons for, policy from the large recent literature on happiness across many disciplines, including economics. Layard defines "happiness" to mean "feeling good—enjoying life and wanting the feeling to continue" and by "unhappiness" he means "feeling bad—and wishing things were different" (Layard 2005: 12). He also explicitly defends utilitarianism in something like the original form it took in Jeremy Bentham's statement of it.[4] On Layard's account, it is the view that "the right action is the one which produces the greatest overall happiness" (Layard 2005: 112).

The definition of adaptation which underlies the recent literature on happiness in applied psychology, which Layard cites a great deal, runs as follows:

---

[4] Bentham (1970: 12–13) writes that "an action is conformable to the principle of utility . . . when the tendency it has to augment the happiness of the community is greater than any it has to diminish it".

"adaptation...refers to any action, process, or mechanism that reduces the effects (perceptual, physiological, attentional, motivational, hedonic and so on) of a constant or repeated stimulus" while "[h]edonic adaptation is adaptation to stimuli that is affectively relevant" (Frederick and Loewenstein 1999: 302). It should be clear that this definition of "adaptation" is quite distinct from those operating in the writings of Elster and Sen. Nonetheless, this definition encompasses the notion of adaptation used in the well-known claim that people increase their aspirations in line with rising incomes, thus dampening any extra satisfaction derived from increases in income (see, for example, Easterlin 1974, 2001). As people's income repeatedly increases, any mechanism, action or process—such as an adjustment of aspirations—which reduces the effects of such increases on levels of satisfaction or happiness can be seen as "adaptation". Unlike Elster's concept of adaptive preferences this notion is not restricted to "sour grapes"; in contrast to Sen's examples, it is not necessarily about the way in which underdogs adjust. As we saw earlier, one key respect in which Elster's and Sen's discussions are similar is that adaptation or adjustment of attitudes—desires, preferences or aspirations—occurs in response to some *limit* in freedom, whether it be some limit in what is feasible (in Elster's case), or some limit in a person's opportunities which makes her an underdog (in Sen's case). By contrast, in the happiness literature adaptation can occur in response to *expansions* in what is feasible or attainable.[5]

There are some peculiar implications of this conceptual difference when one compares Layard's work with Sen's and Elster's. Perhaps the most striking emerges in Elster's discussion of the Industrial Revolution. Elster suggests that if people's aspirations rose in this context, it would mean that they are *released from adaptive preferences* and may be frustrated as their hopes rise, even though they might become more free or autonomous. This same rise in aspirations would, of course—in the modern literature on happiness, including Layard's work—be seen as *adaptation*. Indeed, Elster implicitly acknowledges the possibility that people are not content with ever higher levels of income and sees it as a form of *addictive*, rather than *adaptive*, preference. He writes that "there may come a point beyond which the frustrating search for material welfare no longer represents a liberation from adaptive preferences, but rather enslavement to addictive preferences" (Elster 1983: 136).

The possibilities of confusion arising from such diverse uses of "adaptation" are considerable. Nonetheless, in spite of the confusion there is sometimes a convergence of ideas. One example of this occurs in Layard's discussion of the fact that people "adapt" to higher levels of income by raising their aspirations. He starts

---

[5] Indeed, in this literature, there is a distinction between "upwards" and "downwards" adaptation—which would, for example, cover the distinct cases of whether aspirations adjust upwards or downwards in response to a change in material circumstances. See, for example, Clark (forthcoming).

from a utilitarian assumption that happiness is the only ultimate end or value. Adaptation is then good or bad depending on whether it does, or does not, promote happiness. In the case of adaptation to higher levels of material prosperity, it dampens happiness and is bad. Indeed, the moral that Layard draws from empirical research is that "income is addictive!" He goes on to add that "[s]ince most people do not foresee the addictive effects of income and spending, taxation has a useful role, just as it has with other forms of addiction like smoking" (Layard 2005: 229). Layard's conclusion is prefigured in Elster's discussion of the addictive pursuit of material prosperity.

The relevance of Sen's writings for Layard's work emerges starkly when one considers the conclusions Layard draws from the empirical literature on happiness in the context of physical and mental impairments. Sen clearly sees the disabled as potentially falling under the category of underdogs who might learn to be happy with or cheerfully accept their situation.[6] On this point, the psychological literature on adaptation suggests that Sen is right to be concerned and indeed there is strong evidence of "adaptation" in as much as some people who have become seriously impaired (e.g. paraplegic or quadriplegic as a result of an accident) report surprisingly high levels of happiness (Frederick and Lowenstein 1999: 312). Sen's key argument is that the metric of happiness may provide a flawed measure of the quality of life in this sort of case and can be misleading in evaluating the quality of life and egalitarian claims. He would suggest that we should be concerned with what people can do or be, and consider adapting the environment or in other ways increasing the opportunities open to them. So, in the case of the disabled, we should be concerned with the extent to which the social environment allows the disabled to do or to be certain things, such as gain access to public spaces or find work.

To see the relevance of Sen's arguments, consider Layard's discussion of disability and mental illness. Layard writes that "we ought to be specially concerned about those misfortunes to which it is difficult to adapt. For example, persistent mental illness is impossible to adapt to" (Layard 2005: 121). He also thinks that one reason health "never comes through as the top determinant of happiness ... may be partly because people have a considerable ability to adapt to physical limitations" (69). One might conclude that since it is difficult to adapt to some forms of mental illness, but quite easy to adapt to serious physical impairments, we ought to be less concerned about the physically impaired than about those with specific mental illnesses. Layard himself concludes that "people can never adapt to chronic pain or to mental illness—feelings that come from inside themselves rather than limitations on their external activities. The control of such suffering must be one of our top

---

[6] See his lecture on "Equality of What?", in which the earliest version of the capability approach was articulated (Sen 1982: 367).

priorities" (69). On this view, one would be less concerned about cases where humans tend to adapt to misfortunes. One might even take a positive view of such adaptation—as a sign of "fitness"—and not give priority to action to improve the quality of life of people who suffer from certain misfortunes. Equally, one might not give priority to, or even pursue actions to, adapt the environment they live in. In the case of people with certain impairments, I find this conclusion very unattractive.

Does Layard have a plausible response to the adaptation problem? Layard adopts a robust approach in defence of his brand of utilitarianism (2005: 120 ff.). He accepts the fact that the poor or oppressed might—as Sen would have it—adapt to their living conditions. But Layard believes that this does not lead to neglect of the poor, since the rich adapt even more (to higher levels of income) and there is a case for redistribution, so that his utilitarian approach is "pro-poor". He goes on to argue that the poor and oppressed do dislike poverty and oppression, and indeed that is why we worry about these phenomena. So the claim must be that while people adapt to poverty, they do not adapt "completely"—they still dislike poverty. Finally, he claims that "Ethical theory should surely focus on what people feel, rather than what people think is good for them. If we accept the Marxist idea of 'false consciousness,' we play God and decide what is good for others, even if they will never feel it to be so" (121). These claims are very bluntly expressed, and while Layard neither expands on nor defends them, they do pick up on a very general concern with Sen's writings. The claim is that those who reject a happiness- or "utility"-based view because they do not always take at face value what people report about how they feel or how satisfied or happy they say they are—because of concerns relating to adaptation or "false consciousness"—must decide what is good for others, and thus be paternalistic. This claim has been made more carefully in some of the more philosophical literature on Sen's work (particularly Sugden 2006). I cannot here expand on what Sen has to say about "false consciousness" (on this see Qizilbash 2007b) or on how he responds to claims that his views on adaptation lead to some generalized form of paternalism (see Sen 2006). It is worth noting nonetheless that because of his utilitarian commitments, Layard himself presupposes that happiness is the ultimate good—and that is a philosophical pre- sumption or doctrine rather than a claim based on any examination of people's views or feelings. The fact that happiness researchers use survey questionnaires to consult people's feelings does not make much difference, since nothing in the capability approach excludes consulting people's views, and indeed applications of the approach do sometimes use survey questionnaires with a view to gaining information on the functionings or capabilities people value (see, *inter alia*, Klasen 2000; Qizilbash and Clark 2005; Clark and Qizilbash forthcoming).[7] Furthermore,

---

[7] This is one of a range of reasons why it can be argued that in fact the adaptation problem also applies to Sen's capability approach. On this see: Nussbaum (1988); Sumner (1996); Qizilbash (1997); Qizilbash and Clark (2005); Clark (2007); and Clark and Qizilbash (2008).

some of the policies which emerge from Layard's utilitarian approach might themselves be seen as "paternalistic" if they are motivated by a view of what is good for people, quite aside from what they think or feel. For example, a policy of increasing taxes on those at high income levels with a view to promoting happiness might be regarded as "paternalistic" because Layard claims that people do not properly anticipate how limited an impact ever-increasing income has on happiness, and so he makes an "expert" judgement about what is and is not good for them. So issues about "paternalism" arise in Layard's work as well, even if he does not invoke "false consciousness" (see Qizilbash 2007b).

Layard also links happiness to species survival. While in his classic statement of classical utilitarianism Bentham famously wrote that "Nature has placed mankind under the governance of two sovereign masters, *pain* and *pleasure*" (Bentham 1970: 33), Layard tells us that happiness is "supremely important" because it is our "overall motivational device". Without this drive, he tells us, "we humans would have perished long ago". He adds that "what makes us feel good (sex, food, love, friendship and so on) is generally good for survival. And what causes pain is bad for survival (fire, dehydration, poison, ostracism)", so that by seeking to feel good and avoiding pain "we have survived as a species" (Layard 2005: 24). Happiness—on his view—drives us because of its beneficial effects on species survival.

It is unsurprising that elements of what Sen terms the Darwinian view of progress emerge in Layard's work alongside his utilitarianism. So Layard writes that

[b]y using our brains we have conquered nature. We have defeated most vertebrates and many insects and bacteria. In consequence we have increased our numbers from a few thousand to a few billion in a very short time—an astonishing achievement. The challenge now is to use our mastery over nature to master ourselves and to give us all more of the happiness we all want.   (Layard 2005: 27)

Since Layard endorses utilitarianism and one aspect of the Darwinian view of progress—in as much as he clearly judges progress partially in terms of reproductive success—it is unsurprising that Layard sees adaptation in a positive light when it promotes happiness and thus presumably (on his view) species survival. While it is hard to separate out Layard's Darwinism and his utilitarianism—and hence to separate out the quality-of-species and quality-of-life views in his work—it is easy to see why adaptation to poverty or disability is not seen as a problem on his view. It is thus not surprising that when people with physical impairments adapt to their misfortunes, his response is not—as in recent work on the capability approach and disability (see Sen 2004 and Nussbaum 2006 *inter alia*)—to be concerned about changing the social environment to allow them to do and be various things.

V. Binmore's Contractarian
View of Justice

Ken Binmore's rich and voluminous writings on game theory and the social contract (Binmore 1994, 1998, 2005) articulate a distinct contractarian view of justice. It simply is not possible to provide a summary of Binmore's complex views here and I restrict myself to specfic aspects of his account which are relevant to this chapter. Binmore's is a contractarian account of justice in as much as morality is understood in terms of a social contract. In developing his account Binmore borrows the concept of the "original position" from John Rawls. In that position, according to Rawls, people agree on principles of justice behind a "veil of ignorance". Behind the veil they do not know, amongst other things, their position in society—their class or social status—or their level of intelligence and position in the distribution of natural assets or even their conception of the good (Rawls 1972: 118–92). However, Binmore does not use Rawls's account of the currency of advantage in terms of which interpersonal comparisons are made behind the veil. Rather he turns to John Harsanyi's famous version of utilitarianism.

Harsanyi's statement of utilitarianism changed over the years (see Harsanyi 1953, 1955, 1977, 1982, 1995). He famously builds on the writings of Adam Smith in supposing that human empathy is the basis of interpersonal comparisons. To make interpersonal comparisons, Harsanyi thinks that we use imaginative sympathy and put ourselves into other people's shoes to see what it is like to be in a particular situation. We can thus make comparisons such as: I prefer to be person A in situation X to being person B in situation Y.[8] This is essentially an *intra*personal comparison—a comparison of two possible lives for one person. To go beyond this to make *inter*personal comparisons, Harsanyi needs more. He thinks that at some deep level we are all similar, so that when the influence of upbringing and various other factors is ironed out our "extended preferences"—our preferences purified from the distortions of taste and upbringing—are essentially the same (Harsanyi 1977: 59). As a consequence, interpersonal comparisons should come out the same on the basis of extended preferences whoever makes them. Nonetheless, since the influence of upbringing and other factors is not ironed out in real life, this account may not help with how we actually make interpersonal comparisons.

Unlike Harsanyi, Binmore does not attempt to iron out the differences in preferences which arise from upbringing and so on. Instead he builds on Harsanyi's own observation that "[i]n actuality, interpersonal utility comparisons between people of similar cultural background, social status and personality are likely to show a high degree of interobserver validity" (Binmore 1994: 62). In the light

---

[8] Similar arguments were put forward by William Vickrey, Kenneth Arrow and Amartya Sen. See Sen (1996: 13–15)

of this, Binmore supposes that preferences are malleable to some degree and are formed through social evolution. If people's "empathetic preferences"—Binmore's term for the preferences they have when they perform acts of empathy—diverge and are fixed in the "short run", in the "medium run" they are variable. Once social evolution has operated—through learning and imitation—people's empathetic preferences will converge to the point that they are identical (Binmore 1994: 64–6, 86–7). On his account, behind the veil of ignorance, people make interpersonal comparisons using these identical preferences. So Binmore is able to use Harsanyi's notion of preferences formed through empathy while using a "naturalistic" account of how people come to have identical empathetic preferences and so also the same standard in making interpersonal comparisons of utility.

What are the implications of Sen's writings on adaptation and evolution for Binmore's theory? If "empathetic preferences' are formed through evolutionary pressures with a view to survival, then Sen's discussion of the quality-of-species view suggests that their formation and satisfaction may not reflect a decent quality of life or indeed be connected with welfare at all. They may reflect "fitness", but still have little to do with the quality of a person's life. This point may not pose any serious worry for Binmore's account, since he does not claim that satisfaction of empathetic preferences constitutes welfare. Instead he adopts a "revealed preference" account of "utility" which is purely descriptive and codifies behavior while merely demanding consistency (Binmore 2005: 117–18). This account notoriously does not provide a plausible account of well-being (see e.g. Qizilbash 1996: 63) or even of value (see Broome 1978). Indeed, Binmore does not follow Harsanyi (1982, 1995) in claiming that the preferences used in his account should be informed or rational so that their satisfaction might connect with value or welfare.

Even setting aside the standard worries about a revealed preference view, the adaptation problem arises for Binmore's account because he accepts the malleability of preferences. To be sure, Binmore does not claim that preferences are *entirely* malleable. Rather he accepts that "our preference for clean and healthy foods seems likely to be fairly resistant to change". By contrast, "people's preferences among life-styles are very much a construct of *social* evolution, and hence highly vulnerable to modifying influences. Indeed, we seem to have a built-in urge to imitate the behaviour of those around us, and the capacity to learn to like what we are accustomed to do" (Binmore 1996: 63). The notion of learning invoked here is clearly akin to a form of adaptation in as much as it is a variety of habituation. Indeed, Binmore uses the term "learning" in a less restrictive sense than Elster does. Furthermore, what Binmore thinks of as preferences which evolve through social evolution may include what Elster calls "adaptive preferences" as well as the cases Sen cites when he discusses adaptation. Sen would thus no doubt be worried by the use of socially evolved preferences in an account of justice.

Binmore might remind us that his account makes no presumption that the satisfaction of empathetic preferences constitutes welfare or advantage. His revealed preference account allows for *any* form of motivation, so that preferences need not be self-interested or even link with the person's own interests, however broadly these are construed. Indeed, he makes no claim that interpersonal comparisons of "utility" are interpersonal comparisons of welfare or even of advantage. But then, it is not obvious that Binmore's account is a standard "justice as mutual advantage" account of the "standard" contractarian sort, in which reasonable or rational self-interested agents agree on a social contract or agreement for mutual advantage.

Let us suppose then that Binmore's account is "non-standard". He is aware that because empathetic preferences are shaped by social evolution, they can be influenced by the distribution of power in society. In relation to his concept of "empathy equilibrium"—in which nobody has an incentive to pretend that their empathetic preferences are other than they actually are—he writes that such an equilibrium can be thought of

as encapsulating the cultural history of a society that led people to adopt one standard of interpersonal comparison rather than another. It is true that this history will be shaped by the way in which power is distributed in the society under study, but this is the kind of bullet we have had to bite a great deal already.   (Binmore 2005: 126)

The standard of interpersonal comparisons may thus be shaped by inequalities of power between men and women in some particular culture. It may be "culturally relative" and indeed Binmore explicitly defends "relativism" in the light of a variety of objections (Binmore 2005: 47–53). He may claim that there is no "non-relative" standpoint from which we can judge that the standard(s) operating within a culture is (are) inappropriate for making interpersonal comparisons. Indeed, he may suggest that Sen mistakenly attempts to adopt such a standpoint in stating his adaptation problem in relation to dominated housewives and other underdogs in some societies who are "mentally conditioned" and accept some "pro-inequality apologia". Thus, I expect that the key aspect of Binmore's view which would come into play in responding to the problem that inequalities can distort preferences, desires or perceptions would be relativism.[9] Sen himself rejects relativism, notably in his paper co-authored with Martha Nussbaum (Nussbaum and Sen 1989), and it goes well beyond the scope of this paper to evaluate Binmore's defense of relativism in relation to Sen's view of it.

Nonetheless, there is another basic issue raised by the fact that the standard of interpersonal comparisons can be molded by power inequalities. Rawls's original position—which, as we saw, Binmore invokes—was constructed with a view to removing, as far as possible, the influences of inequalities of status when deciding on principles of justice. If people's empathetic preferences behind the veil can be shaped by, or adapt to, an unequal distribution of power, that seems to undermine

---

[9]   Having said this, it should be noted that Binmore explicitly accuses Sen of paternalism when he casually refers to "modern paternalists like Amartya Sen" (2005: 122). Indeed, it is likely that Binmore would raise this issue of "paternalism" in responding to issues about adaptation.

the motivation for using the original position in a theory of justice. This problem arises for Binmore in as much as his is a modern contractarian account in which the original position is presumably supposed to negate the effects of inequality of status.

VI. Conclusions

Sen's scattered discussions of adaptation do not provide a systematic account of this phenomenon. They differ from Elster's account of "adaptive preferences" not only because they do not focus on sour grapes but also because they tend often to invoke the necessity of survival for various underdogs. When these remarks are read in combination with Sen's discussions of the Darwinian view of progress their implications for modern normative economics—whether this focuses on happiness as in Layard's writings, or takes the form of a contractarian view of justice of the sort that Binmore adopts—are clearer. In Layard's case, the policy conclusions he draws from the happiness literature confirm worries that Sen raises. While Layard's main defense in the face of the adaptation problem suggests that Sen's view is paternalistic, Layard's own writings can be seen as paternalistic. In Binmore's account, on the other hand, the empathetic preferences used to make interpersonal comparisons are not clearly linked to people's interests, so that the satisfaction of these preferences does not necessarily constitute well-being or advantage. The fact that these preferences can be molded by social evolution means that inequalities of power within a culture can influence the social contract agreed in the original position. Even if Binmore defends relativism, the influence of power inequalities on the currency of interpersonal comparisons would appear, to some extent, to undermine the basic motivation for the use of the original position. The adaptation problem thus poses significant difficulties for both these contemporary accounts in normative economics.

References

BENTHAM, J. (1970), *An Introduction to the Principles of Morals and Legislation*, ed. J. H. Burns and H. L. A. Hart (London: Athlone Press).

BINMORE, K. (1996), *Game Theory and the Social Contract. Volume 1: Playing Fair* (Cambridge, Mass.: MIT Press).

—— (1998), *Game Theory and the Social Contract. Volume 2: Just Playing* (Cambridge, Mass.: MIT Press).

BINMORE, K. (2005), *Natural Justice* (Oxford: Oxford University Press).

BROOME, J. (1978), "Choice and Value in Economics", *Oxford Economic Papers*, 30: 313–30.

CLARK, D. (forthcoming), "Adaptation, Poverty and Well-Being: Some Issues and Obser-vations with Special Reference to the Capability Approach and Development Studies", *Journal of Human Development.*

—— and QIZILBASH, M. (2008), "Core Poverty, Vagueness and Adaptation: A New Method-ology and Some Results for South Africa", *Journal of Development Studies*, 44: 519–44.

CRISP, R., and MOORE, A. (1996), "Welfarism and Moral Theory", *Australasian Journal of Philosophy*, 74: 598–613.

CROCKER, D. (1992), "Functioning and Capability: The Foundations of Sen's and Nussbaum's Development Ethic", *Political Theory*, 20: 584–612.

EASTERLIN, R. (1974), "Does Economic Growth Improve the Human Lot? Some Empirical Evidence", in P. A. David and M. W. Reder (eds), *Nations and Households in Economic Growth* (New York: Academic Press), 89–125.

—— (2001), "Income and Happiness: Towards a Unified Theory", *Economic Journal*, 111: 465–84.

ELSTER, J. (1982), "Sour Grapes: Utilitarianism and the Genesis of Wants", in A. Sen and B. Williams (eds), *Utilitarianism and Beyond* (Cambridge: Cambridge University Press), 219–38.

—— (1983), *Sour Grapes: Studies in the Subversion of Rationality* (Cambridge: Cambridge University Press).

—— (1989), "The Market and the Forum: Three Varieties of Political Theory", in J. Elster and A. Hylland (eds), *Foundations of Social Choice Theory* (Cambridge: Cambridge University Press), 103–32.

FREDERICK, S., and LOEWENSTEIN, G. (1999), "Hedonic Adaptation", in D. Kahneman, E. Diener and N. Schwartz (eds), *Well-Being: The Foundations of Hedonic Adaptation* (New York: Russell Sage Foundation), 302–73.

HARSANYI, J. (1953), "Cardinal Utility in Welfare Economics and the Theory of Risk-Taking", *Journal of Political Economy*, 61: 434–5.

—— (1955), "Cardinal Welfare, Individualistic Ethics and Interpersonal Comparisons of Utility", *Journal of Political Economy*, 63, 309–21.

—— (1977), *Rational Behavior and Bargaining Equilibrium in Games and Social Situations* (Cambridge: Cambridge University Press).

—— (1982), "Morality and the Theory of Rational Behavior", in A. Sen and B. Williams (eds), *Utilitarianism and Beyond* (Cambridge: Cambridge University Press), 39–62.

—— (1995), "A Theory of Prudential Values and a Rule Utilitarian Theory of Morality", *Social Choice and Welfare*, 12: 319–33.

KLASEN, S. (2000), "Measuring Poverty and Deprivation in South Africa", *Review of Income and Wealth*, 46: 33–58.

LAYARD, R. (2005), *Happiness: Lessons from a New Science* (London: Penguin).

NUSSBAUM, M. (1988), "Nature, Function and Capability: Aristotle on Political Distribu-tion", *Oxford Studies in Ancient Philosophy*, 6, (suppl. vol.): 145–84.

—— (2000), *Women and Human Development: The Capabilities Approach* (Cambridge: Cambridge University Press).

—— (2006), *Frontiers of Justice: Disability, Nationality, Species Membership* (Cambridge, Mass.: Belknap Press).

—— and Sen, A. (1989), "Internal Criticism and Indian Rationalist Traditions", in M. Krausz (ed.), *Relativism: Interpretation and Confrontation* (Notre Dame, Ind.: University of Notre Dame Press), 299–325.

Qizilbash, M. (1996), "The Concept of Well-Being", *Economics and Philosophy*, 14: 51–73.

—— (1997), "A Weakness of the Capability Approach with Respect to Gender Justice", *Journal of International Development*, 9: 251–63.

—— (2006a), "Capability, Happiness and Adaptation in Sen and J.S. Mill", *Utilitas*, 18: 20–32.

—— (2006b), "Well-Being, Adaptation and Human Limitations", *Philosophy*, 59 (suppl.): 83–109.

—— (2007a), "Social Choice and Individual Capabilities", *Politics, Philosophy and Economics*, 6: 169–92.

—— (2007b), "Utilitarianism, 'Adaptation' and Paternalism", paper presented at the conference on "Poverty and Capital", University of Manchester, July 2007.

—— and Clark, D. (2005), "The Capability Approach and Fuzzy Poverty Measures: An Application to the South African Context", *Social Indicators Research*, 74: 103–39.

Rawls, J. (1972), *A Theory of Justice* (Oxford: Oxford University Press).

Sen, A. (1982), *Choice, Welfare and Measurement* (Oxford: Blackwell).

—— (1984), *Resources, Values and Development* (Oxford: Blackwell).

—— (1987), *On Ethics and Economics* (Oxford: Blackwell).

—— (1992), *Inequality Re-examined* (Oxford: Oxford University Press).

—— (1993a), "Capability and Well-Being", in M. Nussbaum and A. Sen (eds), *The Quality of Life* (Oxford: Oxford University Press), 30–53.

—— (1993b), "Positional Objectivity", *Philosophy and Public Affairs*, 22: 83–135.

—— (1997), *On Economic Inequality*, expanded edn (Oxford: Clarendon Press).

—— (1999), *Development as Freedom* (Oxford: Oxford University Press).

—— (2002), *Rationality and Freedom* (Cambridge, Mass.: Belknap Press).

—— (with B. Agarwal, J. Humphries and I. Robeyns) (2003), "Continuing the Conversation", *Feminist Economics*, 9: 319–32.

—— (2004), "Disability and Justice", paper presented at the Second International World Bank Disability Conference, Washington.

—— (2006), "Reason, Freedom and Well-Being", *Utilitas*, 18: 80–96.

Sugden, R. (2006), "What We Desire, What We Have Reason to Desire, Whatever We Might Desire: Mill and Sen on the Value of Opportunity", *Utilitas*, 18: 33–51.

Sumner, L. (1996), *Welfare, Happiness and Ethics* (Oxford: Clarendon Press).

CHAPTER 5

RIGHTS AND INTERESTS

T. M. SCANLON

I. INTRODUCTION

As Amartya Sen writes, "There is something deeply attractive in the idea that every person anywhere in the world, irrespective of citizenship or territorial legislation, has some basic rights, which others should respect" (2004: 315).[1] This idea is attractive in part because these rights seem to state the moral case for creating and maintaining legal institutions and social practices that protect and promote crucial aspects of human well-being. To serve this critical purpose it is important that rights themselves should be, as Sen says, independent of existing laws and social practices. It is also important that these rights have special normative force—that claims about rights should be something more than claims that "It would be better if…" Moreover, if rights are to serve the purpose I have mentioned, they need to be able to stand against appeals to what would be good to have happen—they need to "trump" such appeals, as Ronald Dworkin (1977) says. This is because actions, laws and policies that violate individual rights—such as imprisonment without trial, torture of detainees, invasions of privacy, and curtailment of freedom of expression—are often held to be justified on the ground that they are necessary in order to produce better consequences, or to prevent very bad ones.

---

[1] As will be evident to the reader, this essay owes much to Sen's writings on rights. It also owes much to my conversations with him, particularly in the seminar on rights that we gave jointly with Richard Tuck at Harvard University in the fall term of 2006.

But these seemingly essential features of rights—their special normative force, their independence of established institutions, and their independence of direct appeals to what would yield the best consequences—naturally give rise to skepticism. If rights are not justified either by their enactment by legitimate institutions or by the good consequences of respecting them, how are they justified? Where does their supposed special normative force come from?

Skepticism about rights can take several different forms. One form is an instance of a more general skepticism about all moral claims. (Skepticism of this kind would be one way of arriving at the view that the only rights are legal rights.) More commonly, skepticism about rights flows from a consequentialist moral outlook. On such a view, there are moral truths, but no moral *rights*: all true moral claims are claims about what leads to the best consequences. (This could lead to a different version, perhaps Bentham's version, of the idea that the only rights are legal rights.)

A third challenge to rights, which I will be concerned with in this paper, questions whether rights are a distinctive and important moral category within a non-consequentialist moral framework. Against the background of a consequentialist view, in which the basic moral requirement is to act so as to produce the best possible consequences, rights which constrain the pursuit of such consequences may be controversial, but they have, or at least claim to have, a distinctive and well-defined role in moral thinking. But what distinct role is there for rights within a moral framework that takes duties and obligations as morally basic? If rights can be defined as certain complexes of duties and the absence of duties, what reason is there to speak of rights at all? Claims about rights may be at most a convenient way of referring to moral facts that can be stated correctly, and more fundamentally, in other terms.

II. The Structure of Rights

There is fairly wide agreement among philosophers writing about rights that claims about rights involve, on the one hand, claims about duties that particular agents have and, on the other, claims about the values that these duties protect or promote, which ground the claim that there are such duties. Joseph Raz (1986: 166), for example, writes that " 'X has a right' if and only if X can have rights, and, other things being equal, an aspect of X's well-being (his interest) is a sufficient reason for holding some other person(s) to be under a duty." Similarly, Judith Thomson (1990: 41) holds that rights in the strict sense are claims that have duties as correlates, and that we have such claims on others just in case we are subject to moral law and have inherently individual interests—those interests that, in her view, play a crucial role in justifying the claims and the correlative duties. I myself have maintained that claims about rights are claims about the necessary and feasible limitations on the discretion to act of individual or institutional agents (Scanlon 1978). Much earlier, Mill wrote (*Utilitarianism*: 327) that a moral right is a claim of an individual that society ought to protect (that is, that needs to be protected if overall utility is to be promoted).

The details of these formulations differ in important ways. But they all agree in identifying two elements in claims about rights: duties that constrain certain agents, and interests or values in terms of which these duties are justified. My main concern in this paper will be with the relation between these two elements. Most of what I have to say will apply to all of the views of rights that I have mentioned, but I will have mainly my own view in mind. In my view, a claim that there is a right involves two claims. The first is the claim that certain interests are of great importance. The second is a claim that duties imposing limits on the discretion of individuals or institutional agents to act in certain ways are necessary to protect these interests, and that there are such constraints which are feasible—that is to say, which provide this protection an acceptable cost to other interests. The second claim depends on empirical claims about how agents are likely to behave in the absence of such constraints and about what the effects of general adherence to these constraints will be.

Claims about rights vary in how specific they are about the duties in question. Some (what I will call *defined rights claims*) identify these duties quite clearly. Familiar claims about the rights of freedom of expression, or the right not to be imprisoned without trial, have this character. Other rights claims (what I will call *abstract rights claims*) merely identify the interests at stake and assert that there is a need for duties to protect them and that *some* duties of this sort can and should be found which have a tolerable cost in other terms. As Sen (2004: 327) emphasizes, the duties that a rights claim holds to be necessary need not be enshrined in law. It can also be important, and in some cases sufficient, that these rights be generally recognized and respected by individuals as moral constraints on their conduct.

III. IS THIS ACCOUNT CONSEQUENTIALIST, OR INSTRUMENTAL?

All of the views I have mentioned hold that the duties which a right involves are held to be justified by the fact that if they are enshrined in law or otherwise recognized they will serve to protect certain important interests. This rationale may suggest that all of these views are at base consequentialist or, at least, forms of "rule consequentialism". But this is not necessarily the case. The defining feature of a consequentialist view is that it takes the goodness of states of affairs as its single ultimate ground of justification. My account of rights (Scanlon 1978) admits of a consequentialist interpretation, and when I first presented that view I interpreted it in this way. But this now seems to me a mistake. Although my account can be given a consequentialist interpretation, it can also be understood within a contractualist moral framework, which takes as basic not the value of the state of affairs that an action or policy would lead to but rather the justifiability of an action or policy to every individual (Scanlon 1998). On this interpretation the basic claim underlying a right is not that constraints on the discretion of individual or institutional agents is necessary in order to prevent consequences that are bad in themselves, but rather that it would be reasonable for individuals to reject institutions or principles of individual conduct that do not incorporate such constraints.

Related to the charge of consequentialism is the idea that accounts of rights like Raz's and mine are instrumentalist—that is, on such an account rights are merely means for the prevention of certain results rather than fundamental moral considerations. On a consequentialist interpretation of the view I have offered, this charge would have merit, since according to consequentialism only one thing is of fundamental moral significance—the goodness of states of affairs—and everything else is of importance only as a means of achieving this. On a contractualist account, however, things are quite different. In a contractualist view, claims about rights are justified in the same way as claims about duties or about right and wrong generally, namely with reference to what would be allowed by principles that individuals could not reasonably reject. So rights are as fundamental as any other category of right and wrong. This does, however, raise the possibility that rights might "disappear" in the third way I mentioned above: that there may be nothing distinctive about rights claims as compared with other claims about right and wrong.

IV. What is Distinctive about Rights?

Even if all rights involve correlative duties, not all duties correspond to rights. As Frances Kamm says (2007: 239, citing Feinberg 1970), "In a world without rights held by other people, there could still be duties". One could, for example, have a duty to do what will promote the best consequences simply because of the value of those consequences, not in virtue of anyone's claim that one do this. The duties involved in rights, by contrast, are duties *owed to* particular individuals.

Some writers appear to suggest that this *individual directed* aspect of rights is accounted for by the nature of the values that justify them. It appears that in Raz's view, for example, what is special about the duties that define rights is that they are justified by certain interests of individuals. Thomson's reference to "inherently individual interests" suggests something similar.

Interests underlying many rights do have this individual-directed character. This seems to be so, for example, in the case of the right to privacy, which is a set of duties (not to pry, observe and so on) which are justified by their role in protecting the legitimate interest that individuals have in being able to control who can observe or know about certain aspects of their lives.

In the case of privacy, the individual interests that justify the right are also the interests that are interfered with when that right is violated—the interests of the individual whose right is violated. The same may be true of the values justifying many other rights. But it does not seem to be true of all commonly recognized rights. As Raz (1986: 179) notes, it does not seem to be true in the case of the right of freedom of expression. What justifies this right is not simply the individual interest that is interfered with when this right is violated—the interest that individuals have in being able to speak and write what they think on certain topics. These individual interests are no doubt important. But the values that justify the right of freedom of expression, and make it so important, include other interests, such as the interest that others have in not having the information available to them filtered by government censorship, the interest we all have in scientific and cultural progress, and the interest that citizens have in a well-functioning democracy, and in having governmental power checked by the reactions of an informed electorate. These are all, at base, individual interests, but they are interests in having a system that functions in a certain way—interests in the maintenance of certain public goods. An important part of the idea behind the right of freedom of expression is that these public goods are unacceptably threatened if governments have the power to regulate expression in certain ways.

Here it may be helpful to compare the case for this right with moral claims arising from other public goods, such as avoiding the consequences of global climate change. If these consequences are severe, then any set of principles that left individuals and institutions free to act in the ways that will have these results would be one that affected individuals could reasonably reject: some constraints on this discretion to act are needed. If this is all that is said, and no specific set of constraints is specified, let alone generally adopted, then what we have is analogous to what I called above an abstract rights claim. In this situation, would I be acting wrongly if I made no effort to curb my consumption of fossil fuels? Perhaps so, although in the absence of a general change in behavior by others my doing this alone would have no significant impact on the problem. What is clearer is that I would be acting wrongly in not doing what I can to bring about such a change, by making known my willingness to go along with that change, encouraging others to do so, contributing to organizations that advocate such a change in policy and so on.[2] But even if it

---

[2] These correspond to the imperfect duties which Sen mentions (2004: 339–41), to do what one can to try to get human rights effectively recognized. I agree that these imperfect duties are real and important. But I would distinguish them from the duties that make up the right itself.

would be wrong not to do these things, it is less clear that in failing to do so I would be violating anyone's rights.

Now suppose that some specific set of constraints, which distribute the burdens fairly, are quite widely accepted as the way of dealing with this problem, and widely followed. We would then have something at least analogous to what I called above a defined right. In such a situation it is much clearer that it would be wrong for me to violate the recognized constraints, just as it is wrong to violate any fair practice that is widely followed as the way to provide some important public good. But would we say that if I fail to obey these constraints I am violating the rights of others? It is not clear to me that we would. Perhaps the answer depends on the form taken by the constraints in question. If they specify that (absent special justification) someone driving alone should pick up others who are standing at designated spots waiting for rides, then it might be said that in failing to do this I violate a right of those who are standing there. But we might not say that I am violating a right when I violate a constraint against taking unnecessary car trips, or driving a gas-guzzling vehicle. If not, then, returning to the example of freedom of expression, we might say that freedom of expression is called a right, despite the role of "public goods" elements in its justification, because the means by which these goods are provided centrally assign to individuals a claim to be allowed to speak (like the claim to be given a ride). But it would seem that I *owe* it to others not to violate the constraints on driving as well as owing it to them to pick them up when they are waiting. So this difference, if it is one, does not amount to a distinction between those duties that are and those that are not owed to others.

If not all of the constraints required to provide important public goods correspond to rights, it would seem to follow that my account of rights—defined as constraints on discretion that are necessary and feasible to prevent unacceptable consequences—is too broad, or at least that it covers more than what are generally called rights. This is an instance of the possibility that rights might not have any distinct role within a larger class of deontological requirements. If there is something that is special about the duties that define rights, it is not clear to me what it is, or how important it is to mark this distinction.

V. Why Do Rights Constrain the Pursuit of Overall Utility?

One thing that is often cited as distinctive about rights is the fact that they constrain or "trump" considerations of overall welfare. But this property is shared by duties in general, so this is not what is special about rights, if anything is. Whether this trumping character is special to rights or not, however, it is something that an account of rights needs to explain. The account I have been discussing does this, on at least two levels.

First, on a contractualist interpretation of the account of rights I am offering, the ultimate justification of rights is non-aggregative. The basic question is not whether a principle defining certain duties would produce the most total welfare, but whether it (or alternatives to it) would affect individuals in what they could reasonably reject. So the ability of rights to act as trumps over appeals to aggregate welfare derives from a larger moral framework within which there are limits to what individuals can be asked to undergo for the sake of others.

Second, as Mill recognized long ago (*Utilitarianism*: 327 ff.), among the central conditions for human well-being are certain forms of assurance that one will have control over one's own life in important ways and not be subject to certain forms of interference by others. Principles defining rights of privacy and bodily security are obvious examples of principles that provide this. The word "assurance" is important here. What people have reason to want is not only that interference of these kinds should rarely occur, but also that they have reasonably reliable assurance that it will not, so that they can plan, invest and so on. A principle regulating interference with the bodies, lives or property of others which allows exceptions to be justified whenever the advantages of a particular intervention will exceed the costs of that particular intervention to the person who is interfered with fails to take account of this value of assurance, and therefore fails to provide assurance of the relevant kind. In order to take account of the value of assurance in the right way we need to look not just at the balance of costs and benefits in each instance, but rather at how it would be possible to live if a certain principle were generally accepted.

As I have said, providing assurance of this kind is a central function of many of the most commonly recognized rights, such as rights of privacy and bodily integrity.[3] So perhaps what is thought to be special about moral rights is not just that they are owed to individuals, or based on individual interests of some kind, but that they protect *these particular* interests in liberty and security. Whether this marks a morally important distinction between rights and other duties will depend on whether these particular interests are always more important than other interests that constraining duties might protect or promote.

A third reason why rights may be defined in ways that limit the pursuit of general welfare should be mentioned, if only to distinguish it from the first two. The harms that might be prevented by interfering with individuals' privacy, their right to speak, or even their freedom of movement and bodily integrity, are often particularly immediate and even dramatic. They are therefore more salient in the minds of

---

[3] These forms of assurance are what Mill calls "security". His argument for rights based on the importance of security at least appears to proceed within the framework of what we would now call a consequentialist theory. It is a matter of controversy how far such an argument can succeed (see Lyons 1977, 1984).

decision-makers than the longer-range value of providing assurance of the kinds I have mentioned. Experience supports the conclusion that even conscientious agents are likely to overestimate these immediate harms and are therefore likely to interfere with individual interests more than even an accurate calculation of aggregate welfare would support. One remedy is to provide a measure of protection against errors of this kind by defining rights in a particularly rigid way. This strategy is often explicitly invoked in arguments about *legal* rights, such as freedom of expression, which, it is sometimes held, should err on the side of protection because of the likelihood of this kind of mistake. It is an interesting question whether a similar argument is valid in the case of moral rights: whether these rights should be defined more broadly than would be ideal because of the likelihood that more narrowly drawn rights would be misapplied, and would therefore not provide the protection needed. I am inclined to believe that they should not. This means, for example, that in deciding what exceptions there should be to the principles that define rights (for example, in deciding when an individual's home can be invaded, or his or her telephone conversations monitored), we should consider what would be the case if agents did these things when they had good grounds for believing that that exception applied. We need not consider the likelihood that agents will believe that an exception applies when in fact they have insufficient reason to think that this is so.

Whether moral rights should take account of error in this way is a controversial point about which I am somewhat uncertain. I mention it here in order to distinguish it from the first two explanations I offered for the ability of rights to constrain the pursuit of overall welfare. Whatever may be true of legal rights, the utility-constraining character of moral rights does not depend on the assumption that rights need to be defined broadly as a protection against errors in judgement.

VI. Rights and Interests

Rights often take their names from the important interests they protect. The "right to privacy" is a prime example of this phenomenon. But it is important not to identify rights simply with these eponymous interests. If rights are identified with interests, they lose the edge and special force that they are supposed to have: claims about rights become merely claims about what it would be good to have happen (or bad to allow to happen). If they are to maintain their special force, claims about rights must at least assert the need for duties of some kind that would protect the interests that justify them.

On the other hand, although claims about rights (at least what I have called defined rights claims) are given content by the duties they assert, rights cannot simply be identified with these duties either. The duties that define rights are always incompletely specified. So even defined rights claims need to be interpreted, and the rights they assert need to be adjusted as conditions change. The interests that underlie and justify rights provide the basis for this process of interpretation and adjustment. They are, so to speak, the anchor of rights.

VII. Against "Balancing" of Rights

Another reason for being clear about the relation between rights and the underlying values and interests that they serve is to avoid confusion about the idea that rights conflict, and need to be "balanced" against one another when this occurs. Sen (2004: 322) writes that one thing that needs to be determined in an agreement about human rights is "how the different types of rights should be weighed against one another and their respective demands integrated together". This observation is subject to two quite different interpretations. On one interpretation, suggested perhaps by the idea of "integrating" mentioned in the second conjunct, what is involved is specifying more clearly the content of each right, in particular the exceptions that it admits of. As I will make clear in what follows, this kind of integration seems to me essential, and unavoidable. On the other interpretation, suggested by the idea of "weighing" mentioned in the first conjunct of Sen's remark, what is needed is a ranking of rights, which determines which right is to prevail in cases of conflict. I will argue that rights do not need to be balanced in this way, and that it is a mistake to think that this is how we should proceed in cases of conflict.

What are called "conflicts of rights" are often mentioned. It is sometimes said, for example, that the right to privacy conflicts with the demands of national security or law enforcement, and therefore needs to be balanced against these concerns. The right to freedom of expression is also sometimes said to conflict with the right to a fair trial, or with the right to one's reputation, and balancing of these rights is said to be called for. These examples involve two different kinds of putative conflict. In some cases what is involved is a conflict between a right and some interest taken to be important. This is so, for example, when it is claimed that there is a conflict between national security and the right to privacy or between national security and freedom of expression. Security from foreign attack may be an important interest, but it is not a right. In other cases, such as the conflict between freedom of expression and the right to a fair trial, the conflict that is alleged is between two different rights.

Consider first how conflicts of the first kind (between rights and important interests) are understood within the account of rights that I have been advocating. On my view, the claim that there is a right is a claim that certain limitations on the discretion to act of individual and institutional agents are *necessary* if important interests are to be adequately protected, and *feasible* as a way of providing this protection. This claim of feasibility is that the cost these limitations impose on our other interests is acceptable given the importance of the interests being protected. When it is claimed that freedom of expression must be restricted because it conflicts with national security, what is claimed is that, when it is understood in a certain way, the right of freedom of expression is not feasible—that is to say, the limitations it would impose on the power of government officials to restrict expression on the ground that it reveals information vital to the national defense are too stringent, and have unacceptable costs. To claim this, on the account I am defending, is to claim that the right of freedom of expression is not as broad as we might have thought that it was—that we were mistaken about what this right covers.

In order to decide whether this is so, one needs to do more than compare, or balance, the importance of national defense and the interests that freedom of expression protects. One must also answer important empirical questions about how a more extensive power of government to regulate expression in the interest of national security might be defined, and how such power would be used. For example, what are the consequences of having an "official secrets act"? Are governments likely to use it as a way of concealing information simply because it would be politically embarrassing? Is there any way of restricting the availability of genuinely dangerous information that would be less threatening to our interests in freedom of expression?

This element of institutional design in what are called cases of balancing explains why rights can sometimes be properly limited for the sake of relatively unimportant interests but not for the sake of more important ones. Opportunities to speak can be limited for the sake of peace and quiet (for example, by banning sound trucks after certain hours) but not to prevent social unrest, even though the consequences of this unrest may be much more severe than the loss of some sleep. This is because there are ways of allowing but limiting the power to restrict speech on the basis of time, place and manner so that this power does not seriously threaten the interests that freedom of expression is designed to protect. By contrast, the power to restrict expression whenever it is likely to provoke violent counter-protest poses a serious threat to these interests.

This analysis is easily extended to cases of alleged conflict between rights, rather than between a right and some interest. For example, we not only have an important interest in our good reputation; this interest is also protected by a right, which includes the legal power to sue others for defamation. But the situation that gave rise to the landmark case *New York Times v. Sullivan* showed that if this power is not restricted, government officials can use it to block criticism of the way they perform their duties by threatening to bring libel suits against newspapers if they publish such criticism.[4] Put in the terms I have been using, what the US Supreme Court decided in this case was that an unrestricted right to sue for defamation whenever a newspaper publishes a not entirely accurate article which reflects badly on one's character or performance is not a feasible way to protect the interest in reputation. It is not feasible because it presents too great a threat to the interests that the right of freedom of expression is designed to protect. So the right to one's reputation cannot be understood to include this unrestricted power, and has to be understood in some more limited way.

Note that insofar as this process involves balancing, what are balanced are interests—in some but not all cases, interests that call for the protection of rights. In addition to this balancing, the process involves a significant element of empirical calculation and institutional design: finding ways to redefine the rights in question so that they protect the relevant interests at feasible cost.[5] Perhaps this is what Sen had in mind in saying that we need to determine how the demands of various rights can be "integrated together".

This is quite different, however, from the idea that in cases of conflict we refer to a ranking of rights which assigns them different degrees of stringency or weight, and give priority to rights with greater weight. There are several problems with this idea. The first is that it is not clear how the weight or stringency of a right is to be understood. As Kamm (2007: 246, 251) observes, the stringency of a right is not identical with the interest it protects, although it may depend in part on this interest. So the stringency of rights seems to be a special kind of deontological force, which should guide us in cases of conflict. For reasons given above, it seems to me unnecessary to posit this somewhat puzzling moral property of relative stringency in order to explain our thinking about cases in which rights appear to conflict. Moreover, as others have pointed out, it is difficult to construct an ordering of rights which fits with our considered judgements about how these conflicts should be resolved (Waldron 1989; Kamm 2007: 248–67). This is brought out, for example, by the phenomenon mentioned above of a stringent right, such as the right of freedom of expression, being limited for the sake of "less stringent" rights, or for the sake of interests, such as our interest in peace and quiet.

My conclusion is that there is no need for such ranking of relative stringency, or any need to speak at all of balancing rights. The only balancing is balancing of interests. Rights are not balanced, but are defined, or redefined, in the light of the balance of interests and of empirical facts about how these interests can best be protected.

---

[4] *New York Times v. Sullivan*, 376 US 254 (1964).

[5] After *New York Times v. Sullivan*, this process went on for some time as the Supreme Court experimented with various ways to limit the right to sue for libel, such as restricting it in the case of public officials, or that of public figures, or those involved in public issues (Tribe 1978: 633–48).

REFERENCES

DWORKIN, R. (1977), *Taking Rights Seriously* (Cambridge, Mass.: Harvard University Press).

FEINBERG, J. (1970), "The Nature and Value of Rights", *Journal of Value Inquiry*, 4: 263–7.

KAMM, F. (2007), *Intricate Ethics* (Oxford: Oxford University Press).

LYONS, D. (1977), "Human Rights and the General Welfare", *Philosophy and Public Affairs*, 6: 113–29.

—— (1984), "Utility and Rights" in J. Waldron (ed.), *Theories of Rights* (New York: Oxford University Press), 110–36.

MILL, J. S., *Utilitarianism and Other Essays*, ed. A. Ryan (London: Penguin Books 1987).

New York Times Co. v. Sullivan (1964), 376 US 254.

RAZ, J. (1986), *The Morality of Freedom* (Oxford: Clarendon Press).

SCANLON, T. (1978), "Rights, Goals and Fairness", in S. Hampshire (ed.), *Public and Private Morality* (Cambridge: Cambridge University Press), 93–125.

—— (1998), *What We Owe to Each Other* (Cambridge, Mass.: Harvard University Press).

SEN, A. (2004), "Elements of a Theory of Human Rights", *Philosophy and Public Affairs*, 32: 315–56.

THOMSON, J. (1990), *The Realm of Rights* (Cambridge, Mass.: Harvard University Press).

TRIBE, L. (1978), *American Constitutional Law* (Mineola, NY: Foundation Press).

WALDRON, J. (1989), "Rights in Conflict", *Ethics*, 99: 503–19.

CHAPTER 6

ELEMENTS OF A THEORY OF THE RIGHT TO DEVELOPMENT

ARJUN SENGUPTA

I. INTRODUCTION

THE right to development (RTD) was adopted by the United Nations through a Declaration in 1986, at first as a resolution falling short of a consensus but later in 1993, at Vienna, with full consensus of all governments. The United Nations community, however, continued to debate this for many years. As the Independent Expert on the Right to Development (1998–2003), with the specific task of clarifying the concept to assist in its implementation, I presented six reports to the Human Rights Commission, which were thoroughly discussed by an Inter-Governmental Working Group.[1] Their salient features were also published in several articles (Sengupta 2002, 2004, 2006b[2]). In writing these reports and articles,

The author is grateful to Ms Avani Kapur for research assistance.

[1] All these reports and discussions are available on the UN website at <http://unhchr.ch/html/menu2/7/b/mdev.htm> and have also been published in Franciscans International (2003).

[2] As there were some printing mistakes in Sengupta 2006b, the Harvard Book Store has brought out a corrected version of the paper on their website, available at <www.hup.harvard.edu/catalog/ANDDEV.html>.

I was overwhelmingly influenced by Sen's writings on rights and development, although Sen may not approve of all my arguments.

Sen himself has not written much about the right to development except for his article in the Nobel Symposium volume, where he says that the right to development "can be seen as a conglomeration of a collection of claims, varying from basic education, health care, and nutrition to political liberties, religious freedoms, and civil rights for all" (Sen 2006b: 5). This comes close to my definition of RTD as a vector of all the different human rights, the value of which improves if at least one right improves and no right deteriorates. Sen's defense of that right, however, is limited to countering objections to its justiciability and feasibility. He does not think that human rights become ineffective if they are not justiciable in a court of law. Nor does he think that complete feasibility is a necessary condition for the cogency of human rights. As I shall argue in the later sections of this article, however, neither of these two defenses is crucial for the vindication of the right to development.

In this chapter I recast my arguments along the lines of Sen's article on "Elements of a Theory of Human Rights" (Sen 2004), in which he considers six questions which he thinks a theory of human rights must address:

1. What kind of a statement does a declaration of human rights make?
2. What makes human rights important?
3. What duties and obligations do human rights generate?
4. Through what forms of actions can human rights be promoted, and in particular, must legislation be the principal, or even necessary, means of implementation of human rights?
5. Can economic and social rights (the so-called "second generation" rights) be reasonably included among human rights?
6. Last but not least, how can proposals of human rights be defended or challenged, and how should their claim to a universal status be assessed? (Sen 2004: 318–19).

Since the right to development is supposed to be a human right, I try to address all these questions comprehensively, though not necessarily in the same sequence.

II. The Characteristics of Human Rights and the Right to Development

According to Sen, human rights are primarily ethical demands. They may inspire legislation, but that will be "a further fact, rather than a constitutive characteristic of human rights" (Sen 2004: 318). For the human rights community, on the other hand, human rights are essentially "legal rights", which implies that right-holders can claim the rights from identified duty-bearers who have "binding obligations" to provide, or to adopt policies to provide, the right. There must also be appropriate mechanisms for enforcing these obligations. Though one does not have to go to the lengths of legal positivists, who consider legal rights as "exclusive paradigms of rights", so that "moral rights are degenerate or spurious" (Nickel 2007: 29), for human rights activists the ability to claim a right, and a mechanism of enforcement of the corresponding obligations, are crucial for their admissibility as a right. For example, Feinberg asserts that the characteristic use of rights is to be "claimed, demanded, affirmed and insisted upon" and that "Having rights, of course, makes claiming possible, but it is claiming that gives rights their special moral signif-icance...Having rights enables us to 'stand up like men', to look others in the eye, and to feel in some fundamental way the equal to anyone" (Feinberg 1970: 252). But for claiming to be effective it must be directed against some agents or authorities who can be held responsible for the denial or fulfillment of the objects of claim. Feinberg, therefore, differentiates between two essential aspects of rights, "claiming to" and "claiming against". While "claiming to" may be guided by moral considerations, "claiming against" calls for identification of the duty-bearers and a mechanism for enforcement.

Clearly, "claiming to" is important, and must be supported by ethical demands and moral entitlements. In fact, philosophers, like McCloskey (1976), consider rights essentially as "an entitlement to do, to demand, to enjoy, to be, to have done" in terms of some freedom, power, protection or benefits for which people have a very strong moral reason, even without identifying duty-bearers against whom the claims are made. Feinberg also admits the importance of the ability to make valid claims which can mobilize appropriate actions. But he would call them "manifesto rights" and not "full-fledged rights" (Feinberg 1970: 255). For a full-fledged right, the duty-bearers against whom such claims can be made have to be identifiable.

The human rights community perceives rights as a legal and enforceable entitle-ment because for them realizing human rights is a political project, established with the adoption of the United Nations Charter in 1945. The international community has tried to formulate and enforce international laws to prevent governments from committing atrocities similar to the Holocaust. The Charter, which became the most important international treaty in the post-war period, imposed obligations on all member governments to promote "universal respect for, and the observance of, human rights and fundamental freedoms" of all individuals (UN 1945: ch. 9, art. 55). It was followed by the formulation of a universally applicable Bill of Rights, beginning with the Universal Declaration of Human Rights (UN 1948), and then, in 1966, the International Covenant on Civil and Political Rights (ICCPR) and the International Covenant on Economic, Social and Cultural Rights (ICESCR). The Declaration was not a treaty in itself but was essentially a set of proposed standards and norms of behavior which all "nations" were expected to respect and observe. Later, to make these standards and norms into "binding obligations", they were incorporated into international law, setting up appropriate enforcement mechanisms through the two Covenants.

In the course of adopting these standards, procedural considerations concerning the bargains and trade-offs in the negotiations were more important than the ethical principles. So, even when a standard could not be justified as a norm of paramount importance, a necessary characteristic of human rights, it was accepted as part of a treaty if adopted through a due process. For example, a provision in the ICESCR referring to "rest, leisure and reasonable limitation of working hours and periodic holidays with pay, as well as remuneration for public holidays", was incorporated as Article 7(4), despite being criticized as unworthy of consideration as a human right, because at that time many country delegations, pressured by their trade union movements, considered this provision to be very important.

Such a formulation of human rights progressed through three stages.

1. There had to be a norm-creating process, a mechanism or a procedure, which allowed all members of the international community to recognize these rights, after full deliberation over all the implications.

2. There had to be a process of incorporating these standards within the legal systems, either in international law or within domestic systems.

3. There had to be a detailed discussion about the methods of implementing these rights or the way in which the governments can fulfill their obligations, setting up mechanisms to monitor the exercise of these obligations and to take corrective action.

In all three of these stages, the importance of considering ethical demands and the acceptance of the corresponding moral rights was not ignored. The norm-creating process, in particular, was dominated by what Sen describes as "articulations of ethical demands", when underlying ethical arguments have to survive open and informed scrutiny. As Sen puts it, "the invoking of such an interactive process of critical scrutiny, open to information (including that about other societies), as well as to arguments coming from far as well as near, is a central feature of the theory of human rights" (Sen 2004: 320–1). The records of the discussion at the inter-governmental meetings towards the adoption of the different Covenants relating to norms acceptable as human rights clearly demonstrates the actual practice of this principle.

In the second stage—incorporating these principles in a legal system—ethical considerations often played a major role. Negotiations were influenced by the principle, proposed by Louis Henkin, that "how human beings are treated anywhere, concerns everyone, everywhere" (Henkin 1989: 129). The limits of this concern and the extent to which the international community can transgress the principles of national sovereignty and get involved in the rights of people living in other nation-states dominated the discussions. Though the Covenants set up their own mechanisms of monitoring, review and redressal of wrongs, they still did not recognize the right of an individual to appeal to an international arbitrator or judicial mechanism. Individuals have to appeal to the mechanism set up by the domestic legal system. Although the International Covenants have included a provision that member nations must incorporate these principles within their domestic legal systems, only a few countries have actually done so.

The implementation of these rights at the third stage depends very much on alternative, non-legislated domestic monitoring and redressal mechanisms, reviews by treaty bodies or international peer pressure exerted through inter-governmental human rights forums and civil society organizations, and—on rare occasions— coercive sanctions following due procedures, in case state parties refuse to honor their obligations. Sometimes, redressal may be achieved through the route Sen describes as "agitation and advocacy", which are built entirely on arguments for ethical demands—by persuading or "naming and shaming" the violators to ensure their compliance. But the ultimate aim is to change domestic laws or amend domestic constitutions to incorporate the human rights standards as binding obligations.

Failure of legislating the rights in a domestic legal system is not always due to a lack of political will. For these rights, the corresponding obligations often cannot be precisely formulated as responsibilities of identified duty-bearers. This is particularly true of economic, social and cultural rights, where the related obligations are often "imperfect" and need to go through several stages of review and refinement to pinpoint them on specific duty-bearers. To accommodate this fact, the human rights community, from early days, has differentiated between "legal" and "justiciable" rights. Legal rights are, essentially, rights which generate corresponding obligations that are "binding" on the respective duty-bearers. They are "binding" in the sense that, once the obligations are specified, the duty-bearers must do whatever is required of them, and not just, as Sen would say, "give reasonable consideration" to taking appropriate action, as would be the case with moral rights. Justiciability, on the other hand, is a method of enforcing those obligations through a judicial system, following legislation, wherein specified duty-bearers are subjected to judicial review and reprimand.

When human rights are implemented in domestic law, they are usually described as constitutional rights and are enforceable by the judiciary. As James Nickel states, "The paradigm of legal implementation at the national level for a human right has two parts: (i) enactment in abstract terms in a constitution or bill of rights, and (ii) enactment in more specific terms in statutes that become part of the day-to-day law of the realm" (Nickel 2007: 50). He adds,

Enactment in effective national or international law is perhaps the most important means of implementing human rights. But legal enactment is neither necessary nor sufficient for the realization of human rights. Legal enactment is not always necessary because in some lucky societies the attitudes of the public and of government officials are so supportive of particular rights that no enforcement is necessary. And it is not always sufficient because legal enactment in a showcase bill of rights does little or nothing to realize a right.

(Nickel 2007: 50)

This corroborates Sen's observation that, "while legislation is an important domain of public action, there are other ways and means which are also important and often effective in advancing the cause of recognized human rights" (Sen 2004: 343). His identification of three routes for advancing "the implementation of human rights" (Sen 2004: 342–5)—namely, "recognition" (the ethical force of human rights is made more powerful in practice through giving it a social recognition and an acknowledged status even when no enforcement is instituted), "agitation" (organized advocacy and the urging of compliance with human rights by civil society through public support and through criticism of violations) and "legislation" (enacting laws to make these rights justiciable)—are essentially the same routes followed by the human rights community. But the effectiveness of such campaigns should not be dependent only on the strength of persuasion and appeal to the duty-bearers' moral principles. There must be some method of enforcement if compliance by duty-bearers is not voluntarily forthcoming, because obligations to satisfy such rights, unlike ethical demands, are binding. Agitation and advocacy are not the only alternatives to justiciability. Other mechanisms of ensuring compliance have also been worked out through legislative committees, local dispute-settlement mechanisms, and administrative systems. If such alternative mechanisms exist, one need not depend only on courts of law to secure redress.

This discussion is important for understanding a basic feature of the right to development. It may not be very easy to make such a right justiciable through comprehensive legislation, as it involves the implementation of a number of different rights, often over a period of time, through "progressive realization". This requires actions of diverse duty-bearers whose actions, in turn, are often contingent upon steps taken by other duty-bearers. So, the enforcement mechanism for RTD may have to be built upon a coordinated system of legislation (for specific aspects of different rights), with administrative measures and dispute-settlement mechanisms, as well as public discussion, with or without agitation. But that should in no way exclude RTD from a system of rights, particularly because in the complex world of today, most rights have to be implemented in a similar manner, by combining different routes of implementation.

II.1 Human Rights

To establish the existence of a right to development, one has to examine critically some of the basic characteristics of any right. The post-war recognition of human rights as a political project opened up the possibility of expanding the domain of rights, the so-called "inflation" of rights. Different societies, at different points of time, depending on their changes in perceptions and political configurations, have identified gross atrocities that compromise human dignity and have proposed new rights applicable to these new situations (Alston 1984).

It is therefore necessary to have a systematic method of selecting claims that deserve to be recognized as human rights. For this I had suggested applying Sen's notions of the "legitimacy critique" and the "coherence critique" of human rights (Sen 2001: 228–31). For an object of a claim to qualify as a right, it must satisfy both the legitimacy test, in terms of being a moral value of paramount importance and resulting from an acceptable norm-creating process, and the coherence test, which links the right to the possible identification of related duties assignable to specified duty-bearers. The plausibility of these duties will depend on (1) whether they enhance the likelihood of realizing the right—the higher the likelihood, the more plausible the duties—and (2) whether their opportunity cost, in terms of the alternative values that may have to be sacrificed by performing these duties, is reasonable.

On the basis of the theory and practice of human rights, it is possible to characterize human rights as follows:

1. All human rights protect and promote certain freedoms of individual members of the society—those sufficiently valuable for the society as a whole to be included as its foundational norms. The classical approach, following Hohfeld (1964), of identifying rights with claims of interests, liberties, powers and immunities, and even means to achieve them, can be effectively subsumed under the notion of freedom. Indeed, in accordance with Sen's approach it is now possible to identify each of the rights recognized in the Universal Declaration and in the Covenants with a freedom, in a manner that enhances the appeal of the right, or what Sen describes as its "social influenceability" (Sen 2004: 319). These rights involve both the "opportunities" and the "process" aspects of freedom, implying that both the "outcomes" and the "process" of realizing them must be consistent with human rights standards.

2. While rights are claims to freedom, not all freedoms can be claimed as rights. They must be important enough to justify others in accepting the obligation to fulfill them. In other words, if R is a human right recognized by a society, and claimed by an individual or a group of individuals, then (1) it should be possible to establish that the enjoyment of R protects and promotes corresponding freedoms; and (2) there should be an acceptable procedure, through public discussion, of a norm-creating and constitution-making process for assessing the value of R and its recognition.

3. The third aspect of human rights relates to the corresponding obligations. In classical human rights theory, based on Hohfeld's claims-rights and the

interpersonal approach, any right claimed by a party entails a co-relative duty of a second party, the performance of which will ensure the fulfillment of that right (Cranston 1983). In this classical approach, the obligation usually rests with state authorities, as most rights are seen as negative rights, such as civil and political rights, which can be secured quite feasibly by negative duties such as non-intervention or withdrawal of state action.

This perspective has changed significantly in the modern approach to human rights, as rights, once recognized by society, are seen as "the basis of a justified claim that a society has a duty to protect" (Winston 2003). As Winston states, incorporating the definitions proposed by Raz, Feinberg and Shue, rights are

claims that call forth duties from other members of society directed towards the rightholder. The corresponding duties of the society can be ascribed to various different agents, e.g., governments, individuals, or in some cases, non-governmental organizations such as private agencies or corporations. What is important about rights is that they give their holders a basis for claiming that other agents within society have certain *duties* which they are bound to fulfill with respect to their (i.e. the right-holder's) enjoyment of certain goods. Rights, in short, ground duties of others which benefit the right-holder.

(Winston 2003; emphasis is in original).

From this perspective, state authorities become one of the agents, while the role of other duty-bearers is no less important. But state authorities are recognized as "primary duty-bearers" because (1) in most cases the state's actions have the largest impact on the fulfillment of rights and (2) states have the capacity to persuade other actors, through incentives or disincentives, to carry out their obligations in a coordinated manner.

Rights today entail obligations to "respect, protect, promote and fulfill", by all the duty-bearers, irrespective of the nature of the right, often resulting in complementary actions of all agents.[3] Some agents may have a greater role in ensuring "respect" and "protection" of rights. Others may be more responsible for "promoting" and "fulfilling" them.

This has a number of implications which are equally important for the right to development. First, it is no longer plausible to categorize rights as either "negative" or "positive", as almost all rights have both negative and positive elements. "Respecting" a right usually involves the negative duty for duty-bearers of non-interference and allowing the right-holders to exercise their rights. But "protecting, promoting and fulfilling" these rights involves both these elements.

This can be illustrated by taking one example of a civil and political right and another of an economic, social and cultural right, namely freedom from torture

---

[3] This general framework was first proposed by Eide *et al.* (1984) and later used in the first study for the UN on the Right to Food through the Sub-Commission on the Promotion and Protection of Human Rights (UN 1989) and subsequently adopted by the CESCR in General Comment no. 12 (1999).

and the right to food, respectively. The right to freedom from torture implies that states should not only refrain from torturing, but also ensure that others in society do not torture. For both these ends, appropriate penal laws have to be enacted, with provisions made for pursuing offenders through administrative and judicial mechanisms, including the setting up of prisons and appropriate courts of law. In the earlier literature on human rights, negative and positive rights were associated with "costless" and "expensive" methods of implementation. But today, even that distinction has disappeared, since states pursue different goals accepted by their society. Not to torture a suspected offender may appear to be costless for states. But if the offender is a terrorist who could potentially inflict huge costs on society and torture is a method of preventing this, in order to respect the right not to be tortured, the state must be prepared to accept alternatives to torture, however costly they may be. Refraining from torture then no longer remains costless for the state.

For the right to food, the combination of negative and positive duties involved in satisfying this right are quite obvious. That right must be respected, protected, promoted, and fulfilled not only by the state's own actions, but also by many other agents in the society.[4]

Secondly, there is rarely a one-to-one correspondence between a duty and a right. Almost all duties have to be seen in probabilistic terms as having a high likelihood of realizing the relevant rights. A state may take firm action, but the actions of other agents and of course exogenous developments may neutralize the effects. Therefore, all duties have to be reckoned in terms of a policy of actions, considering an agent's own action, together with the reaction of other agents and exogenous developments. Furthermore, all rights have to be "progressively" realized, not only because of resource constraints, but because duties relating to protecting, promoting and fulfilling the rights cannot be performed immediately. The policies which can implement a right, therefore, not only have to be coordinated with the actions of every agent cross-sectionally at a point of time, but also over a period of time.

Human rights activists are often very wary of talking about programs or policies instead of immediate actions. But it must be realized that the adoption and execution of policies by duty-bearers, while maintaining consistency with current and future actions of other duty-bearers and exogenous developments, follows logically from the modern approach to human rights. That does not imply any dilution of the duty-bearer's responsibilities. It only implies that, having determined which policies have the highest likelihood of realization (after assessment of alternatives and available information), the duty-bearers, particularly the state authorities, must make the best possible efforts, in transparent and accountable ways, taking some actions immediately and others in a phased manner over a period of time. The

---

[4] There is a huge literature on this subject, beginning with Eide *et al.* (1984) and an early comprehensive approach in Alston and Tomasevski (eds) (1984). I have also examined the right to food in Sengupta (2006b).

Maastricht Guidelines, generally accepted as a guide to the progressive realization of rights, call for working out targets for different parties for fulfilling the rights. It may not always be possible to identify a unique policy that has the "maximum" likelihood of fulfilling a right, as the informational basis often does not exist. But the state must establish that its policies have a very high likelihood of achieving the desired results and should also be willing to adopt a better solution for implementing the right if that is demonstrated by the reviewing authorities (or the judiciary, in the case of legislative rights).

In analyzing the scope of these duties, Sen's discussions of "perfect" and "imperfect" obligations can be very helpful. I have invoked them in delineating the duties of all agents, in terms of direct duties and indirect duties, and linking them to "perfect" and "imperfect" obligations. Direct duties have a direct impact on the fulfillment of the rights. There is a positive correspondence between the performance of a direct duty by a duty-bearer, and an increased likelihood of ensuring the enjoyment of the right by the right-holder. Indirect duties are duties that complement direct duties or are contingent upon the duties performed by other agents of the society. As such, direct duties are similar to what Sen describes as the Kantian concept of "perfect obligation", i.e. "a specific duty of a particular agent for the realization of that right". Indirect duties, however, are not exactly the same as an "imperfect obligation", where "the claims are addressed generally to anyone who can help, even though no particular person or agency may be charged to bring about the fulfillment of the rights involved" (Sen 2001: 230). So long as the agents do not have a "perfect obligation" of performing "direct duties" and no other specific duties can be assigned to them, they may have "imperfect obligations". But if they are assigned some indirect duties, then, following due procedures, they have "binding obligations" to perform those duties. Not all of these duties may have an outcome that can be predicted with certainty, because their effectiveness depends upon what other agents do and what contingencies develop. Nevertheless, the assignment of indirect duties to agents converts their imperfect obligations into binding ones, whereby non-compliance can be subjected to corrective measures.

In a program for implementing a human right, a primary duty-bearer, like the state, has the perfect obligation of carrying out the direct duties. But they also have the duty of adopting policies to coordinate the actions of other duty-bearers and assign them clearly specified indirect duties, which they cannot reasonably refuse to perform as members of society. For example, a program for imposing taxes on some agents of society or directing them to follow some specified course of action must be complied with if it increases the likelihood of fulfilling the rights.

Reference is often made to Onora O'Neill's claim that welfare rights which are related to economic, social and cultural rights cannot be regarded as rights, as they are not accompanied by specified perfect obligations so long as they are not institutionalized. She says that "some advocates of universal economic, social and cultural rights go no further than to emphasize that they *can* be institutionalized, which is true. But the point of difference is that they *must* be institutionalized: if they are not there is no right" (O'Neill 1996: 131–2; emphasis in the original).

Most authors have tried to answer this point simply by insisting that if such institutionalization is necessary, it should be an obligation corresponding to that right, and if it cannot be carried out as a direct duty of an agent, it requires coordination of actions of other duty-bearers over a period of time. However, institutionalization may then at times remain unfulfilled or uncertain, so the theoretical possibility of institutionalization cannot suffice to make the right feasible and therefore legally binding (Cranston 1983). How then can welfare rights be recognized as human rights so long as institutionalization has not been carried out, even though it is possible in principle?

This problem will not arise if rights are taken to be what Sen identifies as a moral right or an ethical demand, since even a demonstration of the possibility of institutionalization in principle should then suffice to establish, again in principle, that the duty-bearers have the obligation to satisfy the rights. As Sen puts it,

why should complete feasibility be a condition of cogency of human rights when the objective is to work toward expanding both their feasibility and their actual realization? The understanding that some rights are not fully realized and may not even be fully realizable under the present circumstances does not, in itself, entail anything like the conclusion that these are, therefore, not rights at all. Indeed, the promotion of human rights proceeds on the understanding that there is much to be promoted, including the expansion of feasibility of the recognized rights.   (Sen 2006: 6)

For a human rights activist who sees these rights as legal rights with "binding obligations", such an answer cannot be entirely satisfactory. What happens to these rights when they are not feasible? How can one assign "binding duties" on agents when there are no duties that could fulfill those rights? In such a situation, there seems no alternative but to describe these rights as moral rights or "manifesto rights" and not full-fledged rights as discussed earlier. Only when appropriate institutional changes have been made, or when methods of making such changes which the identified duty-bearers can carry out have been recognized, can such rights become full-fledged rights, with the complete specification of rights and obligations.

A way out of this difficulty can be suggested by invoking Sen's notion of "meta-rights". I consider this a major contribution of Sen to the theory of rights, though he has not pursued it very far since elaborating it in his article "The Right Not to be Hungry" (Sen 1984).

According to Sen, "a *meta-right* to something, *x*, can be defined as the right to have policies, $p(x)$, that genuinely pursue the objective of making the right to *x* realizable" (1984: 70). Sen then goes on to say, "If *this* right were accepted, then the effect will [be] ... to give a person the right to demand that policy be directed towards securing the objective of making the right [to x] a realizable right, even if that objective cannot be immediately achieved. It is a right of a different kind: not to x, but to p(x) ... [which is] a meta-right to x" (1984: 70; emphasis in original).

Our discussion above suggests that, so long as a right is realizable or corresponding policies exist to realize it, albeit over time through "progressive realization", the right is genuine. But it may be difficult to impute responsibility for the failure of realization to specific duty-bearers, according to the provisions of a legal right, when the outcomes of such policies are subject to probabilities and contingencies. The right, even if it qualifies as a legal right, would then not be identical to other legal rights in terms of monitoring, or reprimanding the duty-bearers for non-compliance. But a meta-right would not suffer from such infirmities. It would derive its justification from the right to which it is a meta-right. Moreover, the duty-bearers responsible for implementing different elements of that policy, taken as a meta-right, would be clearly identifiable and therefore could be held responsible for non-compliance, not in terms of the ultimate objective, but in terms of carrying out the specific policies assigned to them.

Of course, to qualify as a meta-right, p(x) has to be formulated in a transparent manner, delineating the responsibilities of the duty-bearers. But, once so formulated, it would permit the right-holders to claim that the state must see to it that the right is achieved and that all the duty-bearers comply with their obligations.

It can thus be argued that for all rights which can only be achieved progressively, through changing institutions or the growth of resources, the meta-right to them, as policies to achieve them, with appropriate assignment of responsibilities to identified duty-bearers, would conform more readily to the operationalization of the rights according to human rights standards.

One final point regarding the nature of human rights relates to the identification of the right-holder. In the human rights literature, the right-holder is usually assumed to be an individual. This is not just because traditionally rights discourse has been associated with individualism, but mainly because the privileges or freedoms can be enjoyed only by an individual. Logically, however, there is no bar to a group of individuals claiming a right, if a mechanism of sharing the benefits of that right can be worked out. Indeed, the notion of a group in discussions on group rights is based on a mechanism of reconciling different individuals' enjoyment of the right. If there is a procedure for forming a collective of individuals, it should also be possible to work out a method of reconciling the claims of different individuals for enjoying the same right.

While rights are supposed to be enjoyed individually, they are often exercised collectively, even when some individuals do not claim or enjoy these rights. For example, in the right not to be tortured or the right to food, the state's policies seldom aim at specific individuals. But once these rights are established, any individual member of the society who is in a position to claim the rights can enjoy them. The reference to being "in a position to claim" does not limit the scope of the right or violate the principle of universality, because often the rights are designed for specific groups of individuals who are qualified to make these claims. For example, the right to a midday meal for schoolchildren, which is often a part of the overall right to food, can only be claimed by schoolchildren. Similarly, minority rights or rights of indigenous people can be enjoyed only by claimants belonging to these groups. Thus, the human rights literature can take into account the notion of group rights, collective rights and rights of minorities and indigenous people without violating the principles of non-discrimination and universality of human rights.

The last point to note here is procedural qualification. There must be a method by which an improvement in the realization of the right can be clearly recognized. As rights are freedoms reflecting expansion of opportunities, it is necessary to construct an index or indicator for each right. An increase in the value of this indicator or index can then be regarded as an improvement in the enjoyment of the right. The construction of such an indicator is a complex exercise, as often a right consists in a complex of benefits which may not move in the same direction in response to any specific policy. Moreover, rights refer not only to outcomes, but also the processes by which these outcomes are reached, related to equity, non-discrimination, participation, accountability and transparency (ENPAT), which must be reflected in the manner in which the rights are realized (the outcome and process aspects of freedom).

In any practical situation, however, the exercise of constructing indicators reflecting both the expansion of availability and rights-based access can only be approximate, based on the consensus judgement of the individuals involved. This exercise can be continually improved, but at any point in time, there must be an agreement about the nature of the indicator among the members of the society that recognize the right.

II.2 The Right to Development

These discussions of the characteristics of a right are relevant for characterizing the right to development. The definition of the right to development was provided by the 1986 United Nations Declaration on the Right to Development, and later confirmed in other international declarations. As rights must go through an accepted norm-creating process, the inter-governmental agreement on the text of the Declaration, adopted by the United Nations, is the first step in that process. Since RTD has not been incorporated in any international treaty or covenant, it cannot be considered a full-fledged right. But efforts have been made by the international community to analyze the implications of the Declaration and to facilitate the recognition of RTD as a full-fledged right, either through a treaty or custom, or just administrative measures and the advocacy and agitation of civil society.

Article I, Paragraph 1 of the Declaration on the Right to Development states, "the right to development is an inalienable human right by virtue of which every human person and all peoples are entitled to participate in, contribute to, and enjoy economic, social, cultural and political development, in which all human rights and fundamental freedoms can be fully realized". The Article spells out three principles: (1) RTD is a human right, (2) there is a process of economic, social, cultural and political development in which all human rights and fundamental freedoms can be fully realized, and (3) by virtue of this right, every human person is entitled to participate in, contribute to and enjoy that process of development.

This definition can be reformulated in a way that can satisfy the conditions necessary for the operationalization of this right. First, it should allow the construction of an appropriate indicator for RTD whose increase (or decrease) reflects an improvement (or a regression) in the enjoyment of that right. Second, the right should satisfy the test of legitimacy, both in terms of its normative justification, making it binding on all its members, and in terms of the procedural requirement of that acceptance. Third, it should satisfy the coherence test—the corresponding obligations of all members, and particularly the state, should be clearly identified and assigned to specific duty-bearers.

The Preamble to the Declaration defines development as "a regular improvement of 'well-being' for all people in the society" and, in accordance with the discussions at the time of its adoption, the "well-being" of a society can be defined as the level of the population's enjoyment of the different rights and fundamental freedoms. "Well-being" can then be expressed as

$$W = (R_1, R_2, \ldots, R_n; F_1, F_2, \ldots, F_k),$$

where R's are rights and F's are freedoms not yet recognized as rights. Development can then be expressed as

$$D = (dR_1, dR_2, \ldots, dR_n; dF_1, dF_2, \ldots, dF_k).[5]$$

This would involve a complex exercise of constructing the indicators for R and F in order to reflect the extent of the enjoyment of these rights and freedoms by the population. Clearly, such an exercise would depend upon some kind of social consensus about the weights of the different elements of the rights and freedoms and a method of their aggregation (for more on this see Malhotra 2006).

I draw a distinction between rights and freedoms even though each of them is a constituent element of the "well-being" of the people. Rights are claims to certain freedoms satisfying Sen's tests as mentioned above, while freedoms are associated

[5] More appropriately, development should be expressed as

$$D = (dR_{it}, dF_{jt}), i = 1, 2, \ldots, n, j = 1, 2, \ldots, k \quad \text{and} \quad t = 1, 2, \ldots, T.$$

Accordingly, dR_i would be seen as an average, or an agreed pace of improvement of R_i over a given period T.

with opportunities, or freedoms to be and to do. It is possible to incorporate these within Sen's capability approach, wherein capabilities are essentially freedoms. But for operational purposes it may be easier to identify each of these freedoms separately, and then build up specific indicators for them. For example, the right to food can be expressed in terms of specific indicators combining all the different aspects of freedom from hunger, such as availability of food, midday meals for school children, etc., so that an increase in the value of these specific indicators reflects an improvement in the enjoyment of the overall right.

When no account is taken of the recognition of some freedoms as rights, one would see development as

$$D = (dF_1, dF_2, \ldots, dF_n),$$

i.e. as a process of expansion of different freedoms. Indeed such a notion of development as freedom is the foundational basis of the right to development. A process of development as an expansion of freedoms is described as a "rights-based development", when some of these freedoms are recognized as rights. RTD is the right to that process of rights-based development. It can be expressed as

$$D_R = (dR_1, dR_2, \ldots, dR_n \text{ and } dF_j)$$

when F_j's are freedoms not yet recognized as rights.

Looking at RTD in this way allows us to capture the essential characteristics of a right. For example, it should be possible to say when D_R is increasing if, through consensus, we can attach weights to all these different rights and aggregate them. A simpler, and often more useful approach, is a vector definition which describes RTD as a vector of improvement of the different rights, which improves if any one of these rights improves and no right deteriorates (i.e. all $dR_i > 0$). It would of course not allow assessment of how much RTD is improving but, for most practical purposes, even an indication that RTD is improving as a result of certain policies undertaken should be sufficient to design a policy for implementing that right.

A vector definition is also consistent with some well-established characteristics of human rights. First, human rights are interdependent, implying that all R_i's are functions of R_j's, along with other exogenous variables, with the constraint that $\delta R_i / \delta R_j \geq 0$. This non-negativity constraint follows from the notion that an improvement of one right cannot lead to a deterioration of another right. The characteristic that rights are indivisible does not mean that a right cannot be split into different elements, because most rights are composed of different characteristics. It only means that if one constituent element of that right improves, no other element of that right can deteriorate, and thereby disintegrate the right. RTD seen as a vector would imply that all the component rights must satisfy this requirement.

In the rights literature, statements are often made that there cannot be any trade-off between rights (except in special circumstances), because rights are associated with human dignity, which cannot be traded off with any other norms, however desirable they may be (Basu 2003). In any situation where scarce resources are involved in the fulfillment of any right, such a blanket denial of trade-off may create many problems. But in the RTD framework, this problem can be avoided, because even if there cannot be any trade-off between the levels of the enjoyment of one right *vis-à-vis* another, it is still possible to have a trade-off between the increments of those rights. Thus, the pace of realization of one right may be different from that of another, provided the level of enjoyment of any right does not deteriorate.

Looking at RTD as a composite of improvements in the different rights facilitates the process of its recognition. Although RTD as such, is not recognized as part of a treaty or covenant, it has as its components rights already recognized, either in ICCPR or ICESCR. For each of these rights, the obligations can be specified and assigned to identified duty-bearers, including, of course, the state authorities. The fulfillment of RTD would essentially mean the fulfillment of the component rights in different phases, in different countries. Therefore, obligations for implementing RTD can also be fully specified, as a sequential improvement of different recognized rights. Indeed in the Maastricht Guidelines, the idea of progressive realization has been specified as the "targeted improvement of realization" of different rights over a period. The target of improvement of R_i's at time t can be represented as dR_{it}'s (see n. 5 above).

Similarly, the debate whether RTD is a collective right is not so relevant, as most of the rights are provided collectively, through public policy, and the provision of the right would normally be targeted to all the individuals who are in a position to claim that right. In this argument, there is no room for the proposition that RTD is the right of a developing country. Instead, RTD should be seen as a right exercised collectively and enjoyed by individuals in all countries, whether developing or developed.

However, when RTD is exercised as a right to a rights-based process of development, the corresponding obligations have to be more than just the obligation of realizing the individual component rights. Thus, if a society recognizes RTD, which is a right to a process of development consistent with human rights standards, the corresponding obligations not only consist of the obligations of realizing the individual component rights, but also an obligation of coordinating them into a development program, to enable a clear value-addition to that process. This development program can be described as,

$$P_d = (P_1, P_2, P_3, \ldots, P_n),$$

where P_i's are policies for implementing the ith right and P_d is a combination of all these P_i's which maximizes the likelihood of realizing all the rights. In practice, such a maximizing exercise is somewhat imprecise, and based more on judgement than on the mathematics of optimization. But when there are several programs or P_d's that will realize the different R_i's to different extents, it will be necessary to choose from amongst these programs, through a consensual procedure, one which is most acceptable to the society, and which can be taken as an obligation corresponding to the implementation of RTD.

The literature on RTD describes that obligation as assigned to the primary duty-bearer, namely the state authorities, for designing, adopting and implementing a development policy, and coordinating the different policies for realizing the different rights at different phases over time. The value-addition in this process is that a coordinated set of policies taking into account the interdependence of different rights, and the scarcity of physical and institutional resources, will result in a higher value of outcomes of the different rights than if the component rights are pursued in isolation from each other.

For example, the "right to food" can be fulfilled much better if, at the same time, several other rights such as a "right to an adequate standard of living", "right to employment", "right to social security" and even the "right to health" are fulfilled together. The process is further facilitated if the fulfillment of several other liberty rights are associated with that process.

The only issue that remains in the identification of RTD is whether such a development policy exists. Those who advocate the recognition of RTD believe that it does exist for any country at any particular time, although the pace of realization of that right will be progressive. Their arguments are strengthened by the prospect that RTD, which has been espoused by an Inter-Governmental Declaration on the Right to Development, may eventually become a part of international law. In that case, the international community would accept the responsibility of assisting the individual countries through a supply of resources and technology and by adjusting the rules of international trade and finance, thereby enhancing the likelihood of realizing RTD.

III. DEVELOPMENT POLICY
AS A META-RIGHT

Sen's notion of a meta-right is particularly relevant in this context. An appropriately formulated development policy can be considered as a meta-right to RTD. That, in Sen's language, would enable, "one to claim that the state must see to it that [this right] be achieved, and if isn't then to claim, as Dworkin puts it, that the people as a whole would be justified in amending the Constitution . . . or perhaps in rebelling or overthrowing the present form of Government entirely" (Sen 1984: 71). Although RTD can be seen as a valid right satisfying the tests of legitimacy and coherence, it may not be possible to fulfill it immediately. The feasibility of this right, even over a period, would then very much depend upon the implementability of an appropriately designed development policy. If such a development policy is accepted as a meta-right, all agents in society would have either "perfect" or "imperfect" obligations converted into direct and indirect duties, and would be obliged to perform them. The responsibilities of each of these agents could be subjected to monitoring and review with appropriate corrective policies.

In order to formulate such a development policy, RTD has to be redefined in a narrower form which enables faster realization than the broader version of realizing all of the rights in a phased manner over a period of time. It has been proposed that instead of targeting all of the the rights, a society may choose the progressive realization of some "basic rights", at least in the first stage. The notion of basic rights was introduced by Henry Shue (1980), in terms of life, liberty and subsistence. This can be defined, more generally, as those rights whose fulfillment is the precondition for the realization of other rights. Again, the choice of these "basic rights" will have to be decided by social consensus, because when all the rights are interdependent, the fulfillment of any one right can influence the realization of another right. A judgement has to be made about which rights will have the maximum probability of achieving other rights. This depends on the existing conditions of an economy, as well as the preference for different freedoms. In general, one would identify four or five rights as "basic rights" for development such as the "right to food", "right to health", "right to education" and "right to employment", along with some civil rights that allow people to claim the other rights.

This does not mean that RTD can be limited only to these basic rights, ignoring other rights. For that reason, it has been suggested that economic growth consistent with human rights standards, or G^*, can be used as a proxy for realizing other rights and can be included as a constituent element of the right to development. RTD can then be described as

$$D_R = (dR_1^*, dR_2^*, \ldots, dR_k^*; G^*),$$

where R_j^* are the basic rights and G^* is the rights-based process of economic growth.

It should be reiterated that recognizing G^* as a constituent element of RTD in no way compromises the instrumental character of income growth, which is now well recognized in the development literature. All that is assumed here is that a rights-based economic growth has a high likelihood of fulfilling the different rights and fundamental freedoms and is often a necessary condition for realizing them. It is also important to stress that such economic growth must be consistent with human rights standards. A positive relationship between the fulfillment of rights and freedoms and economic growth may only exist if that growth is (1) specially designed to ensure that inequality does not increase and (2) participatory and accountable. Again, the method of determining how a process of economic growth can be consistent with rights, following the principles of ENPAT, would be a complex exercise, but approximate indicators can be worked out towards that end.

A development policy as a meta-right to realize this right would then consist of coordinating policies of not only realizing the basic rights, but also achieving a rights-based process of economic growth. Recognizing the characteristics of that rights-based growth, respecting the principles of participation, accountability and transparency, would change the perspective of the usual policies for raising income growth in a country and may imply a whole new approach to realizing economic development. It is important to remember, however, that although rights-based economic growth would improve the likelihood of the realization of these basic rights along with other rights and freedoms, the objective of RTD is served only when specific targets are proposed for the realization of these basic rights, with specific corresponding policies appropriately coordinated.

IV. CONCLUSION

Instead of trying to summarize all of the arguments of this rather long and complex chapter, I should like to conclude by identifying a major implication of recognizing development policy as a meta-right to RTD. When development is seen only as a phased realization of different rights, the international community may often consider their responsibility as a charity, and providing assistance, as their "imperfect obligation". The rights have to be implemented by the concerned state authorities of different countries and international assistance can be provided only if national authorities have already done their best and require the international community just to complement their efforts. But when RTD is recognized as a part of international law, and G* or a rights-based process of economic growth is accepted as a constituent element of that right, the obligations of the international community go far beyond charitable assistance. This is because, in this age of globalization, no national authority has the flexibility to apply policies to increase their economic growth without taking into account the actions and reactions of the international community, or without any active process of international cooperation. Whether in the area of trade or finance, technology transfer or institutional reforms, the interdependence of international economies is now so substantive that no country can follow an independent policy of economic growth. If the international community accepts the responsibility of helping a country to realize its RTD, it must adopt appropriate policies to help these countries, or at least not neutralize the effects of their national policies.

International cooperation has been accepted in human rights law as an obligation of the international community, at least of the major nations and international institutions. But very rarely have these obligations been recognized as "perfect obligations" binding them to act directly or indirectly. The RTD framework works out a mechanism described as a "Development Compact" whereby a developing country attempting to realize RTD can claim that some of the nations and international institutions whose policies have a large impact on the economic development of that country must enter into a "compact" of mutual cooperation that is binding on all of them.[6] The relationship between a developing country and the international community in all the different forums will then have to be seen in a new perspective. Development will then be the outcome of a partnership between the international community and the developing country concerned. A "compact" will be the expression of the mutual acceptance of corresponding obligations.

REFERENCES

ALSTON, P. (1988), "Making Space for New Human Rights: The Case for the Right to Development", *Harvard Human Rights Yearbook*, 3: 3–40.

—— (1984), "Conjuring Up New Human Rights: A Proposal for Quality Control", *American Journal of International Law*, 78: 607–21.

—— and TOMASEVSKI, K. (eds) (1984), *The Right to Food* (Boston: M. Nijhoff).

BASU, K. (2003), "The Economics and Law of Sexual Harassment in the Workplace", *Journal of Economic Perspectives*, 17: 141–57.

CRANSTON, M. (1983), "Are There Any Human Rights?", *Daedalus*, 112: 1–17.

—— (1979), "What are Human Rights?", in W. Laqueur and B. Rubin (eds), *The Human Rights Reader* (New York: Penguin Books).

EIDE, A. *et al.* (1984), *Food as a Human Right* (Tokyo: United Nations University).

FEINBERG, J. (1970), "The Nature and Value of Rights", *Journal of Value Inquiry*, 4: 243–57.

FRANCISCANS INTERNATIONAL (2003), *Reflections on the First Four Reports of the Independent Expert on the Right to Development* (Geneva: Franciscans International).

HENKIN, L. (1989), "International Human Rights as Rights", in M. E. Winston (ed.), *The Philosophy of Human Rights* (Belmont, California: Wadsworth).

HOHFELD, W. (1964), *Fundamental Legal Conceptions* (New Haven: Yale University Press).

MALHOTRA, R. (2006), "Towards Implementing the Right to Development: A Framework for Indicators and Monitoring Methods", in B. A. Andreassen and S. P. Marks (eds), *Development as a Human Right; Legal, Political and Economic Dimensions*, a Nobel Symposium Book (Cambridge, Mass.: Harvard University Press).

McCLOSKEY, H. J. (1976), "Rights: Some Conceptual Issues", *Australian Journal of Philosophy*, 54: 99–115.

---

[6] This has been spelt out in my First and Second Report on the Right to Development (see n. 1 above) and also in Alston (1988).

NICKEL, J. (2007), *Making Sense of Human Rights*, 2nd edn (Malden, Mass.: Blackwell Publishing).

O'NEILL, O. (1996), *Towards Justice and Virtue: A Constructive Account of Practical Reasoning* (Cambridge: Cambridge University Press).

SEN, A. (2006), "Human Rights and Development", in B. A. Andreassen and S. P. Marks (eds), *Development as a Human Right: Legal, Political and Economic Dimensions*, a Nobel Symposium Book (Cambridge, Mass.: Harvard University Press).

—— (2004), "Elements of a Theory of Human Rights", *Philosophy and Public Affairs*, 32: 315–56.

—— (2001), *Development as Freedom* (New York: Oxford University Press).

—— (2000), "Consequential Evaluation and Practical Reason", *Journal of Philosophy*, 97: 477–502.

—— (1985a), "The Rights as Goals", Austin Lecture, in S. Guest and A. Milne (eds), *Equality and Discrimination: Essays in Freedom and Justice* (Stuttgart: Franz Steiner Verlag).

—— (1985b), "Rights and Capabilities", in T. Honderich (ed.), *Morality and Objectivity* (London: Routledge).

—— (1984), "The Right Not to be Hungry", in P. Alston and K. Tomasevski (eds), *The Right to Food* (Boston: M. Nijhoff).

SENGUPTA, A. (2007), "The Right to Food in the Context of the Right to Development", in W. B. Eide and U. Kratch (eds), *Food and Human Rights in Development. Volume 2: Evolving Issues and Emerging Applications* (Antwerp and Oxford: Intersentia).

—— (2006), "The Human Right to Development", in B. A. Andreassen and S. P. Marks (eds), *Development as a Human Right: Legal, Political and Economic Dimensions*, a Nobel Symposium Book (Cambridge, Mass.: Harvard University Press).

—— (2004), "The Human Right to Development", *Oxford Development Studies*, 32: 179–203.

—— (2002), "On the Theory and Practice of the Right to Development", *Human Rights Quarterly*, 24: 837–89.

SHUE, H. (1980), *Basic Rights* (Princeton: Princeton University Press).

UN (1989), *Right to Adequate Food as a Human Right*, Human Rights Study Series 1 (New York: United Nations).

—— (1948), *Universal Declaration on Human Rights*, available at <www.un.org.overview/rights.htm>.

—— (1945), *United Nations Charter*, available at <www.un.org/aboutun/charter>.

Universal Declaration on Human Rights. available online at <www.un.org/overview/rights.htm>.

WINSTON, M. E. (2003), "On the Indivisibility and Interdependence of Human Rights", paper delivered at the 20th World Congress of Philosophy; available online at <www.bu.edu/wcp/Papers/Huma/HumaWins.htm>.

—— (ed.) (1989), *The Philosophy of Human Rights* (Belmont, Calif.: Wadsworth Publishing).

PART II

·····································

AGENCY, AGGREGATION AND SOCIAL CHOICE

·····································

CHAPTER 7

....

RATIONAL CHOICE ON GENERAL DOMAINS

....

WALTER BOSSERT
KOTARO SUZUMURA

I. INTRODUCTION

....

THE question whether observed (individual or social) choice behavior can be generated by some notion of optimization of an underlying objective is one of the most fundamental issues in the analysis of economic decisions. The basic question to be addressed is the following. Given some observed (or, at least, observable) choices from feasible sets, does there exist a preference relation (possibly with some additional properties) such that, for each choice situation under consideration, the set of chosen objects is given by some set of "best" elements according to this relation? There are two basic forms of rationalizability, namely, *greatest-element*

This paper was presented at the 2005 Canadian Economic Theory Conference in Vancouver, the 2005 Asian Decentralization Conference in Seoul, the 2005 Central European Program in Economic Theory Workshop in Udine, the University of Namur, the University of Northern Illinois and the 2007 Japanese–French Seminar on Social Choice Theory and Welfare Economics in Caen. We thank Kaushik Basu and Yongsheng Xu for comments. Financial support, through grants from the Social Sciences and Humanities Research Council of Canada, the Fonds pour la Formation de Chercheurs et l'Aide à la Recherche of Quebec and a Grant-in-Aid for Scientific Research from the Ministry of Education, Culture, Sports, Science and Technology of Japan, is gratefully acknowledged.

rationalizability and *maximal-element rationalizability*. Greatest-element rationalizability requires the existence of a relation such that, for any feasible set in the domain of a choice function, the set of chosen elements coincides with those elements of the feasible set that are at least as good as all feasible alternatives. Maximal-element rationalizability, on the other hand, demands the existence of a relation such that the set of chosen objects consists of all undominated elements in the feasible set, that is, all elements such that there exists no feasible alternative that is strictly preferred.

In addition to the basic type of rationalizability (in terms of greatest elements or in terms of maximal elements), we can require the rationalizing relation to be endowed with certain fundamental properties. Two standard requirements are *reflexivity* and *completeness,* which we refer to as *richness* properties because they require a relation to contain at least certain pairs of alternatives. Furthermore, it is customary to impose *coherence* properties such as *transitivity, consistency, quasi-transitivity* or *P-acyclicity*; see section II for formal definitions of these properties.

Revealed preference theory has its origins in the theory of consumer demand, where the choices to be analyzed are those of a competitive consumer from budget sets. This area of research has been developed in contributions such as those of Samuelson (1938; 1947: ch. 5; 1948; 1950) and Houthakker (1950).

It was Uzawa (1957) and Arrow (1959) who considered alternative choice situations by introducing the general concept of a choice function defined on the domain of some specified subsets of a universal set of alternatives. In this setting, Sen (1971), Schwartz (1976), Bandyopadhyay and Sengupta (1991), to name but a few, characterized notions of rational choice under various coherence conditions imposed on rationalizing relations. Most notably, the theory of rational choice could be greatly simplified if the domain of a choice function was rich enough to include all finite subsets of the universal set by the equivalence between several revealed preference axioms, for example, the weak axiom of revealed preference and the strong axiom of revealed preference. Recollect that the subtle difference between these axioms had been regarded as lying at the heart of the integrability problem for a competitive consumer.

It is clear, however, that the above-described assumption regarding the class of possible choice situations to be considered restricts the applicability of the results obtained. Thus, it is of great interest to examine what the logic of rational choice—and nothing else—entails in general, irrespective of the domain of a choice function. A crucial step along this line was taken by Richter (1966; 1971), Hansson (1968) and Suzumura (1976a; 1977; 1983: ch. 2), who assumed the domain of a choice function to be an arbitrary family of non-empty subsets of an arbitrary non-empty universal set of alternatives without any further structural assumptions.

While the theory of rational choice on general domains is well developed if a rationalizing relation is assumed to be transitive, much less is known when weaker coherence properties are imposed. The case of consistent rationalizability has been addressed recently in Bossert, Sprumont and Suzumura (2005a). Furthermore, some versions of maximal-element rationalizability (and, thus, those versions of greatest-element rationalizability that are equivalent to them) have been characterized in Bossert, Sprumont and Suzumura (2005b), but a comprehensive treatment of rationalizability on general domains in the presence of quasi-transitivity or P-acyclicity is still missing. An analysis of some conditions that are necessary and others that are sufficient for some forms of quasi-transitive or P-acyclical rationalizability can be found in Suzumura (1983) and Bossert, Sprumont and Suzumura (2006), but full characterizations of most of these concepts remain to be provided.

The purpose of this paper is to develop a unified approach, thereby providing characterizations of all relevant notions of rationalizability on general domains. Thus, the results of this paper provide systematic answers to some important open questions in the literature on rational choice and revealed preference. It may be worth pointing out that answering these open questions has relevance more substantial than simply filling in logical lacunae in the literature. Recollect that assuming the rationalizing weak preference relation to be transitive evokes strong empirical criticism. There are many experimental studies which suggest that the imperfect discriminatory power of human beings leads to non-transitive indifference, and Armstrong (1948: 3) went as far as to assert: "That indifference is not transitive is indisputable, and the world in which it were transitive is indeed unthinkable." Thus, to liberate the theory of rationalizable choice functions from the assumption of transitive indifference may be an important step for the sake of making the theoretical edifice of more empirical relevance than otherwise.

Our basic definitions and some preliminary observations are collected in section II. Section III introduces our different notions of rationalizability and examines their logical relationships on arbitrary domains. Section IV is devoted to our unified approach to rationalizability, which leads to the characterization of all versions of rationalizability defined in section III. Section V concludes the chapter.

II. Preliminaries

We consider a non-empty (but otherwise arbitrary) universal set of alternatives X, and we let $R \subseteq X \times X$ be a (binary) relation on X. The *asymmetric factor* $P(R)$ of R is defined by

$$P(R) = \{(x, y) \in X \times X \mid (x, y) \in R \text{ and } (y, x) \notin R\},$$

and the *symmetric factor* $I(R)$ of R is defined by

$$I(R) = \{(x, y) \in X \times X \mid (x, y) \in R \text{ and } (y, x) \in R\}.$$

If R is interpreted as a *weak preference relation*, that is, $(x, y) \in R$ means that x is considered at least as good as y, then $P(R)$ and $I(R)$ can be interpreted as the *strict preference relation* and the *indifference relation* corresponding to R, respectively. The *diagonal relation* on X is given by

$$\Delta = \{(x, x) \mid x \in X\}.$$

Let $\mathbb{N}$ denote the set of positive integers. The following properties of a binary relation R are of importance in this paper:

Reflexivity. For all $x \in X$,

$$(x, x) \in R.$$

Completeness. For all $x, y \in X$ such that $x \neq y$,

$$(x, y) \in R \text{ or } (y, x) \in R.$$

Transitivity. For all $x, y, z \in X$,

$$[(x, y) \in R \text{ and } (y, z) \in R] \Rightarrow (x, z) \in R.$$

Quasi-transitivity. For all $x, y, z \in X$,

$$[(x, y) \in P(R) \text{ and } (y, z) \in P(R)] \Rightarrow (x, z) \in P(R).$$

Consistency. For all $K \in \mathbb{N} \setminus \{1\}$ and for all $x^0, \ldots, x^K \in X$,

$$(x^{k-1}, x^k) \in R \text{ for all } k \in \{1, \ldots, K\} \Rightarrow (x^K, x^0) \notin P(R).$$

P-acyclicity. For all $K \in \mathbb{N} \setminus \{1\}$ and for all $x^0, \ldots, x^K \in X$,

$$(x^{k-1}, x^k) \in P(R) \text{ for all } k \in \{1, \ldots, K\} \Rightarrow (x^K, x^0) \notin P(R).$$

A reflexive and transitive relation is called a *quasi-ordering* and a complete quasi-ordering is called an *ordering*.

In what follows, we refer to reflexivity and completeness as *richness conditions*. This term is motivated by the observation that the properties in this group require that, at least, some pairs must belong to the relation under consideration. In the case of reflexivity, all pairs of the form (x, x) are required to be in the relation, whereas completeness demands that, for any two distinct alternatives x and y, at least one of (x, y) and (y, x) must be in R. Clearly, the reflexivity requirement is equivalent to the set inclusion $\Delta \subseteq R$.

On the other hand, transitivity, quasi-transitivity, consistency and P-acyclicity are referred to as *coherence conditions*. They require that if certain pairs belong to R, then certain other pairs must belong to R as well (as is the case for transitivity and for quasi-transitivity) or certain other pairs cannot belong to R (which applies to the cases of consistency and of P-acyclicity). Quasi-transitivity and consistency are independent. A transitive relation is quasi-transitive, and a quasi-transitive relation is P-acyclical. Moreover, a transitive relation is consistent, and a consistent relation is P-acyclical. The reverse implications are not true in general. However, the distinction between transitivity and consistency disappears for a reflexive and complete relation; see Suzumura (1983: 244). Thus, if a relation R on X is reflexive, complete and consistent, then R is transitive, hence an ordering.

Transitivity is *the* classical coherence requirement on preference relations, and its significance in theories of individual and collective choice is obvious. Quasi-transitivity was introduced by Sen (1969; 1970: ch. 1*), and it has been employed in numerous approaches to the theory of individual and social choice, including issues related to rationalizability. P-acyclicity has the important property that it is not only sufficient for the existence of undominated choices from any arbitrary finite subset of a universal set, but it is also necessary for the existence of such choices from all possible finite subsets of the universal set; see Sen (1970: ch. 1*).

Violations of transitivity are quite likely to be observed in practical choice situations. For instance, Luce's (1956) well-known coffee–sugar example provides a plausible argument against assuming that indifference is always transitive: the inability of a decision-maker to perceive "small" differences in alternatives is bound to lead to intransitivities. As this example illustrates, transitivity frequently is too strong an assumption to impose in the context of individual choice. In the context of collective choice, it is even more evident that the plausibility of transitivity can be questioned. The concept of consistency, which is due to Suzumura (1976b), is of particular interest in this context. To underline its importance, note that this property is exactly what is required to prevent the problem of a "money pump". If consistency is violated, there exists a preference cycle with at least one strict preference. In this case, an agent with such preferences is willing to trade (where "willingness to trade" is assumed to require that the acquired alternative is at least as good as the relinquished alternative) an alternative x^K for another alternative x^{K-1}, x^{K-1} for an alternative x^{K-2}, and so on until we reach an alternative x^0 such that the agent *strictly prefers* getting back to x^K to retaining possession of x^0. Thus, at the end of a chain of exchanges, the agent is willing to pay a positive amount in order to get back to the alternative it had in its possession in the first place—a classical example of a money pump.

There is yet another reason for the importance of the concept of consistency. As an auxiliary step, a relation R' is said to be an *extension* of a relation R if and only if (i) $R \subseteq R'$; and (ii) $P(R) \subseteq P(R')$. Conversely, R is said to be a *subrelation* of R' if and only if R' is an extension of R. The following classical theorem, which is a variant of the basic theorem due to Szpilrajn (1930), specifies a sufficiency condition for the existence of an extension that is an ordering, to be called an *ordering extension*. This convenient variant of Szpilrajn's theorem was stated by Arrow (1951: 64) without a proof, whereas Hansson (1968) provided a full proof on the basis of Szpilrajn's original theorem.

Theorem 1. *Any quasi-ordering R on X has an ordering extension.*

It was shown by Suzumura (1976b; 1983: ch. 1; 2004) that *a relation R has an ordering extension if and only if it is consistent.*

The *transitive closure* $tc(R)$ of a relation R on X is defined by

$$tc(R) = \{(x, y) \in X \times X \mid \exists K \in \mathbb{N} \text{ and } x^0, \dots, x^K \in X \text{ such that}$$
$$x = x^0, (x^{k-1}, x^k) \in R \text{ for all } k \in \{1, \dots, K\} \text{ and } x^K = y\}.$$

Clearly, for any relation R, $R \subseteq tc(R)$. Furthermore, R is transitive if and only if $R = tc(R)$. Therefore, $tc(R)$ is a transitive superset of R for any R. The crucial importance of the transitive closure of a relation R lies in its property of being the *unique* smallest transitive relation containing R.

Analogously, the *consistent closure* $sc(R)$ of a relation R is defined by

$$sc(R) = R \cup \{(x, y) \mid (x, y) \in tc(R) \text{ and } (y, x) \in R\}.$$

We have $R \subseteq sc(R)$ for any relation R, and the set inclusion is satisfied with an equality if and only if R is itself consistent. Moreover, just as $tc(R)$ is the unique smallest transitive relation containing R, $sc(R)$ is the *unique* smallest consistent relation containing R.

To illustrate the definition of the consistent closure and its relationship to the transitive closure, consider the following examples. Let $X = \{x, y, z\}$, and define two relations R and R' on X by $R = \{(x, x), (x, y), (y, y), (y, z), (z, x), (z, z)\}$ and $R' = \{(x, y), (y, z)\}$. We obtain $sc(R) = tc(R) = X \times X$, $sc(R') = R'$ and $tc(R') = \{(x, y), (y, z), (x, z)\}$. Thus, the consistent closure of R coincides with the transitive closure thereof, whereas the consistent closure of R' is a strict subset of the transitive closure thereof. More generally, for any relation R on X, $sc(R)$ is always a subset of $tc(R)$. Thus, for any relation R,

$$R \subseteq sc(R) \subseteq tc(R).$$

Let $\mathcal{X}$ be the set of all non-empty subsets of X. We now introduce the concepts of greatestness and maximality with respect to a relation. Suppose R is a relation on X and $S \in \mathcal{X}$. The set $G(S, R)$ of all R-*greatest elements* of S is defined by

$$G(S, R) = \{x \in S \mid (x, y) \in R \text{ for all } y \in S\} \qquad (1)$$

and the set $M(S, R)$ of all R-*maximal elements* of S is defined by

$$M(S, R) = \{x \in S \mid (y, x) \notin P(R) \text{ for all } y \in S\}.$$

As is straightforward to verify, $G(S, R) \subseteq M(S, R)$ for all relations R on X and for all $S \in \mathcal{X}$. Furthermore, if R is reflexive and complete, then $G(S, R) = M(S, R)$; for relations R that are not reflexive or not complete, the set inclusion can be strict.

A *choice function* is a mapping that assigns, to each feasible set in its domain, a subset of this feasible set. This subset is interpreted as the set of chosen alternatives.

The domain of the choice function depends on the choice situation to be analyzed, but it will always be a set of subsets of $\mathcal{X}$, that is, an element of $\mathcal{X}$. We assume this subset of $\mathcal{X}$ to be non-empty to avoid degenerate situations. Thus, letting $\Sigma \subseteq \mathcal{X}$ be a non-empty domain, a choice function defined on that domain is a mapping $C : \Sigma \to \mathcal{X}$ such that, for all $S \in \Sigma$, $C(S) \subseteq S$. The *image of Σ under C* is given by $C(\Sigma) = \cup_{S \in \Sigma} C(S)$.

The *direct revealed preference relation R_C* of a choice function C with domain Σ is defined as

$$R_C = \{(x, y) \in X \times X \mid \exists S \in \Sigma \text{ such that } x \in C(S) \text{ and } y \in S\}.$$

III. DEFINITIONS OF RATIONALIZABILITY

There are two basic forms of rationalizability properties that are commonly considered in the literature. The first is *greatest-element rationalizability*, which requires the existence of a relation such that, for any feasible set, every chosen alternative is at least as good as every alternative in the set. Thus, this notion of rationalizability is based on the view that chosen alternatives should weakly dominate all feasible alternatives. *Maximal-element rationalizability*, on the other hand, demands the existence of a relation such that, for each feasible set, there exists no alternative in this set that is strictly preferred to any one of the chosen alternatives. Hence, this version of rationalizability does not require chosen alternatives to weakly dominate all elements of the feasible set but, instead, demands that they are not strictly dominated by any other feasible alternative.

In addition to one or the other of these two concepts of rationalizability, we have a choice regarding the properties that we require a rationalizing relation to possess. We consider the standard richness conditions of *reflexivity* and *completeness* and, in addition, the coherence properties of *transitivity, quasi-transitivity, consistency* and *P-acyclicity*. By combining each version of rationalizability with one or both (or none) of the richness conditions and with one (or none) of the coherence properties, various definitions of rationalizability are obtained. Some of these definitions are equivalent, others are independent, and some are implied by others. To get an understanding of what each of these definitions entails, we summarize all logical relationships between them in this section.

A choice function C is *greatest-element rationalizable, G-rationalizable* for short, if there exists a relation R on X, to be called a *G rationalization* of C, such that $C(S) = G(S, R)$ for all $S \in \Sigma$. Analogously, a choice function C is *maximal-element rationalizable, M-rationalizable* for short, if there exists a relation R on X, to be called an *M-rationalization* of C, such that $C(S) = M(S, R)$

for all $S \in \Sigma$. If a rationalization R is required to be reflexive and complete, the notion of greatest-element rationalizability coincides with that of maximal-element rationalizability because, in this case, $G(S, R) = M(S, R)$ for all $S \in \mathcal{X}$. Without these properties, however, this is not necessarily the case. Greatest-element rationalizability is based on the idea of chosen alternatives weakly dominating all alternatives in the feasible set under consideration, whereas maximal-element rationalizability requires chosen elements not to be strictly dominated by any other feasible alternative.

The following theorem presents a fundamental relationship between the direct revealed preference relation and a G-rationalization of a choice function. This observation, which is due to Samuelson (1938; 1948), states that any G-rationalization of a G-rationalizable choice function must respect the direct revealed preference relation of this choice function. This observation follows immediately from combining the definitions of the direct revealed preference relation R_C and of G-rationalizability. Moreover, an analogous result is valid for the relationship between G-rationalizability by a consistent relation and the consistent closure of R_C (see Bossert, Sprumont and Suzumura 2005a) and for the transitive closure of R_C and G-rationalizability by a transitive relation (see Richter 1971).

Theorem 2. *Suppose $C: \Sigma \to \mathcal{X}$ is a choice function with an arbitrary non-empty domain $\Sigma \subseteq \mathcal{X}$ and R is a relation on X.*

   (i) *If R is a G-rationalization of C, then $R_C \subseteq R$.*
   (ii) *If R is a consistent G-rationalization of C, then $sc(R_C) \subseteq R$.*
   (iii) *If R is a transitive G-rationalization of C, then $tc(R_C) \subseteq R$.*

Analogous set inclusions are not valid for M-rationalizability: an M-rationalization does not necessarily have to respect the direct revealed preference relation because chosen alternatives merely have to be undominated within the feasible set from which they are chosen.

Depending on the additional properties that we might want to impose on a rationalization (if any), different notions of rationalizability can be defined. For simplicity of presentation, we use the following convention when formulating a rationalizability axiom. We distinguish three groups of properties of a relation, namely, *rationalization* properties, *richness* properties and *coherence* properties. The first group consists of the two rationalizability properties of G-rationalizability and M-rationalizability, the second of the two requirements of reflexivity and completeness and, finally, the third of the axioms of transitivity, quasi-transitivity, consistency and P-acyclicity. Greatest-element rationalizability is abbreviated by G, M is short for maximal-element rationalizability, R stands for reflexivity and C is completeness. Transitivity, quasi-transitivity, consistency and P-acyclicity are denoted by T, Q, S and A, respectively. We identify the property or properties to be satisfied within each of the three groups and separate the groups by hyphens.

If none of the properties within a group is required, this is denoted by using the symbol $\emptyset$. Either greatest-element rationalizability or maximal-element rationalizability may be required. In addition to imposing one of the two richness properties only, reflexivity and completeness may be required simultaneously and we may require rationalizability properties without either of the two. We only consider notions of rationalizability involving at most one of the coherence properties at a time. As is the case for the richness properties, imposing none of the coherence properties is a possibility. Formally, a rationalizability property is identified by an expression of the form α-β-γ, where $\alpha \in \{G, M\}$, $\beta \in \{RC, R, C, \emptyset\}$ and $\gamma \in \{T, Q, S, A, \emptyset\}$. For example, greatest-element rationalizability by a reflexive, complete and transitive relation is denoted by G-RC-T, maximal-element rationalizability by a complete relation is M-C-$\emptyset$, greatest-element rationalizability by a reflexive and consistent relation is G-R-S and maximal-element rationalizability without any further properties of a rationalizing relation is M-$\emptyset$-$\emptyset$. Clearly, according to this classification, there are $2 \cdot 4 \cdot 5 = 40$ versions of rationalizability.

We now provide a full description of the logical relationships between these different notions of rationalizability. This result synthesizes contributions due to Bossert, Sprumont and Suzumura (2005a; 2005b; 2006) and, therefore, we do not provide a proof; see the original papers for details. For convenience, a diagrammatic representation is employed. All axioms that are depicted within the same box are equivalent, and an arrow pointing from one box b to another box b' indicates that the axioms in b imply those in b', and the converse implication is not true. In addition, of course, all implications resulting from chains of arrows depicted in the diagram are valid.

Theorem 3. *Suppose $C: \Sigma \to \mathcal{X}$ is a choice function with a general non-empty domain $\Sigma \subseteq \mathcal{X}$. Then*

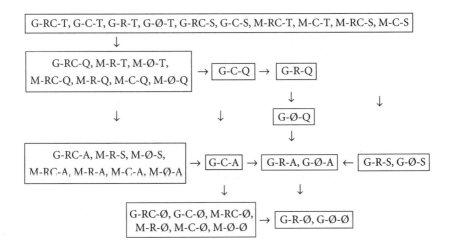

Although the equivalences established in the above theorem reduce the number of distinct notions of rationalizability from a possible 40 to 11, there remains a relatively rich set of possible definitions. In particular, note that none of the coherence properties of transitivity, quasi-transitivity, consistency and P-acyclicity is redundant: eliminating any one of them reduces the number of distinct definitions, and so does the elimination of the versions not involving any coherence property.

Furthermore, it is worth pointing out an important and remarkable difference between G-rationalizability by a transitive or a consistent relation, on the one hand, and G-rationalizability by a quasi-transitive or a P-acyclical relation, on the other. In the case of G-rationalizability with transitivity or consistency, the reflexivity requirement is redundant in all cases. That is, irrespective of whether or not completeness is imposed as a richness condition, any version of G-rationalizability with transitivity or consistency and without reflexivity is equivalent to the definition that is obtained if reflexivity is added. This observation applies to the case where no coherence property is imposed as well. In contrast, G-rationalizability by a complete and quasi-transitive relation is not equivalent to G-rationalizability by a reflexive, complete and quasi-transitive relation, and the same is true for the relationship between G-rationalizability by a complete and P-acyclical relation and G-rationalizability by a reflexive, complete and P-acyclical relation. In addition, while G-rationalizability by a P-acyclical relation and G-rationalizability by a reflexive and P-acyclical relation are equivalent, there is yet another discrepancy in the quasi-transitive case: G-rationalizability by a quasi-transitive relation is not the same as G-rationalizability by a reflexive and quasi-transitive relation.

In the case of M-rationalizability, only four distinct notions of rationalizability exist, although, in principle, there are 20 definitions, as in the case of G-rationalizability. This means that there is a dramatic reduction of possible definitions due to the equivalences established in Theorem 3. Note that, within the set of definitions of M-rationalizability, there is a substantial degree of redundancy. In particular, it is possible to generate all versions of M-rationalizability with merely two coherence properties: any of the combinations of transitivity and consistency, transitivity and P-acyclicity, or quasi-transitivity and consistency is sufficient to obtain all four notions of M-rationalizability (provided, of course, that the option of not imposing any coherence property is retained). Moreover, reflexivity is redundant in all forms of M-rationalizability, irrespective of the coherence property imposed (if any), including quasi-transitivity and P-acyclicity: any version of M-rationalizability without reflexivity is equivalent to the version obtained by adding this richness property.

There is an interesting feature that distinguishes the notions of transitive or consistent M-rationalizability from those involving quasi-transitivity, P-acyclicity or none of the coherence properties. All four M-rationalizability properties involving quasi-transitivity are equivalent, and so are all four notions involving P-acyclicity as well as the four versions without any coherence property. In contrast, there are two distinct notions of transitive M-rationalizability and two distinct notions of consistent M-rationalizability.

As is apparent from Theorem 3, M-rationalizability does not add any new versions of rationalizability, provided that all definitions of G-rationalizability involving all of the four combinations of coherence properties are present. Therefore, we can, without loss of generality, restrict attention to G-rationalizability in the characterization results stated in the following section.

IV. CHARACTERIZATIONS

This section constitutes the main contribution of the chapter. We present necessary and sufficient conditions for all notions of G-rationalizability. Some of these forms of G-rationalizability have been characterized before; see, for instance, Richter (1966), Hansson (1968) and Suzumura (1977) for the case of G-RC-T and its equivalents, Richter (1971) for the case of G-R-Ø and G-Ø-Ø, and Bossert, Sprumont and Suzumura (2005a) for the case of G-R-S and G-Ø-S. However, for the sake of motivating our new systematic approach, we provide alternative axiomatizations of these well-known notions of rationalizability. The main results stated in the remainder of the chapter are extremely general because they apply to any general domain, and they provide characterizations of all notions of rationalizability, including those that have not been axiomatized before.

The characterizations of rationalizability presented in this chapter involve relatively complex formulations of necessary and sufficient conditions. The reason is that there is no such thing as a unique *smallest* quasi-transitive relation or a unique *smallest* P-acyclical relation containing a given arbitrary relation, and similar ambiguities exist in the absence of coherence properties when completeness is imposed. In contrast, any relation R has a well-defined transitive closure, which is the unique *smallest* transitive superset of R, and a well-defined consistent closure, which is the unique *smallest* consistent superset of R. Intuitively, when moving from R to its transitive or consistent closure, pairs are added that are *necessarily* in any transitive or consistent superset of R. As soon as there exist alternatives $x^0, \ldots, x^K$ connecting two alternatives x and y via a chain of weak preferences, transitivity demands that the pair (x, y) is included in any transitive relation that contains R. Analogously, a chain of that nature implies that if, in addition, the pair (y, x) is in R, (x, y) must be added if the resulting relation is to be consistent. In contrast, there are no necessary additions to a relation in order to transform it into a quasi-transitive relation by augmenting it. For instance, suppose we have $(x, y) \in P(R)$, $(y, z) \in P(R)$ and $(z, x) \in P(R)$. In order to define a quasi-transitive relation that contains R, *at least two* of the three strict preferences must be converted into indifferences but *any two* will do. Thus, there is no unique smallest quasi-transitive superset R. Similarly, if we have a P-cycle, a P-acyclical superset of R merely has to have the property that at least *one* of the pairs along the cycle, representing a strict preference, must be converted into an indifference. But, without further information, there is nothing that forces this indifference on a specific pair along the cycle. As a consequence, there is, in general, no unique smallest P-acyclical superset of an arbitrary relation R. The same difficulty arises when G-rationalizability involving completeness without any coherence conditions is considered: there exists no unique smallest complete superset of a given incomplete relation. It is for this reason that we must introduce some novel concepts in order to be able to formulate necessary and sufficient conditions for the definitions of rationalizability considered in this paper. The fact that this new approach to the whole issue of rationalizability can cover the well-known cases, too, testifies to its general usefulness in this arena.

We are now ready to introduce our new approach to rationalizability. Let $C \colon \Sigma \to \mathcal{X}$ be a choice function with an arbitrary non-empty domain $\Sigma \subseteq \mathcal{X}$, and define

$$\mathcal{A}_C = \{(S, y) \mid S \in \Sigma \text{ and } y \in S \setminus C(S)\}.$$

For a choice function C such that $\mathcal{A}_C \neq \emptyset$, let

$$\mathcal{F}_C = \{f \colon \mathcal{A}_C \to X \mid f(S, y) \in S \text{ for all } (S, y) \in \mathcal{A}_C\}.$$

The set $\mathcal{A}_C$ consists of all pairs of a feasible set and an element that belongs to the feasible set but is not chosen by C. If $C(S) = S$ for all $S \in \Sigma$, the set $\mathcal{A}_C$ is empty; in all other cases, $\mathcal{A}_C \neq \emptyset$. The functions in $\mathcal{F}_C$ have an intuitive interpretation. They assign a feasible element to each pair of a feasible set S and an alternative y that is in S, but not chosen from S. Within the framework of G-rationalizability, the intended interpretation is that $f(S, y)$ is an alternative in S that can be used to prevent y from being chosen in the sense that y is not at least as good as $f(S, y)$ according to a G-rationalization. Clearly, the existence of such an alternative for each (S, y) in $\mathcal{A}_C$ is a necessary condition for G-rationalizability.

We begin with the rationalizability property G-R-Ø (and, of course, its equivalents). To do so, we introduce a crucial property of a function $f \in \mathcal{F}_C$ which proves instrumental in our subsequent axiomatization. It imposes a restriction on the relationship between a choice function C and a function $f \in \mathcal{F}_C$.

Direct exclusion (DRE). For all $(S, y) \in \mathcal{A}_C$, for all $T \in \Sigma$ and for all $x \in T$,

$$f(S, y) = x \Rightarrow y \notin C(T).$$

The interpretation of this condition is intuitive. According to the definition of G-rationalizability, if $x = f(S, y) \in S$ is responsible for y being prevented from being chosen in S, then y is not at least as good as x according to a G-rationalization of C. This being the case, y cannot possibly be chosen from any set containing x. This is because, according to G-rationalizability, such a choice would require that y be at least as good as x, which we have just ruled out. Thus, provided that $\mathcal{A}_C$ is non-empty, the existence of a function f satisfying DRE is clearly necessary for G-rationalizability even if no richness or coherence properties are imposed on a rationalization. Conversely, this requirement is also sufficient for G-R-$\emptyset$ and G-$\emptyset$-$\emptyset$, so that we obtain the following theorem. (See Richter (1971) for an alternative characterization of G-$\emptyset$-$\emptyset$ that is not formulated in terms of the existence of a function $f \in \mathcal{F}_C$.)

Theorem 4. *Suppose $C \colon \Sigma \to \mathcal{X}$ is a choice function with a general non-empty domain $\Sigma \subseteq \mathcal{X}$. C satisfies any of G-R-$\emptyset$ and G-$\emptyset$-$\emptyset$ if and only if, whenever $\mathcal{A}_C \neq \emptyset$, there exists $f \in \mathcal{F}_C$ satisfying DRE.*

Proof. By Theorem 3, it is sufficient to consider G-$\emptyset$-$\emptyset$.

To prove the "only if" part of the theorem, let R be a G-rationalization of C, and suppose $\mathcal{A}_C \neq \emptyset$. We define a function $f \in \mathcal{F}_C$ as follows. Consider any $(S, y) \in \mathcal{A}_C$. The assumption that R is a G-rationalization of C implies the existence of $x \in S$ such that $(y, x) \notin R$. Let $f(S, y) = x$. We show that the function f satisfies DRE. Suppose $(S, y) \in \mathcal{A}_C$, $T \in \Sigma$ and $x \in T$ are such that $f(S, y) = x$. By the definition of f, we obtain $(y, x) \notin R$. Because R is a G-rationalization of C, it follows that $y \notin C(T)$.

We now prove the "if" part of the theorem. If $\mathcal{A}_C = \emptyset$, $R = X \times X$ is clearly a G-rationalization of C. If $\mathcal{A}_C \neq \emptyset$, there exists a function $f \in \mathcal{F}_C$ satisfying DRE. Define

$$R = \{(x, y) \in X \times X \mid \nexists S \in \Sigma \text{ such that } (S, x) \in \mathcal{A}_C \text{ and } f(S, x) = y\}.$$

To prove that R is a G-rationalization of C, let $S \in \Sigma$ and $x \in S$.

Suppose $x \in C(S)$. If there exists $y \in S$ such that $(x, y) \notin R$, it follows from the definition of R that there exists $T \in \Sigma$ such that $(T, x) \in \mathcal{A}_C$ and $f(T, x) = y$. But this contradicts the property DRE and, therefore, $x \in G(S, R)$.

Now suppose $x \notin C(S)$. Let $y = f(S, x)$. By definition of R, we obtain $(x, y) \notin R$ and thus $x \notin G(S, R)$. ∎

The intuition underlying the definition of R in the above proof is quite transparent. If $x = f(S, y)$, it follows that y cannot be at least as good as x. That R is indeed a G-rationalization of C follows because f satisfies DRE.

Next, we examine the consequences of adding completeness as a property of a G-rationalization. The following condition prevents a function $f \in \mathcal{F}_C$ itself from exhibiting incoherent behavior, without reference to its relationship with a choice function.

Direct irreversibility (DRI). For all $(S, y), (T, x) \in \mathcal{A}_C$,

$$[f(S, y) = x \text{ and } x \neq y] \Rightarrow f(T, x) \neq y.$$

The existence of a function f with this property is a consequence of requiring a G-rationalization to be complete, given the interpretation of f referred to above. Suppose $f(S, y) = x$ and $f(T, x) = y$ with distinct $x, y \in X$. According to the interpretation of f, this means that x is responsible for keeping y out of $C(S)$ and y is responsible for keeping x out of $C(T)$. By definition of G-rationalizability, this means that, according to a G-rationalization, x fails to be at least as good as y and, at the same time, y is not at least as good as x. But this is in conflict with the completeness requirement.

Conversely, the existence of a function f with the two properties DRE and DRI is sufficient for G-C-Ø and its equivalents. The resulting characterization is a variant of a theorem due to Bossert, Sprumont and Suzumura (2005b).

Theorem 5. *Suppose* $C: \Sigma \to \mathcal{X}$ *is a choice function with a general non-empty domain* $\Sigma \subseteq \mathcal{X}$. *C satisfies any of* G-RC-Ø, G-C-Ø, M-RC-Ø, M-R-Ø, M-C-Ø, M-Ø-Ø *if and only if, whenever* $\mathcal{A}_C \neq \emptyset$, *there exists* $f \in \mathcal{F}_C$ *satisfying DRE and DRI.*

Proof. Using Theorem 3, it is sufficient to treat the case of G-C-Ø.

To prove the "only if" part of the theorem, let R be a complete G-rationalization of C, and suppose $\mathcal{A}_C \neq \emptyset$. We define a function $f \in \mathcal{F}_C$ as in the proof of Theorem 4. We show that the function f has the required properties.

To show that the property DRE is satisfied, we have only to follow the similar reasoning as in the proof of Theorem 4.

To establish the property DRI, let $(S, y), (T, x) \in \mathcal{A}_C$ and suppose $f(S, y) = x$ and $x \neq y$. The definition of f again implies $(y, x) \notin R$. If $f(T, x) = y$, we obtain $(x, y) \notin R$, a contradiction to the completeness of R. Thus, $f(T, x) \neq y$.

We now prove the "if" part of the theorem. If $\mathcal{A}_C = \emptyset$, $R = X \times X$ clearly is a complete G-rationalization of C. If $\mathcal{A}_C \neq \emptyset$, there exists a function $f \in \mathcal{F}_C$ satisfying DRE and DRI. Define

$$R = \{(x, y) \in X \times X \mid \nexists S \in \Sigma \text{ such that } (S, x) \in \mathcal{A}_C \text{ and } f(S, x) = y\}.$$

To prove that R is complete, suppose $x, y \in X$ are such that $x \neq y$, $(x, y) \notin R$ and $(y, x) \notin R$. By definition, there exist $S, T \in \Sigma$ such that $(S, x), (T, y) \in \mathcal{A}_C$, $f(S, x) = y$ and $f(T, y) = x$, contradicting the property DRI.

To show that R is a G-rationalization of C, we may invoke reasoning similar to that employed in the proof of Theorem 4. ∎

The intuition underlying the definition of R in this result is quite straightforward. If $x = f(S, y)$ for distinct $x, y \in X$, it follows that y cannot be at least as good as x and, because of the completeness requirement, this means that x must be better than y. The completeness of the resulting relation R is a consequence of the assumption that f possesses the property DRI and, moreover, R is a G-rationalization of C because f satisfies the property DRE.

Next, we characterize the rationalizability properties that are equivalent to G-$\emptyset$-A. As a consequence of adding P-acyclicity as a requirement on a rationalization and removing the completeness condition, the property of direct irreversibility has to be replaced by the following revelation irreversibility axiom.

Revelation irreversibility (RI). For all $K \in \mathbb{N}$ and for all $(S^0, x^0), \ldots, (S^K, x^K) \in \mathcal{A}_C$,

$$\left[f(S^k, x^k) = x^{k-1} \text{ and } (x^{k-1}, x^k) \in R_C \text{ for all } k \in \{1, \ldots, K\} \text{ and } (x^K, x^0) \in R_C \right]$$

$$\Rightarrow f(S^0, x^0) \neq x^K.$$

Revelation irreversibility differs from direct irreversibility in two ways. First, its conclusion applies to chains of relationships between alternatives via f and not only to direct instances thereof. Moreover, the axiom is conditional on any two consecutive elements in the chain being related not only through f, but also by means of a direct revealed preference according to C. As is straightforward to verify, DRI and RI are independent.

The property RI is a consequence of the P-acyclicity of a G-rationalization. To see that this is the case, note first that, according to the interpretation of f, $f(S^k, x^k) = x^{k-1}$ means that x^k cannot be at least as good as x^{k-1} according to a G-rationalization. Furthermore, because the direct revealed preference relation has to be respected by any G-rationalization, x^{k-1} must be at least as good as x^k, thus leading to a strict preference of x^{k-1} over x^k. Thus, a violation of the property RI immediately yields a violation of the P-acyclicity of a G-rationalization. Again, the existence of a function f with the requisite properties not only is necessary but also sufficient for the rationalizability definitions under consideration.

Theorem 6. *Suppose $C \colon \Sigma \to \mathcal{X}$ is a choice function with a general non-empty domain $\Sigma \subseteq \mathcal{X}$. C satisfies any of G-R-A, G-$\emptyset$-A if and only if, whenever $\mathcal{A}_C \neq \emptyset$, there exists $f \in \mathcal{F}_C$ satisfying DRE and RI.*

Proof. By Theorem 3, it is sufficient to treat the case of G-$\emptyset$-A.

Suppose C satisfies G-$\emptyset$-A and let R be a P-acyclical G-rationalization of C. Suppose $\mathcal{A}_C \neq \emptyset$. The assumption that R G-rationalizes C implies that, for any pair $(S, y) \subset \mathcal{A}_C$, there exists $x \in S$ such that $(y, x) \notin R$. Define $f(S, y) = x$. That f satisfies the property DRE follows as in the previous theorem.

To establish the property RI, suppose $K \in \mathbb{N}$ and $(S^0, x^0), \ldots, (S^K, x^K) \in \mathcal{A}_C$ are such that $f(S^k, x^k) = x^{k-1}$ and $(x^{k-1}, x^k) \in R_C$ for all $k \in \{1, \ldots, K\}$

and, moreover, $(x^K, x^0) \in R_C$. By the definition of f, we obtain $(x^k, x^{k-1}) \notin R$ for all $k \in \{1, \ldots, K\}$. By Theorem 2, $(x^{k-1}, x^k) \in R$ for all $k \in \{1, \ldots, K\}$ and, thus, $(x^{k-1}, x^k) \in P(R)$ for all $k \in \{1, \ldots, K\}$. If $f(S^0, x^0) = x^K$, it follows that $(x^0, x^K) \notin R$ by definition. Because $(x^K, x^0) \in R_C$ implies $(x^K, x^0) \in R$ by Theorem 2, we obtain $(x^K, x^0) \in P(R)$. If $K = 1$, this contradicts the observation that $(x^K, x^0) \notin R$, which follows from the hypothesis $f(S^1, x^1) = x^0$ and the definition of f. If $K > 1$, we obtain a contradiction to the P-acyclicity of R. Therefore, $f(S^0, x^0) \neq x^K$ and the property RI is satisfied.

We now prove the "if" part of the theorem. If $\mathcal{A}_C = \emptyset$, $R = X \times X$ is a P-acyclical G-rationalization of C. If $\mathcal{A}_C \neq \emptyset$, there exists a function $f \in \mathcal{F}_C$ satisfying the properties DRE and RI. Define

$$R = R_C \cup \{(x, y) \in X \times X \mid (y, x) \in R_C \text{ and}$$

$$\nexists S \in \Sigma \text{ such that } (S, x) \in \mathcal{A}_C \text{ and } f(S, x) = y\}.$$

To demonstrate that R is P-acyclical, suppose $K \in \mathbb{N} \setminus \{1\}$ and $x^0, \ldots, x^K \in X$ are such that $(x^{k-1}, x^k) \in P(R)$ for all $k \in \{1, \ldots, K\}$. Consider any $k \in \{1, \ldots, K\}$. By definition,

$$[(x^{k-1}, x^k) \in R_C \text{ or } \{(x^k, x^{k-1}) \in R_C \text{ and } \nexists T^k \in \Sigma \text{ such that}$$

$$(T^k, x^{k-1}) \in \mathcal{A}_C \text{ and } f(T^k, x^{k-1}) = x^k\}]$$

and

$$(x^k, x^{k-1}) \notin R_C \text{ and } \{(x^{k-1}, x^k) \notin R_C \text{ or } \exists S^k \in \Sigma \text{ such that}$$

$$(S^k, x^k) \in \mathcal{A}_C \text{ and } f(S^k, x^k) = x^{k-1}\}.$$

Because $(x^k, x^{k-1}) \notin R_C$ must be true,

$$(x^k, x^{k-1}) \in R_C \text{ and } \nexists T^k \in \Sigma \text{ such that } (T^k, x^{k-1}) \in \mathcal{A}_C \text{ and } f(T^k, x^{k-1}) = x^k$$

cannot be true. Therefore, $(x^{k-1}, x^k) \in R_C$ must be true, which, in turn, implies that $(x^{k-1}, x^k) \notin R_C$ cannot be true. Therefore, it follows that

$$(x^{k-1}, x^k) \in R_C \text{ and } \exists S^k \in \Sigma \text{ such that } (S^k, x^k) \in \mathcal{A}_C \text{ and } f(S^k, x^k) = x^{k-1}.$$

Using the same argument, it follows that $(x^K, x^0) \in P(R)$ implies that $(x^K, x^0) \in R_C$ and there exists $S^0 \in \Sigma$ such that $(S^0, x^0) \in \mathcal{A}_C$ and $f(S^0, x^0) = x^K$. This contradicts the property RI and thus $(x^K, x^0) \notin P(R)$ and R is P-acyclical.

We complete the proof by showing that R is a G-rationalization of C. Let $S \in \Sigma$ and $x \in S$.

Suppose $x \in C(S)$. This implies $(x, y) \in R_C$ and, by part (i) of Theorem 2, $(x, y) \in R$ for all $y \in S$. Hence, $x \in G(S, R)$.

Now suppose $x \notin C(S)$. Thus, $(S, x) \in \mathcal{A}_C$. Let $y = f(S, x)$. If $(x, y) \in R_C$, there exists $T \in \Sigma$ such that $y \in T$ and $x \in C(T)$. Because $y \in S$, this contradicts the property DRE. Therefore, $(x, y) \notin R_C$ and, together with the observations that $(S, x) \in \mathcal{A}_C$ and $y = f(S, x)$, it follows that $(x, y) \notin R$ and hence $x \notin G(S, R)$. ∎

As usual, any G-rationalization R has to respect the direct revealed preference relation R_C. Furthermore, the construction of R employed in the above theorem converts all strict direct revealed preferences into indifferences whenever this is possible without conflicting with the interpretation of the function f. This is done to reduce the potential for conflicts with P-acyclicity as much as possible. That the resulting relation satisfies the required properties follows from the properties of f.

In order to accommodate completeness as well as P-acyclicity, we replace the property RI with the following property of distinctness irreversibility.

Distinctness irreversibility (DSI). For all $K \in \mathbb{N}$ and for all $(S^0, x^0), \ldots,$ $(S^K, x^K) \in \mathcal{A}_C$,

$$\left[f(S^k, x^k) = x^{k-1} \text{ and } x^{k-1} \neq x^k \text{ for all } k \in \{1, \ldots, K\} \text{ and } x^K \neq x^0 \right] \Rightarrow$$
$$f(S^0, x^0) \neq x^K.$$

Clearly, distinctness irreversibility implies direct irreversibility (set $K = 1$ to verify this claim). Although RI and DSI by themselves are independent, DSI implies RI in the presence of DRE. To see that this is the case, suppose f violates RI. Then there exist $K \in \mathbb{N}$ and $(S^0, x^0), \ldots, (S^K, x^K) \in \mathcal{A}_C$ such that $f(S^k, x^k) = x^{k-1}$ and $(x^{k-1}, x^k) \in R_C$ for all $k \in \{1, \ldots, K\}$, $(x^K, x^0) \in R_C$ and $f(S^0, x^0) = x^K$. If any two consecutive elements in this cycle are distinct, we immediately obtain a contradiction to DSI. If $x^{k-1} = x^k$ for all $k \in \{1, \ldots, K\}$, it follows that $f(S^0, x^0) = x^0$ and $(x^0, x^0) \in R_C$. By definition of R_C, there exists $T \in \Sigma$ such that $x^0 \in C(T) \subseteq T$, contradicting DRE.

The property of DSI rather than of RI must be added to DRE if a rationalization is to be complete in addition to being P-acyclical. If DSI is violated, the completeness of a G-rationalization and the interpretation of f together imply that a G-rationalization must have a strict preference cycle, which immediately yields a contradiction to the P-acyclicity requirement. The following theorem establishes that the existence of a function f satisfying DRE and DSI is necessary and sufficient for the rationalizability properties that are equivalent to G-C-A.

Theorem 7. *Suppose* $C : \Sigma \to \mathcal{X}$ *is a choice function with a general non-empty domain* $\Sigma \subseteq \mathcal{X}$. *C satisfies* G-C-A *if and only if, whenever* $\mathcal{A}_C \neq \emptyset$, *there exists* $f \in \mathcal{F}_C$ *satisfying* DRE *and* DSI.

Proof. First, suppose C satisfies G-C-A and let R be a complete and P-acyclical G-rationalization of C. Suppose $\mathcal{A}_C \neq \emptyset$. The assumption that R G-rationalizes C implies that, for any pair $(S, y) \in \mathcal{A}_C$, there exists $x \in S$ such that $(y, x) \notin R$. Define $f(S, y) = x$.

The proof that f satisfies DRE can be given as in the proof of Theorem 4.

To establish the property DSI, suppose $K \in \mathbb{N}$ and $(S^0, x^0), \ldots, (S^K, x^K) \in \mathcal{A}_C$ are such that $f(S^k, x^k) = x^{k-1}$ and $x^{k-1} \neq x^k$ for all $k \in \{1, \ldots, K\}$ and, furthermore, $x^K \neq x^0$. By the definition of f, it follows that $(x^k, x^{k-1}) \notin R$ for all $k \in \{1, \ldots, K\}$. Because R is complete and $x^{k-1} \neq x^k$ for all $k \in \{1, \ldots, K\}$ by assumption, it follows that $(x^{k-1}, x^k) \in P(R)$ for all $k \in \{1, \ldots, K\}$. If $f(S^0, x^0) = x^K$, it follows that $(x^0, x^K) \notin R$ by definition and, by the assumption $x^K \neq x^0$ and the completeness of R, we obtain $(x^K, x^0) \in P(R)$. If $K = 1$, this contradicts the observation that $(x^K, x^0) \notin R$, which follows from the hypothesis $f(S^1, x^1) = x^0$ and the definition of f. If $K > 1$, we obtain a contradiction to the P-acyclicity of R. Therefore, $f(S^0, x^0) \neq x^K$.

We now prove the "if" part of the theorem. If $\mathcal{A}_C = \emptyset$, $R = X \times X$ is a complete P-acyclical G-rationalization of C. If $\mathcal{A}_C \neq \emptyset$, there exists a function $f \in \mathcal{F}_C$ satisfying the properties DRE and DSI. Define

$$R = \{(x, y) \in X \times X \mid \nexists S \in \Sigma \text{ such that } (S, x) \in \mathcal{A}_C \text{ and } f(S, x) = y\}.$$

We prove that R is complete. By way of contradiction, suppose $x, y \in X$ are such that $x \neq y$, $(x, y) \notin R$ and $(y, x) \notin R$. By the definition of R, this implies that there exist $S, T \in \Sigma$ such that $(S, x), (T, y) \in \mathcal{A}_C$, $f(S, x) = y$ and $f(T, y) = x$. Because $x \neq y$, this contradicts the property DSI. Thus, R is complete.

To show that R is P-acyclical, suppose $K \in \mathbb{N} \setminus \{1\}$ and $x^0, \ldots, x^K \in X$ are such that $(x^{k-1}, x^k) \in P(R)$ for all $k \in \{1, \ldots, K\}$. By the definition of R, this implies that there exist $S^1, \ldots, S^K \in \Sigma$ such that $(S^k, x^k) \in \mathcal{A}_C$ and $x^{k-1} = f(S^k, x^k)$ for all $k \in \{1, \ldots, K\}$. Moreover, for all $k \in \{1, \ldots, K\}$, there exists no $T^k \in \Sigma$ such that $(T^k, x^{k-1}) \in \mathcal{A}_C$ and $x^k = f(T^k, x^{k-1})$. This implies $x^{k-1} \neq x^k$ for all $k \in \{1, \ldots, K\}$. If $(x^K, x^0) \in P(R)$, there exists $S^0 \in \Sigma$ such that $(S^0, x^0) \in \mathcal{A}_C$ and $x^K = f(S^0, x^0)$. Furthermore, there exists no $T^0 \in \Sigma$ such that $(T^0, x^K) \in \mathcal{A}_C$ and $x^0 = f(T^0, x^K)$. This implies $x^0 \neq x^K$ and we obtain a contradiction to the property DSI. Thus, $(x^K, x^0) \notin P(R)$ and R is P-acyclical.

It remains to be shown that R is a G-rationalization of C. Let $S \in \Sigma$ and $x \in S$.

Suppose $x \in C(S)$. If there exist $y \in S$ and $T \in \Sigma$ such that $(T, x) \in \mathcal{A}_C$ and $f(T, x) = y$, we obtain a contradiction to the property DRE. Thus, by definition, $(x, y) \in R$ for all $y \in S$ and hence $x \in G(S, R)$.

Now suppose $x \notin C(S)$. Let $y = f(S, x)$. By the definition of R, this implies $(x, y) \notin R$ and, therefore, $x \notin G(S, R)$. ∎

The intuition underlying the definition of R in this result is quite straightforward. If $x = f(S, y)$, it follows that y cannot be at least as good as x and, because of the completeness assumption, this means that x must be better than y whenever $x \neq y$. The resulting relation has all the required properties as a consequence of the properties of f.

Our last set of rationalizability properties which involves P-acyclical G-rationalizations is that containing G-RC-A. Because reflexivity is added as a requirement, an unconditional version of irreversibility is called for.

Indirect irreversibility (II). For all $K \in \mathbb{N}$ and for all $(S^0, x^0), \ldots, (S^K, x^K) \in \mathcal{A}_C$,

$$f(S^k, x^k) = x^{k-1} \text{ for all } k \in \{1, \ldots, K\} \Rightarrow f(S^0, x^0) \neq x^K.$$

Clearly, indirect irreversibility implies all of the irreversibility conditions introduced earlier. The full force of the axiom is needed because, as opposed to the G-rationalizability property G-C-A, its conclusion must hold not only for chains of distinct alternatives but, due to the added reflexivity assumption, for any chain. We obtain the following characterization which, with a slightly different proof, can be found in Bossert, Sprumont and Suzumura (2005b).

Theorem 8. *Suppose* $C \colon \Sigma \to \mathcal{X}$ *is a choice function with a general non-empty domain* $\Sigma \subseteq \mathcal{X}$. *C satisfies any of* G-RC-A, M-R-S, M-Ø-S, M-RC-A, M-R-A, M-C-A, M-Ø-A *if and only if, whenever* $\mathcal{A}_C \neq \emptyset$, *there exists* $f \in \mathcal{F}_C$ *satisfying* DRE *and* II.

Proof. Invoking Theorem 3 again, it is sufficient to consider G-RC-A.

We first prove the "only if" part of the theorem. Let R be a reflexive, complete and P-acyclical G-rationalization of C. Suppose $\mathcal{A}_C \neq \emptyset$ and define a function $f \in \mathcal{F}_C$ as in the proof of Theorem 4.

The proof that f satisfies DRE can be given as in the proof of Theorem 4.

To establish the property II, suppose $K \in \mathbb{N}$ and $(S^0, x^0), \ldots, (S^K, x^K) \in \mathcal{A}_C$ are such that $f(S^k, x^k) = x^{k-1}$ for all $k \in \{1, \ldots, K\}$. By definition, $(x^k, x^{k-1}) \notin R$ for all $k \in \{1, \ldots, K\}$. Because R is reflexive, we have $x^{k-1} \neq x^k$ for all $k \in \{1, \ldots, K\}$ and, thus, the completeness of R implies $(x^{k-1}, x^k) \in P(R)$ for all $k \in \{1, \ldots, K\}$. If $f(S^0, x^0) = x^K$, it follows analogously that $(x^K, x^0) \in P(R)$. If $K = 1$, this contradicts the hypothesis $(x^K, x^0) \notin R$, and if $K > 1$, we obtain a contradiction to the P-acyclicity of R. Therefore, $f(S^0, x^0) \neq x^K$.

Next, we prove the "if" part of the theorem. If $\mathcal{A}_C = \emptyset$, $R = X \times X$ is clearly a reflexive, complete and P-acyclical G-rationalization of C. If $\mathcal{A}_C \neq \emptyset$, there exists a function $f \in \mathcal{F}_C$ satisfying DRE and II. Define

$$R = \{(x, y) \in X \times X \mid \exists S \in \Sigma \text{ such that } (S, x) \in \mathcal{A}_C \text{ and } f(S, x) = y\}.$$

To prove that R is reflexive, suppose, by way of contradiction, that there exists $x \in X$ such that $(x, x) \notin R$. By definition, there exists $S \in \Sigma$ such that $(S, x) \in \mathcal{A}_C$ and $f(S, x) = x$. Letting $K = 1$, $S^0 = S^K = S$ and $x^0 = x^K = x$, we obtain a contradiction to the property II.

To verify the completeness and P-acyclicity of R, we may invoke the corresponding part of the proof of Theorem 7, coupled with the fact that II implies DSI.

It remains to be shown that R is a G-rationalization of C. The method used in the proof of Theorem 4 can be invoked for this purpose as well. ∎

The intuition underlying the definition of R in this result is as follows. If $x = f(S, y)$, it follows that y cannot be at least as good as x and, because of reflexivity and completeness, this means that x must be better than y. As opposed to the previous result, f satisfies II rather than merely DSI and, as a consequence, R is reflexive in addition to being complete and P-acyclical.

We now turn to rationalizability properties involving quasi-transitivity as the coherence property to be satisfied by a G-rationalization. We begin with G-∅-Q. According to Theorem 6, the existence of a function f satisfying DRE and RI is necessary and sufficient for G-∅-A. If P-acyclicity is strengthened to quasi-transitivity, the following additional property of f is required.

Revelation exclusion (RE). For all $K \in \mathbb{N}$, for all $(S^1, x^1), \ldots, (S^K, x^K) \in \mathcal{A}_C$, for all $S^0 \in \Sigma$ and for all $x^0 \in S^0$,

$$\left[f(S^k, x^k) = x^{k-1} \text{ and } (x^{k-1}, x^k) \in R_C \text{ for all } k \in \{1, \ldots, K\} \right] \Rightarrow x^K \notin C(S^0).$$

Revelation exclusion is necessary to ensure that a G-rationalization is quasi-transitive as opposed to merely P-acyclical. As illustrated earlier, the conjunction of $f(S^k, x^k) = x^{k-1}$ and $(x^{k-1}, x^k) \in R_C$ implies, given the interpretation of f, that a G-rationalization must exhibit a strict preference. Following the resulting chain of strict preferences, quasi-transitivity demands that x^0 is strictly preferred to x^K according to the rationalization. This is incompatible with $(x^K, x^0) \in R_C$ and, thus, RE must be satisfied. We obtain the following characterization.

Theorem 9. *Suppose $C: \Sigma \to \mathcal{X}$ is a choice function with a general non-empty domain $\Sigma \subseteq \mathcal{X}$. C satisfies G-∅-Q if and only if, whenever $\mathcal{A}_C \neq \emptyset$, there exists $f \in \mathcal{F}_C$ satisfying DRE, RI and RE.*

Proof. Suppose C satisfies G-∅-Q and let R be a quasi-transitive G-rationalization of C. Suppose $\mathcal{A}_C \neq \emptyset$ and define a function $f \in \mathcal{F}_C$ as in the proof of Theorem 4.

The proof that f satisfies DRE can be given as in the corresponding part of the proof of Theorem 4.

To establish the property RI, we have only to invoke the corresponding part of the proof of Theorem 6, coupled with the fact that quasi-transitivity implies P-acyclicity.

To show that f satisfies RE, suppose $K \in \mathbb{N}$, $(S^1, x^1), \ldots, (S^K, x^K) \in \mathcal{A}_C$, $S^0 \in \Sigma$ and $x^0 \in S^0$ are such that $f(S^k, x^k) = x^{k-1}$ and $(x^{k-1}, x^k) \in R_C$ for all $k \in \{1, \ldots, K\}$. By the definition of f, $(x^k, x^{k-1}) \notin R$ and by Theorem 2, $(x^{k-1}, x^k) \in R$ for all $k \in \{1, \ldots, K\}$. Thus, $(x^{k-1}, x^k) \in P(R)$ for all $k \in \{1, \ldots, K\}$ and the quasi-transitivity of R implies $(x^0, x^K) \in P(R)$. Therefore, $(x^K, x^0) \notin R$ and, because R is a G-rationalization of C, we obtain $x^K \notin C(S^0)$.

Now suppose that there exists $f \in \mathcal{F}_C$ satisfying DRE, RI and RE whenever $\mathcal{A}_C \neq \emptyset$. If $\mathcal{A}_C = \emptyset$, $R = X \times X$ is a quasi-transitive G-rationalization of C and we are done. If $\mathcal{A}_C \neq \emptyset$, there exists a function $f \in \mathcal{F}_C$ satisfying the properties DRE, RI and RE. Define

$$R = R_C$$

$$\cup \{(x, y) \in X \times X \mid (y, x) \in R_C \text{ and } \nexists S \in \Sigma \text{ such that } (S, x) \in \mathcal{A}_C \text{ and}$$

$$f(S, x) = y \text{ and } \nexists K \in \mathbb{N}, x^0 \in X \text{ and } (S^1, x^1), \ldots, (S^K, x^K) \in \mathcal{A}_C$$

$$\text{such that } y = x^0, x^{k-1} = f(S^k, x^k) \text{ and } (x^{k-1}, x^k) \in R_C \text{ for all}$$

$$k \in \{1, \ldots, K\} \text{ and } x^K = x\}$$

$$\cup \{(x, y) \in X \times X \mid \exists K \in \mathbb{N}, x^0 \in X \text{ and } (S^1, x^1), \ldots, (S^K, x^K) \in \mathcal{A}_C$$

$$\text{such that } x = x^0, x^{k-1} = f(S^k, x^k) \text{ and } (x^{k-1}, x^k) \in R_C \text{ for all}$$

$$k \in \{1, \ldots, K\} \text{ and } x^K = y\}.$$

To prove that R is quasi-transitive, suppose $x, y, z \in X$ are such that $(x, y) \in P(R)$ and $(y, z) \in P(R)$. By definition, $(x, y) \in R$ implies

$$(x, y) \in R_C \tag{2}$$

or

$$(y, x) \in R_C \text{ and } \nexists S \in \Sigma \text{ such that } (S, x) \in \mathcal{A}_C \text{ and } f(S, x) = y \text{ and}$$

$$\nexists K \in \mathbb{N}, x^0 \in X \text{ and } (S^1, x^1), \ldots, (S^K, x^K) \in \mathcal{A}_C \text{ such that } y = x^0, \tag{3}$$

$$x^{k-1} = f(S^k, x^k) \text{ and } (x^{k-1}, x^k) \in R_C \text{ for all } k \in \{1, \ldots, K\} \text{ and } x^K = x$$

or

$$\exists K \in \mathbb{N}, x^0 \in X \text{ and } (S^1, x^1), \ldots, (S^K, x^K) \in \mathcal{A}_C \text{ such that } x = x^0, \tag{4}$$

$$x^{k-1} = f(S^k, x^k) \text{ and } (x^{k-1}, x^k) \in R_C \text{ for all } k \in \{1, \ldots, K\} \text{ and } x^K = y.$$

Analogously, $(y, x) \notin R$ implies

$$(y, x) \notin R_C \tag{5}$$

and

$$(x, y) \notin R_C \text{ or } \exists S \in \Sigma \text{ such that } (S, y) \in \mathcal{A}_C \text{ and } f(S, y) = x \text{ or}$$

$$\exists K \in \mathbb{N}, x^0 \in X \text{ and } (S^1, x^1), \ldots, (S^K, x^K) \in \mathcal{A}_C \text{ such that } x = x^0, \tag{6}$$

$$x^{k-1} = f(S^k, x^k) \text{ and } (x^{k-1}, x^k) \in R_C \text{ for all } k \in \{1, \ldots, K\} \text{ and } x^K = y$$

and

$$\nexists K \in \mathbb{N}, x^0 \in X \text{ and } (S^1, x^1), \ldots, (S^K, x^K) \in \mathcal{A}_C \text{ such that } y = x^0, \tag{7}$$

$$x^{k-1} = f(S^k, x^k) \text{ and } (x^{k-1}, x^k) \in R_C \text{ for all } k \in \{1, \ldots, K\} \text{ and } x^K = x.$$

Because (5) must be true, (3) must be false. Therefore, it follows that (2) or (4) is true and that (6) is true. Because (2) and $(x, y) \notin R_C$ are incompatible, it follows that we must have

$$\text{(2) and } \exists S \in \Sigma \text{ such that } (S, y) \in \mathcal{A}_C \text{ and } f(S, y) = x \tag{8}$$

or

$$\text{(2) and (4)} \tag{9}$$

or (4). Clearly, (8) implies (4) and (9) implies (4) trivially. Thus, (4) follows in all possible cases. Analogously, $(y, z) \in P(R)$ implies

$$\exists L \in \mathbb{N}, y^0 \in X \text{ and } (T^1, y^1), \ldots, (T^L, y^L) \in \mathcal{A}_C \text{ such that } y = y^0, \tag{10}$$

$$y^{\ell-1} = f(T^\ell, y^\ell) \text{ and } (y^{\ell-1}, y^\ell) \in R_C \text{ for all } \ell \in \{1, \ldots, L\} \text{ and } y^L = z.$$

Letting $M = K + L$, $z^0 = x^0$, $(U^m, z^m) = (S^m, x^m)$ for all $m \in \{1, \ldots, K\}$ and $(U^m, z^m) = (T^{m-K}, y^{m-K})$ for all $m \in \{K+1, \ldots, K+L\}$, (4) and (10) together imply

$$x = z^0, z^{m-1} = f(U^m, z^m) \text{ and } (z^{m-1}, z^m) \in R_C \text{ for all } m \in \{1, \ldots, M\} \tag{11}$$

and $z^M = z$.

Therefore, by the definition of R, $(x, z) \in R$. Suppose we also have $(z, x) \in R$. This implies

$$(z, x) \in R_C \tag{12}$$

or

$(x, z) \in R_C$ and $\not\exists S \in \Sigma$ such that $(S, z) \in \mathcal{A}_C$ and $f(S, z) = x$ and

$$\not\exists K \in \mathbb{N}, x^0 \in X \text{ and } (S^1, x^1), \ldots, (S^K, x^K) \in \mathcal{A}_C \text{ such that } x = x^0, \tag{13}$$

$$x^{k-1} = f(S^k, x^k) \text{ and } (x^{k-1}, x^k) \in R_C \text{ for all } k \in \{1, \ldots, K\} \text{ and } x^K = z$$

or

$$\exists K \in \mathbb{N}, x^0 \in X \text{ and } (S^1, x^1), \ldots, (S^K, x^K) \in \mathcal{A}_C \text{ such that } z = x^0, \tag{14}$$

$$x^{k-1} = f(S^k, x^k) \text{ and } (x^{k-1}, x^k) \in R_C \text{ for all } k \in \{1, \ldots, K\} \text{ and } x^K = x.$$

If (12) is true, (11) yields a contradiction to the property RE. (13) immediately contradicts (11). Finally, if (14) applies, combining it with (11), we are led to a contradiction to the property RI. Thus, R is quasi-transitive.

To show that R is a G-rationalization of C, let $S \in \Sigma$ and $x \in S$. Suppose $x \in C(S)$. This implies $(x, y) \in R_C \subseteq R$ for all $y \in S$ and, therefore, $x \in G(S, R)$. Now suppose $x \notin C(S)$. Thus, $(S, x) \in \mathcal{A}_C$. Let $y = f(S, x)$ and suppose $(x, y) \in R$. If $(x, y) \in R_C$, there exists $T \in \Sigma$ such that $y \in T$ and $x \in C(T)$. This contradicts the property DRE. If (3) applies, it follows that there exists no $S \in \Sigma$ such that $(S, x) \in \mathcal{A}_C$ and $y = f(S, x)$, an immediate contradiction to our hypothesis. Finally, if (4) applies, we obtain a contradiction to the property RI. Thus, $(x, y) \notin R$ and hence $x \notin G(S, R)$. ■

In the above proof, the components of R are constructed by including all pairs that are necessarily in this relation and then invoking the properties of f to ensure that R satisfies all of the requirements. In particular, as is the case whenever G-rationalizability is considered, the direct revealed preference relation R_C has to be respected. To avoid as many potential conflicts with quasi-transitivity as possible, any strict revealed preference is converted into an indifference whenever possible without contradiction. Finally, any chain of strict preference imposed by the conjunction of relationships imposed by f and by the direct revealed preference criterion has to be respected due to the quasi-transitivity requirement.

If reflexivity is added to quasi-transitivity as a further requirement on a G-rationalization, the function f must possess an additional property as well. This is accomplished by imposing the following axiom.

Self-irreversibility (SI). For all $(S, x) \in \mathcal{A}_C$,

$$f(S, x) \neq x.$$

According to the interpretation of f, $f(S, x) = x$ means that x is excluded from $C(S)$ because x fails to be considered at least as good as itself by a G-rationalization. Clearly, this is incompatible with the reflexivity of a G-rationalization and, thus, self-irreversibility is an additional necessary requirement to be satisfied by f. This leads to the following theorem.

Theorem 10. *Suppose* $C \colon \Sigma \to \mathcal{X}$ *is a choice function with a general non-empty domain* $\Sigma \subseteq \mathcal{X}$. C *satisfies G-R-Q if and only if, whenever* $\mathcal{A}_C \neq \emptyset$, *there exists* $f \in \mathcal{F}_C$ *satisfying* DRE, RI, RE *and* SI.

Proof. Suppose C satisfies G-R-Q and let R be a reflexive and quasi-transitive G-rationalization of C. Suppose $\mathcal{A}_C \neq \emptyset$ and define a function $f \in \mathcal{F}_C$ as in the proof of Theorem 4.

To prove that f satisfies DRE, we may invoke the method of proof used in establishing the corresponding part of Theorem 4.

To prove that f satisfies RI and RE, we may invoke the method of proof used in establishing the corresponding parts of Theorem 6 and Theorem 9.

To prove that SI is satisfied, suppose there exists $(S, x) \in \mathcal{A}_C$ such that $f(S, x) = x$. By the definition of f, this implies $(x, x) \notin R$, contradicting the reflexivity of R.

Suppose that, whenever $\mathcal{A}_C \neq \emptyset$, there exists $f \in \mathcal{F}_C$ satisfying DRE, RI, RE and SI. If $\mathcal{A}_C = \emptyset$, $R = X \times X$ is a reflexive and quasi-transitive G-rationalization of C and we are done. If $\mathcal{A}_C \neq \emptyset$, there exists a function $f \in \mathcal{F}_C$ satisfying DRE, RI, RE and SI. Define

$$R = R_C \cup \Delta$$

$$\cup \{(x, y) \in X \times X \mid (y, x) \in R_C \text{ and } \not\exists S \in \Sigma \text{ such that } (S, x) \in \mathcal{A}_C \text{ and}$$

$$f(S, x) = y \text{ and } \not\exists K \in \mathbb{N}, x^0 \in X \text{ and } (S^1, x^1), \dots, (S^K, x^K) \in \mathcal{A}_C$$

$$\text{such that } y = x^0, x^{k-1} = f(S^k, x^k) \text{ and } (x^{k-1}, x^k) \in R_C \text{ for all}$$

$$k \in \{1, \dots, K\} \text{ and } x^K = x\}$$

$$\cup \{(x, y) \in X \times X \mid \exists K \in \mathbb{N}, x^0 \in X \text{ and } (S^1, x^1), \dots, (S^K, x^K) \in \mathcal{A}_C$$

$$\text{such that } x = x^0, x^{k-1} = f(S^k, x^k) \text{ and } (x^{k-1}, x^k) \in R_C \text{ for all}$$

$$k \in \{1, \dots, K\} \text{ and } x^K = y\}.$$

Clearly, R is reflexive because $\Delta \subseteq R$.

The rest of the proof is essentially the same as in the proof of Theorem 9. ∎

If completeness rather than reflexivity is added to quasi-transitivity, we obtain a stronger rationalizability condition; see Theorem 3. As a consequence, the property RI of f in Theorem 9 is replaced by DSI and, instead of RE, the following requirement is imposed.

Distinctness exclusion (DSE). For all $K \in \mathbb{N}$, for all $(S^1, x^1), \dots, (S^K, x^K) \in \mathcal{A}_C$, for all $S^0 \in \Sigma$ and for all $x^0 \in S^0$,

$$[f(S^k, x^k) = x^{k-1} \text{ and } x^{k-1} \neq x^k \text{ for all } k \in \{1, \dots, K\}] \Rightarrow x^K \notin C(S^0).$$

In the presence of DRE, RE is implied by DSE. Suppose f violates RE. If all x^k are identical, we obtain an immediate contradiction to DRE. If there exists a $k \in \{1, \dots, K\}$ such that $x^{k-1} \neq x^0$, we can without loss of generality assume that all of them are pairwise distinct (otherwise, the chain can be reduced to one involving pairwise distinct elements), which leads to a violation of DSE.

The strengthening of revelation exclusion to distinctness exclusion is necessary as a consequence of adding completeness to quasi-transitivity. If $f(S^k, x^k) = x^{k-1}$ and $x^{k-1} \neq x^K$, the interpretation of f and the completeness of a G-rationalization together imply that x^{k-1} is strictly preferred to x^k. Following this chain of strict preferences, quasi-transitivity demands that x^0 is strictly preferred to x^K, which is not compatible with $(x^K, x^0) \in R_C$. The corresponding characterization result is stated in the following theorem.

Theorem 11. *Suppose* $C: \Sigma \to \mathcal{X}$ *is a choice function with a general non-empty domain* $\Sigma \subseteq \mathcal{X}$. *C satisfies G-C-Q if and only if, whenever* $\mathcal{A}_C \neq \emptyset$, *there exists* $f \in \mathcal{F}_C$ *satisfying DRE, DSI and DSE.*

Proof. We first prove that G-C-Q implies the existence of $f \in \mathcal{F}_C$, which satisfies DRE, DSI and DSE whenever $\mathcal{A}_C \neq \emptyset$. Let R be a complete and quasi-transitive G-rationalization of C. Define a function $f \in \mathcal{F}_C$ as in the proof of Theorem 4.

To prove that f satisfies DRE and DSI, we may invoke the method of proof used in establishing the corresponding parts of Theorem 4 and Theorem 7, coupled with the fact that quasi-transitivity implies P-acyclicity.

To prove that f satisfies DSE, let $K \in \mathbb{N}$, $(S^1, x^1), \ldots, (S^K, x^K) \in \mathcal{A}_C$, $S^0 \in \Sigma$ and $x^0 \in S^0$ be such that $f(S^k, x^k) = x^{k-1}$ and $x^{k-1} \neq x^k$ for all $k \in \{1, \ldots, K\}$. By definition, $(x^k, x^{k-1}) \notin R$ for all $k \in \{1, \ldots, K\}$ and the completeness of R implies $(x^{k-1}, x^k) \in P(R)$ for all $k \in \{1, \ldots, K\}$. R being quasi-transitive, it follows that $(x^0, x^K) \in P(R)$ and thus $(x^K, x^0) \notin R$. Because R is a G-rationalization of C, we obtain $x^K \notin C(S^0)$.

Now suppose that, whenever $\mathcal{A}_C \neq \emptyset$, there exists $f \in \mathcal{F}_C$ satisfying DRE, DSI and DSE. If $\mathcal{A}_C = \emptyset$, $R = X \times X$ is a complete and quasi-transitive G-rationalization of C and we are done. If $\mathcal{A}_C \neq \emptyset$, there exists a function $f \in \mathcal{F}_C$ satisfying DRE, DSI and DSE. Define

$$R = \{(x, y) \in X \times X \mid \exists K \in \mathbb{N}, x^0 \in X \text{ and } (S^1, x^1), \ldots, (S^K, x^K) \in \mathcal{A}_C$$

$$\text{such that } y = x^0, x^{k-1} = f(S^k, x^k) \text{ and } x^{k-1} \neq x^k \text{ for all } k \in \{1, \ldots, K\} \text{ and}$$

$$x^K = x\} \setminus \{(x, x) \in \Delta \mid \exists S \in \Sigma \text{ such that } (S, x) \in \mathcal{A}_C \text{ and } f(S, x) = x\}.$$

To prove that R is complete, suppose, by way of contradiction, that there exist $x, y \in X$ such that $x \neq y$, $(x, y) \notin R$ and $(y, x) \notin R$. By definition, this implies that there exist $K, L \in \mathbb{N}$, $x^0, y^0 \in X$ and $(S^1, x^1), \ldots, (S^K, x^K), (T^1, y^1), \ldots, (T^L, y^L) \in \mathcal{A}_C$ such that $y = x^0$, $x^{k-1} = f(S^k, x^k)$ and $x^{k-1} \neq x^k$ for all $k \in \{1, \ldots, K\}$, $x^K = x$, $x = y^0$, $y^{\ell-1} = f(T^\ell, y^\ell)$ and $y^{\ell-1} \neq y^\ell$ for all $\ell \in \{1, \ldots, L\}$ and $y^L = y$. Letting $M = K + L - 1$, $(U^0, z^0) = (T^L, y^L)$, $(U^m, z^m) = (S^m, x^m)$ for all $m \in \{1, \ldots, K\}$ and $(U^m, z^m) = (T^{m-K}, y^{m-K})$ for all $m \in \{K + 1, \ldots, K + L - 1\}$, it follows that $z^{m-1} = f(U^m, z^m)$ and $z^{m-1} \neq z^m$ for all $m \in \{1, \ldots, M\}$ and $z^M = f(U^0, z^0)$, contradicting the property DSI.

Next, we show that R is quasi-transitive. Suppose $x, y, z \in X$ are such that $(x, y) \in P(R)$ and $(y, z) \in P(R)$. This implies that $x \neq y$ and $y \neq z$ and, by the definition of R, there exist $K, L \in \mathbb{N}$, $x^0, y^0 \in X$ and $(S^1, x^1), \ldots, (S^K, x^K)$, $(T^1, y^1), \ldots, (T^L, y^L) \in \mathcal{A}_C$ such that $x = x^0$, $x^{k-1} = f(S^k, x^k)$ and $x^{k-1} \neq x^k$ for all $k \in \{1, \ldots, K\}$, $x^K = y$, $y = y^0$, $y^{\ell-1} = f(T^\ell, y^\ell)$ and $y^{\ell-1} \neq y^\ell$ for all $\ell \in \{1, \ldots, L\}$ and $y^L = z$. Letting $M = K + L$, $z^0 = x^0$, $(U^m, z^m) = (S^m, x^m)$ for all $m \in \{1, \ldots, K\}$ and $(U^m, z^m) = (T^{m-K}, y^{m-K})$ for all $m \in \{K + 1, \ldots, K + L\}$, it follows that $(z, x) \notin R$. Because R is complete, we obtain $(x, z) \in P(R)$.

Finally, we prove that R is a G-rationalization of C. Let $S \subseteq \Sigma$ and $x \in S$.

Suppose first that $x \in C(S)$ and, by way of contradiction, that there exists $y \in S$ such that $(x, y) \notin R$. If $x = y$ and there exists $S \in \Sigma$ such that $(S, x) \in \mathcal{A}_C$ and $f(S, x) = x$, we obtain a contradiction to the property DRE. If there exist $K \in \mathbb{N}$,

$x^0 \in X$ and $(S^1, x^1), \ldots, (S^K, x^K) \in \mathcal{A}_C$ such that $y = x^0$, $x^{k-1} = f(S^k, x^k)$ and $x^{k-1} \neq x^k$ for all $k \in \{1, \ldots, K\}$ and $x^K = x$, letting $S^0 = S$ yields a contradiction to the property DSE. Therefore, $x \in G(S, R)$. Thus, $C(S) \subseteq G(S, R)$.

Now suppose $x \notin C(S)$. Let $y = f(S, x)$. By definition, this implies $(x, y) \notin R$ and hence $x \notin G(S, R)$. Thus, $G(S, R) \subseteq C(S)$. ∎

The G-rationalization R employed in this proof is less complex because of the completeness assumption—an absence of a weak preference for one of two distinct alternatives implies a strict preference for the other. In addition, whenever an element x is not chosen in a set S because, according to f, x is not at least as good as itself, the pair (x, x) cannot be in R. Because R is also required to be quasi-transitive, chains of strict preference have to be respected as well. In order to arrive at a complete and quasi-transitive G-rationalization of C, we define R to be composed of all pairs $(x, y) \in X \times X$ such that y does not have to be strictly preferred to x according to the above-described criterion. The properties of f ensure that R is indeed a complete and quasi-transitive G-rationalization of C.

Now we consider the rationalizability property G-RC-Q. Because reflexivity *and* completeness are required, both the exclusion axiom and the irreversibility condition to be employed are unconditional—whenever it is the case that $f(S^k, x^k) = x^{k-1}$, the conjunction of reflexivity and completeness, together with the interpretation of f, implies that x^{k-1} must be strictly preferred to x^k by a G-rationalization. Quasi-transitivity demands that any chain of strict preferences from x^0 to x^K be respected and thus x^0 must be strictly preferred to x^K. This immediately rules out $(x^K, x^0) \in R_C$ (as required by the axiom IE introduced below) and $f(S^0, x^0) = x^K$ (see II).

Indirect exclusion (IE). For all $K \in \mathbb{N}$, for all $(S^1, x^1), \ldots, (S^K, x^K) \in \mathcal{A}_C$, for all $S^0 \in \Sigma$ and for all $x^0 \in S^0$,

$$f(S^k, x^k) = x^{k-1} \text{ for all } k \in \{1, \ldots, K\} \Rightarrow x^K \notin C(S^0).$$

Clearly, indirect exclusion implies all of the exclusion properties introduced earlier. We can now state the following result which, with an alternative proof, has been established in Bossert, Sprumont and Suzumura (2005b).

Theorem 12. *Suppose* $C \colon \Sigma \to \mathcal{X}$ *is a choice function with a general non-empty domain* $\Sigma \subseteq \mathcal{X}$. *C satisfies any of G-RC-Q, M-R-T, M-Ø-T, M-RC-Q, M-R-Q, M-C-Q, M-Ø-Q if and only if, whenever* $\mathcal{A}_C \neq \emptyset$, *there exists* $f \in \mathcal{F}_C$ *satisfying* II *and* IE.

Proof. In view of Theorem 3, it is sufficient to treat the case of G-RC-Q.

We first prove that G-RC-Q implies the existence of an $f \in \mathcal{F}_C$ which satisfies II and IE provided that $\mathcal{A}_C \neq \emptyset$. Let R be a reflexive, complete and quasi-transitive G-rationalization of C. Define a function $f \in \mathcal{F}_C$ as in the proof of Theorem 4.

To check that II is satisfied, we have only to see the proof of the corresponding part of Theorem 8, coupled with the fact that quasi-transitivity implies P-acyclicity.

To show that any such function f satisfies IE, suppose $K \in \mathbb{N}$, $(S^1, x^1), \ldots, (S^K, x^K) \in \mathcal{A}_C$, $S^0 \in \Sigma$ and $x^0 \in S^0$ are such that $f(S^k, x^k) = x^{k-1}$ for all $k \in \{1, \ldots, K\}$. By definition, $(x^k, x^{k-1}) \notin R$ for all $k \in \{1, \ldots, K\}$. Because R is reflexive, it must be the case that $x^{k-1} \neq x^k$ for all $k \in \{1, \ldots, K\}$. Thus, the completeness of R implies $(x^{k-1}, x^k) \in P(R)$ for all $k \in \{1, \ldots, K\}$. R being quasi-transitive, it follows that $(x^0, x^K) \in P(R)$ and, thus, $(x^K, x^0) \notin R$. Because R is a G-rationalization of C, we obtain $x^K \notin C(S^0)$.

Now suppose that, provided $\mathcal{A}_C \neq \emptyset$, there exists $f \in \mathcal{F}_C$ satisfying II and IE. If $\mathcal{A}_C = \emptyset$, $R = X \times X$ is a reflexive, complete and quasi-transitive G-rationalization of C and we are done. If $\mathcal{A}_C \neq \emptyset$, there exists a function $f \in \mathcal{F}_C$ satisfying II and IE. Define

$$R = \{(x, y) \in X \times X \mid \exists K \in \mathbb{N}, x^0 \in X \text{ and } (S^1, x^1), \ldots, (S^K, x^K) \in \mathcal{A}_C$$

$$\text{such that } y = x^0, x^{k-1} = f(S^k, x^k) \text{ for all } k \in \{1, \ldots, K\} \text{ and } x^K = x\}.$$

To see that R is reflexive, let $x \in X$. If $(x, x) \notin R$, there exist $K \in \mathbb{N}$, $x^0 \in X$ and $(S^1, x^1), \ldots, (S^K, x^K) \in \mathcal{A}_C$ such that $x = x^0$, $x^{k-1} = f(S^k, x^k)$ for all $k \in \{1, \ldots, K\}$ and $x^K = x$. Letting $S^0 = S^K$, we obtain a contradiction to II. Thus, we must have $(x, x) \in R$.

To establish the completeness of R, suppose $x, y \in X$ are such that $x \neq y$, $(x, y) \notin R$ and $(y, x) \notin R$. By definition, this implies that there exist $K, L \in \mathbb{N}$, $x^0, y^0 \in X$ and $(S^1, x^1), \ldots, (S^K, x^K), (T^1, y^1), \ldots, (T^L, y^L) \in \mathcal{A}_C$ such that $y = x^0$, $x^{k-1} = f(S^k, x^k)$ for all $k \in \{1, \ldots, K\}$, $x^K = x$, $x = y^0$, $y^{\ell-1} = f(T^\ell, y^\ell)$ for all $\ell \in \{1, \ldots, L\}$ and $y^L = y$. Letting $M = K + L - 1$, $(U^0, z^0) = (T^L, y^L)$, $(U^m, z^m) = (S^m, x^m)$ for all $m \in \{1, \ldots, K\}$ and $(U^m, z^m) = (T^{m-K}, y^{m-K})$ for all $m \in \{K + 1, \ldots, K + L - 1\}$, it follows that $z^{m-1} = f(U^m, z^m)$ for all $m \in \{1, \ldots, M\}$ and $z^M = f(U^0, z^0)$, contradicting II.

Next, we show that R is quasi-transitive. Suppose three alternatives $x, y, z \in X$ are such that $(x, y) \in P(R)$ and $(y, z) \in P(R)$. This implies that there exist $K, L \in \mathbb{N}$, $x^0, y^0 \in X$ and $(S^1, x^1), \ldots, (S^K, x^K), (T^1, y^1), \ldots, (T^L, y^L) \in \mathcal{A}_C$ such that $x = x^0$, $x^{k-1} = f(S^k, x^k)$ for all $k \in \{1, \ldots, K\}$, $x^K = y$, $y = y^0$, $y^{\ell-1} = f(T^\ell, y^\ell)$ for all $\ell \in \{1, \ldots, L\}$ and $y^L = z$. Letting $M = K + L$, $z^0 = x^0$, $(U^m, z^m) = (S^m, x^m)$ for all $m \in \{1, \ldots, K\}$ and $(U^m, z^m) = (T^{m-K}, y^{m-K})$ for all $m \in \{K + 1, \ldots, K + L\}$, it follows that $(z, x) \notin R$. Because R is complete, we obtain $(x, z) \in P(R)$. Thus, R is quasi-transitive.

It remains to show that R is a G-rationalization of C. Let $S \in \Sigma$ and $x \in S$.

Suppose first that $x \in C(S)$. If there exists $y \in S$ such that $(x, y) \notin R$, it follows that there exist $K \in \mathbb{N}$, $x^0 \in X$ and $(S^1, x^1), \ldots, (S^K, x^K) \in \mathcal{A}_C$ such that $y = x^0$, $x^{k-1} = f(S^k, x^k)$ for all $k \in \{1, \ldots, K\}$ and $x^K = x$. Letting $S^0 = S$, we obtain a contradiction to IE. Therefore, $x \in G(S, R)$.

Now suppose $x \notin C(S)$. Let $y = f(S, x)$. By definition, this implies $(x, y) \notin R$ and hence $x \notin G(S, R)$. ∎

The definition of the relation R in the above proof is based on the following intuition. Recall that f is intended to identify, for each feasible set S and for each element y of S that is not chosen by C, an alternative x in S such that y is not at least as good as x. Because G-rationalizability by a reflexive and complete relation is considered in the above theorem, the absence of a weak preference of y over x is equivalent to a strict preference of x over y, that is, $(x, y) \in P(R)$. In consequence, we must have a strict preference of an alternative x over an alternative y according to a reflexive and complete G-rationalization whenever x is identified by f to be responsible for keeping y out of the set of chosen alternatives from S. Because R is also required to be quasi-transitive, chains of strict preference have to be respected as well. In order to arrive at a reflexive, complete and quasi-transitive G-rationalization of C, we define R to be composed of all pairs $(x, y) \in X \times X$ such that y does not have to be strictly preferred to x according to the above-described criterion. The properties of f ensure that R indeed is a reflexive, complete and quasi-transitive G-rationalization of C.

We conclude this section with characterizations of G-R-S and G-RC-T (and, of course, their equivalents). Their axiomatizations are simpler than those analyzed thus far because there are well-defined consistent and transitive closure operations whose existence facilitates the formulation of the requisite properties of f.

In the case of consistent G-rationalizability, the following property of f is relevant.

Consistent-closure irreversibility (CCI). For all $(S, x) \in \mathcal{A}_C$ and for all $y \in S$,

$$(x, y) \in sc(R_C) \Rightarrow f(S, x) \neq y.$$

CCI requires that the consistent closure of the direct revealed preference relation R_C be respected as established in part (ii) of Theorem 2: if a pair of alternatives (x, y) is in this consistent closure, then (x, y) must be in any consistent G-rationalization of C and, as a consequence, y cannot be the element that keeps x from being chosen from a set in which both are present. The existence of a function f with this property is also sufficient for G-R-S and G-Ø-S. An alternative characterization of this rationalizability notion can be found in Bossert, Sprumont and Suzumura (2005a).

Theorem 13. *Suppose* $C\colon \Sigma \to \mathcal{X}$ *is a choice function with a general non-empty domain* $\Sigma \subseteq \mathcal{X}$. *$C$ satisfies any of* G-R-S, G-Ø-S *if and only if, whenever* $\mathcal{A}_C \neq \emptyset$, *there exists* $f \in \mathcal{F}_C$ *satisfying* CCI.

Proof. In view of Theorem 3, it is sufficient to treat the case of G-Ø-S.

We first prove that G-Ø-S implies the existence of a function $f \in \mathcal{F}_C$ which satisfies CCI provided that $\mathcal{A}_C \neq \emptyset$. Let R be a consistent G-rationalization of C. Define a function $f \in \mathcal{F}_C$ as in the proof of Theorem 4. To show that f satisfies CCI, suppose $(S, x) \in \mathcal{A}_C$ and $y \in S$ are such that $(x, y) \in sc(R_C)$. By part (ii) of Theorem 2, it follows that $(x, y) \in R$ and, thus, $f(S, x) \neq y$ by definition of f.

Now suppose that, provided $\mathcal{A}_C \neq \emptyset$, there exists $f \in \mathcal{F}_C$ satisfying CCI. If $\mathcal{A}_C = \emptyset$, $R = X \times X$ is a consistent G-rationalization of C and we are done. If $\mathcal{A}_C \neq \emptyset$, there exists a function $f \in \mathcal{F}_C$ satisfying CCI. Define

$$R = sc(R_C).$$

Clearly, R is consistent. We complete the proof by showing that it is a G-rationalization of C. To that end, suppose $S \in \Sigma$ and $x \in S$.

Suppose first that $x \in C(S)$. This implies $(x, y) \in R_C \subseteq sc(R_C) = R$ for all $y \in S$ and thus $x \in G(S, R)$.

Now suppose $x \in G(S, R)$. By definition, $(x, y) \in sc(R_C)$ for all $y \in S$. If $(S, x) \in \mathcal{A}_C$, CCI implies $f(S, x) \neq y$ for all $y \in S$, contrary to the existence of f. Thus, $(S, x) \notin \mathcal{A}_C$ which implies $x \in C(S)$ by definition. ∎

Our final result provides an analogous characterization of G-RC-T and its equivalents. All that needs to be done is to replace consistent closure with transitive closure in the relevant property of f.

Transitive-closure irreversibility (TCI). For all $(S, x) \in \mathcal{A}_C$ and for all $y \in S$,

$$(x, y) \in tc(R_C) \Rightarrow f(S, x) \neq y.$$

Analogously to CCI, TCI requires that the transitive closure of the direct revealed preference relation R_C be respected as established in part (iii) of Theorem 2: if a pair of alternatives (x, y) is in the transitive closure of R_C, then (x, y) must be in any transitive G-rationalization of C and, as a consequence, y cannot be the element that keeps x from being chosen from a set in which both are present. The existence of a function f with this property is also sufficient for G-Ø-T and all of its equivalent properties. Alternative characterizations of this rationalizability notion can be found in Richter (1966; 1971), Hansson (1968) and Suzumura (1977).

Theorem 14. *Suppose* $C\colon \Sigma \to \mathcal{X}$ *is a choice function with a general non-empty domain* $\Sigma \subseteq \mathcal{X}$. *$C$ satisfies any of* G-RC-T, G-C-T, G-R-T, G-Ø-T, G-RC-S, G-C-S,

M-RC-T, M-C-T, M-RC-S, M-C-S *if and only if, whenever* $\mathcal{A}_C \neq \emptyset$, *there exists* $f \in \mathcal{F}_C$ *satisfying* TCI.

Proof. In view of Theorem 3, it is sufficient to treat the case of G-Ø-T.

We begin by proving that G-Ø-T implies the existence of a function $f \in \mathcal{F}_C$ which satisfies TCI provided that $\mathcal{A}_C \neq \emptyset$. Let R be a transitive G-rationalization of C. Define a function $f \in \mathcal{F}_C$ as in the proof of Theorem 4. To show that f satisfies TCI, suppose $(S, x) \in \mathcal{A}_C$ and $y \in S$ are such that $(x, y) \in tc(R_C)$. By part (iii) of Theorem 2, it follows that $(x, y) \in R$ and, thus, $f(S, x) \neq y$ by definition of f.

Now suppose that, provided $\mathcal{A}_C \neq \emptyset$, there exists $f \in \mathcal{F}_C$ satisfying TCI. If $\mathcal{A}_C = \emptyset$, $R = X \times X$ is a transitive G-rationalization of C and we are done. If $\mathcal{A}_C \neq \emptyset$, there exists a function $f \in \mathcal{F}_C$ satisfying TCI. Define

$$R = tc(R_C).$$

Clearly, R is transitive. We complete the proof by showing that it is a G-rationalization of C. To that end, suppose $S \in \Sigma$ and $x \in S$.

Suppose first that $x \in C(S)$. This implies $(x, y) \in R_C \subseteq tc(R_C) = R$ for all $y \in S$ and thus $x \in G(S, R)$.

Now suppose $x \in G(S, R)$. By definition, $(x, y) \in tc(R_C)$ for all $y \in S$. If $(S, x) \in \mathcal{A}_C$, TCI implies $f(S, x) \neq y$ for all $y \in S$, contrary to the existence of f. Thus, $(S, x) \notin \mathcal{A}_C$, which implies $x \in C(S)$ by definition. ∎

For the sake of easy reference, our characterization theorems are summarized in Figure 7.1. Each row corresponds to a rationalizability property and each column

	DRE	DRI	RI	DSI	II	RE	SI	DSE	IE	CCI	TCI	Theorem
G-R-Ø	*											4
G-RC-Ø	*	*										5
G-R-A	*		*									6
G-C-A	*			*								7
G-RC-A	*					*						8
G-Ø-Q	*		*			*						9
G-R-Q	*		*			*	*					10
G-C-Q	*			*				*				11
G-RC-Q	*					*			*			12
G-R-S										*		13
G-RC-T											*	14

Fig. 7.1. **Rationalizability and properties of** f

except for the last (which identifies the relevant theorem) represents a property of a function f as defined earlier. An asterisk in a cell means that the corresponding property of f is used in the characterization of the corresponding rationalizability requirement.

V. CONCLUDING REMARKS

Ever since Samuelson (1938) embarked on the construction of revealed preference theory for a competitive consumer, the theory of rational choice has been engaged in the exercise of Occam's Razor. It was in the work of Richter (1966) that this exercise of shaving off inessential details culminated in the axiomatization of rational choice functions on general domains. Although Richter's seminal work in 1966 was complemented by successive works by Hansson (1968), Richter (1971), Suzumura (1976a; 1977; 1983: ch. 1), and Bossert, Sprumont and Suzumura (2005a), there remained a wide spectrum of rationalizability concepts to be axiomatized in this general area. The task of this chapter has been to fill in this conspicuous lacuna in the literature.

The conditions employed in our axiomatizations involve existential clauses. This is sometimes seen as a shortcoming, but this objection by itself does not stand on solid ground: there is nothing inherently undesirable in an axiom involving existential clauses. If the argument is that existential clauses are difficult to verify in practice, this is easily countered by the observation that universal quantifiers are no easier to check algorithmically than existential quantifiers. At least in the case of existential clauses, a search algorithm can terminate once one object with the desired property is found. In this respect, our conditions do not compare less favorably with those that are required for many forms of rationalizability, where universal quantifiers play a dominant role.

We suspect that a major reason behind the reluctance to accept existential clauses in the context of rational choice may be that conditions involving existential requirements are seen as being close to the rationalizability property itself, because the desired property is expressed in terms of the existence of a rationalization. This is (except for obvious cases) a matter of judgement, of course. Our view is that the combinations of the axioms employed in the characterizations of the weak forms of rationalizability represent an interesting and insightful way of separating the properties which are necessary and sufficient for each class of weak rationalizability. Furthermore, the axioms we use appear to be rather clear and the roles they play in the respective results have very intuitive interpretations. Finally, we should observe that the mathematical structures encountered here are similar to those appearing in dimension theory, which addresses the question of how many orderings are required to express a quasi-ordering as the intersection of those orderings. Consequently, closely related complexities cannot but arise. In fact, existential clauses appear in many of the characterization results in that area; see, for example, Dushnik and Miller (1941).

In concluding this chapter, some remarks on further problems to be explored are in order. Because we do not impose any restrictions on the domain of a choice function (other than non-emptiness), our results are extremely general. As a result, our theorems can be of relevance in whatever context of rational choice as purposive behavior we may care to specify, which is an obvious merit of our general approach. Note, however, that this approach may overlook some meaningful further directions to explore by being insensitive to the structural properties of the domain which may make perfect sense in the specific chosen contexts. Some consequences of an important example of such structural properties, namely, set-theoretic *closedness* assumptions, are examined in Bossert and Suzumura (2007a), but there are many others that one might want to analyze in future work.

Ever since Sen (1993) criticized the notion of internal consistency of choice, there exists a widespread perception that the standard rationalizability approach to the theory of choice has difficulties coping with the existence of external social norms. On the face of it, Sen's argument may seem to go squarely against the theory of rationalizability. However, Bossert and Suzumura (2007b) developed a new concept of *norm-conditional rationalizability* and built a bridge between rationalizability theory and Sen's criticism. In essence, what emerges from the Bossert–Suzumura theory is the peaceful co-existence of a norm-conditional rationalizability theory, which is a variant of the theory of rational choice on general domains, with Sen's elaborated criticism against internal consistency of choice.

REFERENCES

ARMSTRONG, W. E. (1948), "Uncertainty and the Utility Functions", *Economic Journal*, 58: 1–10.

ARROW, K. J. (1951), *Social Choice and Individual Values* (New York: Wiley; 2nd edn 1963).

—— (1959), "Rational Choice Functions and Orderings", *Economica*, 26: 121–7.

BANDYOPADHYAY, T., and SENGUPTA, K. (1991), "Revealed Preference Axioms for Rational Choice", *Economic Journal*, 101: 202–13.

BOSSERT, W., SPRUMONT, Y., and SUZUMURA, K. (2005a), "Consistent Rationalizability", *Economica*, 72: 185–200.

———— (2005b), "Maximal-Element Rationalizability", *Theory and Decision*, 58: 325–50.

———— (2006), "Rationalizability of Choice Functions on General Domains without Full Transitivity", *Social Choice and Welfare*, 27: 435–58.

—— and SUZUMURA, K. (2007a), "Domain Closedness Conditions and Rational Choice", *Order*, 24: 75–88.

————(2007b), *Social Norms and Rationality of Choice*, Working Paper, Institute of Economic Research, Hitotsubashi University.

DUSHNIK, B., and MILLER, E. W. (1941), "Partially Ordered Sets", *American Journal of Mathematics*, 63: 600–10.

HANSSON, B. (1968), "Choice Structures and Preference Relations", *Synthese*, 18: 443–58.

HOUTHAKKER, H. S. (1950), "Revealed Preference and the Utility Function", *Economica*, 17: 159–74.

LUCE, R. D. (1956), "Semiorders and the Theory of Utility Discrimination", *Econometrica*, 24: 178–91.

RICHTER, M. K. (1966), "Revealed Preference Theory", *Econometrica*, 41: 1075–91.

—— (1971), "Rational Choice", in J. S. Chipman, L. Hurwicz, M. K. Richter and H. F. Sonnenschein (eds), *Preferences, Utility, and Demand* (New York: Harcourt Brace Jovanovich), 29–58.

SAMUELSON, P. A. (1938), "A Note on the Pure Theory of Consumer's Behaviour", *Economica*, 5: 61–71.

—— (1947), *Foundations of Economic Analysis* (Cambridge, Mass.: Harvard University Press; 2nd edn 1983).

—— (1948), "Consumption Theory in Terms of Revealed Preference", *Economica*, 15: 243–53.

—— (1950), "The Problem of Integrability in Utility Theory", *Economica*, 17: 355–85.

SCHWARTZ, T. (1976), "Choice Functions, 'Rationality' Conditions, and Variations of the Weak Axiom of Revealed Preference", *Journal of Economic Theory*, 13: 414–27.

SEN, A. K. (1969), "Quasi-Transitivity, Rational Choice and Collective Decisions", *Review of Economic Studies*, 36: 381–93.

—— (1970), *Collective Choice and Social Welfare* (San Francisco: Holden-Day).

—— (1971), "Choice Functions and Revealed Preference", *Review of Economic Studies*, 38: 307–17.

—— (1993), "Internal Consistency of Choice", *Econometrica*, 61: 495–521.

SUZUMURA, K. (1976a), "Rational Choice and Revealed Preference", *Review of Economic Studies*, 43: 149–58.

—— (1976b), "Remarks on the Theory of Collective Choice", *Economica*, 43: 381–90.

—— (1977), "Houthakker's Axiom in the Theory of Rational Choice", *Journal of Economic Theory*, 14: 284–90.

—— (1983), *Rational Choice, Collective Decisions and Social Welfare* (New York: Cambridge University Press).

—— (2004), *An Extension of Arrow's Lemma with Economic Applications*, Working Paper, Institute of Economic Research, Hitotsubashi University.

SZPILRAJN, E. (1930), "Sur l'extension de l'ordre partiel", *Fundamenta Mathematicae*, 16: 386–9.

UZAWA, H. (1957), "Notes on Preference and the Axiom of Choice", *Annals of the Institute of Statistical Mathematics*, 8: 35–40.

CHAPTER 8

SOME REMARKS ON THE RANKING OF INFINITE UTILITY STREAMS

BHASKAR DUTTA

I. INTRODUCTION

THERE is a long tradition in welfare economics and moral philosophy, dating back at least to Sidgwick (1907), that all generations must be treated alike. Perhaps the most forceful assertion of this idea comes from Ramsey (1928), who declared that any argument for preferring one generation over another must come "merely from the weakness of the imagination". The "equal treatment of all generations" or the intergenerational equity principle has been formalized in the subsequent literature as the *Axiom* of *Anonymity*, which requires that two infinite utility streams be judged indifferent to one another if one can be obtained from the other through a permutation of utilities of a *finite* number of generations. Since it also seems "natural" to require that any social evaluation of infinite utility streams respond positively to an increase in the utility of any generation, the Pareto Axiom is also desirable. Unfortunately, Diamond (1965) showed that there is no social welfare

This paper was written while I was visiting the Indian Statistical Institute, New Delhi. I am most grateful to Kaushik Basu, Tapan Mitra and Arunava Sen for helpful discussions and comments.

function satisfying these axioms along with a continuity axiom. In a more recent paper, Basu and Mitra (2003) prove a more general result by showing that the continuity axiom is superfluous.

These impossibility results are for social welfare *functions*. For many purposes, it is sufficient to have a social welfare *ordering* which allows for comparisons of all infinite utility streams. In an important paper, Svensson (1980) showed that such an ordering satisfying Anonymity and the Pareto axioms does exist. However, Svensson's proof is non-constructive. He constructs a *pre-order*[1] satisfying Anonymity and the Pareto axioms, and then appeals to Szpilrajn's Lemma, which guarantees the existence of an ordering extension of any pre-order. Since it is possible to show the existence of an ordering satisfying the two basic axioms, a natural step forward is to explore the existence issue of orderings satisfying additional properties. Several recent papers have taken this route. For instance, Asheim and Tungodden (2004) and Bossert *et al.* (2007) provide characterizations of different infinite-horizon versions of the leximin principle. An infinite-horizon version of utilitarianism is characterized by Basu and Mitra (2007).[2]

Like Svensson (1980), these papers also construct pre-orderings satisfying desirable properties and then invoke Szpilrajn's Lemma to assert the existence of an ordering. Of course, it is one thing to *know* that different infinite utility streams can be compared consistently, and quite another thing to know *how* to make such comparisons. The latter requires explicit knowledge of the form of the ordering extension. Unfortunately, there is no constructive proof of these existence theorems. Indeed, Zame (2007) demonstrates that an ordering satisfying the two basic axioms cannot be explicitly described!

In this note, I describe some of the recent pre-orders which have been proposed in the literature. Analogous to the literature on the rankings of social states for finite societies, these pre-orders are the infinite-horizon versions of classic utilitarianism and the leximin principles. There are basically two different ways in which leximin and utilitarianism have been extended to the infinite-horizon context. I use some simple examples to illustrate how these different approaches compare with one another, and argue informally that one method is perhaps better than the other.

I then go on to explore a consequence of imposing *separability axioms*[3] on social welfare orderings. It is known that no ordering can satisfy the Pareto Axiom and a *strong anonymity* axiom which requires that two utility streams be judged indifferent if one is obtained from another by means of a permutation of an infinite number of generations. But how severe is this violation? Is there any *systematic*

---

[1] A pre-order is a binary relation satisfying reflexivity and transitivity. A pre-order which is also *complete* is an ordering.

[2] See Fleurbaey and Michel (2003), Hara *et al.* (forthcoming) and Asheim *et al.* (2007) for other possibility theorems.

[3] Separability means that the ranking of two utility streams should not depend on the utility levels of generations who are indifferent between the two utility streams.

bias in how generations are treated? Since we do not know the exact form of the various ordering extensions, these questions have remained unanswered. I show that over a limited class of comparisons, separability along with a weaker version of the Pareto Axiom implies that the social welfare ordering must exhibit *time preference*.[4] In other words, there is indeed a systematic bias in the way in which different generations are treated.

II. THE FRAMEWORK

Let $\mathbb{N}$ be the set of natural numbers. Let $\mathbb{R}_+$ be the set of non-negative real numbers, and denote $X \equiv \mathbb{R}_+^{\mathbb{N}}$. Then X is the set of infinite utility sequences. A typical element of X is an infinite-dimensional vector $x = (x_1, x_2, \ldots, x_n, \ldots)$, and the interpretation is that x_n represents the utility experienced by generation n.

Let s be a *finite* sequence with elements from $\mathbb{R}_+$. Then, s_∞ denotes the infinite sequence in which s is repeated infinitely often, while $(s)_k$ will denote the sequence in which s is repeated k times. For any $n \in \mathbb{N}$ and $k \in \mathbb{R}_+$, $(k)_n$ denotes the finite sequence in which k is repeated n times.

For any $x \in X$, let $x^{-n} = (x_1, \ldots, x_n)$ be the first n terms of the sequence x, and x^{+n} be the sequence $(x_{n+1}, \ldots)$. Hence $x = (x^{-n}, x^{+n})$.

Given any $x \in X$ and $n \in \mathbb{N}$, let $\tilde{x}_n$ be the permutation of x^{-n} which ensures that $\tilde{x}^{-n}$ is a *non-decreasing* sequence; let $I(x^{-n}) = x_1 + x_2 + \ldots + x_n$.

I will use the following notation for vector inequalities on X. For any $x, y \in X$, (i) $x \geq y$ if $x_n \geq y_n$ for all $n \in \mathbb{N}$; (ii) $x > y$ if $x \geq y$ and $x \neq y$.

A *social welfare relation* (henceforth SWR) is a binary relation on X which is *reflexive* and *transitive*. For any SWR R, the interpretation is that if xRy, then x is considered to be at least as good as y. The symmetric and asymmetric components of R are denoted by the binary relations I and P. Of course, for any $x, y \in X$, xIy if xRy and yRx, while xPy if xRy and not yRx. A *social welfare ordering* (henceforth SWO) is an SWR which is also *complete*.

An SWR R is a *subrelation* to another SWR R' if for all $x, y \in X$, (i) xIy implies $xR'y$ and (ii) xPy implies $xP'y$. If R is a subrelation to R', then R' is an *extension* of R.

A finite permutation of $\mathbb{N}$ is a bijection $\sigma : \mathbb{N} \to \mathbb{N}$ such that there exists $m \in \mathbb{N}$ with $\sigma(n) = n$ for all $n \in \mathbb{N} \setminus \{1, \ldots, m\}$. Let $\sigma(x)$ denote the utility sequence which results from a finite permutation σ of x. I will use Σ to define the set of all finite permutations of $\mathbb{N}$.

---

[4] Banerjee and Mitra (2007) show that a Paretian social welfare function on the domain of infinite utility streams must also exhibit a preference for the present over the future.

Two fundamental axioms in the recent literature on intergenerational social welfare rankings are the Strong Pareto principle and Finite Anonymity. These are defined below.

$Strong\ Pareto$: For all $x, y \in X$, if $x > y$ then xPy.

$Finite\ Anonymity$: For all $x \in X$, and for all $\sigma \in \Sigma$, $xI\sigma(x)$.

The Suppes–Sen $grading\ principle$ is the SWR R_S defined on X as follows:

For all $x, y \in X$, xR_Sy iff $\exists \sigma \in \Sigma$ such that $\sigma(x) \geq y$.

The grading principle R_S is transitive but not complete, and hence is not an SWO. However, it is a subrelation of any SWR satisfying the Strong Pareto and Finite Anonymity axioms. Svensson (1980) established the existence of an SWO satisfying these two axioms by invoking Szpilrajn's Lemma to conclude that some extension of R_S must be an SWO.

III. Utilitarian and Leximin Relations

Since it is possible to show the existence of SWOs satisfying the two basic assumptions, a natural step forward has been to explore the possibilities of having social welfare orderings satisfying additional assumptions. In the context of a finite society, much of the literature has focused on axiomatic characterizations of utilitarian and leximin social welfare orderings.[5] Several recent papers have taken this route in the ranking of infinite utility streams. For instance, Asheim and Tungodden (2004) and Bossert $et\ al.$ (2007) provide characterizations of different infinite-horizon versions of the leximin principle. Infinite-horizon versions of utilitarianism are characterized by both Basu and Mitra (2007) and Asheim and Tungodden (2004). However, as I have mentioned earlier, none of these papers actually $constructs$ an SWO satisfying these axioms, as they all use some version of Szpilrajn's Lemma to demonstrate the existence of SWOs. This section contains an informal discussion of the various rules, focusing partly on the difficulty which may arise if comparisons are based solely on social welfare relations.

Consider, for example, different formulations of infinite-horizon utilitarianism. Basu and Mitra (2007) define what they call the $utilitarian$ SWR R_U as follows:

$$\forall x, y \in X, xR_Uy \text{ iff } \exists n \in \mathbb{N} \text{ such that } (I(x^{-n}), x^{+n}) \geq (I(y^{-n}), y^{+n}).$$

---

[5] d'Aspremont and Gevers (2002) is an elegant survey of this literature.

A different and more traditional method of comparing infinite utility streams (without using discounting) is by employing the *overtaking* principle. There are two versions of the overtaking criterion—the *catching up* criterion and the *overtaking* criterion. Denote the corresponding SWRs as R_C and R_O. The formal definitions follow:

$$\forall x, y \in X, x R_C y \text{ iff } \exists \bar{n} \in \mathbb{N} \text{ such that } I(x^{-n}) \geq I(y^{-n}) \forall n \geq \bar{n}.$$

$$\forall x, y \in X, x R_O y \text{ iff either } (i) \exists \bar{n} \in \mathbb{N} \text{ such that } I(x^{-n}) > I(y^{-n}) \forall n \geq \bar{n}$$

$$\text{or } (ii) \exists \bar{n} \in \mathbb{N} \text{ such that } I(x^{-n}) = I(y^{-n}) \forall n \geq \bar{n}.$$

There are different extensions of the Rawlsian leximin criterion to the infinite case. In order to define these extensions, it is useful to define the leximin criterion on *finite* utility streams. So, let s and r be two finite sequences both of length k, with $\tilde{s}$ and $\tilde{r}$ being the permutations of s and t which ensure that they are non-decreasing sequences. Then,

$$s R_l^k r \text{ iff } \tilde{s} = \tilde{r} \text{ or } \exists j < k \text{ such that } \tilde{s}_i = \tilde{r}_i \forall i < j \text{ and } \tilde{s}_j > \tilde{r}_j.$$

One version of the infinite-horizon leximin rule, due to Asheim and Tungodden (2004), is the following:

$$\forall x, y \in X, x R_L^1 y \text{ iff } \exists \bar{n} \in \mathbb{N} \text{ such that } \forall n \geq \bar{n}, x^{-n} R_l^n y^{-n}.$$

An alternative formulation of infinite-horizon leximin is due to Bossert *et al.* (2007). They define the following SWR:

$$\forall x, y \in X, x R_L^2 y \text{ iff } \exists n \in \mathbb{N} \text{ such that } x^{-n} R_l^n y^n \text{ and } x^{+n} \geq y^{+n}.$$

These definitions demonstrate that there have been essentially two ways of extending utilitarianism and leximin to the infinite horizon. First, one can define one utility stream x to be at least as good as another utility stream y according to the utilitarian (respectively leximin) principle if there is some period $\bar{n}$ such that *all* finite truncations of x of length greater than $\bar{n}$ are deemed to be at least as good as the corresponding finite truncations of y according to the finite version of utilitarianism (respectively leximin). The catching up and overtaking criteria in the case of utilitarianism, and R_L^1 in the case of leximin, fall into this category. Alternatively, one can declare x to be better than y if there is some finite truncation of x of length n which is better than that of y according to the utilitarian (or leximin) criterion *and* x^{+n} is at least weakly Pareto-preferred to y^{+n}. The utilitarian SWR R_U and the leximin SWR R_L^2 belong to this category.

The relationship between these two categories is clear. Consider, for instance, the two leximin criteria. If $x R_L^2 y$, then from some period onwards, no term in the sequence x is smaller than the corresponding term in y. So, if the truncation of x is better than the truncation of y prior to this period according to the leximin criterion, then x must come out better than y in *all* subsequent comparisons.

Hence, $x R_L^1 y$ must be true. A similar argument holds for R_U on the one hand and R_O, R_C on the other hand. These "facts" are summarized below.

Proposition 1. (i) R_U *is a subrelation of* R_O, *which in turn is a subrelation of* R_C. (ii) R_L^2 *is a subrelation of* R_L^1.

Leximin and utilitarianism are of course very different criteria, and much has been written about the two classes in the finite context. Clearly, a different kind of comparison can also be made in the ranking of infinite utility streams. For instance, is R_U a "better" representative of utilitarianism than R_O? Or what about R_L^1 versus R_L^2?

Consider, first, the comparison between different representatives of utilitarianism. Clearly, R_U is more conservative in declaring one social state to be preferred to another. So, at first sight, it may seem that R_U is less likely to jump to erroneous conclusions in so far as strict preference is concerned. Indeed, this is precisely the point made by Basu and Mitra (2007) in the context of an example which is almost identical to Example 1 below.

However, comparisons between social welfare relations can sometimes be slightly misleading. For suppose R_U is unable to compare two alternative utility streams, while R_O can do so. Do we "complete" R_U by declaring the two states to be indifferent? This can be problematic, as I demonstrate in Example 1. The problem arises because what matters is not the SWR R_U itself, but its *ordering extension(s)*. In principle, an SWR may have more than one ordering extension. Also, if R is a subrelation of R', then the ordering relation of R' must also be an ordering extension of R, although the converse may not be true.[6]

Given any SWR R, let $\bar{R}$ denote some ordering extension of R. Of course, $R = \bar{R}$ if R is an SWO.

Consider the following example:

Example 1. *Let* $x = (2, (1, 0)_\infty)$, $y = ((1, 0)_\infty)$, *and* $z = (1, (1, 0)_\infty)$.

Then $x P_O y$ but neither $x R_U y$ nor $y R_U x$. Basu and Mitra (2007: 360) actually argue that this is a virtue of R_U because "there are an infinite number of future generations who rank x below y". But now let us consider $\bar{R}_U$. Suppose $x \bar{I}_U y$. Then the same intuitive reasoning must force us to conclude that $y \bar{I}_U z$. But now we are in trouble because x Pareto-dominates z and so $x P_U z$, leading to $x \bar{P}_U z$. Transitivity decrees that $x \bar{P}_U y$. Hence, the ordering extension of R_U must express a strict preference between x and y even if R_U itself prefers to remain silent!

In fact, this example demonstrates the following impossibility theorem:

Veto Power of Infinitely Many Generations (VPIMG): For all $x, y \in X$, if $|\{n \in \mathbb{N} | x_n > y_n\}| = \infty$, then $x \bar{R} y$.

---

[6] In fact, if the ordering extension of R' is the *only* ordering extension of R, then there is nothing to choose between R and R'.

Theorem 1. *There is no SWO satisfying VPIMG and the Strong Pareto Principle.*

Proof. Consider x, y, z defined in Example 1. If $\bar{R}$ satisfies Strong Pareto and VPIMG, then $x\bar{P}z$ from Strong Pareto, and $y\bar{I}z$ and $y\bar{I}x$. This is a violation of transitivity. ∎

Remark 1. *Notice that this impossibility is precipitated even without any appeal to the Finite Anonymity condition.*

Basu and Mitra (2007) also argue that a "robustness" check on an SWR is to check whether the ranking between pairs of infinite utility streams provided by the SWR is preserved for discount factors close to 1 in the discounted present-value social welfare function. They then construct an ingenious example of a pair of alternatives x and y such that $xP_O y$ but not $xR_U y$, and the discounted present value of y is strictly higher than that of x *for every* $\delta \in (0, 1)$. In their example, the limiting values as $\delta \to 1$ exist and are equal. Basu and Mitra argue that this implies that x and y should be deemed indifferent.

However, apart from the fact that discounting even as a robustness check goes against the spirit of Anonymity, it is not clear that the two utility streams would be deemed indifferent according to $\bar{R}_U$. Moreover, as the next example demonstrates, R_U may fail to pass judgement on a pair of utility streams even when the discounted present value of one is strictly higher than that of another for all discount factors.

Example 2. *Choose numbers $b > a > 0$, and let $x = (2b, 0)_\infty$ while $y = (b, a)_\infty$.*

In this case, every finite truncation of x has a higher sum than that of y and so x is preferred to y according to the overtaking criterion and hence the catching up criterion. But R_U cannot compare x and y, since an infinite number of generations prefer y to x, although for all $\delta \in (0, 1)$, $\sum_{n=1}^{\infty} \delta^{n-1}(x_n - y_n) > 0$.

Of course, being able to pass judgement is not necessarily a virtue. This is illustrated in the next example.

Example 3. *Let $x = (1, 0)_\infty$, while $y = (0, 1)_\infty$.*

In this example, x and y are non-comparable according to the overtaking criterion, but the catching up criterion declares x to be strictly preferred to y. In the first stream, generations in odd periods get a utility of 1. The role of the "rich" and "poor" generations is reversed in the second utility stream, with generations in even periods getting the higher utility. Clearly, a social welfare ordering satisfying any intuitive notion of intergenerational equity should declare the two utility sequences to be indifferent. Notice that R_C does satisfy Finite Anonymity, but not the stronger version, which requires that two utility streams be judged indifferent if one is obtained from another by means of a permutation of an infinite number of generations.[7]

I come now to a comparison of the two versions of the leximin principle. Consider again Example 1. Suppose $n > 2$ and n is even. Then $\tilde{x}^{-n}$ will have $n/2 - 1$ 0s, followed by $n/2$ 1s and one 2. If n is odd, then $\tilde{x}^{-n}$ will have $(n-1)/2$ 0s followed by the same number of 1s and finally 2. On the other hand, for n even, $\tilde{y}^{-n}$ will have an equal number of 0s and 1s. For n odd, $\tilde{y}^{-n}$ will have $(n+1)/2$ 0s and $(n-1)/2$ 1s. So for all finite truncations, $x^{-n} P_l^n y^{-n}$ and hence $x P_L^1 y$. On the other hand, for no n will x^{+n} Pareto-dominate y^{+n} and so R_L^2 cannot compare the two. However, R_L^2 implicitly gives veto power to coalitions of infinitely many generations. Theorem 1 demonstrates the problem with this principle.

However, the following example suggests that perhaps R_L^1 declares strict preference even when it should not.

Example 4. *Let $x = (0, 2_\infty)$ and $y = 1_\infty$.*

The SWR R_L^2 cannot compare the two utility streams. But for all n, $\tilde{x}^{-n} = (0, 2, \ldots, 2)$ while $\tilde{y}^{-n} = (1, \ldots, 1)$. Hence, $y P_L^1 x$. Notice however that except for $t = 1$, $\tilde{x}_t^{-n} > \tilde{y}_t^{-n}$. Nevertheless, y is declared to be better than x. It is known that while the finite-horizon leximin rule has no individual as a dictator, it is characterized by "positional dictatorship" of the worst-off rank. The extreme importance given to one rank is obviously less defensible when there are an infinity of positions.

IV. SEPARABILITY

In the context of a *finite* society, the axiomatic literature on the characterization of interpersonally comparable social welfare rankings such as leximin and classic utilitarianism uses a *separability condition* which requires that the ranking of two utility or welfare vectors should be independent of the utility levels of "unconcerned" individuals, that is individuals who have the same levels of utility in the two vectors. In this section, I explore some consequences of using the Separability Axiom in the ranking of infinite utility streams.

There are different ways of formalizing separability when there are an infinite number of generations. A particularly weak version of separability is to require that

---

[7] However, no SWR satisfies Strict Pareto and Strong Anonymity. See also the next section, where a separability axiom along with a weaker version of the Pareto principle also results in x being declared better than y.

if the "first" generation has the same utility level in two utility streams, then the ranking of these two utility streams can only depend on the utility sequences from period two onwards:

$$\textit{Separability}: \forall a \in \mathbb{R}_+, \forall x, y \in X, (a, x)R(a, y) \leftrightarrow xRy.$$

This condition, under the name of *Stationarity*, has been used extensively in the literature on the utility ranking of infinite consumption streams.[8]

A stronger form of separability extends the definition to infinite sets of unconcerned individuals. That is, suppose the comparison is between $x = (3, 0, 1)_\infty$ and $y = (2, 0, 2)_\infty$. Then, all generations $t = 2 + 3r$ where $r = 0, 1, \ldots$ have the same utility in x and y. So the stronger form of separability requires that the ranking between x and y coincide with that between $(3, 1)_\infty$ and 2_∞.

I need some more notation to define this stronger form of separability. Given any $x \in X$ and $T \subset \mathbb{N}$, let x_{-T} denote the subsequence of x which takes values only in $\mathbb{N} - T$. For any $x, y \in X$, let $T(x, y) = \{n \in \mathbb{N} | x_n = y_n\}$.

$\textit{Strong Separability}$: For all $x, y \in X, xRy \leftrightarrow x_{-T(x,y)}Ry_{-T(x,y)}$.

A possible reason for objecting to the Strict Pareto condition is that when there are an infinite number of generations, one utility stream should not be judged strictly superior to another if just a single individual is better off and all others are indifferent. A much weaker requirement is a "non-perversity" condition which states that the social ranking must not respond negatively to an increase in individual utilities. This condition is formalized below.

$$\textit{Monotonicity}: \forall x, y \in X, \text{ if } x > y, \text{ then } xRy.$$

Even if a single individual's strict preference (along with other individuals' indifference) should not translate into social strict preference, it may be argued that if a sufficiently large but finite number of individuals strictly prefer x to y and all others are indifferent, then x should be strictly preferred to y. This is the *Finite Pareto Principle*.

$\textit{Finite Pareto Principle}$: There is $\bar{n} \in \mathbb{N}$ such that $\forall x, y \in X$, if $|\{i \in \mathbb{N} | x_i > y_i\}| \geq \bar{n}$ and $x > y$, then xPy.

The three versions of utilitarian pre-orderings as well as the leximin pre-order R_L all satisfy Separability. Since they satisfy the Strict Pareto condition, they obviously satisfy Monotonicity and the Finite Pareto Principle. Notice, however, that Szpilrajn's Lemma cannot be used to assert the existence of an SWO satisfying these three conditions. Consider, for instance, $\bar{R}_U$, the ordering extension of R_U. The fact that R_U satisfies Separability does not rule out the existence of a pair x, y in X and

---

[8] See for instance Koopmans (1960); Fishburn and Rubinstein (1982). A slightly stronger condition has been labeled the "Independent Futures" condition by Fleurbaey and Michel (2003).

a in $\mathbb{R}_+$ such that the pairs (x, y) and $(a + x, a + y)$ are non-comparable according to R_U, but $x\bar{R}_U y$ and $(a, y)\bar{P}_U(a, x)$! Of course, it is not easy to check whether such a pair exists, since we do not know the functional nature of $\bar{R}_U$.

In the following, I describe a characteristic of any SWO satisfying Separability, Monotonicity and the Finite Pareto Principle *if* such an ordering exists. I show that Separability and Strong Separability imply *time preference* within a limited class of comparisons, with the stronger form of Separability leading to time preference for a larger class of comparisons. I will first describe the type of comparisons which result in time preference.

Throughout this section, I restrict attention to utility sequences which are infinite repetitions of finite sequences. That is, comparisons are between sequences of the form s_∞ and s'_∞.

Now consider two finite sequences $s = (p, (0)_k)$ and $s' = ((0)_k, p)$ where $p > (0)_k$ for some integer k. So, s and s' are both sequences of length $2k$, where x is the sequence in which the terms $p_1, \ldots, p_k$ occur first followed by a sequence of k zeroes. In y, the first k terms are 0, followed by the sequence p. Also, note that each p_i is non-negative with at least one term being strictly positive. Of course, any social welfare relation in the finite context satisfying Anonymity must declare s and s' to be socially indifferent, while discounting will imply that s is better than s'. One can also say that in the comparison of infinite utility streams, the social rule exhibits time preference if it declares that s_∞ is strictly preferred to s'_∞. The next proposition shows that any SWO satisfying Monotonicity, Separability and the Finite Pareto Principle must exhibit this kind of time Preference.

Proposition 2. *Suppose R is an SWO satisfying Monotonicity, the Finite Pareto Principle and Separability. Then xPy if $x = (p, (0)_k)_\infty$, $y = ((0)_k, p)_\infty$ where $p > (0)_k$ for some integer k.*

Proof. Consider any SWO R satisfying Monotonicity and Separability. Choose any x and y satisfying the conditions in the proposition.

I show that R cannot satisfy the Finite Pareto Principle when yRx.

Define $z = (p, x)$.

Step 1: I first prove that yRx implies zIy.

Notice that $x \equiv (p, y)$ and $y = ((0)_k, x)$.

Since yRx, the repeated application of Separability ensures that $(p, y)R(p, x)$. Hence, xRz.

Since $p > (0)_k$, Monotonicity ensures that $(p, x)R((0)_k, x)$. So zRy. Hence, from transitivity, xRy. So xIy. This in turn ensures that xIz and so zIy.

Now, define $z^n = ((p)_n, x)$ so that $z^1 \equiv z$. Also, define $y^n = ((0)_{kn}, p)$ so that $y^1 \equiv y$.

Step 2: I now show that $z^n I z^{n+1}$ and $y^n I y^{n+1}$.

Now,

$$z^n = ((p)_n, x)$$

$$= ((p)_n, p, y).$$

From repeated use of Separability,

$$((p)_{n+1}, x) I ((p)_{n+1}, y).$$

Using Separability again,

$$z^{n+1} \equiv ((p)_{n+1}, x) I (p_{n+1}, y) \equiv z^n.$$

Similarly,

$$y^{n+1} = ((0)_{k(n+1)}, x)$$

$$= ((0)_{kn}, y).$$

Making repeated use of Separability,

$$y^{n+1} \equiv ((0)_{kn}, x) I ((0)_{kn}, x) \equiv y^n.$$

Steps 1 and 2 establish the theorem. Step 1 shows that $z^1 I y^1$. Step 2 shows that for all $n \in \mathbb{N}$, $z^1 I z^n$ and $y^1 I y^n$. Hence, for all $n \in \mathbb{N}$, $z^n I y^n$. This shows that the Finite Pareto Principle is violated, since $(p)_n > (0)_{kn}$. ∎

The following proposition follows easily from the earlier one.

Proposition 3. *Suppose R is an SWO satisfying Monotonicity, the Finite Pareto Principle and Strong Separability. Then xPy if $x = (p, (0)_k)_\infty$, $y = ((0)_k, p)_\infty$ where $p > (0)_m$ for some integers m, k with $m \le k$.*

Proof. Of course, Strong Separability implies Separability and so the case of $m = k$ has been proved already. So, take any m, k with $m < k$ and $x = (p, (0)_k)_\infty$ and $y = ((0)_k, p)_\infty$ where $p > (0)_m$.

Since $m < k$, $x_n = y_n = 0$ for all $n = m + 1, \ldots, k - 1, 2(m + 1), \ldots, 2(k - 1),$ $\ldots, t(m + 1), \ldots, t(k - 1), \ldots$ Using Strong Separability, xRy iff $x'Ry$ where $x' = (p, (0)_m)_\infty$ and $y' = ((0)_m, p)_\infty$. Since p is also of length m, we know from Proposition 2 that $x'Py'$. Hence, xPy. ∎

Corollary: *If $x = (1, 0)_\infty$ and $y = (0, 1)_\infty$, then xPy.*

This is obviously a gross violation of intergenerational equity! It shows that any SWO satisfying the stipulated properties must exhibit some form of time preference. Notice that R_C does rank $(1, 0)_\infty$ over $(0, 1)_\infty$. But, as I have remarked in the previous section, this is an unappealing feature of the catching up criterion. This section shows, however, that this is also an inevitable cost associated with the Separability Axiom.

REFERENCES

ASHEIM, G. B., BUCHHOLZ, W., and TUNGODDEN, B. (2001), "Justifying Sustainability", *Journal of Environmental and Economic Management*, 41: 252–68.

—— TUNGODDEN, B. (2004), "Resolving Distributional Conflicts between Generations", *Economic Theory*, 24: 221–30.

—— MITRA, T., and TUNGODDEN, B. (2007), "A New Equity Condition for Infinite Utility Streams and the Possibility of Being Paretian", in J. Roemer and K. Suzumura (eds), *Intergenerational Equity and Sustainability* (London: Palgrave-Macmillan).

BANERJEE, K., and MITRA T. (2007), "On the Impatience Implications of Paretian Social Welfare Functions", *Journal of Mathematical Economics*, 43: 236–48.

BASU, K., and MITRA, T. (2003), "Aggregating Infinite Utility Streams with Intergenerational Equity: The Impossibility of Being Paretian", *Econometrica*, 71: 1557–63.

—— —— (2007), "Utilitarianism for Infinite Utility Streams: A New Welfare Criterion and its Axiomatic Characterization", *Journal of Economic Theory*, 133: 350–73.

BOSSERT, W., SPRUMONT, Y., and SUZUMURA, K. (2007), "Ordering Infinite Utility Streams", *Journal of Economic Theory*, 135: 579–89.

D'ASPREMONT, C., and GEVERS, L. (2002), "Interpersonal Comparability of Welfare and Social Choice Theory", in K. J. Arrow, A. K. Sen and K. Suzumura (eds), *Handbook of Social Choice Theory* (Amsterdam: Elsevier).

DIAMOND, P. (1965), "The Evaluation of Infinite Utility Streams", *Econometrica*, 33: 170–7.

FISHBURN, P., and RUBINSTEIN, A. (1982), "Time Preference", *International Economic Review*, 23: 677–94.

FLEURBAEY, M., and MICHEL, P. (2003), "Intertemporal Equity and Extension of the Ramsey Principle", *Journal of Mathematical Economics*, 39: 777–802.

HARA, C., SHINOTSUKA, T., SUZUMURA, K., and XU, Y. (forthcoming), "Continuity and Egalitarianism in the Evaluation of Infinite Utility Streams", *Social Choice and Welfare*.

KOOPMANS, T. C. (1960), "Stationary Ordinal Utility and Impatience", *Econometrica*, 28: 287–309.

RAMSEY, F. P. (1928), "A Mathematical Theory of Saving", *Economic Journal*, 38: 543–59.

SEN, A. K. (1971), *Collective Choice and Social Welfare* (Edinburgh: Oliver and Boyd).

—— (1977), "On Weights and Measures: Informational Constraints in Social Welfare Analysis", *Econometrica*, 45: 1539–72.

SIDGWICK, H. (1907), *Methods of Ethics* (London: Macmillan).

SUPPES, P. (1966), "Some Formal Models of Grading Principles", *Synthese*, 6: 284–306.

SVENSSON, L.-G. (1980), "Equity Among Generations", *Econometrica*, 48: 1251–6.

ZAME, W. R. (2007), "Can Utilitarianism be Operationalized?", *Theoretical Economics*, 2: 187–202.

CHAPTER 9

INDIVIDUAL CHOICES IN A NON-CONSEQUENTIALIST FRAMEWORK

A PROCEDURAL APPROACH

WULF GAERTNER

YONGSHENG XU

I. MOTIVATION AND SOME EXAMPLES

IN choosing a right action among several feasible ones, a consequentialist moral theory requires that the action producing the best outcome be chosen, as judged from a non-moral and agent-neutral point of view. A welfarist goes further in asserting that the goodness of an outcome depends exclusively on its effect on the

It is a great pleasure and honor to dedicate this piece of work to Amartya Sen. Actually, one of Amartya's many striking examples turned out to be the starting point for our analysis in this chapter. Helpful comments by Nick Baigent, Carmen Bevia, Marc Fleurbaey and Kotaro Suzumura are gratefully acknowledged.

welfare of the indidivuals involved and that the assessment of the outcome must then be based on this effect. It is probably true to say that most of welfare economics is welfarist in particular and consequentialist in general. In other words, what really matters in analyses of welfare are outcomes in terms of individual and social welfare. However, as Suzumura and Xu (2001: 424) write, "there do exist people who care not only about welfaristic features of the consequences, but also about non-welfaristic features of the consequences or even non-consequential features of the decision-making procedure through which these consequences are brought about" (see also Suzumura and Xu forthcoming). This basically reflects a view that, in choosing a right action, there are certain norms and obligations that are *agent-relative*. This view is often called *non-consequentialism*. According to a non-consequentialist, "actions are based on reasons and principles, and some important moral principles hold that the agent's relation to various persons (or other beings) in the outcomes she affects is critically important" (Darwall 2003: 5). Within a firm, for example, most employees will probably prefer that major organizational changes be carried out after some general discussion that involves the staff and not at the bidding of the board of directors. In the political sphere, many people will most likely prefer that a new policy be brought about through public debate and not clandestinely.

In bargaining theory and expected utility theory analogous phenomena exist. Let E_1 and E_2 be two economic environments that yield identical utility allocations or utility-possibility sets, i.e. $S(E_1) = S(E_2)$. If f stands for a particular bargaining solution, we obtain $f(S(E_1)) = f(S(E_2))$ as a fundamental principle of bargaining analysis. Both information on how the underlying commodity allocations came about, and information on how the set of feasible utility allocations was arrived at, are aspects that do not matter under f. One could, again, argue that these features should matter, at least under certain circumstances. In expected utility theory à la von Neumann–Morgenstern, a one-stage lottery and a multi-stage lottery are judged to be equivalent utility-wise as long as the outcomes and the net cumulative probability of each outcome are the same.

Coming back to bargaining theory, to Nash's (1950) solution in particular, his condition of independence of irrelevant alternatives requires that if the solution for a certain set of utility allocations S is still possible or feasible for some subset $S' \subseteq S$, then this solution should also resolve the bargaining problem for S'. In other words, this particular shrinkage of the bargaining set itself is of no relevance.

In experimental game theory of ultimatum games, the model often specifies that the responder's behavior is only responsive to the division rule proposed by the proposer. The procedure or process from which the proposer chooses the division rule is not relevant to how the responder reacts. However, there has been an increasing recognition on the part of experimental economists that the responder's behavior differs depending on whether the division rule is selected by the proposer from a larger set of feasible division rules or the same division rule is chosen by the proposer from a singleton set consisting of just one division rule (in other words, the responder has no choice but to pick the given rule).

In several recent studies on experimental games, players have been observed to care about outcomes as well as procedures through which those outcomes are brought about (see, for example, Rabin 1993, 2002; Bolton, Brandts and Ockenfels 2005; Shor 2006; Cox, Friedman and Gjerstad 2007; and Cox, Friedman and Sadiraj 2008;). It may also be noted that, in empirical measurement of happiness, it has been found that people are concerned about both outcomes and procedures, especially participation rights in making decisions (see, for example, Frey and Stutzer 2004).

Traditional choice theory does not consider procedural aspects or those aspects are deemed insignificant for choice. Let there be a finite set of alternatives X and strict subsets $A \subset X$. Furthermore, let $\mathcal{N}$ be a finite set of distinct procedures (concerning production of the objects or their availability or both). In what follows, $C(\cdot)$ stands for a choice function. If procedures do not matter, we get

$$C([A, i]) = C([A, j]) \neq \emptyset$$

for all $A \subset X$ and any $i, j \in \mathcal{N}, i \neq j$. This result could be called *consequentialist* in our framework, since, obviously, the only thing which is of relevance is the set of objects A (and not the aspect of how A came about). On the other hand, *non-consequentialism* in our framework would hold if for at least one $A \subset X$, one would have $C([A, i]) \neq C([A, j])$ for $i \neq j$, or for at least one $A \subset X$ and for at least one procedure $i \in \mathcal{N}, C([A, i]) = \emptyset$.

In the following sections, we wish to discuss non-consequentialist features of decision-making—in particular, procedural aspects. We shall try to develop a theoretical framework that, we hope, will be able to deal with these characteristics appropriately. To the best of our knowledge, there is only one other paper that explicitly tackles procedural aspects of choice: a recent piece by Arlegi and Dimitrov (2007) which analytically examines the role of procedures within the context of freedom of choice. The point that procedures obviously matter in various contexts is often made in passing. It is explicitly dealt with in the analysis of individual rights exercising within social choice theory. The choice of a particular game form can be seen as the definite choice of a particular system of rights for the individuals concerned. Different rights systems based on a different conferment of rights may lead to different social outcomes—the procedural aspect within such conversions is immediate (see e.g. Suzumura 1996 and Sen 2002).

The structure of this chapter is as follows. In section II, we shall discuss another example, argue in favor of a non-consequentialist approach and introduce some basic structure. Section III presents definitions and axioms and offers a first result. Section IV argues that information about how objects "fare" under different procedures should enter the process of choice. Section V introduces a finer structure where aspects of various production methods are considered as well. Section VI proposes an ordering over shrinking procedures and section VII concludes the chapter. All proofs are given in an Appendix at the end of the chapter.

II. Another Example and the Basic Structure

We wish to start out by discussing a situation we have described before (Gaertner and Xu 2004). It is a modification of an example given by Sen (1988, 1997). Let us consider a country with a finite set of newspapers, some highly political, others only marginally so. Among the first, there is one daily paper which is considered to be the government's mouthpiece, but with undeniable editorial qualities nevertheless. The person we consider chooses this paper among all the available papers. Let us imagine that for some reason, the government decides to ban all papers except for its mouthpiece. The person we observe now decides to refrain from choosing. In other words, her choice set with respect to papers is the empty set. So if n is the mouthpiece and k stands for the procedural aspect of a government ban, we would have $C([\{n\}, k]) = \emptyset$, $n \in S$, where S denotes the set of newspapers before government intervention.[1]

Note that the newspaper example is just one case. A government may ration the supply of certain consumer goods under the pretext that resources are scarce or industry has only limited capacities. The reader will remember that in economies of the Soviet type there was a notorious scarcity of certain consumer goods. The state's emphasis was on nurturing and extending heavy industry, military weapons in particular.

It seems that once such a procedural approach is taken, it is possible to follow various paths. One of the directions would be to argue that an alternative x, for which $C([\{x\}, i]) = \emptyset$ for some $i \in \mathcal{N}$, should *never* be picked under the same i. In other words, for any $A \subset X$ such that $x \in A$, $x \notin C([A], i)$. One could say, however, that this requirement is too strict, so that whenever there is at least

---

[1] One could have modeled the described situation differently by adding the alternative "to choose nothing" as an additional option of choice. In this case, if a, b, c and d were different newspapers and $\{\emptyset\}$ would be the option to choose nothing, a, let us say, would be picked from the "full menu". However, if a and $\{\emptyset\}$ were the only alternatives left, $\{\emptyset\}$ would be chosen. Then a very basic property of "internal consistency" (Sen 1993), viz. contraction consistency, is violated. We shall not pursue this alternative approach any further in the present work.

one other alternative y available under procedure i for which it is not true that $C([\{y\}, i]) = \emptyset$, then x would be choosable. This argument could be modified again by saying that an alternative x for which $x \notin C([\{x\}, i])$ would need a "sufficient or minimal number" of other objects around in order to be chosen. In our example above, one could reason that if a couple of other papers were left undisturbed under the ban (i.e. under the given procedure i), mouthpiece n would perhaps still be picked. This last direction was followed at greater length in our earlier paper (Gaertner and Xu 2004).

It also seems plausible to argue that the government mouthpiece would, perhaps, still be chosen by an individual if it was left as the only available newspaper after a major natural disaster or as the only paper available after a series of bankrupcies in the press industry due to financial mismanagement. This last observation points in one of the directions we are pursuing in this chapter, namely that bits of information about how a certain alternative fares "choice-wise" under various procedures should be taken into consideration. The following sections will be more explicit.

Let us pause for a moment and discuss a fundamental objection to the approach on which we are about to embark. From the examples given above, it should be clear that some decision-makers (not all of them) seem to care about one or several characteristics of a choice procedure which indicates that these characteristics are of relevance for them. Should not these characteristics then be included in a proper description of an alternative or in a proper description of the consequences of an action? These consequences then should not only refer to the decision-maker alone but also to every other person that can be affected, both today and in future times.

This objection, which reflects a consequentialist position, raises the issue of a complete or all-encompassing description of an alternative or action. Could a more comprehensive description of alternatives and actions render the special emphasis on procedural aspects superfluous? An answer to this question involves several aspects. First of all, it may be difficult or impossible to have a full description of all relevant features of an alternative or all relevant aspects of the consequences of a decision-maker's action. Informational constraints may be one reason for this, and by no means the only one. There are also practical reasons why alternatives may be incompletely described. But even if alternatives and actions could be fully specified, they may not be of ultimate interest. Some of the aspects that would render the description of an alternative or action complete depend on information that is so private that, in some cases, the decision-making agents themselves may not be fully aware of all the facets that affect their choices. Therefore, it may be difficult, perhaps impossible, to determine which particular comprehensively described alternative or action has been chosen. What can be determined without much difficulty, however, is which *incompletely* described alternative or action has been picked. In other words, alternatives that are exchanged on markets, claims that are made in contracts and actions that are required in strategic situations are, because of informational reasons, necessarily described incompletely. Baigent and Gaertner (1996: 241) write in a related context that "even a brief glance at the standard economics literature establishes beyond doubt that it is such partial descriptions (commodity bundles, tax schedules, etc.) that are the alternatives of ultimate interest".

There is another aspect which has to be considered. Let us assume that the procedural characteristics have been integrated into a proper description of particular objects. Then at the time of choice, trade-off relationships among different characteristics would have to be considered. A helpful example may be the choice of a car, where different features such as speed, luxury, gas consumption and other aspects are weighed against each other. However, it seems to us that in the case of procedural characteristics, such trade-off relationships very often are not considered. Children's toys which were manufactured in prisoners' camps appear to belong to a different category than "normal" toys. The same seems to hold for carpets woven by children or diamonds mined by children or women. Individuals may decide that these aspects are of no relevance for them. Consequently, there will be no consideration at all in terms of possible trade-offs between characteristics. On the other hand, these procedural aspects do matter for others, actually matter very much, and then again, there is no weighing among different features that describe particular objects or alternatives. In the latter case, it is possible to argue that procedural aspects are considered quite separately. They may even receive lexicographic priority. This then comes close to assigning them a separate role or status.

Having said all this, we have to ask how procedural aspects can be formalized adequately. Given sets X and $\mathcal{N}$ as they were defined in section I, let K be the set of all non-empty subsets of X and $K \times \mathcal{N}$ be the cartesian product of K and $\mathcal{N}$. The elements of $K \times \mathcal{N}$ will be denoted by $[A, i]$, $[B, j]$, etc. The intended interpretation of $[A, i]$ is that the subset A is brought about or produced by the procedure i. A choice function C is a mapping from $K \times \mathcal{N}$ to $K \cup \{\emptyset\}$ such that for all $A \in K$, all $i \in \mathcal{N}$, $C([A, i]) \subseteq A$. In addition, we define $C([\emptyset, i]) = \emptyset$. Note that we shall allow $C([A, i]) = \emptyset$ for some $A \in K$. The emptiness of a choice set can be regarded as an inaction. The individual considered refuses to choose anything from the set of choosable elements. It should be clear from our discussions so far that we interpret $C([A, i])$ as follows. Given a subset A, which is brought about or produced by a procedure i, $C([A, i]) \subset A$ is the set of alternatives that the individual would like to pick from A given i. Let R be a weak ordering (reflexive, transitive and complete) over X. For all $A \subset K$, define $\hat{C}(A, R) = \{x \in A | xRy$ for all $y \in A\}$. $\hat{C}(\cdot)$ specifies the set of best elements according to ordering R. Furthermore, we define $\hat{C}(\emptyset, R) = \emptyset$.

III. Definitions, Axioms and
a First Result

As a first step, we concentrate on those elements x in A such that the choice set of the singleton $\{x\}$ under procedure i is empty. More precisely, given any procedure $i \in \mathcal{N}$, we collect all those objects $x \in X$ for which $C([\{x\}, i]) = \emptyset$.

Definition 1. *Given a choice function C, for all $i \in \mathcal{N}$, all $A \in K$, define $W(A, i) = \{x \in A | C([\{x\}, i]) = \emptyset\}$.*

$W(A, i)$ consists of all those elements x in A that under procedure i are not chosen from the singleton set. We now propose a way in which elements of $W(A, i)$ can be "treated" when the set of choosable elements A contains more than a single element. Analogous to previous discussions (Arrow 1959; Sen 1977), the following notion of rationalizability of choice functions, which was first proposed in Gaertner and Xu (2004), is introduced in this extended framework.

Definition 2. *A choice function C is LP-rationalizable iff for all $i \in \mathcal{N}$, there exists an ordering R_i over X such that for all $A \in K$, $C([A, i]) = \hat{C}(A - W(A, i), R_i)$ if $W(A, i) = A$ and $C([A, i]) = \hat{C}(A, R_i)$ if $W(A, i) \neq A$.*

Definition 2 says that elements from $W(A, i)$ are potential candidates for choice as long as at least one other alternative outside of $W(\cdot)$ is available. This is a requirement that expresses a "limited protest".

An example may help to clarify the implication of Definition 2. Let $X \supset A = \{x, y, z\}$. Furthermore, let us assume that $W(A, i) = \{x, y\}$ according to Definition 1. Then, according to Definition 2, since $W(A, i) \neq A$, the issue of rationalizability concerns all three elements of A. If A only contained elements x and y, $C([A, i])$ would be equal to the empty set.

Our first axiom expresses the idea that if two options x and y are not picked from singleton sets, given procedure i, then if one of them is not chosen from set $A \subset X$, it continues not to be picked if the other option is added to set A.

Weak Protest Consistency (WPC): For all i in $\mathcal{N}$, all A in K, all x in A and all y in X, if x and y are not chosen from singleton sets, given procedure i, then x is not chosen from $[A \cup \{y\}, i]$ whenever x is not chosen from $[A, i]$.

One may object to axiom WPC that it is already too strong. If alternatives x and y, let us say, are such that each of them is not picked from the corresponding singleton set, it would seem unnatural, so the argument goes, to choose nothing from the set $\{x, y\}$, when this set is generated by procedure i. We do not find this argument very convincing. If x and y, again, are newspapers and both happen to be the government's mouthpieces, should one be willing to choose one of them just because of the fact that procedure i was "kind enough" to leave a choice between two papers? Consider a modification of this example. Suppose there is a left-wing newspaper and a right-wing newspaper. The procedure is such that the leftist paper is the only newspaper published when the leftist party rules the country, and the right-wing paper is the only paper when the right-wing party is in power. The procedure obviously is the *same* under both regimes. When both newspapers are available, neither party seems to be dominant. In such a situation where political power is more equalized, there obviously is a *different* procedure which provides for "balanced" opinion. Axiom WPC loses its bite and does not apply.

The following axiom captures an intuition similar to that contained in axiom WPC. If nothing is picked from a set A because of protest, and if the option x is not picked from the singleton set $\{x\}$, then x continues not to be picked if x is added to set A.

Protest-Expansion Consistency (PEC): For all i in $\mathcal{N}$, all A in K and all x in X, if
$\quad C([A, i]) = \emptyset$ and $C[\{x\}, i] = \emptyset$, then x is not chosen from $[A \cup \{x\}, i]$.

It is clear that axiom PEC is both conceptually and formally weaker than axiom WPC.

The next axiom is rather innocuous. It guarantees the non-emptiness of the choice set, given set A and procedure i, if there exists at least one element that does not belong to $W(A, i)$.

Non-empty Choice of No-Protest Situations (NCNP): For all i in $\mathcal{N}$ and all A in K,
$\quad$ if there exist x, y in A such that it is not the case that both objects belong
$\quad$ to $W(A, i)$, then $C([A, i]) \neq \emptyset$.

The third axiom is a consistency requirement when the set of choosable options contracts. It is a straightforward modification (weakening) of Arrow's (1959) rationality condition.

Restricted Arrow Condition (RAC): For all i in $\mathcal{N}$ and all A and A' in K, if $A' \subseteq A$
$\quad$ and there exists x in A' such that the choice from $[\{x\}, i]$ is not empty,
$\quad$ then $C([A', i]) = A' \cap C([A, i])$ whenever $C([A, i]) \cap A' \neq \emptyset$.

In section I, we asserted that traditional choice theory does not consider procedural aspects. This statement can be turned around by saying that conventional choice theory defines conditions of consistency independently of the underlying procedure. In Arrow's rationality condition from 1959, for example, it does not matter at all whether the transition from superset A to subset A', let us say, was caused by procedure i or procedure j or some other process, nor would the consistency requirement be affected in any way if the shrinkage from A to A' were generated by procedure i and the transition from A' to A'' were caused by some other procedure j. In other words, the traditional consistency conditions are stronger than our requirement, since they are implicitly defined for all i, j in $\mathcal{N}$.

The first result we wish to offer is the following. The proof is given in the Appendix.

Theorem 1. *A choice function C is LP-rationalizable iff it satisfies axioms PEC, NCNP and RAC.*

The reader should note that a similar result, where the axiom PEC is replaced by the axiom WPC from above, is obtained in Gaertner and Xu (2004).

IV. Information from other Procedures

So far, we have confined our theoretical analysis to cases where only one procedure at a time is considered. However, as indicated in section II, it may be important for a person to ask whether a certain alternative would, perhaps, not be chosen under several other procedures or even not be picked under any procedure at all. In our newspaper example, we argued that an individual may refuse to pick the only paper left after the government has introduced a ban on all other political papers. Our individual may also decide not to buy the only political paper left if the other papers have been bought up by the government and turned into completely apolitical ones. Another case would be a situation where the rulers of a country declared that because of an emergency situation, it would be a waste of scarce resources if more than one daily paper (their own, of course) appeared. However, as mentioned before, the individual would, perhaps, continue to acquire the government's mouthpiece if the other papers had been destroyed by a major disaster or went out of business due to financial mismanagement. In other words, we now introduce some degree of interdependence among different procedures that permits additional information to enter the process of choice.

In line with the foregoing arguments, let us consider the following refinement. For all elements $x \in X$, we define the set of procedures $N(x)$ with the property that x is not picked from the singleton set. More formally, for all $x \in X$, $N(x) = \{i \in \mathcal{N} | C([\{x\}, i]) = \emptyset\}$. Next, the individual is supposed to compare the cardinality of $N(x)$ with some x-specific threshold level $q(x) > 0$ which defines a level of tolerance for the choosing individual. In other words, if $\#N(x)$ is larger than $q(x)$, $x \in A$ has "failed sufficiently" under various procedures and will be deleted from further choice. For all $A \subset K$, $\Gamma'(A)$ collects all those elements from A that have this property. So we obtain $\Gamma'(A) = \{x \in A | \#N(x) > q(x)\}$. It is obvious that the introduction of the threshold level $q(x)$ only makes sense if the procedures we consider can be clearly defined. Our various examples, we hope, demonstrated that this is what we have in mind. So in our newspaper example, the government ban on other papers, a government buyout of other papers, and financial mismanagement among the other papers leading to their bankruptcy, are instances of clearly defined procedures.

Using the newly introduced notions above, we can now define the concept of LP'-rationalizability, introduced in Gaertner and Xu (2004).

Definition 3. *A choice function C is LP'-rationalizable iff, $\forall i \in \mathcal{N}$, there exists an ordering R_i over X such that $\forall A \in K$, $C([A, i]) = \hat{C}(A - W(A, i), R_i)$ if $W(A, i) = A$ and $C([A, i]) = \hat{C}(A - \Gamma'(A), R_i)$ if $W(A, i) \neq A$.*

Furthermore we define

Protest Consistency Based on a Threshold (TPC): For all $i \in \mathcal{N}$, all $x \in X$ and all $A \in K$, if $x \notin C([\{x\}, i])$ and $N(x)$ contains more elements than $q(x)$, then $x \notin C([A \cup \{x\}, i])$.

This condition states that an alternative that is rejected from the singleton set under a sufficient number of procedures will never be chosen when the set of choosable elements expands, under any procedure i.

The following result gives the characterization of a choice function being LP'-rationalizable. Its proof is given in the Appendix.

Theorem 2. *A choice function C is LP'-rationalizable iff it satisfies TPC, PEC, NCNP and RAC.*

We note that in Theorem 2, axiom PEC may be replaced by axiom WPC (see Gaertner and Xu 2004).

V. A FINER STRUCTURE

Up to now, we have presented two aspects of non-standard rationalizability of a choice function originating from Gaertner and Xu (2004), where the focus is on procedures or processes that shrink the universal set X of all conceivable alternatives to particular feasible subsets $S, S', \dots$ of X. We did not discuss the aspect of production methods as such that give rise to alternatives contained in a feasible set; moreover, we did not look at the interaction between those production methods and processes that shrink the set X to alternative feasible subsets of X. In order to do all this, we need a finer structure within which we hope to be able to carry out our analysis. Before embarking on this, we should be a little more explicit on what we mean by "the aspect of production methods as such".

In standard microeconomic analysis, production of inputs and outputs is more or less entirely reduced to a technological process. This is justified in many cases but not in all situations, since there are production methods that are not innocuous. Carpets woven by children, children's toys manufactured in prisoners' camps, gold mined by children and hard labor done by women are activities that cannot just simply be reduced to different forms of technology, since standards of human dignity and humanity and of safety are immediately involved. Quite a few people but, of course, not everybody has reservations against these forms of production. Coal mining in China, carried out by men, would be another case in point, though at first glance it looks rather harmless. These phenomena have to be put in relation to urgent wants and non-availability or scarcity of badly needed objects. Just consider again our last example. Coal mining with high fatality rates may be viewed differently under severe shortages of energy supply than "under normal circumstances". The fact that there is no general or unanimous view on these issues does not mean that they should be neglected. We now turn to these aspects and propose some analysis.

Let X again be a finite set of all conceivable alternatives. We now wish to describe these alternatives in more detail. Following Debreu (1959), we specify production methods that generate physical commodities or alternatives. Therefore, let T be the set of all relevant production methods. We assume that T can be partitioned into three non-empty subsets T^1, T^2 and $T^3 (T = T^1 \cup T^2 \cup T^3)$, with the interpretation that T^1 consists of those production methods that are *never* acceptable for a choosing individual, T^2 comprises those production methods that are *always* acceptable, and T^3 consists of those methods whose acceptability is contingent *on other things*. Consequently, a commodity or an alternative from the universal set X henceforth specifies the underlying production method in an explicit form. For example, we now distinguish between coal mined by men and coal mined by women (or children), carpets woven by women or by children, or road construction done by men or by women. For ease of presentation, we assume that $X = O \times T$, where O stands for the set of all features of commodities or alternatives other than T. As a consequence, alternatives in X can be denoted by (x_0, τ), (y_0, τ'), etc., where $x_0, y_0 \in O$ and $\tau, \tau' \in T$.

Next, we focus on possible procedures that give rise to a feasible subset from a given set of commodities or alternatives. For this purpose, let N stand for the set of procedures that narrow down a given set S to some proper subsets of S. We assume that N can be partitioned into procedures N^1, which we describe as interventionist procedures (such as dictatorship, wars, and other kinds of imposed interferences) and N^2, which we decompose into interventionist but "not directly man made" procedures (natural catastrophes, large-scale accidents) and non-interventionist procedures such as the market system or a given legal system. A legal system, for example, may in some general way forbid the production of articles manufactured by children or may disallow certain agricultural products based on genetic manipulation. We assume that neither N^1 nor N^2 is empty and that they completely exhaust N, i.e., $N = N^1 \cup N^2$.

We now wish to consider a relationship between procedures that determine the availability of certain subsets and those generated subsets themselves. With K again being the set of *all* non-empty subsets of X, we distinguish between elements from N^1 generating $K^1 \subset K$ and elements from N^2 generating $K^2 \subset K$, where normally $K^1 \cap K^2 \neq \emptyset$. In general, it may not be possible to generate all elements of K from either N^1 alone or from N^2 alone. Also, an interventionist procedure such as dictatorship may bring about subsets from K that would be highly unlikely under a market system or a legal system which belong to N^2 (an imposed rationing of commodities, for example). Given the distinction between N^1 and N^2, it should be clear that all elements of the cartesian product $K^1 \times N^1$ and all elements of the cartesian product $K^2 \times N^2$ are potentially feasible.

Given our definition of X from above, we consider $A \subset O$ and $\tau \in T$. Then $(A \times \{\tau\})$, $(A' \times \{\tau'\})$ are subsets of X, where $\tau, \tau' \in T$ are the underlying production methods. These subsets can be generated by shrinking procedures from either N^1 or N^2. So we may, for example, have triples of the form $(A \times \{\tau\}; i)$ with $i \in N^1$ and $(A' \times \{\tau'\}; j)$ with $j \in N^2$, where subset $(A \times \{\tau\})$ belongs to K^1 and $(A' \times \{\tau'\})$ belongs to K^2. A choice function C chooses nothing or picks an alternative $(a, \tau) \in (A \times \{\tau\})$ from $(A \times \{\tau\}; i)$. For example, we may find that coal mined by women is an acceptable choice in the case of a war (an interventionist procedure from N^1) but unacceptable under elements from N^2.

More generally, given $O \times T$, K^h and N^h, $h \in \{1, 2\}$, a choice function C is a mapping from $K^h \times N^h$ to $K^h \cup \{\emptyset\}$ such that for all $(A \times \{\tau\}) \in K^h$, all $i \in N^h$, $C([A \times \{\tau\}; i]) \subseteq (A \times \{\tau\})$. In addition, we define $C([\emptyset, i]) = \emptyset$. In the present framework, we again allow $C([A \times \{\tau\}; i]) = \emptyset$ for some $(A \times \{\tau\}) \in K^h$, $h \in \{1, 2\}$. Let R be a weak ordering (reflexive, transitive and complete) over X. For all $(A \times \{\tau\}) \in K^h$, we define $\hat{C}(A \times \{\tau\}, R) = \{(a, \tau) \in (A \times \{\tau\}) | (a, \tau) R(b, \tau) \forall (b, \tau) \in (A \times \{\tau\})\}$. $\hat{C}(\cdot)$ specifies again the set of best elements, given ordering R. Furthermore, we define $\hat{C}(\emptyset, R) = \emptyset$.

In the sequel, we wish to propose another notion of rationalizability of choice functions, reflecting our newly extended framework. We start by introducing an axiom that can be considered as rather uncontroversial. However, it would not lead us very far within our current project.

A1. *Unacceptable for Choice* (UC): For all $(A \times \{\tau\}; i)$ from either $K^1 \times N^1$ or $K^2 \times N^2$, if $\tau \in T^1$ and $(a, \tau) \in (A \times \{\tau\})$, then $(a, \tau) \notin C([A \times \{\tau\}; i])$.

Once a commodity or option has been produced by a production method from T^1, it will never be chosen, independent of whether the feasible set of objects was generated by an element from N^1 or N^2.

We shall now elaborate the idea that an individual may find the variety of choosable objects left over by a shrinking procedure unsatisfactory or "too thin". The individual has set up a cardinality requirement or threshold level below which objects that do not meet this requirement are not acceptable for choice. Let $k(a, \tau; i)$ be such a threshold level. It is object-specific and will, in general, depend both on $\tau \in T$ and on $i \in N^h$. For example, the threshold level may, *ceteris paribus*, be more demanding for $\tau \in T^3$ than for $\tau \in T^2$ and may also, *ceteris paribus*, be higher for $i \in N^1$ than for $j \in N^2$.

In the following, we shall restrict our analysis to elements $(A \times \{\tau\}; i) \in K^1 \times N^1$ with $\tau \in T^2 \cup T^3$. A similar analysis can, of course, be done for elements from $K^2 \times N^2$. In order to avoid complications, we shall henceforth assume that (i) $(O \times \{\tau\}; i) \in K^1 \times N^1$ for all $\tau \in T^2 \cup T^3$ and all $i \in N^1$, and (ii) for all $A \subseteq O$, all $\tau \in T^2 \cup T^3$ and all $i \in N^1$, $(A \times \{\tau\}; i) \in K^1 \times N^1$.

A2. *Restricted Protest Consistency* (RPC): $\forall \tau \in T^2 \cup T^3$, $\forall (A \times \{\tau\}; i) \in K^1 \times N^1$, if $(a, \tau) \in (A \times \{\tau\})$ and $\#(A \times \{\tau\}) < k(a, \tau; i)$, then $(a, \tau) \notin C([A \times \{\tau\}; i])$.

An explanation for this type of choice behavior was given above. If an element from $(A \times \{\tau\})$ does not meet its alternative-specific threshold level, it will not be acceptable for choice.

We next define what we shall call "k-cardinal rationalizability".

Definition 4. *A choice function C is k-cardinally rationalizable iff for all $\tau \in T \backslash T^1$, there exists an ordering R_i over K^1 such that for all $(A \times \{\tau\}; i) \in K^1 \times N^1$, $C([A \times \{\tau\}; i]) = \hat{C}(A \times \{\tau\} - \Omega(A, \tau; i), R_i)$, where $\Omega(A, \tau; i) = A \times \{\tau\}$ if $\#(A \times \{\tau\}) < k(a, \tau; i)$ and $\Omega(A, \tau; i) = \emptyset$ if $\#(A \times \{\tau\}) \geq k(a, \tau; i)$.*

Elements that do not meet the cardinality requirement are eliminated and are, therefore, no longer objects of potential choice. They comprise the set $\Omega(A, \tau; i)$.

Next, we reformulate Sen's (1977) well-known expansion consistency condition β for present purposes.

A3. *Expansion Consistency* (EXC): For all $\tau \in T \backslash T^1$, for all $(A \times \{\tau\}; i)$, $(B \times \{\tau\}; i) \in K^1 \times N^1$ with $(B \times \{\tau\}) \subseteq (A \times \{\tau\})$, if $(a, \tau), (b, \tau) \in C([B \times \{\tau\}; i])$, then $(a, \tau) \in C([A \times \{\tau\}; i])$ iff $(b, \tau) \in C([A \times \{\tau\}; i])$.

If elements (a, τ) and (b, τ) were chosen from set $B \times \{\tau\}$, given $i \in N^1$, then either both elements are to be chosen from the larger set $A \times \{\tau\}$ or neither of the two will be picked.

Furthermore, we consider

A4. *Restricted Contraction under $N^1(a^{N^1})$*: For all $\tau \in T \backslash T^1$, for all $(A \times \{\tau\}; i)$, $(B \times \{\tau\}; i) \in K^1 \times N^1$, if $(a, \tau) \in (B \times \{\tau\}) \subseteq (A \times \{\tau\})$ and

$(a, \tau) \in C([A \times \{\tau\}; i])$,   then $\#(B \times \{\tau\}) \geq k(a, \tau; i) \longrightarrow (a, \tau) \in C([B \times \{\tau\}; i])$.

A5. *Consistency of Empty Choice* (CEC): For all $\tau \in T \backslash T^1$, $\forall (A \times \{\tau\}; i)$, $(B \times \{\tau\}; i) \in K^1 \times N^1$, if $(B \times \{\tau\}) \subseteq (A \times \{\tau\})$ and $C([A \times \{\tau\}; i]) = \emptyset$, then $C([B \times \{\tau\}; i]) = \emptyset$.

A6. *Non-Emptiness* (NE): For all $\tau \in T \backslash T^1$ and for all $(A \times \{\tau\}) \subseteq (O \times \{\tau\})$, if there exists $(a, \tau) \in A \times \{\tau\}$ such that $k(a, \tau; i) \leq \#(A \times \{\tau\})$, then $C([A \times \{\tau\}; i]) \neq \emptyset$.

A4 formulates contraction consistency within the new structure. If (a, τ) was picked from the set $A \times \{\tau\}$ under procedure $i \in N^1$, (a, τ) will still be chosen from subset $B \times \{\tau\}$ if the cardinality requirement $k(a, \tau; i)$ is met.

A5 requires consistency of no choice when one goes from larger sets to smaller sets, but note that this is required only for procedures i within N^1.

A6 says something very obvious: if for any set $A \times \{\tau\}$, at least one element (a, τ) meets the threshold level, the choice set from this set is non-empty.

We can now formulate the following result; its proof is also given in the Appendix.

Theorem 3. *A choice function C is k-cardinally rationalizable iff it satisfies RPC, EXC, α^{N^1}, CEC and NE.*

VI. An Ordering Over
Different Procedures

Do people have orderings over procedures? At first glance, it does not appear plausible that individuals have a ranking over procedures *per se*. People judge procedural aspects on the basis of their implications for choice.

In section I, we referred to the game-form format, applied in social choice theory in order to formulate different types of individual rights exercising. Different game forms may represent different conferments of rights, and the ensuing consequences may be quite diverse in terms of externalities and infringement. Consequently, individuals can be assumed to have preferences over different rights systems.

Much closer to our preceding analysis is the following situation. One procedure j is preferred to another procedure i if the former procedure yields set A, while the latter procedure leads to B, and B is fully contained in A. This is a relatively simple case. How about the following? Procedure j leads to A, procedure i yields B, the inclusion property does not hold, and every element in A is considered to be at least as good as every element in B. An ordering with respect to procedures j and i will be straightforward as long as both procedures are deemed "innocuous". What can be said if j yields A while i leads to B, A is larger than B, but procedure j has certain "bad" features that procedure i does not have? The evaluation of procedures now gets somewhat more complicated.

This chapter has discussed several aspects, the shrinkage of sets in particular, which involve a restriction of choice, limiting a person's freedom to choose. A priori, it is not clear at all how an ordering over procedures can be derived in such cases. Our final point in this paper is to make at least one small proposal.

In the second half of the previous section, we focused on the set N^1 of interventionist man-made procedures, related to production methods from $T^2 \cup T^3$. We introduced a threshold level for richness or variety of choice $k(a, \tau; i)$. We argued that elements from the set $(A \times \{\tau\})$, given $i \in N^1$ and $\tau \in T^2 \cup T^3$, should only be picked if "sufficiently many" choosable objects were available. If $k(a, \tau; i)$ is an indirect measure and requirement for richness, it should vary with the type of procedure. One could, for example, argue that the stronger the outside intervention with respect to the availability of objects, the stricter the variety requirement should be; or put differently, the stronger the interference, the higher an individual will set the threshold level $k(a, \tau; i)$. So this level should be lower for elements from N^2, the set of procedures which do not come about through direct man-made intervention. Thus, if $(a, \tau) \in (A \times \{\tau\})$ meets the cardinality requirement under elements i from N^1, it meets the cardinality requirement under elements j from N^2 *a fortiori*. These bits of information may allow us to construct an ordering over procedures. For a given $\tau \in T^2 \cup T^3$ and $(a, \tau) \in (A \times \{\tau\})$, we wish to define a preference relation $\mathcal{R}$ over procedures $i \in N^1$ and $j \in N^2$ in the following way: $< j > \mathcal{R} < i >$ iff $k(a, \tau; j) \leq k(a, \tau; i)$. Due to its construction, the relation $\mathcal{R}$ will be complete and transitive.

One can introduce finer partitions, both with respect to N^1 and N^2, and use the threshold level again as the basis for an ordering over shrinking procedures. Thus, if we have $N^1 = N^{11} \cup N^{12}$ and $N^2 = N^{21} \cup N^{22}$ with indices i, j, l, m referring to subsets $N^{11}, N^{12}, N^{21}, N^{22}$ respectively, one can establish a complete ordering on the basis that in general $k(a, \tau; i) > k(a, \tau; j) > k(a, \tau; l) > k(a, \tau; m)$. Thus, the strictest level requirement is attached to elements from N^{11} (strong interventionist measures taken by a dictator or oligarchy, say) and the weakest level requirement is attached to elements from N^{22} (e.g. shrinkages due to the market mechanism or to instances of democratic legislation). It is unlikely that there will be any level requirement at all in the latter case. Since the levels $k(a, \tau; i)$ are object-specific and consider the underlying production method, they do not represent abstract index numbers. Of course, more complicated constructions seem possible.

VII. Concluding Remarks

In various choice situations, an individual may have good reasons to consider non-consequential features of decision problems, procedural aspects in particular. This non-consequential attitude towards decision-making is certainly different from the standard approach in the theory of rational choice and calls for an unconventional investigation into an individual's choice behavior. In traditional microeconomic analysis, an "all-encompassing" utility function takes all possible consequences into consideration, for everyone who can be affected, including future generations. This is quite demanding. The present chapter has proposed a different framework that enables us to examine various issues of non-consequentialism reflected in an individual's choices.

In our theoretical framework, we have analyzed several types of choice behavior that cannot be rationalized within the standard approach. A common thread in this non-standard approach is the notion that an individual may choose to pick nothing from feasible sets of alternatives if those feasible sets are brought about in particular ways that are deemed unacceptable. This emptiness of a choice set is in sharp contrast to the non-emptiness of a choice set almost universally assumed in the standard framework. It reflects the procedural concern of the individual under consideration: if the way that gives rise to various feasible subsets is not acceptable according to the individual's subscribed view, the individual may register a protest by refusing to choose any alternative from the given feasible subset even though some alternatives in the set would have a positive value for this person. Starting from this "position", we have moved onward to other considerations which require more information. Richness of available choice is one of them, information on how an object fares under different procedural conditions is another. Depending on the context, we have proposed various notions of rationalizability of a choice function that we have characterized axiomatically.

APPENDIX

Proof of Theorem 1. It can be checked that if a choice function C is LP-rationalizable, then it satisfies axioms PEC, NCNP and RAC. Therefore, we have only to show that if a choice function C satisfies PEC, NCNP and RAC, then it is LP-rationalizable.

Let C be the choice function that satisfies PEC, NCNP and RAC. Let $i \in \mathcal{N}$. First, we note that for all $A \subset K$, if $C([\{a\}, i]) = \emptyset$ for all $a \in A$, then, by PEC, $C([A, i]) = \emptyset$. Note also that the above observation is independent of any underlying binary relations. If $C([\{x\}, i]) = \emptyset$ for all $x \in X$, then define the binary relation R_i over X as follows: $x I_i y$ for all $x, y \in X$. Clearly, given PEC, the R_i thus defined is LP-rationalizable. Now, suppose that for some $x \in X$, $C([\{x\}, i]) \neq \emptyset$. Given NCNP, $C([X, i]) \neq \emptyset$. We first define $X_1, X_2, \ldots,$ X_k as follows: $X_1 = C([X, i])$, $X_2 = C([X - X_1, i])$, $\ldots$, $X_k = C([X - \cup_{j=1}^{k-1} X_j, i])$ and k is such that $W(X_k, i) \subseteq X_k$, $C([X_k, i]) \neq \emptyset$ and $C([X - \cup_{j=1}^{k} X_j, i]) = \emptyset$. Now define the binary relation R_i as follows: for all $x, y \in X$, $[x R_i y$ iff $x \in X_m$ and $y \in X_n$ where $m \leq n]$. Clearly, R_i as defined above is reflexive, transitive and complete. Next, we show that C is LP-rationalizable; that is, for all $A \in K$, $C([A, i]) = \hat{C}(A - W(A, i), R_i)$ if $W(A, i) = A$ and $C([A, i]) = \hat{C}(A, R_i)$ if $W(A, i) \neq A$.

Consider $A \in K$ such that $W(A, i) = A$. Let $A = \{a_1, \cdots, a_p\}$. Since $W(A, i) = A$, for all $a \in A$, $C([\{a\}, i]) = \emptyset$. In particular, $C([\{a_1\}, i]) = \emptyset$. Then, by the repeated use of PEC, we must have $C([A, i]) = \emptyset$. On the other hand, $\hat{C}(A - W(A, i), R_i) = \hat{C}(\emptyset, R_i) = \emptyset$. Therefore, in this case, $C([A, i]) = \hat{C}(A - W(A, i), R_i)$.

Now, consider $A \in K$ such that $W(A, i) \neq A$. Clearly, there exists $x \in A$ such that $C([\{x\}, i]) = \{x\}$. It is then clear that $W(X, i) \neq X$. From the definition of R_i, clearly, $C([X, i]) = \hat{C}(X, R_i)$. It is also clear that, from the definition of R_i, $C([X_j, i]) = \hat{C}(X_j, R_i)$ for all $j = 1, \ldots, k$. We now show that $\hat{C}(A, R_i) = C([A, i])$ in this case.

(1) Let $a \in C([A, i])$. By RAC, noting that $C([\{x\}, i]) = \{x\}$, it must be true that $a \in C([\{a, x, y\}, i])$ for all $y \in A$. Suppose to the contrary that $a \notin \hat{C}(A, R_i)$. Then, from the definition of R_i, there exists $b \in A$ such that $b \in X_p$ and $a \in X_q$ with $p < q$. Note that $C([X_p, i]) = \hat{C}(X_p, R_i)$. We must have $b \in C([X_p, i])$. Consider $C([\{a, b, x\}, i])$. If $x P_i b$, then $x \in C([X_m, i])$ where $m < p$. By RAC, $\{x\} = C([\{x, a, b\}, i])$, a contradiction. If $x I_i b$, then $x \in C([X_p, i])$. By RAC, $\{x, b\} = C([\{x, a, b\}, i])$, a contradiction. If $b P_i x$, then, by RAC, $\{b\} = C([\{x, a, b\}, i])$, another contradiction. Hence, $a \in \hat{C}(A, R_i)$.

(2) Let $a \in \hat{C}(A, R_i)$. Then, from the definition of R_i, for all $y \in A$, $a R_i y$. Let X_p be such that $a \in C([X_p, i])$. Then, noting that $C([\{x\}, i]) = \{x\}$, by RAC, we must have $a \in C([A, i])$. Therefore, C is LP-rationalizable. ∎

Proof of Theorem 2. The necessity part of the theorem can be easily checked. We show its sufficiency.

Let C be the choice function that satisfies TPC, PEC, NCNP and RAC. Let $i \in \mathcal{N}$. We distinguish two cases: (i) $C([X, i]) = \emptyset$ and (ii) $C([X, i]) \neq \emptyset$. In case (i), we define the binary relation R_i over X as follows: $x I_i y$ for all $x, y \in X$. Then, by PEC, the R_i defined above is LP'-rationalizable. In case (ii), let $X' = X - \Gamma'(X)$. By TPC and NCNP, $C([X', i]) \neq \emptyset$. Define $X_1', X_2', \ldots, X_k'$ as follows: $X_1' = C([X', i])$, $X_2' = C([X' - X_1', i])$, $\ldots$, $X_k' = C([X' - \cup_{j=1}^{k-1} X_j', i])$ and k is such that $W(X_k', i) \subseteq X_k'$, $C([X_k', i]) \neq \emptyset$ and $C([X - \cup_{j=1}^{k} X_j', i]) = \emptyset$. The remainder of the proof of the result is similar to that of Theorem 1. Therefore, we omit it. ∎

Proof of Theorem 3. It can easily be checked that if a choice function C is k-cardinally rationalizable, then it satisfies axioms RPC, EXC, α^{N^1}, CEC and NE. Therefore, we only have to show that if a choice function C satisfies RPC, EXC, α^{N^1}, CEC and NE, then it is k-cardinally rationalizable.

Note that at the beginning of our formal analysis, we defined $C([\emptyset; i]) = \emptyset$ and $\hat{C}(\emptyset, R) = \emptyset$, where R is a weak ordering.

Let C be the choice function that satisfies RPC, EXC, α^{N^1} and CEC. Let $(A \times \{\tau\}; i) \in K^1 \times N^1$ with $\tau \in T\backslash T^1$. We distinguish the following two cases: (i) $C([O \times \{\tau\}; i]) = \emptyset$ and (ii) $C([O \times \{\tau\}; i]) \neq \emptyset$. In case (i), due to CEC, $C([B \times \{\tau\}; i]) = \emptyset$ for all $(B \times \{\tau\}) \subseteq$

$(O \times \{\tau\})$. In other words, no $(a, \tau) \in (B \times \{\tau\}) \subseteq (O \times \{\tau\})$ meets its cardinality requirement $k(a, \tau; i)$. We define the binary relation R_i over $O \times \{\tau\}$ as follows: $(a, \tau) I_i (b, \tau)$ for all $(a, \tau), (b, \tau) \in O \times \{\tau\}$. Clearly, R_i is reflexive, complete and transitive. It is also clear from the definition of $\Omega(A, \tau; i)$ that $\Omega(A, \tau; i) = A \times \{\tau\}$ for all $A \times \{\tau\} \subseteq O \times \{\tau\}$ so that $\hat{C}(A \times \{\tau\} - \Omega(A, \tau; i), R_i) = \emptyset = C([A \times \{\tau\}; i])$ for all $(A \times \{\tau\}) \in K^1$. Hence C is k-cardinally rationalizable.

In case (ii), we define $A_1, A_2, \ldots, A_p$ as follows: $A_1 = C([O \times \{\tau\}; i])$, $A_2 = C([O \times \{\tau\} - A_1; i])$, $\ldots$, $A_{p-1} = C([O \times \{\tau\} - \cup_{m=1}^{p-2} A_m; i])$, $A_p = O \times \{\tau\} - \cup_{m=1}^{p-1} A_m$, where p is such that $A_{p-1} \neq \emptyset$, $O \times \{\tau\} - \cup_{m=1}^{p-1} A_m \neq \emptyset$ and $C([O \times \{\tau\} - \cup_{m=1}^{p-1} A_m; i]) = O \times \{\tau\} - \cup_{m=1}^{p-1} A_m$ or $C([O \times \{\tau\} - \cup_{m=1}^{p-1} A_m; i]) = \emptyset$. Now define the binary relation R_i over $O \times \{\tau\}$ as follows: $(a, \tau) R_i (b, \tau)$ iff $(a, \tau) \in A_m$ and $(b, \tau) \in A_n$, where $m \leq n$. From its construction, R_i is reflexive, complete and transitive. Also, from the construction and by NE, we have $C([O \times \{\tau\}; i]) = \hat{C}(O \times \{\tau\} - \Omega(O, \tau; i), R_i)$. Next we show that $C([A \times \{\tau\}; i]) = \hat{C}(A \times \{\tau\} - \Omega(A, \tau; i), R_i)$ for all $(A \times \{\tau\}; i) \in K^1 \times N^1$. Let $(A \times \{\tau\}; i) \in K^1 \times N^1$. Let $(a, \tau) \in C([A \times \{\tau\}; i])$. Given that $(a, \tau) \in C([A \times \{\tau\}; i])$, obviously, $\#(A \times \{\tau\}) \geq k(a, \tau; i)$. Hence, $(a, \tau) \notin \Omega(A, \tau; i)$. By EXC and a^{N^1}, we are back in the classical case of contraction and expansion consistency. From the definition of R_i, $(a, \tau) R_i (b, \tau)$ for all $(b, \tau) \in A \times \{\tau\}$. Therefore, $(a, \tau) \in \hat{C}(A \times \{\tau\} - \Omega(A, \tau; i), R_i)$. This shows that $C([A \times \{\tau\}; i]) \subseteq \hat{C}(A \times \{\tau\} - \Omega(A, \tau; i), R_i)$. Suppose next that $(a, \tau) \in \hat{C}(A \times \{\tau\} - \Omega(A, \tau; i), R_i)$. From the definition of $\Omega(A, \tau; i)$ and by condition RPC, for all $(c, \tau) \in \Omega(A, \tau; i)$, $(c, \tau) \notin C([A \times \{\tau\}; i])$. From the definition of R_i, there exist m, n with $m \leq n$ such that $(a, \tau) \in A_m$ and for all $(b, \tau) \in (A \times \{\tau\} - \Omega(A, \tau; i))$, $(b, \tau) \in A_n$. Then, by a^{N^1} and EXC, $(a, \tau) \in C([A \times \{\tau\}; i])$ follows from standard rationalizability. Hence, $\hat{C}(A \times \{\tau\} - \Omega(A, \tau; i), R_i) \subseteq C([A \times \{\tau\}; i])$. Therefore, $C([A \times \{\tau\}; i]) = \hat{C}(A \times \{\tau\} - \Omega(A, \tau; i), R_i)$. That is, C is k-cardinally rationalizable. ∎

References

ARLEGI, R., and DIMITROV, D. (2007), *On Procedural Freedom of Choice*, discussion paper, Department of Economics, Public University of Navarra.

ARROW, K. J. (1959), "Rational Choice Functions and Orderings", *Economica*, 26: 121–7.

BAIGENT, N., and GAERTNER, W. (1996), "Never Choose the Uniquely Largest: A Characterization", *Economic Theory*, 8: 239–49.

BOLTON, G. E., BRANDTS, J., and OCKENFELS, A. (2005), "Fair Procedures: Evidence from Games Involving Lotteries", *Economic Journal*, 117: 1054–76.

COX, J. C., FRIEDMAN, D., and GJERSTAD, S. (2007), "A Tractable Model of Reciprocity and Fairness", *Games and Economic Behavior*, 59: 17–45.

———— and SADIRAJ, V. (2008), "Revealed Altruism", *Econometrica*, 76: 31–69.

DARWALL, S. (2003), *Consequentialism* (London: Blackwell Publishing).

DEBREU, G. (1959), *Theory of Value* (New York: John Wiley).

FREY, B. S., and STUTZER, A. (2004), "Beyond Outcomes: Measuring Procedural Utility", *Oxford Economic Papers*, 57: 90–111.

GAERTNER, W., and XU, Y. (2004), "Procedural Choice", *Economic Theory*, 24: 335–49.

NASH, J. (1950), "The Bargaining Problem", *Econometrica*, 18: 155–62.

RABIN, M. (1993), "Incorporating Fairness into Game Theory and Economics", *American Economic Review*, 83: 1281–302.

—— (2002), "A Perspective on Psychology and Economics", *European Economic Review*, 46: 657–85.

SEN, A. K. (1977), "Social Choice Theory: A Re-Examination", *Econometrica*, 45: 53–89.

—— (1988), "Freedom of Choice: Concept and Content", *European Economic Review*, 32: 269–94.

—— (1993), "Internal Consistency of Choice", *Econometrica*, 61: 495–521.

—— (1997), "Maximization and the Act of Choice", *Econometrica*, 65: 745–79.

—— (2002), "Processes, Liberty and Rights", the Arrow Lectures, in A. K. Sen (ed.), *Rationality and Freedom* (Cambridge, Mass.: Harvard University Press), ch. 21.

SHOR, M. (2006), *Rethinking the Fairness Hypothesis: Procedural Justice in Simple Bargaining Games*, working paper, Owen Graduate School of Management, Vanderbilt University.

SUZUMURA, K. (1996), "Welfare, Rights, and Social Choice Procedures: A Perspective", *Analyse und Kritik*, 18: 20–37.

—— and XU, Y. (2001), "Characterizations of Consequentialism and Non-Consequentialism", *Journal of Economic Theory*, 101: 423–36.

—— —— (forthcoming), "Consequentialism and Non-Consequentialism: The Axiomatic Approach", in P. Anand, P. K. Pattanaik and C. Puppe (eds), *Handbook of Rational and Social Choice* (Oxford: Oxford University Press).

CHAPTER 10

THE METHOD OF MAJORITY DECISION AND RATIONALITY CONDITIONS

SATISH K. JAIN

An important problem in the context of social decision rules which do not possess the property of yielding a rational (transitive, quasi-transitive or acyclic) social binary weak preference relation for every profile of individual weak preference relations is that of characterizing sets of binary relations defined over the set of alternatives which are such that if in a profile every individual's weak preference relation belongs to one of these sets then the social weak preference relation generated by the social decision rule is invariably rational. In other words, if $\mathcal{B}$ is a set of binary relations defined over the set of alternatives then the question is that of formulating conditions which would characterize non-empty subsets D of $\mathcal{B}$ which are such that if every individual's binary weak preference relation in a profile belongs to D then the social binary weak preference relation generated by the profile satisfies a particular rationality condition. In the social choice literature pertaining to domain

The author wishes to thank Rajendra Kundu, Taposik Banerjee, Papiya Ghosh and Anirban Mitra for helpful comments.

restrictions, a condition which completely characterizes all non-empty subsets D with the property that whenever every individual's binary weak preference relation belongs to D the social binary weak preference relation generated by the social decision rule satisfies a particular rationality condition is called an Inada-type necessary and sufficient condition for that rationality condition. In general, for any social decision rule, the characterizing conditions for a particular rationality condition depend on the number of alternatives, the number of individuals and the set B whose non-empty subsets are the objects of study. In the context of any social decision rule, the most important of these problems is obviously that of formulating Inada-type necessary and sufficient conditions when B is the set of all logically possible orderings of the set of alternatives.

In the context of formulating characterizing conditions for social rationality, the method of majority decision has been extensively studied.[1] For the case when B consists of all logically possible orderings of the set of alternatives, contributions by Black (1948, 1958), Arrow (1963), Inada (1964, 1969), Sen (1966, 1970), Sen and Pattanaik (1969), Pattanaik (1971) and Kelly (1974) have resulted in the establishment of the following propositions:

(i) A sufficient condition for transitivity under the method of majority decision (MMD) is that the condition of extremal restriction (ER) holds over every triple of alternatives. If the number of alternatives is at least three and the number of individuals is even and greater than one then the satisfaction of ER over every triple is also an Inada-type necessary condition for transitivity under MMD.

(ii) A sufficient condition for quasi-transitivity under MMD is that at least one of the three conditions of limited agreement (LA), value-restriction (VR) and extremal restriction holds over every triple of alternatives. If the number of social alternatives is at least three and the number of individuals is at least five, then the satisfaction of ER, VR or LA over every triple is also an Inada-type necessary condition for quasi-transitivity under MMD.

In this chapter, Inada-type necessary and sufficient conditions are derived for the cases not covered by propositions (i) and (ii). Given that the number of alternatives is at least three, these cases are: Inada-type necessary and sufficient condition for transitivity when the number of individuals is odd and greater than one, for quasi-transitivity when the number of individuals is four, and for quasi-transitivity when the number of individuals is three.

If Inada-type necessary and sufficient conditions are formulated in terms of disjunction of more than one condition, then for proving the necessity part one first has to find all different ways in which all the conditions figuring in the disjunction could be violated together. This makes the proof of the necessity part of a

---

[1] For an excellent survey of the literature on domain conditions see Gaertner (2001).

characterization theorem both long and tedious. For this reason, in this chapter all Inada-type characterization theorems are formulated in terms of a single condition.

By combining propositions (i) and (ii) with the results of this chapter, the conditions for transitivity and quasi-transitivity under MMD, when the number of alternatives is at least three, can be stated as follows:

(a) If the number of individuals is even and greater than one then an Inada-type necessary and sufficient condition for transitivity under MMD is that the condition of extremal restriction holds over every triple of alternatives.

(b) If the number of individuals is odd and greater than one then an Inada-type necessary and sufficient condition for transitivity under MMD is that the condition of weak Latin Square partial agreement (WLSPA) holds over every triple of alternatives.

(c) If the number of individuals is at least 5 then an Inada-type necessary and sufficient condition for quasi-transitivity under MMD is that the condition of Latin Square partial agreement (LSPA) holds over every triple of alternatives.

(d) If the number of individuals is four, then an Inada-type necessary and sufficient condition for quasi-transitivity under MMD is that the condition of weak extremal restriction (WER) holds over every triple of alternatives.

(e) If the number of individuals is three, then an Inada-type necessary and sufficient condition for quasi-transitivity under MMD is that the condition of Latin Square linear ordering restriction (LSLOR) holds over every triple of alternatives.

The logical relationships among the five conditions which figure in propositions (a)–(e) are given by:

ER implies WLSPA;
WLSPA implies LSPA, LSPA itself being logically equivalent to the disjunction of
    VR, ER and LA;
LSPA implies WER; and
WER implies LSLOR.

It is possible to reformulate extremal restriction in a way that makes it possible to interpret it as a "partial agreement" condition and the other four conditions as its weakened versions. In the reformulated version of ER what is required is that if a set of orderings of a triple contains a linear ordering of the triple, then in any ordering belonging to the set which is of the same Latin Square as the one associated with the linear ordering, the alternative which is the best in the linear ordering must be considered to be at least as good as the alternative which is the worst in the linear ordering. WLSPA requires fulfillment of ER if a weak Latin Square involving a linear ordering exists. LSPA requires fulfillment of ER in case a Latin Square involving a linear ordering exists. WER requires that in case there is a linear ordering of the triple in question, then it must not be the case that there is an ordering of the triple in which the worst alternative of the linear ordering is uniquely best, there is an ordering of the triple in which the best alternative of the linear ordering is uniquely worst, and both these orderings belong to the same Latin Square which is associated with the linear ordering. LSLOR merely requires that there be no Latin Square involving more than one linear ordering. The formulation of extremal restriction as a "partial agreement" condition and of the other four conditions as weakened versions of extremal restriction make it possible to prove Inada-type necessary and sufficient conditions for transitivity and quasi-transitivity for various cases essentially on the basis of a couple of elementary observations elaborated in Lemmas 1–4 of this chapter, resulting in both considerable simplification of proofs and a unified framework. The simplification which is attained because of the "Latin Square approach" adopted in this chapter is even greater in the case when one deals with reflexive, connected and quasi-transitive binary relations rather than orderings.

For the case when $\mathcal{B}$ consists of all logically possible reflexive, connected and quasi-transitive binary relations over the set of alternatives, contributions by Inada (1970), Fishburn (1970) and Pattanaik (1970) have established that a sufficient condition for quasi-transitivity under MMD is that at least one of the four conditions of dichotomous preferences (DP), antagonistic preferences (AP), generalized limited agreement (GLA) and generalized value-restriction (GVR) holds over every triple of alternatives. If the number of social alternatives is at least three and the number of individuals is at least five, then the satisfaction of DP, AP, GLA or GVR over every triple is also an Inada-type necessary condition for quasi-transitivity under MMD. For the remaining cases Inada-type necessary and sufficient conditions are derived in this chapter. When the number of alternatives is at least three, the Inada-type necessary and sufficient conditions for quasi-transitivity for the cases of at least five individuals, for four individuals, for three individuals and for two individuals are respectively: satisfaction over every triple of Latin Square partial agreement-Q (LSPA-Q),[2] of weak extremal restriction-Q (WER-Q), of Latin Square linear ordering restriction-Q (LSLOR-Q), and of Latin Square intransitive relation restriction-Q (LSIRR-Q). It turns out that the absence of Latin Squares involving intransitive relations is crucial for quasi-transitivity. Indeed, conditions LSPA-Q, WER-Q and LSLOR-Q are merely conjunctions of the requirement that there be no Latin Square involving an intransitive relation with LSPA, WER and LSLOR respectively. Thus the requirements for quasi-transitivity are the same when

---

[2] As both LSPA-Q and (DP ∨ AP ∨ GLA ∨ GVR) are Inada-type necessary and sufficient conditions when the number of individuals is at least five, it follows that they are logically equivalent. In Jain (1986) it is inferred that strict Latin Square partial agreement (SLSPA) is logically equivalent to (DP ∨ AP ∨ GLA ∨ GVR). Thus, LSPA-Q is logically equivalent to SLSPA. The formulation in terms of LSPA-Q, rather than SLSPA, has the advantage of making the condition for the case when individual weak preference relations are quasi-transitive directly comparable with the condition for the case when individual weak preference relations are transitive.

individual binary weak preference relations are quasi-transitive as when they are transitive, except for the added requirement that there be no Latin Square involving an intransitive relation. Needless to say, this way of formulating conditions results in considerable simplification of proofs as well as clearer understanding of domain conditions by making the conditions for the case when individual weak preference relations are quasi-transitive directly comparable to the case when individual weak preference relations are transitive. LSIRR-Q, the weakest of the four conditions, merely requires that there be no Latin Square consisting of two intransitive relations or one intransitive relation and one linear ordering.

The chapter is divided into five sections. The first section introduces the Latin Square framework within which the Inada-type necessary and sufficient conditions are formulated. Section II deals with the Inada-type necessary and sufficient conditions for transitivity and section III with conditions for quasi-transitivity when individual binary weak preference relations are orderings. The fourth section contains characterization theorems for quasi-transitivity when individual binary weak preference relations are reflexive, connected and quasi-transitive. The concluding section is concerned with the question of formulating conditions for acyclicity defined only over triples. The main theorem of this section essentially demonstrates that for any non-trivial set of binary relations B containing intransitive binary relations, no condition defined only over triples can be an Inada-type necessary and sufficient condition for acyclicity.

I. Notation and Definitions

The set of social alternatives and the finite set of individuals constituting the society are denoted by S and L respectively. We assume $\#S = m \geq 3$ and $\#L = n \geq 2$. Each individual $i \in L$ is assumed to have a binary weak preference relation R_i on S. We denote asymmetric parts of binary relations R, R_i, R_j, R^s etc. by P, P_i, P_j, P^s etc. respectively; and symmetric parts by I, I_i, I_j, I^s etc. respectively.

We define a binary relation R on a set S to be (i) reflexive iff $(\forall x \in S)(xRx)$, (ii) connected iff $(\forall x, y \in S)(x \neq y \rightarrow xRy \vee yRx)$, (iii) anti-symmetric iff $(\forall x, y \in S)(xRy \wedge yRx \rightarrow x = y)$, (iv) transitive iff $(\forall x, y, z \in S)(xRy \wedge yRz \rightarrow xRz)$, (v) quasi-transitive iff $(\forall x, y, z \in S)(xPy \wedge yPz \rightarrow xPz)$, (vi) acyclic iff $(\forall x_1, x_2, \ldots, x_n \in S)(x_1 P x_2 \wedge x_2 P x_3 \wedge \ldots \wedge x_{n-1} P x_n \rightarrow x_1 R x_n)$, where n is a positive integer ≥ 3, (vii) an ordering iff it is reflexive, connected and transitive, and (viii) a linear ordering iff it is reflexive, connected, anti-symmetric and transitive. Throughout this chapter it will be assumed that for each $i, i \in L$, R_i is reflexive and connected.

We denote by C the set of all reflexive and connected binary relations on S, by A the set of all reflexive, connected and acyclic binary relations on S, by Q the set of all reflexive, connected and quasi-transitive binary relations on S, and by T the set of all reflexive, connected and transitive binary relations (orderings) on S. We denote by $N()$ the number of individuals having the preferences specified within the parentheses. The method of majority decision (MMD) f, a function from $G \subseteq C^n$ to C, $f : G \mapsto C$, is defined by: $(\forall(R_1, \ldots, R_n) \in G)(\forall x, y \in S)[xRy \leftrightarrow N(xP_iy) \geq N(yP_ix)]$, where $R = f(R_1, \ldots, R_n)$.

Let $A \subseteq S$ and let R be a binary relation on S. We define restriction of R to A, denoted by $R|A$, by $R|A = R \cap (A \times A)$. Throughout this paper D will denote a non-empty set of binary relations defined over the set of alternatives S. We define restriction of D to A, denoted by $D|A$, by $D|A = \{R|A \mid R \in D\}$.

A set of three distinct alternatives will be called a triple of alternatives. Let R be a binary relation on S and let $A = \{x, y, z\} \subseteq S$ be a triple of alternatives. We define $R \in C$ to be unconcerned over A iff $(\forall a, b \in A)(aIb)$. R is defined to be concerned over A iff it is not unconcerned over A. We denote by n_A the number of individuals who are concerned over the triple A. We define in A, according to R, x to be best iff $(xRy \wedge xRz)$; to be medium iff $[(yRx \wedge xRz) \vee (zRx \wedge xRy)]$; to be worst iff $(yRx \wedge zRx)$; and to be proper medium iff $[(yPx \wedge xRz) \vee (yRx \wedge xPz) \vee (zPx \wedge xRy) \vee (zRx \wedge xPy)]$.

Weak Latin Square (WLS): Let $A = \{x, y, z\} \subseteq S$ be a triple of alternatives and let R^s, R^t, R^u be binary relations on S. The set $\{R^s|A, R^t|A, R^u|A\}$ forms a weak Latin Square over A iff ($\exists$ distinct $a, b, c \in A$) [(in $R^s|A$ a is best and b is medium and c is worst) $\wedge$ (in $R^t|A$ b is best and c is medium and a is worst) $\wedge$ (in $R^u|A$ c is best and a is medium and b is worst)]. The above weak Latin Square will be denoted by $WLS(abca)$.

Remark 1. $R^s|A, R^t|A, R^u|A$ *in the definition of weak Latin Square need not be distinct.* $\{xIyIz\}$ *forms a weak Latin Square over the triple* $\{x, y, z\}$.

Remark 2. *If* $R^s|A, R^t|A, R^u|A$ *are orderings over* A, *then the set* $\{R^s|A, R^t| A, R^u|A\}$ *forms a weak Latin Square over* A *iff* ($\exists$ *distinct* $a, b, c \in A)[aR^sbR^sc \wedge bR^tcR^ta \wedge cR^uaR^ub]$.

Latin Square (LS): Let $A = \{x, y, z\} \subseteq S$ be a triple of alternatives and let R^s, R^t, R^u be binary relations on S. The set $\{R^s|A, R^t|A, R^u|A\}$ forms a Latin Square over A iff ($\exists$ distinct $a, b, c \in A$) [(in $R^s|A$ a is best and b is proper medium and c is worst) $\wedge$ (in $R^t|A$ b is best and c is proper medium and a is worst) $\wedge$ (in $R^u|A$ c is best and a is proper medium and b is worst)]. The above Latin Square will be denoted by $LS(abca)$.

Remark 3. *If $R^s|A$, $R^t|A$, $R^u|A$ are orderings over A, then the set $\{R^s|A, R^t|A, R^u|A\}$ forms a Latin Square over A iff $R^s|A$, $R^t|A$, $R^u|A$ are concerned over A and $(\exists$ distinct $a, b, c \in A)$ $[a R^s b R^s c \wedge b R^t c R^t a \wedge c R^u a R^u b]$.*

Remark 4. *From the definitions of weak Latin Square and Latin Square, it is clear that if $R^s|A$, $R^t|A$, $R^u|A$ are orderings and concerned over A then they form a Latin Square iff they form a weak Latin Square.*

Let $A = \{x, y, z\} \subseteq S$ be a triple of alternatives. For any distinct $a, b, c \in A$, we define:

$$T[WLS(abca)] = \{R \in \mathcal{T}|A \mid (a R b R c \vee b R c R a \vee c R a R b)\}.$$

$$T[LS(abca)] = \{R \in \mathcal{T}|A \mid R \text{ is concerned over } A \wedge (a R b R c$$
$$\vee b R c R a \vee c R a R b)\}.$$

$$Q[LS(abca)] = \{R \in \mathcal{Q}|A \mid (a \text{ is best and } b \text{ is proper medium and } c \text{ is worst in}$$
$$R) \vee (b \text{ is best and } c \text{ is proper medium and } a \text{ is worst in } R)$$
$$\vee (c \text{ is best and } a \text{ is proper medium and } b \text{ is worst in } R)\}.$$

Thus we have:

$$T[WLS(xyzx)] = T[WLS(yzxy)] = T[WLS(zxyz)] = \{xPyPz, \ xPyIz, \ xIyPz,$$
$$yPzPx, \ yPzIx, \ yIzPx, \ zPxPy, \ zPxIy, \ zIxPy, \ xIyIz\}.$$

$$T[WLS(xzyx)] = T[WLS(zyxz)] = T[WLS(yxzy)] = \{xPzPy, \ xPzIy, \ xIzPy,$$
$$zPyPx, \ zPyIx, \ zIyPx, \ yPxPz, \ yPxIz, \ yIxPz, \ xIyIz\}.$$

$$T[LS(xyzx)] = T[LS(yzxy)] = T[LS(zxyz)] = T[WLS(xyzx)] - \{xIyIz\}.$$

$$T[LS(xzyx)] = T[LS(zyxz)] = T[LS(yxzy)] = T[WLS(xzyx)] - \{xIyIz\}.$$

$$Q[LS(xyzx)] = Q[LS(yzxy)] = Q[LS(zxyz)] = \{xPyPz, \ xPyIz, \ xIyPz,$$
$$yPzPx, \ yPzIx, \ yIzPx, \ zPxPy, \ zPxIy, \ zIxPy, \ (xPy,$$
$$yIz, zIx), \ (yPz, zIx, xIy), \ (zPx, xIy, yIz)\}.$$

$$Q[LS(xzyx)] = Q[LS(zyxz)] = Q[LS(yxzy)] = \{xPzPy, \ xPzIy, \ xIzPy,$$
$$zPyPx, \ zPyIx, \ zIyPx, \ yPxPz, \ yPxIz, \ yIxPz,$$
$$(yPx, xIz, zIy), \ (xPz, zIy, yIx), \ (zPy, yIx, xIz)\}.$$

Now we define several restrictions on sets of orderings.

Extremal restriction (ER): $D \subseteq \mathcal{T}$ satisfies ER over the triple $A \subseteq S$ iff ($\forall$ distinct $a, b, c \in A$) $[(\exists R \in D|A)\ (aPbPc) \rightarrow (\forall R \in D|A \cap T[LS(abca)])(aRc)]$. D satisfies ER iff it satisfies ER over every triple contained in S.[3]

Thus, the satisfaction of extremal restriction by D over the triple A requires that in case $D|A$ contains a linear ordering of A then in every ordering in $D|A$ which belongs to the same Latin Square as the linear ordering, the alternative which is the best in the linear ordering must be at least as good as the alternative which is the worst in the linear ordering.

Weak Latin Square partial agreement (WLSPA): $D \subseteq \mathcal{T}$ satisfies WLSPA over the triple $A \subseteq S$ iff ($\forall$ distinct $a, b, c \in A$)$[(\exists R^s, R^t, R^u \in D|A)(aP^sbP^sc \wedge bR^tcR^ta \wedge cR^uaR^ub) \rightarrow (\forall R \in D|A \cap T[LS(abca)])(aRc)]$. D satisfies WLSPA iff it satisfies WLSPA over every triple contained in S.

The satisfaction of weak Latin Square partial agreement by D over the triple A requires that in case $D|A$ contains a weak Latin Square involving a linear ordering of A, then in every ordering in $D|A$ which belongs to the same Latin Square, the alternative which is the best in the linear ordering must be at least as good as the alternative which is the worst in the linear ordering.

Latin Square partial agreement (LSPA): $D \subseteq \mathcal{T}$ satisfies LSPA over the triple $A \subseteq S$ iff ($\forall$ distinct $a, b, c \in A$)$[(\exists R^s, R^t, R^u \in D|A)(R^s, R^t, R^u$ are concerned over $A \wedge aP^sbP^sc \wedge bR^tcR^ta \wedge cR^uaR^ub) \rightarrow (\forall R \in D|A \cap T[LS(abca)])(aRc)]$. D satisfies LSPA iff it satisfies LSPA over every triple contained in S.

The satisfaction of Latin Square partial agreement by D over the triple A requires that in case $D|A$ contains a Latin Square involving a linear ordering of A, then in every ordering in $D|A$ which belongs to the same Latin Square, the alternative which is the best in the linear ordering must be at least as good as the alternative which is the worst in the linear ordering.

Weak extremal restriction (WER): $D \subseteq \mathcal{T}$ satisfies WER over the triple $A \subseteq S$ iff $\sim (\exists$ distinct $a, b, c \in A)(\exists R^s, R^t, R^u \in D|A)(aP^sbP^sc \wedge bR^tcP^ta \wedge cP^uaR^ub)$. D satisfies WER iff it satisfies WER over every triple contained in S.

The satisfaction of weak extremal restriction by D over the triple A requires that $D|A$ must not contain a Latin Square which is such that one of the orderings involved in the formation of the Latin Square is a linear ordering and in the other two orderings the alternative which is the worst in the linear ordering is preferred to the alternative which is the best in the linear ordering.

Latin Square linear ordering restriction (LSLOR): $D \subseteq \mathcal{T}$ satisfies LSLOR over the triple $A \subseteq S$ iff $\sim (\exists$ distinct $a, b, c \in A)(\exists R^s, R^t, R^u \in D|A)(R^s, R^t, R^u$ are

---

[3] Although the definition of extremal restriction given here is quite different from the usual one, it can easily be checked that the two definitions are equivalent to each other.

concerned over $A \wedge aP^sbP^sc \wedge bP^tcP^ta \wedge cR^uaR^ub)$. D satisfies LSLOR iff it satisfies LSLOR over every triple contained in S.

The satisfaction of Latin Square linear ordering restriction by D over the triple A requires that $D|A$ must not contain a Latin Square involving more than one linear ordering.

Remark 5. *From the definitions of the five conditions above it is clear that ER implies WLSPA; WLSPA implies LSPA; LSPA implies WER; and WER implies LSLOR.*

Next, we define four restrictions on sets of reflexive, connected and quasi-transitive binary relations.

Latin Square partial agreement-Q (LSPA-Q): $D \subseteq Q$ satisfies LSPA-Q over the triple $A \subseteq S$ iff $[[(\forall R^s, R^t, R^u \in D|A)(R^s, R^t, R^u$ form a Latin Square over $A \rightarrow R^s, R^t, R^u$ are orderings over $A)] \wedge [(\forall$ distinct $a, b, c \in A)[(\exists R^s, R^t, R^u \in D|A \cap T|A)(R^s, R^t, R^u$ are concerned over $A \wedge aP^sbP^sc \wedge bR^tcR^ta \wedge cR^uaR^ub) \rightarrow (\forall R \in D|A \cap T[LS(abca)])(aRc)]]]$. D satisfies LSPA-Q iff it satisfies LSPA-Q over every triple contained in S.

The satisfaction of Latin Square partial agreement-Q by D over the triple A requires that there be no Latin Square contained in $D|A$ involving an intransitive binary relation, and that $D|A \cap T|A$ satisfy Latin Square partial agreement.

Weak extremal restriction-Q (WER-Q): $D \subseteq Q$ satisfies WER-Q over the triple $A \subseteq S$ iff $[[(\forall R^s, R^t, R^u \in D|A)(R^s, R^t, R^u$ form a Latin Square over $A \rightarrow R^s, R^t, R^u$ are orderings over $A)] \wedge \sim (\exists$ distinct $a, b, c \in A)(\exists R^s, R^t, R^u \in D|A \cap T|A)(aP^sbP^sc \wedge bR^tcP^ta \wedge cP^uaR^ub)]$. D satisfies WER-Q iff it satisfies WER-Q over every triple contained in S.

The satisfaction of weak extremal restriction-Q by D over the triple A requires that there be no Latin Square contained in $D|A$ involving an intransitive binary relation, and that $D|A \cap T|A$ satisfy weak extremal restriction.

Latin Square linear ordering restriction-Q (LSLOR-Q): $D \subseteq Q$ satisfies LSLOR-Q over the triple $A \subseteq S$ iff $[[(\forall R^s, R^t, R^u \in D|A)(R^s, R^t, R^u$ form a Latin Square over $A \rightarrow R^s, R^t, R^u$ are orderings over $A)] \wedge \sim (\exists$ distinct $a, b, c \in A)(\exists R^s, R^t, R^u \in D|A \cap T|A)(R^s, R^t, R^u$ are concerned over $A \wedge aP^sbP^sc \wedge bP^tcP^ta \wedge cR^uaR^ub)]$. D satisfies LSLOR-Q iff it satisfies LSLOR-Q over every triple contained in S.

The satisfaction of Latin Square linear ordering restriction-Q by D over the triple A requires that there be no Latin Square contained in $D|A$ involving an intransitive binary relation, and that $D|A \cap T|A$ satisfy Latin Square linear ordering restriction.

Latin Square intransitive relation restriction-Q (LSIRR-Q): $D \subseteq Q$ satisfies LSIRR-Q over the triple $A \subseteq S$ iff $\sim (\exists R^s, R^t \in D|A)[(R^s, R^t$ form a Latin Square over

$A) \wedge (R^s$ is intransitive) $\wedge (R^t$ is intransitive $\vee R^t$ is a linear ordering)]. D satisfies LSIRR-Q iff it satisfies LSIRR-Q over every triple contained in S.

The satisfaction of Latin Square intransitive relation restriction-Q by D over the triple A requires that there be no Latin Square contained in $D|A$ consisting of two intransitive relations or of one intransitive relation and one linear ordering.

Remark 6. *It is clear from the definitions of the above four conditions that LSPA-Q implies WER-Q; WER-Q implies LSLOR-Q; and LSLOR-Q implies LSIRR-Q.*

II. Conditions for Transitivity when Individual Binary Weak Preference Relations are Transitive

This section is concerned with characterizing sets of orderings $D \in 2^T - \{\emptyset\}$ which are such that every logically possible $(R_1, \ldots, R_n) \in D^n$ gives rise to a transitive social binary weak preference relation under MMD. If the number of individuals is even and greater than one then extremal restriction constitutes a characterizing condition (Theorem 1); and when the number of individuals is odd and greater than or equal to three then weak Latin Square partial agreement constitutes a characterizing condition (Theorem 2). Both these results follow directly from two elementary observations about MMD elaborated in Lemmas 1 and 2.

Lemma 1. *Let* $f : \mathcal{G} \mapsto \mathcal{C}$, $\mathcal{G} \subseteq \mathcal{C}^n$, *be the method of majority decision. Let* $(R_1, \ldots, R_n) \in \mathcal{G}$ *and* $R = f(R_1, \ldots, R_n)$. *Then we have:*

  (i) $(\forall distinct\ x, y \in S)[xRy \rightarrow N(xR_iy) \geq \frac{n}{2}]$.
  (ii) $(\forall distinct\ x, y \in S)[xPy \rightarrow N(xR_iy) > \frac{n}{2}]$.

Proof. As each R_i, $i \in L$, is connected, it follows that for any distinct $x, y \in S$ we have:

$$N(xR_iy) + N(yR_ix) \geq n. \tag{1}$$

Now,

$$xRy \rightarrow N(xR_iy) \geq N(yR_ix), \text{ and} \tag{2}$$

$$xPy \rightarrow N(xR_iy) > N(yR_ix). \tag{3}$$

(i) follows from (1) and (2), and (ii) follows from (1) and (3). ∎

Lemma 2. *Let* $f : \mathcal{G} \mapsto \mathcal{C}$, $\mathcal{G} \subseteq \mathcal{T}^n$, *be the method of majority decision. Let* $(R_1, \ldots, R_n) \in \mathcal{G}$ *and* $R = f(R_1, \ldots, R_n)$. *Let* $A = \{x, y, z\} \subseteq S$ *be a triple of alternatives and suppose* xPy, yRz *and* zRx. *Then we have:*

(i) $(\exists i \in L)[xP_i y P_i z \vee y P_i z P_i x \vee z P_i x P_i y]$.

(ii) $(\exists i, j, k \in L)[R_i | A, R_j | A, R_k | A \in T[LS(xyzx)] \wedge x P_i y \wedge y P_j z \wedge z P_k x]$.

Proof. To begin with we note:

$$xPy \rightarrow N(x P_i y) > N(y P_i x). \tag{1}$$

$$yRz \rightarrow N(y P_i z) \geq N(z P_i y). \tag{2}$$

$$zRx \rightarrow N(z P_i x) \geq N(x P_i z). \tag{3}$$

(1), (2) and (3) imply respectively:

$$N(z P_i x P_i y) + N(z I_i x P_i y) + N(x P_i z P_i y) + N(x P_i z I_i y) + N(x P_i y P_i z)$$
$$> N(z P_i y P_i x) + N(z I_i y P_i x) + N(y P_i z P_i x) + N(y P_i z I_i x) + N(y P_i x P_i z). \tag{4}$$
$$N(x P_i y P_i z) + N(x I_i y P_i z) + N(y P_i x P_i z) + N(y P_i x I_i z) + N(y P_i z P_i x)$$
$$\geq N(x P_i z P_i y) + N(x I_i z P_i y) + N(z P_i x P_i y) + N(z P_i x I_i y) + N(z P_i y P_i x). \tag{5}$$
$$N(y P_i z P_i x) + N(y I_i z P_i x) + N(z P_i y P_i x) + N(z P_i y I_i x) + N(z P_i x P_i y)$$
$$\geq N(y P_i x P_i z) + N(y I_i x P_i z) + N(x P_i y P_i z) + N(x P_i y I_i z) + N(x P_i z P_i y). \tag{6}$$

Adding (4), (5) and (6), we obtain:

$$N(x P_i y P_i z) + N(y P_i z P_i x) + N(z P_i x P_i y) > N(x P_i z P_i y) + N(z P_i y P_i x)$$
$$+ N(y P_i x P_i z). \tag{7}$$

Adding (7) to (4), (5) and (6) we obtain respectively:

$$2N(z P_i x P_i y) + 2N(x P_i y P_i z) + N(z I_i x P_i y) + N(x P_i y I_i z) > 2N(z P_i y P_i x)$$
$$+ 2N(y P_i x P_i z) + N(z I_i y P_i x) + N(y P_i x I_i z). \tag{8}$$
$$2N(x P_i y P_i z) + 2N(y P_i z P_i x) + N(x I_i y P_i z) + N(y P_i z I_i x) > 2N(x P_i z P_i y)$$
$$+ 2N(z P_i y P_i x) + N(x I_i z P_i y) + N(z P_i y I_i x). \tag{9}$$
$$2N(y P_i z P_i x) + 2N(z P_i x P_i y) + N(y I_i z P_i x) + N(z P_i x I_i y) > 2N(y P_i x P_i z)$$
$$+ 2N(x P_i z P_i y) + N(y I_i x P_i z) + N(x P_i z I_i y). \tag{10}$$

(7)–(10) imply respectively:

$$N(xP_iyP_iz) + N(yP_izP_ix) + N(zP_ixP_iy) > 0. \tag{11}$$

$$N(zP_ixP_iy) + N(xP_iyP_iz) + N(zI_ixP_iy) + N(xP_iyI_iz) > 0. \tag{12}$$

$$N(xP_iyP_iz) + N(yP_izP_ix) + N(xI_iyP_iz) + N(yP_izI_ix) > 0. \tag{13}$$

$$N(yP_izP_ix) + N(zP_ixP_iy) + N(yI_izP_ix) + N(zP_ixI_iy) > 0. \tag{14}$$

$$(11) \to (\exists i \in L)(xP_iyP_iz \vee yP_izP_ix \vee zP_ixP_iy). \tag{15}$$

$$(12) \to (\exists i \in L)(R_i|A \in T[LS(xyzx)] \wedge xP_iy). \tag{16}$$

$$(13) \to (\exists j \in L)(R_j|A \in T[LS(xyzx)] \wedge yP_jz). \tag{17}$$

$$(14) \to (\exists k \in L)(R_k|A \in T[LS(xyzx)] \wedge zP_kx). \tag{18}$$

(15)–(18) establish the lemma.   ∎

Theorem 1. *Let* $\#S \geq 3$ *and* $\#L = n = 2k, k \geq 1$. *Let* $D \subseteq T$. *Then the method of majority decision* f *yields transitive social* $R, R = f(R_1, \ldots, R_n)$, *for every* $(R_1, \ldots, R_n) \in D^n$ *iff* D *satisfies the condition of extremal restriction.*

Proof. Suppose f does not yield transitive social R for every $(R_1, \ldots, R_n) \in D^n$. Then

$$(\exists(R_1, \ldots, R_n) \in D^n)(\exists x, y, z \in S)(xPy \wedge yRz \wedge zRx).$$

This, by Lemma 2, implies that:

$$(\exists i \in L)(xP_iyP_iz \vee yP_izP_ix \vee zP_ixP_iy), \text{ and} \tag{1}$$

$$(\exists i, j, k \in L)[R_i|\{x, y, z\}, R_j|\{x, y, z\}, R_k|\{x, y, z\} \in T[LS(xyzx)]$$

$$\wedge xP_iy \wedge yP_jz \wedge zP_kx]. \tag{2}$$

(1) and (2) imply that D violates ER, which establishes the sufficiency of ER.

Let $D \subseteq T$ violate ER. This implies that

$$(\exists x, y, z \in S)(\exists R^s, R^t \in D)[xP^syP^sz \wedge (yR^tzP^tx \vee zP^txR^ty)].$$

Now consider any $(R_1, \ldots, R_n) \in D^n$ such that $\#\{i \in L \mid R_i = R^s\} = \#\{i \in L \mid R_i = R^t\} = k = \frac{n}{2}$. MMD then yields $(xIy \wedge yPz \wedge xIz)$ or $(xPy \wedge yIz \wedge xIz)$ depending on whether $R^t|\{x, y, z\}$ is yR^tzP^tx or zP^txR^ty. In either case transitivity is violated, which establishes the theorem.   ∎

Theorem 2. *Let* $\#S \geq 3$ *and* $\#L = n = 2k + 1, k \geq 1$. *Let* $D \subseteq T$. *Then the method of majority decision* f *yields transitive social* $R, R = f(R_1, \ldots, R_n)$, *for every* $(R_1, \ldots, R_n) \in D^n$ *iff* D *satisfies the condition of weak Latin Square partial agreement.*

Proof. Suppose f does not yield transitive social R for every $(R_1, \ldots, R_n) \in D^n$. Then

$$(\exists(R_1, \ldots, R_n) \in D^n)(\exists x, y, z \in S)(xPy \wedge yRz \wedge zRx).$$

xPy, yRz and zRx imply, by Lemma 1, respectively:

$$N(xR_iy) > \frac{n}{2}. \tag{1}$$

$$N(yR_iz) \geq \frac{n}{2}. \tag{2}$$

$$N(zR_ix) \geq \frac{n}{2}. \tag{3}$$

As n is odd, (2) and (3) imply, respectively:

$$N(yR_iz) > \frac{n}{2} \text{ and} \tag{4}$$

$$N(zR_ix) > \frac{n}{2}. \tag{5}$$

$$(1) \wedge (4) \rightarrow (\exists i \in L)(xR_iyR_iz). \tag{6}$$

$$(4) \wedge (5) \rightarrow (\exists i \in L)(yR_izR_ix). \tag{7}$$

$$(5) \wedge (1) \rightarrow (\exists i \in L)(zR_ixR_iy). \tag{8}$$

By Lemma 2 we have:

$$(\exists i \in L)(xP_iyP_iz \vee yP_izP_ix \vee zP_ixP_iy), \text{ and} \tag{9}$$

$$(\exists i, j, k \in L)[R_i|\{x, y, z\}, R_j|\{x, y, z\}, R_k|\{x, y, z\} \in T[LS(xyzx)]$$
$$\wedge xP_iy \wedge yP_jz \wedge zP_kx]. \tag{10}$$

(6)–(10) imply that WLSPA is violated, which establishes the sufficiency of WLSPA. Now, let $D \subseteq T$ violate WLSPA. This implies that

$$(\exists x, y, z \in S)(\exists R^s, R^t, R^u \in D)[(xP^syP^sz \wedge yR^tzP^tx \wedge zR^uxR^uy)$$
$$\vee (xP^syP^sz \wedge yR^uzR^ux \wedge zP^txR^ty)].$$

Consider any $(R_1, \ldots, R_n) \in D^n$ such that $\#\{i \subset L \mid R_i = R^s\} = \#\{i \in L \mid R_i = R^t\} = k = \frac{n-1}{2}$, and $\#\{i \in L \mid R_i = R^u\} = 1$. MMD then yields $[xRy \wedge yRz \wedge zRx \wedge \sim (yRx \wedge xRz \wedge zRy)]$, violating transitivity, which establishes the theorem. ■

III. CONDITIONS FOR QUASI-TRANSITIVITY WHEN INDIVIDUAL BINARY WEAK PREFERENCE RELATIONS ARE TRANSITIVE

This section is concerned with characterizing sets of orderings $D \in 2^T - \{\emptyset\}$ which are such that every logically possible $(R_1, \ldots, R_n) \in D^n$ gives rise to a quasi-transitive social binary weak preference relation under MMD. If the number of individuals is greater than or equal to five then Latin Square partial agreement constitutes a characterizing condition (Theorem 3); if the number of individuals is four then weak extremal restriction constitutes a characterizing condition (Theorem 4); and if the number of individuals is three then Latin Square linear ordering restriction constitutes a characterizing condition (Theorem 5). All three of these theorems follow directly from Lemmas 2 and 4. Lemma 4 is a simple consequence of Lemma 3, which is similar to Lemma 1.

Lemma 3. *Let* $f : \mathcal{G} \mapsto \mathcal{C}$, $\mathcal{G} \subseteq \mathcal{C}^n$, *be the method of majority decision. Let* $(R_1, \ldots, R_n) \in \mathcal{G}$ *and* $R = f(R_1, \ldots, R_n)$. *Then we have:*

(i) $(\forall \text{ distinct } x, y, z \in S)[xRy \rightarrow N(R_i \text{ concerned over } A = \{x, y, z\}$
$\wedge xR_iy) \geq \frac{n_A}{2}]$, *and*

(ii) $(\forall \text{ distinct } x, y, z \in S)[xPy \rightarrow N(R_i \text{ concerned over } A = \{x, y, z\}$
$\wedge xR_iy) > \frac{n_A}{2}]$.

Proof. Let $A = \{x, y, z\} \subseteq S$ be a triple of alternatives.

$$xRy \rightarrow N(xP_iy) \geq N(yP_ix), \text{ and} \tag{1}$$

$$xPy \rightarrow N(xP_iy) > N(yP_ix). \tag{2}$$

Adding $N(R_i \text{ concerned over } A \wedge xI_iy)$ to both sides of the inequalities of (1) and (2) we obtain:

$$xRy \rightarrow N(R_i \text{ concerned over } A \wedge xR_iy) \geq N(R_i \text{ concerned over } A \wedge yR_ix), \tag{3}$$

and

$$xPy \rightarrow N(R_i \text{ concerned over } A \wedge xR_iy) > N(R_i \text{ concerned over } A \wedge yR_ix). \tag{4}$$

As each R_i, $i \in L$, is connected, it follows that:

$$N(R_i \text{ concerned over } A \wedge xR_iy) + N(R_i \text{ concerned over } A \wedge yR_ix) \geq n_A. \tag{5}$$

(i) follows from (3) and (5); and (ii) follows from (4) and (5). ∎

Lemma 4. *Let* $f : \mathcal{G} \mapsto \mathcal{C}$, $\mathcal{G} \subseteq \mathcal{T}^n$, *be the method of majority decision. Let* $(R_1, \ldots, R_n) \in \mathcal{G}$ *and* $R = f(R_1, \ldots, R_n)$. *Let* $A = \{x, y, z\} \subseteq S$ *be a triple of* *alternatives and suppose* xPy, yPz *and* zRx. *Then we must have:* $(\exists i, j, k \in L)[R_i, R_j, R_k$ *are concerned over* $\{x, y, z\} \wedge xR_iyR_iz \wedge yR_jzR_jx \wedge zR_kxR_ky]$.

Proof. By Lemma 3, xPy, yPz and zRx imply respectively:

$$N(R_i \text{ concerned over } A \wedge xR_iy) > \frac{n_A}{2}. \tag{1}$$

$$N(R_i \text{ concerned over } A \wedge yR_iz) > \frac{n_A}{2}. \tag{2}$$

$$N(R_i \text{ concerned over } A \wedge zR_ix) \geq \frac{n_A}{2}. \tag{3}$$

$$(1) \wedge (2) \rightarrow (\exists i \in L)(R_i \text{ concerned over } A \wedge xR_iyR_iz). \tag{4}$$

$$(2) \wedge (3) \rightarrow (\exists j \in L)(R_j \text{ concerned over } A \wedge yR_jzR_jx). \tag{5}$$

$$(3) \wedge (1) \rightarrow (\exists k \in L)(R_k \text{ concerned over } A \wedge zR_kxR_ky). \tag{6}$$

(4)–(6) establish the lemma. ∎

Theorem 3. *Let* $\#S \geq 3$ *and* $\#L = n \geq 5$. *Let* $D \subseteq \mathcal{T}$. *Then the method of majority decision* f *yields quasi-transitive social* R, $R = f(R_1, \ldots, R_n)$, *for every* $(R_1, \ldots, R_n) \in D^n$ *iff D satisfies the condition of Latin Square partial agreement.*

Proof. Suppose f does not yield quasi-transitive social R for every $(R_1, \ldots, R_n) \in D^n$. Then $(\exists(R_1, \ldots, R_n) \in D^n)(\exists x, y, z \in S)(xPy \wedge yPz \wedge zRx)$. By Lemmas 4 and 2 we obtain:

$(\exists i, j, k \in L)(R_i, R_j, R_k$ are concerned over $\{x, y, z\} \wedge xR_iyR_iz \wedge yR_jzR_jx$

$\quad \wedge zR_kxR_ky)$. $\tag{1}$

$(\exists i \in L)(xP_iyP_iz \vee yP_izP_ix \vee zP_ixP_iy)$. $\tag{2}$

$(\exists i, j, k \in L)[R_i|\{x, y, z\}, R_j|\{x, y, z\}, R_k|\{x, y, z\} \in T[LS(xyzx)]$

$\quad \wedge xP_iy \wedge yP_jz \wedge zP_kx]$. $\tag{3}$

(1)–(3) imply that LSPA is violated, which establishes the sufficiency of LSPA.

Now, let $D \subseteq \mathcal{T}$ violate LSPA. This implies that

$(\exists x, y, z \in S)(\exists R^s, R^t, R^u \in D)[(xP^syP^sz \wedge yR^tzP^tx \wedge zP^uxR^uy)$

$\vee (xP^tyP^tz \wedge yR^szP^sx \wedge zR^uxP^uy) \vee (xP^tyP^tz \wedge yP^uzR^ux \wedge zP^sxR^sy)]$.

If $n = 3k, k \geq 2$, consider any $(R_1, \ldots, R_n) \in D^n$ such that $\#\{i \in L \mid R_i = R^s\} = k + 1$, $\#\{i \in L \mid R_i = R^t\} = k$ and $\#\{i \in L \mid R_i = R^u\} = k - 1$; if $n = 3k + 1, k \geq 2$, consider any $(R_1, \ldots, R_n) \in D^n$ such that $\#\{i \in L \mid R_i = R^s\} = k + 1$, $\#\{i \in L \mid R_i = R^t\} = k$ and $\#\{i \in L \mid R_i = R^u\} = k$; and if $n = 3k + 2, k \geq 1$, consider any $(R_1, \ldots, R_n) \in D^n$ such that $\#\{i \in L \mid R_i = R^s\} = k + 1$, $\#\{i \in L \mid R_i = R^t\} =$

$k + 1$ and $\#\{i \in L \mid R_i = R^u\} = k$. In each case MMD yields social R violating quasi-transitivity over $\{x, y, z\}$, which establishes the theorem. ∎

Theorem 4. *Let $\#S \geq 3$ and $\#L = n = 4$. Let $D \subseteq \mathcal{T}$. Then the method of majority decision f yields quasi-transitive social R, $R = f(R_1, \ldots, R_4)$, for every $(R_1, \ldots, R_4) \in D^4$ iff D satisfies the condition of weak extremal restriction.*

Proof. Suppose f does not yield quasi-transitive social R for every $(R_1, \ldots, R_4) \in D^4$. Then $(\exists(R_1, \ldots, R_4) \in D^4)(\exists x, y, z \in S)(xPy \wedge yPz \wedge zRx)$. By Lemmas 4 and 2 we obtain:

$$(\exists i, j, k \in L)(R_i, R_j, R_k \text{ are concerned over } \{x, y, z\} \wedge xR_iyR_iz$$

$$\wedge yR_jzR_jx \wedge zR_kxR_ky). \tag{1}$$

$$(\exists i \in L)(xP_iyP_iz \vee yP_izP_ix \vee zP_ixP_iy). \tag{2}$$

$$(1) \rightarrow (\exists i, j, k \in L)(xP_iz \wedge yP_jx \wedge zP_ky). \tag{3}$$

$$(\exists j \in L)(yP_jx) \wedge xPy \rightarrow N(xP_iy) \geq 2 \wedge N(xR_iy) = 3 \wedge N(yP_ix) = 1. \tag{4}$$

$$(4) \rightarrow N(R_i \text{ concerned over } \{x, y, z\} \wedge yR_izR_ix) = 1 \wedge N(zP_iyP_ix) = 0$$

$$\wedge N(yP_ixP_iz) = 0. \tag{5}$$

$$(\exists k \in L)(zP_ky) \wedge yPz \rightarrow N(yP_iz) \geq 2 \wedge N(yR_iz) = 3 \wedge N(zP_iy) = 1. \tag{6}$$

$$(6) \rightarrow N(R_i \text{ concerned over } \{x, y, z\} \wedge zR_ixR_iy) = 1 \wedge N(xP_izP_iy) = 0. \tag{7}$$

$$(1) \wedge (5) \wedge (7) \rightarrow N(xR_iyR_iz) = 2 \wedge N(R_i \text{ concerned over } \{x, y, z\}$$

$$\wedge xR_iyR_iz) \geq 1 \wedge N(R_i \text{ concerned over } \{x, y, z\} \wedge yR_izR_ix) = 1$$

$$\wedge N(R_i \text{ concerned over } \{x, y, z\} \wedge zR_ixR_iy) = 1. \tag{8}$$

$$zRx \wedge N(xP_iz) = 1 \wedge (4) \wedge (6) \wedge (8) \rightarrow (\exists i, j, k \in L)[(xP_iyP_iz$$

$$\wedge yP_izP_ix \wedge zR_ixP_iy) \vee (xP_iyP_iz \wedge yP_izR_ix \wedge zP_ixP_iy)]$$

$$\rightarrow \text{ WER is violated.} \tag{9}$$

$$zRx \wedge N(xP_iz) = 2 \wedge (4) \wedge (6) \wedge (8) \rightarrow (\exists i, j, k \in L)(xP_iyP_iz$$

$$\wedge yR_jzP_jx \wedge zP_kxR_ky) \vee (\exists i, j, k, l \in L)(xP_iyI_iz \wedge xI_jyP_jz$$

$$\wedge yP_kzP_kx \wedge zP_lxP_ly)$$

$$\rightarrow \text{ WER is violated.} \tag{10}$$

(9) and (10) establish that WER is violated, which proves sufficiency of WER.
    Suppose $D \subseteq \mathcal{T}$ violates WER. This implies that

$$(\exists x, y, z \in S)(\exists R^s, R^t, R^u \in D)(xP^syP^sz \wedge yR^tzP^tx \wedge zP^uxR^uy).$$

Consider any $(R_1, \ldots, R_4) \in D^4$ such that $\#\{i \in L \mid R_i = R^s\} = 2$, $\#\{i \in L \mid R_i = R^t\} = 1$ and $\#\{i \in L \mid R_i = R^u\} = 1$. MMD then yields $(xPy \wedge yPz \wedge zIx)$, which violates quasi-transitivity. This establishes the theorem. ∎

Theorem 5. *Let $\#S \geq 3$ and $\#L = n = 3$. Let $D \subseteq \mathcal{T}$. Then the method of majority decision f yields quasi-transitive social R, $R = f(R_1, R_2, R_3)$, for every $(R_1, R_2, R_3) \in D^3$ iff D satisfies the condition of Latin Square linear ordering restriction.*

Proof. Suppose f does not yield quasi-transitive social R for every $(R_1, R_2, R_3) \in D^3$. Then

$$(\exists (R_1, R_2, R_3) \in D^3)(\exists x, y, z \in S)(xPy \wedge yPz \wedge zRx).$$

By Lemma 4 we have:

$$(\exists i, j, k \in L)(R_i, R_j, R_k \text{ are concerned over } \{x, y, z\} \wedge xR_iyR_iz$$

$$\wedge yR_jzR_jx \wedge zR_kxR_ky) \tag{1}$$

$$\rightarrow (\exists i, j, k \in L)(xP_iz \wedge yP_jx \wedge zP_ky). \tag{2}$$

$$xPy \wedge (\exists j \in L)(yP_jx) \wedge (1) \rightarrow (\exists i, j, k \in L)(R_i, R_j, R_k \text{ are concerned}$$

$$\text{over } \{x, y, z\} \wedge xP_iyR_iz \wedge yR_jzR_jx \wedge zR_kxP_ky). \tag{3}$$

$$yPz \wedge (\exists k \in L)(zP_ky) \wedge (3) \rightarrow (\exists i, j, k \in L)(xP_iyP_iz \wedge yP_jzR_jx$$

$$\wedge zR_kxP_ky). \tag{4}$$

$$zRx \wedge (\exists i \in L)(xP_iz) \wedge (4) \rightarrow (\exists i, j, k \in L)[(xP_iyP_iz \wedge yP_jzP_jx$$

$$\wedge zR_kxP_ky) \vee (xP_iyP_iz \wedge yP_jzR_jx \wedge zP_kxP_ky)]. \tag{5}$$

(5) implies that LSLOR is violated, which establishes the sufficiency of LSLOR. Suppose $D \subseteq \mathcal{T}$ violates LSLOR. This implies that

$$(\exists x, y, z \in S)(\exists R^s, R^t, R^u \in D)[xP^syP^sz \wedge yP^tzP^tx \wedge (zP^uxR^uy \vee zR^uxP^uy)].$$

Consider any $(R_1, R_2, R_3) \in D^3$ such that $\#\{i \in L \mid R_i = R^s\} = \#\{i \in L \mid R_i = R^t\} = \#\{i \in L \mid R_i = R^u\} = 1$. MMD then yields $(xRy \wedge yPz \wedge zPx)$ or $(xPy \wedge yPz \wedge zRx)$ depending on whether R^u over $\{x, y, z\}$ is zP^uxR^uy or zR^uxP^uy. As quasi-transitivity is violated in either case the theorem is established. ∎

IV. Conditions for Quasi-Transitivity when Individual Binary Weak Preference Relations are Quasi-Transitive

In this section sets of reflexive, connected and quasi-transitive binary relations $D \in 2^Q - \{\emptyset\}$ which are such that every logically possible $(R_1, \ldots, R_n) \in D^n$ gives rise to a quasi-transitive social binary weak preference relation under MMD are characterized. If the number of individuals is greater than or equal to five then Latin Square partial agreement-Q constitutes a characterizing condition (Theorem 6); if the number of individuals is four then weak extremal restriction-Q constitutes a characterizing condition (Theorem 7); if the number of individuals is three then Latin Square linear ordering restriction-Q constitutes a characterizing condition (Theorem 8); and if the number of individuals is two then Latin Square intransitive relation restriction-Q constitutes a characterizing condition (Theorem 9). The theorems essentially follow from Lemma 5, which is the counterpart of the conjunction of Lemmas 2 and 4 for the case when individual binary weak preference relations are quasi-transitive.

Lemma 5. *Let* $f : \mathcal{G} \mapsto \mathcal{C}$, $\mathcal{G} \subseteq \mathcal{Q}^n$, *be the method of majority decision. Let* $(R_1, \ldots, R_n) \in \mathcal{G}$ *and* $R = f(R_1, \ldots, R_n)$. *Let* $A = \{x, y, z\} \subseteq S$ *be a triple of alternatives and suppose* xPy, yPz *and* zRx. *Then we have:*

(i) $(\exists i, j, k \in L)[R_i|A, R_j|A, R_k|A \text{ form Latin Square } LS(xyzx) \text{ over} A]$.

(ii) $(\exists i \in L)[xP_iyP_iz \vee yP_izP_ix \vee zP_ixP_iy \vee (xP_iy \wedge yI_iz \wedge xI_iz) \vee (yP_iz \wedge zI_ix \wedge yI_ix) \vee (zP_ix \wedge xI_iy \wedge zI_iy)]$.

(iii) $(\exists i, j, k \in L)[R_i|A, R_j|A, R_k|A \in Q[LS(xyzx)] \wedge (xP_iy \vee R_i|A \text{ is intransitive}) \wedge (yP_jz \vee R_j|A \text{ is intransitive}) \wedge (zP_kx \vee R_k|A \text{ is intransitive})]$.

Proof. To begin with we note:

$$xPy \rightarrow N(xP_iy) > N(yP_ix). \tag{1}$$

$$yPz \rightarrow N(yP_iz) > N(zP_iy). \tag{2}$$

$$zRx \rightarrow N(zP_ix) \geq N(xP_iz). \tag{3}$$

(1), (2) and (3) imply respectively:

$$N(zP_ixP_iy) + N(zI_ixP_iy) + N(xP_i\sigma P_iy) + N(xP_i\sigma I_iy') + N(xP_iy'P_iz)$$
$$+ N(xP_iy \wedge yI_iz \wedge xI_iz) > N(zP_iyP_ix) + N(zI_iyP_ix) + N(yP_izP_ix)$$
$$+ N(yP_izI_ix) + N(yP_ixP_iz) + N(yP_ix \wedge xI_iz \wedge yI_iz). \tag{4}$$

$$N(x P_i y P_i z) + N(x I_i y P_i z) + N(y P_i x P_i z) + N(y P_i x I_i z) + N(y P_i z P_i x)$$
$$+ N(y P_i z \wedge z I_i x \wedge y I_i x) > N(x P_i z P_i y) + N(x I_i z P_i y) + N(z P_i x P_i y)$$
$$+ N(z P_i x I_i y) + N(z P_i y P_i x) + N(z P_i y \wedge y I_i x \wedge z I_i x). \tag{5}$$

$$N(y P_i z P_i x) + N(y I_i z P_i x) + N(z P_i y P_i x) + N(z P_i y I_i x) + N(z P_i x P_i y)$$
$$+ N(z P_i x \wedge x I_i y \wedge z I_i y) \geq N(y P_i x P_i z) + N(y I_i x P_i z) + N(x P_i y P_i z)$$
$$+ N(x P_i y I_i z) + N(x P_i z P_i y) + N(x P_i z \wedge z I_i y \wedge x I_i y). \tag{6}$$

By adding (4) and (5) we obtain:

$$2N(x P_i y P_i z) + N(x P_i y I_i z) + N(x I_i y P_i z) + N(x P_i y \wedge y I_i z \wedge x I_i z)$$
$$+ N(y P_i z \wedge z I_i x \wedge y I_i x) > 2N(z P_i y P_i x) + N(z P_i y I_i x) + N(z I_i y P_i x)$$
$$+ N(z P_i y \wedge y I_i x \wedge z I_i x) + N(y P_i x \wedge x I_i z \wedge y I_i z). \tag{7}$$

$$(7) \rightarrow N(x P_i y P_i z) + N(x P_i y I_i z) + N(x I_i y P_i z) + N(x P_i y \wedge y I_i z \wedge x I_i z)$$
$$+ N(y P_i z \wedge z I_i x \wedge y I_i x) > 0. \tag{8}$$

$$(8) \rightarrow (\exists i \in L)[\text{in } R_i | A \ x \text{ is best } \wedge \ y \text{ is proper medium } \wedge z \text{ is worst}]. \tag{9}$$

Analogously we can show that:

$$(5) \wedge (6) \rightarrow (\exists j \in L)[\text{in } R_j | A \ y \text{ is best} \wedge z \text{ is proper medium} \wedge x \text{ is worst}]. \tag{10}$$

$$(6) \wedge (4) \rightarrow (\exists k \in L)[\text{in } R_k | A \ z \text{ is best} \wedge x \text{ is proper medium} \wedge y \text{ is worst}]. \tag{11}$$

(9), (10) and (11) imply:

$$(\exists i, j, k \in L)[R_i | A, R_j | A, R_k | A \text{ form Latin Square } LS(xyzx) \text{ over } A]. \tag{12}$$

Adding (4), (5) and (6), we obtain:

$$N(x P_i y P_i z) + N(y P_i z P_i x) + N(z P_i x P_i y) + N(x P_i y \wedge y I_i z \wedge x I_i z)$$
$$+ N(y P_i z \wedge z I_i x \wedge y I_i x) + N(z P_i x \wedge x I_i y \wedge z I_i y) > N(z P_i y P_i x)$$
$$+ N(y P_i x P_i z) + N(x P_i z P_i y) + N(z P_i y \wedge y I_i x \wedge z I_i x)$$
$$+ N(y P_i x \wedge x I_i z \wedge y I_i z) + N(x P_i z \wedge z I_i y \wedge x I_i y). \tag{13}$$

$$(13) \rightarrow N(x P_i y P_i z) + N(y P_i z P_i x) + N(z P_i x P_i y) + N(x P_i y \wedge y I_i z$$
$$\wedge x I_i z) + N(y P_i z \wedge z I_i x \wedge y I_i x) + N(z P_i x \wedge x I_i y \wedge z I_i y) > 0. \tag{14}$$

$$(14) \rightarrow (\exists i \in L)[x P_i y P_i z \vee y P_i z P_i x \vee z P_i x P_i y \vee (x P_i y \wedge y I_i z \wedge x I_i z)$$
$$\vee (y P_i z \wedge z I_i x \wedge y I_i x) \vee (z P_i x \wedge x I_i y \wedge z I_i y)]. \tag{15}$$

Adding (4) and (13) we obtain:

$$2N(zP_ixP_iy) + N(zI_ixP_iy) + 2N(xP_iyP_iz) + N(xP_iyI_iz)$$

$$+ 2N(xP_iy \land yI_iz \land xI_iz) + N(yP_iz \land zI_ix \land yI_ix)$$

$$+ N(zP_ix \land xI_iy \land zI_iy) > 2N(zP_iyP_ix) + N(zI_iyP_ix)$$

$$+ 2N(yP_ixP_iz) + N(yP_ixI_iz) + 2N(yP_ix \land xI_iz \land yI_iz)$$

$$+ N(xP_iz \land zI_iy \land xI_iy) + N(zP_iy \land yI_ix \land zI_ix). \tag{16}$$

$$(16) \rightarrow (\exists i \in L)[R_i|A \in Q[LS(xyzx)] \land (xP_iy \lor R_i|A \text{ is intransitive})]. \tag{17}$$

Analogously we can show that:

$$(5) \land (13) \rightarrow (\exists j \in L)[R_j|A \in Q[LS(xyzx)] \land (yP_jz \lor R_j|A \text{ is intransitive})]. \tag{18}$$

$$(6) \land (13) \rightarrow (\exists k \in L)[R_k|A \in Q[LS(xyzx)] \land (zP_kx \lor R_k|A \text{ is intransitive})]. \tag{19}$$

(17)–(19) imply:

$$(\exists i, j, k \in L)[R_i|A, R_j|A, R_k|A \in Q[LS(xyzx)] \land (xP_iy \lor R_i|A \text{ is intransitive})$$

$$\land (yP_jz \lor R_j|A \text{ is intransitive}) \land (zP_kx \lor R_k|A \text{ is intransitive})]. \tag{20}$$

(12), (15) and (20) establish the lemma. ∎

Theorem 6. *Let $\#S \geq 3$ and $\#L = n \geq 5$. Let $D \subseteq Q$. Then the method of majority decision f yields quasi-transitive social R, $R = f(R_1, \ldots, R_n)$, for every $(R_1, \ldots, R_n) \in D^n$ iff D satisfies the condition of Latin Square partial agreement-Q.*

Proof. Suppose f does not yield quasi-transitive binary relation R for every $(R_1, \ldots, R_n) \in D^n$, $D \subseteq Q$. Then $(\exists (R_1, \ldots, R_n) \in D^n)(\exists x, y, z \in S)(xPy \land yPz \land zRx)$. Denote $\{x, y, z\}$ by A. By Lemma 5 we obtain:

(i) $(\exists i, j, k \in L)[R_i|A, R_j|A, R_k|A$ form Latin Square $LS(xyzx)$ over $A]$.

(ii) $(\exists i \in L)[xP_iyP_iz \lor yP_izP_ix \lor zP_ixP_iy \lor (xP_iy \land yI_iz \land xI_iz) \lor (yP_iz \land zI_ix \land yI_ix) \lor (zP_ix \land xI_iy \land zI_iy)]$.

(iii) $(\exists i, j, k \in L)[R_i|A, R_j|A, R_k|A \in Q[LS(xyzx)] \land (xP_iy \lor R_i|A \text{ is intransitive}) \land (yP_jz \lor R_j|A \text{ is intransitive}) \land (zP_kx \lor R_k|A \text{ is intransitive})]$.

If $(\exists i \in L)[R_i|A \in Q[LS(xyzx)] \land R_i|A \text{ is intransitive}]$ then in view of (i) there is a Latin Square involving an intransitive binary relation, which would imply violation of LSPA-Q. (1)

If $\sim (\exists i \in L)[R_i|A \in Q[LS(xyzx)] \land R_i|A \text{ is intransitive}]$ then (i)–(iii) imply that there exist $R_i|A, R_j|A, R_k|A \in T[LS(xyzx)]$, of which at least one is a linear ordering over A, which form a Latin Square; and furthermore $(\exists i, j, k \in L)[R_i|A, R_j|A, R_k|A \in T[LS(xyzx)] \land xP_iy \land yP_jz \land zP_kx]$. This implies that LSPA-Q is violated. (2)

(1) and (2) establish the sufficiency of LSPA-Q.

Suppose $D \subseteq Q$ violates LSPA-Q. Then there is some triple $A = \{x, y, z\}$ over which LSPA-Q is violated. Violation of LSPA-Q over the triple A implies that there exists a Latin Square over A involving an intransitive binary relation or LSPA is violated over A. If LSPA is violated over A then by Theorem 3 there exists $(R_1, \ldots, R_n) \in D^n$ for which $R = f(R_1, \ldots, R_n)$ violates quasi-transitivity. If there exists a Latin Square over A involving an intransitive binary relation then we must have:

$$(\exists \text{ distinct } a, b, c \in \{x, y, z\})(\exists R^s, R^t \in D)[[(aP^sb \wedge bI^sc \wedge aI^sc) \wedge (bP^tc$$

$$\wedge cI^ta \wedge bI^ta)] \vee [(aP^sb \wedge bI^sc \wedge aI^sc) \wedge (bR^tcR^ta \wedge R^t|A \text{ is concerned})]].$$

Consider any $(R_1, \ldots, R_n) \in D^n$ such that $\#\{i \in L \mid R_i = R^s\} = n - 1$, $\#\{i \in L \mid R_i = R^t\} = 1$. Then in each case MMD yields an R which violates quasi-transitivity. ∎

Theorem 7. *Let $\#S \geq 3$ and $\#L = n = 4$. Let $D \subseteq Q$. Then the method of majority decision f yields quasi-transitive social R, $R = f(R_1, \ldots, R_4)$, for every $(R_1, \ldots, R_4) \in D^4$ iff D satisfies the condition of weak extremal restriction-Q.*

Proof. Suppose f does not yield quasi-transitive social R for every $(R_1, \ldots, R_4) \in D^4$, $D \subseteq Q$. Then

$$(\exists (R_1, \ldots, R_4) \in D^4)(\exists x, y, z \in S)(xPy \wedge yPz \wedge zRx).$$

Denote $\{x, y, z\}$ by A. By Lemma 5 we obtain:

$$(\exists i, j, k \in L)[R_i|A, R_j|A, R_k|A \text{ form Latin Square } LS(xyzx) \text{ over } A]. \quad (1)$$

$$(\exists i \in L)[xP_iyP_iz \vee yP_izP_ix \vee zP_ixP_iy \vee (xP_iy \wedge yI_iz \wedge xI_iz)$$

$$\vee (yP_iz \wedge zI_ix \wedge yI_ix) \vee (zP_ix \wedge xI_iy \wedge zI_iy)]. \quad (2)$$

If $(\exists i \in L)[R_i|A \in Q[LS(xyzx)] \wedge R_i|A \text{ is intransitive}]$ then in view of (1) there is a Latin Square involving an intransitive binary relation, which would imply violation of WER-Q. $\quad (3)$

If $\sim (\exists i \in L)[R_i|A \in Q[LS(xyzx)] \wedge R_i|A \text{ is intransitive}]$ then (1) and (2) imply that there exist $R_i|A, R_j|A, R_k|A \in T[LS(xyzx)]$ which form a Latin Square over A, with at least one of them being a linear ordering. $\quad (4)$

$$(4) \rightarrow (\exists i, j, k \in L)(xP_iz \wedge yP_jx \wedge zP_ky). \quad (5)$$

$$(\exists j \in L)(yP_jx) \wedge xPy \rightarrow N(xP_iy) \geq 2 \wedge N(xR_iy) = 3 \wedge N(yP_ix) = 1. \quad (6)$$

$$(6) \rightarrow N(R_i \text{ concerned over } \{x, y, z\} \wedge yR_izR_ix) = 1 \wedge N(zP_iyP_ix) = 0$$

$$\wedge N(yP_ixP_iz) = 0 \wedge N(yP_ix \wedge xI_iz \wedge yI_iz) = 0. \quad (7)$$

$$(\exists k \in L)(zP_ky) \wedge yPz \rightarrow N(yP_iz) \geq 2 \wedge N(yR_iz) = 3 \wedge N(zP_iy) = 1. \quad (8)$$

$$(8) \rightarrow N(R_i \text{ concerned over } \{x, y, z\} \wedge zR_ixR_iy) = 1 \wedge N(xP_izP_iy) = 0$$

$$\wedge N(zP_iy \wedge yI_ix \wedge zI_ix) = 0. \quad (9)$$

$$(4) \wedge (7) \wedge (9) \rightarrow N(xR_iy \wedge yR_iz \wedge xR_iz) = 2 \wedge N(R_i \text{ concerned over}$$

$$\{x, y, z\} \wedge xR_iyR_iz) \geq 1 \wedge N(R_i \text{ concerned over } \{x, y, z\}$$

$$\wedge yR_izR_ix) = 1 \wedge N(R_i \text{ concerned over } \{x, y, z\} \wedge zR_ixR_iy) = 1. \quad (10)$$

$$zRx \wedge N(xP_iz) = 1 \wedge (6) \wedge (8) \wedge (10) \rightarrow (\exists i, j, k \in L)[(xP_iyP_iz$$

$$\wedge yP_izP_ix \wedge zR_ixP_iy) \vee (xP_iyP_iz \wedge yP_izR_ix \wedge zP_ixP_iy)$$

$$\rightarrow \text{ WER-Q is violated.} \quad (11)$$

$$zRx \wedge N(xP_iz) = 2 \wedge (\exists i \in L)(xP_iz \wedge zI_iy \wedge xI_iy) \wedge (6) \wedge (8) \wedge (10)$$

$$\rightarrow (\exists i, j, k \in L)(xP_iyP_iz \wedge yP_izP_ix \wedge zP_ixP_iy)$$

$$\rightarrow \text{ WER-Q is violated.} \quad (12)$$

$$zRx \wedge N(xP_iz) = 2 \wedge \sim (\exists i \in L)(xP_iz \wedge zI_iy \wedge xI_iy) \wedge (6) \wedge (8) \wedge (10)$$

$$\rightarrow (\exists i, j, k \in L)(xP_iyP_iz \wedge yR_jzP_jx \wedge zP_kxR_ky)$$

$$\vee (\exists i, j, k, l \in L)(xP_iyI_iz \wedge xI_jyP_jz \wedge yP_kzP_kx \wedge zP_lxP_ly)$$

$$\rightarrow \text{ WER-Q is violated.} \quad (13)$$

(3), (11), (12) and (13) establish the sufficiency of WER.

Suppose $D \subseteq Q$ violates WER-Q. Then there is some triple $A = \{x, y, z\}$ over which WER-Q is violated. Violation of WER-Q over the triple A implies that there exists a Latin Square over A involving an intransitive binary relation or WER is violated over A. If WER is violated over A then by Theorem 4 there exists $(R_1, \ldots, R_4) \in D^4$ for which $R = f(R_1, \ldots, R_4)$ violates quasi-transitivity. If there exists a Latin Square over A involving an intransitive binary relation then we must have:

$$(\exists \text{ distinct } a, b, c \in \{x, y, z\})(\exists R^s, R^t \in D)[[(aP^sb \wedge bI^sc \wedge aI^sc) \wedge (bP^tc$$

$$\wedge cI^ta \wedge bI^ta)] \vee [(aP^sb \wedge bI^sc \wedge aI^sc) \wedge (bR^tcR^ta \wedge R^t|A \text{ is concerned})]].$$

Consider any $(R_1, \ldots, R_4) \in D^4$ such that $\#\{i \in L \mid R_i = R^s\} = 3$ and $\#\{i \in L \mid R_i = R^t\} = 1$. Then in each case MMD yields an R which violates quasi-transitivity. ∎

Theorem 8. *Let $\#S \geq 3$ and $\#L = n = 3$. Let $D \subseteq Q$. Then the method of majority decision f yields quasi-transitive social R, $R = f(R_1, R_2, R_3)$, for every $(R_1, R_2, R_3) \in D^3$ iff D satisfies the condition of Latin Square linear ordering restriction-Q.*

Proof. Suppose f does not yield quasi-transitive social R for every $(R_1, R_2, R_3) \in D^3$. Then

$$(\exists(R_1, R_2, R_3) \in D^3)(\exists x, y, z \in S)(xPy \wedge yPz \wedge zRx).$$

Denote $\{x, y, z\}$ by A. By Lemma 5 we have:

$$(\exists i, j, k \in L)[R_i|A, R_j|A, R_k|A \text{ form Latin Square } LS(xyzx) \text{ over } A]. \quad (1)$$

If $(\exists i \in L)[R_i|A \in Q[LS(xyzx)] \wedge R_i|A$ is intransitive] then in view of (1) there is a Latin Square involving an intransitive binary relation, which would imply the violation of LSLOR Q. $\quad (2)$

$$\sim (\exists i \in L)[R_i|A \in Q[LS(xyzx)] \wedge R_i|A \text{ is intransitive}] \wedge (1) \wedge n = 3$$

$$\rightarrow (\forall i \in L)(R_i|A \text{ is transitive}). \quad (3)$$

$$(3) \wedge (1) \rightarrow (\forall i \in L)(R_i|A \text{ is transitive}) \wedge (\exists i, j, k \in L)(R_i|A, R_j|A, R_k|A$$

$$\text{form Latin Square } LS(xyzx) \text{ over } A). \quad (4)$$

Now, by proceeding as in Theorem 5 one can show that (4) implies that LSLOR is violated; which coupled with (2) establishes the sufficiency of LSLOR-Q for quasi-transitivity.

Suppose $D \subseteq Q$ violates LSLOR-Q. Then there is some triple $A = \{x, y, z\}$ over which LSLOR-Q is violated. Violation of LSLOR-Q over the triple A implies that there exists a Latin Square over A involving an intransitive binary relation or LSLOR is violated over A. If LSLOR is violated over A then by Theorem 5 there exists $(R_1, R_2, R_3) \in D^3$ for which $R = f(R_1, R_2, R_3)$ violates quasi-transitivity. If there exists a Latin Square over A involving an intransitive binary relation then we must have:

$$(\exists \text{ distinct } a, b, c \in \{x, y, z\})(\exists R^s, R^t \in D)[[(aP^s b \wedge bI^s c \wedge aI^s c) \wedge (bP^t c$$

$$\wedge cI^t a \wedge bI^t a)] \vee [(aP^s b \wedge bI^s c \wedge aI^s c) \wedge (bR^t c R^t a \wedge R^t|A \text{ is concerned})]].$$

Consider any $(R_1, R_2, R_3) \in D^3$ such that $\#\{i \in L \mid R_i = R^s\} = 2$ and $\#\{i \in L \mid R_i = R^t\} = 1$. Then in each case MMD yields an R which violates quasi-transitivity. ■

Theorem 9. *Let $\#S \geq 3$ and $\#L = n = 2$. Let $D \subseteq Q$. Then the method of majority decision f yields quasi-transitive social R, $R = f(R_1, R_2)$, for every $(R_1, R_2) \in D^2$ iff D satisfies the condition of Latin Square intransitive relation restriction-O.*

Proof. Suppose f does not yield quasi-transitive social R for every $(R_1, R_2) \in D^2$. Then

$$(\exists(R_1, R_2) \in D^2)(\exists x, y, z \in S)(xPy \wedge yPz \wedge zRx).$$

$$xPy \rightarrow N(xP_iy) \geq 1 \wedge N(xR_iy) = 2. \tag{1}$$

$$yPz \rightarrow N(yP_iz) \geq 1 \wedge N(yR_iz) = 2. \tag{2}$$

$$(1) \wedge (2) \wedge zRx \rightarrow (\exists i, j \in L)[[xP_iyP_iz \wedge (zP_jx \wedge xI_jy \wedge zI_jy)]$$

$$\vee [(xP_iy \wedge yI_iz \wedge xI_iz) \wedge (yP_jz \wedge zI_jx \wedge yI_jx)]]$$

$$\rightarrow \text{LSIRR-Q is violated.}$$

Suppose $D \subseteq Q$ violates LSIRR-Q. Then there is some triple $A = \{x, y, z\}$ over which LSIRR-Q is violated. Violation of LSIRR-Q over the triple A implies that

$$(\exists \text{ distinct } a, b, c \in \{x, y, z\})(\exists R^s, R^t \in D)[[(aP^sb \wedge bI^sc \wedge aI^sc)$$

$$\wedge (bP^tc \wedge cI^ta \wedge bI^ta)] \vee [(aP^sb \wedge bI^sc \wedge aI^sc) \wedge bP^tcP^ta]].$$

Consider any $(R_1, R_2) \in D^2$ such that $\#\{i \in L \mid R_i = R^s\} = \#\{i \in L \mid R_i = R^t\} = 1$. Then in each case MMD yields an R which violates quasi-transitivity. ∎

V. CONDITIONS FOR ACYCLICITY

Unlike transitivity and quasi-transitivity, the condition of acyclicity is not defined over triples. Consequently, there is no reason to expect existence of conditions defined only over triples which can completely characterize all D, $D \subseteq B$, $B \subseteq C$, which are such that all logically possible $(R_1, \ldots, R_n) \in D^n$ give rise to acyclic social R, $R = (R_1, \ldots, R_n)$, under MMD. In fact, if $B = Q$, then the subsets $D \subseteq B$ which are such that all logically possible $(R_1, \ldots, R_n) \in D^n$ give rise to acyclic social R under MMD cannot be characterized by a condition defined only over triples, as the following theorem shows.

Theorem 10. *Let f be the method of majority decision; and let $\#S = m \geq 4$ and $\#L = n \geq 2$. Let $\mathcal{D}_Q = \{D \subseteq Q \mid (\forall (R_1, \ldots, R_n) \in D^n)(R = f(R_1, \ldots, R_n) \text{ is acyclic})\}$. Then, there does not exist any condition α defined only over triples such that D, $D \in 2^Q - \{\emptyset\}$, belongs to $\mathcal{D}_Q$ iff it satisfies condition α.*

Proof. Let condition α defined only over triples be such that D, $D \in 2^Q - \{\emptyset\}$, belongs to $\mathcal{D}_Q$ iff it satisfies condition α. Let $S = \{x, y, z, w, t_1, \ldots, t_{m-4}\}$. Consider $D = \{(xPy, yIz, xIz; x, y, zPwPt_1P \ldots Pt_{m-4}), (yPz, zIx, yIx; x, y, z PwPt_1P \ldots Pt_{m-4})\}$. It is immediate that MMD yields acyclic R for every $(R_1, \ldots, R_n) \in D^n$; and consequently it follows that $D \in \mathcal{D}_Q$. As condition α is defined only over triples, it follows that D must satisfying α over every triple of alternatives. Therefore it follows that if $A \subseteq S$ is a triple and $(\exists \text{ distinct } a, b, c \in A)[D|\{a, b, c\} = \{(aPb \wedge bIc \wedge aIc), (aIb \wedge bPc \wedge aIc)\} \vee D|\{a, b, c\} = \{aPbPc, aIbPc\}]$ then D would satisfy α over A.

Now consider the following $(R_1, \ldots, R_n)$:

$(x P_1 y, y I_1 z, z P_1 w, w I_1 x, x I_1 z, y I_1 w; \; x, y, z, w P_1 t_1 P_1 \ldots P_1 t_{m-4}).$

$(\forall i \in L - \{1\})(x I_i y, y P_i z, z I_i w, w P_i x, x I_i z, y I_i w; \; x, y, z, w P_i t_1 P_i \ldots P_i t_{m-4}).$

The R yielded by MMD for the above configuration is $(x P y, y P z, z P w, w P x,$ $x I z, y I w; \; x, y, z, w P t_1 P \ldots P t_{m-4})$, which violates acyclicity. Now, for every triple of alternatives $A \subseteq S$ we have

$(\exists \text{ distinct } a, b, c \in A)[\{R_i | A \mid i \in L\} = \{(a P b, b I c, a I c), (b P c, c I a, b I a)\}$

$\vee \{R_i | A \mid i \in L\} = \{a P b P c, a I b P c\} \vee \{R_i | A \mid i \in L\} = \{a P b P c\}$

$\vee \{R_i | A \mid i \in L\} = \{a I b P c\}].$

Therefore, it follows that either $\{(a P b \wedge b I c \wedge a I c), (a I b \wedge b P c \wedge a I c)\}$ or $\{a P b P c, a I b P c\}$ must be violating a, contradicting the earlier conclusion that both of these sets satisfy a. This contradiction establishes the theorem.   ∎

From the above theorem the following corollary follows immediately.

Corollary 1. *Let f be the method of majority decision; and let $\#S = m \geq 4$ and $\#L = n \geq 2$. Let $\mathcal{D}_A = \{D \subseteq \mathcal{A} \mid (\forall (R_1, \ldots, R_n) \in D^n)(R = f(R_1, \ldots, R_n) \text{ is acyclic})\}$. Then, there does not exist any condition a defined only over triples such that $D, D \in 2^A - \{\emptyset\}$, belongs to $\mathcal{D}_A$ iff it satisfies condition a.*

If the number of individuals is greater than or equal to 11 then the sets $D \subseteq \mathcal{T}$ which are such that all logically possible $(R_1, \ldots, R_n) \in D^n$ give rise to acyclic social R under MMD, however, can be characterized by a condition defined only over triples. The following theorem can easily be proved.

Theorem 11. *Let $\#S \geq 3$ and $\#L = n \geq 11$. Let $D \subseteq \mathcal{T}$. Then the method of majority decision f yields acyclic social R, $R = f(R_1, \ldots, R_n)$, for every $(R_1, \ldots, R_n) \in D^n$ iff D satisfies the condition of Latin Square partial agreement.*[4]

As far as the remaining cases are concerned, there is no uniformity among them. In some cases it can be shown that no condition defined only over triples can be a characterizing condition, while in some other cases it is possible to formulate a characterizing condition defined only over triples. For instance, it can be shown that if the number of individuals is four then there does not exist any condition defined only over triples which can characterize the sets of orderings which invariably give rise to acyclic social R. On the other hand the validity of Theorem 11 can be shown for $n = 9$ as well.[5]

---

[4] See Sen and Pattanaik (1969) and Kelly (1974).   [5] See Kelly (1974).

REFERENCES

ARROW, K. J. (1963), *Social Choice and Individual Values*, 2nd edn (New York: Wiley).

BLACK, D. (1948), "On the Rationale of Group Decision-Making", *Journal of Political Economy*, 56: 23–34.

—— (1958), *The Theory of Committees and Elections* (Cambridge: Cambridge University Press).

FISHBURN, P. C. (1970), "Conditions for Simple Majority Decision Functions with Intransitive Individual Indifference", *Journal of Economic Theory*, 2: 354–67.

GAERTNER, W. (2001), *Domain Conditions in Social Choice Theory* (Cambridge: Cambridge University Press).

INADA, K.-I. (1964), "A Note on the Simple Majority Decision Rule", *Econometrica*, 32: 525–31.

—— (1969), "The Simple Majority Decision Rule", *Econometrica*, 37: 490–506.

—— (1970), "Majority Rule and Rationality", *Journal of Economic Theory*, 2: 27–40.

JAIN, S. K. (1986), "Special Majority Rules: A Necessary and Sufficient Condition for Quasi-Transitivity with Quasi-Transitive Individual Preferences", *Social Choice and Welfare*, 3: 99–106.

KELLY, J. S. (1974), "Necessity Conditions in Voting Theory", *Journal of Economic Theory*, 8: 149–60.

PATTANAIK, P. K. (1970), "On Social Choice with Quasitransitive Individual Preferences", *Journal of Economic Theory*, 2: 267–75.

—— (1971), *Voting and Collective Choice* (Cambridge: Cambridge University Press).

SEN, A. K. (1966), "A Possibility Theorem on Majority Decisions", *Econometrica*, 34: 491–9.

—— (1970), *Collective Choice and Social Welfare* (San Francisco: Holden-Day).

—— and PATTANAIK, P. K. (1969), "Necessary and Sufficient Conditions for Rational Choice Under Majority Decision", *Journal of Economic Theory*, 1: 178–202.

CHAPTER 11

CONVEXITY AND SEPARABILITY IN REPRESENTING CONSENSUS

ISAAC LEVI

I. CONSENSUS IN GROUP DECISION-MAKING AND DOUBT IN INDIVIDUAL DECISION-MAKING

TONY is finally fed up with the Iraq War and wants out. He ranks the option of Cut and Run higher than a Phased Withdrawal and this in turn higher than Stay the Course. George remains loyal to Stay the Course. He ranks this higher than Phased Withdrawal and this in turn higher than Cut and Run. Tony is the junior partner in this decision but George cannot ignore Tony's preferences. They need to reach some sort of consensus.

Originally both Tony and George evaluated these options in terms of the values or utilities of the possible consequences of these options and the probabilities that these consequences will be realized conditional on the options being implemented. Their assessments of the expected utilities for the options coincided.

But now Tony has become pessimistic about the prospects of staying the course. He has reassessed his probabilities and, hence, his expected utilities. Even though

Tony and George continue to share the same evaluation of possible consequences, they disagree in their evaluation of the options due to a difference in their probability judgements concerning these possible consequences.

Tony and George need to reach some agreement as to what to do. If they were not powerful men eager to get their own way, they might consider pursuing a joint deliberation.

In a joint deliberation, the parties to the dispute identify a potential point of view accessible to both of them encompassing just the opinions they currently share in common. These opinions include the full beliefs, probability judgements and value judgements embedded in their initial points of view that express agreement. Where their initial views differ, they adopt attitudes that express suspension of judgement.

Each of the parties is prepared, at least for the sake of the argument, to take for granted the judgements they already share and to entertain the views of their interlocutors that conflict with their own as discussable items in their subsequent deliberations. By each of them adopting this point of view as their consensus at the beginning of inquiry, George and Tony can engage in a joint deliberation without begging questions in order to settle the issues concerning which they disagree. Or, if circumstances prevent further inquiry before a decision is to be taken, George and Tony can choose an option that is admissible for choice according to that same consensus.

A representation of the initial consensus adopted by George and Tony could also represent the point of view of a single agent. If, in the case before us, Howard were to recognize the probability judgements p_G endorsed by George and the probability judgements p_T endorsed by Tony as entertainable for use in evaluating expected utility, Howard would recognize as *admissible for choice* Tony's preferred option, Cut and Run, and George's favorite, Stay the Course. Strictly speaking, for Howard neither of these options would maximize expected utility categorically or be categorically optimal. Given Howard's state of doubt, both options would be admissible with respect to expected utility because each of them maximizes expected utility among the available options according to the common utility function and a probability function that Howard has not ruled out as impermissible for use in calculating expected utility.

Nonetheless, Stay the Course and Cut and Run are not tied for optimality according to either of the expected utility functions under consideration. And even if there is some other probability function that is permissible according to the consensus perspective reached by George and Howard such that both options are optimal with respect to expected utility when that probability function is used to calculate expected utility, it would be wrong to conclude that the two options are *categorically* equipreferred—i.e. equipreferred according to all permissible expectation evaluations considered. Both are admissible for choice. Yet they are non-comparable with respect to expected utility. In spite of having these attitudes, the common view of George and Tony or the point of view adopted by Howard would be rationally coherent.

George and Tony agree that the decision problem they face may be represented in *state functional form*. That is to say, the set A of options available for choice are representable by functions from possible circumstances or states in set H to hypotheses about consequences in some set O of possible consequences. They agree as to what the set of available options is, what the possible states are and what are the possible consequences.[1]

George and Tony also share a common utility function for the consequences $u(o_{ij})$, where o_{ij} represents the relevant consequences of option a_i under circumstances h_j. They disagree concerning their credal or subjective probability judgements:

> p_G = George's credal probability for the circumstances in H given the choice of an option.
>
> p_T = Tony's credal probability for the circumstances in H given the choice of an option.
>
> $E_G(a_i)$ = the expected utility of a_i when p_G is used. This expected utility is determined by the probability–utility pair $<p_G, u>$.
>
> $E_T(a_i)$ = the expected utility when p_T is used. It is determined by the probability–utility pair $<p_T, u>$.

The disagreement between George and Tony regarding expected utilities and credal probabilities could in some cases be due to a disagreement concerning what they fully believe. But if George and Tony are to form a consensus for the sake of the deliberation, they should shift to a common state of full belief. If a difference in their credal states remains, it must be due to differences in their *confirmational commitments* (Levi 1980: §4.3). I assume that a rational agent is committed to a set of rules specifying the credal state the agent should be in given the agent's state of full belief for every potential state of full belief K in the agent's space K of potential states of full belief. Any such system of rules is representable by a function from potential states in K to credal states in the set B of states of credal states. If K is the shared state of full belief, {$p_{George} = C_{George}(K)$ and $p_{Tony} = C_{Tony}(K)$}. Throughout this discussion, I shall assume that the agents involved are making appraisals relative to a common state of full belief. On the assumption that the confirmational commitments of the parties involved satisfy the Bayesian requirement of *confirmational conditionalization* (Levi 1980: 81), it becomes possible to derive credal states for the consensus state of full belief for each of the parties to the deliberation—such as George and Tony.

---

[1] See Levi (1980) for some initial reflection on what I now call representation of a decision problem in state functional form. Improvements are proposed in Levi (1986) and, thanks to criticism from Leeds (1990) and Seidenfeld (1993), in Levi (1999). It should not be assumed that all decision problems are representable in state functional form.

In such a deliberation, George and Tony should retreat, at least for the sake of the argument, from their own opinionated probability judgements[2] $C_G(K) = \{p_G\}$ and $C_T(K) = \{p_T\}$ relative to the consensus state of full belief K to a point of view $C_{GT}(K)$ where both credal probability judgements p_T and p_G (at least) are recognized as *permissible to use in computing expected utilities for the options* according to the common state of full belief K (Levi 1974, 1980, 1986).

Consequently, when seeking to maximize expected utility, both E_T and E_G are permissible functions to maximize when considering the group decision by Tony and George. In effect, the group is understood to be an agent whose full beliefs are the shared full beliefs of Tony and George, whose credal probability judgements are the system of permissible credal probability judgements warranted by a consensus confirmational commitment, and whose utility judgements are those permissible in consensus. As I have noted, the judgements of the group agent could be the views of the personal agent Howard in doubt concerning p_G and p_T.

In general, agent X's *credal state* B_X is representable by a set of conditional subjective or credal probability functions each member of which is *permissible* according to X. Y's credal state B_Y is representable by a different set of conditional probability functions—those permissible according to Y. In consensus, their credal state B_{XY} includes as permissible at the very minimum those conditional probability functions permissible according to X and those permissible according to Y.

X's evaluation of consequences of the options is represented by a set of permissible utility functions defined over the set O of consequences. This is the *extended value structure EV(O)*. In the George-and-Tony predicament, $EV(O)$ is a singleton (i.e. unique up to a positive affine transformation) that is the same for both George and Tony.[3]

X's evaluation of the options in set A of available options is represented by a set of *permissible expected utility functions V(A)* or the corresponding set of permissible probability–utility pairs. *V(A) is the value structure for A.*

It should be emphasized that the set A of available options is the set that the decision-maker is committed to judging available and relevant for choice *given*

---

[2] Some authors regard a view to be opinionated to the extent that the agent judges some propositions to carry credal probability 1. But assigning credal probability 1 is no more and no less opinionated than assigning any numerically determinate credal probability to a proposition. In both cases, a credal probability is taken to be uniquely permissible. The agent is perfectly free of doubt. Unlike some, I do not deplore such opinionation automatically. Sometimes opinionation may be warranted and sometimes not. Opinionation of this kind should not be confused with incorrigibility or immunity from revision.

[3] The set O of outcome propositions (or the appropriate descriptions) should be basic in the sense of Levi (1999): if an element o of O that is consistent with K_a^+, where a is an element of A, then refining o into further propositions consistent with K_a^+ yields propositions that are equipreferred. In this sense the space of possible outcomes O represents the set of possible outcome descriptions that specify all consequence of information that the decision-maker cares about. This requirement meets a difficulty posed by Leeds (1990) and Seidenfeld (1993).

the decision-maker's full beliefs and the judgements of serious possibility supported by them as well as the goals and values that define the agent's problem. An act of a given type *a* is available for choice by X according to X if and only if X fully believes that X is able to implement *a* through X's deliberation, X fully believes that if X chooses to implement *a*, *a* will be implemented, and X judges it seriously possible that X will implement *a* (see Levi 1986: §4.3, 1997: ch. 2). In addition, implementing *a* must be judged by X to be relevant to the solution of the problem X is facing. Similar remarks obtain *mutatis mutandis* concerning the decision-maker's judgements about what constitute the states in *H*, the set *O* of relevant potential consequences and the permissible utility functions defined over *O* in the extended value structure $EV(O)$, the set *B* of permissible credal probabilities and the value structure $V(A)$.

II. VALUE STRUCTURES REPRESENTED BY SETS OF PREMISSIBLE EXPECTED UTILITIES AND BY CATEGORICAL PREFERENCE

An agent's *value commitments* (Levi 1986: §1.2) may be characterized by two components: a *scope specification* that identifies features of the set of options, states and consequences and a *constraint* on the value structure. This constraint may come as a restriction directly imposed on the set of permissible utility functions in the extended value structure that together with the agent's credal state constrains the agent's value structure. Or the constraint may be directly imposed on the value structure, in which case the space *O* of relevant consequences collapses into the set of available options and the extended value structure $EV(O)$ coincides with the value structure $V(A)$. In both cases, the value structure $V(A)$ is representable as a set of permissible expected utility functions.

A rationally coherent value commitment imposes a maximally specific constraint on *O* if and only if it recognizes exactly one utility function (satisfying von Neumann–Morgenstern requirements) to be permissible. In the typical case, however, rationally coherent value commitments are not maximally specific. The constraints on the extended value structure $EV(O)$ (or when appropriate the value structure $V(A)$) allow for several permissible utility (expected utility) functions. As we have seen in the George-and-Tony example, these permissible utilities can represent a consensus between the competing views of George and Tony or a state of suspense or doubt in a single agent (Howard).

Consider first the direct imposition of constraints on the set of options, as when the value commitment prohibits breaking promises. In such cases, the domain of the value commitment is the set of decision problems where at least one of the options is breaking a promise. The value commitment requires that options of promise-breaking be ranked below options where promise-breaking is avoided. There are any number of value structures understood as sets of permissible expected utility functions that meet this constraint.

In other settings, constraints are directly imposed on the set of permissible utility functions in the extended value structure $EV(O)$ on the space O of consequences. These in turn conspire with the agent's full beliefs and credal state to determine a set of permissible expected utility functions $V(A)$.

It is commonplace in discussions of rational choice to utilize evaluations of options in A by a comparison of options that induces either a weak ordering or, if not that, a partial or a quasi-ordering. Such evaluations of options in terms of a weak ordering, partial ordering or quasi-ordering of available options are also representable by sets of permissible (expected) utility functions. But representations by sets of permissible expected utility functions cannot always be captured by exclusive reliance on rankings of the set of available options. Reporting evaluations of the options in A by means of a quasi-ordering or a weak ordering may (and I think often does) suppress relevant information.

For example, if $A = \{x, y, z\}$, all three options might be non-comparable due to a conflict between an evaluation that assigns x the expected utility of 1, z the expected utility of 0 and y some value r and an evaluation assigning $x = 0$, $y = r$ and $z = 1$. In one case, $r \geq 0.5$. y is "second best" according to both utility functions. In another, $r < 0.5$ and y is second worst according to both utility functions. And there are other possibilities which, like the second-best case, are not second worst. They are all compatible with all three options being non-comparable, all things considered.

If we do not consider the set of permissible expected utility functions in the value structure but merely the comparisons that, in this case, yield total non-comparability, we are not in a position even to discuss whether the recommended choice in the first case is the same as or different from what it is in the other. Yet it seems clear that when the intermediate option is second worst, it ought to be rejected, whereas in the other cases the intermediate option is not ruled out. Perhaps ordinalist representations are fully adequate; but if they are, it must be explained why the clear difference between second-worst and not-second-worst cases is irrelevant to rational choice.

Representing rationally coherent evaluations of options by sets of expected utility functions does impose some constraints in the name of rationality on the kinds of ranking comparisons that are allowable. Option x is *categorically weakly preferred* (strictly, equipreferred) *to* y according to the decision-maker if and only if every expected utility function in $V(A)$ permissible according to the decision-maker ranks x at least as good as (better than, equally as good as) y. Otherwise x and y are categorically non-comparable (Levi 1986: §6.5).[4]

Categorical preference so understood captures the notion of doubt and consensus that I contend is relevant to contexts where several agents must engage in a joint deliberation and need to take into account conflicting evaluations of the options, or a single agent is in earnest doubt concerning competing evaluations.[5]

Categorical preference so conceived should *require* that categorical weak, strict and equi- preference *all* be transitive. Categorical weak preference cannot coherently be acyclic but not transitive. There should be no case of consensus where transitivity of weak preference, strict preference or equipreference breaks down.

III. CATEGORICAL OR INTERSECTION STRICT PREFERENCE VERSUS THE ASYMMETRIC FACTOR OF CATEGORICAL WEAK PREFERENCE

In Sen (2002), he discussed *intersection preference*. Sen defined IPAIR as the intersections of strict preferences and indifference (i.e. equipreference) relations in sets of what I am calling permissible rankings (Sen 2002: 674). These correspond exactly to categorical strict and categorical equi- preference. One can then define IPAIR weak preference by the set of ordered pairs satisfying categorical or intersection strict preference or equipreference. But IPAIR weak preference has categorical strict preference as an asymmetrical factor and categorical equipreference as the symmetrical factor. When x is strictly preferred to y according to some permissible rankings in the value structure and equipreferred according to others, x apparently is not IPAIR-comparable with y. So the IPAIR notion of weak preference is not categorical weak preference. IPAIR weak, strict and equi- preference when taken together fail to capture the consensus that categorical weak, strict and equi- preference characterizes.

---

[4] Since $V(A)$ is a set of expected utility functions, mixtures of the available options in A can be evaluated at least for the sake of argument by taking their expected values. So the categorical preference relations just described can be made to apply to the elements of the "mixture set" M[A] of all value-neutral roulette lotteries where the payoffs are implementations of members of A. $V(M[A])$ is determined by $V(A)$.

[5] I discuss categorical preference in Levi (1986: §6.5). It corresponds to what Sen calls the "intersection" of multiple preference rankings in papers published in 1991, one of which appears as ch. 22 of Sen (2002). What is noteworthy about this notion is that strict preference is *not* the asymmetric factor of weak preference. In this respect it differs from the usual versions of "paretian" agreement. See the following text for more discussion.

Sen also introduces IQOR, which is based on categorical weak preference or the intersection of all permissible weak preference relations. He then defines strict preference as the asymmetric factor of categorical weak preference. This is not the categorical (or intersection) strict preference, although the symmetric factor is categorical equipreference.

So neither IPAIR nor IQOR can be used to characterize the shared agreements in the consensus value structure $V(A)$. Both representations insist on taking strict preference to be the asymmetric factor of a weak preference. The consequence is that the requirements of unanimity are compromised either by the weak preference used as in IPAIR or by the strict preference used as in IQOR. Sen recognizes this point but seems committed (without argument) to retaining the usual factorization of weak preference into strict and equi- preference.

Retaining the factorization of weak preference into strict and equi- preference is compelling when the value structure is a weak order so that there is no incompleteness. But incompleteness in some cases poses obstacles that make the retention of the factorization undesirable if one is seeking to capture the notion of a consensus in the evaluation of the options.

In his extended discussion of intersection preference and its problems, Sen is concerned with the evaluation of different opportunity subsets of a large set X for which a set of permissible (or reasonable) weak orderings is given. The two methods for comparing such opportunity sets make use of the categorical (intersection) weak preference (Sen 2002: 674–5). He also points out that if one wants a strict ordering of these opportunity sets, one can use either the categorical strict ordering or the asymmetric factor strict preference.

The issue here, however, is not the comparison of different opportunity sets but a choice among elements in a given opportunity set, "menu", or set of available options in consensus. One choice criterion, the one favored by Sen, requires options admissible for choice to be *maximal* among the available options.

In defining maximal x in a set S (Sen 2002: 182), Sen stipulates that no member of S is strictly preferred to x where strict preference is the asymmetric factor of the weak preference relation. If we want the preferences to represent consensus or shared agreements among the permissible weak orderings of the options, Sen himself has pointed out that we cannot always guarantee that the categorical strict preference is an asymmetric factor of the categorical strict preference.

Rather than compromising the requirements for consensus as shared agreement, it seems sensible to abandon the requirement that the strict preference used to define maximality is the asymmetric factor of categorical weak preference. Categorical strict preference can be used to define maximality. Maximal elements are assured in all finite sets of options. In the pairwise choice between x and y described above, both x and y are maximal and, according to maximality, admissible for choice. As we shall see, the recommendation is in agreement with the recommendation that choices between options be E-admissible.

To adopt this approach does not preclude consideration of other preference relations for other purposes. But where choice among the options available is relative to a consensus among the several permissible valuations in the conflicted value structure and a criterion like maximality is to be used, the weak, strict and equi-preference relation ought all to be categorical. In that case, strict preference cannot in general be the asymmetric factor of weak preference. It seems desirable, therefore, to abandon Sen's use of the asymmetric factor of categorical (i.e. intersectional) weak preference to determine maximality.

To be sure, categorical preference does not capture all the information about the evaluation of A conveyed by the value structure. But it captures all the information required for applying maximality while remaining faithful to the demand that consensus be represented. It captures precisely that information representing the currently settled features concerning the ranking of elements of A. We shall shortly consider the ways in which the categorical preference falls short of capturing relevant information.

An example may help illustrate these points. Suppose Maya has a choice between option x of traveling first class on airline 1 and option y of traveling coach class on airline 2. She prefers traveling first class to coach but is indifferent between traveling on airlines 1 and 2. So she categorically weakly prefers option x to option y, does not categorically weakly prefer y to x and yet does not categorically strictly prefer x to y.

Although x is not categorically strictly preferred to y in this type of case, according to the definition of strict IQOR preference as the asymmetric factor of weak preference (in this case, categorical weak preference), x is strictly preferred to y. If this understanding of preference is plugged into Sen's definition of maximality, option x is uniquely maximal. But IQOR maximality does not represent judgements made at the onset of deliberation where the shared agreements at the beginning of deliberation are taken into account. According to at least one permissible ranking both options are admissible for choice. In consensus, that point of view ought not to be declared inadmissible.[6] IPAIR maximality and categorical maximality recognize both options as maximal and, hence, admissible. They do better in representing shared agreements. But IPAIR maximality judges x and y to be non-comparable whereas categorical maximality recognizes x to be weakly preferred to y so that x and y are comparable. IPAIR and categorical preference render the same verdict regarding maximality; but categorical maximality is exclusively based on the shared agreements in the value structure.

---

[6] There is a difference between a consensus as a shared agreement reached by acknowledging the several points of view in contention and a consensus as a partial or complete resolution of the conflicts between these points of view. That is one of the important differences between consensus at the beginning of inquiry and consensus at the end of inquiry. Even if only one permissible ranking recognizes y as optimal, it should be counted as admissible for choice in consensus at the beginning of inquiry.

IV. Maximality, E-Admissibility and the Second Worst

Setting aside these niceties, even if a maximality criterion is based on a categorical weak preference derived from the decision-maker's value structure $V(A)$, maximality is at best necessary but not sufficient for rational choice. To see this, consider elaborations of the scenario involving George and Tony:

Second Worst. According to George's initial point of view, Phased Withdrawal is almost as bad as Cut and Run. Stay the Course is far superior to both. Tony takes the position that Phased Withdrawal is almost as bad as Stay the Course and that Cut and Run is vastly superior.

Not Second Worst. This is any case where Phased Withdrawal is closer to the best according to at least one permissible evaluation.

In the Second Worst case, the consensus must rule out Phased Withdrawal. In the Not Second Worst case, the consensus must recognize all three options as admissible.

Maximality requires treating both cases alike. All three options count as admissible. But in the Second Worst case, Phased Withdrawal should be inadmissible whereas when Phased Withdrawal is second best according to at least one of the two parties, Phased Withdrawal should be admissible for choice. Insensitivity to the difference between Second Worst and Not Second Worst seems to me to be a fatal defect in the maximality criterion, whether we understand by this categorical or non-categorical maximality. We should consider a criterion for choice that avoids this defect. E-admissibility is worth considering for this purpose:

An option is *E-admissible* if and only if it is optimal according to at least one permissible probability–utility pair or permissible expected utility function in the value structure $V(A)$ for the options in A derived from the state of full belief K, credal state B and extended value structure $EV(O)$.

V. E-Admissibility, the Second Worst, Separability of Probability and Value, and the Cross-Product Rule

Whether E-admissibility can be used to register the required sensitivity depends on how the set of expected utility functions in $V(A)$ that X is committed to judging permissible is constituted. In consensus between George and Tony, it seems non-controversial that the expected utility functions George and Tony initially endorsed separately should both count as permissible provided the state of full belief is shared in common. This parallels the case of suspension of judgement between truth-value-bearing claims where both claims are recognized as serious possibilities rather than one of them being ruled out in favor of the other.

But permissible expected utility functions are not possibly true hypotheses. In suspense, we do not require that *only* George's and Tony's expected utility functions should be permissible. That response is tantamount to treating the two expected utility functions as truth-value-bearing alternative possibilities exactly one of which is true. In any case, if these are the only permissible expected utility functions in the consensus value structure, the distinction between second best and second worst is just as surely lost as it is if maximality is the choice criterion.

It appears that once George's and Tony's expected utility functions are countenanced as permissible, other expected utility functions should be judged permissible as well if sensitivity to the second best/second worst distinction is to be available. But which expected utility functions should be required to be permissible in addition to George's and Tony's? The sensitivity of E-admissibility to the difference between second-best and second-worst cases depends on the answer to this question.

A permissible expected utility function evaluates the options actually available to a decision-maker or to a group of decision-makers such as X and Y. However, such a function evaluates mixtures of available options as well. Whether such mixed options are available to a decision-maker or not, the decision-maker can judge whether a mixed option would be ranked above, below or equal to an option actually available according to a permissible expected utility function *were* that mixture included among the available options. If George had the option of participating in a roulette lottery where the chance of implementing Stay the Course is c, Phased Withdrawal is d and Cut and Run is $e(c + d + e = 1$ and c, d, e are all non-negative reals), the expected value of the lottery would be cE_G(Stay the Course) $+ dE_G$(Phased Withdrawal) $+ eE_G$(Cut and Run) provided that the decision-maker does not impute some value or disvalue to gambling, so that the lottery is value-neutral as far as the decision-maker is concerned. The evaluation of such a value-neutral lottery is thus assumed to have the *mixture property* (Levi 1986: §5.3). This assumption is relevant to determining which expected utility functions other than E_G and E_T preserve the relevant comparisons required for consensus. Not only must the comparisons that are common to George and Tony and explicit in the preferences among the available options be preserved, but so should their agreements regarding such hypothetical comparisons that are involved in considering mixtures.

Requiring the preservation of these comparisons has no impact on the determination of which options are maximal; but it is important for capturing the consensus articulated in the value structure $V(A)$.

Thus, in the Second Worst case, there is no mixture of Stay the Course and Cut and Run whose expected utility is less than the expected value of Phased Withdrawal, according to George's expected utility function or according to Tony's. In the Not Second Worst case, there is at least one such mixed option. We should expect this feature to be preserved in any other expected utility function that is recognized as permissible. This means that no permissible expected utility function should rank Phased Withdrawal as optimal in a three-way choice. Phased Withdrawal cannot be E-admissible.

Turn then to a case that is not second worst. In that event, there is a mixture of Stay the Course and Cut and Run whose expected utility is inferior to the expected utility of Phased Withdrawal according to both George's expected utility and Tony's. Consider then a weighted average of George's and Tony's expected utility functions where the weights are the chances of Stay the Course and Cut and Run in the mixture. Phased Withdrawal will rank above the other two pure options according to this expected utility. This expected utility ought to be permissible if all expected utilities preserving the unanimous comparisons in the mixture set are countenanced as permissible.

Keep in mind that we are looking for a way to represent the shared agreements between George and Tony with respect to their value structures in a context where George and Tony share an extended value structure $EV(O)$ but adopt different (strictly Bayesian) credal states. This suggests that we should consider adding to the permissible expected utility functions all those expected utility functions that preserve the evaluations of options concerning which the expected utility functions for George and Tony agree. Each of these expected utilities generates a weak ordering over the set of all value-neutral mixtures of options in A, so satisfaction of this condition for consensus has the form of a Pareto unanimity condition. In that case, the set of such functions are characterizable by the set of weighted averages of the expected utility for X and the expected utility for Y and, hence, is convex.[7]

Now if X and Y are George and Tony, who share an extended value structure, this argument seems quite compelling. In that case, not only can we conclude that $V(A)$ is convex but so is the credal state—i.e. the set of permissible probability functions.

---

[7] Levi (1986) and Seidenfeld, Kadane and Schervish (1989) point this out. The *weighted average principle* of Levi (1986) stipulates that a weighted average of permissible expected utility functions for the mixture set $M[A]$ of a set A of available options is also permissible. This principle was shown to be unacceptable in Seidenfeld, Kadane and Schervish (1989) in cases where X and Y not only differ in their credal states but also in their value structures. In cases where X and Y share a common value structure or share a common credal state, one can consistently mandate the weighted average principle in the name of characterizing consensus. Seidenfeld, Schervish and Kadane (2007) have recently argued against endorsing the weighted average principle even in these cases. I agree that one can resist the weighted average principle if one does not require a consensus at the beginning of joint deliberation of the sort that the weighted average principle requires. I also think that Seidenfeld, Kadane and Schervish are wrong to resist.

Similarly, if X and Y agree in their credal probability state but not in their extended value structures, the value structure is arguably convex and so is the extended value structure.

However, as Seidenfeld, Schervish and Kadane (aka SSK) (1989) point out, when X and Y differ both in credal state and extended value structure, the only two expected utility functions preserving Pareto unanimity are X's and Y's. Convexity obviously fails.

As SSK themselves observe, they presuppose that the consensus being sought between X and Y requires the permissibility of the probability–utility pairs for X and for Y and any other probability–utility pairs that preserve the shared agreements between these pairs. It turns out that as a general rule, there are no other such probability–utility pairs.

Perhaps, however, we are looking at the characterization of consensus from the wrong end of the telescope. Instead of focusing directly on the shared agreements between the value structures for X and Y, we should attend to the shared agreements between X's and Y's states of credal probability judgement and between X's and Y's extended value structures. Once X and Y agree on their full and probabilistic beliefs and also on their goals and values, they can reason to agreement as to how to evaluate their options.

From this perspective, the consensus value should recognize as permissible not only X's probability–utility pair $<p_X, u_X>$ and Y's probability–utility pair $<p_Y, u_Y>$ but also the probability–utility pairs $<p_X, u_Y>$ and $<p_Y, u_X>$ formed by combining X's probability with Y's utility and Y's probability with X's utility. Those who resist this idea should ask themselves the following question: in a consensus value structure, should $<p_X, u_Y>$ and $<p_Y, u_X>$ be ruled out as impermissible?

If we take seriously the notion that X and Y assign credal probabilities to hypotheses on the basis of the common state of full belief K but different confirmational commitments, and that X's (Y's) endorsement of a confirmational commitment is a separate matter from X's (Y's) endorsement of a value commitment licensing utility assignments to the consequences in O, there are four value structures that must be brought into consensus: the value structure generated by $<p_X, u_X>$, by $<p_Y, u_Y>$, by $<p_X, u_Y>$, and by $<p_Y, u_X>$. The consensus between X and Y (or the state of suspense for a single agent) ought to require the permissibility of these four probability–utility pairs and all probability–utility pairs that preserve the robust paretian consensus between them (Levi 1997: 181 ff.).

This type of consensus guarantees that the set of permissible credal probabilities in the consensus will be the convex hull of the credal states of X and Y. Similarly, the set of permissible utility functions in the consensus will be the convex hull of the extended value structures of X and Y.

The consensus value structure will not be a convex set of expected utility functions or probability–utility pairs. But the consensus value structure is derived from a consensus credal state and a consensus extended value structure, both of which are required to be convex. The convex hull of any pair of probability–utility pairs in this cross-product that share a common probability (utility) is a subset of the consensus value structure. The value structure is obtainable by taking the cross-product of the set of permissible probabilities in the consensus credal state and the set of permissible utilities in the extended value structure and forming the cross-product.

This *cross-product rule* allows the credal state and the extended value structure to vary independently of one another, as it does according to the story about Tony's change of heart, where Tony's credal state changes without any change in his extended value structure. In this sense, probability and utility are taken to be separable.

In the general setting we are now considering, where X and Y start with different credal states and value structures, a second-worst case now becomes one where in a three-way choice between a, b and c, a is ranked over b over c according to $<p_X, u_X>$ and c is ranked over b over a according to $<p_Y, u_X>$, with b second worst according to both expected utility functions and, in addition, similar rankings obtain for $<p_X, u_Y>$ and $<p_Y, u_Y>$ respectively. In this second-worst case, b fails to be E-admissible provided that the value structure is derived via the cross-product rule from the convex hull of X and Y's credal states and the convex hull of their value structures. According to maximality all three options ought to be admissible for choice, as they are according to E-admissibility and maximality alike when the second-worst condition fails.

Although the value structure in consensus need not, in general, be convex, its derivability from a convex credal state and a convex extended value structure via the cross-product rule is enough to insure that when E-admissibility is applied as the choice rule, second-worst options will be ruled out as inadmissible and not-second-worst options will be recognized as admissible. E-admissibility and robust paretian considerations suffice to insure recognition of the distinction that maximality cannot recognize.

VI. SEPARABILITY, SECOND WORST
AND IRRELEVANCE

Seidenfeld, Schervish and Kadane do not endorse separability of credal state and extended value structure and the cross-product rule as conditions on consensus in value structure. According to SSK, the identification of consensus should begin with insisting that Tony's expected utility function and George's expected utility function should be counted as permissible and consensus derived from this. Like Sen, SSK attach primacy to the value structure and the choice function based on it rather than the beliefs and values of the agents whose views are being brought into consensus.

Nonetheless, SSK and I agree that choice functions should satisfy the requirements of E-admissibility rather than maximality. E-admissibility exhibits a sensitivity to the second worst/not second worst distinction that maximality lacks. When combined with the cross-product rule and the convexity of credal states and value structures, E-admissibility always rules out second-worst options and always acknowledges the E-admissibility of not-second-worst options.

According to Seidenfeld, Schervish and Kadane, however, middle options that are second worst are sometimes E-admissible and sometimes not. That is because they resist the requirements of credal and extended value structure convexity and the use of the cross-product condition. They think that these requirements are insensitive to certain important types of consensus—in particular, those concerning irrelevance. Space does not permit a considered discussion of the details of their important arguments or my contention that consensus concerning irrelevance or independence of probabilities is a consensus about statistical probabilities and ought to be thought of as part of a consensus state of full belief.

This discussion has considered three criteria of choice that may be deployed when value structures do not provide a complete ranking of the available options: maximality, E-admissibility with convexity of credal state and extended value structure, and E-admissibility without a convexity requirement.

Sen's championing of maximality, we have seen, is insensitive to differences in decision problems that I have labeled differences between three-way choices where one option is second worst according to both rival assessments of expected utility, and three-way choices where the "middle option" is second best according to at least one of these assessments. E-admissibility displays such sensitivity provided that convexity in the credal state and extended value structure is required.

Seidenfeld, Schervish and Kadane have probed two lines of criticism that call into question the requirement that the credal state be convex.

As I have already reported, Seidenfeld, Kadane and Schervish (1989) reject the approach I have taken, which treats the credal state and extended value structure as separable and derives consensus in the value structure from consensus in credal state and extended value structure. However, they acknowledge the pull of the case for convexity when there is agreement concerning the extended value structure or concerning the credal state. In Seidenfeld, Schervisch and Kadane (2007), they reject the convexity requirement even for these special cases. They insist that sometimes consensus concerning probabilistic relevance needs to be represented in the credal state rather than as a question of fact concerning stochastic independence—something that cannot be achieved if convexity of the credal state is required. So they are prepared to retain E-admissibility but give up the requirement of convexity for credal states.

But giving up the convexity requirement for credal states undermines the case for the convexity of the credal state and extended value structure and thereby weakens the case for E-admissibility as compared to maximality. If the position of SSK is taken seriously, the case for maximality has also to be reconsidered.

Seidenfeld, Schervish and Kadane (2007) discuss the following example. X and Y are confronted with a choice between three options for treating a patient:

T_1 Treating the patient according to protocol for non-allergic patients.
T_2 Treating the patient according to protocol for allergic patients.
T_3 For a fee, letting the weather determine which treatment to adopt: if the weather is sunny, treat as allergic, if cloudy treat as non-allergic.

The decision matrix can be represented as follows where A = patient allergic and S = sunny weather:

	AS	A~S	~AS	~A~S
T_1	0.00	0.00	1.00	1.00
T_2	1.00	1.00	0.00	0.00
T_3	0.99	0.01	0.01	0.99

Agent X has a credal probability distribution of 0.08, 0.32, 0.12 and 0.48 over the four states and agent Y has a credal distribution of 0.48, 0.12, 0.32 and 0.08.

If the consensus credal state for X and Y is the convex hull of the credal states for X and for Y, the 50–50 weighted average of the two credal distributions—0.28, 0.22, 0.22, 0.28—is a permissible distribution and according to that distribution the expected value of T_3 is 0.5478, whereas the expected values of the other two options is 0.5. So T_3 is E-admissible, as are the other two options. But if the only two permissible distributions are those of X and Y, then only T_1 and T_2 are E-admissible.

Seidenfeld, Schervish and Kadane maintain that T_3 is an unacceptable option. It recommends treating the patient for an allergy depending on whether the weather is sunny or not. This recommendation is made in spite of the experts' agreement that the state of the weather has nothing to do with whether the patient is allergic. Insisting on convexity fails to preserve this important consensus.

But what do the experts agree about that is being neglected? To claim that the weather has nothing to do with whether the patient suffers from an allergy is to take a stand on a question of fact. The experts agree that weather and the medical condition of the patient are stochastically independent of one another. That is to say: the chance of the patient being in the allergic condition while the weather is sunny is equal to the product of chance of the patient being in the allergic condition and the chance of the weather at the time being sunny.

This consensus concerns statistical probabilities, which are truth-value-bearing claims. The two probability distributions represent the full beliefs concerning the statistical probability of a patient suffering from an allergy while the weather is sunny. Identifying a consensus between X and Y is specifying the set of seriously possible hypotheses as to what the true statistical probability is. This consensus is represented by a set of probability distributions but these distributions do not represent a consensus credal state for X and Y. The set of distributions represents possibly true hypotheses about the true joint chance distribution of a patient being allergic (or not) while the weather is sunny or cloudy. Unlike a set of credal probability distributions representing a consensus credal state, a set of statistical probability distributions representing a consensus in full belief need not be convex.

Notice that the shared agreement about chances or statistical probabilities is a contraction of both X's initial state of full belief and Y's initial state of full belief and hence differs from the cases we have considered thus far, where X and Y share the same state of full belief at the outset and the focus in reaching consensus in credal state relative to that state of full belief.

Such consensus concerning statistical probabilities does not by itself determine how to evaluate the treatment options. Assessing the permissible expectations of the three options in consensus calls for determining the permissible credal probabilities of the patient to be treated being allergic or not allergic. These credal probabilities may be derived via "direct inference" from information about statistical probabilities together with the available information concerning the circumstances under which the patient is presented to the physicians. Space does not permit detailed elaboration of this oft-told tale. According to a plausible model of the situation, the consensus credal state for the joint space constructed from {allergic, not allergic} and {sunny, not sunny} could be the convex hull of the distributions for X and Y as according to the SSK version.

Now the extreme points of this set of permissible distributions exhibit independence in credal probability of allergic condition and the weather, which is a common feature of the views of X and Y. But this independence is not exhibited in the permissible probability distributions in the interior of the convex hull. So SSK might insist that the consensus credal state does not capture the shared agreement in credal probability judgement concerning probabilistic independence. Even if SSK were right about this, consensus in judgements of probabilistic independence is captured when the probabilities are chances. Consensus in credal state focuses on probability judgements relevant to decision-making.

So let us consider the option T_3. There are two ways to understand this option and to evaluate its expectations. One can use the datum of the weather as *evidence* for reaching a decision as to how to treat the patient. Or one can use the datum as *input* into a program which selects the treatment.

According to the first way, once one obtains the information about the weather and expands one's initial state of full belief, each of the permissible unconditional probabilities concerning the presence or absence of allergy is updated in conformity with confirmational conditionalization and Bayes' Theorem to yield a new set of permissible probabilities for the presence or absence of allergy. The set of permissible probabilities that the patient is allergic is the same prior to finding out the state of the weather and afterward. This is so even if the convexity requirement is imposed on credal states.[8] So the datum used as evidence is irrelevant to both X and Y. Neither one of them would pay to obtain the datum and would rest content with choosing T_1 or T_2 using the credal state for the allergic condition prior to finding out the weather.

If, however, one uses the datum as input into a program for selecting a treatment prior to finding out the weather, one can describe the payoffs (with the penalty SSK mention) and the program becomes E-admissible. But that does not make the information about the weather relevant information. Using data as input is not using it as information. To gain the benefit of using this program, the decision-maker must not find out what the weather is until the program is implemented. Finding out the information is poisonous to the implementation of the program precisely because the datum is irrelevant and, hence, useless information. So X and Y could allow implementation of this program to be E-admissible without acknowledging the datum to be relevant information to the treatment of patients with and without allergies.

The permissible probabilities in the consensus credal state prior to ascertaining the weather are not intended to represent the consensus regarding stochastic independence. That consensus is expressed in the state of full belief. However, the uselessness of deploying the data as evidence is supported by the confirmational irrelevance of the information about the weather. The sense in which the datum about the weather does not alter the unconditional credal probability about medical status which is relevant to determining the uselessness of the datum as evidence is captured by the notion that information about the weather is *confirmationally irrelevant* (Levi 1980) or *epistemologically irrelevant* (Walley 1990) to the question of the presence of allergy. The set of permissible unconditional probability distributions over the hypotheses (the patient has the allergy, the patient does not have the allergy) relative to K where it is not settled as to whether the weather is sunny or not and relative to the expansion of K by adding information about the weather remains the same.

There is a long tradition of advocacy for using data as input in statistical decision-making. C. S. Peirce was one proponent. J. Neyman and E. S. Pearson initiated the classical program in statistics using this idea. This tradition insists that there is an advantage in using data as input over using it as evidence, especially in situations where using the data as evidence renders it confirmationally or epistemically

---

[8] The unconditional probability that the patient is allergic is the marginal distribution in the joint space for allergy and weather. Conditioning on the weather (sunny or cloudy) gives the same probability as the updated one in the case of the extreme points of the initial convex credal state. If we start with an interior point of the initial credal state, the updated credal probability will be different. However, if we consider the set of permissible probability distributions for allergic/not allergic before updating and afterwards, they are the same. In determining E-admissibility, it is the set of permissible distributions for being allergic or not that matters. In that sense, the datum about weather when used as evidence is irrelevant to the issue of the patient's condition.

irrelevant. Indeed, this idea is a cornerstone of an important rationale for classical non-Bayesian approaches to statistical reasoning.

One may wish, as Bayesians do, to call into question the practice of using data as input. But I cannot see that taking one side or the other on this issue calls into question the convexity requirement on credal states. Advocates of the use of the "forward look" and Bayesian critics agree that using data as evidence in such cases is useless because it is confirmationally irrelevant. The issue under dispute is the practice of using data as input. But apologists for doing so, like me, do not think that allowing the practice make such data confirmationally relevant.

In my judgement, when the argument of SSK is taken seriously as it should be, it should be rejected in favor of retaining E-admissibility, separability of probability and utility, and convexity of credal states.

There is more that needs to be said to provide a complete report on the current state of this debate and to support the position I have endorsed. But conceptualizing consensus has to be a centerpiece of any articulate account of the intelligent conduct of problem-solving inquiry. When I began thinking about this matter in the late 1960s, I did not anticipate the complexities that the formal characterization of suspension of judgement, doubt and consensus must confront. Thanks to Sen, Seidenfeld, Kadane and Schervish, I have learned much about the complexities of this project even if I honor their contributions by disagreeing with their conclusions.

REFERENCES

GOODMAN, J. (1988), "Existence of Compromises in Simple Group Decisions", unpub. Ph.D. thesis, Carnegie Mellon University.

LEEDS, S. (1990), "Levi's Decision Theory", *Philosophy of Science*, 57: 158–68.

LEVI, I. (1974), "On Indeterminate Probabilities", *Journal of Philosophy*, 71: 391–418; repr. in Levi (1997).

—— (1980), *The Enterprise of Knowledge* (Cambridge, Mass.: MIT Press).

LEVI, ISAAC (1984), *Decisions and Revisions* (Cambridge: Cambridge University Press).

—— (1985), "Imprecision and Indeterminacy in Probability Judgment", *Philosophy of Science*, 36: 331–40.

—— (1986), *Hard Choices* (Cambridge: Cambridge University Press).

—— (1988), "Possibility and Probability", *Erkenntnis*, 31: 365–86.

—— (1990), "Consensus and Pareto Unanimity", *Journal of Philosophy*, 87, 481–92; repr. in Levi (1997).

—— (1997), *The Covenant of Reason* (Cambridge: Cambridge University Press).

—— (1999), "Value Commitments, Value Conflict and the Separability of Belief and Value", *Philosophy of Science*, 66: 509–33.

MONGIN, P. (1995). "Consistent Bayesian Aggregation", *Journal of Economic Theory*, 66: 313–51.

SEIDENFELD, T. (1993), "Outline of a Theory of Partially Ordered Preferences", *Philosophical Topics*, 21: 173–89.

—— KADANE, J., and SCHERVISH, M. (1989), "On the Shared Preferences of Two Bayesian Decision Makers", *Journal of Philosophy*, 86: 225–44.

—— SCHERVISH, M., and KADANE, J. S. (2007), "Coherent Choice Functions under Uncertainty", paper presented to the Fifth International Symposium on Imprecise Probabilities and their Applications, Prague.

SEN, A. K. (2002), *Rationality and Freedom* (Cambridge, Mass.: Harvard University Press).

WALLEY, P. (1990), *Statistical Reasoning with Imprecise Probabilities* (London: Chapman and Hall).

CHAPTER 12

....

RIGHTS, INDIVIDUAL PREFERENCES AND COLLECTIVE RATIONALITY

....

PRASANTA K. PATTANAIK

I. INTRODUCTION

....

SEN's theorem on the impossibility of a Paretian liberal (Sen 1970a, 1970b), which introduced the first formal formulation of individual rights in welfare economics, constitutes one of the central results in welfare economics. Over the last four decades or so, a voluminous literature on individual rights has developed, drawing inspiration from Sen's theorem. In this paper, I seek to clarify two distinct, though related, issues which have often come up in this literature.[1] I discuss these two issues specifically in the context of what have been called individual rights to liberty in "private" matters,[2] a class of rights much emphasized by Sen. First, what is the role

---

[1] For helpful discussions about rights over many years, I am grateful to Kaushik Basu, Rajat Deb, Wulf Gaertner, the late Stig Kanger, Maurice Salles, Amartya Sen, Robert Sugden, Kotaro Suzumura and Yonsgeng Xu.

[2] See, for example, Riley (1989, 1990), who calls such rights "rights to liberty in purely private matters".

of individual preferences over alternative social states in our notion of individual rights to liberty in private affairs? Earlier, a number of writers, including me, have felt that the notion of individual rights has very little to do with individual preferences. I now believe that this position needs qualification as well as further clarification. Secondly, in the literature on social choice, it is usual to require that, given the preferences of individuals in a society, social choices from different sets of feasible social alternatives should satisfy certain consistency conditions or conditions of collective rationality. What are the implications of individual rights for collective rationality? If we want individuals to have rights at all, can we expect social choices to satisfy the properties of collective rationality so familiar in the literature on social choice? This question, which was first raised by Sugden (1985b), does not seem to have received much attention in the literature on rights. The point is, however, of crucial importance in many ways. In particular, it clarifies our understanding of what an individual's rights in private matters can or cannot be expected to do to protect an individual's preferences with respect to such matters. One of the conclusions that emerges from my discussion is that there can be alternative interpretations of Sen's original theorem on the impossibility of a Paretian liberal and that some of these interpretations are intuitively more attractive than certain others.

The plan of the chapter is as follows. In section II, I introduce some basic notation and definitions. Section III deals with the role of individual preferences in our conception of individual rights to liberty in private affairs. Section IV discusses the problem of collective rationality when individuals are granted rights. In section V, I comment on some alternative interpretations of the formulation of individual rights to be found in Sen (1970a, 1970b).

II. The Notation and Some Basic Definitions

II.1 Individual Preferences and Social Alternatives

Let $N = \{1, 2, \ldots, n\}$ denote the set of individuals constituting a society. An individual whose rights are under consideration will be called the *principal individual*.

X denotes the set of all conceivable social states. A social state (or, equivalently, a social alternative) is a description of the state of affairs in a society. The concept of a social state can be interpreted in a very broad fashion so as to include a description of institutions such as the structure of rights.[3] Alternatively, it can be interpreted, as

---

[3] For such a broad interpretation, see Arrow (1963: 90–1) and Pattanaik and Suzumura (1996: 197) among others.

in much of welfare economics, in a relatively narrow fashion. I shall use this narrow interpretation so that the description of the rights structure will not be included in the notion of a social state.

$\Re$ denotes the set of all orderings defined over X. The elements $(R_1, \ldots, R_n), (R_1', \ldots, R_n'), \ldots$ of $\Re^n$ will be interpreted as profiles of individual preference orderings with R_i, R_i', etc., denoting the ordering of individual i in the relevant profile of orderings. For all $i \in N$, and all $x, y \in X$, $x P_i y$ if and only if $(x R_i y$ and not $y R_i x)$.

I shall assume a particular structure for the set, X, of all conceivable social states. The motivation for this structure arises from the following consideration. In his early contributions on individual rights, Sen (1970a, 1970b) was mainly concerned with an individual's right to liberty with respect to matters in her private life, such as her right to sleep on her back or on her stomach, her right to read or not to read a book, her right to have her walls painted pink or white, and so on, though the literature that followed Sen (1970a, 1970b) often considered rights in general. For brevity, I shall call individual rights to liberty in private affairs[4] p-rights. I shall focus on p-rights which have a relatively simple formal structure, though some of the things that I say apply to a much wider range of rights. In the case of most p-rights, the principal individual can ensure for himself a certain state of affairs relating to his private life. Depending on the nature of the right, the state of affairs may be sleeping on his back, practicing Buddhism, having his walls painted pink, etc. The individual may also have a combination of what, from an intuitive point of view, are really different rights. In that case, the alternative states of affairs relating to his private life that the individual can ensure may be more complex, such as sleeping on his back *and* having his walls painted pink *and* practicing Hinduism, sleeping on his back *and* having his walls painted white *and* practicing Buddhism, etc. Given his p-rights, typically the principal individual ensures a feature or state of affairs relating to his private life by simply choosing that feature or state of affairs directly.[5] In discussing such rights I shall use the following formal framework first introduced by Gibbard (1974). For all $i \in N$, the set of all conceivable (mutually exclusive) features or states of affairs relating to the private life of individual i will be denoted by X_i ($\infty > \#X_i \geq 2$). There are some aspects of a social state which do not relate to anybody's personal life; these are what may be called the public aspects of a social state. The (non-empty) set of all alternative descriptions of the public aspects will be denoted by X_0. I assume that $X = X_0 \times X_1 \times \ldots \times X_n$. Let

---

[4] Note that I am using the concept of an individual's private affairs as a primitive and, hence, undefined, notion. The issue of how one should conceptualize "private affairs" is, however, important and deserves independent analysis

[5] Of course, the principal individual's p-right imposes certain obligations on other individuals; I am assuming that other individuals fulfill these obligations and that the fulfillment of these obligations by other individuals figures in the description of the public aspects of the relevant social state.

$\mathbb{Z}$ denote the set of all subsets A of X such that $A = A_0 \times A_1 \times \ldots \times A_n$ for some non-empty subsets $A_0, A_1, \ldots$, and A_n of $X_0, X_1, \ldots$, and X_n, respectively. I shall assume that $\mathbb{Z}$ is the set of all possible feasible sets of social states with which the society may be confronted. For every $A \in \mathbb{Z}$, A will be said to be decomposable into $A_0, A_1, \ldots$, and A_n if and only if $A_0, A_1, \ldots$ and A_n are the (unique) non-empty subsets of $X_0, X_1, \ldots$, and X_n, respectively, such that $A = A_0 \times A_1 \times \ldots \times A_n$. Let $A \in \mathbb{Z}$ be decomposable into $A_0, A_1, \ldots$, and A_n. Then, for all $i \in N$, A_{-i} will denote $A_0 \times A_1 \times \ldots \times A_{i-1} \times A_{i+1} \times \ldots \times A_n$. Given $A \in \mathbb{Z}$, a_{-i}, a'_{-i}, etc. will denote the elements of A_{-i}. For all $x_{-i} \in X_{-i}$ and all $y_i \in X_i$, (x_{-i}, y_i) will denote $z \in X$ such that, for all $j \neq i$, $z_j = x_j$ and $z_i = y_i$. For all $x, y \in X$ and all $i \in N$, x and y will be said to be i-variants if and only if $x_i \neq y_i$ and, for all $k \in \{0, 1, \ldots, n\} - \{i\}$, $x_k = y_k$.

II.2 Social Ranking Rules and Social Choice Rules

A *social ranking rule* is a function f which, for every profile $(R_1, \ldots, R_n) \in \mathfrak{R}^n$, specifies exactly one reflexive and connected binary relation R defined over X (the binary relation R has the usual interpretation as the society's weak preference relation over X). A *social choice rule* is a function C which, for every profile $(R_1, \ldots, R_n) \in \mathfrak{R}^n$ and every $A \in \mathbb{Z}$, specifies exactly one non-empty subset, $C(A, R_1, \ldots, R_n)$, of A. $C(A, R_1, \ldots, R_n)$ is to be interpreted as the set of social states "chosen" by the society when the set of feasible social alternatives is A and the profile of individual orderings is $(R_1, \ldots, R_n)$. The social ranking rule and the social choice rule can be thought of as two alternative ways of conceptualizing the social decision process. Sen's (1970a, 1970b) original formulation of rights was in the framework of a social ranking rule, but this formulation was later translated into the language of social choice rules. As we shall see in section V, the specific way in which this translation is carried out is of considerable intuitive importance.

III. Rights and Individual Preferences

III.1 The Formal Structure of p-Rights

p-rights constitute a subclass of what Feinberg (1973, 1980) calls active rights. The active rights of an individual, say, i, typically take the following form:

$$i \text{ can see to it that } \gamma_{i1}; i \text{ can see to it that } \gamma_{i2}, \ldots; \tag{1}$$

and

for every individual $j \neq i$, j has a set of obligations, $\Delta^{ij} = \{\delta_1^{ij}, \delta_2^{ij}, \ldots, \}$,

imposed on j by i's active rights.   (2)

In the case of p-rights, $\gamma_{i1}, \gamma_{i2}, \ldots$ indicate alternative states of affairs relating to i's private life. For example, if the right we are considering is the right to choose a shirt of any color from one's wardrobe and if only red, blue, and yellow shirts are available to i, then γ_{i1} in (1) may stand for "i wears a red shirt", γ_{i2} may stand for "i wears a blue shirt", and so on. Similarly, if j ($j \neq i$) happens to be i's employer, then δ_1^{ij} may denote j's obligation not to fire i from his job for wearing a yellow shirt, δ_2^{ij} may denote j's obligation not to harass i for wearing a red shirt, and so on (it is possible that i's active rights do not impose any obligation on a specific individual j, in which case Δ^{ij} will be empty). While (1) reflects the power that i enjoys under the right, (2) usually incorporates the immunities that i has under the right.[6] Sometimes the structure of p-rights may be somewhat more complex insofar as it may involve other intuitive dimensions, such as claims of power and immunity.[7] Consider, for example, the right to eat a vegetarian diet. It is possible to think of this right as including the principal individual's claim against the producers of processed food to have information about whether the processed food sold by them contains any non-vegetarian ingredients, with a corresponding obligation of the producers of processed food to supply such information. In that case, there will be a claim aspect of the principal individual's right to be a vegetarian[8]—an aspect which will be reflected by suitably incorporating in (2) the obligation of producers of processed food to reveal whether the food marketed by them contains any non-vegetarian components.

Note that neither (1) nor (2) has any reference to the principal individual's preferences, desires, intentions or motives. The position with regard to the other individuals in this respect is, however, different. Going back to the example of the right to practice any religion, note that the obligation that i's right to practice any religion imposes on i's employer is not that i's employer must not fire i for any reason whatsoever but that he must not fire i to punish him for practicing a particular religion. Thus, the obligations of individuals other than the principal individual cannot be described by just listing in an "objective fashion" the actions that they may or may not take; the motives, intentions and desires underlying their actions may be important in deciding whether they are doing something that violates i's right to practice any religion.

---

[6] See Hohfeld (1913) and Kanger and Kanger (1972).
[7] See Kanger and Kanger (1972) for a discussion of the notions of power, immunity, claim, and freedom that may be involved in rights.
[8] Cf. Sen's (1996: 158) comments on the right to choose one's diet.

The point is quite general. All active rights, including p-rights, grant certain immunities to the principal individual and these immunities are reflected in the obligation of other individuals not to do certain things to penalize the principal individual for exercising in a particular fashion the powers given to him by the rights. Thus, even when we are concerned only with the formal structure of active rights, the desires and motives behind the actions of individuals other than the principal individual would seem to be relevant.[9] It does, however, seem true that the primary individual's preferences do not enter into the articulation of the structure of active rights in terms of (1) and (2).

Finally, as I have mentioned earlier, one characteristic of p-rights of an individual i, which distinguishes them from many other active rights of i, is that typically, under her p-rights, i herself directly chooses one of the features of the social state, namely, the feature relating to his private affairs.

III.2 Two Alternative Approaches to p-Rights

When one says that i's right to practice the religion of her choice has a structure for which appropriately specified versions of (1) and (2) hold, one is simply making a statement about how we use, in ordinary language, the phrase "the right to practice the religion of one's choice". If someone just says that, in the USA, a person has the right to be a Christian or a Muslim or a Hindu, we would normally understand him as saying that, in the USA, a person can adopt any one of these religions with immunity from certain types of punitive actions by other individuals. Thus, in some ways, the analysis of the structure of p-rights in terms of (1), (2), etc. is analogous to the analysis of what we mean when we make the moral statement that John ought to do θ. In both cases, we are concerned with the formal structure of important words in our language. Several philosophers and legal theorists, including Hohfeld (1913) and Kanger and Kanger (1972), focus on the formal structure of rights; and so does the more recent game-form representation of rights.[10] I shall call this approach to the notion of rights the *form-based approach*; it is primarily concerned with the formal structure of rights and proceeds to understand it by analyzing how we use the word "rights" in different contexts.

The form-based approach to rights, by its very nature, is limited in its scope. It cannot answer a host of substantive questions about rights. In particular, it cannot answer substantive questions of the following type:

[9] This is a point that I did not quite appreciate until I listened to a seminar presentation of Martin van Hees. See van Hees (1990) for a published version of this point. See also Pattanaik and Xu (2007), where it is discussed in some detail.

[10] See Gärdenfors (1981), Sugden (1985a), Seidl (1986) and Gaertner, Pattanaik and Suzumura (1992) among others. The conceptual origin of the game-form approach to rights lies in Nozick (1974: 164–6), though Nozick did not explicitly use the concept of a game form.

(a) Why should people have the right to practice the religions of their choice? Are there circumstances under which people should be denied this right?

(b) If people are given the right to practice the religions of their choice, how would they exercise their right and what would be the outcomes?

(c) How does the society decide whether or not people should have the right to practice the religions of their choice?

One can, however, approach the notion of p-rights, or the notion of rights in general, from perspectives other than that of the form-based approach. For example, in formulating the notion of p-rights, one can focus on the purpose(s) that p-rights are intended to serve rather than the formal structure of these rights. I believe that Sen's (1970a, 1970b) classical formulation of rights reflects a *purpose-based approach* to p-rights.

III.3 The Purpose of p-Rights and Individual Preferences

What purposes are p-rights intended to serve? Alternatively, how do we justify p-rights? This, of course, is a general version of question (a) in section III.2. At the risk of emphasizing the obvious, it may be useful to distinguish this issue from the issue of how a society should choose a particular system of p-rights, given the individuals' preferences with respect to alternative systems of p-rights and the social outcomes that may emerge from them (see question (c) in section III.2)—an issue that has been discussed in some detail in Pattanaik and Suzumura (1992). If most individuals in a society prefer to have a rights structure that empowers every individual in the society to practice whatever religion he/she likes, at one level that may constitute an adequate reason for that society's decision to give individuals that right. Nevertheless, if individual i holds the ethical belief that every person in India should have the right to practice whatever religion he/she wants to practice, and if i is asked to justify his ethical position, then it would hardly be considered an adequate response from i if he simply appeals to the fact that most people in India believe that every individual in India should have that right (see Dworkin's distinction between "a thin theory" about how a political constitution is to be selected in a society where people have different preferences over constitutions, and a full theory about the ethical justification of these alternative constitutions: Dworkin 1984: 157). Thus, the question of how society should aggregate the different opinions of individuals so as to choose a particular set of p-rights to be given to individuals is very different from the question of how we can justify p-rights or what constitutes the purpose of p-rights. It is the latter question with which I am concerned here.

It is clear that one major purpose of giving such rights to an individual, i, is so that i's desires and preferences with respect to matters in i's private life will prevail and will not be overruled by the possibly contrary desires, with respect to matters

in i's private life, of individuals other than i. To use Dworkin's terminology, i's
p-rights can be viewed as i's "trumps" against the intrusive desires of other people
about i's private life. I shall presently come to the important issue of what exactly is
meant by i's preferences with respect to his private affairs, but first I would like to
note that, while upholding the individual's preferences with respect to his private
life is a major goal of p-rights, it may not be the only goal. Consider a society where
the central planner is aware of every individual's preferences and chooses the social
state in such a way that every individual's preferences with respect to her private life
are respected (in whatever way we choose to interpret the notion of an individual's
preferences with respect to her private life being respected). In general, one may feel
that such a society does not entirely achieve what one believes to be the purpose of
rights to liberty in private affairs. We may believe that one of the purposes of such
rights is to ensure that an individual has the liberty to make choices in matters
relating to her private life herself. In that case, it may not be enough that the private
affairs of an individual are arranged according to the desires of the individual; we
may also attach value to the objective that the individual should be able to arrange
those matters in that fashion *herself*. Thus, p-rights may have purposes or justi-
fications that go beyond the objective of ensuring that an individual's preferences
about matters regarding her private life will be respected. I shall, however, focus
exclusively on the objective of respecting the individual's preferences about private
matters.

What exactly is meant by respecting an individual's preferences with respect to
matters regarding her private life? The answer is not obvious. It will not do to say
simply that the purpose of i's right to choose the color of his shirt is to ensure that
whatever "preference" i may have over his shirts of different colors will prevail. The
reason is that whether i "prefers" a white shirt over a blue shirt or the other way
round may very well depend on whether j is wearing a white shirt or a blue shirt.[11]
Consider the following requirements for a social choice rule, which seek to capture
in different ways the implications of respecting the preferences of an individual, i,
with respect to her private affairs.

There exist i-variant $x, y \in X$ such that, for all $(R_1, \ldots, R_n) \in \Re^n$, and all

$A \in \mathbb{Z}$, if $x, y \in A$, then $[x P_i y$ implies $y \notin C(A, R_1, \ldots, R_n)]$

and $[y P_i x$ implies $x \notin C(A, R_1, \ldots, R_n)]$. $\qquad$ (3)

For all i-variant $x, y \in X$, all $(R_1, \ldots, R_n) \in \Re^n$, and all $A \in \mathbb{Z}$,

if $x, y \in A$, then $[x P_i y$ implies $y \notin C(A, R_1, \ldots, R_n)]$ and

$[y P_i x$ implies $x \notin C(A, R_1, \ldots, R_n)]$. $\qquad$ (4)

---

[11] To use the terminology of Hammond (1982), i's preferences may not be "privately
unconditional".

There exist i-variant $x, y \in X$ such that, for all $(R_1, \ldots, R_n) \in \mathfrak{R}^n$,

[if $x P_i y$, then $C(\{x, y\}, R_1, \ldots, R_n) = \{x\}$, and, if $y P_i x$,

then $C(\{x, y\}, R_1, \ldots, R_n) = \{y\}$]. (5)

For all i-variant $x, y \in X$ and all $(R_1, \ldots, R_n) \in \mathfrak{R}^n$, [if $x P_i y$, then

$C(\{x, y\}, R_1, \ldots, R_n) = \{x\}$, and, if $y P_i x$, then

$C(\{x, y\}, R_1, \ldots, R_n) = \{y\}$]. (6)

For all $A \in Z$ and all $(R_1, \ldots, R_n) \in \mathfrak{R}^n$, if there exists $x_i \in A_i$ such that, for

all $u_{-i} \in A_{-i}$ and all $y_i \in A_i - \{x_i\}$, $(a_{-i}, x_i) P_i (a_{-i}, y_i)$, then

$C(A, R_1, \ldots, R_n) \subseteq \{z \in A : \text{for all } a_{-i} \in A_{-i} \text{ and all}$

$y_i \in A_i - \{z_i\}, (a_{-i}, z_i) P_i (a_{-i}, y_i)\}$. (7)

(3) requires the existence of social states x and y such that: x and y differ only with respect to some aspect of i's private life; if x and y are both feasible and i strictly prefers x to y, then y does not emerge as a social outcome; and if x and y are both feasible and i strictly prefers y to x, then x does not emerge as a social outcome. (4) requires that, for all social states x and y such that x and y differ only with respect to some aspect of i's private life, if x and y are both feasible and i strictly prefers x to y, then y does not emerge as a social outcome, and if x and y are both feasible and i strictly prefers y to x, then x does not emerge as a social outcome. Clearly (4) is stronger than (3). (5) requires the existence of at least two distinct social states x and y such that: x and y differ only with respect to some aspect of i's private life; if x and y are the only two feasible social alternatives and i strictly prefers x to y, then x emerges as the sole social outcome; and if x and y are the only two feasible social alternatives and i strictly prefers y to x, then y emerges as the sole social outcome. (6) is much stronger than (5) since (6) states that, for all distinct social states x and y such that x and y differ only with respect to some aspect of i's private life, if x and y are the only two feasible social alternatives and i strictly prefers x to y, then x emerges as the sole social outcome, and if x and y are the only two feasible social alternatives and i strictly prefers y to x, then y emerges as the sole social outcome. What (7) basically requires is this. Suppose the set of feasible social alternatives is given by $A \in Z$. Suppose the preference profile is such that, for some $x_i \in A_i$, x_i "strictly dominates" every $y_i \in A_i - \{x_i\}$, i.e. for every $a_{-i} \in A_{-i}$ and every $y_i \in A_i - \{x_i\}$, i strictly prefers (a_{-i}, x_i) to (a_{-i}, y_i). Then every social state that emerges as a social outcome must have such "strictly dominant" x_i as i's personal feature. The implication relations among (3), (4), (5), (6) and (7) are given in Fig. 12.1.

Suppose we identify any one of (3), (4), (5), (6) and (7) as reflecting a purpose that p-rights are intended to serve. To take a specific example, let it be (3). Then there are two different ways in which we can use (3) in a purpose-based approach

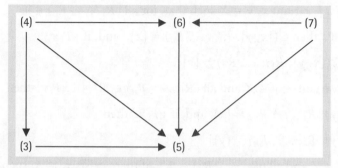

Fig. 12.1. Relations between conditions (3) through (7)

to p-rights. First, one can say that p-rights for any individual i must be *defined* in such a way that they will imply (3), so that, if (3) does not hold, one will say that i does not enjoy any p-rights. Alternatively, one can take (3) simply as a purpose which i's p-rights are intended to serve, without treating (3) as something implied by i's p-rights by definition. In the second case, we retain a conception of p-rights that is independent of the purpose(s) which p-rights are intended to serve, and therefore, if (3) does not hold, we say that it may be either because i does not have any p-rights at all or because i has p-rights, as we conceive them independently, but they do not serve the purpose of ensuring (3). The second route would seem to be more attractive. After all, when we talk about the purpose of p-rights, our language itself suggests that we have a conception of p-rights which is independent of what we may think to be their purpose. It seems to me that some amount of conceptual flexibility will be lost if, by definition, we conflate the concept of a p-right and the purposes that the p-right is supposed to serve. I shall therefore take the second route, but the reasoning that follows will not be much different if we choose to take the first route.

In considering whether p-rights serve the purpose of ensuring that a specific statement in the set consisting of (3) through (7) will hold, one needs to make some assumptions about how p-rights are exercised. This is obvious, since statements (3) through (7) are formulated in terms of what social alternatives should or should not be chosen by a society depending on the principal individual's preferences over social states, and without making assumptions about how, given a preference profile, the individuals exercise their p-rights, it is not possible to say what social outcome will or will not emerge in a society that abides by these rights. Nor is there any obvious comprehensive answer to the question of how people exercise their rights, given their preferences over social states. For our purpose, however, we do not need a comprehensive answer to this question.

Consider first (7), which implies both (6) and (5). Consider a society which has a system of p-rights with the structure described in section III.1. Then:

(i) given a set, A ($A \in \mathbb{Z}$), of feasible social alternatives, for every $i \in N$, (1) and (2) hold, with γ_{i1}, γ_{i2}, etc. being interpreted as elements of A_i and with corresponding interpretations of the set of obligations Δ^{ij} for every individual $j \neq i$; and

(ii) every individual i herself directly chooses an element of A_i and thereby ensures that that element will be realized.

Assume that an individual, i, knows what is the set, A, of feasible social alternatives. Now suppose there exists $x_i \in A_i$, such that, for every $a_{-i} \in A_{-i}$, i strictly prefers (x_i, a_{-i}) to (y_i, a_{-i}) for all $y_i \in A_i$. Then, given the mild assumption that i knows that A is the set of feasible social states, it seems most plausible that i will choose x_i, which "strictly dominates" every other element in A_i. Therefore, it is reasonable to say that, if (7) constitutes a purpose of giving i the right to liberty in private affairs, then such rights will indeed achieve that purpose. Since (7) implies (6) and (5), a similar conclusion holds for (6) and (5) too. I now believe that the purpose of p-rights implicit in Sen's (1970a, 1970b) original formulation is best understood in terms of (5). It is true that (5) constitutes a very weak version of what one may mean by respecting i's preferences with respect to his private affairs, but given that Sen (1970a, 1970b) was proving an impossibility result, this weakness of (5) is a strength of the theorem. Outside impossibility results, however, one may like to have a condition that captures as much of our intuition about respecting an individual's preferences regarding private matters as possible. In such contexts (7), which is stronger than (5) and (6) but is still intuitively compelling, has an edge over both (5) and (6).

The case of (3) and (4) is different from that of (7), (6) and (5). Consider (3), which has been discussed at considerable length in the literature on rights. Gaertner, Pattanaik and Suzumura (1992) use an example to show how p-rights may not be able to ensure (3), which is weaker than (4). I reproduce the example, which I shall use for a different purpose later. In the Gaertner–Pattanaik–Suzumura example, we have two individuals, 1 and 2, each of whom has a blue shirt and a white shirt. The right under consideration is the right to choose the color of one's shirt. The public features are all assumed to be fixed (it is implicitly assumed that no individual does anything to penalize the other individual for whatever shirt the other individual may choose) and the two individuals choose their respective shirts simultaneously and independently. Assume that (3) holds for $i = 1$ and for some some i-variant $x, y \in A_1 \times A_2 = \{w, b\} \times \{w, b\}$—say, for $x = (w, w)$ and $y = (b, w)$. Since the public features are assumed to be fixed, a social state is completely described by the shirts that both individuals choose. There are four social states: (w, b) (i.e. white shirt for 1 and blue shirt for 2), (b, w), (w, w) and (b, b). The four social states and the two individuals' ordinal utilities from each of these social states are given in Table 12.1.

It is assumed that neither individual knows anything about the other individual's preferences and so the notion of Nash equilibrium does not apply here (note that a Nash equilibrium in pure strategies does not exist here). In choosing his shirt, each individual is assumed to follow the "maximin" principle and, accordingly, 1 chooses

Table 12.1. The right to choose the color of one's shirt: Gaertner, Pattanaik and Suzumura's example

	2	
1	w	b
w	10,8	7,9
b	8,10	9,7

b and 2 chooses w. As a result, (b, w) emerges as the social outcome. This contradicts our assumption that (3) holds for $i = 1$, $x = (w, w)$ and $y = (b, w)$. A similar contradiction arises for any other specification of i-variants $x, y \in A_1 \times A_2$. Since we intuitively feel that, in this example, each individual is fully enjoying his right to choose the color of his shirt, it seems that giving individual i a right to liberty in matters relating to his private life does not ensure that (3) will hold. Of course, the same conclusion holds for the stronger statement (4). Thus, it follows that, if one considers (3) or (4) to be a purpose that i's rights to liberty in private matters is intended to serve, then such rights cannot serve that purpose.[12] In the following section, I discuss the intuitive origin of the difficulty that arises if we consider (3) or (4) to be a purpose of giving p-rights to an individual i, a difficulty that does not arise in the case of (5), (6) or (7).

IV. Collective Rationality and Rights

A basic idea that recurs in much of the literature on social choice is that, given the profile of individual orderings, social choice from different feasible sets must satisfy certain consistency conditions. Numerous conditions of collective rationality have been discussed in the literature. For our purpose, however, it will be enough to consider one of the most widely used conditions, Chernoff's condition, and some weaker variants of it.

[12] Note that, if one chooses to *define* i's p-rights in such a way that the definition implies (3) or (4), then the same example will show that the definition does not conform to our intuitions about p-rights.

Let C be a social choice rule. Then:

C satisfies Chernoff's condition if and only if, for all $(R_1, \ldots, R_n) \in \mathfrak{R}^n$ and for all

$A, B \in \mathbb{Z}$, if $A \subseteq B$, then for all $x \in (A - C(A, R_1, \ldots, R_n))$,

$x \in (B - C(B, R_1, \ldots, R_n))$; [13]

and

C satisfies non-reversal if and only if for all $(R_1, \ldots, R_n) \in \mathfrak{R}^n$, all $A, B \in \mathbb{Z}$,

and all $x, y \in X$, if $x, y \in A \subseteq B$ and $\{x\} = C(A, R_1, \ldots, R_n)$,

then $\{y\} \neq C(B, R_1, \ldots, R_n)$. [14]

Chernoff's condition requires that, given a profile of individual orderings, a social state which belongs to a feasible set but is socially rejected for that feasible set must continue to be socially rejected if the feasible set is expanded by adding some more social states. Non-reversal is weaker than Chernoff's condition. Non-reversal requires that, given a profile of individual orderings, if, to start with, x is the only option to be socially chosen from a given set of feasible alternatives which contains y ($y \neq x$), then, after an expansion of the set of feasible social alternatives, y must not be the only socially chosen option.

Note that, though (5) is strictly weaker than (3), (5) and Chernoff's condition together imply (3). So, if p-rights can ensure (5) but not (3), then the reason clearly lies with Chernoff's condition. Indeed, a slight extension of the Gaertner–Pattanaik–Suzumura example reproduced above shows that, for some preference profiles and for certain plausible rules of behavior, the outcomes that result from p-rights can run afoul of the following condition, which is weaker than non-reversal:

For all $(R_1, \ldots, R_n) \in \mathfrak{R}^n$, all $B \in \mathbb{Z}$, and all i-variant $x, y \in B$,

$\quad$ if $x P_i y$ and $C(\{x, y\}, R_1, \ldots, R_n) = \{x\}$, then $C(B, R_1, \ldots, R_n) \neq \{y\}$.   (8)

To see this, recall that, in the example of Gaertner, Pattanaik and Suzumura, the two individuals' exercise of their respective rights leads the society to choose (b, w) when the set of feasible social alternatives is $\{(w, w), (b, b), (w, b), (b, w)\}$. Now assume that individual 2 has only one shirt, w, while individual 1 continues to have two shirts, w and b, so that the set of feasible social states is now $\{(w, w), (b, w)\}$. Assume that the two individuals' preferences over $\{(w, w), (b, b), (w, b), (b, w)\}$ are the same as before. Then it is clear that, in this new situation, 1 will choose w and

---

[13] This condition, originally due to Chernoff (1954), has been called Property α by Sen (1970b: 17).

[14] This is a somewhat stronger version of a condition introduced by Sugden (1985b: 167); the weaker condition of Sugden assumes that the set A figuring in the statement of non-reversal here is a two-element set.

Table 12.2. The right to choose the color of one's shirt: a second example

1	2		
	w	b	r
w	0,0	0,0	4,0
b	3,0	3,0	3,3
r	0,0	3,5	0,0

the social outcome will be (w, w). This, of course, violates (8). Sugden (1985b) has made the same point in a somewhat different framework. In Sugden's example, the right involved is the right to marry another consenting person. This right, however, does not fit very well into our framework, since it does not empower an individual to determine the arrangement of her private affairs by herself: individual i cannot, by herself, see to it that she will marry j, though, if j has already agreed to marry i should i want to marry j, then i can see to it that she will marry j.

In constructing their example, Gaertner, Pattanaik and Suzumura assume that the individuals are completely ignorant about each other's preferences and follow the maximin rule in choosing their actions. The use of the maximin rule does not seem unreasonable if the individuals are completely ignorant about each other's preferences, so that they do not even have probabilistic beliefs about the other individual's preferences. What happens if we allow for complete information? In the presence of complete information and with very plausible notions of game-theoretic equilibrium, one can still show that, for some preference profile, the social outcomes that result from the exercise of p-rights can violate non-reversal. Consider the following variant of the shirt-choice example. To start with, we assume that each of the two individuals has three shirts: white (w), blue (b) and red (r). There are now nine feasible social alternatives: (w, w), (b, r), etc. The ordinal utility numbers of the two individuals for each of the nine feasible outcomes are shown in Table 12.2.

It is easy to check that if the two individuals follow the behavioral rule underlying the notion of dominance solvability, then (w, r) will be the social outcome. Now suppose the situation changes so that, the preference profile remaining the same, 1 has two shirts, w and r, while 2 continues to have three shirts, w, b, and r. Then we have a set of six feasible social alternatives, which constitutes a proper subset of the set of nine social alternatives we started with. Again, if both individuals follow the logic of dominance solvability, then the social outcome in the new situation will be (r, b). This violates non-reversal.[15]

---

[15] A similar example has been used by Dasgupta, Kumar and Pattanaik (2000) to show how a player's choices of strategies in games can violate very basic conditions of "consistency".

The fact that, for some preference profile, the exercise of p-rights can lead to violations of very weak consistency conditions for social outcomes in different situations is not really surprising. After all, given p-rights, we have a social decision procedure which is at least partly decentralized and under which each individual, through his choice of a personal feature, independently determines only one of the many aspects of the social outcome. There does not seem to be any clear intuitive reason why, for every plausible behavioral rule (reflected in some plausible game-theoretic concept of equilibrium) for the individuals concerned, such a decentralized decision-making procedure will satisfy consistency conditions such as Chernoff's condition and non-reversal. If the violation of such consistency conditions is a serious problem, the problem seems to be inherent in p-rights.

V. THE IMPOSSIBILITY
OF A PARETIAN LIBERAL

In light of my preceding discussion, I now consider some alternative versions of Sen's (1970a, 1970b) theorem on the impossibility of the Paretian liberal in its original form. Though the theorem is a part of our folklore in welfare economics, I restate it here, since I need to refer to the exact conditions involved in the theorem. Recall that Sen's theorem was proved in a framework where no specific structure was imposed on X or any other set of feasible social states; in particular, in Sen's framework, there was no assumption regarding "decomposability" of sets of feasible social alternatives. I restate Sen's theorem as follows, using the framework I have employed above:

Theorem 1. *(Sen 1970a, 1970b). There does not exist any social ranking rule which satisfies the following conditions simultaneously:*

P*-acyclicity: for every profile* $(R_1, \ldots, R_n) \in \Re^n$, *the asymmetric factor, P, of R is acyclic;*

minimal liberalism: *there exist at least two distinct individuals, j and k, and $x, y, z, w \in x$, such that x and y are j-variants, z and w are k-variants, and [for all $(R_1, \ldots, R_n) \in \Re^n$, (if $x P_j y$, then $x P y$), (if $y P_j x$, then $y P x$), (if $z P_k w$, then $z P w$), and (if $w P_k z$, then $w P z$)];*

weak Pareto criterion: *for every profile $(R_1, \ldots, R_n) \in \Re^n$ and for all $x, y \in X$, if $x P_i y$ for all $i \in N$, then $x P y$.*

Theorem 1 uses the social ranking rule as the basic concept. For a social choice rule, the following theorem is the exact counterpart of Theorem 1.

Theorem 2. *There does not exist any social choice rule which satisfies all of the following conditions:*

> *for all $(R_1, \ldots, R_n) \in \Re^n$, there exists a reflexive and connected binary relation*
>
> R, *defined over X, such that the asymmetric factor, P, of R is acyclic,*
>
> *and for all $A \in \mathbb{Z}$, $C(A; R_1, \ldots, R_n)$ is the set of R-greatest elements in A;* $\quad$ (9)
>
> *there exist distinct $j, k \in N$ such that (5) holds for $i = j$ and $i = k$;* $\qquad$ (10)
>
> *for every profile $(R_1, \ldots, R_n) \in \Re^n$ and for all $\{x, y\} \in Z$, if $x P_i y$*
>
> *for all $i \in N$, then $C(\{x, y\}; R_1, \ldots, R_n) = \{x\}$.* $\qquad$ (11)

We know that the impossibility result in Theorem 2 can be strengthened by weakening (9) to Chernoff's condition while leaving (10) and (11) intact, thus generating this theorem:

Theorem 3. *There does not exist any social choice rule C which satisfies Chernoff's condition, (10) and (11).*

We also know that Theorem 3 can be strengthened to this:

Theorem 4. *There does not exist any social choice rule which satisfies the following conditions simultaneously:*

> *there exist distinct $j, k \in N$ such that (3) holds for $i = j$ and $i = k$;* $\qquad$ (12)
>
> *for all $(R_1, \ldots, R_n) \in \Re^n$, all $A \in Z$, and all $x, y \in A$, if $x P_i y$ for all*
>
> $i \in N$, *then $y \notin C(A; R_1, \ldots, R_n)$.* $\qquad$ (13)

Thus, in passing from Theorem 2, which is the exact choice-based counterpart of the original version of Sen's theorem stated in terms of a social ranking, to Theorem 4, one steadily strengthens the impossibility result, which, for the purpose of the negative result, is an analytical gain. It is, however, important to note that when, in passing from Theorem 3 to Theorem 4, we replace Chernoff's condition, (10), and (11) by (12) and (13), we introduce a major change from an intuitive point of view, though (12) is strictly weaker than Chernoff's condition and (10) taken together, and (13) is strictly weaker than Chernoff's condition and (11) taken together. This is because, while one can very plausibly take (10) to be a minimal purpose of giving p-rights to at least two individuals, it is difficult to give such an interpretation to (12), which involves (3). We are then left with two conditions in Theorem 4 such that neither of the conditions can be linked to p-rights very well. Many writers, including me in the past, have viewed (3) as an essential component of Sen's purpose-based approach to the p-rights of an individual.[16] There is, however, no compelling reason to do so. It seems much more appropriate to interpret Sen's purpose-based formulation in terms of (5) rather than (3). If we take (3) to be a purpose of giving p-rights to i, then we shall set up a goal that the p-rights of i, in general, cannot achieve. In contrast, as a minimal purpose of giving p-rights to individual i, (5) seems unexceptionable.

References

ARROW, K. J. (1963), *Social Choice and Individual Values* (New York: Wiley).

CHERNOFF, H. (1954), "Rational Selection of Decision Functions", *Econometrica*, 22: 422–43.

DASGUPTA, I., KUMAR, S., and PATTANAIK, P. K. (2000), "Consistent Choice and Falsifiability of the Maximization Hypothesis", in R. Pollin (ed.), *Capitalism, Socialism, and Radical Political Economy* (Cheltenham: Edward Elgar).

DWORKIN, R. (1984), "Rights as Trumps", in J. Waldron (ed.), *Theories of Rights* (Oxford: Oxford University Press).

FEINBERG, J. (1973), *Social Philosophy* (Englewood Cliffs, NJ: Prentice Hall).

—— (1980), *Rights, Justice and the Bounds of Liberty: Essays in Social Philosophy* (Princeton, NJ: Princeton University Press).

GAERTNER, W., PATTANAIK, P. K., and SUZUMURA, K. (1992), "Individual Rights Revisited", *Economica*, 59: 161–77.

GÄRDENFORS, P. (1981), "Rights, Games and Social Choice", *Noûs*, 15: 341–56.

GIBBARD, A. (1974), "A Pareto Consistent Libertarian Claim", *Journal of Economic Theory*, 7: 388–410.

HAMMOND, P. (1982), "Liberalism, Independent Rights and the Pareto Principle", in L. J. Cohen, J. Łoś, H. Pfeiffer and K.-P. Podewski (eds), *Logic, Methodology and the Philosophy of Science* (Amsterdam: North-Holland).

HAMMOND, P. (1996), "Game Forms versus Social Choice Rules as Models of Rights", in K. J. Arrow, A. Sen and K. Suzumura (eds), *Social Choice Re-examined*, vol. 2 (New York: St Martin's Press).

HOHFELD, W. N. (1913), "Some Fundamental Legal Conceptions as Applied in Judicial Reasoning", *Yale Law Journal*, 23: 16–59.

KANGER, S., and KANGER, H. (1972), "Rights and Parliamentarism", in R. E. Olson and A. M. Paul (eds), *Contemporary Philosophy in Scandinavia* (Baltimore: Johns Hopkins Press).

NOZICK, R. (1974), *Anarchy, State and Utopia* (Oxford: Basil Blackwell).

PATTANAIK, P. K., and SUZUMURA, K. (1996), "Individual Rights and Social Evaluation: A Conceptual Framework", *Oxford Economic Papers*, 48: 194–212.

---

[16] Sen has sometimes used (12)—see, for example, Sen (1970a: n. 4, 1983)—and has endorsed (3) as a possible formulation of an individual's rights to liberty in her personal sphere (in particular, see Sen 1983: 9).

PATTANAIK, P. K., and Y. XU (forthcoming), "Conceptions of Rights and Freedom in Welfare Economics: A Re-Examination", in P. Dumouchel and R. Gotoh (eds), *Against Injustice: Ethics, Economics and the Law* (Cambridge: Cambridge University Press).

RILEY, J. (1989), "Rights to Liberty in Purely Private Matters: Part I", *Economics and Philosophy*, 5: 121–66.

—— (1990), "Rights to Liberty in Purely Private Matters: Part II", *Economics and Philosophy*, 6: 27–64.

SEIDL, C. (1986), "The Impossibility of Non-Dictatorial Tolerance", in D. Bös and C. Seidl (eds), *Journal of Economics*, Supplementum 5, *Welfare Economics of the Second Best*, 211–25.

SEN, A. K. (1970a), "The Impossibility of a Paretian Liberal", *Journal of Political Economy*, 78: 152–7.

—— (1970b), *Collective Choice and Social Welfare* (San Francisco: Holdenday).

—— (1983), "Liberty and Social Choice", *Journal of Philosophy*, 80: 5–28.

—— (1996), "Rights: Formulations and Consequences", *Analyse & Kritik*, 18, 153–70.

SUGDEN, R. (1985a). "Liberty, Preference, and Choice", *Economics and Philosophy*, 1: 213–29.

—— (1985b), "Why be Consistent? A Critical Analysis of Consistency Requirements", *Economica*, 52: 167–83.

VAN HEES, M. (1996), "Individual Rights and Legal Validity", *Analyse & Kritik*, 18, 81–95.

C H A P T E R 13

....

IRRELEVANT ALTERNATIVES

....

KEVIN ROBERTS

I. INTRODUCTION

....

CONDITIONS imposing an independence from "irrelevant alternatives" play a central role both in what may be termed individual choice theory and in social choice theory. The purpose of this chapter is to examine different aspects of independence, to assess whether independence can be defended, and to examine the consequences of weaker notions of independence, particularly ones based upon the extent of independence being determined endogenously by the problem.

Consistency of choice is often associated with some notion that there is an independence of irrelevant alternatives (Sen 1970: ch. 1*).[1] Nash (1950), in the presentation of his bargaining solution, uses a notion of independence relating to a consistency of choice. This has been referred to as "independence of irrelevant alternatives" (IIA) by Luce and Raiffa (1957). The arguments in favor of such a condition are different from those relating to another notion of independence, invoked originally by Arrow (1963), and incorporated into a major part of social theory since that time.[2] This, of course, also goes under the name of "independence of irrelevant alternatives". An attempt will be made in the next section to clarify

---

[1] It is worthy of note that this text is now as old as was Amartya Sen when he wrote this classic of social choice theory.

[2] Sen (1977) surveys the results incorporating independence under different informational structures; for a more recent discussion of different structures, see Fleurbaey and Hammond (2004).

the differences between these conditions and the arguments for and against each of them. It will be suggested that whilst Nash IIA relates to the nature of the choice problem, Arrow IIA relates to the informational requirements underlying choice.[3] This requirement may imply that irrelevant alternatives become relevant, even when social choice is based upon some desire for independence. Examples of this will be developed in section III.

In social choice problems, an Arrow IIA condition is very powerful. Consider the original Arrow impossibility theorem. Arrow sought to aggregate a set of individual orderings into a social ordering, subject to the requirements that (1) aggregation is possible whatever the set of individual orderings—a condition of unrestricted domain U; (2) aggregation respects the weak Pareto criterion P; and (3) Arrow IIA is satisfied so that the social ordering over a subset of alternatives is independent of the ranking of alternatives outside the subset. The only aggregation rule satisfying U, P and IIA is a dictatorship, social value reflecting one of the individual orderings. Whilst all three conditions play a role, the role of IIA is noteworthy. Condition U relates only to the domain of application of the aggregation rule, even though it is as demanding as it can be in this regard. Condition P serves only to rule out uninteresting rules, as is demonstrated by Wilson's (1972) characterization of the possibilities under U and IIA.[4] Given the power of IIA, it is not a condition to be invoked lightly.

If there are reasons to believe that IIA as a blanket condition is too strong, the question arises as to how it could be weakened. Even with the informational structure of the Arrow problem, there are many aggregation rules satisfying U and P. With richer informational structures, there is a further embarrassment of riches.[5] Is there a halfway house which incorporates some desirable elements of independence without invoking something as strong as Arrow IIA? Recent work by Campbell and Kelly (forthcoming) suggests that imposing an independence condition which states that there are some alternatives, specified exogenously, which are irrelevant in any ranking can be a condition almost as strong as IIA. Another approach is needed.

Section IV takes such an approach. First, a strong condition of neutrality is imposed, in essence forcing aggregation rules to be welfarist, independently of other conditions.[6] Within the Arrow informational structure, the nature of aggregation rules is investigated. An independence condition is introduced which determines irrelevant alternatives endogenously. A characterization theorem is then presented,

---

[3]   When we speak of Arrow IIA, we mean a condition lifted from the informational constraints of aggregation based upon a set of individual orderings. See Sen (1977).

[4]   Specifically, one individual's ordering is dictatorial in that other individual orderings are essentially disregarded. This restriction admits rules which negate the single individual ordering, giving an anti-dictatorship, ones which are imposed, and ones based upon dictatorship. Some combination of these rules is also possible.

[5]   See the discussion in Sen (1977).

[6]   For the most part, we also restrict attention to anonymous rules.

showing that the aggregation rule must be the Borda rule. This serves as an alternative characterization to that provided by Young (1974), which was based upon consistency with respect to decisions of sub-populations.[7] Given that the Borda rule is often presented as an example of a rule that rides roughshod over notions of independence, it is interesting to see it emerge from an attempt to embody some element of independence. In other work, Young (1988, 1995) has used a condition, referred to as stability or local independence of irrelevant alternatives, which is an endogenous condition. Whilst the formal setting is similar in his work to that studied here, the interpretation of the social ranking is different and his condition does not seem appropriate in our setting (see section IV below).

Section V extends some of our analysis to a richer information structure where interpersonal comparisons are permitted. Concluding remarks follow in section VI.

II. Independence of Irrelevant Alternatives

We start by investigating the nature of choice through the use of choice functions. Let S be a domain of social states, taken to be the set of all outcomes that could be envisaged. A decision-maker chooses from some subset X of S, and $C(X, S)$ is a non-empty subset of X—the choice set of the decision-maker. The function C is the choice function which captures the process of choice.

As we have written it, C has two arguments, X and S. S describes the possible universe in the sense that information about states in S is potentially available and could inform a decision-maker concerning the 'best' choice from X. In particular, in a social choice problem, information could include the well-being of individuals in states. We could think of S as being a subset of some more universal set T. Then, as S varies, so the information available to a decision-maker could change. The set X describes the currently feasible alternatives. With fixed S, varying X varies the set of alternatives available but the information available to the decision-maker is unchanged.

One notion of IIA relates to the idea that the choice set for some set of available alternatives should change with the set of alternatives only if chosen elements become excluded or alternatives are added which 'dominate' the chosen alternatives.

---

[7] Campbell and Kelly (2006) lament the fact that all characterization theorems of the Borda rule utilize an axiom based upon sub-populations. The present result shows that another approach is possible.

One way of expressing this condition is

IIA1:   Let $X \subset Y$. Either $C(X, S) = C(Y, S) \cap X$ or $C(Y, S) \cap X$ is empty.

The "either" part of this statement corresponds to the idea that elements in Y/X do not "dominate" $C(X, S)$ and the "or" part corresponds to the idea that elements in Y/X do "dominate". A justification for IIA1 could come from the idea that the value of an outcome is to be judged only by the consideration of features related to that outcome rather than a value in part related to what else could have been chosen. An example of the latter would be a choice function which tries to avoid outcomes where individuals fare poorly compared to how they would have fared if other available alternatives had been chosen. Thus, IIA1 is one way of capturing a consequentalist or end-state approach to decision-making.

More conventional properties of a choice function than IIA1 are the following (see Sen 1970: ch. 1*):

Property α: Let $x \in X \subset Y$. If $x \in C(Y, S)$ then $x \in C(X, S)$.

Property β: Let $x, y \in X \subset Y$. If $x, y \in C(X, S)$ then $x \in C(Y, S)$

$\leftrightarrow y \in C(Y, S)$.

These properties, often referred to as contraction and expansionist consistency conditions, are well-known and possess well-known properties.[8] Define a base relation R as a ranking of states such that $x R y$ if $x \in C(\{x, y\}, S)$. Then α implies that if $x \in C(X, S)$ then $x \in C(\{x, y\}, S)$ for all $y \in X$, so $x R y$ for all $y \in X|x$. Thus $C(X, S)$ is drawn from the best states under the ranking R. Moreover, under β, the ranking R must be transitive. For assume that $x R y$, $y R z$ and $z P x$. Applying α, this rules out $x \in C(\{x, y, z\}, S)$. If $y \in C(\{x, y, z\}, S)$ then, applying β, $y R x$ and this together with $x R y$ implies $x \in C(\{x, y, z\}, S)$, which is a contradiction. Applying β again, if $z \in C(\{x, y, z\}, S)$ then $z R y$ and this together with $y R z$ implies $x \in C(\{x, y, z\}, S)$, a contradiction. Thus $C(\{x, y, z\}, S)$ is empty, another contradiction. The implication is that $x R y$ & $y R z \Rightarrow x R z$ so that the base relation is transitive.

What is the connection between IIA1 and the properties α and β? We have:

Proposition 1. *IIA1 is equivalent to α and β taken together.*

Proof. Assume IIA1. If $C(Y, S) \cap X$ is empty, the antecedents of α and β do not apply. If $C(Y, S) \cap X$ is non-empty then there is an $x \in X \subset$ such that $x \in C(Y, S)$. By IIA1, $x \in C(X, S)$ giving α. If there is also a $y \in C(X, S)$ then IIA1 implies that $y \subset C(Y, S) \cap X$, giving β.

---

[8] Property α is the independence of irrelevant alternatives condition used in Nash (1950).

Now assume α and β. If $C(Y, S) \cap X$ is non-empty then α implies that if $x \in C(Y, S) \cap X$ then $x \in C(X, S)$. Thus $C(Y, S) \cap X \subseteq C(X, S)$. Also, as $x \in C(X, S)$ and $x \in C(Y, S)\beta$ implies that if $y \in C(X, S)$ then $y \in C(Y, S) \cap X$. Thus $C(X, S) \subseteq C(Y, S) \cap X$. IIA1 follows. ∎

The implication of this is that standard consistency conditions of choice are equivalent to an attempt to treat unchosen available alternatives as irrelevant. That the underlying base relation is transitive is a manifestation of the fact that choice is based, for instance, upon a consequentialist approach to the evaluation of states. If the base relation underlying a choice function fails to be transitive then this does not necessarily imply that choice is "irrational"; it could be *prima facie* evidence that a non-consequentialist approach is being adopted.

So far, we have considered how $C(X, S)$ varies with changes in X. What about changes in S? Consider changes which permit the set of available alternatives to stay fixed at X. This can be interpreted as changes in the information which could be used to inform the choice to be made from the set X. If these (unavailable) alternatives are to be irrelevant then we have:

IIA2:   For some X, consider any $S_1, S_2 \subset T$ such that $X \subseteq S_1 \cap S_2$.

Then $C(X, S_1) = C(X, S_2)$.

IIA1 and IIA2 are independent conditions relating to the different arguments of the function C. One implication of IIA2 is that if $X \subseteq S$ then $C(X, S) = C(X, X)$, so that the choice function is determined once choices where all alternatives are available has been pinned down. IIA2 may be thought of as the appropriate independence condition behind Arrow's IIA condition.[9] In terms of the base relation R underlying C, the binary ranking of x and y is determined independently of unavailable alternatives in the domain, irrespective of the information that could be imparted from the knowledge of such alternatives.

If unavailable states may provide information about what would be a good choice, so an argument is provided for not invoking IIA2. In the next section we look at how information from other states could be introduced naturally into a choice problem. Then we will look at possibilities when IIA2 is not invoked. However, if IIA2 is not invoked then a decision-maker may need to be aware of information from the whole domain of alternatives. This is problematic, not least because of the fact that the domain is unconstrained by the set X of alternatives that can be chosen. Related to this, the set S may contain states which could never arise as an available alternative in a choice problem. In any particular problem where the set of available alternatives is X, these hypothetical alternatives are not dissimilar to

[9] The structure of the problem studied by Arrow assumes a fixed domain but permits the (welfare) information associated with states to vary. But with unavailable alternatives being irrelevant, the separate conditions will place the same restrictions on a choice function.

any alternative outside the set X. Thus, if IIA2 is not invoked then an awareness of hypothetical alternatives could be used as information to inform choices that have to be made.

III. Unavailable Alternatives and Information Extraction

Consider the well-known Borda rule which determines a ranking of states based upon a set of individual rankings of the states—from each individual ranking, no points are awarded to the lowest-ranked state, one to the second lowest, etc.;[10] the aggregate ranking is then based upon the aggregate points received by a state. This procedure may be viewed as being applied across the domain of states S.[11] The aggregate ranking R can then be interpreted as creating a choice function over any subset of states X:

$$C^B(X, S) = \{x : x \in X \text{ and } xRy \ \forall y \in X\}.$$

The ranking R, by its construction, is a transitive ordering and C^B satisfies IIA1. The Borda rule is thus consistent with a consequentialist decision-making process.

But C^B clearly fails IIA2: R over X depends upon the ranking of states outside X, as is obvious from its construction. However, the rule may be interpreted as a utilitarian rule, which is consequentialist, with information being extracted from knowledge of states outside X. The decision-maker would like to base decisions on utility information that incorporates interpersonally comparable utility differences. But with only a set of rankings of utility for each individual and no richer welfare information, the assignment of points as in the Borda rule can be justified as a reasonable approach in the context of what is, to the utilitarian decision-maker, extreme parsimony of information. In essence, ignorance leads to the equal treatment of the utility difference between adjacently ranked states.

The Borda rule places equal information weight on all unavailable states—the set S/X. This has the unfortunate implication that if hypothetical states are introduced then they are to be given equal weight. An augmentation of the rule would be to use a points system which reduces the power of information in some states in determining the social ordering. One example of this is that if S is divided into S_1 and S_2 then, taking one individual's ranking, if x and y are adjacently ranked then

---

[10]   If a number of states are ranked as indifferent then they can share equally the points that would have been awarded if they had been strictly ranked.

[11]   This is sometimes referred to as the broad Borda rule.

their points difference is unity if $x, y \in S_1$ but one-half otherwise. Hypothetical alternatives could be assigned to S_2 and be given a low weight, particularly if individual rankings over such states have to be created by the decision-maker, perhaps through some process of introspection.

Consider now a problem where the decision-maker is utilitarian and the information available relates to a ranking of intrapersonal and interpersonal utility differences. For instance, if $u(x, i)$ is utility in state x of individual i then information may take the form:

$$u(x, 1) - u(y, 1) > u(y, 2) - u(x, 2) > u(y, 3) - u(x, 3) > 0.$$

It is a common belief that a ranking of utility differences is sufficient to determine a utilitarian ranking. However, if IIA2 is invoked then, in a three-person society and with the above ranking of differences, it is impossible to determine which state gives the higher sum of utilities. In fact, the only non-dictatorial rule that satisfies IIA1, IIA2 and the Pareto criterion for all rankings is a rule that gives equal utility weight to two individuals and zero weight to all other individuals.[12] But if IIA2 is not invoked then information can be gleaned from non-available states to provide further information concerning available states. For the above utility difference ranking, assume that there is a state z where

$$u(z, 2) - u(y, 2) = u(y, 3) - u(x, 3).$$

Using this we have

$$\sum_{i=1,3} [u(x, i) - u(y, i)] = (u(x, 1) - u(y, 1)) - (u(z, 2) - u(x, 2)).$$

Thus, the sum of utilities is greater in state x than in state y if 1's utility difference between y and x is greater than 2's utility difference between x and z. We therefore see that information involving a non-available state can be used to make consequentialist choices between available states. In principle, state z could be a hypothetical state.

How does this example differ from our information-acquisition interpretation of the Borda rule? In the Borda-rule case, available information is ordinal and the construction of an interpersonally comparable cardinal index of utility is, in major part, conjectural. However, in the utility difference example, there is nothing conjectural and exact restrictions upon utility differences between two states are provided by invoking information from other states.

---

[12] See Roberts (forthcoming).

IV. Social Choice without Independence

The purpose of this section is to examine aggregation rules that allow unavailable alternatives to influence the social ranking. It will be assumed that IIA1 is satisfied and, instead of investigating possible choice functions, we concentrate on an examination of transitive base relations underlying choice functions. We will also restrict attention to an informational structure based upon a set of individual orderings defined over a set of domains S being all subsets of some set T. The cardinality of T is assumed to be sufficiently large.[13] If IIA2 is invoked then one is quickly led to the Arrow impossibility theorem. Here, we dispense with such a condition and invoke strictly weaker conditions.

If R_i is individual i's ordering then we seek a rule $f(< R_i >_{i=1,n})$ which is a single ordering. f is a function of S and orderings defined over this S. Most of the conditions imposed upon f relate to a fixed S; the exception is EIIA, defined below. For convenience, it will be assumed that there is no indifference in the individual orderings—each R_i is a strict order, P_i. As IIA2 is not imposed, we impose some other strong conditions. In particular, we impose a strong condition of neutrality which makes the rule insensitive to any features of the problem other than the individual rankings. Let $\pi : S \rightarrow S$ be a permutation of states. Define the ordering $R(\pi, R)$ as

$$x R(\pi, R) y \text{ iff } \pi(x) R \pi(y).$$

A standard neutrality condition is

Neutrality (N): If π is a permutation of states then, for all $< R_i >$,

$$R(\pi, f(< R_i >)) = f(< R(\pi, R_i) >).$$

We will also exploit a stronger notion of neutrality:

Strong neutrality (SN): If π is a permutation of states, $\pi(x) = x$ and $\pi(y) = y$, and j is any individual, then

$$f(< R_i >)|_{\{x,y\}} = f(< R_i' >)|_{\{x,y\}},$$

where $R_i = R_i' \ \forall i \neq j$ and $R_j' = R(\pi, R_j)$.

Strong neutrality says that a permutation of *one* individual's ranking which preserves the position of states x and y gives rise to an invariance in the social ranking over $\{x, y\}$.[14] This condition rules out the possibility that the social ranking

---

[13] This is for convenience of proofs. When this is not the case, proofs are more involved.

[14] SN is different from a condition sometimes called strong neutrality which embodies independence. The condition SN bears a relation to N similar to that which a condition sometimes called strong anonymity bears to anonymity. See section V below.

over $\{x, y\}$ is influenced by a correlation across individuals of the hierarchical ranking of states other than x and y. Under an independence condition like IIA2, SN is always satisfied—it relates to neutrality only with respect to alternatives outside the choice set. A consequentialist decision-maker, seeking to use information from irrelevant states to inform his choices, is unlikely to find SN objectionable and the examples of section III lend support to SN.

We will also impose standard conditions on f:

Unrestricted domain (U): f is defined for all individual strict orders over all subsets S of a set T.

Pareto (P): $x P_i y \ \forall i \Rightarrow x \ P \ y$ where P is the strict preference derived from $f(<R_i>)$.

Anonymity (A): Let σ be a permutation of the set of individuals. Then

$$f(<R_i>) = f(<R_{\sigma(i)}>).$$

An endogenous independence condition will be added later.

We start by considering the determinants of the social ordering over some pair of states x and y within some fixed set S where $|S| = m$.[15] Condition N will then ensure that the same determinants apply to all pairs. Assume that all states are labeled $z_1, \ldots, z_m$ and that individual preferences satisfy

$$z_k P_i z_\ell \quad \forall i, \quad \forall k > \ell,$$

where states x and y are excluded from this requirement. Under this restriction, individual preferences are totally determined by where x and y lie in each individual's ordering. Let

$$v_i(x) = |k : x P_i z_k|.$$

$v_i(y)$ is defined symmetrically. In this restricted problem, the social ranking is determined by the vector $v(x)$ and $v(y)$, where v_i is an integer between zero and $m - 1$. By N the social ranking is independent of the pair $\{x, y\}$ or the labeling of other states. Thus, the pairwise social ranking can be viewed as a function of the vectors v, the domain of this function being $[0, m - 1]^N$. Let this ranking be $\tilde{R}$. As only strict individual preferences are permitted, $\tilde{R}$ cannot rank $v(x)$ and $v(y)$ when $v_i(x) = v_i(y)$ for some i. Thus $\tilde{R}$ is an incomplete ranking.

Now consider an unrestricted problem where each individual has any strict order P_i over S and $R = f(<P_i>)$ is the social ranking. Recall that the social ranking is transitive. Consider the ranking over some pair $\{x, y\}$. Take each individual's ranking in turn and permute the states, other than the states x and y, so that with the labeling of states $z_1, \ldots, z_m$, we have $z_k P z_\ell$ for all $k > \ell$. Notice that $v_i(x)$ and $v_i(y)$ remain unchanged. After each permutation, the social ranking exists, by U,

---

[15] We have yet to impose a condition which relates social rankings with different domains S.

and is unchanged, by SN, so, after all individuals' rankings have been permuted, the social ranking will be determinable by the ranking $\tilde{R}$ applied to $v(x)$ and $v(y)$. The same process can be applied to all pairs of states. We thus have $f\ (<P_i>)|_{\{x,y\}} = \tilde{R}|_{v(x),v(y)}$. If three vectors are pairwise ranked under $\tilde{R}$, transitivity of R implies transitivity of $\tilde{R}$. In particular, if $v\tilde{R}v'$ and $v'\tilde{R}v''$ then $v''Pv$ is ruled out in all cases. Without loss of generality, $\tilde{R}$ can always be extended to ensure that it is reflexive: $v\tilde{R}v$.

We have shown that f can be represented by a ranking $\tilde{R}$:

Proposition 2. *If $f(<P_i>)$ satisfies U, N and SN then the social ranking is representable by a real-valued function W_S such that*

$$x f(<P_i>)y \quad iff \quad v(x)\tilde{R}_S v(y).$$

This implies that the social choice rule is equivalent to a points-based voting rule where the social ranking is based upon the number of states ranked below that state for each individual. We have indexed $\tilde{R}$ by S to denote the fact that, so far, we have kept the state domain of f fixed at S. We note, first, that $xP_i y$ for all i implies $v(x) \gg v(y)$, so if condition P is invoked, $\tilde{R}$ must display strict preference with an increase in all arguments. Second, under A, a permutation of preferences between individuals does not change the social ordering. Thus, if $\sigma(v)$ is some permutation of the vector v then, under A, $v\tilde{R}_S v' \Leftrightarrow \sigma(v)\tilde{R}_S\sigma(v')$ and the ranking will be symmetric.

The representation theorem in Proposition 2 is different from theorems which present an equivalence between social choice rules and rankings defined over utilities achieved in a state (Roberts 1980a). Such theorems critically depend upon an independence condition like IIA2. Here, $v(x)$ and $v(y)$ depend upon the ranking of x and y with all other states in S.

How can aggregation rules be further pinned down? First, one could demand that the rule possessed aggregation consistencies with respect to subsets of the population. This is the approach adopted first by Young (1974) in an environment when IIA2 is not imposed. In the context of the present analysis, a separability condition could be imposed which demands that if an individual is indifferent between x and y then his overall ranking of all states does not influence the social ranking.[16] This separability condition requires the domain of f to be extended to include indifference.[17] Proposition 2 can then be used to impose a restriction of additive separability on $\tilde{R}$.

Taking another route, is it possible to impose any condition which treats some alternatives as irrelevant without being led to dictatorship? If there is an exogenously determined subset of states that are irrelevant in the decision concerning

---

[16] See Deschamps and Gevers (1978) for a use of this condition under IIA2.

[17] This is most easily accomplished by imposing a continuity assumption in the rule f. See, for instance, Maskin (1978).

the pair $\{x, y\}$ then this imposes extreme restrictions on $\tilde{R}$, quickly leading to a dictatorship result.[18] Another approach is to consider some states to be irrelevant on the basis of how they are ranked by individuals—this can be thought of as endogenous independence. In this setting, a state z could be considered irrelevant if everybody ranks $\{x, z\}$ in the same way as they rank $\{y, z\}$. Thus, information from state z brings no information which could permit further discrimination between x and y. Let f be the rule over some domain of states S and let f^+ be the rule when the domain is extended to consider a new state z. We have:

Endogenous Independence of Irrelevant Alternatives (EIIA): Let f be defined over some S, f^+ defined over $S \cup \{z\}$ $z \notin S$. If, for all i, $P_i = P_i^+|_S$ and either $z P_i^+ x \,\&\, z P_i^+ y$ or $x P_i^+ z \,\&\, y P_i^+ z$, then $f(<P_i>) = f^+(<P_i^+>)|_S$.

In terms of the analysis of section II, EIIA is a condition that relates to how the social ranking, and so the implied choice function, changes with changes in S. Thus it is in the spirit of IIA2, though independence is implied only under strict conditions.

Another endogenous independence condition which has appeared in the literature is the condition of stability (Young 1988) or limited independence of irrelevant alternatives (Young 1995). In essence, this condition states that if x and y are adjacent to each other in the social ranking then the ranking of x vis-à-vis y should be independent of other alternatives. Under anonymity, neutrality and Pareto, this directly implies that adjacently ranked states are ranked as under majority rule—see the discussion of majority rule below. In the context of our analysis, it could be thought that information from other states is most valuable in the ranking of x and y when there is little difference between them as judged by the social ranking, so this condition may be inappropriate. One similarity between the two endogenous conditions comes from the fact that states which are overwhelmingly superior or inferior to states x and y are viewed as "irrelevant" under both endogenous independence conditions.

Given that Proposition 2 can be applied, first we investigate the dependence of $\tilde{R}$ on the domain of social states S. If a new state z is added and new preference rankings P_i^+ are such that, for each i, $P_i = P_i^+|_S$ and $z P_i^+ w$ for all $w \in S$, then $v(w)$ is the same for all w in S. Furthermore, EIIA implies that $f(<P_i>) = f^+(<P_i^+>)|_S$, so f and f^+ are both representable by the same ranking $\tilde{R}$. A similar analysis applies with regard to the removal of a state from the domain S. We thus have

Proposition 3. *If $f(<P_i>)$ satisfies U, N, SN and EIIA then it is representable by a ranking $\tilde{R}$ that is independent of the domain of social states over which rankings are defined.*[19]

---

[18] See Campbell and Kelly (forthcoming).
[19] The individual arguments of $\tilde{R}$, the arguments of the vector v, are limited in magnitude by the size of set S minus unity. Thus, for any S, one could set $\tilde{R}_S = \tilde{R}_T$.

Standard IIA2 conditions ensure independence of irrelevant alternatives both with respect to the aggregation rule used and with respect to how the rule operates when faced with a set of available alternatives in the domain S. EIIA ensures that the aggregation rule itself is independent, even though the operation of the rule admits the influence of unavailable alternatives through the way that the function v is constructed.

We have thus far considered the implications of changes to the domain S involving states that dominate available alternatives. Now let us consider the addition of a state which, for some individual i, is dominated by the pair $\{x, y\}$ and, for everybody else, dominates $\{x, y\}$. This change has the effect of increasing $v_i(x)$ and $v_i(y)$ by unity. Similarly, deletion of a state with this property will lead to unity being subtracted from v_i and v_i'. But by combining a series of additions and subtractions, with different individuals affected, we have:

Lemma 1. *Let t be an n-dimensional vector of (positive and negative) integers. Under U, N, SN and EIIA, the representation ranking $\tilde{R}$ satisfies $v\tilde{R}v' \iff (v + t)\tilde{R}(v' + t)$ (whenever the arguments are in the domain of $\tilde{R}$).*

Lemma 1 implies a translation invariance property of the ranking by $\tilde{R}$. It imposes strong restrictions on this ranking and this we now investigate. It is convenient also to invoke A, which permits us to restrict attention to symmetric rankings.

What is implied by Lemma 1? Consider two rankable vectors v and v' such that $\sum v_i = \sum v_i'$. Assume that $v\tilde{P}v'$. Let k be a constant vector such that $k_i = k_j$ for all i, j. This vector is chosen to ensure that the vectors to be created are admissible, i.e. have non-negative arguments.[20] Applying Lemma 1:

$$v + (k - v')\tilde{P}v' + (k - v')$$

$$\Rightarrow v - v' + k\tilde{P}k.$$

Let σ be a circular permutation of vectors such that $\sigma_{i+1}(v) = v_i$ and $\sigma_1(v) = v_n$. Under A, $\tilde{R}$ is symmetric:

$$\sigma(v - v') + k\tilde{P}k$$

(recall that k is a constant vector). Applying Lemma 1 again gives

$$(v - v') + \sigma(v - v') + k\tilde{P}(v - v') + k\tilde{P}k.$$

If the three vectors are pairwise rankable, transitivity and symmetry give

$$\sigma(v - v') + \sigma^2(v - v') + k\tilde{P}k.$$

Repeating the initial permutation $n - 1$ times, we have

$$v - v' + \sigma(v - v') + \cdots + \sigma^{n-1}(v - v') + k\tilde{P}k.$$

---

[20] The magnitude of arguments can be constrained by a more indirect proof. In particular, we could work with v, v' such that $|v_i - v_j| \leq 2$.

But from the construction of σ:

$$v - v' + \sigma(v - v') + \cdots + \sigma^{n-1}(v - v') = \sum v_i - \sum v'_i = 0.$$

Hence $k \; \tilde{P} \; k$, which is a contradiction. Thus we have shown that $v \tilde{I} v'$.

The above argument depends upon each of the $n - 1$ created vectors being rankable with the vector k, i.e. not equal in any argument. This depends upon the form of the vector $v - v'$ and cannot be guaranteed. To overcome this problem, a more cumbersome approach is required. Consider any rankable v, v' with $\sum v_i = \sum v'_i$ and let $w = v - v'$. By A, we can assume that $w_i > 0$, $i \leq m$, and $w_i < 0$, $i > m$. Apply a circular permutation among the first m arguments of the vector so that, after $m - 1$ permutations, we attain a vector with constant positive arguments in its first m places. At each stage, full rankability is retained. A similar circular permutation can be applied amongst the last $n - m$ arguments. The net result is that the ranking of v and v' will be the same as the ranking of two vectors whose difference $\tilde{w}$ takes the form $\tilde{w}_i = \overline{w}$, $i \leq m$, $\tilde{w}_i = -\underline{w}$, $i > m$. It will be the case that $m\overline{w} = (n - m)\underline{w}$.

Take the case where n is even and assume $m < \frac{n}{2}$ (the case $m > \frac{n}{2}$ is symmetric). Consider two vectors such that their difference $\tilde{w}'$ takes the form $\tilde{w}'_i = w'$ $i \leq \frac{n}{2}$, $\tilde{w}'_i = -w'$, $i > \frac{n}{2}$. By A, these vectors must be ranked as indifferent, or $\tilde{w}' + k \tilde{I} \; k$ for some constant vector k. By Lemma 1, $\tilde{w} + \tilde{w}' + k \tilde{I} \; \tilde{w} + k$. Let $w' > \underline{w}$ so the vector $\tilde{w} + \tilde{w}'$ will be strictly positive in its first $\frac{n}{2}$ arguments, strictly negative otherwise. How will $\tilde{w} + \tilde{w}' + k$ be ranked with k? Taking circular permutations among the first $n/2$ arguments, it will be ranked the same as a vector $\tilde{w}'' + k$ where $\tilde{w}''$ has constant positive arguments for $i \leq \frac{n}{2}$, constant negative thereafter. By A, $\tilde{w}'' + k \tilde{I} \; k$, so $\tilde{w} + \tilde{w}' + k \tilde{I} \; k$ and, as $\tilde{w} + k$ and k are rankable, $\tilde{w} + k \tilde{I} \; k$. Thus $v \tilde{I} v'$.

When n is odd, we can consider vectors $\tilde{w}$ where $\tilde{w}'_i = w'$, $i \leq \frac{n+1}{2}$, $\tilde{w}'_i = -\frac{(n+1)}{n-1}w'$ otherwise. Both w' and $\frac{(n+1)w'}{n-1}$ must be integers. It can be checked that a circular permutation amongst all arguments gives rankability at all stages so our initial argument gives us $\tilde{w} + k \tilde{I} \; k$. The argument then follows the lines of the n even case. The net effect is that if $\sum v_i = \sum v'_i$ then $v \tilde{I} v'$.

Finally, when $\sum v_i > \sum v'_i$ we can use a similar analysis to show that, under P, $v \tilde{P} v'$. Thus the ranking $\tilde{R}$, although it is incomplete, is representable itself by a real-valued function $W = \sum v_i$.

Starting with preferences $<P_i>$, if each P_i is used to award zero points to the lowest ranked state, 1 to the next, etc., then the rule represented by W will rank states according to the total number of points awarded to each state—we will have the Borda rule. Collecting together the conditions which underlie the result, we have:

Proposition 4. *If $f(<P_i>)$ satisfies U, N, SN, A, P and EIIA then f is the Borda rule.*

This result is of some interest. First, it provides a characterization of the Borda rule that is different in flavor to previous approaches and is based upon conditions that are easily comparable to conditions much utilized in social choice theory. The only conditions which are not entirely straightforward are SN and EIIA. SN is only a mild strengthening of N and is in the same spirit. EIIA is a weakening of IIA2. Weakening IIA2 but retaining some exogenous independence of 'irrelevant' alternatives is, in essence, as strong as IIA and, as Campbell and Kelly (forthcoming) have shown, there are no rules that satisfy such a condition together with N, A and P.[21] If any independence condition is to be imposed then it needs to incorporate some notion of endogenous independence and EIIA is a weak condition in this regard.[22]

It is also useful to compare Proposition 4 with May's (1952) characterization of simple majority rule. May showed that the unique aggregation rule applied to individual orderings which satisfies N, A, P and a condition capturing IIA2 was majority rule. IIA2 implies that both SN and EIIA are satisfied. However, majority rule is not a permissible rule in Proposition 4 because it can induce cycles in the social ranking—condition U is not satisfied. With a desire for a rule giving rise to transitive orderings, and so satisfaction of IIA1, a natural question to ask is by how much IIA2 must be relaxed before a rule can be found satisfying transitivity. Proposition 4 provides an answer and also tells us that the 'nearest' transitive rule to majority rule in the direction of relaxing independence is the Borda rule.[23]

We now make some further observations relating to Proposition 4. First, it should be stressed that the result applies only to strict individual orderings. With the possibility of indifference, the characterization result still holds over the sub-domain of strict preferences but, when there is indifference, a variety of rules can be utilized.[24] Second, we can consider whether it is possible to relax the conditions in the proposition without a major impact upon the characterization. Condition P is important only in ensuring that the social choice is positively responsive to increases in $\sum v_i$. Condition A is used in a fundamental way in the proof but this relates mostly to the method of proof. If A is not invoked then it is possible to show that $W = \sum \gamma_i v_i$ where the γ_i are positive weights. Proving this seems to be rather more involved than in the anonymity case. We give a brief sketch. Consider extending the domain of possible v vectors to $\mathbb{R}^n$. Taking the set of v such that

[21] Of course, this result is closely related to Arrow's (1963) impossibility theorem.

[22] If no independence condition is to be incorporated then we are left with the representation result of Proposition 2.

[23] If we relax anonymity then Arrow's analysis shows that the "nearest" transitive rule is dictatorship.

[24] With indifference, there are different ways of assigning points to different states which are then aggregated to create the social ordering.

$v\tilde{R}v^*$, one can form the convex hull of this set, $\overline{V}$. Using translation invariance, one can show that no v such that $v^*\tilde{P}v$ is contained in the interior of this set. Similar properties apply to $\underline{V}$, the convex hull of v such that $v^*\tilde{R}v$. A separating hyperplane theorem can be applied to show that a hyperplane separates these sets, given by $\sum \gamma_i v_i =$ constant. This forms an indifference curve in $\mathbb{R}^n$. Translation invariance then implies that the same sloped hyperplane can be used for all v^* and the result follows. The class of rules characterized extends now to weighted Borda rules but no further.

V. INTERPERSONAL COMPARISONS

The results of section IV have been developed under the (welfare) information restriction of ordinality and non-interpersonal comparability. If the information structure is richer then the set of possibilities expands and the potential application of information drawn from 'irrelevant' alternatives is enhanced—recall the discussion in section III. On the other hand, the richer the information structure, the less the need to extract information from 'irrelevant' alternatives. The appeal of any independence condition will thus depend upon the information structure of the problem being investigated.

In this section, we will consider the information structure of ordinality combined with interpersonal comparability: welfare information is captured by an ordinal function $u(x, i)$ defined over state/individual pairs, so $u(x, i) > u(y, j)$ is taken to mean that i in state x has higher welfare than j in state y. Conditions U, P, A, N and SN can be straightforwardly applied in this set-up. It is useful to strengthen the anonymity condition to a condition of strong anonymity which has similarities to the connection between N and SN:

Strong Anonymity (SA): Let σ be a permutation of the set of individuals. If u and u' are such that for some $x \in S$,

$$u(x, i) = u'(x, \sigma(i)) \quad \forall i$$

and

$$u(y, j) = u'(y, j) \quad \forall j, \quad \forall y \in S/x,$$

then $f(u) = f(u')$.

This condition is due to Sen (1977). Importantly, it says that a permutation of individuals in any state does not change the social ranking. A welfarist should be happy with such a condition. Recall that SN related to a permutation of states for some individual. If SA is applied with respect to each state in turn using the same σ then we see that SA implies A but not vice versa.

Conditions SA and SN taken together allow us to impose conditions upon the social ranking f and we adopt an approach similar to that adopted in the previous section. We consider the determinants of the social ordering over some pair of states x and y with different welfare information: $f|_{\{x,y\}}$. Assume that all states are labeled $z_1, \ldots, z_m$ and all individuals are labeled $1, \ldots, n$. Fixing x and y, consider u such that

(i) $\forall z_k \forall i, j, i < j:$ $\quad u(z_k, i) < u(z_k, j)$.

(ii) $\forall z_k, z_\ell \neq x, y, k < \ell,$ $\quad \forall i, j:$ $\quad u(z_k, i) < u(z_\ell, j)$.

Condition (i) says that, in every state, the ordering of individuals by their welfare level is the same. Condition (ii) says that states other than x and y can be ordered by their welfare level: everybody in one state is better off than everybody in another state.

We will consider the function $f|_{\{x,y\}}$ over the sub-domain of individual welfares satisfying (i) and (ii). How large is this sub-domain? All rankings not including x and y are given; for x and y the ranking of individuals in each state are given. Thus u is totally determined given vectors $v(x)$ and $v(x)$ where

$$v_i(x) = |\{k, j\} : u(x, i) > u(z_k, j)|$$

and with $v(y)$ defined symmetrically. Notice that the vector $v(x)$ is restricted to be increasing across its arguments. We note that if u and u' are such that for some $w, x, y, z: u'(w, \cdot) = u(x, \cdot), u'(x, \cdot) = u(w, \cdot), u'(z, \cdot) = u(y, \cdot), u'(y, \cdot) = u(z, \cdot)$ and $u = u'$ over other states, then N gives $f(u)|_{\{x,y\}} = f(u')|_{(w,z)}$, so $f(u)|_{\{x,y\}}$ is determined by $v(x)$ and $v(y)$ not by the identity of x and y. We can therefore define a ranking $\tilde{R}$ over v vectors such that $\tilde{R}|_{v(x),v(y)} = f(u)|_{\{x,y\}}$, where u satisfies (i) and (ii) and $v(x), v(y)$ are distilled from the function u.

We now proceed to show that $\tilde{R}$ determines the ranking of states even when (i) and (ii) are not satisfied. Consider any u. Assume that the lowest state–individual pair not relating x and y is (z, j). Consider a permutation of states which swaps (z, j) for (z_1, j). If u' is the transformed welfare information, $f(u)|_{\{x,y\}} = f(u')|_{\{x,y\}}$ by SN. Now consider a permutation of individuals which swaps (z_1, j) with $(z_1, 1)$. If u'' is the transformed information, SA implies that $f(u'') = f(u')$, so $f(u'')|_{\{x,y\}} = f(u)|_{\{x,y\}}$. Now moving to the second-lowest state–individual pair, a state and then a person permutation can transform the welfare information so that this state–individual pair is $(z_1, 2)$ and if u''' is the transformed welfare information, $f(u''')|_{\{x,y\}} = f(u)|_{\{x,y\}}$. This can be repeated for all state–individual pairs excluding x and y. Finally, a permutation of individuals in state x to give $\tilde{u}(x, i) < \tilde{u}(x, j)$ if $i < j$, and a similar permutation for y, gives us, by SA, transformed welfare information $\hat{u}$ such that $f(\hat{u})|_{\{x,y\}} = f(u)|_{\{x,y\}}$, where $\hat{u}$ satisfies the conditions (i) and (ii). The vectors $\hat{v}(x)$, $\hat{v}(y)$ that apply to $\hat{u}$ relate directly to u: $\hat{v}_i(x)$ is the number of state–individual pairs giving welfare below the i'th lowest welfare levels in state x under u—it relates to a position in the welfare hierarchy in state x rather than a particular individual in state x.

Taking any u, $f(u)|_{\{x,y\}} = \tilde{R}|_{\hat{v}(x),\hat{v}(y)}$ and for three pairwise rankable vectors, $\tilde{R}$ will be transitive. We have

Proposition 5. *If $f(u)$ satisfies U, N, SN and SA then the social ranking is representable by a ranking $\tilde{R}$ such that $xf(u)y$ iff $\bar{v}(x)\tilde{R}\bar{v}(y)$.*

If P is added as a condition then there will be a strict preference with an increase in all arguments. If the ranking can be represented by a real-valued function W, then if $W(v) = v_d$, the social ranking follows the ranking of the d'th lowest welfare position in each state. For example, if $d = 1$ then W is the Rawlsian rule. If W is an affine function requiring separability, then $W = \sum \gamma_i v_i$, which is a generalized Borda rule based upon position in the welfare hierarchy rather than on particular individuals (Sen 1977).

The characterization result in Proposition 5 has not invoked an independence condition. If IIA2 is added then W can be further restricted and it is known from Gevers (1979) and Roberts (1980b) that W must then take on the form $W = v_d$—a positional dictatorship. This can be derived directly or, more simply, by invoking Proposition 5. But if IIA2 is not invoked, is there a reasonable endogenous independence condition that could be imposed? Closest to EIIA is a condition which states that the ranking over $\{x, y\}$ is independent of the welfare information relating to states that are unambiguously dominated or unambiguously dominate states x and y. Consider a change in welfare information which shifts the welfare achieved in some state z from dominating both x and y to being dominated by x and y. Then $\hat{v}(x)$ and $\hat{v}(y)$ will be augmented by unity in all arguments. If this is done τ times then it will be required of W that

$$\hat{v}\tilde{R}\hat{v}' \Longleftrightarrow \hat{v} + (\tau, \tau, \ldots, \tau)\tilde{R}\hat{v}' + (\tau, \tau, \ldots, \tau).$$

This condition is much weaker than the translation invariance property of the previous section—instead of linear indifference surfaces, one indifference surface is almost unrestricted but other indifference surfaces have the property that they are a translation up the 45° line of the initial indifference surface. Further restriction would have to be based upon the imposition of a more restrictive independence condition.

VI. Concluding Remarks

The purpose of this paper has been to explore aspects of the role of "irrelevant" alternatives. One condition deems as irrelevant whether rejected states were or were not available to be chosen. The arguments for and against such a condition appear relatively straightforward. However, changes to the set of potentially available states can lead to a change in the information that is available, and deeming such alternatives irrelevant is to deny the value of information that they may contain. We have seen, by example, how non-available alternatives can provide information about available alternatives.

If 'irrelevant' alternatives are not independent then the issue arises as to whether it is reasonable to impose any sort of independence condition. In the context of a welfare information structure of ordinality and interpersonal non-comparability, we have investigated weakening independence, motivated by the idea that alternatives could be deemed independent if welfare information relating to them is uninformative—the idea of endogenous independence. Adopting such a condition leads to the characterization of a unique aggregation procedure—Borda's rule. This analysis gives insights into the role of independence conditions and into the nature of Borda's rule.

It would be useful to examine further the possibilities with richer information structures. We have seen that some progress is possible under ordinality together with interpersonal comparability, but the general issue that must be faced is that the appropriateness of any independence condition relates to the information structure of the problem being examined.

References

ARROW, K. J. (1963), *Social Choice and Individual Values*, 2nd edn (New York: Wiley).

CAMPBELL, D. E., and KELLY, J. S. (forthcoming), "Social Welfare Functions that Satisfy Pareto, Anonymity, and Neutrality but not IIA", *Social Choice and Welfare*.

DESCHAMPS, R., and GEVERS, L. (1978), "Leximin and Utilitarian Rules: A Joint Characterization", *Journal of Economic Theory*, 17: 143–63.

FLEURBAEY, M., and HAMMOND, P. J. (2004), "Interpersonally Comparable Utility," in S. Barbera, C. Seidl and P. T. Hammond (eds), *Handbook of Utility Theory* (Dordrecht: Kluwer Academic Publishers).

GEVERS, L. (1979), "On Interpersonal Comparability and Social Welfare Orderings", *Econometrica*, 47: 75–90.

LUCE, R. D., and RAIFFA, H. (1957), *Games and Decisions* (New York: Wiley).

MASKIN, E. (1978), "A Theorem on Utilitarianism", *Review of Economic Studies*, 45: 93–6.

MAY, K. O. (1952), "A Set of Independent Necessary and Sufficient Conditions for Simple Majority Rule", *Econometrica*, 20: 680–4.

NASH, J. F. (1950), "The Bargaining Problem", *Econometrica*, 18: 155–62.

ROBERTS, K. (1980a), "Interpersonal Comparability and Social Choice Theory", *Review of Economic Studies*, 47: 421–39.

—— (1980b), "Possibility Theorems with Interpersonally Comparable Welfare Levels", *Review of Economic Studies*, 47: 409–20.

—— (forthcoming), "Social Choice Theory and the Informational Basis Approach", in Morris (ed.), *Amartya Sen*, Cambridge University Press Series on Modern Philosophers (Cambridge: Cambridge University Press).

SEN, A. K. (1970), *Collective Choice and Social Welfare* (San Francisco: Holden-Day).

—— 1977. "On Weights and Measures: Informational Constraints in Social Welfare Analysis", *Econometrica*, 45: 1539–72.

WILSON, R. B. (1972), "Social Choice Theory without the Pareto Principle", *Journal of Economic Theory*, 5: 478–86.

YOUNG, H. P. (1974). "An Axiomatization of Borda's Rule", *Journal of Economic Theory*, 9: 43–52.

—— (1988), "Condorcet's Theory of Voting", *American Political Science Review*, 82: 1231–44.

—— (1995), "Optimal Voting Rules", *Journal of Economic Perspectives*, 9: 51–64.

CHAPTER 14

LIMITED RIGHTS AND SOCIAL CHOICE RULES

MAURICE SALLES

I. INTRODUCTION

THE origin of the tremendous development of studies on rights and freedom within social choice theory and normative economics can be traced back to the famous short paper of Amartya Sen published in 1970 (Sen 1970a; see also his book published the same year, Sen 1970b; Sen 1982, 2002). In Sen's paper, it is shown in the framework of aggregation procedures that there is a conflict between collective rationality embedded in the notion of social decision function (in terms of a transitivity-type of the social preference property—in fact, acyclicity of the asymmetric part of the social preference), Paretianism (a unanimity property) and some slight violation of neutrality (neutrality meaning that the names of options

This paper is dedicated to Amartya Sen. It is a variation on and a tribute to Sen's landmark paper (Sen 1970a). I am grateful to participants at the International Conference on Rational Choice, Individual Rights and Non-Welfaristic Normative Economics, Hitotsubashi University, Tokyo, 11–13 March 2006, for suggesting that the notion of limited rights that was used in Salles (2007) in the framework of aggregation functions would also be studied in the framework of social choice rules. Financial support from the French ANR through contract NT05-1_42582 (3LB) is gratefully acknowledged.

or social states are not to be taken into account), possibly combined with some slightly unequal distribution of power among individuals interpreted as a property of individual liberty. Although since then, rights have been considered within another paradigm, viz. game forms (see for instance Gärdenfors 1981, 2005; Gaertner, Pattanaik and Suzumura 1992; Peleg 1998; Suzumura 2006), and freedom has been mainly analyzed in the context of opportunity sets following the pioneering paper of Pattanaik and Xu (1990) (see also the survey by Barbera, Bossert and Pattanaik 2004), some authors (for instance Saari and Pétron 2006 and Igersheim 2006) have recently revisited the foundational framework of Sen and Gibbard (1974) either by studying the informational structure of the aggregation procedure or by examining the consequences of taking a Cartesian structure to define the set of social states, consequences that take the form of a restriction of individual preferences. The purpose of my paper (Salles 2007) was different. I wished to study formally a weakening of the conditions associated with the notion of individual liberty. I have always considered that this condition was rather strong in Sen's original paper. In fact, the condition is quite strong in the mathematical framework and only the interpretation (the idea of personal sphere), to my view, makes it not only acceptable but obvious. However, there is nothing in the basic mathematical framework that guarantees this personal aspect (in contrast with a suitable Cartesian product structure). In this basic framework, it was however possible to weaken the liberalism conditions which amount to a kind of local dictator to local vetoers. Unfortunately I showed that this weakening did not suffice to offer an interesting escape route from Sen's negative result. Basically, I showed that with the weaker condition, we still had impossibility results, but for social welfare functions or some variants (where the social preference was an interval order or a semiorder).[1] In the present chapter, I explore the effect of a suitable weakening of the liberalism condition within the framework of social choice rules rather than aggregation functions, where a choice function (rather than a social preference) is associated to a profile of individual preferences.[2] Although the mathematical derivations are quite simple, I initially expected to have to use properties of choice functions borrowed from the revealed preference literature as presented, among others, by Arrow (1959, 1984), Fishburn (1975), Jamison and Lau (1973), Schwartz (1976), Sen (1971, 1982) and Suzumura (1976, 1983), but, to my surprise, this was necessary only in a very specific case.

After introducing general definitions and recalling Sen's theorems, I will present new Sen-type impossibility theorems in the social choice rules setting.

---

[1] For these concepts see Fishburn (1985) and Suppes *et al.* (1989).
[2] This social choice rule approach probably originates in Suzumura's works (see e.g. Suzumura 1983).

II. Basic Definitions
and Sen's Theorem

Let X be the set of social states. Nothing specific is assumed for this set unless it is clearly indicated that it is finite. A binary relation, a *preference*, over X is a subset of $X \times X$. It will be denoted by $\succeq$. I will write $x \succeq y$ rather than $(x, y) \in \succeq$. All binary relations considered in this chapter are supposed to be *complete* (for all x and $y \in X$, $x \succeq y$ or $y \succeq x$) and, consequently, *reflexive* (for all $x \in X$, $x \succeq x$). The *asymmetric* part of $\succeq$, denoted $\succ$, is defined (since $\succeq$ is complete) by $x \succ y$ if $\neg y \succeq x$. The *symmetric* part of $\succeq$ is defined by $x \sim y$ if $x \succeq y$ and $y \succeq x$. Intuitively, $x \succeq y$ will mean "x is at least as good as y", $x \succ y$ will mean "x is preferred to y" and $x \sim y$ will mean "there is an indifference between x and y". A preference $\succeq$ is *transitive* if for all x, y and $z \in X$, $x \succeq y$ and $y \succeq z \Rightarrow x \succeq z$. The asymmetric part of $\succeq$, $\succ$, is transitive if for all x, y and $z \in X$, $x \succ y$ and $y \succ z \Rightarrow x \succ z$. The symmetric part of $\succeq$, $\sim$, is transitive if for all x, y and $z \in X$, $x \sim y$ and $y \sim z \Rightarrow x \sim z$. If $x \succeq$ is transitive, $\succ$ and $\sim$ are transitive too. We will say that $\succ$ is *acyclic* if there is no finite subset of X, $\{x_1, \ldots, x_k\}$, for which $x_1 \succ x_2, x_2 \succ x_3, \ldots, x_{k-1} \succ x_k$ and $x_k \succ x_1$. A complete and transitive binary relation is a *complete preorder* (sometimes called "weak ordering"). Let $\mathbb{P}$ denote the set of complete preorders over X, and $\mathbb{A}$ denote the set of complete binary relations over X whose asymmetric part is acyclic.

Let N be the set of individuals. Individual $i \in N$ has her preference given by a complete preorder $\succeq_i$ over X. A *profile* π is a function from N to $\mathbb{P}'$, $\pi : i \mapsto \succeq_i$, where $\mathbb{P}' \subseteq \mathbb{P}$ with $\mathbb{P}' \neq \emptyset$. Let Π' be the set of profiles when the $\succeq_i$'s are in $\mathbb{P}'$ and Π be the set of all profiles when the $\succeq_i$'s are in $\mathbb{P}$. When N is finite and $\#N = n$, a profile is an n-list $(\succeq_1, \ldots, \succeq_n)$ with each $\succeq_i$ in $\mathbb{P}'$. Then $\Pi' = \mathbb{P}'^n$ and $\Pi = \mathbb{P}^n$ ($\mathbb{P}'^n$ and $\mathbb{P}^n$ are n-times Cartesian products of $\mathbb{P}'$ and $\mathbb{P}$). Let 2^X be the set of subsets of X and $2^X_{-\emptyset}$ be the set of non-empty subsets of X.

Definition 1. *A choice function is a function* $C : 2^X_{-\emptyset} \to 2^X_{-\emptyset}$ *such that for all* $S \in 2^X_{-\emptyset}$, $C(S) \subseteq S$.

Given a subset S of elements in X, the choice set $C(S)$ can be interpreted as the elements that are chosen, with the assumption that at least one element is chosen and all chosen elements belong to S. Given X, let $\mathbb{C}$ be the set of choice functions as defined above.

Definition 2. *A social choice function is a function* $f : \Pi' \to \mathbb{C}$.

A social choice function associates a unique choice function, that is a way to select options in each subset of options, to individual preferences (one preference for each individual).

Given a social choice function f, and two (distinct) social states x and $y \in X$,[3] we will say that individual $i \in N$ is (x, y)-c-decisive if for all $\pi \in \Pi'$ and all $S \in 2^X_{-\emptyset}$, $x \succ_i y$ and $x \in S \Rightarrow y \notin C(S)$, where $C = f(\pi)$.

This means that whenever individual i prefers x to y and x is available, y cannot be socially chosen.

Definition 3. *An individual who is (x, y)-c-decisive and (y, x)-c-decisive will be said to be $\{x, y\}$-c-decisive or an $\{x, y\}$-c-strong vetoer.*[4]

I can now define Sen's two liberalism conditions. Let f be a social choice function.

Definition 4 (c-liberalism: general 2-cSV). *For all $i \in N$, there exist a_i and $b_i \in X$ such that i is an $\{a_i, b_i\}$-c-strong vetoer.*

It should be noted that $\mathbb{P}'$ must be large enough to have a non-trivial satisfaction of general 2-cSV: for each individual i it must be possible to have both $a_i \succ_i b_i$ and $b_i \succ_i a_i$. Also, it should be outlined that the condition is rather fair, since each individual is endowed with the same kind of power. The theorem can be proved by using a weaker form of the foregoing condition.

Definition 5 (c-minimal liberalism: minimal 2-cSV). *There exist two individuals i and $j \in N$, and a, b, c, $d \in X$ such that i is an $\{a, b\}$-c-strong vetoer and j is a $\{c, d\}$-c-strong vetoer.*[5]

Of course, the fairness property has disappeared. The options are to be "interpreted" as being specific to the concerned individual, i.e. a and b are specific to individual i. a and b can even be "interpreted" as perfectly identical social states except for some features that are personal to individual i. Clearly general 2-cSV implies minimal 2-cSV.

As previously mentioned, the domain of the social choice function f must be rich enough. This is ensured by the following condition.

Definition 6 (universality: U). *Let f be a social choice function. Universality requires that $\mathbb{P}' = \mathbb{P}$.*

This means that an individual preference can be any complete preorder. There is no restriction imposed by some kind of upper rationality or the existence of

---

[3] They have to be distinct, though saying so is superfluous, since $x \succ_i y$ and $\succ_i$ is asymmetric.

[4] The letter "c", as in c-decisive and c-vetoer, indicates that decisiveness, vetoer, etc. are defined in the social choice functions setting rather than in the more standard aggregation functions setting where the values taken by the aggregation functions are social preferences.

[5] I will justify in sect. IV the "vetoer" label rather than the term "dictator" used in my previous paper (Salles 2007).

inter-individual constraints. The last condition is a weak form of unanimity (the Pareto principle).

Definition 7 (Pareto principle: P). *Let f be a social choice function, $\pi \in \Pi'$, $x, y \in X$, and $S \in 2^X_{-\emptyset}$.[6] If for all $i \in N$, $x \succ_i y$, and $x \in S$, then $y \notin C(S)$, where $C = f(\pi)$.*

Sen's theorem is obtained in this setting without introducing any further properties of social choice functions. In Sen's original setting the theorem was obtained within a large class of aggregation functions (Sen called them *social decision functions*), viz. $\mathbb{A}$-valued aggregation functions that include, among others, social welfare functions *à la* Arrow (1950, 1951, 1963). (See Salles 2007.)

The collective rationality (acyclicity of the asymmetric part of the social preference relation) imposed in the case of a social decision function is rather weak. It has an interesting consequence for the non-emptiness of the set of maximal elements in any finite subset of X (or, since we are considering complete binary relations, for the non-emptiness of maximum elements or possible choices).

Theorem 1. *If there are at least two individuals and if $\#X \geq 2$, there is no social choice function satisfying minimal 2-cSV, U and P.*

An immediate corollary is:

Corollary 1. *If there are at least two individuals and if $\#X \geq 2$, there is no social choice function satisfying general 2-cSV, U and P.[7]*

III. PARTIAL WEAK VETO AND SEN-TYPE THEOREMS

As mentioned in Salles (2007), it is in reading Pattanaik's paper (1996) that I got the impetus to work on this topic. In particular, Pattanaik discusses Sen's possible views regarding a distinction between a conception of rights as the ability to prevent something and a conception of rights as the obligation to prevent something, an obligation which seems to be built into the liberalism conditions. Although I wish to devote some time to introducing modal-theoretic techniques to deal with this distinction, I will be more modest in this chapter and will consider only a weakening of the liberalism conditions. It is, however obvious that this weakening is not a real response to the ability–obligation problem. Nevertheless, at least from a semantic

---

[6] Again, x and y are necessarily distinct.
[7] For a proof see Suzumura (1983) or Pattanaik (1994).

point of view, having a (partial) veto power weaker than the strong veto defined above corresponds rather well to the idea of an ability to prevent something. I will then introduce the notion of partial weak veto and will show how extremely robust Sen's theorem is.

Given a social choice function f, and two (distinct) social states x and $y \in X$, we will say that individual $i \in N$ is (x, y)-c-semi-decisive if for all $\pi \in \Pi'$ and all $S \in 2^X_{-\emptyset}, x \succ_i y$ and $x \in S \Rightarrow (y \in C(S) \Rightarrow x \in C(S))$, where $C = f(\pi)$.

This means that whenever individual i prefers x to y and x is available, if y happens to be socially chosen, then x has to be socially chosen too.

Definition 8. *An individual who is (x, y)-c-semi-decisive and (y, x)-c-semi-decisive will be said to be $\{x, y\}$-c-semi-decisive or an $\{x, y\}$-c-weak vetoer.*

I can now define weak versions of liberalism.

Definition 9 (c-weak liberalism: general 2-cWV). *For all $i \in N$, there exist a_i and $b_i \in X$ such that i is an $\{a_i, b_i\}$-c-weak vetoer.*

Definition 10 (c-minimal weak liberalism: minimal 2-cWV). *There exist two individuals i and $j \in N$, and $a, b, c, d \in X$ such that i is an $\{a, b\}$-c-weak vetoer and j is a $\{c, d\}$-c-weak vetoer.*[8]

I can now state the main result of this paper.

Theorem 2. *If there are at least two individuals, there is no social choice function satisfying U, P and minimal 2-cWV, provided that, in the definition of minimal 2-cWV, $\{a, b\} \neq \{c, d\}$ and provided that $\#X \geq 4$.*

Proof. Let f be a social choice function satisfying U, P and 2-cWV. Suppose first that $\{a, b\} \neq \{c, d\}$, but $\{a, b\} \cap \{c, d\} \neq \emptyset$. Without loss of generality, assume that $a = d$. Consider a profile π such that $a \succ_i b, c \succ_j a$, and for all $k \in N, b \succ_k e$ and $e \succ_k c$, where e is a fourth social state. Note that $a \succ_i b \succ_i e \succ_i c$ and $b \succ_j e \succ_j c \succ_j a$. Let $T = \{a, b, c, e\}$. Then, by condition P, $e \notin C(T)$ and $c \notin C(T)$. Since j is c-semi-decisive over $\{a, c\}$ and $c \succ_j a$, if $a \in C(T)$ then $c \in C(T)$. Since $c \notin C(T), a \notin C(T)$. One is left with b, i.e. $\{b\} = C(T)$. But since i is c-semi-decisive over $\{a, b\}$ and $a \succ_i b$, if $b \in C(T)$, we have also $a \in C(T)$, a contradiction.

Now suppose $\{a, b\} \cap \{c, d\} = \emptyset$, i.e. a, b, c, and d are distinct options. Consider a profile π such that $a \succ_i b, c \succ_j d$, and for all $k \in N, b \succ_k c$ and $d \succ_k a$. Note that $d \succ_i a \succ_i b \succ_i c$ and $b \succ_j c \succ_j d \succ_j a$. Let $T = \{a, b, c, d\}$. Then, by condition P, $a \notin C(T)$ and $c \notin C(T)$. Either b or $d \in C(T)$. But since i is c-semi-decisive over

---

[8] Karni (1974) was probably the first author to propose this kind of weakening of the liberalism condition, in a working paper that is still unpublished. In Karni's paper the condition applies to subsets of alternatives (and in the aggregation functions framework). This paper also includes important comments about the Cartesian product structure and unconditional preferences.

$\{a, b\}$ and $a \succ_i b$, if $b \in C(T)$, then $a \in C(T)$, a contradiction. Then $\{d\} = C(T)$. Since j is c-semi-decisive over $\{c, d\}$ and $c \succ_j d, c \in C(T)$, a contradiction.

Although we need four options, this does not seem to be a very restrictive assumption. For instance, with a basic set of two elements α and β, if we have two individuals 1 and 2, a set of options X in a Cartesian product setting could be given by $\{(\alpha, \alpha), (\alpha, \beta), (\beta, \alpha), (\beta, \beta)\}$, a four-option set.

If $\{a, b\} = \{c, d\}$, the result does not apply. Given a profile π and a non-empty subset S of X, let us define the set of Pareto-dominated options, denoted $D_{Par}(S)$, by $D_{Par}(S) = \{y \in S : \text{there is an } x \in S \text{ such that for all } i \in N, x \succ_i y\}$. Let us suppose that $\{a, b\} = \{c, d\}$. Assume X is finite. We define a social choice function, f_1, in the following way. For a profile π:

$C(\{a, b\}) = \{a\}$ if for all $k \in N, a \succ_k b$,
$C(\{a, b\}) = \{b\}$ if for all $k \in N, b \succ_k a$, and
$C(\{a, b\}) = \{a, b\}$ otherwise.

For $S \neq \{a, b\}$,

(1) if (i) a and $b \in S$, (ii) there is a third alternative in S, say z, such that for all $k \in N, z \succ_k a$, and (iii) $a \succ_i b$ or $a \succ_j b$, then $C(S) = S - (D_{Par}(S) \cup \{b\})$;

(2) if (i) a and $b \in S$, (ii) there is a third alternative in S, say z, such that for all $k \in N, z \succ_k b$, and (iii) $b \succ_i a$ or $b \succ_j a$, then $C(S) = S - (D_{Par}(S) \cup \{a\})$;

(3) $C(S) = S - D_{Par}(S)$ otherwise.

One can verify that $C(S) \neq \emptyset$ for all non-empty S and that the conditions P and minimal 2-cWV are satisfied.

Now if $\#X = 2$, let $X = \{a, b\}$. We can define a social choice function, f_2, in exactly the same way as in the previous case when $\{a, b\} = \{c, d\}$, i.e. for a profile π:

$C(\{a, b\}) = \{a\}$ if for all $k \in N, a \succ_k b$,
$C(\{a, b\}) = \{b\}$ if for all $k \in N, b \succ_k a$, and
$C(\{a, b\}) = \{a, b\}$ otherwise.

If $\#X = 3$, let $X = \{a, b, c\}$. If i and j are c-semi-decisive over the same subset of two options, we can use f_1. If i and j are c-semi-decisive over different subsets of two options—say, i is c-semi-decisive over $\{a, b\}$ and j is c-semi-decisive over $\{b, c\}$—we can define a social choice function, f_3, in the following way. For a profile π:

$C(\{a, b\}) = \{a\}$ if for all $k \in N, a \succ_k b$,
$C(\{a, b\}) = \{b\}$ if for all $k \in N, b \succ_k a$, and
$C(\{a, b\}) = \{a, b\}$ otherwise;
$C(\{b, c\}) = \{b\}$ if for all $k \in N, b \succ_k c$,

$C(\{b, c\}) = \{c\}$ if for all $k \in N, c \succ_k b$, and
$C(\{b, c\}) = \{b, c\}$ otherwise;
$C(\{a, c\}) = \{a, c\} - P_{Par}(\{a, c\})$.

If either for all $k \in N, c \succ_k a$, or for all $k \in N, c \succ_k b$,

$C(\{a, b, c\}) = \{c\}$, and
$C(\{a, b, c\}) = \{a, b, c\} - P_{Par}(\{a, b, c\})$ otherwise.

One can verify that $C(S) \neq \emptyset$ for all non-empty S and that the conditions P and minimal 2-cWV are satified. ∎

Our next theorem is, however, negative with exactly three options, if we want the choice functions to satisfy a rationality property borrowed from the revealed preference literature. A choice function satisfies the weak axiom of revealed preference (WARP) if for S and $T \in 2^X_{-\emptyset}$ with $S \subseteq T$, $C(T) \cap S \neq \emptyset \Rightarrow C(S) = C(T) \cap S$ (see, for instance, Arrow 1959, 1984 and Schwartz 1976).

Definition 11 (weak axiom of revealed preference: WARP). *A social choice function,* $f : \Pi' \to \mathbb{C}$, *is said to satisfy WARP if all choice functions* $C \in \mathbb{C}$ *satisfy WARP.*

Theorem 3. *Let us assume that* $X = \{a, b, c\}$. *Then there is no social choice function satisfying U, P, minimal 2-cWV and WARP, provided that the individuals i and j of the definition of c-2WV are not c-semi-decisive over the same subset of options.*

Proof. Let f be a social choice function satisfying U, P, 2-cWV and WARP. Assume that i is c-semi-decisive over $\{a, b\}$ and j is c-semi-decisive over $\{b, c\}$. Consider a profile π such that $a \succ_i b, b \succ_j c$ and for all $k \in N, c \succ_k a$. Observe that $c \succ_i a \succ_i b$ and $b \succ_j c \succ_j a$. Let $T = \{a, b, c\}$. Since for all $k \in N, c \succ_k a$, by condition P, $a \notin C(T)$. Then $b \in C(T)$ or $c \in C(T)$. If $b \in C(T)$, since $a \succ_i b$ and i is c-semi-decisive over $\{a, b\}$, $a \in C(T)$, a contradiction. As a consequence, $C(T) = \{c\}$. But $\{c\} = C(T) \cap \{b, c\}$. By WARP, one should have $C(\{b, c\}) = \{c\}$. Since j is c-semi-decisive over $\{b, c\}$ and $b \succ_j c, c \in C(\{b, c\}) \Rightarrow b \in C(\{b, c\})$, a contradiction. ∎

Of course, as in Sen's result, it is a straightforward matter to establish corollaries to Theorems 2 and 3 by replacing minimal 2-cWV by general 2-cWV. These corollaries are omitted.

IV. DISCUSSION

In this section, I wish to make some remarks and comments.

First, with Sen-type theorems there is no need to assume that N is finite. Of course, giving practical meaning to infinite N may be hazardous, although in mathematical economics this kind of assumption (even the assumption of a non-countable infinite) is routinely made, for instance to model perfect competition.

Second, compared with the framework in Salles (2007), it is interesting to consider the notions of 2-dictatorship or 2-vetoers. For aggregation functions, Sen's notions of liberalism request that two individuals (or all individuals) be decisive over a subset of two options. This means that, for individual i, and for two options a and b, a is socially preferred to b whenever i prefers a to b, and b is socially preferred to a if (s)he prefers b to a. There is then some compulsory effect on both a and b at the level of the social preference. The preference, be it individual or social, is a kind of global notion. On the other hand, in the social choice function setting, b is not chosen when a is available whenever i prefers a to b (and a is not chosen when a is available whenever i prefers b to a). This means that one option is rejected, but it does not mean that one option is chosen. This is why I have refrained from using the word "dictator" in this context, preferring "strong veto". Of course, when one considers the subset $S = \{a, b\}$, $C(S) = \{a\}$ whenever i prefers a to b. Only in this case have we something that is reminiscent of a local dictatorship. In other cases, the status of a vis-à-vis the choice set remains uncertain. In the present chapter, I have introduced the notion of "weak veto" as a weakening of "strong veto". With weak veto, b is not necessarily rejected when a is available whenever i prefers a to b. But if b is not rejected (that is, if b is chosen), then a has to be chosen too. In the aggregation function setting, the weakening of the liberalism condition consists in requesting that a be socially at least as good as b whenever i prefers a to b etc. Again, in the social choice function framework, it is only in the case of $S = \{a, b\}$ that we have either $C(S) = \{a, b\}$ or $C(S) = \{a\}$ whenever i prefers a to b. In the other cases the status of a is linked to the status of b. If b is not chosen, the status of a is again uncertain.

An important feature of the main result obtained in the present chapter is that it is independent of any properties of the choice functions and is, accordingly, exactly of the same kind as the social choice functions version of Sen's theorem (with the exception of the assumptions on the number of options and on the subsets over which the individuals have a limited weak veto, but I believe that these assumptions are not very restrictive). In Salles (2007), the new results were obtained for specific aggregation functions (social welfare functions, or functions whose values were semi-orders or interval orders). These functions require that the social preferences be "more rational" than the social preferences obtained in the case of Sen's social decision function. (Incidentally, they are even more rational than the aggregation functions whose values are quasi-transitive social preferences, aggregation functions for which a Pareto extension function gives a kind of counter-example with every individual being a (non-limited) vetoer.) It is however rather surprising that the assumptions concerning the number of options and the subsets over which the individuals have a limited weak veto in Theorem 2 of the present chapter are identical to the assumptions made in Theorem 4 in Salles (2007) (for semi-ordered social preferences) and that when $\#X \geq 3$ (this case was dealt with for social welfare functions) we need (for $\#X = 3$) a specific assumption on social choice functions (viz. WARP) that plays a major rôle in rationalizability by complete preorders.

In Salles (2007), I tried to compare Sen-type theorems and Arrovian theorems. I cannot establish this kind of comparison in the present chapter, because Arrovian theorems in the social choice functions setting have recourse to properties of choice functions (path-independence, Chernoff condition, base-acyclicity, etc.).[9]

I will not discuss the non-welfaristic aspects of the new results, since the comments that one can find in many papers by Amartya Sen, in Pattanaik (1994) and in Salles (2007) apply to these results.

V. CONCLUSION

In this paper, Sen's liberalism conditions have been weakened in a social choice functions setting where choice functions are obtained, rather than the case in which social preferences are obtained in an aggregation function framework. The social choice functions setting can be justified to some extent by the claim that rights are the possibility of preventing something from happening. The proposed weakening does not take us very far, since impossibilities will occur for exactly the same kind of functions. In fact Theorem 2 can be considered as a kind of generalization of Sen's theorem (Theorem 1), though due regard should be paid to the specific conditions on the number of options and the subsets of options over which two individuals have a weak veto.

REFERENCES

ARROW, K. J. (1950), "A Difficulty in the Concept of Social Welfare", *Journal of Political Economy*, 58: 328–46.

—— (1951), *Social Choice and Individual Values* (New York: Wiley; 2nd edn 1963).

—— (1959), "Rational Choice Functions and Orderings", *Economica*, 26: 121–7.

—— (1984), *Individual Choice under Certainty and Uncertainty*, vol. 3 of *Collected Papers of Kenneth J. Arrow* (Oxford: Blackwell).

[9] See Blair *et al.* (1976) and Suzumura (1983).

BARBERÀ, S., BOSSERT, W., and PATTANAIK, P. K. (2004), "Ranking Sets of Objects", in S. Barberà, P. J. Hammond and C. Seidl (eds), *Handbook of Utility Theory*, vol. 2 (Dordrecht: Kluwer).

BLAIR, D. H., BORDES, G., KELLY, J. S., and SUZUMURA, K. (1976), "Impossibility Theorems without Collective Rationality", *Journal of Economic Theory*, 13: 361–79.

FISHBURN, P. C. (1975), "Semiorders and Choice Functions", *Econometrica*, 43: 975–7.

—— (1985), *Interval Orders and Interval Graphs* (New York: Wiley).

GAERTNER, W., PATTANAIK, P. K., and SUZUMURA, K. (1992), "Individual Rights Revisited", *Economica*, 59: 161–77.

GÄRDENFORS, P. (1981), "Rights, Games and Social Choice", *Nous*, 15: 341–56.

—— (2005), *The Dynamics of Thought* (Heidelberg: Springer).

GIBBARD, A. (1974), "A Pareto-Consistent Libertarian Claim", *Journal of Economic Theory*, 7: 388–410.

IGERSHEIM, H. (2006), "Invoking a Cartesian Product Structure on Social States: New Resolutions of Sen's and Gibbard's Impossibility Theorems", working paper, CODE, Universitat Autonoma de Barcelona.

JAMISON, D. T., and LAU, L. J. (1973), "Semiorders and the Theory of Choice", *Econometrica*, 41: 901–12.

KARNI, E. (1974), "Individual Liberty, the Pareto Principle and the Possibility of Social Decision Function", working paper, Foerder Institute for Economic Research, Tel-Aviv University.

PATTANAIK, P. K. (1994), "Some Non-Welfaristic Issues in Welfare Economics", in B. Dutta (ed.), *Welfare Economics* (Delhi: Oxford University Press).

—— (1996), "On Modelling Individual Rights: Some Conceptual Issues", in K. J. Arrow, A. K. Sen and K. Suzumura (eds), *Social Choice Reexamined*, vol. 4 (London: Macmillan).

—— and XU, Y. (1990), "On Ranking Opportunity Sets in Terms of Freedom of Choice", *Recherches Economiques de Louvain*, 56: 383–90.

PELEG, B. (1998), "Effectivity Functions, Game Forms, Games, and Rights", *Social Choice and Welfare*, 15: 67–80, repr. in J.-F. Laslier, M. Fleurbaey, N. Gravel and A. Trannoy (eds), *Freedom in Economics: New Perspectives in Normative Economics* (London: Routledge).

SAARI, D. G., and PÉTRON, A. (2006), "Negative Externalities and Sen's Liberalism Theorem", *Economic Theory*, 28: 265–81.

SALLES, M. (2007), "Limited Rights as Partial Veto and Sen's Impossibility Theorem", working paper, University of Caen.

SCHWARTZ, T. (1976), "Choice Functions, 'Rationality' Conditions, and Variations on the Weak Axiom of Revealed Preference", *Journal of Economic Theory*, 13: 414–27.

SEN, A. K. (1970a), "The Impossibility of a Paretian Liberal", *Journal of Political Economy*, 78: 152–7.

—— (1970b). *Collective Choice and Social Welfare* (San Francisco: Holden-Day).

—— (1971), "Choice Functions and Revealed Preference", *Review of Economic Studies*, 38: 307–17.

—— (1976), "Liberty, Unanimity and Rights", *Economica*, 43: 217–45

—— (1982), *Choice, Welfare and Measurement* (Oxford: Blackwell).

—— (2002), *Rationality and Freedom* (Cambridge, Mass.: Harvard University Press).

SUPPES, P., KRANTZ, D. H., LUCE, R. D., and TVERSKY, A. (1989), *Foundations of Measurement*, vol. 2 (New York: Academic Press).

SUZUMURA, K. (1976), "Rational Choice and Revealed Preference", *Review of Economic Studies*, 43: 149–58.

—— (1983), *Rational Choice, Collective Decisions and Social Welfare* (Cambridge: Cambridge University Press).

—— (2006), "Rights, Opportunities, and Social Choice Procedures", in K. J. Arrow, A. K. Sen and K. Suzumura (eds), *Handbook of Social Choice and Welfare*, vol. 2 (Amsterdam: Elsevier).

CHAPTER 15

DOMINANCE CRITERIA FOR CRITICAL-LEVEL GENERALIZED UTILITARIANISM

ALAIN TRANNOY

JOHN A. WEYMARK

I. INTRODUCTION

WHILE Dalton (1920) was the first to ground the measurement of income inequality on social welfare considerations, it was not until the pioneering articles of Kolm (1969), Atkinson (1970), Dasgupta, Sen and Starrett (1973), and Rothschild and Stiglitz (1973) that a systematic attempt was made to provide normative foundations for the measurement of inequality.[1] The theoretical analyses of Atkinson and Kolm,

We thank Mike Hoy for his comments. This research was conducted during a visit of John Weymark to GREQAM. He gratefully acknowledges the financial support of the Ecole des Hautes Etudes en Sciences Sociales, which made this visit possible.

[1] See Sen (1973) for an illuminating discussion of these articles.

are restricted to comparisons of distributions for the same number of individuals. However, as Dasgupta, Sen and Starrett (1973: 184) have observed, in order to make inequality comparisons across countries or time, it is necessary to consider populations of different sizes. A natural way to extend fixed-population results to the variable-population case is provided by Dalton's Principle of Population (Dalton 1920). This principle regards an income distribution and any replication of it as exhibiting the same degree of inequality. The dominance criteria based on Lorenz and generalized Lorenz curves satisfy this population replication principle. Following Dasgupta, Sen and Starrett (1973), it is now standard practice to make comparisons involving different-sized populations on the basis of Dalton's principle.[2] However, by employing this principle, one is implicitly assuming that inequality and social welfare should be thought of in per capita terms and hence that population size is not a concern.

About the same time that the foundations of the modern theory of inequality measurement were being laid, there was a resurgence of interest in population ethics (see, for example, Dasgupta 1969). Particularly influential contributions to this literature were provided by Blackorby and Donaldson (1984) and Parfit (1984).[3] One of their central concerns is determining under what circumstances the addition of a person to a given population should be regarded as welfare-improving. To answer this question, Blackorby and Donaldson (1984) proposed using a generalization of classical utilitarianism called critical-level generalized utilitarianism as a social objective.

To date, the ethical debates about the best way to evaluate distributions of utilities for different population sizes has not had any impact on normatively based inequality measurement. In this chapter, we make an initial attempt at integrating the literatures on population ethics and inequality measurement by investigating the implications for social welfare dominance criteria of making comparisons of distributions of utilities (or any other scalar attribute of well-being, such as income or wealth) using critical-level generalized utilitarian social welfare functions.[4] Dominance criteria based on critical-level generalized utilitarianism provide an alternative to the generalized Lorenz dominance criterion of Tomić (1949), Kolm (1969), Rothschild and Stiglitz (1973), Shorrocks (1983) and Kakwani (1984). Our new dominance criteria are of interest in so far as one would like a measure of social welfare for the population as a whole, rather than some measure of welfare per capita, as is implicitly the case with generalized Lorenz dominance.

---

[2] Aboudi, Thon and Wallace (2008) have recently proposed an alternative to Dalton's principle that involves generalizing the idea of an equalizing transfer so that it applies to transfers between populations of different sizes.

[3] Two recent monographs on population ethics are Broome (2004) and Blackorby, Bossert and Donaldson (2005).

[4] A social welfare function is a real-valued function defined on distributions of utilities.

The generalized Lorenz dominance criterion provides a quasi-ordering of alternative income distributions for homogeneous populations.[5] According to this criterion, one income distribution weakly dominates a second if the generalized Lorenz curve for the former lies nowhere below the generalized Lorenz curve for the latter. With a population of size n, for each fraction k/n of the population, $k = 0, \ldots, n$, a generalized Lorenz curve plots one nth of the total income of the poorest k people against k/n, with linear interpolation used so that the curve is defined for all points $p \in [0, 1]$. This curve is simply the Lorenz curve scaled up by the mean income. This dominance criterion can be applied both when the size of the population is the same in both distributions and when it is not. Replicating a population and its distribution of incomes has no effect on the shape of a generalized Lorenz curve and hence, as we have already noted, the generalized Lorenz criterion satisfies Dalton's Principle of Population.

In homogeneous populations, everyone receives the same utility from a given amount of income. When this is the case, Kakwani (1984) and Shorrocks (1983) have shown that the average utility for one income distribution is no less than the average utility for a second income distribution for all continuous, increasing, concave utility functions if and only if the former distribution generalized-Lorenz-dominates the latter. We shall henceforth refer to this result as the Kakwani–Shorrocks Theorem. More generally, assuming that the social welfare function is invariant to a replication of the distribution of utilities (and hence invariant to a replication of the income distribution), a straightforward extension of an argument developed for Lorenz domination by Dasgupta, Sen and Starrett (1973) shows that it is sufficient for the equivalence between welfare dominance and generalized Lorenz dominance to hold that the social welfare function is increasing, symmetric and quasi-concave for each population size. It is not necessary for the social welfare function to aggregate utilities by taking their average. Note that the replication invariance property of the social welfare function implies that overall social welfare is being measured in per capita terms.

The generalized Lorenz dominance criterion can also be applied to distributions of utility. In this case, the Kakwani–Shorrocks Theorem shows that one distribution of utilities is weakly preferred to a second distribution by all inequality-averse average generalized utilitarian social welfare functions if and only if the former utility distribution generalized-Lorenz-dominates the latter. In its inequality-averse formulation, average generalized utilitarianism applies a common continuous, increasing, concave transform to each person's utility before averaging across individuals to form the social objective function (see Blackorby, Bossert and Donaldson 2005: 171). Average utilitarianism is simply the special case in which this function is defined using the identity transform.

---

[5] A quasi-ordering is a reflexive and transitive binary relation. For a good introduction to generalized Lorenz dominance, see Lambert (2001: ch. 3).

As Blackorby, Bossert and Donaldson (2005: 143) have noted, average utilitarianism "makes some stark trade-offs: an alternative with a population of any size in which each person is equally well off is ranked as worse than an alternative in which a single person experiences a trivially higher utility level". The same observation can also be made about any social welfare function that is defined in per capita terms, such as average generalized utilitarianism. As another example of these questionable trade-offs, consider a poor country that experiences a marginal decrease in utility per capita but in which the distribution of utilities remains unchanged as measured by the Lorenz criterion. According to the generalized Lorenz criterion, there has been a loss in social welfare, even if the population has increased substantially.

Classical utilitarianism does not fare much better, as it suffers from what Parfit (1984: 388) has called the repugnant conclusion. A social welfare ranking of utility distributions is subject to the repugnant conclusion if any distribution in which everyone's utility is positive, no matter how large, is socially worse than some other distribution for a larger population in which everyone's utility is arbitrarily close to zero.[6] Average utilitarianism avoids the repugnant conclusion because the addition of an individual to the population is welfare-improving only if his or her utility exceeds the intial average utility level.

Critical-level generalized utilitarianism was introduced by Blackorby and Donaldson (1984) in order to overcome these problems with average and classical utilitarianism. What distinguishes a critical-level population principle is the existence of a utility level c such that adding a person with this utility to any utility distribution is a matter of social indifference. The objective function for a critical-level generalized utilitarian social welfare function is obtained from the objective function for a generalized utilitarian social welfare function by subjecting the critical level to the same transform that is applied to utilities and subtracting this amount from each person's transformed utility before summing across individuals. By choosing the critical level to be positive, the repugnant conclusion is avoided. In our example of a poor country with declining per capita utility, a critical-level generalized utilitarian may regard this change as a social improvement if the proportion of the added population with utilities above the critical level is sufficiently large.[7]

As noted above, we are interested in developing social welfare dominance criteria for comparing distributions of utilities using inequality-averse critical-level generalized utilitarian social welfare functions. These welfare dominance criteria can be given different interpretations. In one interpretation, there is a social planner whose preferences (as expressed by the social welfare function) agrees with the ethical norms underlying critical-level generalized utilitarianism when this

---

[6] In most formal models of population ethics (e.g. Blackorby, Bossert and Donaldson 2005) zero utility represents a neutral life, with negative utilities corresponding to lives considered to be not worth living.

[7] For a detailed discussion of critical-level generalized utilitarianism and related population principles, see Blackorby, Bossert and Donaldson (2005).

principle exhibits inequality aversion. As in traditional welfare dominance analysis, this planner wants to propose a social welfare ranking that has widespread support, and so he identifies the quasi-ordering that is obtained by taking the intersection of all of the inequality-averse critical-level generalized utilitarian orderings of the utility distributions for a given critical level. Alternatively, we can suppose that every individual agrees that utility distributions should be ranked by a critical-level generalized utilitarian social welfare function, but they disagree about which transform should be applied to the individual utilities before aggregating. By taking the intersection of all such rankings for a given critical level, we obtain the same dominance relation as in the social-planner interpretation of the problem.

Our main objective is to establish an analogue of the Kakwani–Shorrocks Theorem for critical-level generalized utilitarianism. To do this, we introduce a new graphical representation of a distribution called a *generalized concentration curve*. For distributions of utilities, this curve plots the sum of the utilities of the t individuals with the smallest utilities against t. For a given critical level c, we define a dominance criterion based on these generalized concentration curves and show that this dominance criterion identifies the same quasi-ordering of utility distributions as does the critical-level generalized utilitarian dominance criterion described above. We also extend our results to allow for the possibility that the critical level lies within some range, rather than being known for certain. This extension is based on a generalization of critical-level generalized utilitarianism introduced by Blackorby, Bossert and Donaldson (1996) called critical-band generalized utilitarianism.

In section II, we consider welfare dominance based on average generalized utilitarianism and formally state the Kakwani–Shorrocks Theorem. In section III, we present our welfare dominance results for critical-level generalized utilitarianism when the critical level is known. We extend these results in section IV to the case in which the critical level is only known to lie in some interval. In section V, we offer some concluding remarks.

II. Welfare Dominance for Average Generalized Utilitarianism

A utility distribution for a population of size $n \in \mathbb{N}$ is a vector $\mathbf{u} = (u_1, \ldots, u_n) \in \mathbb{R}^n$, where u_i is the ith person's utility, $i = 1, \ldots, n$, and $\mathbb{N}$ is the set of positive integers.[8] The set of possible utility distributions is $\mathcal{U} = \cup_{n \in \mathbb{N}} \mathbb{R}^n$. While we are interpreting the variable whose distribution is of interest to be utility, it can also

---

[8] We shall also have occasion to consider the set of non-negative integers, $\mathbb{N}^*$.

be interpreted as any other scalar attribute of well-being, such as income or wealth, provided that the critical level is defined in terms of this attribute, not utility.[9] For all $\mathbf{u} \in \mathcal{U}$, $n(\mathbf{u})$ denotes the size of the population in $\mathbf{u}$ and $\mathbf{u}_\uparrow$ denotes the vector in which the components of $\mathbf{u}$ have been rearranged in a non-decreasing order. A *social welfare function* is a mapping $W : \mathcal{U} \to \mathbb{R}$.

II.1 Generalized Lorenz Dominance

The *generalized Lorenz curve* for a utility distribution $\mathbf{u} \in \mathcal{U}$ is a function $GL_{\mathbf{u}} : [0, 1] \to \mathbb{R}$ defined as follows. For each $p \in [0, 1]$, let k_p be the smallest integer $k_p \in \{0, \dots, n(\mathbf{u}) - 1\}$ such that $\frac{k_p}{n(\mathbf{u})} \leq p \leq \frac{(k_p+1)}{n(\mathbf{u})}$, and let $\lambda_p \in [0, 1]$ be the unique number for which $p = (1 - \lambda_p)\frac{k_p}{n(\mathbf{u})} + \lambda_p \frac{(k_p+1)}{n(\mathbf{u})}$. Then, for all $p \in [0, 1]$,

$$GL_{\mathbf{u}}(p) = \frac{1}{n(\mathbf{u})} \left[\sum_{i=0}^{k_p} u_{\uparrow i} + \lambda_p [u_{\uparrow k_p+1} - u_{\uparrow k_p}] \right], \tag{2.1}$$

where $u_{\uparrow 0} = 0$.

The generalized Lorenz curve is well defined and convex for all $\mathbf{u} \in \mathcal{U}$. In contrast, the Lorenz curve for $\mathbf{u}$ is not defined if the mean utility is zero and is concave if the mean is negative. If some utilities are negative, then initially a generalized Lorenz curve has a negative slope. For a perfectly equal distribution, the slope is constant and equal to the mean.[10] Note that when $p = \frac{k}{n(\mathbf{u})}$ for some $k \in \{1, \dots, n(\mathbf{u})\}$ (in which case $k_p = k - 1$), the formula in (2.1) simplifies to

$$GL_{\mathbf{u}}(p) = \frac{1}{n(\mathbf{u})} \sum_{i=1}^{k} u_{\uparrow i}. \tag{2.2}$$

The *generalized Lorenz dominance* criterion is the quasi-ordering $\succsim^{\mathrm{GL}}$ on $\mathcal{U}$ for which one utility distribution weakly dominates a second utility distribution if the generalized Lorenz curve for the first distribution lies nowhere below that of the second.[11]

---

[9] In some of these alternative interpretations of the model, it may be natural to require all distributions to be non-negative. The formal results presented here also hold with this restriction. Such a restriction is appropriate when the attribute being considered is wage income, but not when it is income from self-employment or wealth. For example, in their study of Israeli *kibbutzim*, Amiel, Cowell and Polovin (1996) found that the incomes and wealth of some *kibbutzim* were negative for some years in their sample.

[10] See Amiel, Cowell and Polovin (1996) and Jenkins and Jäntii (2008) for further discussion of the properties of a Lorenz curve when $\mathbf{u}$ has one or more negative components.

[11] For any binary relation $\succsim$ on $\mathcal{U}$, the corresponding asymmetric and symmetric factors are denoted by $\succ$ and $\sim$ respectively.

Generalized Lorenz dominance. For all $\mathbf{u}, \mathbf{u}' \in \mathcal{U}$,

$$\mathbf{u} \succsim^{GL} \mathbf{u}' \Leftrightarrow GL_{\mathbf{u}}(p) \geq GL_{\mathbf{u}'}(p) \text{ for all } p \in [0, 1]. \tag{2.3}$$

If $\mathbf{u}, \mathbf{u}' \in \mathbb{R}^n$, then (2.3) simplifies to:

$$\mathbf{u} \succsim^{GL} \mathbf{u}' \Leftrightarrow \sum_{i=1}^{k} u_{\uparrow i} \geq \sum_{i=1}^{k} u'_{\uparrow i} \text{ for all } k \in \{1, \dots, n\}. \tag{2.4}$$

II.2 Average Generalized Utilitarian Dominance

An average generalized utilitarian social welfare function is characterized by a *utility transform* $g: \mathbb{R} \to \mathbb{R}$. The transform g that is applied to the individual utilities permits the social value of utility to diverge from its individual value. We assume that $g \in \mathcal{C}$, the set of increasing concave functions for which $g(0) = 0$.[12] The social welfare function for *average generalized utilitarianism* with utility transform g is given by

$$W_g^A(\mathbf{u}) = \frac{1}{n(\mathbf{u})} \sum_{i=1}^{n(\mathbf{u})} g(u_i), \quad \forall \mathbf{u} \in \mathcal{U}. \tag{2.5}$$

By requiring g to be concave, the social welfare function is weakly inequality-averse. If g is the identity mapping, then W_g^A is the social welfare function for *average utilitarianism*.

Consider any pair of distributions $\mathbf{u}, \mathbf{u}' \in \mathcal{U}$. The change in social welfare ΔW_g^A that results from a change in the distribution from $\mathbf{u}'$ to $\mathbf{u}$ is

$$\Delta W_g^A(\mathbf{u}, \mathbf{u}') = W_g^A(\mathbf{u}) - W_g^A(\mathbf{u}'). \tag{2.6}$$

The *average generalized utilitarian dominance* quasi-ordering $\succsim^A$ on $\mathcal{U}$ is defined by taking the intersection of the orderings of the utility distributions in $\mathcal{U}$ for all average generalized utilitarian social welfare functions. That is, this quasi-ordering identifies the ordered pairs of utility distributions for which the change in social welfare ΔW_g^A is non-negative, no matter how inequality-averse the social welfare function is as measured by the utility transform g.

Average generalized utilitarian dominance. For all $\mathbf{u}, \mathbf{u}' \in \mathcal{U}$,

$$\mathbf{u} \succsim^A \mathbf{u}' \Leftrightarrow \Delta W_g^A(\mathbf{u}, \mathbf{u}') \geq 0 \text{ for all } g \in \mathcal{C}. \tag{2.7}$$

---

[12] As we shall see, the assumption that $g(0) = 0$ is a harmless normalization. If utilities are restricted to be non-negative and thus g is only defined on $\mathbb{R}_+$, in order to ensure that g is continuous it is also necessary to assume that g is continuous at the origin.

II.3 The Kakwani–Shorrocks Theorem

The Kakwani–Shorrocks Theorem shows that one distribution of utilities generalized-Lorenz-dominates a second if and only if the former average-generalized-utilitarian-dominates the latter.[13]

Proposition 1. *For all* $\mathbf{u}, \mathbf{u}' \in \mathcal{U}$, $\mathbf{u} \succsim^{GL} \mathbf{u}' \Leftrightarrow \mathbf{u} \succsim^{A} \mathbf{u}'$.

Proposition 1 is a variable-population extension of the fixed-population version of this theorem due to Tomić (1949).[14] It is instructive to see how it is possible to use Tomić's Theorem to establish Proposition 1. Consider any $\mathbf{u} \in \mathbb{R}^n$ and $\mathbf{u}' \in \mathbb{R}^{n'}$. Let $\hat{\mathbf{u}}$ be the utility distribution obtained by replicating $\mathbf{u}$ n' times. Similarly, $\hat{\mathbf{u}}'$ is obtained by replicating $\mathbf{u}'$ n times. By construction, $\mathbf{u} \sim^{GL} \hat{\mathbf{u}}$ and $\mathbf{u}' \sim^{GL} \hat{\mathbf{u}}'$. Therefore, $\mathbf{u} \succsim^{GL} \mathbf{u}' \Leftrightarrow \hat{\mathbf{u}} \succsim^{GL} \hat{\mathbf{u}}'$. For any $g \in \mathcal{C}$, $W_g^A(\mathbf{u}) = W_g^A(\hat{\mathbf{u}})$ and $W_g^A(\mathbf{u}') = W_g^A(\hat{\mathbf{u}}')$. Hence, $\mathbf{u} \succsim^{A} \mathbf{u}' \Leftrightarrow \hat{\mathbf{u}} \succsim^{A} \hat{\mathbf{u}}'$. Because $\hat{\mathbf{u}}$ and $\hat{\mathbf{u}}'$ are both in $\mathbb{R}^{nn'}$, Tomić's Theorem implies that $\hat{\mathbf{u}} \succsim^{GL} \hat{\mathbf{u}}' \Leftrightarrow \hat{\mathbf{u}} \succsim^{A} \hat{\mathbf{u}}'$. Proposition 1 then follows from these equivalences. Thus, as in Dasgupta, Sen and Starrett (1973) and Shorrocks (1983), replications of two utility distributions are used in order to reduce any variable-population comparison to one in which the population size is fixed.

III. Welfare Dominance for Critical-Level Generalized Utilitarianism

III.1 Critical-Level Generalized Utilitarian Dominance

A critical-level generalized utilitarian social welfare function is characterized by a critical level $c \in \mathbb{R}$ and a utility transform $g \in \mathcal{C}$. For any utility distribution $\mathbf{u} \in \mathcal{U}$, adding an individual to the population with utility level c is a matter of social indifference. The social welfare function for *critical-level generalized utilitarianism*

---

[13] See Kakwani (1984: Theorem 1). This theorem is not stated explictly in Shorrocks (1983), but it follows from the Corollary to his Theorem 2 and his remarks in n. 7 and on p. 8. Neither Kakwani nor Shorrocks assumes that $g(0) = 0$. However, if g does not satisfy this property, it can be made to do so by replacing $g(t)$ with $\overline{g}(t) = g(t) - g(0)$ for all $t \in \mathbb{R}$ without affecting the sum in (2.5).

[14] See Marshall and Olkin (1979: Theorem 4.B.2). Versions of Tomić's Theorem have also been established by Kolm (1969) and Rothschild and Stiglitz (1973). Kakwani and Shorrocks appear to be the first to have applied the generalized Lorenz dominance criterion to populations of different sizes.

with critical level c and utility transform g is given by

$$W_{c,g}(\mathbf{u}) = \sum_{i=1}^{n(\mathbf{u})} [g(u_i) - g(c)], \quad \forall \mathbf{u} \in \mathcal{U}.^{15} \tag{3.1}$$

If g is the identity mapping, then $W_{c,g}$ is the social welfare function for critical-level utilitarianism with critical level c. If, furthermore, $c = 0$, we then have *classical* (total) *utilitarianism*. Analogous to (2.6), for all $\mathbf{u}, \mathbf{u}' \in \mathcal{U}$, let

$$\Delta W_{c,g}(\mathbf{u}, \mathbf{u}') = W_{c,g}(\mathbf{u}) - W_{c,g}(\mathbf{u}'). \tag{3.2}$$

The *critical-level c generalized utilitarian dominance* quasi-ordering $\succsim_c^{CL}$ on $\mathcal{U}$ is defined by taking the intersection of the orderings of the utility distributions in $\mathcal{U}$ for all critical-level generalized utilitarian social welfare functions when the critical level is fixed at c. Analogous to the construction of the average generalized utilitarian dominance relation, this quasi-ordering identifies the ordered pairs of utility distributions for which the change in social welfare $\Delta W_{c,g}$ is non-negative regardless of the degree of inequality aversion exhibited by the social welfare function, i.e. regardless of the degree of concavity of the transform g.

Critical-level c generalized utilitarian dominance. For all $c \in \mathbb{R}$, for all $\mathbf{u}, \mathbf{u}' \in \mathcal{U}$,

$$\mathbf{u} \succsim_c^{CL} \mathbf{u}' \Leftrightarrow \Delta W_{c,g}(\mathbf{u}, \mathbf{u}') \geq 0 \text{ for all } g \in \mathcal{C}. \tag{3.3}$$

For comparisons of two utility distributions with the same population size, average generalized utilitarian and critical-level c generalized utilitarian dominance are equivalent criteria because the terms involving the critical level cancel out in the welfare difference in (3.2) and the sign of the welfare difference in (2.6) is unaffected if average utility is replaced by the sum of utilities. However, this equivalence no longer holds if the two distributions are for populations of different sizes.

III.2 Critical-Level Generalized Concentration Curve Dominance

Generalized Lorenz dominance employs replications of distributions in order to reduce a variable-population comparison to a fixed-population equivalent. However, replicating a utility distribution is not a matter of social indifference for any critical-level generalized utilitarian rule. Nevertheless, adding individuals with utility equal to the critical level is. This observation provides a basis for identifying a new

---

[15] For an axiomatization of this population principle, see Blackorby, Bossert and Donaldson (1998: Theorem 2).

dominance criterion that can be used to establish an analogue to Proposition 1 for critical-level c generalized utilitarian dominance. Furthermore, this criterion coincides with the generalized Lorenz dominance quasi-ordering for fixed-population comparisons.

For any utility distribution, a generalized concentration curve plots the sum of the utilities of the t individuals with the smallest utilities against t, using linear interpolation so that the curve is defined for non-integer values of t. Formally, the *generalized concentration curve* for $\mathbf{u} \in \mathcal{U}$ is the function $GC_{\mathbf{u}}: [0, n(\mathbf{u})] \to \mathbb{R}$ defined as follows. For each $t \in [0, n(\mathbf{u})]$, let k_t be the smallest integer $k_t \in \{0, \ldots, n(\mathbf{u}) - 1\}$ such that $k_t \leq t \leq k + 1$, and let $\lambda_t \in [0, 1]$ be the unique number for which $t - (1 - \lambda_t)k_t + \lambda_t(k_t + 1)$. Then, for all $t \in \lfloor 0, n(\mathbf{u}) \rfloor$;

$$GC_{\mathbf{u}}(t) = \sum_{i=0}^{k_t} u_{\uparrow i} + \lambda_t [u_{\uparrow k_t + 1} - u_{\uparrow k_t}]. \qquad (3.4)$$

The generalized concentration curve is well defined and convex for all $\mathbf{u} \in \mathcal{U}$. If some utilities are negative, then initially this curve has a negative slope. For a perfectly equal distribution, the slope is constant and equal to the common utility value. When $t \in \{1, \ldots, n(\mathbf{u})\}$, (3.4) simplifies to

$$GC_{\mathbf{u}}(t) = \sum_{i=1}^{t} u_{\uparrow i}. \qquad (3.5)$$

The construction of a generalized concentration curve is illustrated in Fig. 15.1. The solid lines in this diagram show the generalized concentration curves for the distributions $\mathbf{u}^1 = (5, 5, 10, 15, 25)$ and $\mathbf{u}^2 = (-20, 0, 20, 40)$.

Had we plotted the fraction of the total utility for the population as a whole that is obtained by the t individuals with the smallest utilities against t, the resulting curve would be formally equivalent to what is known in the literature on the measurement of industrial concentration as a concentration curve (see, for example, Blackorby, Donaldson and Weymark 1982).[16] In this application, firms correspond to individuals and output or sales correspond to incomes. Thus, a generalized concentration curve is obtained from a concentration curve by multiplying by the mean of the variable being considered, just as a generalized Lorenz curve is obtained from a Lorenz curve by multiplying by the mean, at least when the mean is not zero.

For utility distributions $\mathbf{u}, \mathbf{u}' \in \mathbb{R}^n$, the generalized concentration curve for $\mathbf{u}$ lies nowhere below that of $\mathbf{u}'$ if and only if the generalized Lorenz curve for $\mathbf{u}$ lies nowhere below that of $\mathbf{u}'$. However, when the number of individuals differ in two utility distributions, whether their generalized concentration curves cross or not

[16] Strictly speaking, the concentration curves used to measure industrial concentration plot the sum of the t largest utilities against t and hence are concave functions.

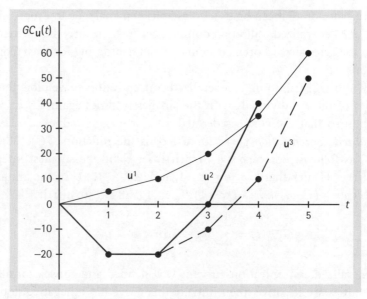

Fig. 15.1. Generalized concentration curves

is of no significance because they have different domains of definition. We are interested in defining a dominance criterion for generalized concentration curves that can be applied to both fixed- and variable-population comparisons when the critical level of utility is a given fixed value c. This is accomplished by regarding generalized concentration curves for two utility distributions with different population sizes as being in the same equivalence class of the dominance relation if the only difference in the two distributions is that one of them has additional individuals with the critical utility level.[17] In order to compare two generalized concentration curves for different populations, we augment the utility distribution for the smaller population with a sufficient number of individuals at the critical level of utility until the population sizes in the two distributions are the same.[18]

[17] In their analysis of the measurement of industrial concentration, Blackorby, Donaldson and Weymark (1982) introduced the corresponding property for concentration curves for the special case in which $c = 0$. They called their property "zero output independence". They did not consider other values of c.

[18] Since writing the first version of this chapter, we have learned that Pogge (2007: 51) has considered a dominance relation in which $\mathbf{u} \in \mathbb{R}^m$ strictly dominates $\mathbf{u}' \in \mathbb{R}^n$ when $m > n$ if (i) the n highest incomes in $\mathbf{u}_\uparrow$ are Pareto-superior to the incomes in $\mathbf{u}'_\uparrow$ (i.e. these two n-vectors are not identical and every component of the truncated version of $\mathbf{u}_\uparrow$ is no smaller than the corresponding component of $\mathbf{u}'_\uparrow$) and (ii) the remaining $(m - n)$ individuals in $\mathbf{u}_\uparrow$ have lives worth living. Except for using the Pareto criterion in a slightly different way, Pogge's proposal is equivalent to augmenting $\mathbf{u}_\uparrow$ with $(m - n)$ individuals with zero utility and then comparing this augmented distribution with $\mathbf{u}_\uparrow$ according to the Pareto criterion. Pogge does not consider critical levels other than zero, nor does he take account of the inequality in the two distributions.

For any $c \in \mathbb{R}$, the *critical-level c generalized concentration curve dominance* criterion is the quasi-ordering $\succsim_c^{GC}$ on $\mathcal{U}$ defined as follows. One utility distribution weakly dominates a second utility distribution according to this criterion if after augmenting the distribution for the smaller population (if necessary) as described above, the generalized concentration curve for the first (possibly augmented) distribution lies nowhere below that of the (possibly augmented) second distribution. To define this dominance criterion formally, we need to introduce some further definitions.

For all $\mathbf{u} \in \mathcal{U}$, $c \in \mathbb{R}$, and $\bar{n} \in \mathbb{N}^*$, the *augmented utility distribution* $\mathbf{u}_{c,\bar{n}}$ is defined by setting $\mathbf{u}_{c,\bar{n}} = (\mathbf{u}, c\mathbf{1}_{\bar{n}})$, where $\mathbf{1}_{\bar{n}}$ is the vector of ones in $\mathbb{R}^n$. Note that $\mathbf{u} = \mathbf{u}_{c,\bar{n}}$ when $\bar{n} = 0$. For all $\mathbf{u}, \mathbf{u}' \in \mathcal{U}$, let $\bar{n}(\mathbf{u}, \mathbf{u}') = 0$ if $n(\mathbf{u}) \geq n(\mathbf{u}')$, and $\bar{n}(\mathbf{u}, \mathbf{u}') = n(\mathbf{u}') - n(\mathbf{u})$ otherwise.

Critical-level c generalized concentration curve dominance. For all $c \in \mathbb{R}$, for all $\mathbf{u}, \mathbf{u}' \in \mathcal{U}$,

$$\mathbf{u} \succsim_c^{GC} \mathbf{u}' \Leftrightarrow GC_{\mathbf{u}_{c,\bar{n}(\mathbf{u},\mathbf{u}')}}(t) \geq GC_{\mathbf{u}'_{c,\bar{n}(\mathbf{u}',\mathbf{u})}}(t) \text{ for all } t \in [0, \max\{n(\mathbf{u}), n(\mathbf{u}')\}]. \quad (3.6)$$

This definition can be illustrated by using the utility distributions in Fig. 15.1. To compare $\mathbf{u}^1$ and $\mathbf{u}^2$, it is necessary to augment $\mathbf{u}^2$ by adding a single individual with the critical utility level c. For concreteness, let $c = 10$. The resulting distribution is $\mathbf{u}^3 = \mathbf{u}_{10,1}^2 = (-20, 0, 20, 40, 10)$. The corresponding concentration curve coincides with that of $\mathbf{u}^2$ for $t \leq 2$ and then shifts to the right for higher values of t, as indicated by the broken line in the diagram. We thus have $\mathbf{u}^1 \succ_{10}^{GC} \mathbf{u}^2$ even though the generalized concentration curves for $\mathbf{u}^1$ and $\mathbf{u}^2$ intersect. It is straightforward to verify that $\mathbf{u}^1 \succ_c^{GC} \mathbf{u}^2$ for all $c \leq 20$. However, if $c > 20$, then $\mathbf{u}^1$ and $\mathbf{u}^2$ are not comparable using this dominance criterion.[19]

III.3 An Equivalence Theorem

We now show that for any value of the critical level c, the quasi-ordering of the utility distributions in $\mathcal{U}$ obtained using critical-level c generalized concentration curve dominance is equivalent to that obtained using the critical-level generalized utilitarian dominance criterion for the same value of the critical level.

---

[19] In this example, there is a critical value $\hat{c}$ that separates the values of c for which the distributions $\mathbf{u}^1$ and $\mathbf{u}^2$ can be ranked according to $\succsim_c^{GC}$ from those values of c for which they cannot. More complicated patterns are also possible. For example, for given $\mathbf{u}, \mathbf{u}' \in \mathcal{U}$, there may exist two critical values $\hat{c}_1, \hat{c}_2$ with $\hat{c}_1 < \hat{c}_2$ such that $\mathbf{u} \succsim_c^{GC} \mathbf{u}'$ if $c \leq \hat{c}_1$ and $\mathbf{u}' \succsim_c^{GC} \mathbf{u}$ if $c \geq \hat{c}_2$, with the ranking indeterminate if $c \in (\hat{c}_1, \hat{c}_2)$. It would be of interest to identify restrictions on the pair of distributions being compared such that their ranking according to $\succsim_c^{GC}$ can be characterized by a small number of critical points, as in these examples.

Proposition 2. *For any $c \in \mathbb{R}$, for all $\mathbf{u}, \mathbf{u}' \in \mathcal{U}$, $\mathbf{u} \succsim_c^{GC} \mathbf{u}' \Leftrightarrow \mathbf{u} \succsim_c^{CL} \mathbf{u}'$.*

Proof. Consider any $c \in \mathbb{R}$ and $\mathbf{u}, \mathbf{u}' \in \mathcal{U}$. From (3.6), we have $\mathbf{u} \succsim_c^{GC} \mathbf{u}' \Leftrightarrow \mathbf{u}_{c,\bar{n}(\mathbf{u},\mathbf{u}')} \succsim_c^{GC} \mathbf{u}'_{c,\bar{n}(\mathbf{u}',\mathbf{u})}$. For a fixed population, it follows from their definitions that generalized Lorenz dominance coincides with critical-level c generalized concentration curve dominance for any value of $c \in \mathbb{R}$. Thus, $\mathbf{u} \succsim_c^{GC} \mathbf{u}' \Leftrightarrow \mathbf{u}_{c,\bar{n}(\mathbf{u},\mathbf{u}')} \succsim^{GL} \mathbf{u}'_{c,\bar{n}(\mathbf{u}',\mathbf{u})}$. To complete the proof, we show that the latter relation holds if and only if $\mathbf{u} \succsim_c^{GC} \mathbf{u}'$.

For any critical-level generalized utilitarian rule, adding an individual with utility equal to the critical level is a matter of social indifference. Hence, $\mathbf{u} \sim_c^{CL} \mathbf{u}_{c,\bar{n}(\mathbf{u},\mathbf{u}')}$ and $\mathbf{u}' \sim_c^{CL} \mathbf{u}'_{c,\bar{n}(\mathbf{u}',\mathbf{u})}$. The transitivity of $\succsim_c^{CL}$ then implies that $\mathbf{u} \succsim_c^{CL} \mathbf{u}' \Leftrightarrow \mathbf{u}_{c,\bar{n}(\mathbf{u},\mathbf{u}')} \succsim_c^{CL} \mathbf{u}'_{c,\bar{n}(\mathbf{u}',\mathbf{u})}$. But for fixed-population comparisons, for any $g \in \mathcal{C}$, an average generalized utilitarian rule with utility transform g ranks utility distributions in exactly the same way as a critical-level generalized utilitarian rule for the same utility transform regardless of the value of the critical level. Therefore, $\mathbf{u}_{c,\bar{n}(\mathbf{u},\mathbf{u}')} \succsim_c^{CL} \mathbf{u}'_{c,\bar{n}(\mathbf{u}',\mathbf{u})} \Leftrightarrow \mathbf{u}_{c,\bar{n}(\mathbf{u},\mathbf{u}')} \succsim^A \mathbf{u}'_{c,\bar{n}(\mathbf{u}',\mathbf{u})}$. By Proposition 1, $\mathbf{u}_{c,\bar{n}(\mathbf{u},\mathbf{u}')} \succsim^A \mathbf{u}'_{c,\bar{n}(\mathbf{u}',\mathbf{u})} \Leftrightarrow \mathbf{u}_{c,\bar{n}(\mathbf{u},\mathbf{u}')} \succsim^{GL} \mathbf{u}'_{c,\bar{n}(\mathbf{u}',\mathbf{u})}$. It then follows from these equivalences that $\mathbf{u} \succsim_c^{CL} \mathbf{u}' \Leftrightarrow \mathbf{u}_{c,\bar{n}(\mathbf{u},\mathbf{u}')} \succsim^{GL} \mathbf{u}'_{c,\bar{n}(\mathbf{u}',\mathbf{u})}$.   ∎

As we have observed, for any value of the critical level c, $\mathbf{u} \succsim_c^{CL} \mathbf{u}' \Leftrightarrow \mathbf{u} \succsim^{GL} \mathbf{u}'$ whenever $n(\mathbf{u}) = n(\mathbf{u}')$. However, when $n(\mathbf{u}) \neq n(\mathbf{u}')$, $\mathbf{u} \succsim_c^{CL} \mathbf{u}'$ is neither a necessary nor a sufficient condition for $\mathbf{u} \succsim^{GL} \mathbf{u}'$. For example, suppose that $n(\mathbf{u}') > n(\mathbf{u})$ and that $\mathbf{u} \sim_c^{CL} \mathbf{u}'$. By Proposition 2, we therefore have $\mathbf{u}_{c,\bar{n}(\mathbf{u},\mathbf{u}')} \sim^{GL} \mathbf{u}'$. However, if $u_i > c$ for all $i \in \{1, \ldots, n(\mathbf{u})\}$, then by Proposition 1, we have $\mathbf{u} \succ^{GL} \mathbf{u}_{c,\bar{n}(\mathbf{u},\mathbf{u}')}$, from which it follows that $\mathbf{u} \succ^{GL} \mathbf{u}'$. A similar argument shows that $\mathbf{u}' \succ^{GL} \mathbf{u}$ if $u_i < c$ for all $i \in \{1, \ldots, n(\mathbf{u})\}$.

Blackorby, Bossert and Donaldson (2003: 375) have introduced a generalization of critical-level generalized utilitarianism called *number-sensitive critical-level generalized utilitarianism* (see also Blackorby, Bossert and Donaldson 2005: 168). With this principle, the critical level is permitted to depend on the population size, but not on the individual utilities. It is straightforward to extend Proposition 2 so that it applies to number-sensitive critical-level generalized utilitarianism. Note that the augmentation procedure used above to convert two distributions into distributions for populations of the same size only involves augmenting the distribution for the smaller population by adding an appropriate number of individuals with the fixed critical level. If, however, the critical level is permitted to depend on population size, then it is these number-sensitive critical levels that are used when adding individuals. For example, if the smaller population contains 10 people and the larger contains 12, then two people are added to the smaller population distribution, one person with the critical level for a population of size 10 and one person with the critical level for a population of size 11.

IV. CRITICAL-BAND GENERALIZED
UTILITARIAN DOMINANCE

Blackorby, Bossert and Donaldson (1996, 2005) have considered a generalization of critical-level c generalized utilitarian dominance that allows for there to be a range of critical levels. Consider any $\underline{c}, \overline{c} \in \mathbb{R}$ with $\underline{c} < \overline{c}$. The interval $[\underline{c}, \overline{c}]$ is interpreted as being the smallest *band* in which it is known that the critical level lies. *Critical-band* $[\underline{c}, \overline{c}]$ *generalized utilitarian dominance* is the quasi-ordering $\succsim_{[\underline{c},\overline{c}]}^{CB}$ obtained by taking the intersection of the critical-level generalized utilitarian quasi-orderings for all $c \in [\underline{c}, \overline{c}]$. In other words, the critical-level generalized dominance criteria must agree for all values of the critical level in this interval in order for this criterion to rank utility distributions.

Critical-band $[\underline{c}, \overline{c}]$ *generalized utilitarian dominance.* For all $\underline{c}, \overline{c} \in \mathbb{R}$ with $\underline{c} < \overline{c}$, for all $\mathbf{u}, \mathbf{u}' \in \mathcal{U}$,

$$\mathbf{u} \succsim_{[\underline{c},\overline{c}]}^{CB} \mathbf{u}' \Leftrightarrow \mathbf{u} \succsim_{c}^{CL} \mathbf{u}' \text{ for all } c \in [\underline{c}, \overline{c}].^{[20]} \tag{4.1}$$

In Proposition 3, we show that this quasi-ordering is equivalent to the quasi-ordering that is obtained by taking the intersection of the critical-level c generalized utilitarian quasi-orderings for the critical levels $\underline{c}$ and $\overline{c}$ that define the endpoints of the band. It then follows from Proposition 2 that this quasi-ordering is also the intersection of the quasi-orderings defined by critical-level c generalized concentration curve dominance for these two values of c.

Proposition 3. *For all* $\underline{c}, \overline{c} \in \mathbb{R}$ *with* $\underline{c} < \overline{c}$, *for all* $\mathbf{u}, \mathbf{u}' \in \mathcal{U}$, *the following conditions are equivalent:*

(i) $\mathbf{u} \succsim_{[\underline{c},\overline{c}]}^{CB} \mathbf{u}'$,

(ii) $\left[\mathbf{u} \succsim_{\underline{c}}^{CL} \mathbf{u}' \text{ and } \mathbf{u} \succsim_{\overline{c}}^{CL} \mathbf{u}' \right]$, *and*

(iii) $\left[\mathbf{u} \succsim_{\underline{c}}^{GC} \mathbf{u}' \text{ and } \mathbf{u} \succsim_{\overline{c}}^{GC} \mathbf{u}' \right]$.

Proof. It follows trivially from the definition of $\succsim_{[\underline{c},\overline{c}]}^{CB}$ that (i) implies (ii).

We now show that (ii) implies (i). Suppose that (ii) holds. Consider any $c \in [\underline{c}, \overline{c}], g \in \mathcal{C}, n, m \in \mathbb{N}, \mathbf{u} \in \mathbb{R}^n$, and $\mathbf{u}' \in \mathbb{R}^m$. There are two cases to consider.

---

[20] In their definition of critical band generalized utilitarian dominance, Blackorby, Bossert and Donaldson (1996, 2005) replace the closed interval $[\underline{c}, \overline{c}]$ with an arbitrary bounded interval. An axiomatization of their version of this population principle may be found in Blackorby, Bossert and Donaldson (2005: Theorem 7.12).

Case 1. Suppose that $n \geq m$. By assumption,

$$\sum_{i=1}^{n} [g(u_i) - g(\bar{c})] \geq \sum_{i=1}^{m} [g(u_i') - g(\bar{c})]. \tag{4.2}$$

Equivalently,

$$\sum_{i=1}^{n} g(u_i) \geq \sum_{i=1}^{m} g(u_i') + (n - m)g(\bar{c}). \tag{4.3}$$

Because $n - m \geq 0$, $c \leq \bar{c}$, and the function g is increasing, (4.3) implies that

$$\sum_{i=1}^{n} g(u_i) \geq \sum_{i=1}^{m} g(u_i') + (n - m)g(c), \tag{4.4}$$

or, equivalently,

$$\sum_{i=1}^{n} [g(u_i) - g(c)] \geq \sum_{i=1}^{m} [g(u_i') - g(c)]. \tag{4.5}$$

Case 2. Suppose that $m > n$. By assumption,

$$\sum_{i=1}^{n} [g(u_i) - g(\underline{c})] \geq \sum_{i=1}^{m} [g(u_i') - g(\underline{c})]. \tag{4.6}$$

Equivalently,

$$\sum_{i=1}^{n} g(u_i) + (m - n)g(\underline{c}) \geq \sum_{i=1}^{m} g(u_i'). \tag{4.7}$$

Because $m - n \geq 0$, $c \geq \underline{c}$, and the function g is increasing, (4.7) implies that

$$\sum_{i=1}^{n} g(u_i) + (m - n)g(c) \geq \sum_{i=1}^{m} g(u_i'), \tag{4.8}$$

which is equivalent to (4.5).

Thus, (4.5) holds in both cases. Because c is an arbitrary element of $[\underline{c}, \bar{c}]$, we have therefore shown that $\mathbf{u} \succsim_c^{CL} \mathbf{u}'$ for all $c \in [\underline{c}, \bar{c}]$. That is, (i) holds.

The equivalence of (iii) with both (i) and (ii) now follows immediately from Proposition 2. ∎

V. Concluding Remarks

Social welfare dominance criteria provide a way of partially ordering distributions based on widely shared value judgements. In practice, the dominance criterion that is most commonly employed is the generalized Lorenz quasi-ordering. This dominance criterion implicitly measures social welfare in per capita terms. More precisely, as the Kakwani–Shorrocks Theorem establishes, it coincides with the averaged generalized utilitarian dominance criterion. However, as we have noted, per capita measures of social welfare make some trade-offs that many would find unpalatable when the size of the population is subject to variation. Critical-level generalized utilitarianism was introduced as a way of overcoming these problems. The critical-level generalized utilitarian welfare dominance criterion introduced here measures differences in social welfare in aggregate, not per capita, terms.

We have also introduced a new geometric construction, the generalized concentration curve for a distribution, that is a natural analogue for critical-level generalized utilitarianism of a generalized Lorenz curve. For a given value of the critical level c, we have used generalized concentration curves to define a new dominance relation, the critical-level c generalized utilitarian quasi-ordering, and shown that it coincides with the critical-level generalized utilitarian quasi-ordering for this value of the critical level, thereby providing an analogue of the Kakwani–Shorrocks Theorem for this population principle. Furthermore, we have used critical-band generalized utilitarianism to extend this result so as to allow for a range of critical levels.

We have framed our discussion in terms of distributions of utilities. However, in empirical applications of our dominance criteria, for practical reasons income is most likely to be chosen as the measure of individual well-being. Implementation of our proposal will then require the specification of a critical income level or critical income band. In this interpretation of our model, the critical level is the level of income for which it is a matter of social indifference to add an additional individual with this amount of income. For most societies, this level will be below the observed average income of the population. It is also likely to be below what is regarded as an appropriate value for an absolute poverty line. Given the lack of an obvious choice for the critical income level, the use of a critical band is an attractive option, as then any distributional comparisons that can be made using our approach to constructing a dominance relation will not be overly sensitive to the exact specification of the critical level. In any event, the choice of the critical level calls for further investigation, which is beyond the scope of this chapter.

Sen (1973: 76) has argued that "[t]reating inequality as a quasi-ordering has much to be commended from the normative as well as the descriptive point of view".

The same can be said for social welfare comparisons. The critical-level and critical-band generalized utilitarian welfare dominance criteria introduced here provide alternatives to generalized Lorenz dominance. They are alternatives that we think have "much to be commended".

REFERENCES

ABOUDI, R., THON, D., and WALLACE, S. (2008), "Inequality Comparisons when the Populations Differ in Size", unpublished manuscript, Bodø Graduate School of Management.

AMIEL, Y., COWELL, F., and POLOVIN, A. (1996), "Inequality Among the Kibbutzim", *Economica*, 63: S63–S85.

ATKINSON, A. B. (1970), "On the Measurement of Inequality", *Journal of Economic Theory*, 2: 244–66.

BLACKORBY, C., BOSSERT, W., and DONALDSON, D. (1996), "Quasi-Orderings and Population Ethics", *Social Choice and Welfare*, 13: 129–50.

————— (1998), "Uncertainty and Critical-Level Population Principles", *Journal of Population Economics*, 11: 1–20.

————— (2003), "The Axiomatic Approach to Population Ethics", *Politics, Philosophy & Economics*, 2: 342–81.

————— (2005), *Population Issues in Social Choice Theory, Welfare Economics, and Ethics* (Cambridge: Cambridge University Press).

—— and DONALDSON, D. (1984), "Social Criteria for Evaluating Population Change", *Journal of Public Economics*, 25: 13–33.

———— and WEYMARK, J. A. (1982), "A Normative Approach to Industrial-Performance Evaluation and Concentration Indices", *European Economic Review*, 19: 89–121.

BROOME, J. (2004), *Weighing Lives* (Oxford: Oxford University Press).

DALTON, H. (1920), "The Measurement of the Inequality of Incomes", *Economic Journal*, 30: 348–61.

DASGUPTA, P. (1969), "On the Concept of Optimum Population", *Review of Economic Studies*, 36: 295–318.

—— SEN, A., and STARRETT, D. (1973), "Notes on the Measurement of Inequality", *Journal of Economic Theory*, 6: 180–7.

JENKINS, S. P., and JÄNTII, M. (2008), "Methods for Summarizing and Comparing Wealth Distributions", in *Construction and Usage of Comparable Microdata on Household Wealth: The Luxemburg Wealth Study* (Rome: Bank of Italy).

KAKWANI, N. (1984), "Welfare Rankings of Income Distributions", in R. L. Basmann and G. F. Rhodes Jr (eds), *Economic Inequality: Measurement and Policy*, vol. 3 of *Advances in Economics* (Greenwich, Conn.: JAI Press), 191–213.

KOLM, S.-C. (1969), "The Optimal Production of Social Justice", in J. Margolis and H. Guitton (eds), *Public Economics: An Analysis of Public Production and Consumption and their Relations to the Private Sector* (London: Macmillan), 145–200.

LAMBERT, P. J. (2001), *The Distribution and Redistribution of Income*, 3rd edn (Manchester: Manchester University Press).

MARSHALL, A. W., and OLKIN, I. (1979), *Inequalities: Theories of Majorization and its Applications* (New York: Academic Press).

PARFIT, D. (1984), *Reasons and Persons* (Oxford: Oxford University Press).

POGGE, T. (2007), *John Rawls: His Life and Theory of Justice* (New York: Oxford University Press).

ROTHSCHILD, M., and STIGLITZ, J. E. (1973), "Some Further Results on the Measurement of Inequality", *Journal of Economic Theory*, 6: 188–204.

SEN, A. (1973), *On Economic Inequality* (Oxford: Clarendon Press).

SHORROCKS, A. F. (1983), "Ranking Income Distributions", *Economica*, 50: 3–17.

TOMIĆ, M. (1949), "Gauss' Theorem Concerning the Center of Gravity and its Application" (in Serbo-Croatian), *Vesnik Društva Mathematicara i Fizicara Narodne Republike Srbije*, 1: 31–40.

PART III

POVERTY, CAPABILITIES AND MEASUREMENT

CHAPTER 16

....

THE
MEASUREMENT OF
CAPABILITIES

PAUL ANAND

CRISTINA SANTOS

RON SMITH

I. INTRODUCTION

....

FROM the variety of conceptions of what constitutes a good life that policy might
promote, we focus on two. One emphasizes the freedoms and rights that people
have, what Amartya Sen calls their capabilities. The other emphasizes individual
well-being derived from what individuals do. The capabilities approach to welfare
has focused on issues of freedom but both freedom and well-being appear in his
formal account of the approach (Sen 1985 and Sen and Nussbaum 1993), in which
he suggests that a person's happiness depends on what the person does, whilst

We particularly wish to thank a number of colleagues who have collaborated on papers that form
part of the project here reported as well as contributors to two related design workshops held at
Wolfson College, Oxford in 2004 and 2005 where the OCAP survey instrument was developed. In
addition, the first author acknowledges funding from the Arts and Humanities Research Board, Grant
no. 17685, and thanks Caterina Laderchi for discussions which helped initiate the research
program.

assessment of a person's advantage should depend, in addition, on the other things that person could do.[1]

These two approaches to quality of life potentially conflict. According to the first view, the right to vote, for example, is a good thing; it makes people capable of doing something, probably something they have reason to value, and it may remain a good thing not only if people do not vote but if people would prefer not to have the right to vote and would feel better if somebody else made decisions for them. According to the second view, what counts is just well-being and if that is greater under a regime in which no one has the right to vote and everyone can avoid the need to make decisions, then policy should not grant the right to vote.

In deciding between these two views, there are many normative questions, but there is an informational issue also. It is far easier to find out whether a particular group of people do or do not have the right to vote than it is to find out whether they would prefer having the vote or not. In principle, these are quite distinct and non-comparable philosophical issues.[2]

In practice, for policy purposes, they might not be so different. If capabilities and well-being were, in fact, highly correlated, then, contrary to the voting example, extending people's capabilities would (on average) increase their well-being. If an expansion of capabilities increased, or at least did not reduce, well-being, it could be argued that policy should be aimed at capabilities development even if well-being maximization is the ultimate objective. These are variants of the information argument above, that it is easier to determine capabilities than well-being; the freedom argument is that since people's tastes differ, policy should extend the range of things that people can do rather than prescribe what they should do. Indeed one could argue that freedom and autonomy have been central to economic thinking and that the emphasis on optimal goods bundles as the source of happiness is inadequate for some policy purposes.

In any case, whether capabilities and well-being are correlated is an interesting and important empirical question and raises a number of issues. How do we measure capabilities? How do we measure well-being? Since we are considering average relations over a sample, what statistical methods can be used to estimate the association between capabilities and well-being over the sample and infer any causal relationship between them? Having measured capabilities and well-being

---

[1] Further theoretical development of this approach can be found in Gaertner and Xu (2005), Nehring and Puppe (2005), Pattanaik and Xu (1998) and van Hees (2004), and a number of key philosophical issues are examined by Carter (1999, 2003). The origins of the capabilities approach in problems of conventional social choice and welfare economics are particularly evident in Sen (1979).

[2] Initially, researchers were pessimistic about the prospects of broadening capability indicators beyond those available through the Human Development Index (see, for example, Brandolini and D'Alessio 1999). However, there are now a number of attempts to do quantitative empirical work in ways that engage with the approach—see for instance Brower et al. (2004), Burchardt and Le Grand (2002), Chiappero-Martinetti (2000), Clark (2003), Klasen (2000), Kuklys (2005), Laderchi (2001) and Schokkaert and Ootegem (1990).

and estimated the relationship between them, can we begin to derive policy implications from these results?

In this chapter, we provide an overview of a research project that tries to address some of these issues. In particular, we focus on the questions of whether and how capabilities can be measured and then go on to consider some of the ways in which capability data can be analyzed. We then focus on three topics that are of particular interest from a capabilities perspective: health and poverty, forms of violence and the correlates of life satisfaction. In each case, there is good theoretical or a priori reason to suppose that the capabilities approach can contribute to our understanding. In the first case, we use latent class analysis to explore capabilities from a multidimensional angle and determine whether there exists, for our national sample, a group of people who are impoverished with respect to their capabilities across the board. Next, we focus on the existence of different types of violence and their impact on well-being and capabilities. We identify a group who are more vulnerable to each type of violence and we identify the causal impact of violence on well-being. Finally, we consider the role of capabilities in life satisfaction (happiness), which many conventional economists have recently shown interest in, and ask whether there is evidence of any detectable relationship between capabilities and life satisfaction across a range of life domains.

Although the project was initially motivated by a desire to determine whether capability indicators can be constructed, a number of related methodological issues have emerged and these will be considered in section IV. One particularly interesting issue that arises as we move from theory to empirical work concerns causality. For instance, it may be that some unobserved variable, e.g. personality, influences both an individual's perceived capabilities and their expressed well-being, so the association between capabilities and well-being is non-causal. However, appropriate data design and data merging allows us to make some headway in addressing questions of causality, as our work on the relationship between expectations of violence and life satisfaction indicates.

II. Capabilities and Well-being: Motivation and Operationalization

Sen's (1985) formalization of the capabilities approach defines two key relations. To begin, Sen suggests that happiness or utility, u_i, of the ith individual is a function of the things a person is or does, i.e.

$$u_i = f_i(\mathbf{f}_i),$$

where $\mathbf{f}$ is a vector of j dimensional functionings (doings or beings) and f_i is a utility function that relates functionings to happiness and varies between individuals, thereby recognizing that preferences are not homogeneous. Sen then goes on to argue that what people can choose is also important for welfare and policy purposes, and proposes that the set of functioning vectors a person could choose given their endowments broadly defined, Q, be taken as a measure of a person's advantage in welfare evaluations. Many researchers have argued that the capabilities approach is difficult to implement in practice because the set Q cannot be enumerated. Our project recognizes that many, if not most, of the welfare statistics available are more accurately conceived as indicators and that the proper economic statistics question is not whether capabilities can be enumerated, but rather whether it is possible to construct statistics that indicate the size of Q in a manner consistent with theory and the accepted methodologies of survey design and social statistics. For what follows, we assume that the empirical measurement challenge is one of developing appropriate indicators.

II.1 Measurement of Capabilities

As a first pass at measuring aspects of Q in practice, a collection of questions, based on a primary data set, that distinguishes between achievements and scope in people's lives was devised (Anand and van Hees 2006). The distinction between scope and achievement offers only one way of measuring capabilities (as distinct from functionings) and it led us to reconsider whether, in fact, there might not be some secondary data that relate more directly to the freedom aspects of capabilities. Using data and questions that exist in secondary data sets, like the BHPS and GSOEP, which are routinely used by economists and social scientists, Anand (2005) and Anand, Hunter and Smith (2005) argued that social and household surveys do already contain data that measure capabilities. At least five kinds of indicators can be identified:

Type 1: Externally oriented questions about opportunity
Type 2: Explicit questions about personal ability aspects of capability
Type 3: Explicit constraint questions
Type 4: Functioning probes combined with questions about reasons
Type 5: Functioning probes combined with a universality assumption

Questions about access to facilities, like the use of a car or van when needed, and questions about the existence of factors preventing people from moving house, illustrate questions capable of generating type 1 and 2 indicators. In some cases, it is possible to use questions about functionings, when combined with reasons, to determine whether a particular behavior or state reflects a person's preference or rather an inability to make certain choices. And in a smaller number of situations, functioning questions, for example about the experience of violent assault, can be assumed to indicate evidence of a reduced capability set.

Whilst such indicators are used frequently in social science and official statistics, economists often question the validity of such data because of their apparent subjectivity. In an ideal world, data based on objective observation would be preferable, but in reality many data sources, including many of the secondary data sources regularly used by economists (e.g. income data from household surveys), are based on self-report. This is almost inevitable if one wants to analyze individual-level data covering a wide range of life domains (given the way social and administrative statistics are collected) and we suggest that two related questions are particularly important when doing so. First, are there any *particular* incentives for data to be biased or noisy, and second, if such problems exist, what is their likely impact on analysis? In many cases, once a person has agreed to take part in a survey, the incentives to misrepresent may not be strong, though of course accurate recall is difficult, with the result that data on relations between variables may underestimate true underlying relations. Furthermore, in regression analyses, there are endogeneity risks associated with using subjective variables from the same respondent on both sides of an equation; our project has considered how this might be tested for and suitable instruments devised (not discussed in this chapter, but see Anand, Hunter and Smith 2005). Finally, and beyond this, many capabilities are inherently subjective. The question "How safe do you feel?" does not have an objective answer, since it depends on probabilities of harm, a person's risk aversion, and a person's behavior: for example, whether they go out at night will also reflect a variety of other factors that influence the costs and benefits of action.

II.2 Measurement of Happiness (Well-Being)

To measure happiness, we note that a growing number of economists have moved beyond the use of income as a utility indicator and examine data on self-reported happiness as a more accurate measure of what Kahneman *et al.* (1997) call "experienced utility" (see, for instance, Frey and Stutzer 2000; Kahneman *et al.* 2004; Layard 2005; Oswald 1997; Winkelmann and Winkelmann 1998).[3] This move is consistent both with utilitarian theory (if not the methods of revealed preference) and the emphasis of the capabilities approach on non-financial aspects of quality of life, though there are normative issues which suggest asymmetries in use. Many utilitarians claim that we should give priority only to those sources of disadvantage to which individuals do not adapt,[4] whilst proponents of the capabilities view point

---

[3] In his *Econometrica* survey, Manksi (2004) concludes that subjective measures fare better in terms of statistical accuracy than might have been supposed. (Recognizing this point about accuracy does not commit one to accepting that evidence of affective adaptation should be used to discount policies aimed at eradicating social and economic problems to which people adapt.)

[4] Where we model life satisfaction as a function of capabilities, the justification is that adaptation to capability changes in circumstances is likely to be neither perfect nor instantaneous. Recent work by Di Tella *et al.* (2007) substantiates this and helps to quantify the rate of adaptation where it takes

out that many women have adapted to inequities in labor markets but that this is not a reason against promoting equality of opportunity. However, there are some adaptations that many would recognize as healthy and desirable from a welfare perspective and yet there is no account of what role adaptation should play. We take the view, therefore, that the role of adaptive preferences in theories of equity and justice has become confounded with the somewhat different methodological issues surrounding subjective data, particularly those to do with noise and bias in estimation, and with endogeneity within regression models. In this project, where a summary measure of well-being is useful, we therefore argue that happiness can play a helpful role, particularly if we account properly for the implications it may have for estimation and model building.

III. Data

The data used in our analysis consist of a quota sample of approximately 1,000 individuals selected at random from a panel constructed to be roughly representative of the adult population in mainland Britain. The survey process was implemented by an opinion polling and market research company, YOUGOV, in the early part of 2005. In keeping with emerging practice, driven largely by data protection constraints and the spread of Internet access and use, the panel consists of people who have previously agreed to be contacted by the company for market research purposes and so cannot be treated as random. That said, we were able to use some replicated substantive and socio-demographic questions from the BHPS, and found that statistically our results were identical, or very close, to those found there, so there is some reason to believe that our results have some representative value in addition to demonstrating the methods developed.

IV. Results

IV.1 Capabilities, Poverty and Health

In the first of our three results sections, we use multivariate non-dependency techniques to understand capability indicators on their own. Such techniques have been used by statisticians and social scientists in a wide range of applications (see Everitt

place, though they find that people tend to adapt more readily to income changes than to changes in status.

Table 16.1a. Fit diagnostics for five latent class models

Number of latent classes	LL	Bayesian Information Criteria	Number of parameters	L2	df	p value
5	−42,505.08	87,706.27	397	72,921.78	493	2.7e-15197
6	−42,274.42	87,598.09	449	72,460.46	441	8.7e-15155
7	−42,130.72	87,663.84	501	72,173.06	389	4.9e-15151
8	−42,130.72	87,786.53	553	71,942.61	337	5.0e-15161
9	−41,813.26	87,853.59	605	71,656.52	285	1.1e-15160

and Dunn 2001). In this case, we use latent class analysis to categorize respondents on the basis of all their capability indicators. This allows us to assess whether there is a group who are poor in capabilities across the board and to examine the covariates of category membership. The results of this exercise appear in Tables 16.1a and 16.1b. To determine the appropriate number of latent classes, we compute models without a covariate matrix, x, and select the model that minimizes the value of the Bayesian Information Criterion. This statistic is generally used, as it provides a measure of fit adjusted for the number of parameters involved. According to this criterion, a model in which there are six latent classes provides the optimal balance between fit and parsimony.

When a variety of six class models as a function of health status is estimated, we observe that variations in health status are always statistically significant predictors of class membership. (Table 16.1b summarizes findings for a series of such models.)

Table 16.1b. Wald statistics for health status and other predictors of latent class membership in a six-class model

Covariate	Model diagnostic statistics				
Health status	51.97, 5.50e-10	31.5533, 7.30e-06	42.5177, 4.60e-08	25.6563, 0.0001	30.7661, 1.00e-05
Household income		31.0012, 9.30e-06	21.9757, 0.00053	26.8417, 6.10e-05	12.0814, 0.034	20.9303, 0.00083
Controls for age	No			Yes	
Personality					
PAGREE				29.036, 2.3e-05	29.3056, 2.00e-05
PCONSC				24.1576, 0.0002	21.8305, 0.00056
POPEN				55.0846, 1.3e-10	60.14, 1.10e-11
PSTABLE				49.8809, 1.50e-09	50.2556, 1.20e-09
PXTRAVT				19.8605, 0.0013	24.708, 0.00016
Controls for regions	No				Yes

Notes: Cell entries indicate respectively the value of the Wald statistic and its associated p value. Controls for age comprise age and its square.

The same is true of household income, though the test statistics tend to be even more significant for health. The status of health as a class predictor appears robust to the introduction of controls, though in the final model summarized, the controls for age and its square are not significant, whereas three of the four regional controls are. This is in marked contrast to equations where capabilities are covariates of life satisfaction (e.g. Anand *et al.* forthcoming) and in which age is always significant but regional controls rarely are. It is noticeable that all five dimensions of personality are statistically significant, a finding in keeping with work reported by Helliwell recently in his work on quality of life based on models of life satisfaction (Helliwell 2006). Clearly, personality is a source of heterogeneity (see also Clark *et al.* 2005) but we are unable to identify further the reasons for this variation. It may be, for example, that people with different personality traits have different opportunities open to them, either as a result of the way in which they themselves cope with adversity or because of the supportive behavior their traits induce in others. Alternatively, it could be that different personalities are associated with different levels of adaptive coping and/or reporting behaviors.

By examining the average capability scores for each group across all the indicators we can begin to assess whether there is a particularly poor group within our sample. In fact, class 6, which accounts for just over 8% of our sample, does indeed appear to be such a group. Generally the average capability indicator scores of class 6 are either the most extreme of all groups or close to being so, with only a small number of modest exceptions. From Table 16.1c, it is possible to compare some of the characteristics (covariate averages) of class 6 with those of other groups. Just over half this group (52.99%) have limited health and this is a notably higher proportion than for any other group. This is also the youngest group on average—perhaps

Table 16.1c. Average covariate characteristics by class

	Class 1	Class 2	Class 3	Class 4	Class 5	Class 6
Class size (% of sample)	23.7%	20.79%	19.05%	18.30%	10.13%	8.02%
Health Status	78.49%	82.96%	85.74%	61.45%	67.95%	47.01%
MGHI	3.19	3.31	3.33	2.93	2.86	2.32
PAGREEABLE	4.73	4.88	5.50	4.93	5.23	4.41
PCONSCIENTIOUS	5.12	5.53	5.87	4.9	5.42	4.7
POPEN	4.86	4.58	5.36	4.60	5.55	5.22
PSTABLE	4.47	4.87	5.32	3.61	4.70	3.41
PEXTRAVERT	4.09	4.07	4.84	3.53	4.14	3.51
MAGE	42.19	46.17	50.63	39.65	47.14	38.14
MMALE	59.73%	54.22%	45.55%	40.73%	10.64%	38.41%
MRMIDWLS	25.05%	29.76%	20.58%	18.30%	18.99%	13.47%
MRNORTH	25.15%	28.93%	28.50%	24.78%	32.82%	38.71%
MRSCOT	10.25%	8.05%	10.64%	12.77%	7.02%	3.45%
MRSOUTH	16.61%	21.57%	27.10%	24.48%	13.09%	29.58%

the opposite of what one might expect, until we recall that the question about health status asks respondents to make a comparative judgement allowing for age norms. Class 6 is also lowest on the income category indicator and just over 60% of class 6 members are female. The group has low scores on four of the personality dimensions with the exception of openness, which is also relatively high in class 5, who, in turn, are only marginally better off than class 6. However, the highest average score for openness is found in class 3, which is possibly the most affluent group, so we cannot infer a simple relation between openness and deprivation. It is also noticeable that capability deprivation displays a geographical bias towards England (especially the south), which may reflect higher levels of health and social care in Wales and Scotland, though there could be a comparison effect in play. Reference class effects have been found to be empirically significant in the literature on income and life satisfaction (see Clark, Frijters and Shields 2006 for example) and it could also be that capability deprivation is felt more keenly in the south of England because ambient capability levels are higher on average.

IV.2 Violence, Vulnerability and Life Satisfaction

In this second results section, we draw on an analysis of capability indicators concerning data relating to the experience and subjective risk of violence (Anand and Santos 2007), an issue that Nussbaum (2000) and Sen (2006) have both done much to highlight. This section shows how our capabilities measurements can generate data which can be used to understand very specific topics, and that future risks which might constrain what a person can do can be measured and used in analysis. In what follows, we concentrate on the different experiences that men and women have of different forms of violence, and the covariates of these experiences and their consequences for quality of life. With this focus we are able to identify a causal impact, through the pathway of expectations, between violence and well-being.

Within our set of capabilities indicators, we have a total of eight variables: two measures of fear of walking around one's locality—during the day and at night— and a further six variables that measure both experienced and perceived risk of violence in three categories (sexual assault, domestic violence and the residual category). Our extensions to the original formal capabilities framework (in Sen 1985) derives from the recognition that there may be significant probabilistic aspects of capabilities between people,[5] and as can be seen from Tables 16.2a and 16.2b, there are significant differences both in the proportions of female and male respondents reporting experience of violence in each category, and in their perceived risks of sexual and domestic violence. To understand the causes, or at least covariates, of

---

[5] The ability to walk about safely at night, much discussed in the literature, provides a good example. Usually the question is not binary but rather turns on the degree of risk that one takes.

Table 16.2a. Self-reported experience of violence by gender
t-test on the equality of means, where data are not assumed to be paired.

	Proportion females	Proportion males	p value
Sexual assault (SA)	0.151	0.048	0.000
Domestic violence (DV)	0.226	0.099	0.000
Both sexual assault and domestic violence	0.062	0.015	0.000
Some other form of violent assault or attack (VA)	0.123	0.339	0.000

experienced violence we present six probit models (see Table 16.2c) in which we use covariate data on age, marital status, income, both individual and household, ethnicity, family size, education, personality, local crime rates and a set of regional dummies.

Being separated is associated with other forms of assault reported by women and domestic violence reported by men, and it is possible that the primary causal link is different between the sexes—separated women are most at risk of other forms of assault, whilst experience of domestic violence by men is more likely to be related to a subsequent separation. However, perhaps the most significant results are those concerning income for women. There is some evidence that domestic violence significantly decreases as household income increases but controlling for this, there is some evidence (not significant) that women with higher personal incomes are more at risk of experiencing domestic violence. We should be particularly cautious about this, as the result is not significant, but it suggests that there may be a resentment effect which causes women with higher incomes than their partners to be at a higher risk. If that is indeed the case, it would suggest that social policy programs designed to reduce domestic violence could not automatically assume that increasing women's income and human capital will reduce their risk, a policy that might otherwise help women escape from violent relations, as Agarwal and

Table 16.2b. Self-reported violence-related capabilities by gender
Wilcoxon rank-sum test on the equality of the distributions.

	Females		Males		p value
	Mean	Median	Mean	Median	
Fear during day (D)	2.155	2	1.925	2	0.000
Fear at night (N)	3.670	3	2.785	3	0.000
Vulnerability to sexual assault (VSA)	3.439	3	1.535	1	0.000
Vulnerability to domestic violence (VDV)	1.585	1	1.328	1	0.000
Likelihood of assault in future (LVA)	3.159	3	3.198	3	0.990

Table 16.2c. Identifying the relatively vulnerable: probit models of reported experiences of violence by gender

	Females			Males		
	SA	DV	VA	SA	DV	VA
35–55 Years Old	0.059	0.185	0.221	−0.161	0.302	0.105
	(0.212)	(0.192)	(0.225)	(0.396)	(0.299)	(0.209)
≥ 55 Years Old	0.123	0.304	−0.094	−0.319	0.094	−0.249
	(0.232)	(0.216)	(0.257)	(0.456)	(0.390)	(0.254)
Separated	0.003	0.503	0.694*	0.278	0.895*	0.087
	(0.288)	(0.259)	(0.277)	(0.408)	(0.360)	(0.318)
No Partner	−0.007	−0.070	0.300	−0.898	0.135	0.218
	(0.218)	(0.202)	(0.232)	(0.484)	(0.364)	(0.221)
£10,000–20,000 Household Income	0.118	−0.440	−0.043	−0.867	0.231	0.031
	(0.291)	(0.263)	(0.287)	(0.533)	(0.435)	(0.371)
£20,000–30,000 Household Income	−0.290	−0.809**	0.153	−0.816	−0.125	−0.090
	(0.325)	(0.275)	(0.311)	(0.661)	(0.524)	(0.405)
≥ £30,000 Household Income	−0.287	−0.663*	0.023	−1.716**	0.025	0.174
	(0.333)	(0.299)	(0.330)	(0.605)	(0.566)	(0.420)
£10,000–20,000 Individual Income	−0.095	0.297	−0.196	0.609	−0.400	0.124
	(0.226)	(0.214)	(0.253)	(0.497)	(0.362)	(0.309)
£20,000–30,000 Individual Income	−0.452	0.462	−0.175	0.006	−0.454	−0.129
	(0.330)	(0.278)	(0.296)	(0.642)	(0.451)	(0.364)
≥ £30,000 Individual Income	0.352	−0.001	−0.362	0.728	−0.691	−0.353
	(0.347)	(0.376)	(0.430)	(0.654)	(0.548)	(0.406)
Non-White British	−0.265	0.379	−0.075	(dropped)	0.439	0.343
	(0.329)	(0.264)	(0.300)		(0.316)	(0.275)
At least 1 Child	−0.174	0.068	−0.389	−0.208	0.304	0.257
	(0.221)	(0.191)	(0.216)	(0.352)	(0.288)	(0.192)
Vocational Diploma	0.362	0.101	0.529	−0.166	−0.217	−0.055
	(0.310)	(0.284)	(0.394)	(0.354)	(0.355)	(0.270)
CSE A Level	0.081	0.148	0.152	(dropped)	−0.411	−0.245
	(0.308)	(0.267)	(0.376)		(0.350)	(0.269)
Graduate	0.231	−0.231	0.355	−0.077	−0.152	−0.103
	(0.309)	(0.288)	(0.389)	(0.394)	(0.352)	(0.285)
Not Employed (At Home)	0.288	−0.012	0.002	−0.045	−0.200	−0.177
	(0.199)	(0.181)	(0.217)	(0.344)	(0.296)	(0.226)
Extraversion	−0.063	−0.165	−0.212	−0.081	−0.258	−0.179
	(0.124)	(0.104)	(0.128)	(0.152)	(0.136)	(0.097)
Agreeableness	0.180*	0.235**	0.257**	0.082	0.248*	0.068
	(0.090)	(0.087)	(0.099)	(0.134)	(0.121)	(0.082)
Conscientiousness	−0.028	0.013	0.150	−0.023	0.183	0.279**
	(0.096)	(0.090)	(0.100)	(0.153)	(0.120)	(0.091)
Emotional Stability	−0.181	−0.025	−0.064	−0.065	−0.112	−0.031
	(0.095)	(0.095)	(0.112)	(0.156)	(0.121)	(0.093)
Openness	−0.075	0.007	−0.020	−0.209	−0.085	−0.048
	(0.095)	(0.085)	(0.097)	(0.150)	(0.115)	(0.090)

(cont.)

Table 16.2c. (Continued)

	Females			Males		
	SA	DV	VA	SA	DV	VA
Local Crime Rates	0.009	−0.008	−0.001	0.006	−0.005	0.004
	(0.007)	(0.007)	(0.008)	(0.004)	(0.007)	(0.005)
South of England excluding London	−0.024	−0.053	−0.363	0.528	0.050	−0.314
	(0.278)	(0.255)	(0.264)	(0.431)	(0.285)	(0.236)
Midlands and Wales	0.109	0.389	0.853**	0.190	−1.224**	−0.415
	(0.260)	(0.244)	(0.274)	(0.524)	(0.399)	(0.231)
North of England	0.043	0.253	−0.388	−0.259	−0.111	−0.190
	(0.247)	(0.236)	(0.245)	(0.503)	(0.270)	(0.219)
Constant	−1.472**	−0.801	−1.253*	−0.647	−0.856	−0.300
	(0.485)	(0.440)	(0.516)	(0.703)	(0.638)	(0.484)
Pseudo-R^2	0.077	0.107	0.106	0.202	0.195	0.094
N	382	389	390	214	330	329

Notes: Significance levels: *5%; **1%.

Marginal effects reported. Standard errors in parentheses.

Reference categories are: <35 Years Old, Married, Other Schooling, £0–£10,000 Gross Household Income, £0–£10,000 Gross Individual Income, White British, No Dependent Children, Other Schooling, Working at least 8hrs/Week, and London.

Panda (2006) has proposed. It is also worth noting that of all the personality traits, being agreeable is a significant risk for women especially, and this in turn may mean that behavioral therapies could play a significant role alongside economic issues in violence reduction programs.

Ultimately, we were interested in assessing the impact of experienced violence and the threat of violence on well-being. Table 16.2d shows the results. We find that the measures of experience of violence, with the exception of domestic violence for women, are not significant.

However, it is particularly noteworthy that the risk of violence *is* significant. In the case of all three forms of violence, the coefficients are significant, though the pattern is not the same for men, a fact that might suggest either that the impact on quality of life of fear of violence is more severe for women or that the average severities of experiences of violence are particularly different for men and women. There is not much evidence that income has an impact on life satisfaction here, though there is some evidence that household income does have an impact for men. Being without a partner, being non white British and introversion all have a negative effect that is statistically significant. Crime rates are also significant but in the wrong direction, suggesting, perhaps, that crime rates are correlated with the existence of other local resources that make an area more attractive to live

Table 16.2d. Ordered probit models of well-being deprivation by gender

	Females		Males	
	Experience only	Both	Experience only	Both
Victim of Sexual Assault	−0.133	−0.264	0.044	0.002
	(0.170)	(0.176)	(0.312)	(0.318)
Victim of Domestic Violence	0.366*	0.275	0.240	0.260
	(0.152)	(0.160)	(0.235)	(0.250)
Victim of Any Other Form of	0.056	−0.062	−0.011	−0.039
Violence	(0.189)	(0.193)	(0.149)	(0.153)
Vulnerability to Sexual Assault		0.290**		0.106
		(0.096)		(0.123)
Vulnerability to Domestic Violence		0.302**		−0.023
		(0.116)		(0.156)
Likelihood of Future Violence of		0.290**		0.092
Any Other		(0.103)		(0.092)
35–55 years old	0.061	0.294	−0.041	−0.013
	(0.156)	(0.164)	(0.186)	(0.188)
≥ 55 years old	−0.379*	−0.053	−0.314	−0.250
	(0.174)	(0.186)	(0.219)	(0.223)
Separated	0.092	0.077	0.471	0.441
	(0.227)	(0.231)	(0.275)	(0.277)
No Partner	0.402*	0.404*	0.426*	0.429*
	(0.165)	(0.167)	(0.194)	(0.195)
£10,000–20,000 Household Income	−0.105	−0.130	−0.356	−0.344
	(0.225)	(0.229)	(0.317)	(0.319)
£20,000–30,000 Household	0.088	0.061	−0.702*	−0.667
Income	(0.235)	(0.238)	(0.347)	(0.349)
≥ £30,000 Household Income	−0.348	−0.362	−0.714	−0.668
	(0.253)	(0.258)	(0.368)	(0.370)
£10,000–20,000 Individual Income	0.050	0.096	−0.066	−0.064
	(0.173)	(0.176)	(0.263)	(0.264)
£20,000–30,000 Individual Income	−0.303	−0.276	−0.227	−0.254
	(0.225)	(0.229)	(0.305)	(0.305)
≥ £30,000 Individual Income	−0.102	0.008	−0.344	−0.386
	(0.281)	(0.287)	(0.341)	(0.342)
Non-White British	0.211	0.329	0.625*	0.593*
	(0.226)	(0.232)	(0.268)	(0.270)
At least 1 Child	−0.161	−0.138	0.115	0.129
	(0.158)	(0.161)	(0.168)	(0.170)
Vocational Diploma	−0.083	−0.195	0.065	0.068
	(0.238)	(0.244)	(0.243)	(0.243)
CSE A Level	−0.152	−0.250	−0.095	−0.082
	(0.229)	(0.234)	(0.247)	(0.249)
Graduate	−0.236	−0.252	−0.168	−0.135
	(0.237)	(0.241)	(0.253)	(0.255)
Not Employed (At Home)	0.094	0.123	−0.334	−0.332
	(0.152)	(0.155)	(0.189)	(0.190)

(cont.)

Table 16.2d. (*Continued*)

	Females		Males	
	Experience only	Both	Experience only	Both
Extraversion	−0.314***	−0.324***	−0.321***	−0.320***
	(0.082)	(0.084)	(0.087)	(0.087)
Agreeableness	0.119	0.089	0.061	0.052
	(0.072)	(0.073)	(0.072)	(0.072)
Conscientiousness	−0.078	−0.042	0.065	0.062
	(0.076)	(0.077)	(0.077)	(0.077)
Emotional Stability	0.060	0.052	−0.023	−0.021
	(0.074)	(0.076)	(0.080)	(0.081)
Openness	−0.082	−0.100	−0.006	0.001
	(0.070)	(0.071)	(0.077)	(0.078)
Local Crime Rates	−0.005	−0.008	−0.010	−0.011*
	(0.006)	(0.006)	(0.006)	(0.006)
South of England excluding London	0.244	0.376	0.059	0.065
	(0.205)	(0.211)	(0.210)	(0.210)
Midlands and Wales	−0.407*	−0.403*	0.259	0.243
	(0.201)	(0.205)	(0.200)	(0.202)
North of England	−0.111	−0.063	0.206	0.197
	(0.194)	(0.198)	(0.193)	(0.194)
Pseudo-R^2	0.093	0.135	0.110	0.113
N	379	379	327	327

Notes: Significance levels: *5%; **1%; ***0.1%.

Standard errors in parentheses. All variables are described in the Appendix.

Reference categories are: <35 Years Old, Married, Other Schooling, £0–£10,000 Gross Household Income, £0–£10,000 Gross Individual Income, White British, No Dependent Children, Other Schooling, Working at least 8hrs/Week, and London.

in—shops, pubs and local services encourage people to reside in an area but they also provide opportunities for criminal activity to take place.

IV.3 Capabilities, Life Satisfaction and Gender Differences

In this third and final analysis we employ all 60-plus capability indicators to model life satisfaction. As we noted, if happiness depends on what people do or are, then it should also depend on what it is they are free to do or to be. Alternatively, one could argue that our analysis amounts to testing which capabilities matter most to the population from which our sample respondents are drawn—and that the significant capabilities are those to which utilitarians would give priority, because they affect people's welfare. Such capabilities would certainly be interesting, because they are of importance both to advocates of the capabilities approach and to defenders of traditional utilitarian approaches to welfare.

In column (1) of Table 16.3a, we present the results of a regression model that was derived by backwards elimination, starting with all 60-plus indicators to arrive at a model with 17 in which all are significant covariates of happiness.[6] Self-assessed life expectancy is not a significant correlate of life satisfaction (mirroring results elsewhere—see for instance Deaton 2007) but the results show, nevertheless, that a wide range of capability dimensions are significant correlates of happiness. GHOLIDAY and BSHELTER, the ability to afford a week's annual holiday or live in adequate accommodation, could arguably both be taken as indicators of income, but this is less true of the remaining 15 indicators, which cover issues that might broadly be described as abilities to socialize, live autonomously, be respected, and use skills and talents. There has been much debate within economics about whether income brings happiness and if so under what circumstances; our findings seem rather clearly to support those who, like Sen, have argued that material status is only one factor amongst many that determines human welfare.

To explore the robustness of this finding, we add in a variety of controls (see the rest of Table 16.3a). Similar results are obtained for the ordered logit and ordered probit models but we follow the practice of presenting the OLS versions to facilitate interpretation of results. We do not have panel data, which would allow for person-specific controls, but we do have data on what psychologists call the "big five" dimensions of personality and it is apparent that the patterns of coefficient significance do not change much when these controls are added in. The same can be said for the fits obtained for the more general models. Happiness according to this picture is a function of a variety of dimensions of what people are able to do, and income seems to play only a limited role.

One further analysis worth remarking on concerns model estimation for sub-populations. Table 16.3b presents the results for the data partitioned by gender, and could be seen either as contributing to our assessment of robustness, or more substantively, as contributing to the exploration of gender differences in the capabilities–happiness relationship. In general the signs of the coefficients are the same for men and women, though the pattern of significant coefficients has notable differences. Particularly obvious is the fact that BSHELTER is significant for women but not men, which could reflect a biologically oriented difference. However, when we examine a similar depooled exercise the coefficient is only significant for young people, which in turn suggests that it is younger women who are particularly sensitive to quality of accommodation, possibly because of their concerns about the implications it has for child-rearing. Almost equally striking is the fact that

---

[6] A variety of other controls are used, including two which control for labour-force work status.

Table 16.3a. Regression of subjective well–being on capabilities, with demographics and personality controls

Variable	(1) Capabilities				(2) Capabilities and demographics				(3) Capabilities and personality				(4) Capabilities, demographics and personality			
	Coefficient	Standard error	t stat	p value	Coefficient	Standard error	t stat	p value	Coefficient	Standard error	t stat	p value	Coefficient	Standard error	t stat	p value
BSHELTER	0.27	0.09	2.93	0.00	0.29	0.10	2.99	0.00	0.22	0.09	2.37	0.02	0.23	0.09	2.43	0.02
CDASALTP	−0.17	0.08	−2.01	0.04	−0.13	0.09	−1.53	0.13	−0.17	0.08	−2.03	0.04	−0.14	0.09	−1.69	0.09
CSEXSAT	0.25	0.07	3.33	0.00	0.21	0.08	2.86	0.00	0.25	0.07	3.47	0.00	0.22	0.07	2.91	0.00
ELOVE	0.08	0.03	3.03	0.00	0.08	0.03	2.94	0.00	0.08	0.03	3.16	0.00	0.08	0.03	2.99	0.00
EFEELING	0.1	0.03	4.14	0.00	0.11	0.03	4.14	0.00	0.10	0.03	3.68	0.00	0.10	0.03	3.62	0.00
ESTRAIN	−0.13	0.04	−3.24	0.00	−0.10	0.04	−2.48	0.01	−0.11	0.04	−2.72	0.01	−0.08	0.04	−2.09	0.04
FGOOD	0.09	0.03	3.17	0.00	0.10	0.03	3.56	0.00	0.08	0.03	3.01	0.00	0.09	0.03	3.37	0.00
FPLAN	0.2	0.02	5.10	0.00	0.13	0.02	5.26	0.00	0.10	0.02	4.17	0.00	0.11	0.02	4.25	0.00
FEVALUATE	−0.06	0.03	−2.15	0.03	−0.06	0.03	−2.16	0.03	−0.03	0.03	−1.23	0.22	−0.03	0.03	−1.22	0.22
FROLE	0.36	0.05	6.89	0.00	0.38	0.05	7.35	0.00	0.35	0.05	6.72	0.00	0.37	0.05	7.15	0.00
GCONCERN	0.09	0.03	2.69	0.01	0.12	0.04	3.26	0.00	0.11	0.04	3.01	0.00	0.13	0.04	3.38	0.00
GHOLIDAY	0.27	0.08	3.28	0.00	0.21	0.09	2.49	0.01	0.25	0.08	3.08	0.00	0.20	0.08	2.35	0.02
GWORTH	0.35	0.04	7.86	0.00	0.37	0.05	8.00	0.00	0.29	0.05	6.36	0.00	0.31	0.05	6.65	0.00
JRACEWP	−0.54	0.17	−3.18	0.00	−0.55	0.17	−3.24	0.00	−0.58	0.17	−3.46	0.00	−0.59	0.17	−3.49	0.00
JRACEWF	0.08	0.03	2.26	0.02	0.07	0.03	2.18	0.03	0.07	0.03	2.23	0.03	0.07	0.03	2.16	0.03
MDSWORKF	−0.23	0.09	−2.41	0.02	−0.25	0.10	−2.43	0.02	−0.24	0.09	−2.61	0.01	−0.28	0.10	−2.74	0.01

	Model 1				Model 2				Model 3				Model 4			
	B	SE	t	p	B	SE	t	p	B	SE	t	p	B	SE	t	p
JSEARCH	-0.05	0.02	-2.20	**0.03**	-0.04	0.02	-1.70	0.09	-0.06	0.02	-2.38	**0.02**	-0.04	0.02	-1.75	0.08
JSKILLSW	0.08	0.03	2.61	**0.01**	0.07	0.03	2.33	**0.02**	0.07	0.03	2.60	**0.01**	0.07	0.03	2.30	**0.02**
MWORK	-0.32	0.16	-2.01	**0.05**	-0.36	0.17	-2.17	**0.03**	-0.35	0.16	-2.19	**0.03**	-0.37	0.16	-2.28	**0.02**
MMALE					-0.04	0.07	-0.61	0.54					-0.08	0.07	-1.06	0.29
MAGE					-0.02	0.01	-1.64	0.10					-0.02	0.01	-1.41	0.16
MAGE2					0.00	0.00	1.38	0.17					0.00	0.00	1.12	0.26
MGHI					0.07	0.03	2.40	**0.02**					0.06	0.03	2.09	**0.04**
MRSOUTH					-0.20	0.10	-1.96	**0.05**					-0.18	0.10	-1.75	0.08
MRMIDWLS					0.00	0.10	-0.04	0.97					0.04	0.10	0.36	0.72
MRNORTH					-0.17	0.10	-1.71	0.09					-0.14	0.10	-1.43	0.15
MRSCOT					-0.04	0.13	-0.30	0.77					0.00	0.13	0.00	1.00
PXTRAVRT									0.08	0.03	3.04	0.00	0.07	0.03	2.74	**0.01**
PAGREEBL									-0.04	0.03	-1.41	0.16	-0.04	0.03	-1.17	0.24
PCONSCS									-0.04	0.03	-1.54	0.13	-0.03	0.03	-1.22	0.22
PSTABLE									0.11	0.03	4.19	0.00	0.12	0.03	4.42	0.00
POPEN									-0.04	0.03	-1.16	0.25	-0.03	0.03	-1.02	0.31
R^2	0.54				0.55				0.56				0.57			
Adjusted R^2	0.53				0.54				0.55				0.55			
Log likelihood	-999.39				-990.71				-983.08				-974.19			
Observations	778				778				778				778			

Table 16.3b. Model estimates for sub-samples by gender

Variable	Female					Male				
	OLS coefficient	Standard error	t stat	p value	Ordered logit p value	OLS coefficient	Standard error	t stat	p value	Ordered logit p value
BSHELTER	0.39	0.13	3.05	0.00	0.01	0.02	0.15	0.14	0.89	0.96
CDASALTP	−0.18	0.10	−1.75	0.08	0.19	−0.18	0.17	−1.10	0.27	0.36
CSEXSAT	0.14	0.11	1.29	0.20	0.09	0.29	0.11	2.70	0.01	0.00
ELOVE	0.12	0.03	3.54	0.00	0.00	0.02	0.04	0.62	0.54	0.20
EFEELING	0.04	0.04	1.00	0.32	0.38	0.16	0.04	3.91	0.00	0.00
ESTRAIN	−0.04	0.05	−0.69	0.49	0.07	−0.16	0.06	−2.44	0.02	0.01
FGOOD	0.16	0.04	3.93	0.00	0.00	0.05	0.04	1.37	0.17	0.44
FPLAN	0.11	0.04	3.17	0.00	0.00	0.09	0.04	2.52	0.01	0.03
FEVALUATE	−0.03	0.04	−0.90	0.37	0.48	−0.02	0.04	−0.62	0.54	0.70
FROLE	0.41	0.07	5.91	0.00	0.00	0.30	0.08	3.64	0.00	0.00
GCONCERN	0.13	0.05	2.60	0.01	0.03	0.08	0.06	1.32	0.19	0.30
GHOLIDAY	0.12	0.11	1.09	0.28	0.37	0.27	0.14	2.00	0.05	0.02
GWORTH	0.32	0.06	5.09	0.00	0.00	0.28	0.07	3.92	0.00	0.01
JRACEMP	−0.23	0.26	−0.88	0.38	0.54	−0.73	0.23	−3.24	0.00	0.00
JRACENF	0.04	0.05	0.87	0.39	0.34	0.07	0.05	1.56	0.12	0.04
MDSWORKF	−0.40	0.14	−2.89	0.00	0.00	−0.11	0.15	−0.73	0.47	0.23
JSEARCH	−0.03	0.04	−0.87	0.38	0.11	−0.05	0.03	−1.37	0.17	0.02
JSKILLSW	0.02	0.04	0.44	0.66	0.37	0.11	0.04	2.63	0.01	0.00
MWORK	−0.03	0.23	−0.13	0.90	0.57	−0.75	0.25	−3.02	0.00	0.00

MAGE	-0.03	0.02	-1.92	0.06	0.06	0.01	0.02	0.80	0.42	0.55
MAGE2	0.00	0.00	1.19	0.24	0.16	0.00	0.00	-0.58	0.56	0.41
MGHI	0.03	0.04	0.89	0.37	0.36	0.10	0.04	2.30	0.02	0.04
MRSOUTH	-0.16	0.14	-1.14	0.25	0.20	-0.17	0.15	-1.14	0.26	0.17
MRMIDWLS	0.14	0.14	0.99	0.32	0.34	-0.11	0.15	-0.71	0.48	0.30
MRNORTH	-0.13	0.13	-1.00	0.32	0.45	-0.12	0.14	-0.82	0.41	0.23
MRSCOT	0.13	0.18	0.73	0.47	0.74	-0.12	0.18	-0.63	0.53	0.47
PXTRAVRT	0.08	0.03	2.39	0.02	0.02	0.03	0.04	0.78	0.44	0.53
PAGREEBL	-0.06	0.04	-1.34	0.18	0.24	0.00	0.05	-0.08	0.93	0.80
PCONSCS	-0.07	0.04	-1.80	0.07	0.03	0.00	0.04	0.01	0.99	0.80
PSTABLE	0.13	0.04	3.52	0.00	0.00	0.14	0.04	3.32	0.00	0.00
POPEN	-0.01	0.04	-0.32	0.75	0.90	-0.05	0.05	-1.13	0.26	0.30
R^2	0.61				0.58					
Adjusted R^2	0.58				0.54					
Log likelihood	-505.9				-445.0					
Observations	418				360					

experiencing racial discrimination at work in the past is significant for men but not for women, a result that is consistent with a number of possibilities we cannot separate out. For example, it could be that discrimination is more severe for men than for women, but equally it could be that it is merely more salient for men, perhaps because they are less likely to suffer from other forms of discrimination, like gender discrimination, at work. Alternatively, it could be that racial discrimination at work is something men experience for longer, as their workforce participation rates are higher. Clearly there are differences between men and women but combined with the fact that some variables which are significant covariates of happiness for both men and women—like FROLE, which measures abilities to play a useful role in life—suggest that where there are differences they are determined by environmental factors, and that there are levels of abstraction at which concepts are equally significant between the sexes. Clearly these practical issues are rather important for designing and interpreting empirical work, and indicate the need for additional inputs when one is trying to operationalize a theory such as that developed in Sen (1985).

V. Concluding Remarks

This chapter has reported on a research project in which economists, philosophers and psychologists have sought to address the purported dearth of information about people's capabilities and to use the data developed to assess welfare. The capabilities approach has already been highly influential in shaping the evolution of the Human Development Index, and in our program of work, we have focused on developing and analyzing instruments that could, in principle, be used to broaden its scope significantly. The research reported here illustrates the feasibility, though non-triviality, of the tasks involved and has highlighted a number of statistical issues, though a number remain. We summarize below the more significant points.

First, it is important to recognize that both capabilities and subjective well-being may be multi-dimensional. We have shown how many of the more significant dimensions of capability can be measured, but it is worth acknowledging that these capability indicators may be particularly closely related to satisfaction with particular areas of life. Our work on violence is related: capabilities are inherently multi-dimensional but in looking at experiences of violence, we were able to isolate one set of capabilities and infer its impact on overall well-being, and how it spreads to other dimensions and culminates in a relative deprivation of well-being. This highlights the fact that capabilities can be operationalized in different ways: a *global* perspective sees how dimensions are intertwined whilst a *partial* perspective analyzes the total effect in a single area only. Beyond the research discussed here, such analyses remain largely unexplored at this point, though it is worth highlighting the existence of work by Kuklys (2005) in which she demonstrates how satisfaction with financial income can be used to generate econometric estimates of the cost of disability.

Secondly, we have highlighted the importance, and practical measurability, of personality. If there is heterogeneity between people in terms of the rate at which they convert resources into welfare, then personality is likely to be a significant contributor to variations in these conversion factors, and we have shown how these can be partially treated in the absence of panel data. Thirdly, we have begun to explore the causes of capabilities, though clearly there is further work to be done. Fourthly, we have shown that latent variable methods, traditionally used in statistics but increasingly employed in economics, can play a valuable role in helping to understand patterns in observations that would otherwise be hard to detect by virtue of the high number of dimensions on which human capabilities can vary. Fifthly and finally, we have presented linear additive models of subjective well-being, although some philosophical characterizations suggest that a lexicographic approach would be more appropriate. However, our additive models, used widely in empirical work, appear to serve quite well and this in turn suggests that a piecemeal approach to policy could be feasible—even if one cannot address all of the sources of impoverishment and misery, addressing some will help.

There remain areas of application where further questions could be devised, but the questions developed and analyzed to date nonetheless illustrate which economic statistics the capabilities approach requires for its operationalization within quantitative empirical work. In many cases, the empirical associations are not what one would immediately expect, and while we have suggested possible explanations, they must be speculative. However, these surprising quantitative associations are useful in that they suggest ways of developing theory and pursuing related psychological investigations, quantitative or otherwise.

APPENDIX: CAPABILITIES, QUESTIONS AND VARIABLES

I. Main capabilities indicators from OCAP (2005 version)

Main corresponding question(s)	Variable name and response code
1. Given your family history, dietary habits, lifestyle and health status, until what age do you expect to live?	ALIFEXP years
2. Does your health in any way limit your daily activities compared to most people of your age?	BHEALTH 1 if N, 0 otherwise
3. Are you able to have children?	BPEPRODT 1 if Y or N*, 0
4. Do you eat fresh meat, chicken or fish at least twice a week?	BNOURISH 1 if Y or N*, 0
5. Is your current accommodation adequate or inadequate for your current needs?	BSHELTER 1 if A, 0
6. Are you prevented from moving home for any reason?	BCANMOVE 0 if Pa, 1
7. Please indicate how safe you feel walking alone in the area near your home during the daytime.	CSAFEDAY 1–7(Cs)
8. Please indicate how safe you feel walking alone in the area near your home after dark.	CSAFENYT 1–7(Cs)
9. Have you ever been the victim of some other form of violent assault or attack [i.e. not domestic violence or sexual assault]?	CVASALPT 1 if Y, 0
10. How likely do you think it is that you will be a victim of violent assault or attack in the future?	CVASALTF 1–7(El)
11. Have you ever been a victim of sexual assault?	CSASALTP 1 if Y, 0
12. Please indicate how vulnerable you feel to sexual assault or attack.	CSASALTF 1–7(El)
13. Have you ever been a victim of domestic violence?	CDASALPT 1 if Y, 0
14. Please indicate how vulnerable you feel to domestic violence in the future.	CDASALPF 1–7(Vv)
15. Do you have sufficient opportunities to satisfy your sexual needs?	CSEXSAT 1 if Y, 0
16. Even if you don't need or have never needed any of the following [contraception, abortion or infertility treatment], are you prohibited from using any of the following for any reason (e.g. religious beliefs, family pressure)?	CCHOICE 1 if Y, 0
17. What is the highest educational or work-related qualification you have?	DQUAL 1 if A+, 0
18. How often do you use your imagination and/or reasoning in your day-to-day life?	DIMAGINE 1–7(At)

Main corresponding question(s)	Variable name and response code
19. I am free to express my political views.	DXPRSPOL 1–7(As)
20. I am free to practice my religion as I want to.	DXPRSRLG 1–7(As)
21. Have you recently been able to enjoy your normal day-to-day activities?	DENDJOY2 1–4(Mm)
22. How difficult do you find it to make friendships which last with people outside work?	EFRIENDS 1–7(Ee)
23. At present, how easy or difficult do you find it to enjoy the love, care and support of your immediate family?	ELOVE 1–7(Ee)
24. Do you find it easy or difficult to express feelings of love, grief, longing, gratitude and anger compared to most people of your age?	EFEELING 1–7(Ee)
25. Have you recently lost much sleep over worry?	ENOSLEEP 1–4(Mm)
26. Have you recently felt constantly under strain?	ESTRAIN 1–4(Mm)
27. My idea of a good life is based on my own judgement.	FGOOD 1–7(As)
28. I have a clear plan of how I would like my life to be.	FPLAN 1–7(As)
29. How often, if at all, do you evaluate how you lead your life and where you are going in life?	FEVALUATE 1–7(At)
30. Outside of work, have you recently felt that you were playing a useful part in things?	FROLE 1–4(Mm)
31. I respect, value and appreciate other people.	GCONCERN 1–7(As)
32. Do you normally have at least one week's (seven days') annual holiday away from home?	GHOLIDAY 1 if Y, 0
33. Do you normally meet up with friends or family for a drink or a meal at least once a month?	GMEAL 1 if Y, 0
34. Do you tend to find it easy or difficult to imagine the situation of other people (i.e. to put yourself in others' shoes)?	GIMAGINE 1–7(Ee)
35. Have you recently been thinking of yourself as a worthless person?	GWORTH 1–4(Ml)
36–41. Outside of any employment or work situation, have you ever experienced discrimination because of your race, sexual orientation, gender, religion, age?	GRACEP 0 if N, 1 GSEXOP 0 if N, 1 GGENP 0 if N, 1 GRELIGNP 0 if N, 1 GAGEP 0 if N, 1

Main corresponding question(s)	Variable name and response code
42–46. Outside of any employment or work situation, how likely do you think it is that in the future you will be discriminated against because of your race, sexual orientation, gender, religion, age?	GRACEF 1–7(Eu) GSEXOF 1–7(Eu) GGENF 1–7(Eu) GRELIGNF 1–7(Eu) GAGEF 1–7(Eu)
47. I appreciate and value plants, animals and the world of nature.	HSPECIES 1–7(As)
48. Have you recently been enjoying your recreational activities?	IPLAY 1–4(Mm)
49. I am able to participate in the political activities that affect my life if I want to.	JPARTPOL (As)
50. For which of the following reasons, if any, have you not bought your home? [U = forced not to for reasons of affordability or difficulty obtaining mortgage, 1 = home owner or chose not to buy for other reasons.]	JOWN 0 if U, 1
51–55. When seeking work in the past, have you ever experienced discrimination because of your race, sexual orientation, gender, religion, age?	JRACEWP 1 if Y, 0 JSEXOWP 1 if Y, 0 JGENDWP 1 if Y, 0 JRLIGNWP 1 if Y, 0 JAGEWP 1 if Y, 0
56–60. When seeking work in the future, how likely do you think it is that you will experience discrimination because of your race, sexual orientation, gender, religion, age?	JRACEWF 1–7(Eu) or 0[a] JSEXOWF 1–7(Eu) or 0[a] JGENDWF 1–7(Eu) or 0[a] JRLIGNWF 1–7(Eu) or 0[a] JAGEWF 1–7(Eu) or 0[a]
61. How likely do you think it is that within the next 12 months you will be stopped and searched by the police when it is not warranted?	JSEARCII 1–7(Eu) or 0[a]

Main corresponding question(s)	Variable name and response code
62. To what extent does your work make use of your skills and talents?	JSKILLSW 1–7(At) or 0^b
63. At work, have you recently felt that you were playing a useful part in things?	JROLEW 1–4(Mm) or 0^b
64. Do you tend to find it easy or difficult to relate to your colleagues at work?	JREALTEW 1–7(Ee) or 0^b
65. At work, are you treated with respect?	JRESPECTW 1–7(At) or 0^b

Note: The terms 1–4, 1–7 indicate 4- and 7-point scales; following each maximum is an abbreviation denoting the semantic anchor used for that point.

Key

A	Adequate	Eu	Extremely unlikely
As	Agree strongly	Ml	Much less than usual
At	All the time	Mu	Much more than usual
A+	A level or above	N	No
Cs	Completely satisfied	N*	No for reasons of choice
Ee	Extremely easy	Pa	Prevented for reasons of affordability
El	Extremely likely	Vv	Very vulnerable
		Y	Yes

[a] Variable = 0 if there is no intention to work in future (MDSWORKF = 1, 0 if there is no such intention).
[b] Variable = 0 if the respondent is out of work (MWORK = 1, 0 if out of work).

II. Key to controls

Socio-Demographic

MMALE	Gender (1 if female, 0 if male)
MAGE	Age (in years)
MAGE2	Age squared
MGHI	What is your gross household income?
MRSOUTH	South of England excluding London
MRMIDWLS	Midlands and Wales
MRNORTH	North of England
MRSCOT	Scotland

"Big Five" personality dimensions[c]

PXTRAVRT	I see myself as extraverted, enthusiastic.
	I see myself as reserved quiet.
PAGREEBL	I see myself as critical, quarrelsome.
	I see myself as sympathetic, warm.
PCONSCS	I see myself as dependable, self-disciplined.
	I see myself as disorganized, careless.

PSTABLE	I see myself as anxious, easily upset.
	I see myself as calm, emotionally stable.
POPEN	I see myself as open to new experience, complex.
	I see myself as conventional, uncreative.

c Measured by scores on the "big five" dimensions of personality. In each case, subjects are asked to say whether they agree with two statements relating to a dimension of personality; responses are then combined to generate an overall score for each of the five dimensions.

REFERENCES

AGARWAL, B., and PANDA, P. (2006), "Toward Freedom from Domestic Violence: The Neglected Obvious", *Journal of Human Development*, 8: 359–88.

ALKIRE, S. (2002), "Dimensions of Human Development", *World Development*, 30: 119–205.

ANAND, P., and DOLAN, P. (2005), "Equity Capabilities and Health: Special Issue Introduction", *Social Science and Medicine*, 60: 219–22.

—— and VAN HEES, M. (2006), "Capabilities and Achievements", *Journal of Socio-Economics*, 35: 268–84.

—— HUNTER, G., DOWDING, K., GUALA, F., and VAN HEES, M. (forthcoming), "The Development of Capability Indicators", *Journal of Human Development*.

—— —— and SMITH, R. (2005), "Capabilities and Wellbeing: Evidence Based on the Sen–Nussbaum Approach to Welfare", *Social Indicators Research*, 79: 9–55.

—— and SANTOS, C. (2007), "Violence, Gender Inequalities and Life Satisfaction", *Révue d'Economie Politique*, 117: 135–60.

—— and WAILOO, A. (2000), "Utilities vs. Rights to Publicly Provided Goods: Arguments and Evidence from Health Care Rationing", *Economica*, 67: 543–78.

BRANDOLINI, A., and D'ALESSIO, G. (1998), "Measuring Wellbeing in the Functioning Space", plenary paper given to the 13th International Economics Association Congress, Buenos Aires.

BROWER, W. B. F., VA EXEL, N., JOB, A., and STOLK, E. A. (2004), "Acceptability of Less than Perfect Health States", *Social Science and Medicine*, 60: 237–46.

BURCHARDT, T., and LE GRAND, J. (2002), *Constraint and Opportunity: Assessing Employment Capability* (London: ESRC Research Centre for the Analysis of Social Exclusion, London School of Economics).

CARTER, I. (1999), *A Measure of Freedom* (Oxford: Oxford University Press).

—— (2003), "Functionings Capabilities and the Non-Specific Value of Freedom", unpubl. paper, Nuffield College, Oxford.

CHIAPPERO-MARTINETTI, E. (2000), "A Multi-Dimensional Assessment of Wellbeing Based on Sen's Functioning Approach", *Rivista Internazionale di Scienze Sociali*, 107: 208–39.

CLARK, A., ETILE, F., POSTEL-VINAY, F., SENIK, C., and VAN DER STRAETEN, K. (2005), "Heterogeneity in Reported Wellbeing", *Economic Journal*, 115: 118–32.

CLARK, A. E., FRIJTERS, P., and SHIELDS, M. A. (2006), *Income and Happiness: Evidence, Explanations and Economic Implications*, Paris-Jourdan Sciences Economiques Working Paper 2006-24 (Paris: Paris-Jourdain Sciences Economiques).

CLARK, D. A. (2003), "Concepts and Perceptions of Human Wellbeing: Some Evidence from South Africa", *Oxford Development Studies*, 31: 173–96.

DI TELLA, R., HAISKEN-DE NEW, J. P., and MACCULLOCH, R. (2007), *Happiness Adaptation to Income and to Status in an Individual Panel*, NBER Working Paper 13159 (Cambridge, Mass.: NBER).

EVERITT, B. S., and DUNN, G. (2001), *Applied Multivariate Data Analysis* (London: Hodder Arnold).

FREY, B., and STUTZER, A. (2000), "Happiness, Economy and Institutions", *Economic Journal*, 110: 918–38.

GAERTNER, W., and XU, Y. (2005), "Alternative Proposals to Measure the Standard of Living When its Development Over Time is Uncertain", paper presented at the Annual American Economic Association Conference, Philadelphia.

GOSLING, S. D., and RENTFROW, W. B. S. (2003), "A Very Brief Measure of the Big-Five Personality Domains", *Journal of Research in Personality*, 37: 504–28.

HELLIWELL, J.-F. (2006), "Wellbeing, Social Capital and Public Policy", *Economic Journal*, 116: 35–45.

KAHNEMAN, D., KRUGER, A. B., SCHKADE, D., SCHWARZ, N., and STONE, A. (2004), "Toward National Wellbeing Accounts", *American Economic Review*, 94: 429–34.

——— WAKKER P. P., and SARIN, R. (1997), "Back to Bentham? Explorations of Experienced Utility", *Quarterly Journal of Economics*, 112: 375–406.

KUKLYS, W. (2005), *Amartya Sen's Capability Approach: Theoretical Insights and Empirical Applications*, Studies in Choice and Welfare (Berlin, Springer-Verlag).

——— and ROBEYNS, I. (2005), "Sen's Capability Approach to Welfare Economics", paper presented at the Annual American Economic Association Conference, Philadelphia.

LADERCHI, C. R. (2001), *Do Concepts Matter? An Empirical Investigation of the Differences between a Capability Approach and a Monetary Assessment of Poverty*, Discussion Paper, Queen Elizabeth House (Oxford: Queen Elizabeth House).

LAYARD, R. (2005), *Happiness: Lessons from a New Science* (London: Allen Lane).

LAYTE, R., NOLAN, B., and WHELAN, C. T. (2000), "Targeting Poverty: Lessons from Monitoring Ireland's National Anti-Poverty Strategy", *Journal of Social Policy*, 29: 553–75.

MANSKI, C. F. (2004), "Measuring Expectations", *Econometrica*, 72: 1329–76.

NEHRING, K., and PUPPE, C. (2002), "A Theory of Diversity", *Econometrica*, 70: 1155–98.

NUSSBAUM, M. C. (2000), *Women and Human Development: The Capabilities Approach* (Cambridge: Cambridge University Press).

——— and SEN, A. K. (1993), *The Quality of Life* (Oxford: Clarendon Press).

OSWALD, A. J. (1997), "Happiness and Economic Performance", *Economic Journal*, 107: 1815–31.

PATTANAIK, P., and XU, Y. (1998), "On Preference and Freedom", *Theory and Decision*, 44: 173–98.

QIZILBASH, M. (2004), *On the Arbitrariness and Robustness of Multi-Dimensional Poverty Rankings*, UNU-WIDER Research Paper 2004/37 (Tokyo: United Nations University).

ROBEYNS, I. (forthcoming), "Selecting Capabilities for Quality of Life Measurement", *Social Indicators Research*.

SCHOKKAERT, E., and VAN OOTEGEM, L. (1990), "Sen's Concept of the Living Standard Applied to the Belgium Unemployed", *Recherches Economiques de Louvain*, 56: 429–50.

SEN, A. K. (1979), "Personal Utilities and Public Judgements: Or What's Wrong with Welfare Economics", *Economic Journal*, 89: 537–58.

—— (1985), *Commodities and Capabilities* (Amsterdam: North-Holland).

—— (2006), *Identity and Violence: The Illusion of Destiny* (London: Allen Lane).

VAN HEES, M. (2004), "Freedom of Choice and Diversity of Options: Some Difficulties", *Social Choice and Welfare*, 22: 253–66.

WINKELMANN, L., and WINKELMANN, R. (1998), "Why are the Unemployed so Unhappy?", *Economica*, 65: 1–15.

CHAPTER 17

ON ULTRAPOVERTY

SUDHIR ANAND

CHRISTOPHER HARRIS

OLIVER LINTON

I. INTRODUCTION

In an influential series of articles written for the World Bank, Michael Lipton introduced and discussed the concept of ultrapoverty. He distinguished the "poor" from the "ultrapoor", claiming that "sharp discontinuities exist between poor and ultra-poor, but not between poor and non-poor" (Lipton 1988: 46). His definition of ultrapoverty was in terms of a "double-eighty" criterion, viz. calorie intake below 80% of FAO/WHO (1973) calorie requirements, and expenditure on food above 80% of total expenditure (or income). Lipton's definition of poverty was also in terms of two food adequacy standards: calorie intake at 80–100% of requirements, and expenditure on food above 70% of income. It should be noted that the ultra-poor are *not* a subset of the poor—see Figure 17.1.

In the context of developing countries, it is natural to focus on food adequacy as the primary indicator of extreme deprivation—and hence "ultrapoverty". Food is, after all, the most important basic need for human survival and functioning. The most pressing dimension of food consumption, especially for people who are

This paper was initiated in the programme on hunger and poverty led by Amartya Sen at the World Institute of Development Economics Research (WIDER), Helsinki, in the 1990s. The authors are extremely grateful to Amartya Sen for helpful discussions and suggestions, and would also like to thank Ravi Kanbur and seminar participants at Oxford, Harvard, Yale and Berkeley for comments.

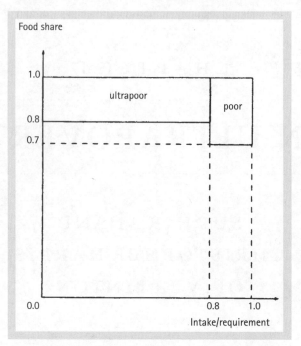

Fig. 17.1. Lipton's definition of poverty and ultra-poverty

severely deprived of it, is energy or calorie intake. Nutrition does, of course, have many other dimensions apart from calories—such as protein and micronutrients (minerals and vitamins). But for those whose food consumption is low, protein intake is usually correlated with calorie intake (McLaren 1974; Payne 1975; Poleman 1981; World Bank 1986). It makes sense, therefore, to restrict attention to calories in attempting to define ultrapoverty.

A major problem now arises: people *differ* in their calorie requirements. To some extent one can allow for this by taking account of the variation in calorie require-ments with easily observable characteristics such as age and sex. But significant inter- (and intra-)individual differences in requirements will still remain. To take a concrete example, consider two workers of the same age, sex and body weight: a well-paid office worker and a manual laborer. The former could have a low calorie intake because he does not need any more food, whereas the latter could have a low calorie intake because he cannot afford any more food (although he needs it).[1]

Lipton argues that, of two individuals with the same calorie intake, the individual with the higher calorie requirement will be more subject to nutritional stress, and

---

[1] Apart from activity level, other sources of variation in requirements are individual differences in basal metabolic rate (given weight and height), in efficiency of food-to-work conversion (e.g. variations caused by parasitic disease), in climate, and so on.

will therefore assign a greater priority to food. This will be reflected in a higher food share.[2] He thereby arrives at a *double* criterion: an individual is ultrapoor if he has a low calorie intake *and* a high food share.

It remains to specify what is meant by a low calorie intake and a high food share. Lipton (1983: p. iii) suggests that 80% of FAO/WHO (1973) calorie requirements normally suffices to avoid undernutrition (though not hunger), adducing several reasons for reducing the norms by 20%. In food share space he specifies an 80% cut-off on the basis of what he argues to be an empirical regularity. He assembles evidence to show that the food share–expenditure curve is fairly flat at low levels of expenditure (Bhanoji Rao 1981), and asserts that "20% or so of outlay for non-food essentials seems fairly non-compressible" (Lipton 1983: 40), because of expenditure committed to items such as rent and transportation to work.[3]

According to Lipton, the moderately poor, unlike the ultrapoor, are prepared to forgo food and cheap calories in order to fulfill other needs (for non-food items and tastier—and hence dearer—calories). For the moderately poor this indicates that "poverty is *perceived* as non-threatening to nutrition" (Lipton 1983: 44). His motivation for the distinction between ultrapoverty and poverty is that "crudely, the ultra-poor are usually *forced* into undernourishment; the poor often, and the less-poor sometimes, *choose* what *may* be undernourishment (but what is more probably discomfort or hunger) in preference to the grinding boredom of diets dominated by the cheapest foods" (Lipton 1983: 45).

The aim of this chapter is to evaluate Lipton's concept of ultrapoverty. In order to do this, we relate ultrapoverty to the widely used welfare indicator "household total expenditure per capita" in the context of a high-quality household budget survey in a low-income country: the Sri Lanka Consumer Finance Survey (CFS) 1981/82, conducted by the Central Bank of Ceylon.[4] Two of the present authors have analyzed this survey extensively in other publications (e.g. Anand and Harris 1989, 1990, 1994).

The indicator "total expenditure" measures a household's command over commodities, and is well founded in the economic theory of the consumer (Deaton and Muellbauer 1980): it represents "money-metric utility". Although total expenditure is corrected for household size, no adjustment is made for household composition.

---

[2] It is not immediately clear why food share is the most appropriate measure of nutritional inadequacy. A better measure of stress might be the average calorie price of food consumed— individuals suffering from nutritional inadequacy might be expected to seek cheaper sources of calories. Another measure would be the starchy–staple ratio. It would be interesting to explore these alternative measures of stress in the way in which we explore food share in the present chapter.

[3] It is by no means clear why the irreducible minimum of non-food expenditure should be a *percentage* of total expenditure. Indeed, it might seem more plausible to express the irreducible minimum of non-food expenditure in absolute terms.

[4] We could, alternatively, have related it to "household food expenditure per capita", which Anand and Harris (1990) argue to be a good welfare indicator. However, here we use household total expenditure per capita, as it commands wide assent.

There is no agreed or standard methodology for estimating equivalence scales (Deaton and Muellbauer 1986), and using even fairly extreme equivalence scales seems to make little difference compared to the simple correction for household size (Anand and Harris 1989). Thus, we regard total expenditure per capita as a good general-purpose indicator, which will have discriminatory power not only between the poor and the rich, but also among the poor and among the rich. For ease of exposition we shall often refer to total expenditure per capita simply as "expenditure".

CFS 1981/82, which sampled some 8,000 households using a stratified two-stage design, collected detailed information on food expenditure and quantities consumed (200 items), on non-food (non-durable) expenditure (139 items), and on durable expenditure (41 items). Moreover, demographic and socio-economic information was collected on each household member (including employment status and labor and non-labor income from 17 sources), as well as data on housing conditions, amenities and some household equipment. The survey data on food expenditure and quantities have been thoroughly cleaned, before using the food quantities to estimate calorie consumption (see Anand and Harris 1987). A description of the survey is contained in Statistics Department, Central Bank of Ceylon (1984); a detailed assessment can be found in Anand and Harris (1985).

The plan of this chapter is as follows. Section II relates calorie intake to total expenditure per capita, through non-parametric regression of household calorie intake adjusted partially for requirements (age, sex, and moderate activity). The aim is to determine how much welfare information is contained in calorie intake, especially at low levels of intake (say around 80% of average requirement for age, sex and activity). Section III moves on to the second variable in Lipton's definition of ultrapoverty, namely food share. Again, non-parametric regression is used to determine whether the food share–expenditure curve is flat at low values of expenditure, and if so whether the food/outlay ratio is 80% at such low values. Our purpose is also to assess the amount of welfare information contained in food share. Section IV is devoted to ultrapoverty. It aims to determine whether the use of a second criterion (food share) is justified in defining ultrapoverty, by estimating the welfare information this contains orthogonal to the welfare information contained in the first criterion (calorie intake). Here we make use of some non-expenditure variables available in the data set, such as housing, amenities and household durable equipment. Section V is in conclusion.

II. The Intake–Expenditure Curve

Lipton's food adequacy standard is a sufficient calorie intake relative to requirement. However, information is rarely available on individuals' energy requirements. Household budget surveys typically do not collect data on individual heights, weights or metabolic efficiency—and they seldom collect data on time use and activity levels. From survey data we can at best make only a rough allowance for requirements, by assigning to individuals the average requirements for their age, sex and activity group (ASAG). With information on age and sex from CFS 1981/82, and assuming a "moderate" level of activity for everyone, we use the FAO/WHO (1973) recommended energy requirements, adapted for Sri Lanka by the Medical Research Institute, Colombo.

Our measure of calorie intake relative to requirement for a household will be the total calories it consumes divided by the total requirements of its members as determined by their age and sex groups for moderate (including some discretionary) activity. This is tantamount to using a "calorie equivalence scale" to correct for the different calorie needs of a household's members. Hence our measure of calorie intake relative to requirement for a household is just calorie intake per equivalent calorie adult. For ease of exposition, we shall usually abbreviate this to "intake". Thus if a household is meeting its FAO/WHO (1973) requirements exactly, its intake will be unity; if it is meeting 80% of its requirements, its intake will be 0.8.

The purpose of the present section is to relate intake to expenditure. As we are interested mainly in the ordinal rather than the cardinal information contained in expenditure—e.g. the percentile of the expenditure distribution (rather than the rupee expenditure) at which intake attains a given level—we have opted to use expenditure percentiles as our independent variable.[5] This choice also confers advantages for the non-parametric regression estimator: it gives an equi-spaced design in which fixed window and nearest neighbor procedures are essentially the same. Specifically, keeping the bandwidth constant ($h = 0.05$) at each point of the horizontal axis leads to the same number of observations (754) in each window (except near the endpoints). Furthermore, the 100 points at which the regression is calculated are the percentiles themselves.

In Figure 17.2 we have estimated the density function of intake for households from CFS 1981/82. After cleaning the data, the sample size used here and for all other estimations in this paper is 7,547 households. The method of estimation was to use a fixed window kernel estimator (Silverman 1986) at each of 100 equally spaced points along the intake axis, employing a quadratic (Epanechnikov) kernel and a bandwidth of 0.05 times the intake range (implying 754 observations on average in each window). The estimated density function of intake turns out to have a long upper tail. This is perhaps as one would expect, given that intake is bounded below by zero (the minimum level of intake to requirement in this sample is 0.19 and the maximum level 4.06; the median level is 1.09).

The positively skewed shape of the density function of intake will tend to imply that the mean is an upwardly biased estimate of the location of the distribution. One way of correcting for this is to take the logarithm of intake, and the estimated

---

[5] Regressions estimated on this basis will reflect not only the underlying behavioral relationship but also the existing distribution of households by total expenditure per capita in the sample.

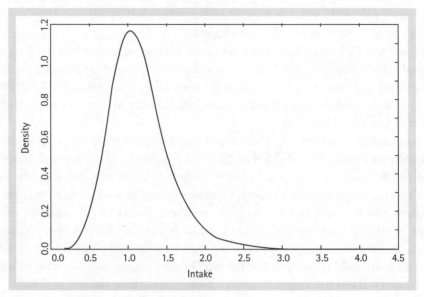

Fig. 17.2. Density function of intake

density of log(intake) does indeed approximate the normal distribution (not shown here). However, if one considers the conditional intake distribution at each level of expenditure—as is necessary in estimating a regression between intake and expenditure—one would expect a priori the skewness of the intake distribution to vary, with greater skewness at lower values of expenditure. Hence, in estimating the intake–expenditure relationship, we have preferred not to take the logarithm of intake, but rather to use more robust measures of the location of the conditional distribution of intake given expenditure, namely the median, the 20th percentile and the 80th percentile. This choice has the further (expositional) advantage that Lipton's ultrapoverty criterion is couched in terms of intake rather than log(intake).

Figure 17.3 plots the non-parametric quantile regressions between intake and expenditure percentile. The median regression shows the intake–expenditure curve to be upward-sloping and concave relative to expenditure percentile. The regressions for the 20th and 80th percentiles show that the spread of the distribution of intake increases with expenditure. The concavity suggests that the signal content of intake—as measured by the slope of the intake–expenditure curve—decreases with expenditure. The increasing spread suggests that the noise content of intake increases with expenditure. Overall, then, it would appear that intake is a more potent welfare indicator at low levels of expenditure than at high levels.

We pursue this idea in two different ways. First we use a simple, direct method which estimates moving Spearman correlation coefficients at each percentile of expenditure. We calculate the Spearman rank correlation coefficient between intake and expenditure percentile for the (754) observations falling in a window (except at the endpoints, where slightly fewer observations are employed) of fixed bandwidth ($h = 0.05$) around each percentile. We also calculate the 95% confidence intervals

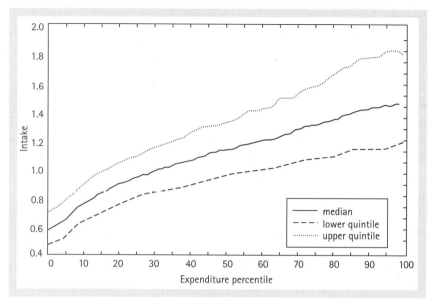

Fig. 17.3. Quantile regressions of intake on expenditure percentile

for the Spearman coefficient at each percentile under the null hypothesis of zero correlation. (The confidence interval depends only on the total number of observations in each window, and is therefore the same at each interior percentile; this is an advantage of our decision to transform the independent variable to expenditure percentiles.) The results of this exercise are shown in Figure 17.4.

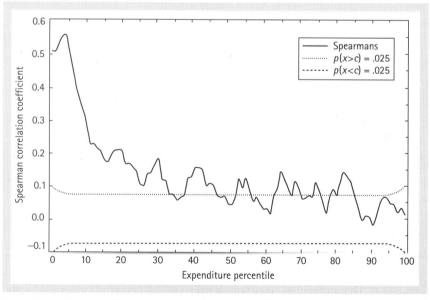

Fig. 17.4. Moving Spearman correlation coefficients between intake and expenditure

The estimates of the moving Spearman coefficient in Figure 17.4 are remarkable. Up to about the 35th percentile, the relationship between intake and expenditure is significantly positive, with the Spearman coefficient declining in value as one moves to higher percentiles. But beyond the 35th percentile the relationship is no longer uniformly significant. Moreover, these results are not a consequence of undersmoothing, i.e. using too narrow a bandwidth. The overall window size is already quite large, containing 10% of the sample (or 754 observations) for each estimate of the Spearman coefficient (except at the endpoints of the percentile range). Of course, the intake–expenditure relationship is positive on average (i.e. positive Spearman coefficients on average), as the basic median regression in Figure 17.3 would indicate.

The second way to pursue the idea that intake is locally a more powerful welfare indicator at low rather than high levels of expenditure is to estimate the first derivative of the regression function (in this case the median). This is done in Figure 17.5 (again using a bandwidth of $h = 0.05$), which also shows the 95% confidence interval for the derivative at each point under the null hypothesis of the derivative being zero. (In this case, unlike in Figure 17.4, the size of the confidence interval varies at each point because we allow for heteroskedasticity.)

The results are in general agreement with those for the moving Spearman plot in Figure 17.4. The derivatives are significantly positive up to approximately the 25th percentile, after which they bounce in and out of significance. On average, the derivative is positive, as the basic median regression in Figure 17.3 would suggest.

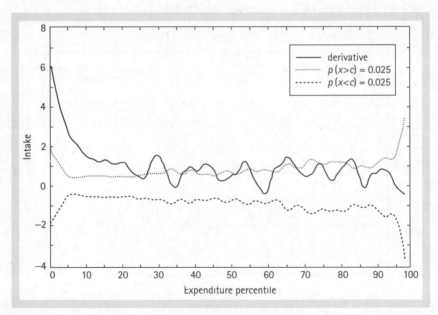

Fig. 17.5. Derivative of median intake with respect to expenditure percentile

Overall, Figures 17.3–17.5 suggest that intake contains a significant amount of low-end welfare information, and relatively little high-end welfare information. It may therefore be possible to use it to distinguish between the poor and the remainder of the population and to discriminate among the poor. To the extent that expenditure is a reliable indicator, the results also suggest that intake contains relatively little high-end welfare information.

III. THE FOOD SHARE–EXPENDITURE CURVE

Lipton's second criterion in the definition of ultrapoverty is based on a high share of food in total expenditure (or income). As we suggested in Section I, the motivation behind this is that an individual's struggle to attain nutritional adequacy will be indicated by a high food share as his or her calorie requirements begin to override other considerations. The use of food share is thus an attempt to address the issue of requirements at the level of the individual (or household).

In this section, we relate food share to expenditure, in much the same way as the previous section related intake to expenditure. The objective is to assess the value of food share as a welfare indicator, but in passing we shall have opportunity to comment on Engel's Law and on Lipton's hypothesis about the flatness of the food share–expenditure curve at the bottom. The empirical analysis here is again based on non-parametric regression.

Figure 17.6 presents the estimate of the density function of food share for the sample of 7,547 households from CFS 1981/82. (The same kernel and number of points were used as in Figure 17.2, with the bandwidth in Figure 17.6 of $h = 0.05$.) As in the case of calorie intake, the skewed shape (in this case negative) of the marginal density of food share tends to imply that the mean is a biased estimate (in this case downwardly) of the location of the distribution. One way of correcting for this is to take a logistic transform of food share—not a logarithmic one, as in the case of calorie intake, because food share is bounded above by unity. (The estimated density of logit(food share), not shown here, is quite symmetric—indeed almost normal.) A more direct way, as before, is simply to use the median and other quantiles of the food share distribution rather than the mean. This also has the expositional advantage that it is in terms of food share—and not in terms of logit(food share)—that Lipton's ultrapoverty criterion is couched.

Figure 17.7 shows the quantile regressions of food share as a function of expenditure percentile. According to these regressions, food share would appear to be a decreasing concave function of expenditure. Median food share appears to be about 0.8 for the poorest households, and its decline from that level is very gradual as one

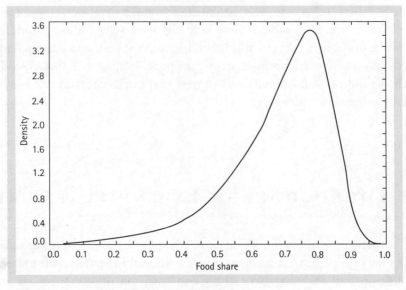

Fig. 17.6. Density function of food share

moves to better-off households. Thus even at the 40th percentile of expenditure, the median food share is still 0.75. It would also seem that the spread of the food share distribution increases with expenditure.

Since the signal content of food share—as measured by the slope of the food share–expenditure curve—increases with expenditure, and the noise content of

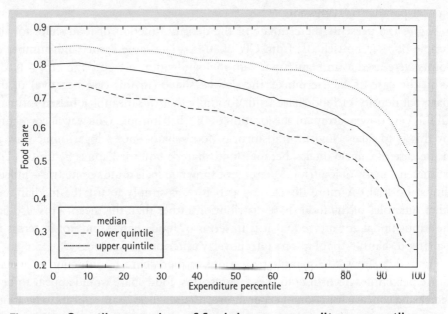

Fig. 17.7. Quantile regressions of food share on expenditure percentile

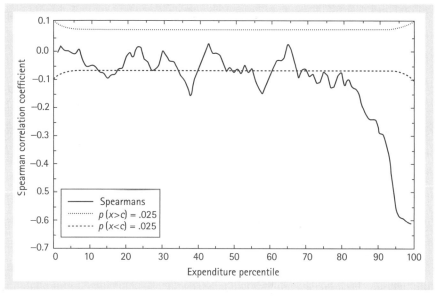

Fig. 17.8. Moving Spearman correlation coefficients between food share and expenditure

food share—as measured by the spread of the distribution of food share—also increases, the behavior of the overall strength of the statistical relationship between food share and expenditure is ambiguous. In order to obtain a more precise assessment of the strength of the food share–expenditure relationship along the expenditure percentile range, we again calculate moving Spearman correlation coefficients (Figure 17.8) and median derivatives (Figure 17.9). As Figure 17.8 shows, the moving Spearmans generally lie within the 95% confidence interval around zero correlation up to the 70th expenditure percentile, and from the 80th percentile onwards we observe a clear-cut negative relationship.

This interpretation concerning the strength of the food share–expenditure relationship along the percentile range is corroborated by the median derivative estimates in Figure 17.9 (using a bandwidth of $h = 0.05$). The median derivatives generally remain within the 95% confidence interval around zero up to the 70th expenditure percentile, and after the 80th percentile they are significantly negative. Figures 17.8 and 17.9 confirm that the relationship between food share and expenditure is significant and negative only in the top 30% of the expenditure distribution.

We conclude that at low levels of food share, food share contains a significant amount of welfare information. It may therefore be possible to use it to discriminate between the rich and the remainder of the population, and to discriminate among the rich. The results of the present section do not tell us whether food share contains a significant amount of welfare information at high levels of food share. However, to the extent that expenditure is a reliable indicator, they do suggest that food share contains relatively little information at high levels of food share.

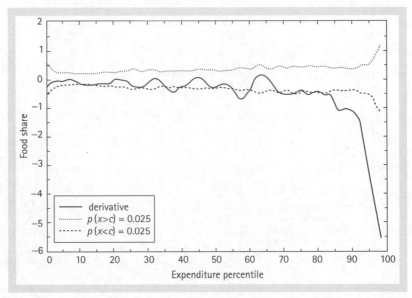

Fig. 17.9. Derivative of median food share with respect to expenditure percentile

Figures 17.7–17.9 can also be used to comment on various aspects of the literature on Engel's Law (Engel 1895). Engel's Law was formulated on the basis of his estimate of this relationship on Belgian data; the law states that food share decreases with total expenditure or income. Some researchers have attempted to test Engel's Law on primary data from surveys by use of parametric regression techniques (e.g. Deaton 1980; see also Houthakker 1957). Others have attempted to test it on secondary data (Bhanoji Rao 1981; Lipton 1983) by computing the food share for published expenditure or income classes—a simple non-parametric technique analogous to estimating a histogram. Figure 17.7 suggests that food share is negatively related to expenditure throughout the expenditure range. This is consistent with Engel's Law. On the other hand, Figures 17.8 and 17.9 suggest that the relationship between food share and expenditure is weak at low levels of expenditure—which is consistent with Lipton's view that the curve is flat in this region.

IV. Ultrapoverty

In sections II and III we showed that intake has power as a welfare indicator for low (but not high) levels of intake, and food share has power as a welfare indicator for low (but not high) levels of food share; and that intake and food share are consistent with expenditure being a reasonable overall welfare indicator. Hence there might be some merit in Lipton's proposal to use an aggressive (i.e. low) calorie intake cut-off, but little to justify his use of an aggressive (i.e. high) food share cut-off.

If the secondary criterion of food share is to be used, then it should be applied conservatively, and not aggressively. In other words, it may be possible to identify the poor by using an aggressive calorie intake cut-off of 0.8, and then to eliminate from this group those who have a food share less than 0.6 (who are more certain to be rich)—rather than to eliminate, according to Lipton's criterion, those who have a food share less than 0.8 (which may include many poor). This is equivalent to defining the ultrapoor as those who have a calorie intake less than 0.8 and a food share greater than 0.6. It is a substantial weakening of Lipton's double-eighty criterion, and may well produce numbers that are not significantly different from those obtained by applying the primary selection criterion of intake by itself.[6]

If a secondary selection criterion is to be employed in addition to intake as the primary selection criterion, it may be better to use expenditure rather than food share. We can even go further and ask whether intake itself should be the primary selection criterion: again, perhaps expenditure might be better. In other words, might we do better to use expenditure as our primary selection criterion instead of intake, or expenditure as our secondary selection criterion instead of food share? Sections II and III do not offer much guidance as to whether intake or expenditure is the better welfare indicator at the bottom of the distribution, or whether food share or expenditure is the better indicator at the top. They also leave open the questions of whether intake contains any information orthogonal to expenditure at the top, and whether food share contains any information orthogonal to expenditure at the bottom.

In this section we use other welfare information from the CFS 1981/82 data set to cast light on these questions. This information is based largely on the quality of housing and the ownership of certain basic household equipment and durable goods. Through linear regression analysis, we shall attempt to determine how well our three indicators—intake, food share and expenditure—are correlated with and explained by various housing and other non-monetary indicators. To use the linear regression model consistently, we need to transform our basic indicators, because they are either bounded below (intake and expenditure) or bounded both below and above (food share).

As we did for the other welfare indicators, we have estimated the density function for expenditure non-parametrically (displayed in Figure 17.10). It is positively

---

[6] In fact, our estimate of ultrapoverty for the CFS 1981/82 data set on Sri Lanka using Lipton's double-eighty criterion is 5.10% of households and 6.83% of individuals; according to the weakened (eighty–sixty) criterion, the estimate is 14.88% of households and 18.63% of individuals. If one uses only the primary selection criterion of calorie intake (less than 0.8), the estimate is 17.13% of households and 21.16% of individuals. Thus, only a relatively small number of anomalous cases (the rich) are eliminated by the secondary selection criterion of food share greater than 0.6.

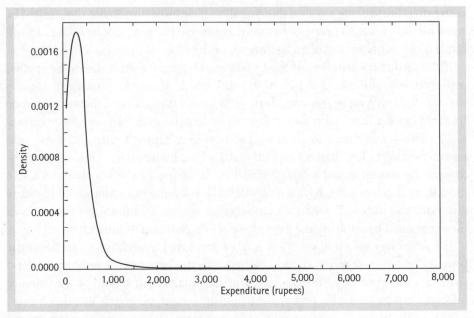

Fig. 17.10. Density function of expenditure

skewed and, to a first approximation, seems to resemble a lognormal distribution. Accordingly, we generated a density estimate for log(expenditure), not shown here, which was roughly normal (with a little positive skewness left, as can be expected of an expenditure distribution which in the upper range is better approximated by the thicker tail of a Pareto density).

We also used the logarithmic function to transform intake; the resulting density function, not shown here, was quite symmetric around the median and resembled a normal distribution even more closely. Finally, for food share we used the logistic transformation because it is bounded both below (by zero) and above (by unity). The logistic function logit ($\cdot$) is defined as: logit (fshr) = log (fshr) $-$ log (1 $-$ fshr), where fshr is food share. The density function of logit(fshr), not shown here, was also quite symmetric around the median, and resembled a normal distribution. These density plots provide strong support for applying our transformations to the three basic indicators before using them as dependent variables in linear regression.

A brief description follows of the housing and other non-monetary variables from CFS 1981/82 that are used to generate welfare information. Since data on the stock of total wealth (physical and financial assets) are not collected in CFS, we are restricted to relying on housing particulars, the availability of certain household equipment and durable goods, and five non-monetary indicators of individuals' educational attainment, employment status and disability.

The variables on housing particulars and availability of household equipment and durable goods are as follows: tenure of accommodation (owned, rented, leased, etc.); number of rooms; floor area; floor type (unprepared earth, prepared clay, cement, wood, other); wall type (wattle and daub, bricks, kabok/metal, mud, wood, cadjan, metal, cement, other); roof type (tiles, asbestos, metal and tar sheet, thatched, other); ceiling (yes–no); toilet facilities (separate, common, none); toilet type (water seal, bucket, cesspit); source of water (pipe-borne inside, pipe-borne outside, own well, common well, other); cooker (electric, gas, kerosene); lighting (electric, kerosene, biogas, other); number of chairs; number of tables; number of beds; radio (yes–no); television (yes–no); sewing machine (yes–no); refrigerator (yes–no); telephone (yes–no); bicycle (yes–no); scooter/motorcycle (yes–no); and car (yes–no).

Variables used at the individual level within the household are as follows: schooling (none, some); literacy (illiterate, literate); educational attainment (no schooling, kindergarten, passed grade 1, passed grade 2, . . ., passed grade 12, undergraduate, graduate); disability (yes, no); and employment status (unemployed, unpaid family worker, casual employee, regular employee, self-employed, employer).

The number of rooms, chairs, tables, etc. and floor area of the house (measured in square meters) are each divided by household size for use as continuous independent variables in the regressions. The individual-level variables are entered in the regressions by summing the numerical values assigned to each variable category across members of the household and dividing by household size, again on a continuous basis.

The regressions use a total of 34 independent variables plus an intercept. The household-level categorical variables were entered as dummies, for which we selected those characteristics of a variable that were likely to discriminate between poor households (e.g. unprepared earth floor, wattle-and-daub wall, no toilet facilities, etc.) and rich households (e.g. cement floor, cement wall, separate toilet facilities, etc.). We also aggregated into a composite variable some yes–no categories which account for a very small percentage of households—e.g. household with a cooker of any type (electric, gas, or kerosene) and household with a consumer durable of any type (television, refrigerator, telephone, scooter/motorcycle, or car).

To begin with, we conducted regressions on the full sample of 7,457 households. The dependent variables in the regressions were log(intake), logit(food share) and log(expenditure). The independent variables were the above-mentioned 34 housing and other non-monetary indicators. Tables 17.1–17.3 contain the parameter estimates, t-ratios and associated significance levels for these three regressions.

For the full sample, the regression results were as follows. The log(expenditure) regression had an R^2 of 0.4653 ($\bar{R}^2$ of 0.4629), the log(intake) regression an R^2 of 0.2279 ($\bar{R}^2$ of 0.2244), and the logit(food share) regression an R^2 of 0.2953 ($\bar{R}^2$ of 0.2921). The same independent variables thus explain a much larger proportion of the total variation of log(expenditure) than that of either of the other two indicators. Although the R^2s of the different regressions are not strictly comparable, we have attempted to achieve a degree of comparability by

Table 17.1. Log(intake) regression on housing and other non-monetary indicators: parameter estimates, t-statistics and associated significance levels

Variable	Parameter estimate	t for H_0: parameter = 0	prob > |t|
Intercept	−0.253543	−8.742	0.0001
Area	0.000120	1.093	0.2744
Beds	0.079135	−6.745	0.0001
Bicycle	0.070055	8.703	0.0001
Ceiling	−0.009287	−0.610	0.5417
Chairs	0.014418	3.917	0.0001
Cooker	0.021284	1.286	0.1984
Disability	0.014341	0.389	0.6976
EdLev	0.010229	3.994	0.0001
EmpType	0.065642	14.404	0.0001
Floor 1	−0.056526	−3.607	0.0003
Floor 3	−0.015668	−1.635	0.1020
Illiteracy	−0.137403	−5.736	0.0001
LatAcc 1	−0.011252	−0.864	0.3875
LatAcc 3	0.001703	0.127	0.8993
Light 1	−0.047861	−3.670	0.0002
NoSch	0.267696	10.829	0.0001
Owship 1	0.015114	1.149	0.2505
Owship 4	0.119042	7.202	0.0001
Radio	0.018103	2.275	0.0229
Roof 1	0.000841	0.085	0.9322
Roof 4	0.001661	0.153	0.8780
Rooms	0.109984	16.666	0.0001
SewMach	0.027381	2.943	0.0033
Tables	−0.003536	−0.265	0.7914
Wall 1	−0.022426	−1.693	0.0904
Wall 2	−0.007395	−0.504	0.6146
Wall 3	0.018994	1.213	0.2251
Wall 4	−0.040958	−2.652	0.0080
Wall 8	0.027155	1.477	0.1397
Water 1	0.007387	0.355	0.7223
Water 2	0.042550	2.731	0.0063
Water 3	0.034223	2.591	0.0096
Water 4	0.007242	0.588	0.5566
Durables	0.028203	1.738	0.0822

transforming the original indicators into approximately similar-looking normal distributions.

The regression results are consistent with expenditure being a decent overall indicator, and with each of intake and food share having relevance in only a part of the welfare range. In this connection it is also worth reporting that all but 7 of the independent variables are significant at the 5% level for the log(expenditure) regression, but 18 are not significant for the log(intake) regression and 17 are not

Table 17.2. Logit(food share) regression on housing and other non-monetary indicators: parameter estimates, t-statistics and associated significance levels

Variable	Parameter estimate	t for H_0: parameter = 0	prob $> |t|$
Intercept	1.510515	25.639	0.0001
Area	0.000023	0.101	0.9194
Beds	0.005053	0.212	0.8321
Bicycle	−0.046416	−2.839	0.0045
Ceiling	−0.102521	−3.317	0.0009
Chairs	−0.028318	−3.788	0.0002
Cooker	−0.188678	−5.614	0.0001
Disability	0.069727	0.930	0.3524
EdLev	0.059365	−11.410	0.0001
EmpType	−0.004433	−0.479	0.6320
Floor 1	0.095023	2.985	0.0028
Floor 3	−0.000807	−0.041	0.9669
Illiteracy	−0.025894	−0.532	0.5947
LatAcc 1	−0.020852	−0.788	0.4304
LatAcc 3	0.033604	1.230	0.2188
Light 1	−0.046299	−1.748	0.0806
NoSch	−0.220610	−4.394	0.0001
Owship 1	−0.025822	−0.967	0.3338
Owship 4	−0.021954	−0.654	0.5132
Radio	−0.084652	−5.238	0.0001
Roof 1	0.004846	0.241	0.8092
Roof 4	0.052886	2.405	0.0162
Rooms	−0.112943	−8.426	0.0001
SewMach	−0.098350	−5.204	0.0001
Tables	−0.096948	−3.570	0.0004
Wall 1	0.007327	0.272	0.7854
Wall 2	−0.066126	−2.217	0.0267
Wall 3	−0.013974	−0.439	0.6603
Wall 4	0.021604	0.689	0.4910
Wall 8	0.008153	0.218	0.8272
Water 1	−0.127276	−3.015	0.0026
Water 2	−0.076126	−2.405	0.0162
Water 3	−0.055297	−2.061	0.0393
Water 4	−0.039790	−1.590	0.1118
Durables	−0.321766	−9.762	0.0001

significant for the logit(food share) regression (Tables 17.1–17.3). Moreover, two variables that have obvious relevance for poor households—illiteracy and mud wall (Wall 4)—are highly significant in the regression for log (intake) but not significant in the regression for logit (food share). Similarly, three variables that have obvious relevance for rich but not poor households—ceiling, cooker and durables—are highly significant in the regression for logit(food share) but not significant in the regression for log(intake). This supports our view that intake has power as

Table 17.3. Log(expenditure) regression on housing and other non-monetary indicators: parameter estimates, t-statistics and associated significance levels

Variable	Parameter estimate	t for H_0: parameter = 0	prob > $|t|$
Intercept	5.046718	123.728	0.0001
Area	0.000204	1.324	0.1855
Beds	0.044164	2.677	0.0074
Bicycle	0.111624	9.860	0.0001
Ceiling	0.070560	3.297	0.0010
Chairs	0.035542	6.866	0.0001
Cooker	0.198293	8.522	0.0001
Disability	−0.082380	−1.587	0.1125
EdLev	0.047724	13.249	0.0001
EmpType	0.099468	15.521	0.0001
Floor 1	−0.049868	−2.263	0.0237
Floor 3	0.035360	2.624	0.0087
Illiteracy	−0.196195	−5.824	0.0001
LatAcc 1	−0.069255	−3.782	0.0002
LatAcc 3	−0.041855	−2.212	0.0270
Light 1	0.045996	2.508	0.0122
NoSch	0.315562	9.078	0.0001
Owship 1	−0.057846	−3.128	0.0018
Owship 4	0.048865	2.102	0.0356
Radio	0.046666	4.171	0.0001
Roof 1	−0.038017	−2.735	0.0062
Roof 4	−0.015553	−1.022	0.3070
Rooms	0.144978	15.621	0.0001
SewMach	0.052301	3.997	0.0001
Tables	0.041704	2.218	0.0266
Wall 1	−0.115392	−6.196	0.0001
Wall 2	−0.016936	−0.820	0.4122
Wall 3	−0.033016	−1.500	0.1337
Wall 4	−0.116373	−5.358	0.0001
Wall 8	0.042986	1.663	0.0964
Water 1	0.144588	4.947	0.0001
Water 2	0.124625	5.688	0.0001
Water 3	0.072208	3.887	0.0001
Water 4	0.027299	1.576	0.1151
Durables	0.290383	12.725	0.0001

an indicator mainly at the bottom of the welfare distribution but not at the top, and that food share has power as an indicator mainly at the top of the welfare distribution but not at the bottom.

We now consider the welfare information content of each of our three basic variables when used as a secondary criterion to define the ultrapoor after an initial group has been identified by means of a (different) primary variable. For example, after identifying those with calorie intake less than 0.8 (à la Lipton), how much extra welfare information do we obtain by using food share as a secondary selection criterion, e.g. those with food share greater than 0.8? Might expenditure provide more welfare information as a secondary selection criterion than food share does?

Since we are mainly interested in the concept behind ultrapoverty, rather than in its particular implementation through the double-eighty criterion, we consider alternative cut-offs to identify the primary group. We identify five different size groups at the bottom of the primary variable distribution: the lowest 10%, 15%, 20%, 25% and 30% of households. We also consider alternative variables to identify the primary group—viz. food share and expenditure—and alternative variables as a secondary selection criterion—viz. intake and expenditure. This allows us to assess whether the variables selected by Lipton for his double criterion are the appropriate ones, and how much information a double criterion adds over a single criterion. In particular, if the extra information obtained by means of a secondary criterion is relatively low, then using it will simply amount to reducing the numbers identified by the primary criterion in an essentially random manner.

Table 17.4 shows the adjusted R^2, or $\bar{R}^2$, of the regressions of the secondary variable on the 34 housing and other non-monetary indicators for each different size group at the bottom of the primary variable distribution. The three transformed welfare indicators—log(intake), logit(food share), and log(expenditure)—are used successively as primary and secondary variables.[7] Thus each panel of Table 17.4 reports the $\bar{R}^2$s of nine separate regressions, whose observations correspond to the subsample size selected by the primary variable for the regression on the secondary variable.

Consider first the use of calorie intake as a primary selection variable. Hardly any of the variation of log(intake) itself is explained by the housing and other non-monetary indicators: as one moves up from a subsample size of 10% to a subsample size of 30%, the $\bar{R}^2$ rises from 0.0215 to 0.0738.[8] Now consider the use of food share or expenditure as a secondary selection criterion. For each subsample size, food share does contain a significant amount of welfare information orthogonal to intake. The $\bar{R}^2$ of logit(food share) regressed on the housing and other non-monetary indicators for the lowest 10% identified by calorie intake is 0.1587; this rises steadily to 0.2302 for the lowest 30%. Thus if one were to use the supplementary selection criterion of food share, there would be some improvement in the group identified by intake alone.[9]

---

[7] Since the logarithmic and logistic functions are monotonic-increasing, the transformed welfare indicators identify exactly the same group at the bottom of the distribution as the untransformed indicators—intake/requirement, food share, and expenditure.

[8] As noted earlier, if one moves up to the full sample, the $\bar{R}^2$ rises to 0.2244. With the same error variance (or root mean-square error), $\bar{R}^2$ is bound to increase as the subsample size is increased because the variance of the dependent variable will be larger.

[9] That improvement would correspond to an improvement in the "purity" of the group identified by calorie intake alone, although this might possibly be at the expense of "comprehensiveness". For definitions of these terms, see Anand and Harris (1992: 200).

Table 17.4. Adjusted R^2s for regressions of secondary selection variable on housing and other non-monetary indicators for alternative subsamples selected at the bottom by primary variable

Subsample	Primary selection variable	Secondary selection variable		
		Log(intake)	Logit(food share)	Log(expenditure)
Lowest 10%	Intake	0.0215	0.1587	0.3196
	Food share	0.2954	−0.0035	0.3726
	Expenditure	0.0591	0.0889	0.0739
Lowest 15%	Intake	0.0386	0.1798	0.3116
	Food share	0.2898	0.0205	0.3669
	Expenditure	0.0579	0.0846	0.0799
Lowest 20%	Intake	0.0486	0.1991	0.3413
	Food share	0.2817	0.0304	0.3543
	Expenditure	0.0611	0.0721	0.0945
Lowest 25%	Intake	0.0682	0.2124	0.3666
	Food share	0.2814	0.0396	0.3562
	Expenditure	0.0742	0.0804	0.1067
Lowest 30%	Intake	0.0738	0.2302	0.3871
	Food share	0.2652	0.0454	0.3407
	Expenditure	0.0758	0.0832	0.1169

But as a secondary selection criterion, expenditure contains far more welfare information. The $\bar{R}^2$ of log(expenditure) regressed on the housing and other non-monetary indicators of the lowest 10% identified by calorie intake is 0.3196; and it rises to as much as 0.3871 for the lowest 30%. This is a particularly impressive performance given that $\bar{R}^2$ for the full sample, as noted earlier, is 0.4629. Thus, as a secondary selection criterion, expenditure clearly outperforms food share.

We now examine food share as a primary selection variable. Again, hardly any of the variance of logit(food share) itself is explained by the housing and other non-monetary indicators. In fact, $\bar{R}^2$ is negative (−0.0035) for the smallest subsample of 10%, and it only rises to 0.0454 for the largest subsample of 30%. This suggests that there may be a considerable amount of information orthogonal to food share if it is used to identify a low welfare group (given that $\bar{R}^2$ for the full sample is 0.2921). It turns out that intake does indeed convey a significant amount of additional welfare information. The $\bar{R}^2$ of log(intake) regressed on the housing and other non-monetary indicators is 0.2954 for the lowest 10% identified by food share. This falls steadily as one increases the size of the lowest group identified by food share; for the lowest 30%, $\bar{R}^2$ is 0.2652. The drop is consistent with calorie intake having less power as an indicator at higher levels of welfare (see section II). Nonetheless, if one were to adduce the supplementary criterion of calorie intake when food share is the primary selection variable, there would be an improvement in the group identified.

Expenditure, however, clearly beats intake as a secondary selection criterion when food share is the primary selection variable. The $\bar{R}^2$ of log(expenditure) regressed on the housing and other non-monetary indicators for the lowest 10% identified by food share is 0.3726, compared with 0.2954 for the log(intake) regression. For the lowest 30%, the comparison is between an $\bar{R}^2$ of 0.3407 and one of 0.2652. We conclude that expenditure outperforms both calorie intake as a secondary selection criterion when food share is the primary selection variable, and food share as a secondary selection criterion when intake is the primary selection variable.

Finally, let us consider expenditure itself as the primary selection variable. As expected, relatively little of the variance of log(expenditure) is explained by the housing and other non-monetary indicators within each subsample: $\bar{R}^2$ rises from 0.0739 for the lowest 10% to 0.1169 for the lowest 30%. Given these levels of fit, it is at least conceivable that intake or food share might possess significant welfare information orthogonal to expenditure at the bottom.

It turns out that the information added by intake or food share is very low if they are used as secondary selection variables. The $\bar{R}^2$s for log(intake) and logit(food share) are of the same order of magnitude as for log(expenditure) in the lowest 10% and lowest 15% subsamples, and markedly smaller when the subsample size is increased. Note that the $\bar{R}^2$ for logit(food share) is uniformly higher than for log(intake)—perhaps reflecting the fact that intake is well correlated with expenditure at the bottom (section II) but food share is not (section III), and is therefore capable of yielding some information orthogonal to it. For the lowest 10% the $\bar{R}^2$ for the logit(food share) regression is 0.0889, compared with 0.0591 for the log(intake) regression and 0.0739 for the log(expenditure) regression. For the lowest 15% these numbers are respectively 0.0846, 0.0579 and 0.0799. In our view these results suggest that the extra information content of food share is too low to justify using it as a secondary selection criterion when total expenditure per capita is the primary selection variable.

V. CONCLUSION

According to Lipton's definition of ultrapoverty, a household is ultrapoor if it satisfies two criteria simultaneously: intake less than 0.8 and food share greater than 0.8. In order to evaluate this definition, we began by evaluating each criterion on its own. In section II we showed there was a positive statistical relationship between intake and expenditure at all levels of expenditure, with the relationship being strongest at low levels of expenditure—perhaps up to the 25th percentile. This suggests that intake contains a significant amount of low-end welfare information, and relatively little high-end welfare information. Intake can thus be used to distinguish between the poor and the non-poor and to discriminate among the poor, but it cannot be used to discriminate among the non-poor.

The findings of section II leave open the question of whether intake contains more or less low-end welfare information than expenditure. The results of section IV suggest that intake contains much less low-end welfare information than expenditure. When intake is regressed on housing and other non-monetary indicators for the subsample consisting of households whose expenditure lies below the 20th percentile, an $\bar{R}^2$ of 0.0611 is obtained. But when expenditure is regressed on housing and other non-monetary indicators for the subsample consisting of households whose intake lies below the 20th percentile, an $\bar{R}^2$ of 0.3413 is obtained. This suggests that intake contains little welfare information orthogonal to the low-end welfare information contained in expenditure, whereas expenditure contains a substantial amount of welfare information orthogonal to the low-end welfare information contained in intake. Overall, then, expenditure would appear to be a better indicator on which to base a poverty criterion than intake.

In section III we showed there was a negative statistical relationship between food share and expenditure at all levels of expenditure. This relationship was weakest at low levels of expenditure, and strengthened as expenditure increased—especially at levels of expenditure above the 80th percentile. This suggests that food share contains a significant amount of high-end welfare information, and relatively little low-end welfare information. Hence food share can be used to distinguish between the rich and the non-rich and to discriminate among the rich, but it cannot be used to discriminate among the non-rich. In particular, since the fall in median food share with expenditure up to the 80th percentile is offset by the rise in the spread of the distribution of food share, it seems likely that the set of households with a food share of 0.8 or more is an almost random cross-section of the set of non-rich households.

The findings of section III leave open the question of whether food share contains *any* low-end welfare information distinct from that contained in expenditure. The results of section IV suggest that food share contains very little low-end welfare information distinct from that contained in expenditure. When food share is regressed on housing and other non-monetary indicators for the subsample consisting of households whose expenditure lies below the 20th percentile, an $\bar{R}^2$ of 0.0721 is obtained. But when expenditure is regressed on housing and other non-monetary indicators for the subsample consisting of households whose food share lies above the 80th percentile, an $\bar{R}^2$ of 0.3543 is obtained. This suggests that food share contains very little welfare information orthogonal to the low-end welfare information contained in expenditure, whereas expenditure contains a substantial amount of welfare information orthogonal to the low-end welfare information contained in food share. Overall, then, expenditure would appear to be a better indicator on which to base a poverty criterion than food share.

In the light of this discussion, neither of Lipton's two criteria would appear to be a good poverty criterion on its own. The discussion does, however, leave open the possibility that together they do constitute a good poverty criterion.[10]

We refer once again to the results of section IV. When food share (expenditure) is regressed on housing and other non-monetary indicators for the subsample consisting of households whose intake lies below the 20th percentile, an $\bar{R}^2$ of 0.1991 (0.3413) is obtained. When intake (expenditure) is regressed on housing and other non-monetary indicators for the subsample consisting of households whose food share lies above the 80th percentile, an $\bar{R}^2$ of 0.2817 (0.3543) is obtained. These results suggest that food share contains a significant amount of welfare information orthogonal to the low-end welfare information contained in intake, and that intake contains a significant amount of welfare information orthogonal to the low-end welfare information contained in food share, but that in both cases expenditure contains more information. Hence, if a *double* criterion is to be employed, it would appear to be better to use a double criterion involving either intake and expenditure or food share and expenditure, but not intake and food share.

Finally, when food share and intake are regressed on housing and other non-monetary indicators for the subsample consisting of households whose expenditure lies below the 20th percentile, $\bar{R}^2$'s of 0.0721 and 0.0611 are obtained, respectively. This suggests that neither intake nor food share contains much welfare information orthogonal to the low-end welfare information contained in expenditure. Hence, the inclusion of a second criterion in addition to an expenditure-based criterion would appear to be of dubious value. On balance, then, an expenditure-based poverty criterion would appear to be superior to any double criterion.

We turn now to other implications of our results. In section II we saw that there is a strong positive relationship between intake and expenditure that persists up to about the 25th expenditure percentile. It may be possible to exploit this relationship to arrive at an alternative definition of ultrapoverty as follows. First, one could calculate an explicit calorie norm using the factorial approach advocated by FAO/WHO/UNU (1985). For example, one could calculate the calorie requirement of an individual who: (1) is below median height (e.g. an individual whose height

---

[10] It may be helpful to illustrate this point. Suppose that $I = W + \epsilon$ and $S = -W + \epsilon$, where I is intake, S is food share, W is welfare, and ϵ is independent of W. If the variance of ϵ is large, then neither I nor S on its own is the basis for a good criterion of poverty. Taken together, however, they do form the basis for a good criterion. For example, the set of households such that $I \leq c$ and $S \geq c$ is a strict subset of the set of households such that $W \leq c$. (The crucial feature of this example is that I and S are strongly positively correlated conditional on W. An indirect test of whether the combined criterion is a good criterion would therefore be to examine the conditional correlation of intake and food share given expenditure. We have preferred to use the more direct tests reported in section IV.)

is equal to the 20th percentile of the distribution of heights in the population); (2) undertakes some limited discretionary activity; but (3) is otherwise unemployed. Secondly, through the non-parametric regression estimate one could find the level of expenditure at which this calorie requirement is attained. Thirdly, one could use this expenditure level as a poverty cut-off. This approach to ultrapoverty has several advantages. First, it is based on a food adequacy standard. Secondly, the basis for the calorie norm is made fully explicit: the norm can therefore be adjusted in a meaningful way if necessary. Thirdly, by making indirect rather than direct use of calorie information—i.e. by using the level of calorie intake predicted on the basis of expenditure rather than raw calorie information—one avoids the difficulties that result from the noisiness of calorie intake itself as a welfare indicator. This approach is closely related to the ideas discussed in Anand and Harris (1992).

In section III we saw that the relationship between food share and expenditure was weak, perhaps for levels of expenditure up to the 80th percentile. This suggests that food share is a poor welfare indicator. Such a conclusion is not entirely unexpected. Both expenditure and food expenditure can be expected to be strong, positive welfare indicators. Food share, by contrast, is the ratio of food expenditure to total expenditure. As such, it responds positively to welfare through food expenditure, and negatively to welfare through total expenditure. Hence its overall response to welfare is likely to be weaker than that of either food expenditure or total expenditure on its own (Anand and Harris 1994: 229).[11]

Taken together, the results of sections II and III suggest the following pattern of behavior by households: at low levels of expenditure, food expenditure and calorie intake rise sharply with expenditure; at intermediate levels of expenditure, food expenditure continues to rise sharply, but calorie intake itself increases relatively little (in other words, the quality of food consumption as measured by average calorie price increases); and at high levels of expenditure, non-food expenditure rises sharply in comparison with food expenditure.

Finally, we conclude with a general point. In trying to understand relationships such as those between intake and expenditure or between food share and expenditure, it is important to examine not how the slope of the regression curve varies, but rather how the local strength of the statistical relationship varies. The shape of the regression curve as such depends on the cardinalizations adopted for the dependent and independent variables, whereas the signal-to-noise ratio does not. We have attempted to get at this idea by examining moving Spearman correlation coefficients and median derivatives, although it is possible to imagine other ways of approaching the same idea.

---

[11] Basically, food share reduces the signal value of, and increases the noise associated with, either food expenditure or total expenditure considered on its own. For an algebraic demonstration, see Anand and Harris (1989).

REFERENCES

ANAND, S., and HARRIS, C. J. (1985), "Living Standards in Sri Lanka, 1973–1981/82", unpubl. MS, St Catherine's College, Oxford.

—— —— (1987), "Changes in Nutrition in Sri Lanka, 1978/79–1981/82", unpubl. MS, World Institute for Development Economics Research, Helsinki.

—— —— (1989), "On the Choice of Welfare Indicator in the Analysis of Poverty: An Illustration Using Sri Lankan Data", unpubl. background paper for the World Bank's *World Development Report 1990: Poverty*, St Catherine's College, Oxford.

—— —— (1990), "Food and Standard of Living: An Analysis Based on Sri Lankan Data", in J. P. Drèze and A. Sen (eds), *The Political Economy of Hunger*, vol. 1 (Oxford: Clarendon Press), 297–350.

—— —— (1992), "Issues in the Measurement of Undernutrition", in S. R. Osmani (ed.), *Nutrition and Poverty* (Oxford: Clarendon Press), 187–217.

—— —— (1994), "Choosing a Welfare Indicator", *American Economic Review*, 84: 226–31.

—— —— and LINTON, O. B. (1993), *On the Concept of Ultrapoverty*, Working Paper 93.02 (Cambridge, Mass.: Harvard Center for Population and Development Studies).

BHANOJI RAO, V. V. (1981), "Measurement of Deprivation and Poverty Based on the Proportion Spent on Food: An Exploratory Exercise", *World Development*, 9: 337–53.

DEATON, A. (1981), *Three Essays on a Sri Lanka Household Survey*, LSMS Working Paper 11 (Washington, DC: World Bank).

—— and MUELLBAUER, J. (1980), *Economics and Consumer Behaviour* (Cambridge: Cambridge University Press).

ENGEL, E. (1895), "Die Lebenskosten belgischer Arbeiter-Familien früher und jetzt", *International Statistical Institute Bulletin*, 9: 1–125.

FAO/WHO (1973), *Energy and Protein Requirements: Report of a Joint FAO/WHO ad hoc Expert Committee*, World Health Organization Technical Report 522 (Geneva: World Health Organization).

FAO/WHO/UNU (1985), *Energy and Protein Requirements. Report of a Joint FAO/WHO/ UNU Expert Consultation*, World Health Organization Technical Report 724 (Geneva: World Health Organization).

HOUTHAKKER, H. S. (1957), "An International Comparison of Household Expenditure Patterns, Commemorating the Centenary of Engel's Law", *Econometrica*, 25: 532–51.

JAMES, W. P. T., and SCHOFIELD, E. C. (1990), *Human Energy Requirements: A Manual for Planners and Nutritionists* (Oxford: Oxford University Press/FAO).

LIPTON, M. (1983), *Poverty, Undernutrition, and Hunger*, World Bank Staff Working Papers 597 (Washington, DC: World Bank).

—— (1988), *The Poor and the Poorest: Some Interim Findings*, World Bank Discussion Papers 25 (Washington, DC: World Bank).

McLAREN, D. (1974), "The Great Protein Fiasco", *Lancet*, 2: 93–8.

PAYNE, P. R. (1975), "Safe Protein-Calorie Ratios in Diets: The Relative Importance of Protein and Energy Intake as Causal Factors in Malnutrition", *American Journal of Clinical Nutrition*, 28: 281–6.

POLEMAN, T. T. (1981), "Quantifying the Nutrition Situation in Developing Countries", *Food Research Institute Studies*, 18: 1–58.

SILVERMAN, B. W. (1986), *Density Estimation* (London: Chapman and Hall).

Statistics Department, Central Bank of Ceylon (1981), "Instructions to Investigators: Consumer Finance and Socio-Economic Survey 1981/82", unpubl. MS, Colombo.

—— (1984), *Report on Consumer Finances and Socio-Economic Survey 1981/82, Sri Lanka* (Colombo: Statistics Department: Central Bank of Ceylon).

World Bank (1986), *Poverty and Hunger* (Washington, DC: World Bank).

World Health Organization (1978), *Habitual Physical Activity and Health*, WHO Regional Publications, European Series no. 6 (Copenhagen: World Health Organization Regional Office for Europe).

CHAPTER 18

·······································

MULTIDIMEN-SIONAL POVERTY ORDERINGS

THEORY AND APPLICATIONS

·······································

FRANÇOIS BOURGUIGNON
SATYA R. CHAKRAVARTY

I. INTRODUCTION

·······································

THE removal of poverty is one of the major aims of economic policy in many countries. In order to evaluate the efficacy of an anti-poverty policy it is necessary to observe the changes in the level of poverty over time. Therefore, the way that the level of poverty is measured is important both for an understanding of poverty and for policy applications. Since the publication of Sen's (1976) pioneering paper

An initial version of this chapter has been presented in various seminars over the last couple of years. We thank participants in these seminars for helpful comments. They are too numerous to be mentioned and duly thanked by name. All remaining errors in this chapter are undoubtedly ours. The findings, interpretations and conclusions expressed in this chapter are entirely those of the authors, and do not necessarily represent the views of the World Bank and its affiliated organizations, or those of the Executive Directors of the World Bank or the governments they represent.

on poverty measurement, a great deal has been written on this subject. Over the last quarter century, research on poverty measurement has focused on two closely related but distinct projects: construction of *measures of poverty* and *poverty orderings*. In both of these, income or consumption expenditure has been regarded as the only attribute of well-being. The first project, following Sen (1976), is an attempt to develop alternative measures of poverty. A poverty measure aggregates the income shortfalls of the poor—persons whose incomes fall below the poverty line, which represents the income necessary to maintain a subsistence standard of living. Several measures of poverty, including the one suggested by Sen (1976), are now available in the literature. They have been surveyed by various researchers (see, for example, Foster 1984; Seidl 1988; Chakravarty 1990; Foster and Sen 1997; and Zheng 1997).

The second project is concerned with rankings of income distributions based on multiple desiderata of poverty measurement. Since quite often the choice of a particular measure of poverty can be arbitrary, so can the conclusions based on that measure. However, it may be possible to reduce the degree of arbitrariness by choosing all poverty measures that satisfy a set of reasonable postulates. That is, instead of choosing individual poverty measures one chooses a set of criteria for poverty measures which in turn implicitly determines a class of measures. One can then check whether all members of this class give the same rank to two income distributions. In a sense this kind of research has grown out of the presence of too many poverty measures. However, the use of a class of measures may not make all income distributions comparable—that is, there may be no unanimous agreement among these measures about the ranking of some income distributions. Thus, while a single measure of poverty completely orders all income distributions, the ordering generated by a family of measures is partial: not all members of the family will rank distributions in precisely the same order. Thus, we are forced to withhold our judgements on relative poverty for some pairs of distributions. Following Zheng (1999), we refer to this notion of ordering as *poverty-measure ordering*. In an important contribution, Atkinson (1987) derived conditions on poverty-measure orderings for subgroup-decomposable poverty measures with a common poverty line. Zheng (1999) extended Atkinson's results to a more restrictive class of poverty measures with the objective of increasing the completeness of poverty orderings. Atkinson (1992) and Jenkins and Lambert (1993) considered poverty-measure orderings when the poverty line is adjusted for differences in family composition.[1]

The definition of a poverty line is crucial for both poverty measures and poverty orderings. The determination of an income or consumption threshold that would define poverty has been an issue of debate for a long time. Quite often a significant degree of arbitrariness is involved in the construction of a poverty line. A single

---

[1] Spencer and Fisher (1992), Jenkins and Lambert (1997, 1998a, 1998b) and Shorrocks (1998) characterized poverty dominance criteria involving poverty incidence, poverty intensity and inequality among the poor.

poverty measure may rank two income distributions differently for two distinct poverty lines. Therefore, it is useful to see if two income distributions can be ranked unanimously by a given measure for all poverty lines in some reasonable interval. This is the second goal of research on partial poverty orderings, which arises from uncertainty about the poverty line. This notion of ordering of distributions by a given poverty measure for a range of poverty lines is called *poverty-line ordering* (Zheng 1999). Foster and Shorrocks (1988a, 1988b) and Foster and Jin (1996) characterized partial poverty-line orderings for several classes of poverty measures.

All these contributions regard income or consumption expenditures as the sole indicator of well-being. But the poverty of an individual also arises from the insufficiency of other attributes of well-being that are necessary to maintain a subsistence level of living. The basic-needs approach considers development as an improvement in an array of human needs, not just income. Well-being is intrinsically multidimensional for the capability–functionings perspective, where functionings refer to the various things a person may value doing (or being), and capability deals with the freedom to choose a particular set of functionings (Sen 1985, 1992). Valued functionings may vary from such elementary ones as health status or life expectancy, literacy, adequate nourishment, the availability of certain public goods and personal income, to very complex activities or personal characteristics, such as participation in community life and having self-respect. This in turn means that poverty is essentially a multidimensional phenomenon and income is just one of its dimensions. It is certainly true that with a sufficiently high income, a person will be able to improve some non-income attributes. But income cannot buy everything. On the one hand, there may not be a market for some goods—for instance, flood-control programs in an underdeveloped economy. On the other hand, even if markets are available, prices may be too high for a person to afford the consumption of different attributes above the corresponding thresholds representing subsistence level. Therefore, poverty should be viewed multidimensionally as the inability to achieve minimally acceptable or subsistence levels of income as well as non-income indicators of welfare. Ravallion (1996) identified four sets of such indicators as ingredients for a sensible approach to poverty measurement (see also Bourguignon and Chakravarty 1999, 2003).[2]

While the literature on income poverty is already quite extensive, research on multidimensional poverty measurement has just begun. Tsui (2002), Chakravarty *et al.* (1998), Bourguignon and Chakravarty (1999, 2003), Chakravarty (2006) and Chakravarty and Silber (2007) have suggested several functional forms for multidimensional poverty indices. Bourguignon and Chakravarty (2003) also examined the shapes of isopoverty contours, taking into account the idea of substitutability or complementarity between attributes, an important issue for multivariate poverty

[2] An example of a multidimensional poverty indicator is the human poverty index suggested by the UNDP (1997). It aggregates country-level deprivations in literacy, life expectancy and decent standard of living.

measures. However, partial poverty orderings in a multidimensional context still remains an important area to be explored. This chapter is a contribution to this area. More precisely, for given poverty threshold levels of attributes of well-being, this paper provides *multidimensional poverty-measure orderings* corresponding to a class of multidimensional poverty measures satisfying a set of intuitively reasonable axioms.

The criteria we obtain generalize, in a sensible way, single-dimensional poverty-line orderings. A simple ordering criterion for two distributions defined in a single dimension is that the proportion of poor is not higher in the first than in the second distribution for all poverty lines below the actual threshold level. This property is extended to more than one dimension by considering all combinations of individual attributes' poverty lines below actual threshold levels.

Atkinson and Bourguignon (1982) demonstrated explicitly how utility should change under a correlation-increasing shift of attributes between two individuals. Using this as a postulate and applying the Atkinson–Bourguignon (1982) dominance results to the comparison of two-dimensional head-count ratios, we show that if the two attributes are substitutes, then comparison should be made only in the region in which individuals lack both the attributes, that is, in the intersection of the sets in which the attribute quantities remain below the corresponding thresholds. On the other hand, if they are complements, the comparison should be in the union of the sets. That is, the definition of who is poor is then shown to depend on whether the various attributes that define multidimensional poverty may be considered as substitutes or complements. Interestingly enough, our study of multidimensional poverty ordering leads to a new view on the definition of multidimensional poverty itself.

It may be important to note that since the poverty limits of different attributes are given exogenously, the notion of poverty we are considering here is of the absolute type and departs from the relative concept of poverty, in which the limits are determined using consumption levels of those attributes in the whole population— typically the median or the mean. For instance, in the case of income poverty, a family with income less than half the median may be regarded as relatively poor. However, the concept of absolute poverty is deemed to be more appropriate in a multidimensional context, even in the income dimension.[3]

In an interesting contribution, Atkinson (2003) brought out key differences between our approach and the "counting approach", the latter concentrating on the number of dimensions in which people suffer deprivation. He also explained how the counting approach can be incorporated in an analytical framework like ours. Duclos *et al.* (2002) considered bivariate poverty orderings under a different set of assumptions. They regarded the attributes only as substitutes. Their

---

[3] Note that when using the median definition, poverty thresholds become essentially ambiguous in a multidimensional setting. Things are less problematic with the mean.

framework differs from ours because they assume the dependence of the poverty line of one attribute on the poverty line of the other and vice-versa, thus implicitly postulating some substitutability among the various dimensions of poverty and, in effect, getting closer to a single-dimensional approach combining the two well-being attributes.

The present chapter is organized as follows. The next section discusses the properties for a multidimensional poverty measure. Section III develops multi-dimensional poverty orderings for classes of poverty measures satisfying some subset of these properties. A graphical illustration of these orderings and their implications are provided in section IV for a simple stylized case. Section V is the conclusion.

II. Properties for a Measure of Multidimensional Poverty

In this section, which relies on some of our previous work, we lay down the postulates for a multidimensional poverty index. As Sen (1976) suggested, two steps are involved in framing a poverty index. The first step is the identification of the poor, that is, the problem of counting the number of poor persons. Once the poor have been identified, the next step is to aggregate the income deviations of the poor from the poverty line into an overall device.

Since in this chapter we are viewing poverty from a multivariate perspective, the identification problem will also be of the multivariate type. For ease of exposition we assume that there are only two attributes, 1 and 2, both supposed to be continuous. For example, attribute 1 could be the level of literacy or schooling and attribute 2 a composite good constituting all the other basic needs of human life. Our analysis in this section easily generalizes to more than two attributes.

Let R_+^2 stand for the non-negative orthant of the two-dimensional Euclidean space R^2. For a set of n persons, the ith person possesses a two-vector $(x_{i1}, x_{i2}) = x_i \in R_+^2$ of attributes. The vector x_i is the ith row of the $n \times 2$ matrix $X \in M^n$, where M^n is the set of all $n \times 2$ matrices whose entries are non-negative real numbers. The jth column x_j of $X \in M^n$ gives the distribution of attribute $j(j = 1, 2)$ among the n persons. Let $M = \cup_{n \in N} M^n$, where N is the set of all positive integers. For any $X \in M$, we write $n(X)$(or n) for the associated population size.

In this multivariate structure, a threshold is defined for each attribute. These thresholds represent the minimal quantities of the two attributes necessary for maintaining a subsistence level of living. Let $z = (z_1, z_2) \in Z$ be the vector of thresholds, where Z is a non-empty subset of R_{++}^2, the strictly positive subset of R_+^2.

In this framework, person i will be considered poor with respect to attribute j if $x_{ij} < z_j$, and non-poor if $x_{ij} \geq z_j$ for all j. The subset of R_+^2 corresponding to the set of persons who are poor with respect to attribute j is denoted by g_j, which we call a single-dimensional poverty space, $SDPS(z_j)$, where $j = 1, 2$. Adding together the numbers of poor in g_1 and g_2 will clearly overestimate the total number of poor. This is because people who are poor in the two dimensions simultaneously will be counted twice. This subset of R_+^2 in which each person's quantities of the two attributes remain below the corresponding threshold values, i.e. $x_{ij} < z_j$ for $j = 1, 2$, will be called the two-dimensional poverty space, $TDPS(z_1, z_2)$. Figure 18.1 illustrates these concepts.

People in $TDPS(z_1, z_2)$ are certainly not rich. Hence, being poor along all dimensions might be a definition of multidimensional poverty. But it is also possible that a person has one attribute, say education, above its threshold, and yet the other attribute, the composite good, lies below the corresponding threshold. Such

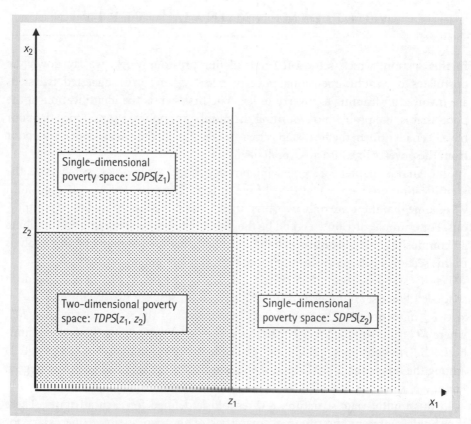

Fig. 18.1. Alternative definitions of poverty in the two–dimensional case

a person should not be called rich because of his/her high education. If we do not allow any trade-offs between the two attributes, one of which is below the threshold and the other above, then another, possibly more satisfactory definition of poverty is that person i is poor if $x_{ij} < z_j$ holds for at least one j. In fact, one of our axioms, Focus, rules out this type of trade-off. As a practical example of this, we note that an old beggar cannot be regarded as rich because of his high longevity.

In terms of $SDPS(z_j)$, the first definition is equivalent to considering all people in the *intersection* of $SDPS(z_1)$ and $SDPS(z_2)$, which is $TDPS(z_1, z_2)$, as poor. In the second definition, poverty is defined by the *union* of the two $SDPS$es. The next section will show that this distinction becomes crucial when considering multi dimensional poverty orderings.

A multidimensional poverty measure P^n is a non-constant real-valued function defined on $M^n \otimes Z$. For any $X \in M^n$, $z \in Z$, the functional value $P^n(X; z)$ gives the extent of poverty associated with the attribute matrix X and the threshold vector z.

Sen (1976) suggested two basic postulates for an income or a consumption poverty measure. They are: (i) the monotonicity axiom: poverty should not decrease given a reduction in the income of a poor individual, and (ii) the transfer axiom: poverty should not decrease if there is a transfer of income from a poor person to anyone with a higher income. Following Sen, variants of these two axioms and several other axioms have been suggested in the literature (see, for example, Foster Greer and Thorbecke 1984; Donaldson and Weymark 1986; Chakravarty 1990; Foster and Shorrocks 1991; and Bourguignon and Fields 1997).

Following Tsui (2002) and Bourguignon and Chakravarty (1999, 2003), we now suggest some properties for an arbitrary measure P^n which are immediate generalizations of an income/consumption poverty measure. All properties apply for any strictly positive n.

Focus (FOC): For any $(X; z) \in M^n \otimes Z$ and for any person i and attribute j such that $x_{ij} \geq z_j$, an increase in x_{ij}, given that all other attribute levels in X remain fixed, does not change the poverty value $P^n(X; z)$.[4]

Normalization (NOM): For any $(X; z) \in M^n \otimes Z$, if $x_{ij} \geq z_j$ for all i and all j, then $P^n(X; z) = 0$.

Monotonicity (MON): For any $(X; z) \in M^n \otimes Z$, any person i and any attribute j such that $x_{ij} < z_j$, an increase in x_{ij}, given that the other attribute levels in X remain fixed, does not increase the poverty value $P^n(X; z)$.

Principle of population (POP): For any $(X; z) \in M^n \otimes Z$, $P^n(X; z) = P^{nm}[X^{(m)}, z]$, where $X^{(m)} = \cup_{i=1}^m X^i$ with $X^i = X$, and $m \geq 2$ is arbitrary.

---

[4] One may imagine a stronger version of this axiom where the condition $x_{ij} \geq z_j$ would apply simultaneously to all j. See Bourguignon and Chakravarty (2003).

Symmetry (SYM): For any $(X; z) \in M^n \otimes Z$, $P^n(X; z) = P^n(\pi X; z)$, where π is any permutation matrix of order n.[5]

Subgroup decomposability (SUD): For $X^i \in M^{n_i}, i = 1, 2, \ldots, k; z \in Z$, $P^n(X; z) = \sum_{i=1}^{k} \frac{n_i}{n} P^{n_i}(X^i; z)$, where $\cup_{i=1}^{m} X^i = X \in M$ and $\sum_{i=1}^{k} n_i = n$.

Continuity (CON): For any $z \in Z$, P^n is continuous on M^n.

Transfers principle (TRP): For any $z \in Z$ and $X, Y \in M^n$, if $X^P = BY^P$ and BY^P is not a permutation of the rows of Y^P, where $X^P(Y^P)$ is the attribute matrix of the poor corresponding to $X(Y)$ and $B = (b_{ij})$ is some bistochastic matrix of appropriate order ($b_{ij} \geq 0$, $\sum_i b_{ij} = \sum_j b_{ij} = 1$), then $P^n(X; z) \leq P^n(Y; z)$.

FOC states that if a person is not poor with respect to an attribute, then giving him more of this attribute does not change the intensity of poverty, even if he/she is poor in another attribute. Thus, FOC rules out trade-off between two attributes in an *SDPS*. So, for example, more education above the threshold is of no use if the composite good is below its threshold. This, however, does not exclude the possibility of a trade-off in *TDPS*. NOM is a cardinality property of the poverty index. It says that if all persons in a society are non-poor in both dimensions, then the index is value zero. According to MON, poverty does not increase if the condition of a poor individual improves in any dimension. According to POP, if an attribute matrix is replicated several times, then poverty remains unchanged. Since by replication we can transform two different-sized matrices into the same size, POP enables us to make inter-temporal and inter-regional poverty comparisons. SYM demands anonymity. Any characteristic other than the attributes under consideration, for instance the names of individuals, is immaterial to the measurement of poverty. CON ensures that minor changes in attribute quantities will not give rise to an abrupt jump in the value of the poverty index. Therefore, a continuous poverty index will not be oversensitive to minor observational errors on basic-need quantities.

According to SUD, if a population is partitioned into several subgroups defined along ethnic, geographical or other lines, then overall poverty is the population-share-weighted average of subgroup poverty levels. The contribution of subgroup i to overall poverty is $n_i P(X^i; z)/n$ and overall poverty will decrease by precisely this amount if poverty in subgroup i is eliminated. Thus, SUD is quite appealing from a policy point of view, in the sense that it enables us to identify the subgroups that contribute most to overall poverty and hence to implement effective anti-poverty policies. Using SUD we can express the poverty index as

$$P^n(X; z) = \frac{1}{n} \sum_{i=1}^{n} P^1(x_i, z) - \frac{1}{n} \sum_{i=1}^{n} p(x_i; z).$$

[5] A square matrix with entries 0 and 1 is called a permutation matrix if each of its rows and columns sums to one.

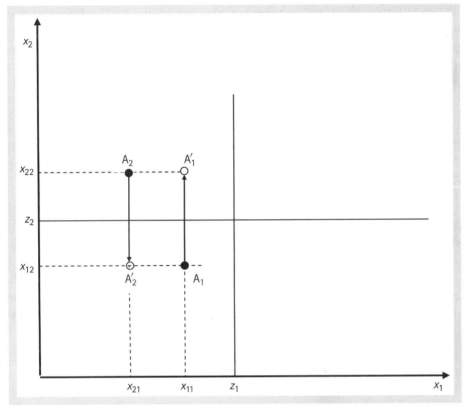

Fig. 18.2. Correlation–increasing shift: $(A_1, A_2) \rightarrow (A'_1, A'_2)$

Since $p(x_i; z)$ depends only on person i's attributes, we call it the "individual poverty function". Finally, TRP shows that if we transform the attribute matrix Y^P of the poor in Y to the corresponding matrix X^P in X by some equalizing operation, then poverty in X will not be higher than poverty in Y. Under SUD, TRP holds if and only if the individual poverty function is convex (Kolm 1977).

Let us now consider a property which expresses the essence of multidimensional measurement through correlation of attributes. By taking into account the association of attributes as captured by the degree of correlation between them, this property also brings out the features which distinguish single-dimensional from multidimensional poverty measurements. To illustrate this property, consider the two-person, two-attribute case in Figure 18.2. Suppose that $x_{11} > x_{21}$ and $x_{12} < x_{22}$. Now consider a shift of attribute 2 from person 2 to person 1. This shift increases the correlation between the attributes, because person 1, who had more of attribute 1, now has more of attribute 2 too. Now suppose that attributes 1 and 2 are *substitutes*, or, in other words, that one attribute may compensate for the lack of another in the definition of individual poverty. Then increasing the correlation between the two attributes must not decrease poverty. Indeed, the shift just defined does not modify the marginal distribution of each attribute but decreases the extent to which the lack of one attribute may be compensated by the availability of the other. A parallel argument will establish that poverty should not increase under a correlation-increasing shift if the two attributes are complements.[6]

We state this principle formally for substitutes as:

Non-decreasing poverty under correlation-increasing shift (NDP): For any $(X, z) \in M^n \otimes Z$, if $Y \in M^n$ is obtained from X by a correlation-increasing shift of an attribute between two persons who are poor in both attributes, then $P^n(X; z) \leq P^n(Y; z)$ if the two attributes are substitutes.

The analogous property, which ensures that poverty does not increase under such a shift when the attributes are complements, is denoted by NIP. Note that NDP and NIP hold only in *TDPS* and the implicit trade-off never allows a person to cross the poverty limit of an attribute.

It may be worthwhile to give an example of a measure that satisfies all of the above postulates. The following general form of a multi-dimensional poverty index which meets these properties has been suggested by Bourguignon and Chakravarty (1999):

$$
P^n_{a,\beta,b}(X;z) = \frac{1}{n} \sum_i \left[I\left(x_{i1} < z_1\right) \left(1 - \frac{x_{i1}}{z_1}\right) + b^{\frac{\beta}{a}} I\left(x_{i2} < z_2\right) \left(1 - \frac{x_{i2}}{z_2}\right)^\beta \right]^{\frac{\beta}{a}},
$$
(1)

where $\alpha \geq 1, \beta \geq 1$ and $b > 0$, and $I(\cdot)$ is an indicator function that takes on the value 1 or 0 according as $x_{ij} < z_j$ or $x_{ij} \geq z_j$. The condition $\alpha \geq 1$ ensures that TRP is satisfied in an *SDPS*. Given $\alpha \geq 1, \beta \geq 1$ guarantees that TRP holds in *TDPS* (z_1, z_2). An increase in the value of β makes the contours of the individual poverty function more convex to the origin. Since in (1) the shortfalls $(z_1 - x_{i1})$ and $(z_2 - x_{i2})$ have been expressed in relative terms (as fractions of z_1 and z_2 respectively), the index satisfies a scale-invariance condition: when all quantities of an attribute as well as its thresholds are multiplied by a positive scalar, poverty remains unchanged. The elasticity of substitution between the two relative shortfalls $(1 - x_{i1}/z_1)$ and $(1 - x_{i2}/z_2)$ is $1/(\beta - 1)$. The parameter b (> 0) shows the importance attached to poverty associated with attribute 2 relative to that attached to attribute 1.

Poverty index (1) is identical to the familiar Foster–Greer–Thorbecke (FGT) or "P_α" index in the two *SDPS*es. In that sense, it is a straight generalization of that single-dimensional poverty measure to the two-dimensional case, with β

---

[6] For further discussions of this issue, see Atkinson and Bourguignon (1982) and Bourguignon and Chakravarty (1999, 2003). Bourguignon and Chakravarty (1999) employed this property to examine the elasticity of substitution between proportional shortfalls of attributes from respective thresholds.

representing the substitutability between the two dimensions in $TDPS$ (z_1, z_2). For $1 \leq \beta \leq a$, the two attributes are substitutes and the measure (1) satisfies NDP. For $\beta = 1$, there is a perfectly elastic trade-off between the attributes in $TDPS$ (z_1, z_2). For $\beta > a$, the measure satisfies NIP since the two attributes are then complements.[7] As $\beta \to \infty$, the resulting index becomes

$$P_{a,\infty}^n(X;z) = \frac{1}{n}\sum_i \left[1 - \min\left(1, \frac{x_{i1}}{z_1}, \frac{x_{i2}}{z_2} \right) \right]^a. \qquad (2)$$

In this case the isopoverty contours are of rectangular shape—the two attributes are perfect complements. Note that the index in (2) requires information only on relative shortfalls of different persons and a poverty aversion parameter.

An alternative of interest arises from the specification

$$P^n(X;z) = \sum_{j=1}^{2}\sum_{i=1}^{n} f_j\left(\frac{x_{ij}}{z_j} \right), \qquad (3)$$

where the real-valued function f_j defined on $(0, \infty)$ is non-increasing, convex and $f_j(t) = 0$ for all $t \geq 1$. As an illustration, we may choose $f_j(t) = -a_j \log t$, where $a_j > 0$ is a constant and $t \in (0, 1)$. We may interpret a_j as the weight given to attribute j in the overall poverty index. Then the resulting index is

$$P^n(x;z) = \sum_{j=1}^{2}\sum_{i=1}^{n} a_j \log\left(\frac{z_j}{\hat{x}_{ij}} \right), \qquad (4)$$

where $\hat{x}_{ij} = \min(x_{ij}, z_j) > 0$. This is a simple multidimensional extension of the well-known Watts index.[8] Note that because of additivity the index in (3) (hence in (4)) is not sensitive to correlation-increasing shift.

III. Multidimensional Poverty Orderings

The concern of this section is the ranking of attribute matrices by a chosen set of poverty measures, assuming that the threshold limits are common. It is assumed at the outset that the poverty index satisfies the following set (S) of properties among the ones listed above: FOC, SYM, POP, SUD and twice-differentiability. The last

[7] Under SUD, attributes are substitutes or complements depending on whether the cross-derivative of the individual poverty function $p(x_1, x_2; z_1, z_2)$ with respect to x_1 and x_2 is positive or negative.

[8] A characterization of this index was developed by Chakravarty and Silber (2007).

property replaces CON. Also, the exposition will be simplified by consideration of a continuous representation of the bivariate distribution, rather than the discrete formulation used until now. The analysis that follows relies on stochastic dominance results originally established by Hadar and Russel (1974) and Levy and Paroush (1974), and extended to multidimensional inequality by Atkinson and Bourguignon (1982).[9]

As this section is formulated in terms of a continuum of population, the suffix i in the vector x_i is dropped, and the distribution of attributes $x = (x_1, x_2)$ in the population is represented by the cumulative distribution function $H(x_1, x_2)$, defined on the $[0, a_1] \times [0, a_2]$ range. The objective is to compare two distributions represented by the distribution functions H and H^*, the difference of which will be denoted by $\Delta H(x_1, x_2)(= H(x_1, x_2) - H^*(x_1, x_2))$.

In view of the SUD property, poverty associated with distribution H may be written as:

$$P(H, z) = \int_0^{a_1} \int_0^{a_2} p(x_1, x_2; z_1, z_2)\, dH,$$

where $p(x_1, x_2; z_1, z_2)$ is the level of poverty associated with a person whose attributes are (x_1, x_2). To simplify notation, the individual poverty functions $p(x_1, x_2; z_1, z_2)$ will be written as $\pi_z(x_1, x_2)$ in what follows. The difference in poverty between distributions H and H^* is then defined as:

$$\Delta P(z) = \int_0^{a_2} \int_0^{a_2} \pi_z(x_1, x_2)\, d\Delta H. \tag{5}$$

The distribution H is then said to (weakly) dominate H^* in the sense of P^c when $\Delta P(z)$ is (non-positive) negative for all individual poverty functions $\pi_z(x_1, x_2)$ belonging to the class P^c.

Note that FOC, NOM and MON imply the following properties (T) for the function $\pi_z(x_1, x_2)$:

$$\pi_z(x_1, x_2) = 0 \text{ for } x_1 \geq z_1 \text{ and } x_2 \geq z_2;$$

$$\pi_{z1}(x_1, x_2) \leq 0 \text{ and } \pi_{z2}(x_1, x_2) \leq 0 \text{ for } x_1 < z_1 \text{ and } x_2 < z_2;$$

$$\pi_{z12}(x_1, x_2) = 0 \text{ for } x_1 \geq z_1 \text{ or } x_2 \geq z_2;$$

where $\pi_{zi}(x_1, x_2)$ is the derivative of $\pi_z(x_1, x_2)$ with respect to x_i and $\pi_{z12}(x_1, x_2)$ is the second cross-derivative. As stated in note 7, NDP requires $\pi_{z12}(x_1, x_2) \geq 0$ in $TDPS(z_1, z_2)$, whereas NIP requires $\pi_{z12}(x_1, x_2) \leq 0$.

---

[9] Kosvevoy (1998) demonstrated equivalence between cone-Lorenz majorization and cone-directional majorization, where a distribution is said to be cone-directional-majorized by another if at any set of prices in a cone the expenditure distribution in the former is less dispersed than in that latter (see also Koshevoy 1995 and Koshevoy and Mosler 1996). This is equivalent to using linear poverty functions. In contrast, we use all possible functions satisfying the desirable axioms.

Following the discussion in the preceding section on the importance of the NIP/NDP properties, three classes of poverty indices will be considered in what follows:

Class P^+: properties (S), MON and NDP.
Class P^-: properties (S), MON and NIP.
Class P^0: properties (S), MON and $\pi_{z12}(x_1, x_2) = 0$ in $TDPS$.

Clearly P^0, which corresponds to the additive individual-poverty function, may be considered as an intermediate case between classes P^+ and P^-.

Following the stochastic dominance literature, integrating (5) by parts and taking into account properties (T) above, we get the following decomposition formula (derived in the Appendix):

$$\Delta P(H, H^*, z) = - \int_0^{z1} \pi_{z1}(x_1, z_2) \, \Delta H_1(x_1) \, dx_1$$

$$- \int_0^{z2} \pi_{z2}(x_1, z_2) \, \Delta H_2(x_2) \, dx_2$$

$$+ \int_0^{z1} \int_0^{z2} \pi_{z12}(x_1, x_2) \, \Delta H(x_1, x_2) \, dx_1 \, dx_2, \tag{6}$$

where $\Delta H_1(x_1)$ stands for the difference in the marginal distribution of attribute 1, i.e. $\Delta H(x_1, a_2)$, and $\Delta H_2(x_2)$ is the analogous notation for attribute 2.

On the basis of (6), the following proposition follows (see Appendix for proof):

Proposition 1. *Let H and H^* be two bivariate distribution functions on the same range $[0, a_1] \times [0, a_2]$. Then the following conditions are equivalent:*

(i) $\Delta P(H, H^*, z) \leq 0$ *for all poverty indices belonging to P^+.*
(ii) *(a)* $\Delta H_i(x_i) \leq 0$ *for all $x_i < z_i$ and for $i = 1, 2$; (b)* $\Delta H(x_1, x_2) \leq 0$ *for all $x_1 < z_1$ and $x_2 < z_2$.*

In other words, poverty dominance under properties (S), MON and NDP requires:

(a) the poverty headcount to be lower in each dimension for all poverty thresholds below the thresholds z_i, that is, one-dimensional dominance in the sense of Atkinson (1987) and Foster and Shorrocks (1988);
(b) the poverty headcount to be lower in $TDPS(x_1, x_2)$ defined by any combination of poverty lines below the thresholds z_i.

Overall dominance thus requires single-dimensional dominance in each dimension plus two-dimensional dominance over the set of persons who are poor simultaneously in all dimensions.

It is also shown in the Appendix that:

$$\Delta P(H, H^*, z) = - \int_0^{z1} \pi_{z1}(x_1, 0) \, \Delta H_1(x_1) \, dx_1 - \int_0^{z2} \pi_{z2}(0, x_1) \, \Delta H_2(x_2) \, dx_2$$

$$+ \int_0^{z1} \int_0^{z2} \pi_{z12}(x_1, x_2)[\, \Delta H(x_1, x_2)$$

$$- \Delta H_1(x_1) - \Delta H_2(x_2)] \, dx_1 \, dx_2. \qquad (7)$$

The decomposition formula (7) leads to a slightly different proposition (again, see Appendix for proof):

Proposition 2. *Let H and H^* be two bivariate distribution functions on the same range $[0, a_1] \times [0, a_2]$. Then the following conditions are equivalent:*

   (i) $\Delta P (H, H^*, z) \leq 0$ *for all poverty indices belonging to P^-.*
   (ii) $\Delta H_1(x_1) + \Delta H_2(x_2) - \Delta H(x_1, x_2) \leq 0$ *for all $x_1 < z_1$ and/or $x_2 < z_2$.*

Note that condition (ii) implies single-dimensional poverty dominance, as in proposition 1(ii.a), when the condition is evaluated at $x_1 = 0$ or $x_2 = 0$. Dominance in two dimensions thus requires single-dimensional dominance, irrespective of whether NDP or NIP holds. The two-dimensional dominance condition for NIP differs from the one obtained under NDP. In the NIP case, dominance requires the poverty headcount not to be higher in the *union*, rather than in the *intersection*, of *SDPS* defined by all possible combinations of poverty lines below the original thresholds.

The difference between the two dominance criteria obtained under NDP and NIP is illustrated in Figure 18.3. Consider any point A in the original *TDPS* (z_1, z_2). NDP dominance requires the poverty headcount corresponding to the area (II) south-west of A not to be greater with distribution H. Clearly, (II) is the *TDPS* corresponding to A, that is, corresponding to poverty lines x_1 and x_2. This region may thus be denoted by *TDPS* (x_1, x_2). Thus, with NDP, the poverty headcount must not be higher with H than with H^* for all possible *TDPS* (x_1, x_2) defined within the original *TDPS* (z_1, z_2). With NIP, the headcount must not be greater in the region consisting of the three areas (I), (II) and (III). This rectangular region actually corresponds to the union of $SDPS$ (x_1) and $SDPS$ (x_2): I + (II) and (II) + (III). Interestingly enough, NDP thus appears to be associated with the *TDPS* definition of poverty whereas NIP is associated with a definition of poverty based on the union on *SDPS*.

The intuition behind Proposition 2 is as follows. Consider the two alternative definitions of poverty shown in Figure 18.1 and an increasing-correlation shift as in Figure 18.2. Then consider all combinations of poverty lines x_1 and x_2 below the original threshold levels z_1 and z_2. In Figure 18.4, these combinations are represented by point B. NDP requires that poverty should not decrease with a

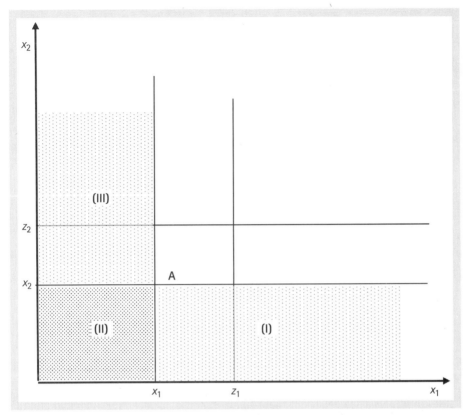

Fig. 18.3. Dominance criterion: poverty headcount must not be higher either in *TDPS* (II) under NDP or in the union of the *SDPS* (I + II + III) under NIP

correlation-increasing shift. If the poverty headcount is required not to decrease for any possible combinations of x_1 and x_2, then the headcount ratio must be defined on the area $TDPS(x_1, x_2)$, which lies south-west of point B. In fact, it can be seen in Figure 18.4 that the correlation-increasing shift does not modify the poverty headcount in $TDPS(x_1, x_2)$ as long as point B is outside the rectangle $A_2 A_2' A_1 A_1'$ and it necessarily increases the poverty headcount if it lies inside that rectangle. To see this, consider a leftward horizontal movement of the point B so that it lies on the left-hand side of the line $A_2 A_2'$. Given that the poverty thresholds are set at (x_1, x_2), the correlation-increasing shift changes the positions of the persons in the sense that person 2, who was rich at B, becomes poor, and the reverse happens for person 1. The shift thus keeps the headcount index unaltered. The other cases can be proven similarly. The opposite occurs when we take the union of $SDPS(x_1)$ and $SDPS(x_2)$: the headcount does not change for all B outside the rectangle but the headcount in the region (I) + (II) + (III) goes down if B is inside the rectangle. The latter result violates NDP, but satisfies NIP.

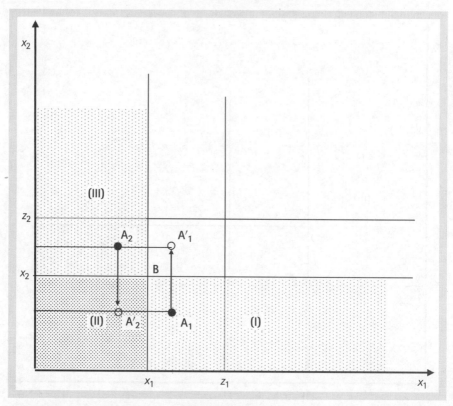

Fig. 18.4. A correlation–increasing shift does not reduce the poverty head-count in the *TDPS* regions (II) but does not increase it in the union of the *SDPS* regions

Coming back to the issue of the definition of two-dimensional poverty discussed earlier, the preceding propositions would seem to imply that overall poverty should be measured over $TDPS(z_1, z_2)$ if the two attributes are taken as substitutes and over the union of $SDPS(z_1)$ and $SDPS(z_2)$ if they are complements. This would be pushing the argument too far, however. The distinction between defining poverty on *TDPS* or the union of the two *SDPS*es arises when considering dominance conditions of one distribution over another. Consideration of head-count ratios in the union or the intersection of areas $SDPS(x_1)$ and $SDPS(x_2)$ arises only within the basic rectangle $[0, z_1] \times [0, z_2]$. Outside that rectangle only one dimension of poverty matters and dominance is taken care of there by the marginal dominance conditions on $\Delta H_1(x_1)$ and $\Delta H_2(x_2)$, as shown in the preceding propositions. (This point is further strengthened and analyzed by Atkinson 2003.)

The relevance of the two single-dimensional dominance conditions appears still more clearly in the limit case, where the two attributes are neither complements nor substitutes. In that case the second cross-derivative of the individual poverty function $\pi_z(x_1, x_2)$ is nil, so that the function is additive:

$$\pi_z(x_1, x_2) = p(x_1, x_2; z_1, z_2) = f_1(x_1; z_1) + f_2(x_2; z_2). \tag{8}$$

One such example is the poverty-gap function, which corresponds to the case $b = 1$, $\alpha = 1$ and $\beta = 1$ in equation (1).

The following proposition is proved in the Appendix:

Proposition 3. *Let H and H* be two bivariate distribution functions on the same range* $[0, a_1] \times [0, a_2]$. *Then the following conditions are equivalent:*

(i) $\Delta P(H, H^*, z) \leq 0$ *for all poverty indices belonging to* P^0.

(ii) $\Delta H_1(x_1) \leq 0$ *for all* $x_1 < z_1$ *and* $\Delta H_2(x_2) \leq 0$ *for all* $x_2 < z_2$.

The preceding propositions give a neat interpretation of the multivariate first-order stochastic dominance results when applied to multidimensional poverty ordering. It is not clear whether second-order stochastic dominance can be employed analogously. The reason behind this is that the second-order dominance criterion involves restrictions on the signs of third- and fourth-order derivatives of the poverty function. The interpretation of these restrictions is not obvious in the poverty context. However, if $\pi_z(x_1, x_2)$ is additive across components, then we have an unambiguous comparability result. Note that under additivity the attributes are treated independently and our result reduces to single-dimensional ordering. In that particular case, it also follows that the transfer principle (*TRP*) leads to the familiar second-order dominance in each dimension, as stated in the following proposition.

Proposition 4. *Let H and H* be two bivariate distributions on the common domain* $[0, a_1] \times [0, a_2]$. *Then the following conditions are equivalent:*

(i) $\Delta P(H, H^*, z) \leq 0$ *for all poverty indices belonging to* P^0 *and satisfying TRP.*

(ii) $\int_0^{x_1} \Delta H_1(u)\, du \leq 0$ *for all* $x_1 < z_1$ *and* $\int_0^{x_2} \Delta H_2(u)\, du \leq 0$ *for all* $x_2 < z_2$.

The proof of this proposition is straightforward. Given additivity of the poverty index P, TRP simply means that $f_1'' \geq 0$ and $f_2'' \geq 0$, that is, each $p_{ii} \geq 0$. A well-known equivalent condition of the criteria stated in clause (ii) of Proposition 4 is that poverty gaps must not be higher under distribution H than under H^* for all poverty lines x_i below the threshold level z_i, where $i = 1, 2$.

IV. A NUMERICAL ILLUSTRATION

To illustrate the preceding propositions and to see how they can be applied, consider the very simple example portrayed in Figures 18.5 to 18.8. The two dimensions of poverty are income and education. The income poverty line is set at $35 per month whereas the education-poor are those with less than 6 years of schooling. To simplify, these two dimensions are further "discretized" into two categories of equal magnitude: from $0 to $17.50 and from $17.50 to $35 on the one hand, and below 3 years of education and from 3 to 5 years on the other hand. Differences in education and income within these categories are simply ignored, but it would be a simple matter to generalize this example to a finer grid.

The initial distribution of a population of 12 individuals is represented by squares. The new distribution is represented by diamonds. Except for one or two cases, diamonds are close to squares and should be considered essentially as identical observations.

The application of the dominance criteria consists of counting the number of observations in the intersection or union of the *SDPS* areas at the vertices of the grid (A_1, A_2, B_1, B_2) within the overall poverty rectangle $[0, 35] \times [0, 6]$. The bottom pair of numbers corresponds to the *TDPS* headcounts in the initial and

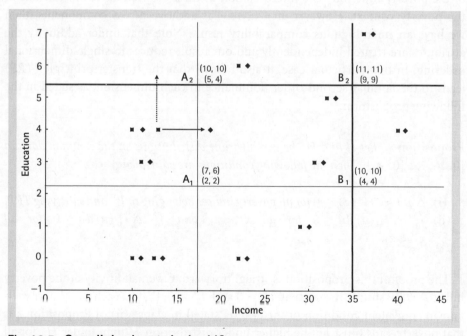

Fig. 18.5. Overall dominant single shift

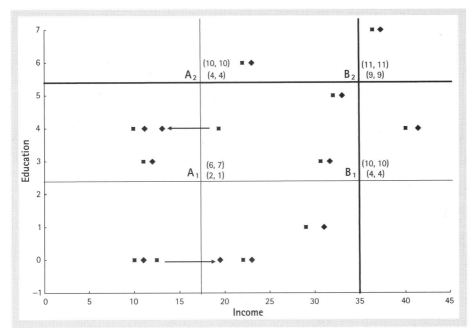

Fig. 18.6. NDP-type dominant double shift

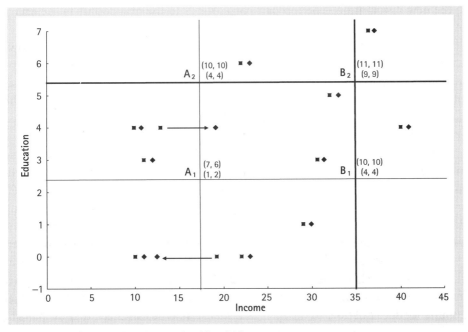

Fig. 18.7. NIP-type dominant double shift

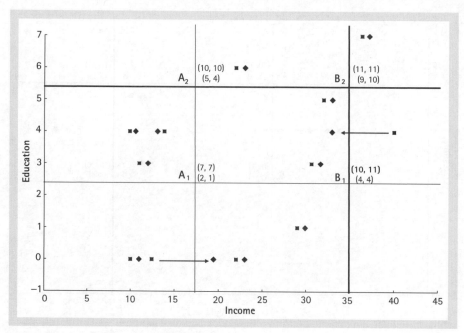

Fig. 18.8. Non-dominant double shift

in the new distribution. The top pair corresponds to the headcounts in the union of the *SDPS* areas.

Figure 18.5 depicts the effects of a dominant single shift. The solid arrow shows a drop in income poverty for one individual in the population. Poverty unambiguously declines, as can be seen from the headcount pairs at A_1, A_2. Note that all dominance criteria are satisfied, whether one considers the intersection or the union of the two *SDPS* areas. The same result would be obtained with the dotted arrow and also if the shift originates above one of the two poverty lines.

Figure 18.6 shows the effect of a "correlation-decreasing" shift. The income of one individual goes up whereas that of another, more educated individual goes down. In agreement with NDP, there is dominance at A_1 when we consider the *TDPS* area, but the dominance criterion is violated at the same point when considering the union-of-*SDPS* criterion. Figure 18.7 shows the opposite case of a correlation-increasing shift that violates the former dominance condition and satisfies the latter.

Finally, Figure 18.8 shows the same type of double and opposite shift but at very different levels of income, with an individual moving from above to below the income poverty line. There cannot be dominance in this case, since marginal dominance does not hold in the income dimension. One can check that the pairs of headcounts in the grid confirm this result. There is an improvement in the bottom pair at A_1 and A_2, but there is a worsening at B_2. Likewise, there is no change in the top pair except a worsening at B_1.

This simple example is useful in showing how the dominance criteria derived in this paper can be practically applied. It is indeed a simple matter to extend it to more complex cases, more numerous populations and a finer grid of sub-poverty lines.

V. CONCLUSION

In income-based poverty measurement it is assumed that individuals in a society are distinguished only by income. But in many cases, in addition to low income a person may have insufficient levels of other attributes of well-being, e.g. literacy and health care. Therefore, a genuine measure of poverty should be based on non-monetary as well as monetary attributes of well-being. A particular measure of poverty will completely rank alternative distributions of attributes of well-being. But two different measures satisfying the same set of postulates may order two distributions differently. Therefore, it seems worthwhile to investigate whether a certain class of poverty indices might uniformly order a set of distributions. This chapter may be regarded as a step in this direction.

A simple generalization of the existing results for first-order income-poverty dominance has been provided. First, two-dimensional dominance of a distribution over another requires one-dimensional dominance for the marginal distribution of each attribute. Second, for all combinations of poverty lines below the original threshold levels, two-dimensional dominance requires the multidimensional poverty headcount not to be higher with the first distribution than with the second. However, the sets on which the headcount is evaluated differ, depending on whether the two attributes may be taken as substitutes or complements. This second requirement is irrelevant in the case where the two attributes are neither complements nor substitutes. In this case, two-dimensional poverty dominance is simply equivalent to one-dimensional poverty dominance for each attribute. It may be noted that our results can be generalized to the n-dimensional case, but for the sake of simplicity we have considered only the two-attribute case.

APPENDIX

Derivation of formula (6)

Integrate by parts the definition of the dominance condition (5) with respect to x_2. This yields:

$$\Delta P\,(H, H^*, z) = \int_0^{a1} \int_0^{a2} \pi_z(x_1, x_2)\, d\,\Delta H$$

$$= \int_0^{a1} \left[\pi_z(x_1, x_2) \int_0^{x2} d\,\Delta H\,(x_1, u_2) \right]_{x_2=0}^{x_2=a_2}$$

$$- \int_0^{a1} \int_0^{a2} \pi_{z2}(x_1, x_2) \left[\int_0^{x2} d\,\Delta H\,(x_1, u_2) \right] dx_2. \tag{9}$$

After evaluating the first square-bracketed term, we get:

$$\Delta P\,(H, H^*, z) = \int_0^{a1} \pi_z(x_1, a_2)\, d\,\Delta H\,(x_1, a_2)$$

$$- \int_0^{a1} \int_0^{a2} \pi_{z2}(x_1, x_2) \left[\int_0^{x2} d\,\Delta H\,(x_1, u_2) \right] dx_2. \tag{10}$$

Integrating the first term by parts yields:

$$\int_0^{a1} \pi_z(x_1, a_2)\, d\,\Delta\,H\,(x_1, a_2) = \left[\pi_z(x_1, a_2)\,\Delta\,H_1(x_1) \right]_{x_1=0}^{x_1=a_1}$$

$$- \int_0^{a1} \pi_{z1}(x_1, a_2)\,\Delta\,H_1(x_1) dx_1, \tag{11}$$

where $H_1(x_1) = H(x_1, a_2)$ is the marginal distribution of x_1 and we have the symmetric notion for x_2.

Integration of the second term of (10) by parts with respect to x_1 leads to:

$$\int_0^{a1} \int_0^{a2} \pi_{z2}(x_1, x_2) \left[\int_0^{x2} d\,\Delta\,H\,(x_1, u_2) \right] dx_2$$

$$= \int_0^{a2} \left[\pi_{z2}(x_1, x_2) \int_0^{x1} \int_0^{x2} d\,\Delta\,H\,(u_1, u_2) \right]_{x_1=0}^{x_1=a_1} dx_2$$

$$- \int_0^{a1} \int_0^{a2} \pi_{z12}(x_1, x_2)\,\Delta\,H(x_1, x_2) dx_1 dx_2. \tag{12}$$

Finally, putting together (11) and (12), and after evaluating the various functions at the bounds of integration intervals, we get:

$$\Delta P\,(H, H^*, z) = \int_0^{a1} \pi_{z1}(x_1, a_2)\,\Delta H_1\,(x_1)$$

$$- \int_0^{a2} \pi_{z2}(a_1, x_2)\,\Delta\,H_2(x_2)$$

$$+ \int_0^{a1} \int_0^{a2} \pi_{z12}(x_1, x_2)\,\Delta\,H(x_1, x_2) dx_1 dx_2. \tag{13}$$

Let us now take into account the following properties implied by (T):

$$\pi_{zi}(x_1, x_2) = 0 \quad \text{for} \quad i = 1, 2, \; x_1 \in [z_1, a_1] \quad \text{and} \quad x_2 \in [z_2, a_2],$$

$$\pi_{z12}(x_1, x_2) = 0 \quad \text{for} \quad x \in [z_1, a_1] \quad \text{or} \quad x_2 \in [z_2, a_2].$$

These conditions are sufficient to replace the bounds a_1 and a_2 in (13) by the poverty thresholds z_1 and z_2. This leads to decomposition (6):

$$\Delta P\,(H, H^*, z) = -\int_0^{z1} \pi_{z1}(x_1, z_2)\Delta H_1\,(x_1)dx_1 - \int_0^{z2} \pi_{z2}(x_1, z_2)\Delta H_2\,(x_2)dx_2$$

$$+ \int_0^{z1}\int_0^{z2} \pi_{z12}(x_1, x_2)\Delta\,H(x_1, x_2)dx_1dx_2.$$

Proof of Proposition 1

The sufficiency part of Proposition 1 is obtained by the following argument. Since the sign of the first derivatives of $\pi_z(x_1, x_2)$ is implied by properties (T) and the sign of the second cross-derivative is implied by NDP, the conditions $\Delta H_1(x_1) \le 0$, $\Delta H_2(x_2) \le 0$, $\Delta H(x_1, x_2) \le 0$ for all $(x_1, x_2) \in [0, z_1] \times [0, z_2]$ make $\Delta P(H, H^*, z)$ non-positive.

Necessity is obtained by exhibiting a particular function $\pi_z(x_1, x_2)$ satisfying properties (S) and NDP and leading to $\Delta P(H, H^*, z) > 0$ whenever one of the three conditions $\Delta H_1(x_1) \le 0$, $\Delta H_2(x_2) \le 0$, $\Delta H(x_1, x_2) \le 0$ is not satisfied on some subset of $[0, z_1] \times [0, z_2]$. The proof of this is not given here.[10]

Derivation of formula (7)

Some modification must be made in the preceding argument. Note first that

$$\pi_{z1}(x_1, z_2) = \pi_{z1}(x_1, 0) + \int_0^{z2} \pi_{z12}(x_1, x_2)dx_2,$$

and, symmetrically:

$$\pi_{z2}(z_1, x_2) = \pi_{z2}(0, x_2) + \int_0^{z1} \pi_{z12}(x_1, x_2)dx_1.$$

Substituting these two expressions into (6), we get (7):

$$\Delta P\,(H, H^*, z) = -\int_0^{z1} \pi_{z1}(x_1, 0)\Delta H_1\,(x_1)dx_1 - \int_0^{z2} \pi_{z2}(0, x_2)\Delta H_2\,(x_2)dx_2$$

$$+ \int_0^{z1}\int_0^{z2} \pi_{z12}(x_1, x_2)[\,\Delta\,H(x_1, x_2) - \Delta\,H_1(x_1) - \Delta\,H_2(x_2)]dx_1dx_2.$$

Proposition 2 then follows from the same arguments as those employed for Proposition 1.

Proof of Proposition 3

Whether one chooses decomposition (6) or (7), additivity of the individual poverty function implies that $\pi_{z12}(x_1, x_2) = 0$. Proposition 3 then follows from the negative sign of the derivatives of the poverty function with respect to its arguments.

---

[10] See Atkinson and Bourguignon (1982) for a proof.

References

ATKINSON, A. B. (1987), "On the Measurement of Poverty", *Econometrica*, 5: 244–63.

—— (1992), "Measuring Poverty and Difference in Family Composition", *Economica*, 59: 1–16.

—— (2003), "Multidimensional Deprivation: Contrasting Social Welfare and Counting Approaches", *Journal of Economic Inequality*, 1: 51–65.

—— and BOURGUIGNON, F. (1982), "The Comparison of Multidimensioned Distributions of Economic Status", *Review of Economic Studies*, 49: 183–201.

BOURGUIGNON, F., and CHAKRAVARTY, S. R. (1999), "A Family of Multidimensional Poverty Measures", in D. J. Slottjee (ed.), *Advances in Econometrics, Income Distribution and Methodology of Science: Essays in Honor of C. Dagum* (New York: Springer-Verlag).

—— —— (2003), "Measurement of Multidimensional Poverty", *Journal of Economic Inequality*, 1: 25–49.

—— and FIELDS, G. (1997), "Discontinuous Losses from Poverty, Generalized Measures and Optimal Transfers to the Poor", *Journal of Public Economics*, 63: 155–75.

CHAKRAVARTY, S. R. (1990), *Ethical Social Index Numbers* (New York: Springer-Verlag).

—— (2006), "An Axiomatic Approach to Multidimensional Poverty Measurement via Fuzzy Sets", in A. Lemmi and G. Betti (eds), *Fuzzy Set Approach to Multidimensional Poverty Measurement* (New York: Springer-Verlag).

—— MUKHERJEE, D., and RANADE, R. (1998), "The Family of Subgroup and Factor-Decomposable Measures of Multidimensional Poverty", *Research on Economic Inequality*, 8: 175–94.

—— and SILBER, J. (2007), "Measuring Multidimensional Poverty: The Axiomatic Approach", in N. Kakwani and J. Silber (eds), *Quantitative Approaches to Multidimensional Poverty* (New York: Palgrave Macmillan).

DONALDSON, D., and WEYMARK, J. A. (1986), "Properties of Fixed Population Poverty Indices", *International Economic Review*, 27: 667–88.

DUCLOS, J.-Y., SHAN, D., and YOUNGER, S. (2002), "Robust Multidimensional Poverty Comparisons", unpubl. MS, Université de Laval.

FOSTER, J. E. (1984), "On Economic Poverty: A Survey of Aggregate Measures", in R. L. Basman and G. F. Rhodes (eds), *Advances in Econometrics*, vol. 3 (Stanford, Conn.: JAI Press).

—— GREER, J., and THORBECKE, E. (1984), "A Class of Decomposable Poverty Measures", *Econometrica*, 52: 761–6.

—— and SEN, A. K. (1997), "On Economic Equality after a Quarter Century", Annex to the enlarged edn of *On Economic Inequality* by A. K. Sen (Oxford: Clarendon Press).

—— and SHORROCKS, A. F. (1988a), "Poverty Orderings", *Econometrica*, 56: 173–7.

—— —— (1988b), "Poverty Orderings and Welfare Dominance", *Social Choice and Welfare*, 5: 175–98.

—— —— (1991), "Subgroup-Consistent Poverty Indices", *Econometrica*, 59: 687–709.

—— and JIN, Y. (1996), "Poverty Orderings for the Dalton Utility-Gap Measures", in S. Jenkins, A. Keptyn and B. van Praag (eds), *The Distributions of Welfare and Household Production: International Perspectives* (Cambridge. Cambridge University Press).

HADAR, J., and RUSSELL, R. R. (1974), "Stochastic Dominance in Choice under Uncertainty", in M. S. Balch, D. L. McFadden and S. Y. Wu (eds), *Essays on Economic Behavior under Uncertainty* (Amsterdam: North-Holland).

JENKINS, S., and LAMBERT, P. J. (1993), "Ranking Income Distributions When Needs Differ", *Review of Income and Wealth*, 39: 337–56.

———— (1997), "Three 'I's of Poverty Curves, with an Analysis of UK Poverty Trends", *Oxford Economic Papers*, 49: 317–27.

———— (1998a), "Three 'I's of Poverty Curves and Poverty Dominance: TIP for Poverty Analysis", *Research on Economic Inequality*, 8: 39–56.

———— (1998b), "Ranking Poverty Gap Distributions: Further TIPs for Poverty Analysis", *Research on Economic Inequality*, 8: 31–8.

KOLM, S. C. (1977), "Multidimensional Egalitarianism", *Quarterly Journal of Economics*, 91: 1–13.

KOSHEVOY, G. (1995), "Multivariate Lorenz Majorization", *Social Choice and Welfare*, 12: 93–102.

—— (1998), "The Lorenz Zonotope and Multivariate Majorizations", *Social Choice and Welfare*, 15: 1–14.

—— and MOSLER, K. (1996), "The Lorenz Zonoid of a Multivariate Distribution", *Journal of the American Statistical Association*, 60: 252–76.

LEVY, H., and PAROUSH, J. (1974), "Toward Multivariate Efficiency Criteria", *Journal of Economic Theory*, 7: 129–42.

RAVALLION, M. (1996), "Issues in Measuring and Modeling Poverty", *Economic Journal*, 106: 1328–43.

SEIDL, C. (1998), "Poverty Measurement: A Survey", in D. Bos, M. Rose and C. Seidl (eds), *Welfare and Efficiency in Public Economics* (New York: Springer-Verlag).

SEN, A. K. (1976), "Poverty: An Ordinal Approach to Measurement", *Econometrica*, 44: 219–31.

—— (1985), *Commodities and Capabilities* (Amsterdam: North-Holland).

—— (1992), *Inequality Re-examined* (Cambridge, Mass.: Harvard University Press).

SHORROCKS, A. F. (1998), "Deprivation Profiles and Deprivation Indices", in S. Jenkins, A. Keptyn and B. van Praag (eds), *The Distributions of Welfare and Household Production: International Perspectives* (Cambridge: Cambridge University Press).

SPENCER, B., and FISHER, S. (1996), "On Comparing Distributions of Poverty Gaps", *Sankhya: The Indian Journal of Statistics B*, 54: 114–26.

TSUI, K. Y. (1997), "Multidimensional Poverty Indices", *Social Choice and Welfare*, 19: 69–93.

UNDP (1997), *Human Development Report* (New York Oxford University Press).

ZHENG, B. (1997), "Aggregate Poverty Measures", *Journal of Economic Surveys*, 11: 123–63.

—— (1999), "On the Power of Poverty Orderings", *Social Choice and Welfare*, 16: 349–71.

CHAPTER 19

EXTERNAL CAPABILITIES

JAMES E. FOSTER

CHRISTOPHER HANDY

I. Introduction

THE capability approach evaluates well-being in terms of a person's ability to achieve certain outcomes, doings and beings, which are collectively called functionings. It measures human development by freedom, which is "the 'capabilities' of people to lead the kind of lives they value" (Sen 1999: 18). The development process is seen as one of expanding capabilities, or giving individuals the freedom to realize more and better functionings.

Although the capability approach is a general framework for evaluating well-being, it has found the most purchase in the literature on human and economic development. This is due in part to its multidimensional focus, which easily accommodates the synergies inherent in development processes. For example, two capabilities commonly identified within the approach are the abilities to achieve health and be well educated. Levy (1991) and others have described in detail the synergistic relationship between nutrition, health and education—namely, undernourished

This paper is based on the undergraduate honors thesis of Christopher Handy, written under the direction of James Foster at Vanderbilt University. We are grateful to Sabina Alkire, Kaushik Basu and John Siegfried for helpful comments, and to the Vanderbilt Undergraduate Summer Research Program for financial support.

children have trouble learning, and the less educated find good health difficult to attain—and this conforms well to the capability framework.[1] As another example, consider Anand and Ravallion (1993), who show that poverty alleviation and public spending on health care explain the entire effect of economic growth on raising life expectancy in poor countries. Whereas a traditional economic approach would tend to focus on income growth, studies informed by the capability approach also investigate the pathway from growth to individual well-being.

Sen's goal in formulating the capability approach was a more realistic understanding of the determinants of a person's well-being. The individual is the basic unit of analysis in the capability approach and, indeed, many of the capabilities described in the literature, such as the ability to read, can be viewed as somehow belonging to the individual.[2] Social influences also play a role in the construction of certain capabilities and can have detrimental or positive effects on individual well-being. For example, Sen has often quoted Adam Smith's observation that while having a linen shirt was not physically essential for doing day labor in eighteenth-century Britain, not having such a shirt would mark the laborer as being somehow different from or below his peers.[3] The linen shirt played a key role in signaling this socially determined capability (or deprivation): society sets a norm and the person has the capability exactly when he is able to meet this standard. Considerable attention has likewise been devoted to publicly provided capabilities intended to benefit the members of society. Examples include the provision of health care, schooling, and public transport by the government or other institutions.

Both of these traditional forms of capabilities—which might be called individual capabilities and socially created capabilities—are centrally important for understanding well-being and development. However, we argue that they do not nearly cover the wide scope of capabilities that are instrumental for development. Consider a farmer who has an Internet connection that allows him to keep track of crop prices at nearby markets, so that he can gain a better price from middlemen or bypass these agents altogether. He regularly shares this information with a second farmer, who lives next door and is his good friend. Clearly, the capabilities of both farmers are enhanced by gaining access to crop prices and other information. But while the capability gained by the first farmer is individual (or perhaps socially created), this is not the case for the second farmer. His expansion depends crucially and contingently on his friendship with the first farmer, so the new capability is hardly an individual capability. It is also not purely a socially created capability, since its provision to the second farmer hinges so importantly on his friend.

---

[1] The government of Mexico created the successful Progresa/Oportunidades program, a contingent cash-transfer program for poor families, to capture these synergies and break the cycle of poverty. See Levy (2006).

[2] Sen adopts what Robeyns (2008) calls "ethical individualism", which "postulates that individuals, and only individuals, are the *ultimate* units of moral concern" while acknowledging the vital role of social structures in creating capabilities. See section IV below.

[3] See, for example, Sen (1983).

Another instructive example is provided by children's health. A young child has almost no individual capability to achieve good health, and so must rely on the care of a parent or other persons. A mother might instruct her child in basic hygiene, keep track of the services offered by a local health center, or undertake a wide range of activities in order to keep the child healthy. But the resulting ability to achieve good health is certainly not an individual capability of the child. The mother's own capability to achieve health may be individual or socially determined—by government provision, perhaps—but the child's is most directly determined by its relationship with the mother.

This chapter introduces the notion of "external capabilities" to describe cases in which a person is able to achieve additional functionings through a direct connection with another person. The standard conception of capabilities already allows an individual's social environment to have an impact on his or her capabilities, and acknowledges the role of institutions and policies in the creation of capabilities. But it makes little use of the fact that the individual's relationships can also matter greatly in this regard. So when the capability approach is used as a tool for analyzing policy, it is likely to capture, for example, a person's expansion in capabilities from becoming literate, but likely to miss the next step, wherein the person's literacy can enhance the capabilities of family and friends. Our goal is to recognize this important class of capabilities.

This chapter proceeds as follows. Section II provides an overview of the capability approach. Section III introduces the notion of external capabilities and explains its role within the capability approach. The fourth section contrasts external capabilities with existing forms of group capabilities and shows that the two concepts are very different. A final section summarizes the argument and presents some suggestions for future research.

II. The Capability Approach

The capability approach is fundamentally a framework for conceptualizing and evaluating well-being. In this capacity it is being employed in a wide range of applications, from formulating and analyzing policies to serving as a component in philosophical theories of justice. The approach was introduced and first developed by Amartya Sen (1980, 1984, 1985a, 1985b, 1987) and continues to mature in the work of Sen and other scholars.[4]

The capability approach aims to give a truer picture of human well-being. It finds fault with the use of utility or primary goods as indicators of well-being,

[4] See Sen (1990, 1992, 1993, 1999); Foster and Sen (1997); Alkire (2002, 2006); Basu and Lopez-Calva (2008); Deneulin and Stewart (2002); Evans (2002); Herrero (1996); Ibrahim (2006); Nussbaum (1988, 1992, 1998, 2000, 2003); Robeyns (2000, 2005, 2008); and Stewart (2005).

and it criticizes economists for switching between the two in their theoretical and empirical work. The approach admits multiple dimensions of human well-being, including market-based capabilities, such as having enough income to purchase food and avoid malnutrition, and non-market capabilities, such as the freedom to participate in the political process.

The capability approach specifies a fairly detailed chain of well-being, summarized by Robeyns (2005) in an excellent survey article. Production activities combine with income to form an individual's means to achieve. These means determine certain goods and services available to the individual, who uses the characteristics of those goods and services to form capabilities. This conversion process is specific to the individual and is influenced by other people, social norms, and various social and environmental factors. For example, a given level of income may translate for one person into the capability of being nourished, but may not allow a pregnant woman to purchase enough food. And for both these individuals, whether that level of income buys enough food may be influenced by weather, geography, government policy, and trade policy in foreign countries. To some degree, the social and environmental context in which the individual chooses and acts can be thought of as having characteristics that produce capabilities, similar to the characteristics of goods and services. These social and environmental influences may also contribute directly to an individual's capabilities, as described in the introduction.

In Sen's (1985a) formulation, each capability represents the ability to achieve a certain doing or being, called a functioning. All of an individual's capabilities together form his or her capability set. The capability set can be thought of as a collection of vectors of functionings from which the individual may choose one achieved vector. This choice is influenced by individual and social factors, similar to how such factors affect the formation of an individual's capabilities. Finally, from the achieved functionings an individual may derive some amount of utility. However, according to Sen (1999: 74) the appropriate space for evaluating well-being is not utility, but "that of substantive freedoms—the capabilities—to choose a life one has reason to value".

The capability approach has been used to motivate improved aggregate measures of well-being and poverty. Probably the best-known example is the Human Development Index (HDI), produced by the United Nations Development Programme (UNDP). This indicator combines data on a country's income, life expectancy, literacy and school enrollment to obtain an overall measure by which countries are ranked in the annual Human Development Report. The Human Poverty Index (HPI), also provided by the UNDP, focuses on deprivations in income, education and health. Both indices go beyond the traditional income basis for evaluation.[5]

---

[5] See Alkire and Foster (2007) for multidimensional poverty measures motivated, in part, by the capability approach.

The capability approach has motivated a number of empirical studies as well.[6] Sen (1985a), using 1980–2 data, investigated GNP, life expectancy and infant mortality in several countries, including Mexico, Brazil and Sri Lanka. He found that while Brazil and Mexico had much higher GNP per capita, Sri Lanka had the best life expectancy and lowest infant mortality. This is evidence that income does not always reflect development, and also that growth in income does not always translate into better living standards, a point Sen has made repeatedly (see e.g. Sen 1999). Ruggeri Laderchi (1997), using 1992 data from Chile, found that income is a poor indicator of deprivation in education, health and child nutrition, and hence that poverty may be quite sensitive to the choice of indicators. Ellman (1994) provided evidence of rapidly increasing mortality rates in the former Soviet countries following the fall of the USSR and showed that this cannot be explained by prices, incomes and consumption.

While the capability approach offers a clearer picture of well-being, it is not a full-fledged theory of justice (Sen 1995, 2004b), in part because it includes no explicit method by which the importance of one capability can be measured against another. Nussbaum (1988, 1992, 1998, 2000, 2003) has attempted to move closer to such a theory by identifying a list of "central human capabilities" that she argues should be guaranteed to all people. A recent list (Nussbaum 2003) contains more than thirty individual capabilities grouped into the following categories: life; bodily health; bodily integrity; senses, imagination and thought; emotions; practical reason; affiliation; other species; play; and control over one's environment. Whether a universal list should exist is a matter of some debate; Nussbaum (2003) argues that the capability approach is powerless without it, while Sen (2004a) has noted the difficulties in and consequences of endorsing such a list.

Two further themes of the capability approach merit special mention. The first is the need to distinguish between the means and the ends of development. The means are production, income, and social and environmental factors that determine or form the inputs for capabilities. The ends are capabilities and achieved functionings. Of course, some ends are also instrumentally important to development—that is, they double as means. Participation in the political process is both a matter of freedom (an end) and a way to influence policy (a means). A friendship may be both intrinsically valuable and a vehicle for further capabilities. And many capabilities feed back into higher income, which is then an input for more capabilities. The second theme is the role of choice in the capability approach. Choice over functionings is viewed as being intrinsically valuable, and Sen recognizes the value of both well-being achievement, which is best represented by functionings, and well-being freedom, which is best represented by the scope and quality of achievable functionings in the capability set.[7]

---

[6] It is also being formalized to provide a sounder basis for theoretical and empirical work. See Sen (1985a); Basu and López-Calva (2008); and Herrero (1996), for example.

[7] The intrinsic value of choice is not unlike Weisbrod's (1964) "option value". For a technical survey on the measurement of freedom, see Foster (2008).

III. EXTERNAL CAPABILITIES

External capabilities are abilities to function that depend on direct human relationships.[8] Specifically, they depend on an individual's access to the capabilities of another person. They frequently require some coordinated action within personal relationships: again, it is more than a single person going to the market to buy food, and more than simply accepting government provision. But the relationships on which they depend are also very often informal: they happen outside group and organizational structures, and in fact often work best when fewer people are involved. Within this framework, the farmer whose friend has an Internet connection has the external capability of access to crop prices through this friendship—specifically, through a direct relationship with someone who has the capability of access to this information. And the child has the external capability of better health through the capabilities of its mother.

Another example of an external capability can be found in the notion of "proximate literacy" developed by Basu and Foster (1998). The idea is that there is a "positive intrahousehold externality" to illiterate family members when at least one member can read and write; and while the authors do not explicitly mention the capability approach in their discussion, their concept effortlessly fits the idea of external capabilities. A person who cannot read may nevertheless have proximate literacy—an external capability—through one or more relationships. Basu and Foster offer a pair of examples where proximate literacy may be beneficial: (1) agricultural extension workers distribute brochures about planting, growing and harvesting high-yield crop varieties, and (2) a new medical center is established nearby, and pamphlets are provided that describe the services offered by the center and give preventative tips. Whether a person reads the information, or has it read to them, the achieved functioning is similar: obtaining information or communicating through reading and writing.[9]

The idea of external capabilities extends naturally to other skills. Consider numeracy: if an individual has some skill but is prevented from entrepreneurship by a lack of proficiency with numbers, a relationship with a numerate person could offer that individual a chance to start a small business. Proficiency in a foreign language is another example. A family may have access to a local Internet kiosk,

[8] The term "external capabilities" has previously been used by Nussbaum (1998) in a very different sense: to recognize the fact that individuals are sometimes prevented by others from using their capabilities. Nussbaum's two examples are suppression of criticism in "repressive nondemocratic regimes" and repression of women. This idea, then, has much in common with the "social conversion factors" discussed by Robeyns (2005). Nussbaum has recognized this and discarded the term.

[9] Whether external capabilities are good substitutes for individual capabilities, or are distinct in important ways, is an interesting question. See the related discussion below. Note that Basu and Foster used the term "proximate illiteracy" rather than "proximate literacy"; the latter term seems more apt in the present context.

but much of the information available online may only be in English. So having a family member who reads English can make this information accessible to the entire family. And for immigrants, having a child who learns the local tongue in school may ease the transition into a new and unfamiliar country. Finally, the skill of technological proficiency can often generate external capabilities. The family and friends of someone who knows computers may be better able to use their own computers because they have direct access to tips and troubleshooting. Sometimes these various skills converge: an individual might use his or her literacy and technological savvy to help others send, receive and read e-mails or text messages.

The range of external capabilities can be dramatically amplified by information and communications technology (ICT). One way ICT does this is by enhancing connections between people. For example, *The Economist* (2001a) recently reported that fishermen in India are using mobile phones to guide their friends to areas where the fishing is best, and to the landing spots where market prices are currently most favorable. At the same time, ICT can augment a person's individual capabilities by providing access to information, and this can expand the external capabilities of that person's friends and family. A second report (*Economist* 2001b) noted that fishermen are now using the Internet to retrieve weather forecasts and satellite images of fish shoals; it is likely that this information is being shared across existing social networks. ICT advances individual capabilities and makes them easier to share as external capabilities.

Another fascinating example of external capabilities and ICT is Kiva, a non-profit organization that allows a person in an industrialized country to extend credit to an entrepreneur in the developing world through the Internet, using a credit card, PayPal, or a checking account. Funds are sent to local microcredit partners and then disbursed to qualified borrowers, and the lender gets updates on the status of the small business using the money. The initial effect for an entrepreneur in the developing world is access to credit through a relationship with another individual—an external capability. If well used, the loan will expand the business and the entrepreneur may have easier access to traditional sources of credit, which is a more individual capability. The loan will also enable the entrepreneur to gain business experience and increase earnings potential—a synergistic expansion of other individual capabilities.

Each of our examples of external capabilities involves sharing—from a person who has a capability to another who lacks it—and it is the willingness to share that creates the external capability where none existed before. But the process by which external capabilities are produced also imposes certain restrictions on them. For example, external capabilities can be inferior to their individual analogs, as suggested by Basu and Foster (1998) in the context of literacy. They also note that the quality of external capabilities may vary depending on the characteristics of the person providing them, drawing on evidence that females are more effective than males in generating literacy externalities in families.[10]

A person who has individual capabilities rather than external capabilities need not face the contingencies or inherent variations in quality associated with external capabilities. But moving to individual capabilities may require a significant investment, such as the long-term commitment of time and effort needed to complete an adult literacy program. In other cases, the repeated sharing that leads to external capabilities may also create individual capabilities over time. A mother who teaches her children good health practices keeps them healthy now while also enabling them to maintain their own health in the future. And as noted above, a rural entrepreneur who successfully borrows through Kiva may eventually advance her enterprise to the point that it can secure reliable funding through traditional credit markets.

As we go from general definition to specific example, it is not always easy to identify a capability. For instance, take the example of the two farmers and the Internet-connected computer, and suppose that the two have always raised different crops. The first farmer makes use of the Internet-connected computer in deciding where to sell his crops. Is the relevant capability access to the Internet, or is it access to the prices of that farmer's specific crops in nearby markets? In the first view, the farmer converts the capability of Internet access into the achieved functioning of knowing crop prices; in the second, the capability and the functioning are identical. Both views are valid descriptions of the farmer's capabilities. But when the external capabilities of the second farmer are considered, the broadly defined capability is the relevant one. His external capability is formed by the first farmer's access to information on the Internet, including the prices of the crops he raises (which have value to the second farmer) and the prices of the crops raised by the first farmer (which have no such value to the second farmer). External capabilities, then, are freedoms to achieve functionings that a person values by accessing the capabilities of other people through relationships.

The idea of external capabilities fits well into the capability approach and preserves the importance placed by the capability approach on the freedom to choose. External capabilities, like other capabilities, ultimately reside in an individual's capability set and may be converted, or not, into functionings at the discretion of the individuals involved. Moreover, an individual has the freedom to choose his or her relationships, and each set of relationships potentially makes available a different set of external capabilities. Of course, as we have noted above, this freedom is tempered by the possibility that the other person may choose not to share or may refuse altogether to form the relationship.

---

[10]   See, for example, Coldwell (1979); Murthi, Guio and Drèze (1995); or Nag (1983). It is not difficult to imagine differences across ages, environments and societies as well.

IV. External Capabilities and Group Capabilities

Several scholars have developed concepts of *group* capabilities, which typically refer to abilities to function that are created through organizations, such as political parties, credit and savings groups, and producer associations. Group capabilities have similarities to our concept of external capabilities. We now present a brief review of the literature on group capabilities in order to compare the two concepts.

Stewart defines group capabilities as "capabilities that belong to groups even though the groups are made up of individuals and the behavior of the group affects individuals". These include "the resource access (political and economic) of the group" and "the way the group operates and the resulting impact on members of the group and on others". Stewart reasons that membership in a group affects people's well-being in three major ways. First, there is a direct impact, both through feelings of inclusion and self-respect and through tying one's own well-being to how well the group is doing (of course, this incurs risks if the group fares poorly). Second, groups are important to well-being instrumentally: through collective action, they confer capabilities that the individual would not have in the absence of membership in the group. As Stewart puts it, "the group capabilities of collective entities are not simply the sum of the individual capabilities of members of the group". Third, groups influence an individual's preference formation and behavior. Stewart writes that a group can be good or bad according to whether it tends to promote desirable or undesirable capabilities. A bad group might create identities that foster violent political conflict, while a good group might organize collective action among the poor (Stewart 2005: 199–200).

Evans (2002: 56) has discussed a similar idea through "collective capabilities". He notes that "for the less privileged attaining development as freedom requires collective action. Organized collectivities—unions, political parties, village councils, women's groups, etc.—are fundamental to 'people's capabilities to choose the lives they have reason to value.' " Evans, like Stewart, also recognizes the impact of groups on the formation of an individual's preferences.

Deneulin and Stewart (2002: 66) argue for the importance of "structures of living together" in the formation of capabilities. These structures represent the organization and properties of society, including "social norms, cultural practices, [and] trust". This notion, then, is a very broad one, going beyond formal groups to the realm of social capital. Deneulin and Stewart assert that these structures are important intrinsically, not merely as they promote individual capabilities. Ibrahim, using Evans's language of collective capabilities, says much the same thing, noting the "intrinsic and instrumental value of social structures". She goes further than Deneulin and Stewart by calling for "shifting the focus of the analysis from the individual to the collectivity" (Ibrahim 2006: 397, 413).

Some of these concepts were originally presented as challenges to the capability approach's focus on the individual. But, as we noted above, the capability approach does recognize social influences. Robeyns (2005) makes sense of this debate by distinguishing among three different types of individualism. First, ethical individualism is the common denominator of liberal philosophy: individuals are ultimately what matter morally. Robeyns notes that within ethical individualism, it is still possible to recognize the importance of social structures and societal properties, but only insofar as they contribute to the well-being of the individual. Second, methodological individualism is, in part, the view that everything can be explained by reference to individuals and their properties. Finally, ontological individualism holds that society is merely the sum of individuals and their properties. Robeyns argues that by recognizing social influences both in the formation of capabilities and in the choice of functionings, the capability approach embraces ethical individualism, but not—and rightly so, in both her opinion and ours—methodological or ontological individualism. Robeyns concludes that groups and social structures can fit into the capability approach, but that the literature on these phenomena may indeed be insufficient.

Alkire (2008), using Robeyns's distinction among different types of individualism, argues that Deneulin's and Stewart's objections do not challenge ethical individualism. She notes that the capability approach can be used in both evaluative and prospective roles. For example, it can be used both to evaluate outcomes or policy options and to shape proposals for policy or social change. Therefore Deneulin and Stewart's argument, properly reinterpreted, is that because the capability approach uses only an individual's capability in evaluation, social influences may well be missed when the capability approach is used in its prospective role.

A common denominator of the various notions of group capabilities mentioned above is that they arise when people organize to create capabilities that none of them would otherwise have. This provides one key distinction between group capabilities and external capabilities. Consider again the example of the two farmers. The second farmer, who learns of crop prices from his Internet-connected friend, does not gain this capability through a well-defined group that is formed for the purpose of generating it. Instead, he receives it from a friend who has access and is willing to share. Moreover, the first farmer will have the capability of accessing the Internet and knowing crop prices regardless of whether he shares the resulting information with his friend. This contrasts with the other central characteristic of group capabilities—they exist or perish with the group. The notion of external capabilities is fundamentally different from previously defined concepts of group capabilities.

V. CONCLUSION

This chapter has introduced the notion of external capabilities and discussed some issues arising from the concept; many others remain to be explored. One potentially important task is to identify likely dimensions for external capabilities. Which types of capabilities are especially well suited to be shared along social networks in this way, and which types are not? It may be that skills (such as literacy) are readily shared, while higher-order capabilities (such as reasoning) are not; or more nuanced understandings may be needed to answer this question. A second issue concerns the persons and relationships associated with external capabilities. Are certain types of people better providers of external capabilities? If so, then for which types of capabilities? Answers to these questions may help in the design of development policies.

A third area for investigation concerns the dynamic implications of external capabilities. External capabilities may be viewed as imperfect substitutes for their more reliable and permanent counterparts, and this can influence investment in future capabilities. On the one hand, the presence of an external capability can be a helpful coping mechanism that eases the pressure of a capability deprivation, providing an interim solution while a person builds individual capabilities. On the other hand, this coping mechanism may discourage the very investments that would reverse the capability deprivation that the external capability addressed. Determining which effect would hold in a given situation could be very useful in policy-making. In particular, it would be interesting to explore whether external capabilities might be an important part of a prospective plan for enhancing capabilities, such as through the use of ICT.

The capability approach has proven valuable in conceptualizing and evaluating well-being, and creating policies that promote development. It recognizes that human well-being is multidimensional and that progress in development involves synergies across those varied dimensions. But as currently presented the capability approach often misses the impact of an individual's relationships on his or her capabilities. In other words, while it succeeds in capturing synergies across *dimensions*, it fails to recognize important synergies across *people*. Our concept of external capabilities remedies this by specifically focusing on the capabilities enjoyed through social networks. It augments the considerable power of the capability approach to provide insight about well-being and to craft policies that make use of that insight.

REFERENCES

ALKIRE, S. (2002), *Valuing Freedoms: Sen's Capability Approach and Poverty Reduction* (New York: Oxford University Press).

—— (2008), "Using the Capability Approach: Prospective and Evaluative Analyses", in S. Alkire, F. Comim and M. Qizilbash (eds), *The Capability Approach: Concepts, Measures, and Applications* (Cambridge: Cambridge University Press).

—— and FOSTER, J. (2007), *Counting and Multidimensional Poverty Measurement*, OPHI Working Paper 7 (Oxford: OHPI).

ANAND, S., and RAVALLION, M. (1993), "Human Development in Poor Countries: On the Role of Private Incomes and Public Services", *Journal of Economic Perspectives*, 7: 133–50.

BASU, K., and FOSTER, J. E. (1998), "On Measuring Literacy", *Economic Journal*, 108(451): 1733–49.

—— and LOPEZ-CALVA, L. (forthcoming), "Functionings and Capabilities", in K. Arrow, A. Sen and K. Suzumura (eds), *Handbook of Social Choice and Welfare*, vol. 2 (Amsterdam: Elsevier).

CALDWELL, J. C., 1979. "Education as a Factor in Mortality Decline", *Population Studies*, 33: 395–413.

DENEULIN, S., and STEWART, F. (2002), "Amartya Sen's Contribution to Development Thinking", *Studies in Comparative International Development*, 37: 61–70.

DREZE, J., and SEN, A. (2002), *India: Development and Participation* (Oxford: Oxford University Press).

Economist (2001a), "Another Kind of Net Work", *The Economist*, 3 Mar. 2001: 59.

—— (2001b), "Fishermen on the Net", *The Economist*, 10 Nov 2001: 8.

ELLMAN, M. (1994), "The Increase in Death and Disease under 'Katastroika' ", *Cambridge Journal of Economics*, 18: 329–55.

EVANS, P. (2002), "Collective Capabilities, Culture, and Amartya Sen's 'Development as Freedom' ", *Studies in Comparative International Development*, 37: 54–60.

FOSTER, J. E. (2008), "Freedom, Opportunity and Well-Being" unpubl. MS, Vanderbilt University.

—— and SEN, A. (1997), *On Economic Inequality: After a Quarter Century*, in A. Sen, *On Economic Inequality* (Oxford: Clarendon Press).

HERRERO, C. (1996), "Capabilities and Utilities", *Economic Design*, 2: 69–88.

IBRAHIM, S. (2006), "From Individual to Collective Capabilities: The Capability Approach as a Conceptual Framework for Self-Help", *Journal of Human Development*, 7: 397–416.

LEVY, S. (1991), *Poverty Alleviation in Mexico*, Policy Research Working Paper 679 (Washington, DC: World Bank).

—— (2006), *Progress Against Poverty: Sustaining Mexico's Progresa-Oportunidades Program* (Washington: Brookings Institution Press).

MURTHI, M., GUIO, A.-C., and DREZE, J. (1995), "Mortality, Fertility and Gender Bias in India", *Population and Development Review*, 21: 745–82.

NAG, M. (1983), "Impact of Social and Economic Development on Mortality: Comparative Study of Kerala and West Bengal", *Economic and Political Weekly*, 18: 877–900.

NUSSBAUM, M. (1988), "Nature, Functioning and Capability: Aristotle on Political Distribution", in J. Annas and R. H. Grimm (eds), *Oxford Studies in Ancient Philosophy: Supplementary Volume* (Oxford: Oxford University Press).

—— (1992), "Human Functioning and Social Justice: In Defense of Aristotelian Essentialism", *Political Theory*, 20: 202–46.

—— (1998), "The Good as Discipline, The Good as Freedom", in D. A. Crocker and T. Linden (eds), *Ethics of Consumption: The Good Life, Justice, and Global Stewardship* (Lanham, Md.: Rowman and Littlefield).

NUSSBAUM, M. (2000), *Women and Human Development: The Capabilities Approach* (Cambridge: Cambridge University Press).

——(2003), "Capabilities as Fundamental Entitlements: Sen and Social Justice", *Feminist Economics*, 9: 33–59.

ROBEYNS, I. (2000), *An Unworkable Idea or A Promising Alternative? Sen's Capability Approach Re-Examined*, CES Discussion Paper 00.30 (Leuven: Katholleke Universiteit).

——(2005), "The Capability Approach: A Theoretical Survey", *Journal of Human Development*, 6: 93–117.

——(2008), "Sen's Capability Approach and Feminist Concerns", in S. Alkire, F. Comim and M. Qizilbash (eds), *The Capability Approach: Concepts, Measures, and Applications* (Cambridge: Cambridge University Press).

RUGGERI LADERCHI, C. (1997), "Poverty and its Many Dimensions: The Role of Income as an Indicator", *Oxford Development Studies*, 25: 345–60.

SEN, A. (1980), "Equality of What?", in S. McMurrin (ed.), *The Tanner Lectures on Human Values* (Salt Lake City: University of Utah Press).

——(1983), "Poor, Relatively Speaking", *Oxford Economic Papers*, 35: 153–69.

——(1984), "Rights and Capabilities", in A. Sen, *Resources, Values and Development* (Cambridge, Mass.: Harvard University Press).

——(1985a), *Commodities and Capabilities* (Amsterdam: North-Holland).

——(1985b), "Well-Being, Agency and Freedom", *Journal of Philosophy*, 82: 169–221.

——(1987), "The Standard of Living", in G. Hawthorn (ed.), *The Standard of Living* (Cambridge: Cambridge University Press).

——(1988), "The Concept of Development", in H. Chenery and T. N. Srinivasan (eds), *Handbook of Development Economics* (Amsterdam: Elsevier).

——(1990), "Justice: Means versus Freedoms", *Philosophy and Public Affairs*, 19: 111–21.

——(1992), *Inequality Re-Examined* (Oxford: Clarendon Press).

——(1993), "Capability and Well-Being", in M. Nussbaum and A. Sen (eds), *The Quality of Life* (Oxford: Clarendon Press).

——(1995), "Gender Inequality and Theories of Justice", in M. Nussbaum and J. Glover (eds), *Women, Culture and Development: A Study of Human Capabilities* (Oxford: Clarendon Press).

——(1997), *On Economic Inequality* (Oxford: Clarendon Press).

——(1999), *Development as Freedom* (New York: Knopf).

——(2004a), "Capabilities, Lists, and Public Reason: Continuing the Conversation", *Feminist Economics*, 10: 77–80.

——(2004b), "Elements of a Theory of Human Rights", *Philosophy and Public Affairs*, 32: 315–56.

STEWART, F. (2005), "Groups and Capabilities", *Journal of Human Development*, 6: 185–204.

WEISBROD, B. A. (1964), "Collective-Consumption Services of Individual-Consumption Goods", *Quarterly Journal of Economics*, 78: 471–7.

CHAPTER 20

ON THE WELFARIST RATIONALE FOR RELATIVE POVERTY LINES

MARTIN RAVALLION

I. INTRODUCTION

THE most common practice for measuring poverty in developing countries aims to set absolute poverty lines, meaning that they have constant purchasing power over commodities. The cost-of-living indices used for this purpose are typically based on the prices observed at each date or location (urban versus rural areas, region, or country), with an allowance for spending on those goods (notably non-food items) for which price data are missing. A poverty measure, such as the headcount index or poverty gap index, is then calculated by deflating actual consumptions or incomes at household level by these poverty lines, which can also be used to adjust for differences in household size and demographic composition. Such measures

The findings, interpretations and conclusions of this paper are those of the author and should not be attributed to the World Bank, its Executive Directors, or the countries they represent.

have become important tools for assessing progress in development and for guiding policy-making.

What are the conceptual foundations of this practice? On reflection, it can be seen that two axioms are crucial, and neither is uncontroversial. The first is the *subgroup additivity axiom*, meaning that aggregate poverty is the sum of all individual levels of poverty in the population. This has long been considered a desirable feature of a poverty measure. It implies that if poverty increases in any subgroup of the population, and does not change for any other group, then aggregate poverty must increase; this is the "subgroup monotonicity axiom" of Foster and Shorrocks (1991). The practice of poverty measurement has largely been confined to additive measures.[1]

But additivity is not universally accepted. Foster and Sen (1997) argue in favor of non-additive functional forms as a means of bringing relativist considerations into poverty measurement; an example is the Sen (1976) measure, based on weights that reflect rank order in the income distribution. Even such non-additive measures, however, need not reflect poor peoples' perceptions of relative deprivation. A simple example will suffice to see why. Consider a society divided into "rich" and "poor", with incomes y^r and y^p, and a fixed poverty line $z \in (y^p, y^r)$. Suppose that poor people experience relative deprivation in that higher y^r makes them worse off at given y^p. Such an increase in y^r will leave measured poverty unchanged, whether one uses the (non-additive) Sen index or any of the many additive measures.

The second axiom has received less attention in the poverty measurement literature, but is arguably more contentious. This says that moving a person between groups, with no absolute loss in her own real consumption, cannot increase aggregate poverty. I shall call this the *subgroup anonymity axiom*. In combination with additivity, this implies that we should use poverty lines that have a constant real value across subgroups.[2]

Anonymity rules out the possibility that a person's poverty depends not just on her own consumption, but is also directly affected by the consumptions of others in some reference group. In other words, it rules out the idea of a "relative poverty line", which is an increasing function of the levels of mean consumption (or income) of the region or country.[3] Subgroup anonymity is thus a crucial assumption justifying current practices in setting poverty lines.

[1] Examples include the widely used Foster–Greer–Thorbecke (1984) class of measures. Atkinson (1987) reviews other measures belonging to the broad class of additive measures.

[2] To see why, let aggregate poverty be $P = \sum p(y_i, z_i)$, where y_i is the real income of person i, and z_i is the (real) poverty line of the group to which i belongs; the function p is strictly decreasing in y and increasing in z. Subgroup anonymity entails that P is unchanged when the group assignment changes; without any change in the y's, the poverty line for person k is simply replaced by that of the new group, $j \neq k$. Given the monotonicity of p in z, it is evident that the only way this is possible is that $z_i = z$ for all i.

[3] This is clearly the most important way that relativist considerations enter poverty measurement, but it is not the only way; for an overview of the concepts found in the literature see Foster (1998).

This chapter critically explores the evidence and arguments for the anonymity axiom. The following section reviews the conceptual foundations of poverty measurement and the sources of interdependence, including the idea of "relative deprivation" (RD), but also recognizes that there are both positive and negative welfare effects for poor people of belonging to a better-off group. Section III asks when RD will be the dominant source of interdependence in a simple economic model combining informal risk-sharing with the idea of a "positional good". Section IV turns to the problems of testing for RD, while section V presents some micro-evidence on the issue for one of the poorest countries, Malawi. Section VI offers some overall conclusions.

II. Conceptual Foundations for Relativism

Real-income comparisons have long been anchored to some underlying absolute space. Economists have traditionally seen "utility" or "welfare" (in most uses they are the same thing) as the relevant absolute space. For example, a "true cost-of-living index" is defined as the monetary cost in a specific setting (data or place) of a fixed-reference utility level relative to its cost at some reference setting (see, for example, Deaton and Muellbauer 1980). A monetary poverty line can be interpreted as the minimum cost of not being deemed absolutely poor in the utility space (Blackorby and Donaldson 1987).

There is scope for debate about what the absolute space should be. Sen has argued that "capabilities" rather than utility or commodities should be seen as absolute; in the context of poverty measurement, this means that "an absolute approach in the space of capabilities translates into a relative approach in the space of commodities" (Sen 1983: 168).

These two views on the relevant absolute space are not inconsistent. Indeed, one can reconcile them by assuming that utility is an interpersonally stable function of capabilities; absolute minima in the latter space can then be transformed into a common utility poverty line (Ravallion 2006). On a priori grounds it would seem far easier to accept that there is a stable function common to all people relating welfare to capabilities than it is to accept that there is such a function defined solely on the commodities consumed. As Sen and others have argued persuasively, the utility value of a given set of commodities must be highly dependent on individual circumstances—a source of heterogeneity that creates much trouble for mainstream approaches to welfare measurement in economics, as discussed further below.

An absolute poverty line in terms of welfare or capabilities does not require that the income poverty line is invariant to context, such as the region or country a person lives in. Indeed, relative poverty lines that rise with mean income are implied whenever levels of welfare (or capabilities) depend on relative consumption. This is consistent with the large body of work which has argued that *relative* economic position is the carrier of welfare, not absolute income or consumption. This is often called the theory of relative deprivation (RD), following Runciman (1966).[4] The importance of RD has long been debated in economics, although early discussions had little or no empirical evidence to draw upon.[5] In more recent times, we have seen mounting evidence of RD effects from a variety of sources, though almost solely for developed countries.[6]

The issue of how much RD matters to poor people is of the utmost importance to policy discussions about how to fight poverty. If welfare depends on both one's own consumption *and* consumption relative to the mean of one's country (say), then a welfare-consistent poverty line will be a relative line, rising with mean consumption. For example, poverty lines in Western Europe have been set at a constant proportion of average income (strictly the median).[7] Relative-deprivation effects in poor countries as strong as those claimed for rich ones would cast serious doubt on the justification for many current development policies, notably the emphasis currently placed on promoting economic growth in poor countries. Negative externalities in consumption from RD would also suggest that poor people face inefficiently *high* incentives to escape poverty, because they do not take account of the negative spillover effects of their income gains on social comparators. On this view, promoting poverty reduction would entail welfare efficiency costs—pointing to a potentially important trade-off for development policy.

However, while RD postulates a negative external effect on the welfare of the poor from an economic gain to the relevant reference group, other theories and evidence point instead to *positive* external effects. The uninsured risks facing poor people, and the scope for falling into permanent destitution, are known to foster various arrangements for mutual support and risk-sharing.[8] Local communities have been

---

[4] There is a large literature; other contributions include Easterlin (1974, 1995); Townsend (1979), van de Stadt *et al.* (1985); Frank (1997); Oswald (1997); Solnick and Hemenway (1998); Walker and Smith (2001); and Alpizar *et al.* (2005).

[5] See, for example, Becker's (1974) discussion of the differing views of Adam Smith and Thorstein Veblen concerning (in effect) the welfare relevance of RD.

[6] Easterlin (1974) used RD to explain why the proportion of people who think they are happy has not changed much over time in the US, despite economic growth. Also see Frank (1997); Oswald (1997); and Blanchflower and Oswald (2004).

[7] This has been a common practice in Western Europe. Although the US government has traditionally used absolute poverty lines, there have been proposals to introduce relative poverty lines; see Citro and Michael (1995) and Betson *et al.* (2000).

[8] There is a large literature, including Ravallion and Dearden (1988); Murgai *et al.* (2002); Ligon *et al.* (2002); Fafchamps and Lund (2003); Maitra and Ray (2003); and Cox *et al.* (2004).

seen to play an important role in these and other sources of positive external effects, such as through employment and local public goods.[9]

The pace of urbanization in a developing country could also be expected to play an important role in the balance of positive and negative external effects. It can be conjectured that community-based risk-sharing and collective action erodes with urbanization; the repeated interactions amongst essentially the same group of people that sustain informal risk-sharing arrangements are clearly more common in village-based societies than in urban areas with more mobile populations.[10] Perceptions of RD, on the other hand, may well be stronger in urban areas.

If the positive externalities are the dominant social effect, with RD playing at best a secondary role, then welfare-consistent relative-poverty measurement will take a radically different form to (say) the standard methods found in the developed-country literature: the income poverty line would *fall* as the mean income of the reference group rises.

To address this issue, and bring relativist considerations into poverty measurement in a scientifically credible way, one first needs to say how "welfare" is to be measured. The tradition in economics has been to try to infer welfare from demand behavior. This approach has met with some severe identification problems, which render it impossible to infer utility from observed consumer demand behavior amongst heterogeneous households without some rather strong assumptions; see, for example, Pollak (1991) and Browning (1993). Even in high-quality surveys (in which an income aggregate is built up from many detailed questions), current incomes are unlikely to reflect very well either past or expected future incomes, both of which are likely to matter to current welfare. Expenditure on current consumption may do a better job in this respect, but will still be an imperfect welfare indicator given that inter-temporal markets do not work perfectly. There are also uncertainties about how best to normalize for heterogeneity in consumption needs, such as heterogeneity stemming from demographic differences between households.

In this light, Sen's advocacy of a capabilities foundation for poverty measurement can be seen as a means of addressing the identification problem, by broadening the information base for assessing welfare. One strand of the poverty measurement literature has used approaches that anchor poverty lines in the income space to attainments of certain basic functionings, notably being sufficiently well nourished to maintain good health and normative activity levels.[11] Here too the measurement problems are far from trivial, such as gauging nutritional attainments and setting

[9] For an interesting perspective on the role of communities see Bowles and Gintis (2002); in a development context, see Mansuri and Rao (2004). Jalan and Ravallion (2002) find evidence of positive externalities for poor rural households living in areas with better-off neighbors (in south-west China).

[10] For supportive evidence see Ravallion and Dearden (1988) (using data for Java).

[11] A critical review of these approaches can be found in Ravallion (1994).

normative activity levels. There is some evidence that, in practice, these methods generate poverty lines with similar properties to relative poverty lines, in which the poverty line is roughly proportional to the mean income of the area of residence (Ravallion and Bidani 1994).

However, there is a risk of anchoring poverty lines to a partial subset of the capabilities that matter to welfare. Nutritional requirements are an example. The high income elasticity that is found for poverty lines anchored to attaining nutritional requirements *alone* can arise from factors that one might well deem to be irrelevant to welfare. For example, tastes often shift to more expensive sources of food energy as real incomes rise with urbanization; shifts in relative prices can also play an important role in this change in consumer behavior as economies develop. The resulting poverty comparisons can then be welfare-inconsistent (Ravallion 1994, 1998).

A potentially important source of information for identifying a more comprehensive welfare metric for anchoring poverty lines is subjective assessments of well-being. In one method, survey respondents state their perceived minimum income for attaining certain subjective-qualitative levels of living (van Praag 1968; Danziger *et al.* 1984; Kapteyn *et al.* 1988). The "consumption adequacy" question of Pradhan and Ravallion (2000) is an alternative approach, with advantages when "income" is not well defined. More general "subjective well-being" questions have also been used; probably the most common example is the satisfaction with life (SWL) question.[12]

The role of such subjective welfare data is not to decide who is better off, but to identify the parameters of an objective welfare metric. SWL is assumed to depend on true objective welfare *plus* other, extraneous factors such as personality traits, "mood effects" and so on. Econometric methods are then used to extract the signal on how objective welfare varies with relevant covariates (see, for example, Kapteyn 1994 and Ravallion and Lokshin 2002).

A body of research along these lines has suggested that there are RD effects on welfare. Past econometric tests have regressed self-rated welfare (satisfaction with life or happiness) on both own income and an estimate of comparison-group income, which is typically the mean income of people living in the same area or working in the same industry or with similar characteristics (age, education, occupation).[13]

Such studies have suggested that welfare-consistent poverty lines need to have a high income elasticity in developed countries. In a recent example, Luttmer (2005) regressed self-assessed happiness in the US on log income and log mean

---

[12] A common form is: "Overall, how satisfied (content, happy) are you with your life? Are you (i) very unsatisfied; (ii) unsatisfied; (iii) neither unsatisfied nor satisfied; (iv) satisfied; (v) very satisfied?"

[13] Examples include Stadt *et al.* (1985); Clark and Oswald (1996); Pradhan and Ravallion (2000); McBride (2001); Ravallion and Lokshin (2002); Blanchflower and Oswald (2004); Kingdon and Knight (2004); Senik (2004); Ferrer-i-Carbonell (2005); and Luttmer (2005).

"neighbors" income, and found that the two coefficients add up to roughly zero, implying that an equal proportionate increase in all incomes (leaving relative inequality unchanged) would have no impact on average happiness. This suggests a welfarist justification for setting the poverty line at a constant proportion of mean income. An equi-proportional increase in all incomes would then leave most poverty measures unchanged. Other studies for developed countries have found income elasticities of the poverty line lower than that suggested by Luttmer's results. Kilpatrick (1973) found that subjective poverty lines over time in the US have an elasticity of about 0.6 to mean income. Hagenaars and van Praag (1985) found an elasticity of about 0.5, using data for eight European countries. But all these studies suggest that the elasticity is appreciably greater than zero.

The use of subjective questions in welfare assessment has been controversial in economics. Sen has criticized the use of subjective assessments of capabilities, notably health; see, for example, Sen (1998). A number of studies have emphasized the potential for reporting biases in self-assessed health.[14] Though less well researched, similar problems arise in self-assessments of overall welfare. Under certain conditions, it is possible to extract a more reliable signal on welfare effects from such data using multiple observations over time for the same person to purge the data of latent idiosyncratic personality traits (Ravallion and Lokshin 2001). Subjective data help solve some of the fundamental identification problems in measuring welfare, but they bring their own problems as well.

III. An Encompassing Theoretical Model

It is assumed that individual utility depends on both own income and the mean income of a reference group of (say) "neighbors". (In the most general formulation utility depends on the complete vector of incomes.) Relative deprivation theories essentially say that utility increases in own income but decreases in the mean of the reference group. However, other sources of economic interdependence suggest that there may be countervailing and strong *positive* forces on welfare stemming from more affluent neighbors. This section begins with a reasonably general "reduced form" model of a relative poverty line, and then outlines a simple theoretical "structural form" model in which both the positive and negative forces co-exist. This allows us to explore the conditions under which RD emerges as the dominant concern.

---

[14] See, for example, Butler *et al.* (1987); Groot (2000); and Lokshin and Ravallion (forthcoming).

III.1 A General Formulation of a Utility-Consistent Relative Poverty Line

To capture the idea of RD in a simple way, we can postulate a standard (cardinal and interpersonally comparable) utility function for a person with income y and other welfare-relevant characteristics x, with the difference that the function also varies with relative income, $r = y/m$, where m is mean income in an appropriate reference population, such as the fellow-citizens of the country in which the person lives.[15] The utility function is

$$u = v(y, r, x). \tag{1}$$

This is smoothly increasing in y and r. The fixed poverty line in utility space is

$$z_u = v(z, z/m, x), \tag{2}$$

where z is the poverty line in income space. Equation (2) defines implicitly the function

$$z = z(m, x, z_u). \tag{3}$$

This shows how the poverty line for "type x" people varies with the m, to keep utility constant. Letting η denote the elasticity of the monetary poverty line with respect to the mean, we find that:

$$\eta \equiv \frac{\partial \ln z}{\partial \ln m} = \frac{1}{1 + mMRS}, \tag{4}$$

where MRS is the marginal rate of substitution between y and r (i.e. $MRS = (\partial v/\partial y)/(\partial v/\partial r)$). The value of η will be somewhere between 0 and 1. This prediction is confirmed by a number of empirical studies of both objective and subjective poverty lines.[16]

Thus we can provide a theoretical rationale for the notion of a poverty line that is absolute in the welfare space, but relative in the income space, as discussed in section II. But where does the direct interdependence embodied in (1) come from? And why is it necessarily a *negative* external effect (whereby having a better-off reference group lowers welfare)? And where is the evidence that it exists? The rest of this essay will take up these issues.

[15] If one defines m as average expenditure on certain "basic goods" then the following argument in the text will generate the type of poverty line proposed by Citro and Michael (1995), though it need not have an elasticity of 1 to m, as assumed by Citro and Michael. But it is unclear why perceptions of RD should exclude certain goods, and particularly "non-basic" goods; this assumption would seem hard to defend.

[16] Ravallion (1998) provides evidence consistent with this property based on cross-country comparisons of how poverty lines used in practice vary with mean consumption. The analyses of subjective poverty lines for the US by Kilpatrick (1973) and for European countries by Hagenaars and van Praag (1985) are also consistent with this prediction.

III.2 An Expository Structural Model of the Sources of Interdependence

The above formulation is too general to provide any insights into the competing (positive and negative) sources of interdependence, and it is only then that we can try to understand why one might find an interaction effect between concerns about RD and one's own level of living. However, it must be acknowledged that there are many possible sources of interdependence, particularly in a developing-country context. The following model pits two stylized sources against each other: interdependence arising from the existence of *positional goods* and interdependence arising from *informal risk-sharing arrangements*.

I will assume that an informal risk-sharing arrangement exists amongst a set of self-interested individuals and I consider two homogeneous groups, one of which draws income y while the other, which we can think of as the "neighbors", gets y^n. The risk-sharing arrangement is in place prior to the realization of an uncertain process that assigns people to these groups at each date. The incomes are random variables, reflecting the risks faced in a (largely rural) developing economy.

Let utility depend on the quantities consumed of two commodities, X_1 and X_2 (to simplify the notation I treat individuals as homogeneous in other respects). Utility from X_1 depends on one's own consumption, but for X_2 it depends on consumption relative to the other group, making it a "positional good". One can think of X_1 as a good that is consumed in private while the consumption of X_2 is public knowledge within the community and so gives status in the specific social context, leading to consumption rivalries.

Utility is $u(X_1, X_2 - X_2^n)$ when neighbors consume X_2^n of the positional good.[17] Utility is strictly increasing and quasi-concave and the budget constraint is

$$X_1 + pX_2 = y + \tau(y, y^n) = Y, \qquad (5)$$

where $\tau(y, y^n)$ is the monetary value of the support (in cash or kind) received by a person with pre-transfer income y in $[y^{min}, y^{max}]$ when the neighbors have the pre-transfer income y^n. (I use lower-case y to denote pre-transfer income and upper-case Y for post-transfer income, and similarly for y^n and Y^n.) I assume that $\tau(y, y^n) > 0$ if $y < y^n$ and $\tau(y, y^n) + \tau(y^n, y) = 0$.

The function τ is decided prior to knowing the actual state-specific incomes. The folk theorem can be used to motivate the risk-sharing arrangement as the outcome of a repeated non-cooperative game in which defectors are penalized by being excluded from the game for ever after. Full risk-sharing (income pooling) requires that $\tau(y, y^n) = y^n - y$, so that everyone ends up with y^n.[18] However, to be feasible,

---

[17] Notice that I am assuming that it is the difference $X_2 - X_2^n$ that matters, not the ratio X_2/X_2^n. This is not essential, though it simplifies the analytics.

[18] This property can be relaxed to allow post-transfer income inequality with full risk-sharing by introducing a risk-free idiosyncratic income component.

the transfers must satisfy the constraint that the gain from continued participation in the risk-sharing arrangement is no less than the gain from defection. When full-risk sharing is not attainable, the equilibrium $\tau(y, y^n)$ is the maximum amount that can be taken from the person with higher realized income without inducing defection, given the cost of that defection (Coate and Ravallion 1993).[19]

There are other possible interpretations of $\tau(y, y^n)$. The positive externality of a higher y^n might arise instead from financing arrangements for a local public good, the quantity of which is subsumed in the direct utility function u. Then $\tau(y, y^n)$ (<0) can be thought of as the charge levied on those who draw the income y in a community with mean income y^n.

The implied demand functions are $X_i[y + \tau(y, y^n), X_2^n, p]$ ($i = 1, 2$) and the corresponding demand functions for the neighbors are $X_i[y^n - \tau(y, y^n), X_2, p]$. I assume that these functions are non-decreasing in incomes, implying marginal propensities to spend that are non-negative and bounded above by unity for both goods and both groups. The indirect utility function is:

$$v(y, y^n) \equiv \tilde{v}[y + \tau(y, y^n), X_2^n, p] = \max[u(X_1, X_2 - X_2^n) | X_1 + pX_2$$
$$= y + \tau(y, y^n)]. \tag{6}$$

(The corresponding utility function for the neighbors is $v(y^n, y)$.) It can be shown that:[20]

$$sign\frac{\partial v}{\partial y^n} = sign\left[\frac{\partial \tau}{\partial y^n} - p\frac{\partial X_2^n}{\partial Y^n}\left(1 + p\frac{\partial X_2^n}{\partial Y^n}\right)^{-1}\right]. \tag{7}$$

This captures the two opposing effects of an increase in neighbor's income: the gain from higher transfer receipts ($\partial \tau/\partial y^n > 0$) versus enhanced relative deprivation ($\partial X_2^n/\partial Y^n > 0$).

Three special cases regarding the range of possible outcomes are instructive.

Case 1: Full risk-sharing. It is plain from (7) that the positive effect will always dominate the RD effect under full risk-sharing. Then $\partial v/\partial y^n > 0$, given that $\partial \tau/\partial y^n = 1$ and $p\partial X_2^n/\partial Y^n \geq 0$ ($p\partial X_2^n/\partial Y^n > -1$ is all that is strictly required). With full risk-sharing, RD cannot be the dominant social effect in this model at any income level.

---

[19] Coate and Ravallion derive $\tau(y, y^n)$ as the solution to a repeated non-cooperative game in which each player faces an independent and uncertain income stream with (y, y^n) as the possible draws. They characterize the solution for the case in which utility depends on own income, and compare this to the optimal insurance scheme. Extending their analysis to the present situation of externalities is not difficult; the simplest approach would assume that utility is separable between own income and neighbor's income.

[20] This result is proved by applying the envelope theorem to (6), then using the first-order condition for X_2, and then solving further using the income derivative of the demand function for X_2^n.

Case 2: Partial risk-sharing with small transfers. With partial risk-sharing, the equilibrium transfer is the maximum that can be sustained without inducing the donor's defection, i.e. $\tau(y, y^n)$ is defined implicitly by equating the donor's benefit from defection with the utility cost of defecting, c:

$$v(y^n, y) - v[y^n - \tau(y, y^n), y] = c \text{ (for } y^n > y).^{21} \tag{8}$$

We can treat c as fixed, implying that

$$\frac{\partial \tau}{\partial y^n} = 1 - \frac{\partial v(y^n, y)/\partial y^n}{\partial v(y^n - \tau, y)/\partial y^n}. \tag{9}$$

It is clear from (9) that for small transfers, the maximum possible τ without inducing defection is unresponsive to changes in y^n. Setting $\partial \tau/\partial y^n = 0$ in (7), it is evident that when efficient risk-sharing is not feasible and transfers are small, RD will dominate ($\partial v/\partial y^n < 0$).

Between these extreme cases, stronger assumptions are needed to determine the direction of the welfare effect with large transfers that fall short of full risk-sharing. Nor can it be presumed that the external effect will have the same sign whatever the level of own income. This is illustrated by the following case.

Case 3: Partial risk sharing, non-negligible transfers and an interaction effect. In this case, the positive externality dominates for the poor, but this shifts at sufficiently high incomes, when RD becomes the dominant social effect. To see how this can happen, notice first that (from equation 7) there are two ways that differences in own income y could affect the balance between the two opposing external effects. The first is through an interaction effect between own income and neighbors' income in the transfer function, and the second is through any own-income effect on neighbors' marginal propensity to consume the positional good. Let us close off the first effect by assuming that the utility function is separable between y and y^n, so that the marginal propensity to transfer, $1 > \partial \tau/\partial y^n > 0$, does not depend on y. The first term on the RHS of (7) is thus a constant. Focusing on the second term in (7), Case 3 assumes that the marginal propensity to consume the positional good is very low at low incomes. The idea here is that when both incomes are very low, social rivalries are likely to be dominated by the attainment of basic needs for survival.[22] So one can set $p\partial X_2^n/\partial Y^n$ sufficiently close to zero at y^{min} such that $\partial v/\partial y^n > 0$. At higher incomes, the social aspect of the positional good starts to influence budget allocations; in particular, I assume that the neighbor's marginal propensity to spend on the positional good rises to near unity at y^{max} (this boundary condition can be relaxed without changing the result). Then $\partial v/\partial y^n < 0$

[21]   Note that $v(y^n, y)$ is the neighbor's utility and recall that $\tau(y, y^n) + \tau(y^n, y) = 0$.
[22]   One does not need a kink in the demand functions, which can still be continuous with continuous first derivatives. All one requires is that the income gradient is sufficiently low at low incomes.

at $y = y^{\max}$. By continuity there will be a unique shift point in the income space, below which $\partial v / \partial y^n > 0$ and above which $\partial v / \partial y^n < 0$.

We will see later that some new micro-evidence on RD in a poor country points to the existence of just such an interaction effect between "own income" and the marginal welfare impact of having better-off friends and neighbors.

IV. Pitfalls in Testing for Relative Deprivation

As was noted in section II, the literature has reported evidence of RD effects in subjective welfare data. However, there are reasons to suspect that past tests are biased toward finding signs of RD when it is not in fact present.

One source of bias is when the mean income of neighbors—strictly it is typically the mean income of survey respondents in a geographic area that includes the respondent—picks up a spatial autocorrelation in income measurement errors. Such spurious social effects would appear to be a common problem in past tests for relative deprivation. Ravallion and Lokshin (2007) attempt to solve the problem by using a better measure of own economic welfare than income, where "better" is judged from the point of view of predicting subjectively assessed welfare. The obvious place to look is the respondent's own perception of economic welfare, which will automatically reflect geographic factors with direct bearing on economic well-being.

A less familiar source of spurious RD effects is that different people are likely to attach different meanings to the categories used in satisfaction or happiness questions.[23] People answer such questions relative to their personal *frame of reference* (FOR), which depends on their own knowledge and experience. And this is likely to be correlated with characteristics of where they live, including mean income. It would seem reasonable to assume that people living in poor areas tend to have more limited knowledge and experience of the full range of levels of living found in the society as a whole. Someone living in a poor village who has gone no further than the county town will undoubtedly rate her economic welfare higher than someone with the same real income living in a city, who sees far greater affluence around her.

In these circumstances, heterogeneity in the frame of reference will translate into corresponding differences in perceived welfare. At given objective circumstances,

---

[23] This is an instance of what is called differential item functioning (DIF) in the literature on educational testing, where DIF exists if students with equal latent ability have different probabilities of giving a correct answer; for an overview of the history and methods of addressing DIF see Angoff (1993).

the person living in the poor area will have higher perceived welfare because she simply does not know that many people live better than she does. Thus the regressions used in this literature would tend to reveal a negative coefficient on neighbors' mean income, even if there is no direct social comparison effect on utility, as postulated by RD theory. The negative regression coefficient reflects the difference in knowledge, which creates a systematic difference in the scale used to assess well-being.

There is a solution to this problem. Ravallion and Lokshin (2007) show that one can reduce the bias by using the respondent's self-assessed economic welfare instead of the objective value, y, for explaining SWL, under the assumption that all subjective measures for a given respondent are subject to the same FOR effect. This is plausible since they are constrained by the same knowledge and experience.

The measurement of comparison-group welfare also poses a problem. In the standard approach in the literature, the researcher must make an a priori judgement about the relevant comparison group. Yet this can vary greatly from person to person. It has been argued that "comparisons are most salient if individuals perceive the reference person or group as in some way similar to themselves" (Kahneman and Varey 1991: 140). But that is based on the individual's own judgement, given idiosyncratic informational and social factors that a researcher would have a very hard time observing in any systematic way. Neither psychological nor economic theories of RD offer much insight into who constitutes the relevant comparison group. The researcher must make some potentially strong identifying assumptions.

A further concern is that differences in the objective economic welfare of one's neighbors can hardly be relevant to RD, or the security that may come from knowing that friends and neighbors are capable of coming to one's aid, *unless* those differences are known and perceived as relevant by the person in question. In accounting for differences in overall well-being, it can be argued that the subjective assessment is likely to matter more than the objective one, such as mean income in the area of residence. The objective measure can be thought of as a proxy (possibly poorly measured) for the true perception of the comparison group's welfare. Assuming classical measurement errors, attenuation biases can be expected, although the errors could also be correlated with the dependent variable in this case, clouding the direction of bias.

These observations motivated Ravallion and Lokshin (2007) to take a different approach that avoids the need to prejudge the comparison group and the precise welfare metric. They used data on the respondent's assessments of the economic welfare of the family's "friends" and "neighbors". This has the advantage that it is tailor-made to the perceptions of the respondent.

This assumes that people report accurately to the interviewer on their perceptions of both their own welfare and that of their friends and neighbors. There may also be systematic (non-random) reporting biases. If RD is a source of disutility then it may well influence the answers given to interviewers. Could this undermine such tests? It is instructive to consider a simple, yet seemingly plausible, model of that bias. Suppose that utility depends on own economic welfare and comparison-group welfare and that RD matters, but to "save face" the respondent hides the true RD from the interviewer. More precisely, assume that the responses are biased in amounts that are directly proportional to the difference between (true) own welfare and that of the comparison group; if the respondent feels poorer than her comparison group then she overstates her own economic welfare and/or understates that of her comparison group. The true parameters are then positively weighted linear combinations of the estimated parameters based on the reported data (Ravallion and Lokshin 2007). Even though one does not know the bias parameters, this model implies that if one finds that both own welfare and comparison-group welfare have positive coefficients then this must also be the case for the true parameters; reporting biases cannot be hiding a true RD effect when no such effect is observed empirically.

V. SOME FINDINGS FROM MALAWI

Malawi is one of the world's poorest countries. Almost 90% of the population live in rural areas, and are mostly smallholders, depending heavily on rain-fed, and risk-prone, agriculture. In the late 1990s, two-thirds of the population lived below the country's poverty line (National Economic Council 2000). Income inequality is high, with a Gini index around 0.50 (World Bank 2005b). As in any risk-prone and poor rural economy, there are various forms of informal insurance and social assistance in rural Malawi.

Ravallion and Lokshin (2007) tested for RD effects on subjective welfare in Malawi using the 2004 round of the Malawi Integrated Household Survey (MIHS), covering a sample of over 11,000 households. The MIHS collects data on consumption of a wide range of food and non-food items, as well as detailed information about the socio-demographic composition of the household, the labor status of the household members, health, educational achievements, various sources of household income including income in kind, and individual wages. A section of the questionnaire asks the opinion of the household head about the household's standard of living, including questions about satisfaction with life.

The measure of overall welfare is provided by answers to the SWL question (see 11. 12 above). The majority of the sample were not satisfied with their lives; 62.5% answered either (i) or (ii) (24.4% gave (i)). Slightly less than one quarter were satisfied; 18.3% gave (iv) as their answer and 5.6% gave (v). (The remainder, 13.6%, reported that they were neither unsatisfied nor satisfied.) These numbers indicate a much lower level of satisfaction with life than found in Western Europe, where 80–90% of the population report that they are satisfied with their lives when asked the same question in surveys (Delhey 2004).

While SWL is the natural choice for identifying a measure of utility, how should we measure economic welfare, as one argument of utility? Ravallion and Lokshin used alternative objective and subjective measures. The most widely used objective measure of economic welfare in developing countries is *consumption expenditure per person (C)*, given by total household expenditure, including spending on food (purchased and home-produced and food received as gifts), non-food items, estimated flow of services from consumer durables, and actual or self-estimated rental cost of housing.[24] Although this is a comprehensive consumption aggregate, there are well-known concerns about how well it reflects welfare, even when this is thought of as the narrower concept of "economic welfare".[25] In that light, one cannot rule out the possibility that the results obtained using consumption as the measure of economic welfare will be biased by correlations between the perceived economic welfare of friends and neighbors and the errors in measuring own welfare using consumption.

For these reasons, Ravallion and Lokshin also used self-assessed economic welfare, based on the *own-economic welfare* (OEW) question, in which respondents are asked: "Imagine six steps, where on the bottom, the first step, stand the poorest people, and on the highest step, the sixth, stand the rich [show a picture of the steps]. On which step are you today?"

One also needs measures of the economic welfare of relevant groups for social comparison or risk-sharing. People in geographic proximity to the respondent are an obvious source of comparators, co-insurers and help in other ways, such as finding employment. Following past practice in the literature, we can use the geographic structure of the sample design to estimate mean consumption of neighbors by mean consumption of all sampled households in the respondent's enumeration area, excluding the respondent.

As noted above, it is not clear that this provides a good measure of the economic welfare of neighbors. However, there is an additional source of information for studying social effects (which appears to have been largely ignored in the literature), namely to ask survey respondents about their comparison groups. Ravallion and Lokshin used questions asking people how they perceive the economic welfare of the two most obvious comparison groups: friends and neighbors. (Workplace comparisons are another possibility, but these are of limited relevance in a poor, largely rural, country such as Malawi.) It is left to the respondent to judge who

---

[24] For details on how the consumption aggregate was formed see World Bank (2005a).
[25] On the identification problem in measures based on consumer demand, see Pollak (1991). Slesnick (1998) surveys alternative empirical approaches. Subjective welfare measures have been seen as a promising route to avoiding the identification problems in deriving a metric of welfare from observed demand behavior; for overviews of this approach see van Praag (1991) and Kapteyn (1994).

their friends and neighbors are, and by what standard their economic status is to be judged. With regard to the respondent's friends, Ravallion and Lokshin use the *friends' economic welfare* (FEW) question: "Imagine six steps, where on the bottom, the first step, stand the poorest people, and on the highest step, the sixth, stand the rich [show a picture of the steps]. On which step are most of your friends today?" The same question is asked about *neighbors' economic welfare* (NEW). The unobserved measure of utility takes the form:

$$u_i = \alpha\mathrm{OEW}_i + \beta^F\,\mathrm{FEW}_i + \beta^N\mathrm{NEW}_i + \gamma^F\,\mathrm{OEW}_i\mathrm{FEW}_i$$

$$+ \gamma^N\mathrm{OEW}_i\mathrm{NEW}_i + \delta\mathrm{FEW}_i\mathrm{NEW}_i + \pi X_i + \epsilon_i. \tag{10}$$

The answers to the SWL question are then interpreted as ordinal responses from this latent continuous variable, and the model is estimated as an ordered probit (OP) (assuming that the error term in (10) is normally distributed).

The results of the tests using objectively assessed neighbors' consumption indicate a positive effect of neighbors' consumption for the bulk of the data. However, this effect declines as own consumption rises (a negative interaction effect), consistent with Case 3 in section II. Using the specification that gave the most precise estimates, the neighborhood consumption effect is positive for 79% of the data points. However, SWL increases with own consumption over the entire range of consumptions found in the data. Splitting the sample between rural and urban areas also reveals marked differences. The external effect of neighbors' consumption and its negative interaction effect with own consumption remain strong in rural areas, but they are only evident in urban areas when one includes geographic dummy variables. In that case one finds that the negative external effect dominates; indeed, the effect of neighbors' consumption is negative for the entire urban sample. By interpretation, RD is the weaker social effect in rural areas, but the dominant one in urban areas.

These results are broadly confirmed using the respondents' own assessments of the welfare of their friends and neighbors. For the (self-assessed) poor, the results are clearly inconsistent with the implications of relative deprivation theory. However, signs of a negative gradient with respect to neighbor's economic welfare emerge at the upper rungs of the own-welfare ladder. Amongst those who feel that they have poor neighbors, having well-off friends results in higher mean SWL. This gradient is more robust as one moves up the NEW ladder.

The estimates of equation (10) suggest that RD does emerge as a concern amongst middle-income and relatively well-off groups. To help interpret the implications for welfare-consistent poverty lines for Malawi, I shall extend the analysis of Ravallion and Lokshin (2005) by using their econometric estimates of (10) to derive the iso-welfare contours (indifference curves), as obtained by calculating the critical value of OEW needed to compensate for differences in FEW and NEW, while holding the expected value of utility constant. This can be interpreted as the utility-consistent

Table 20.1. Poverty lines for own-economic welfare in Malawi, holding utility constant

	Neighbors (NEW)				
	1 (poorest)	2	3	4	5
(a) At the boundary between "unsatisfied" and "neither unsatisfied nor satisfied" Friends (FEW)					
1 (poorest)	2.88	2.85	2.82	2.78	2.74
2	2.82	2.79	2.75	2.70	2.64
3	2.76	2.72	2.66	2.60	2.53
4	2.68	2.62	2.56	2.47	2.36
5	2.58	2.50	2.41	2.29	2.13
(b) At the boundary between "neither unsatisfied nor satisfied" and "satisfied" FEW					
1 (poorest)	4.01	4.05	4.11	4.17	4.24
2	4.06	4.12	4.18	4.26	4.35
3	4.13	4.20	4.27	4.37	4.48
4	4.21	4.29	4.39	4.51	4.67
5	4.31	4.42	4.55	4.72	4.93

Notes: The table gives the value OEW* needed to compensate for each (NEW, FEW) combination, holding the expected value of utility constant. Controls are set to mean points.
Source: Author's calculations.

poverty line in the space of economic welfare corresponding to a fixed-reference utility level (the poverty line in the space of utility). When RD is the dominant social effect, the utility-consistent poverty line will rise with comparison-group economic welfare. However, this shifts when the positive externality is dominant. Fixing the expected value of utility at u^*, one solves for:[26]

$$\mathrm{OEW}_i^* = \frac{u^* - \beta^F \mathrm{FEW}_i - \beta^N \mathrm{NEW}_i - \pi X_i}{\alpha + \gamma^F \mathrm{FEW}_i + \gamma^N \mathrm{NEW}_i}. \tag{11}$$

Table 20.1 provides the values of OEW* at mean points for X and for two reference utility levels (as defined by the middle two cut-off points from the ordered probits reported in Ravallion and Lokshin 2007). The proportion of the population reporting that they are below the lower of these two cut-off points (i.e. that they

[26] I set $\delta = 0$ in equation (11) consistently with the empirical results of Ravallion and Lokshin (2007). Note that OEW* is a continuous variable, unlike OEW.

are either "very unsatisfied" or "unsatisfied") corresponds closely to prevailing estimates of the poverty rate for Malawi.

Focusing first on panel (a) in Table 20.1, one finds that for u^* at the estimated cut-off point below which one is either "very unsatisfied" or "unsatisfied", the value of OEW* tends to fall as FEW rises (at given NEW) and similarly OEW* falls as NEW rises (at given FEW). This pattern reflects the positive utility gains from having better-off friends and neighbors. However, the pattern reverses when one shifts to the higher reference utility level (panel (b)), when the RD effect kicks in. Then the poverty lines in the space of perceived economic welfare start to look like relative poverty lines. However, note that in all cases in Table 20.1, the gradients in OEW* are small; to the nearest ladder rung, the poverty line is at OEW* = 3 for 80% of cases in panel (a) and is OEW* = 4 for 80% of cases in panel (b).

VI. CONCLUSIONS

A relative poverty line that rises with the mean income of a country or region makes sense as a money metric of welfare if poor people experience relative deprivation— a negative externality from living in a well-off place. Yet other theories in development economics point instead to positive external effects arising from institutions for risk-sharing, the provision of local public goods and local employment opportunities, or productivity-enhancing spillovers.

Taking risk-sharing as the source of positive externalities, I have identified conditions under which relative deprivation will dominate the gains from risk-sharing. If full risk-sharing is attainable then the positive effect of an increase in the community's mean income will always dominate relative deprivation. With partial risk-sharing (constrained by the need to avoid defection from the co-insurance group) the outcome is unclear. Under certain conditions, the positive external effect will tend to be the dominant factor for the poor, while relative deprivation will emerge at high incomes. The outcome is an empirical question.

In marked contrast to past empirical work for developed countries, the results discussed here for Malawi do not suggest that economic disparities relative to friends and neighbors are a welfare-relevant concern for most people, and certainly not for the poor. Neither objective nor subjective measures of economic welfare reveal any sign of relative deprivation effects for poor people. Indeed, most of the specifications tested indicate significant *positive* external effects for the bulk of the data, although these effects are largely confined to rural areas. However, the empirical results do indicate the existence of a negative interaction effect between friends' economic welfare and own-economic welfare in rural areas. Thus, relative deprivation does emerge as a concern amongst the relatively well off within this (poor) country.

The evidence presented here offers little support for the idea implied by relative deprivation theory of a poverty line that rises with the mean income of the comparison group. Indeed, the results suggest the opposite; for the bulk of the sampled households, the utility-consistent poverty line will actually fall as the comparison group income increases, although my quantitative estimates do not suggest much gradient. However, the evidence for Malawi is consistent with the idea that relative poverty will be more salient as the economy becomes more urbanized.

These results offer support on welfarist grounds for the emphasis given to absolute level of living in development policy discussions. However, the results also suggest that relative deprivation can be found even in poor but unequal countries, and that it is likely to become more important as such countries develop. It could well be that future measurement practices even in developing countries will need to be more relativist if they are to be consistent with perceptions of welfare on the ground.

References

ALPIZAR, F., CARLSSON, F., and JOHANSSON-STENMAN, O. (2005), "How Much Do We Care about Absolute versus Relative Income and Consumption?", *Journal of Economic Behavior and Organization*, 56: 405–21.

ANGOFF, W. H. (1993), "Perspectives on Differential Item Functioning Methodology", in P. Holland and H. Wainer (eds), *Differential Item Functioning* (Hillsdale, NJ: Lawrence Erlbaum Associates), 3–24.

ATKINSON, A. B. (1987), "On the Measurement of Poverty", *Econometrica*, 55: 749–64.

BECKER, G. S. (1974), "A Theory of Social Interactions", *Journal of Political Economy*, 82: 1063–93.

BETSON, D. M., CITRO, C. F., and MICHAEL, R. T. (2000), "Recent Developments for Poverty Measurement in US Official Statistics", *Journal of Official Statistics*, 16: 87–111.

BLACKORBY, C., and DONALDSON, D. (1987), "Welfare Ratios and Distributionally Sensitive Cost–Benefit Analysis", *Journal of Public Economics*, 34: 265–90.

BLANCHFLOWER, D., and OSWALD, A. (2004), "Well-Being Over Time in Britain and the USA", *Journal of Public Economics*, 88: 1359–86.

BOWLES, S., and GINTIS, H. (2002), "Social Capital and Community Governance", *Economic Journal*, 112(483): 419–36.

BROWNING, M. (1992), "Children and Household Economic Behavior", *Journal of Economic Literature*, 30: 1434–75.

BUTLER, J. S., BURKHAUSER, R., MITCHELL, J., and PINCUS, T. (1987), "Measurement Error in Self-Reported Health Variables", *Review of Economics and Statistics*, 69: 644–50.

CITRO, C. F., and MICHAEL, R. T. (1995), *Measuring Poverty: A New Approach* (Washington, DC: National Academy Press).

CLARK, A. E., and OSWALD, A. J. (1996), "Satisfaction and Comparison Income", *Journal of Public Economics*, 61: 359–81.

COATE, S., and RAVALLION, M. (1993), "Reciprocity without Commitment: Characterization and Performance of Informal Insurance Arrangements", *Journal of Development Economics*, 40: 1–24.

COX, D., HANSEN, B., and JIMENEZ, E. (2004), "How Responsive are Private Transfers to Income? Evidence from a Laissez-Faire Economy", *Journal of Public Economics*, 88: 2193–219.

DANZIGER, S., VAN DER GAAG, J., SMOLENSKY, E., and TAUSSIG, M. (1984), "The Direct Measurement of Welfare Levels: How Much Does It Take to Make Ends Meet?", *Review of Economics and Statistics*, 66: 500–5.

DEATON, A., and MUELLBAUER, J. (1980), *Economics and Consumer Behaviour* (Cambridge: Cambridge University Press).

DELHEY, I. (2004), *Life Satisfaction in an Enlarged Europe* (Dublin: European Foundation for the Improvement of Living and Working Conditions).

EASTERLIN, R. A. (1974), "Does Economic Growth Improve the Human Lot? Some Empirical Evidence", in P. A. David and M. W. Reder (eds), *Nations and Households in Economic Growth: Essays in Honor of Moses Abramovitz* (New York: Academic Press), 89–125.

—— (1995), "Will Raising the Incomes of All Increase the Happiness of All?", *Journal of Economic Behavior and Organization*, 27: 35–47.

FAFCHAMPS, M., and LUND, S. (2003), Risk-Sharing Networks in Rural Philippines. *Journal of Development Economics*, 71: 261–87.

FERRER-I-CARBONELL, A. (2005), "Income and Well-Being: An Empirical Analysis of the Comparison Income Effect", *Journal of Public Economics*, 89: 997–1019.

FOSTER, J. (1998), "Absolute versus Relative Poverty", *American Economic Review: Papers and Proceedings*, 88: 335–41.

—— GREER, J., and THORBECKE, E. (1984), "A Class of Decomposable Poverty Measures", *Econometrica*, 52: 761–6.

—— and SEN, A. (1997), "On Economic Inequality after a Quarter Century", in A. K. Sen (ed.), *On Economic Inequality* (Oxford: Clarendon Press), 107–219.

—— and SHORROCKS, T. (1991), "Subgroup-Consistent Poverty Indices", *Econometrica*, 59: 687–709.

FRANK, R. H. (1997), "The Frame of Reference as a Public Good", *Economic Journal*, 107(445): 1832–47.

GROOT, W. (2000), "Adaptation and Scale of Reference Bias in Self-Assessments of Quality of Life", *Journal of Health Economics*, 19: 403–20.

HAGENAARS, A., and VAN PRAAG, B. (1985), "A Synthesis of Poverty Line Definitions", *Review of Income and Wealth*, 31: 139–54.

JALAN, J., and RAVALLION, M. (2002), "Geographic Poverty Traps? A Micro Model of Consumption Growth in Rural China", *Journal of Applied Econometrics*, 17: 329–46.

KAHNEMAN, D., and VAREY, C. (1991), "Notes on the Psychology of Utility", in J. Elster and J. Roemer (eds), *Interpersonal Comparisons of Well-Being* (Cambridge: Cambridge University Press), 127–63.

KAPTEYN, A. (1994), "The Measurement of Household Cost Functions: Revealed Reference versus Subjective Measures", *Journal of Population Economics*, 7: 333–50.

—— KOOREMAN, P., and WILLEMSE, R. (1988), "Some Methodological Issues in the Implementation of Subjective Poverty Definitions", *Journal of Human Resources*, 23: 222–42.

KILPATRICK, R. (1973), "The Income Elasticity of the Poverty Line", *Review of Economics and Statistics*, 55: 327–32.

KINGDON, G., and KNIGHT, J. (2004), *Community, Comparisons and Subjective Well-Being in a Divided Society,* Working Paper 2004-21 (Oxford: Centre for the Study of African Economies, Oxford University).

LIGON, E., THOMAS, J., and WORRALL, T. (2002), "Informal Insurance Arrangements with Limited Commitment: Theory and Evidence from Village Economies", *Review of Economic Studies*, 69: 209–44.

LOKSHIN, M., and RAVALLION, M. (forthcoming), "Testing for An Economic Gradient in Health Status Using Subjective Data", *Health Economics.*

LUTTMER, E. F. P. (2005), "Neighbors as Negatives: Relative Earnings and Well-Being", *Quarterly Journal of Economics*, 120: 963–1002.

MAITRA, P., and RAY, R. (2003), "The Effect of Transfers on Household Expenditure Patterns and Poverty in South Africa", *Journal of Development Economics*, 71: 23–49.

MANSURI, G., and RAO, V. (2004), "Community-Based and-Driven Development", *World Bank Research Observer*, 19(1): 1–40.

MCBRIDE, M. (2001), "Relative Income Effects on Subjective Well-Being in the Cross-Section", *Journal of Economic Behavior and Organization*, 45: 251–78.

MURGAI, R., WINTERS, P., SADOULET, E., and DE JANVRY, A. (2002), "Localized and Incomplete Mutual Insurance", *Journal of Development Economics*, 67: 245–74.

National Economic Council (2000), *Profile of Poverty in Malawi, 1998: Poverty Analysis of the Malawi Integrated Household Survey* (Lilongwe: National Economic Council, Government of Malawi).

OSWALD, A. J. (1997), "Happiness and Economic Performance", *Economic Journal*, 107(445): 1815–31.

POLLAK, R. (1991), "Welfare Comparisons and Situation Comparisons", *Journal of Econometrics*, 50: 31–48.

PRADHAN, M., and RAVALLION, M. (2000), "Measuring Poverty Using Qualitative Perceptions of Consumption Adequacy", *Review of Economics and Statistics*, 82: 462–71.

RAVALLION, M. (1994), *Poverty Comparisons* (Chur, Switzerland: Harwood Academic Press).

—— (1998), *Poverty Lines in Theory and Practice,* Living Standards Measurement Study Paper 133 (Washington, DC: World Bank).

—— (forthcoming), "Poverty lines", in S. Durlauf and L. Blume (eds), *The New Palgrave Dictionary of Economics*, 2nd edn (London: Palgrave Macmillan).

—— and BIDANI, B. (1994), "How Robust is a Poverty Profile?", *World Bank Economic Review*, 8: 75–102.

—— and DEARDEN, L. (1988), "Social Security in A 'Moral Economy': An Empirical Analysis for Java", *Review of Economics and Statistics*, 70: 36–45.

—— and LOKSHIN, M. (2001), "Identifying Welfare Effects from Subjective Questions", *Economica*, 68(271): 335–57.

—— —— (2002), "Self-Assessed Economic Welfare in Russia", *European Economic Review*, 46(8): 1453–73.

—— —— (2007), *Who Cares About Relative Deprivation?*, Policy Research Working Paper 3782 (Washington, DC: World Bank Development Research Group).

RUNCIMAN, W. G. (1966), *Relative Deprivation and Social Justice* (London: Routledge and Kegan Paul).

SEN, A. K. (1976), "Poverty: an Ordinal Approach to Measurement", *Econometrica*, 44: 219–31.

—— (1983), "Poor, Relatively Speaking", *Oxford Economic Papers*, 35: 153–69.

SEN, A. K. (1985), *Commodities and Capabilities* (Amsterdam: North-Holland).

—— (1997), *On Economic Inequality* (Oxford: Clarendon Press).

—— (1998), "Mortality as an Indicator of Economic Success and Failure", *Economic Journal*, 108(446): 1–25.

SENIK, C. (2004), "When Information Dominates Comparison: Learning from Russian Subjective Panel Data", *Journal of Public Economics*, 88: 2099–123.

SLESNICK, D. T. (1998), "Empirical Approaches to Measuring Welfare", *Journal of Economic Literature*, 36: 2108–65.

SOLNICK, S., and HEMENWAY, D. (1998), "Is More Always Better? A Survey on Positional Concerns", *Journal of Economic Behavior and Organization*, 37: 373–83.

TOWNSEND, P. (1979), *Poverty in the United Kingdom* (Harmondsworth: Penguin Books).

VAN DE STADT, H., KAPTEYN, A., and VAN DE GEER, S. (1985), "The Relativity of Utility: Evidence from Panel Data", *Review of Economics and Statistics*, 67: 179–87.

VAN PRAAG, B. M. S. (1968), *Individual Welfare Functions and Consumer Behavior* (Amsterdam: North-Holland).

—— (1991), "Ordinal and Cardinal Utility: An Integration of the Two Dimensions of the Welfare Concept", *Journal of Econometrics*, 50: 69–89.

WALKER, I., and SMITH, H. (eds) (2001), *Relative Deprivation: Specification, Development and Integration* (Cambridge: Cambridge University Press).

WORLD BANK (2005a), *Note on Construction of Expenditure Aggregate and Poverty Lines for IHS2* (Washington, DC: World Bank Development Research Group).

—— (2005b), *World Development Report: Equity and Development* (New York: Oxford University Press).

CHAPTER 21

....

JUSTICE AS FAIRNESS AND THE CAPABILITY APPROACH

....

INGRID ROBEYNS

I. INTRODUCTION

....

THROUGHOUT his writings, Amartya Sen has acknowledged his intellectual debts
to John Rawls. Yet Sen is also known to be one of Rawls's major critics. Rawls's
theory of justice, which he calls "justice as fairness", and Sen's capability approach
are generally regarded as among the most important and influential rival theories
in contemporary political philosophy. Students and scholars of justice as fairness
and the capability approach are still debating the precise differences between and
merits of the theories.

My aim in this chapter is to assess the different arguments that have been formulated in the debate between Rawls and Sen, and to offer a reinterpretation of the

I would like to thank Eva Kittay Feder, Thomas Pogge, Mozaffar Qizilbash and Robert van der Veen
for comments on the first version of this chapter, and especially Elizabeth Anderson, Harry
Brighouse, Anthony Laden, Roland Pierik and Henry Richardson for very helpful comments and
criticism on the penultimate version. The first version was written while I was a visiting scholar at the
Philosophy Department of Columbia University, and was presented at the 2004 APSA meetings in
Chicago and the 2004 conference of the HDCA in Pavia. I am grateful to the audiences for their
comments. The financial support of the Netherlands Organization for Scientific Research (NWO) is
gratefully acknowledged.

debate. I will put aside Sen's (1970: 135–41) critique of Rawls's difference principle, and move straight to his criticism that social primary goods are too inflexible to be the metric of justice. Rawls has argued that this criticism implies that the capability approach endorses a comprehensive moral doctrine, and therefore cannot be a theory that yields unanimous support in a liberal democracy characterized by reasonable pluralism about such comprehensive doctrines. In addition, Rawls has criticized the capability approach for failing to provide a workable set of criteria of political justice that can be publicly verified. I will discuss these critiques, and argue that the more fundamental underlying disagreement is in the different *kinds* of theory that Rawls and Sen are pursuing.

The analysis of the debate between Rawls and Sen will lead me to the following suggestions. First, it is far from straightforward to compare justice as fairness and the capability approach. While both are profoundly concerned with human freedoms, equality and justice, Rawls and Sen are trying to answer different questions. Second, in order to see in what respect they truly differ, each theory needs to be further developed in opposite directions: the capability approach requires more theoretical elaboration and justification, while justice as fairness has to be developed to show how it would deal with questions of justice in non-ideal circumstances. Thirdly, rather than pitting both theories against each other as rivals, it is possible to understand the capability approach and justice as fairness as complementary and potentially converging theories. That, at least, is what I will try to argue in this chapter.

II. RAWLS'S JUSTICE AS FAIRNESS IN A NUTSHELL

Rawls's theory of justice is situated in the social contract tradition. Society is viewed as a fair system of cooperation between free and equal persons. Justice as fairness asks which political principles individuals would unanimously agree to as just principles to regulate the basic structure of a society, "its main political and social institutions and the way they hang together as one system of cooperation" (Rawls 2001: 8–9). Rawls's theory is therefore a theory of institutional or political justice (Rawls 1999: 76–7; 2001: 50). The decision about the principles of justice is made in the "original position", a hypothetical situation in which the so-called "veil of ignorance" deprives the parties of the information which Rawls holds to be morally irrelevant for deciding about the principles of justice. The parties have no knowledge about their place in society, nor do they have any information about which race, gender or class they would belong to, their conceptions of the good, or their natural abilities. As the parties in the original position have no information about the place in society, circumstances or life plans of the citizens which will live in this just society, the agreement they will reach in the original position regarding the principles of justice will be fair to everyone, as morally irrelevant information cannot influence the choice of those principles.

Rawls conceptualizes citizens as being moved by two higher-order interests: (1) to realize the two powers of moral personality, which are the capacity for a sense of right and justice, and the capacity to form and pursue a conception of the good, and (2) to pursue their determinate conceptions of the good. In his later work Rawls (1982, 1985, 2001) has stressed that justice as fairness does not rely on a metaphysical but on a political account of the person, that is, a characterization of those aspects of personhood that are relevant when deciding on the political principles of society.

The parties in the original position who decide on the principles of justice are assumed to possess certain cognitive abilities that allow them to take part in the decision. In the original position, the parties only decide on the principles of justice, and not on the concrete institutional design and policies that will give these principles content in the actual world. That is done in later stages, when the veil of ignorance is gradually lifted and more and more information becomes available to the parties. The representative parties will choose from a list of possible principles of justice only those principles that it is rational for them to choose. Rawls (2001: 42–3) argues that the parties will choose the following two principles:

1 Each person has the same indefeasible claim to a fully adequate scheme of equal basic liberties, which scheme is compatible with the same scheme of liberties for all (the principle of equal basic liberties).
2 Social and economic inequalities are to satisfy two conditions: first, they are to be attached to offices and positions open to all under conditions of fair equality of opportunity (the principle of fair equality of opportunity); and second, they are to be to the greatest benefit of the least advantaged members of society (the difference principle).

The basic liberties are listed as follows: "freedom of thought and liberty of conscience; political liberties (for example, the right to vote and to participate in politics) and freedom of association, as well as the rights and liberties specified by the liberty and integrity (physical and psychological) of the person; and finally, the rights and liberties covered by the rule of law" (2001: 44). The first principle has priority over the second principle; in addition, the principle of fair equality of opportunity has priority over the difference principle.

Applying the difference principle requires a notion of advantage. Rawls argues that since the parties in the original position do not know which notion of the good life the citizens will endorse, they choose, for general purposes, the so-called social primary goods (1999: 54). In the first version of *A Theory of Justice*, Rawls (1971: 92) defined the primary goods as "things which it is supposed a rational man wants whatever else he wants", and "which he would prefer more of rather than less". Later Rawls shifted this definition to relate them to the higher-order interests of citizens (1982: 164–7; 2001: 57), and defined primary goods as "various social conditions and all-purpose means that are generally necessary to enable citizens adequately to develop and fully exercise their two moral powers, and to pursue their determinate conceptions of the good" (2001: 57). The social primary goods can be classified into five groups (2001: 58–9): (1) the basic rights and liberties; (2) freedom of movement and free choice of occupation; (3) powers and prerogatives of offices and positions of authority and responsibility; (4) income and wealth; and (5) the social bases of self-respect. In response to some of the critiques of the original version of *A Theory of Justice* (1971), Rawls has stressed that it is not actual persons who are assumed to want those primary goods, but rather persons in their capacity as citizens (1982: 164–7).

Finally, Rawls's views have shifted rather drastically over the years. In the first edition of *A Theory of Justice*, Rawls defended his principles of justice as part of what he later came to see as a comprehensive liberal doctrine. Later his work shifted to a *political* conception of justice, whereby the principles are justified by reference to political values only, and not by reference to how they relate to a more comprehensive doctrine. It is therefore not uncommon to distinguish between the "early Rawls" of *A Theory of Justice*, and the "later Rawls" of *Political Liberalism* (1993) and *Justice as Fairness: A Restatement* (2001). The reason for this shift to political liberalism was Rawls's increasing concern that in a democratic society the fact of reasonable pluralism is unavoidable: citizens have various and conflicting reasonable comprehensive doctrines. Rather than merely defending an alternative to utilitarianism, Rawls's goal has switched to showing how, in such a society characterized by pluralism, a common agreement on a set of principles of justice for the basic structure is possible.

III. Social Primary Goods and Human Diversity

Sen's best-known critique of Rawls is that the social primary goods approach ignores the diversity of human beings. In his 1979 Tanner Lecture, Sen argued that

the primary goods approach seems to take little note of the diversity of human beings. . . . If people were basically very similar, then an index of primary goods might be quite a good way of judging advantage. But, in fact, people seem to have very different needs varying with health, longevity, climatic conditions, location, work conditions, temperament, and even body size. . . . So what is involved is not merely ignoring a few hard cases, but overlooking very widespread and real differences.   (Sen 1980: 215–16)

He gives the example of a person unable to walk, whose impairment would not give him a claim to additional resources under Rawls's two principles of justice. The difference principle would not justify any redistribution to the disabled on the grounds of their disability. Rawls responded at first that, while we must acknowledge our moral duties towards the disabled, we should postpone the question of our obligations towards them until we have worked out a robust and convincing theory of justice for the "normal" cases (Rawls 2001: 176).

Yet Sen's critique of the primary goods approach goes beyond the case of the severely disabled. As Sen puts it, the problem does not end with "a few hard cases". As the above quotation illustrates, he believes that the more general problem with the use of primary goods is that they cannot deal adequately with the pervasive differences between people. Primary goods cannot adequately account for differences in people's abilities to convert these primary goods into what they are able to be and to do in their lives. Therefore, so Sen argues, we should focus directly on people's beings and doings, that is, on their capabilities to function. Primary goods are among the valuable means to pursue one's life plan. But the real opportunities or possibilities that a person has to pursue her own life plan are not only influenced by the primary goods that she has at her disposal, but also by a range of factors that determine the extent to which she can turn these primary goods into valuable states of being and doing. Hence, Sen claims that we should focus on the extent of opportunity freedom that a person effectively has, i.e. her capabilities.

How persuasive is Sen's critique of social primary goods as the metric of justice? Let us first look at the special case of the disabled, since this has generated a large literature and a debate of its own. Rawls has indeed stated that in his theory "everyone has physical needs and psychological capacities within the normal range", and therefore he excludes people with severe physical or mental disabilities from the scope of justice as fairness (1999: 83–4; 2001: 170–6). Rawls justifies this by arguing that a theory of justice should in any case apply to "normal cases"—if the theory is inconsistent or implausible for such cases, then it will certainly not be attractive for the more challenging cases, such as people with severe disabilities. We may postpone the question of how to treat people with disabilities to one of the later (legislative) stages of the design of the basic structure of society (1999: 84). However, Sen argues that a theory of justice should not postpone this question in developing the basic structure of the theory. He argues that the "hard cases" of the disabled are just extreme examples, and that the more general problem of differences in needs is pervasive and therefore should be given due attention in a theory of justice. In later work Rawls (2001: 176) no longer argues that the case of justice towards the disabled has to be postponed to the legislative phase, but rather that we have to try to extend justice as fairness to include those cases.

Given this debate, we can ask two questions. First, is it *in principle* possible to include the physical and mentally disabled in Rawls's theory by extending the social contract drawn up in the original position? And if the only way to deal with the case of the disabled is in an ad hoc fashion, should this be considered a problem?

The first question has been investigated by Eva Kittay (1999), Harry Brighouse (2001), Martha Nussbaum (2006), and Henry Richardson (2006), among others. I will not discuss their arguments at length, but will note merely that these philosophers have drawn conflicting conclusions. It emerges from this debate that, *at best*, justice as fairness can accommodate the disabled by modifying some Rawlsian assumptions—and then the key question becomes which of those assumptions need to be altered for the reinterpretation to count as an extension of rather than a departure from the Rawslian framework.

This brings us to the second question. If justice towards the disabled cannot be handled within Rawls's framework, and the only way to deal with the disabled is in an ad hoc fashion, how problematic is that? Brighouse and Nussbaum have argued that we would then no longer be discussing this as a matter of justice, but as a matter of charity or compassion. Kittay and Nussbaum argue that this postponement is deeply problematic, since dependency and care are central to everybody's lives and are crucial factors in determining our quality of life. Moreover, care and dependency are not just "special cases", but are important aspects of human life which at any particular point in time affect a large share of the population, and affect everyone at some point in their lives. Moreover, the distribution of the burdens and benefits of being cared for, and the distribution of the burdens and benefits of caring, are as much concerns of political justice as the distribution of income, wealth, liberties and opportunities.

Rawlsians would take issue with this argument that it is problematic to restrict the scope of a theory of justice. Why, they would ask, is Rawls not entitled to restrict the scope of his theory? One answer to that question is that partial accounts of justice run the risk of giving us distorted principles of justice if there are significant spill-over effects between those domains of justice that are included in the theory and those that are excluded. This is not just a problem for the status of the disabled in Rawls's theory. It is also a problem for other aspects of human diversity that are excluded from the scope of justice as fairness. For example, Rawls stresses that his theory is only a theory of political justice, and does not address the issue of "local justice", i.e. questions of justice within associations and institutions, such as the family. Yet this is unsatisfying, since the literature on gender injustice has clearly demonstrated that one cannot separate the public and the private—or, in Rawls's terms, issues of political justice and local justice—if one wants to develop an adequate account of gender justice or justice for care-givers. In Rawls's theory of political justice, such informal care-givers have no moral grounds on which to claim a just distribution of the burdens of care, since the conceptualization of the parties in the original position and the kind of decisions they have to make exclude these issues from their decisions. Yet in real life, questions of the principles of justice for the basic structure and questions of justice within families and other associations cannot be separated, since these different spheres of life have significant spill-over effects.

The exclusion of the disabled from the scope of justice as fairness has led us to a discussion of the problematic consequences of restrictions of the scope of justice. However, as pointed out before, the disabled are just one category of persons whose needs are not adequately accounted for in justice as fairness. The more general problem, which is primarily related not to the scope of Rawls's theory but rather to his metric of justice, is that "interpersonal variability in the conversion of primary goods into [capabilities] introduces elements of arbitrariness into the Rawlsian accounting of the respective advantages enjoyed by different persons; this can be a source of unjustified inequality and unfairness" (Sen 1990: 112). This will be further illustrated in the following sections, in which we turn to the capability approach.

IV. The Capability Approach to Justice

When Sen first formulated his critique of justice as fairness for not adequately accounting for interpersonal diversity in his 1979 Tanner Lecture, he sketched the outlines of his alternative, the capability approach. Since 1979, the capability approach has been further developed by Sen and others, and presented as an alternative for interpersonal comparisons of well-being to the social primary goods of Rawlsian justice. Before analyzing the debates between capability theorists and Rawlsians, I will briefly summarize the main aspects of the capability approach to justice.

In contrast to justice as fairness, the capability approach is not a theory of justice, and certainly not a theory of *political* justice. Rather, it is a general framework specifying a space for the interpersonal comparison of individual well-being, and can be developed into a wide range of capability theories. Some of these are part of the philosophical literature on social justice (e.g. Anderson 1999; Nussbaum 2000, 2006; Wolff and de-Shalit 2007), while others fall within the domain of welfare and development economics or the other social sciences (e.g. Alkire 2002; Kuklys 2005). The main claim of the capability approach is that in making interpersonal comparisons of advantage, we should focus on people's real or effective opportunities to do what they want to do, and to be who they want to be, instead of focusing on people's holdings of social primary goods or their mental states (as in certain forms of utility). These beings and doings are called a person's functionings, and include such basic functionings as being healthy, being sheltered, not being mentally ill, engaging in social relations, and more complex and specific functionings such as combining a career with a gender-egalitarian family life. Capabilities are the effective opportunities that a person has to attain these functionings.

As already noted, Sen has argued that Rawls fails to account for diversity between individuals in the conversion of these primary goods into valuable states of being and doing. Over time, Sen has discussed three categories of such conversion factors: personal conversion factors (e.g. metabolism, physical condition, sex, reading skills, intelligence), social conversion factors (e.g. public policies, social or religious norms, discriminatory practices, gender roles, societal hierarchies, power relations) and environmental conversion factors (e.g. climate, infrastructure). They all play a role in the conversion of characteristics of goods or other "capability inputs" to the individual's capabilities to functioning.

Do justice as fairness and capability theories of justice have the same subject of justice? Justice as fairness postulates that the subject of justice is the basic structure of society, that is, the set of major societal institutions. The subject of Sen's capability approach to justice could include the basic structure, but would most likely go beyond it. At present, Sen has not presented a fully developed capability theory of justice to be compared with Rawls's theory. Moreover, he has argued that developing a full theory of justice may not be what philosophers should be doing in the first place (Sen 2006). If a capability theory of justice would not just include the basic structure but also pay explicit attention to social norms, widespread attitudes and implicit practices within a certain society, then this theory would be able to account for several injustices which elude a theory that limits itself to the basic structure. An example may serve as an illustration. Rawls has written that the family belongs to the basic structure and therefore needs to be regulated in accordance with the two principles, but that the behavior of the members of the family need not be regulated by such principles. As citizens, members of families have to comply with the principles of political justice; as members of an association, justice as fairness does not cover injustices within the family, since these issues of "local justice" are not on its agenda. Moreover, Rawls postulates that in the "well-ordered" (or fully just) society citizens will be compelled to follow the principles of justice, and thus the behavior of members of social institutions could be very different from the injustice-generating behavior that we observe in reality. Unfortunately, this is an idealization that is not very helpful for thinking about current injustices within families, such as unequal burdens of care or the unequal financial consequences of fatherhood and motherhood. The quality of life of individuals in terms of their capability sets is profoundly affected by the behavior of other family members. Capability theorists of justice would claim that the injustices such behavior generates need to be part of a theory of justice, and not relegated to other parts of moral theory.

The capability approach advocates that prima facie we should be concerned with people's capabilities, and not with their achieved functionings. There are exceptions, however, such as young children and the mentally disabled, as their limited cognitive capacities justify a (partial) focus on achieved functionings instead of capabilities. The basic assumption is that if people have the same opportunities, and their ability to make decisions and bear personal responsibility for their choices is not more restricted than those of other people, then justice should be concerned with their capabilities rather than their achieved functionings.

Sen thus stresses the normative primacy of capabilities rather than achieved functionings because he wants to respect many different notions of the good. Sen holds that people should have effective possibilities to shape their own life and attain a high quality of life, but since in most circumstances we can assume that they are capable of making responsible decisions, it is up to them to choose which capabilities they would effectively like to realize. This core characteristic of the capability approach makes it a liberal theory, just like Rawls's. Yet in contrast to some other liberal theories, the material and non-material circumstances that shape people's opportunity sets, and the circumstances that influence the choices which people make from the capability set, receive a central place in the interpersonal comparisons. The capability approach directs our focus to people's capability sets, but insists that we also need to scrutinize the impact of social norms, the context in which economic production and social interactions take place and how that affects people's well-being, and whether the circumstances in which people choose from their opportunity sets are just. Attention to the importance of social norms and other informal social structures is a crucial characteristic of the capability approach, whereas it is absent from justice as fairness.

V. Is the Capability Approach a Comprehensive Moral Doctrine?

Perhaps Rawlsians would take issue with my claim that the capability approach is a liberal theory, and would argue that it is a comprehensive moral doctrine. For the later Rawls, the distinction between a political conception of justice and a comprehensive moral doctrine is very important: "The idea is that in a constitutional democracy the public conception of justice should be, so far as possible, independent of controversial philosophical and religious doctrines" (Rawls 1985: 223).

According to Sen (1990: 112), Rawls has argued that the capability approach's critique of justice as fairness as being insufficiently sensitive to interpersonal variability in the conversion of primary goods into capabilities presupposes the acceptance of a comprehensive doctrine, and therefore goes against political liberalism. Sen has replied that Rawls's claim that the capability approach must endorse one unique view of the good is mistaken (Sen 1992: 82–3). The capability approach holds that the relevant focus is on people's capability sets, which "stands for the actual freedom of choice a person has over alternative lives that he or she can lead" (Sen 1990: 114). An interpersonal comparison focusing on a set of achieved functionings would imply the endorsement of a comprehensive notion of the good. Yet as Sen has stressed repeatedly, the primary focus of the capability approach to justice is not on achieved functionings, but on capabilities to achieve those functionings.

This reply strikes me as correct. However, one could object that the capability approach ultimately relies on a specification of the list of valuable capabilities, and as such endorses a comprehensive moral doctrine. One may argue that by deciding on the capabilities that are going to count for purposes of social justice, we are already imposing a comprehensive notion of the good life.

A defender of the capability approach to justice could formulate at least two replies. First, one may doubt whether justice as fairness is as uncommitted to any comprehensive doctrine as Rawls argues it to be. For one thing, in his political conception of the person, Rawls postulates that citizens are conceptualized as free and equal persons, and moved by their higher-order interests. Rawls (1985, 1988) claims that these fundamental ideas of justice as fairness are independent of a comprehensive doctrine and can be found in the public culture of a democratic society. Yet by conceptualizing citizens as free and equal persons who are moved by higher-order interests, Rawls is also committing himself to certain comprehensive ideas. I am not at all objecting to these fundamental Rawlsian ideas, but rather doubting whether it is possible to construct a theory of justice that is truly and completely independent of *any* comprehensive ideas. In addition, even if Rawls could construct a fully convincing justification for an index of social primary goods as the metric of justice within political liberalism, the relative weights of those different primary goods would make the index serve the interests of citizens with some comprehensive doctrines better than citizens with other doctrines. This problem would become even more pressing if Rawls were to expand the list of social primary goods to include leisure time and perhaps even states of consciousness such as physical pain, as he has tentatively suggested (Rawls 1988: 257; 2001: 179).

The second line of defense is that the Rawlsian objection may hold for some capability theories of justice, but not necessarily for all. It is well known that Sen has refused to endorse one particular list of capabilities (Sen 2004). Yet other capability theorists have made proposals as to which capabilities matter, including proposals for the domain of justice. Elizabeth Anderson (1999: 36) argues that people should be entitled "to whatever capabilities are necessary to enable them to avoid or escape entanglement in oppressive social relationships" and "to the capabilities necessary for functioning as an equal citizen in a democratic state". Martha Nussbaum (2003, 2006) has proposed and defended what she takes to be a universal list of ten capabilities. Thus, the objection that capability theories of justice could indirectly endorse a comprehensive notion of the good life may *perhaps* be relevant to Anderson's or Nussbaum's theory.[1] Sen has not (yet) developed his capability approach to justice

---

[1] In the case of Anderson's theory, one would need to show that her two general principles for the selection of capabilities imply the introduction of a controversial view of the good. Nussbaum's list of capabilities is more prone to objections of perfectionism. Nussbaum argues that her list can be obtained as the result of an overlapping consensus of people as citizens who have otherwise diverse views of the good life. Yet she has failed to convince some of her critics (e.g. Barclay 2003; Robeyns 2005).

to such a degree that it would allow us to judge whether it becomes a comprehensive political doctrine rather than a form of political liberalism.

The crucial question is whether it is possible to select capabilities without imposing a comprehensive notion of the good life. This is a key question in the development of the capability approach into a theory of social justice, and a full proposal on how this could be done is beyond the scope of the present essay. Let me briefly sketch, however, the outline of an alternative way to select capabilities *for purposes of political justice* that is not vulnerable to the objection that it inadvertently introduces a comprehensive notion of the good.

The first layer of selection would consist in taking stock of comprehensive notions of the good. All liberal theories, including those within political liberalism, endorse some limits to the permissibility of comprehensive moral views of the good life. Capability theorists could similarly specify some principles that legitimate notions of the good life would need to meet. The list of relevant capabilities would then be derived by pulling together all the capabilities of which those legitimate notions of the good life would be composed. As a second layer of selection, one would have to restrict the list of capabilities to those that fall within the domain of political justice, after this domain has been appropriately specified. This is necessary to avoid claims of injustice which fall outside the scope of those claims that one can reasonably put to the government and one's fellow-citizens, such as the claim for free cosmetic surgery by people with a certain facial feature they dislike (Pogge 2002: 204–8). Obviously, a fair process of deliberative democracy would be crucial for these first two stages in the selection process. We would therefore also need to work out the right set of conditions under which such a fair deliberative democratic process could take place. Finally, a third layer of selection would include only objective capabilities, and exclude capabilities that are primarily subjective. For example, Sen has sometimes mentioned being happy as a valuable capability. While happiness can be conceptualized as a capability, it is not a legitimate ground on which citizens can make claims on each other in the public realm.[2] This is not to say that these subjective capabilities are not important, but rather that in the political domain they cannot be the basis for choosing the principles of justice and designing justice-enhancing policies (though they may play a contingent role).[3]

This is an extremely sketchy and tentative proposal, and it would need to be worked out in much more detail to see whether it is viable. Yet to my mind, developing such a line of enquiry may be well worth the effort. Such a criteria-based selection of capabilities would have the advantage of respecting all legitimate comprehensive notions of the good life and thus falling within political liberalism as squarely as justice as fairness. Moreover, by opting for a deliberative democratic

---

[2] The reasons are well known from the critiques of utilitarianism, and need not be rehearsed here.

[3] Note that this procedure would face the same problems regarding the indexing of capabilities as the index of social primary goods would face. Clearly this is a very important issue, but I cannot address it here.

approach, one could avoid the problems of political legitimacy which plague any list that is (rightly or wrongly) perceived as being non-democratic, such as Nussbaum's.

VI. THE PUBLICITY CRITIQUE OF THE CAPABILITY APPROACH

I will now consider one final Rawlsian objection to the capability approach. Since Rawls wants to analyze how people with very different comprehensive moral views on the good life can come to a reasonable agreement on the principles of political justice, he stresses that the conception of justice must be public and the information necessary to make a claim of injustice must be verifiable to all, and preferably easy to collect. A theory of social justice needs a *public* standard of interpersonal comparisons, as otherwise, given the diversity of views between citizen on the good life, the principles of justice will prove unstable (Rawls 1982: 169–70).

Pogge (2002) has suggested that the capability approach cannot meet the publicity criterion. The suggestion is that as capabilities are very hard to measure or assess in such a public fashion, and as their verification would require an enormous amount of information, much of it difficult to obtain, the capability approach is unworkable as a theory of social justice.

The first part of the objection is that a capability-based theory of social justice would require too much information. But it is hard to see why that would count as a decisive argument against a conception of justice. It is true that, all other things being equal, the less information a particular conception of justice requires, the better; but given that Rawls claims justice to be the first virtue of a society, this surely can never be a decisive Rawlsian argument against a particular conception.[4]

The second part of the objection is that the information needed to make interpersonal comparisons has to be publicly verifiable. Given considerations of stability and incentive problems, this is indeed a justified requirement for a plausible conceptualization of justice, and a sufficient reason to ban subjective capabilities from the metric of political justice. But is it really too difficult to know for each individual which capabilities his or her capability set contains, and is it really clear that such evaluation would not rely on publicly verifiable information?

---

[4] An exception may have to be made for information that is either plainly impossible to know, or else is not merely unmeasurable, but also cannot be decently estimated within a reasonable margin of error.

There are two ways to assess the capabilities of a person, and each way can complement the other. The first strategy is to try to measure a person's capabilities directly. However, generally one does not have information on a person's capabilities; one would have to assess her achieved functioning levels and infer her capability set from those levels. So far, empirical studies measuring or estimating capabilities have been limited to comparing group differences in functionings, either using econometric techniques or relying on the assumption that group differences in achieved functionings mirror group differences in their capability sets (Robeyns 2006). However, this technique cannot assess an *individual's* capability set rather than group differences in capability levels.

For the assessment of individual capability sets, another strategy might be more helpful. One could start by analyzing the capability inputs and determinants. These include the basic structure of the society in which the individual lives, as well as interaction with others, and a range of resources broadly defined. Capability inputs also include Rawlsian primary goods. In addition, one would carefully scrutinize the social, environmental and personal conversion factors that affect a certain individual. If one of those conversion factors can be argued to lower the conversion of income (or other primary goods) into valuable capabilities, then this could possibly provide a claim for either extra resources, or other social policies or public goods. Finally, the capability approach would also require the scrutiny of the social constraints on the choices that people make from their capability set, but this can be done as a complementary task to the evaluation of the distribution of resources, and the redistributive and other policies resulting from the analysis of the conversion factors.

If a capability-based theory of social justice carries out the interpersonal comparison of individual advantage in this way, and not by aiming to assess capabilities directly, it not only becomes a standard of justice that is much more public, but its complementarity with an evaluation based on social primary goods becomes much more visible. The capability approach can thus be developed into a theory of justice in a way that incorporates the Rawlsian focus on social primary goods.[5]

Before closing this section, let me mention that it is not entirely obvious to me that the publicity criterion is met by the social primary goods approach. There is a big difference between a formal legal guarantee of rights and opportunities, and an effective guarantee. For example, it is far from straightforward to assess publicly whether a certain basic structure meets the fair equality of opportunity principle, as it is difficult to estimate the influence of social norms, prejudice and stereotypes. Of course, Rawls has postulated that in the fully just society there will be full compliance with the principles of justice; but for a real-world analysis this assumption brushes under the carpet the problem of unconscious injustice in the

---

[5] For further debates on the capability approach and primary goods as metrics of justice, some of which also highlight this potential complementarity, see the contributions to Brighouse and Robeyns (forthcoming).

treatment of women and minorities. While I cannot analyze this issue at length here, I suspect that the publicity criterion is not only a challenge for a capability theory of justice, but also for a primary goods theory when certain idealizing assumptions of justice as fairness are removed.

VII. What is the Purpose of a Theory of Justice?

In his 2006 article "What Do We Want from a Theory of Justice?", Sen asks the question that hangs over much of the analysis in this essay. Rawls and Sen are working towards rather different types of theories of justice, and this can explain many of the differences between justice as fairness and the capability approach.

Justice as fairness is (1) a hypothetical justification of principles of justice, (2) limited to domestic justice and brackets questions of local and global justice, thereby ignoring significant spill-over effects, and (3) an exercise in ideal theory. For capability theorists, the ideal nature of justice as fairness is quite worrisome. Rawlsian ideal theory aims at working out the principles of justice in a *perfectly just* society. Political theorists are divided on the usefulness of ideal theory to deal with issues of existing injustice. Ideal theory sharpens our thinking on justice and serves as a guide that is indispensable in many cases, but it does not tell us how to reach that ideal of justice. Moreover, *in practice* ideal theory too often makes theoretically distorting assumptions about human nature or societal conditions, resulting in theories that provide very little guidance for dealing with actual cases of socio-economic injustice (Robeyns 2008). In justice as fairness, all judgements of actual inequalities are against a background of equal basic liberties and fair equality of opportunity. As Rawls himself notes, this is why justice as fairness does not discuss issues of gender and race, as in the ideal well-ordered society there would be no racial or gender discrimination and fair equality of opportunity would be secured for all (2001: 64–5). In no country in the world, however, is either of these conditions met. In addition, current knowledge about the causes of gender and racial inequalities strongly suggest that these causes cannot be reduced only to violations of the basic liberties. In sum, it is far from clear how useful justice as fairness is for non-ideal circumstances. In contrast, while the capability approach introduces abstractions, it does not rely on idealizations. And most of Sen's writings are concerned with how to think about justice in the non ideal world we currently inhabit. While in principle these two modes of thinking *can* be complementary, in the practice of contemporary theorizing about social justice they conflict in many ways (Robeyns 2008).

Some Rawlsians have argued that theoretical resources within Rawls's work can be used to deal with real-life questions of injustice, such as the subordination of women (Laden 2003). Yet such arguments require further development and interpretation of Rawls's work which not all Rawlsians will consider faithful to Rawls's theory. The debate earlier mentioned on the theoretical possibility of including the severely disabled within justice as fairness illustrates how divided Rawlsians are on the right interpretation of his theory, and on whether a reinterpretation should count as an extension rather than an abandonment of Rawls's work. In any case, much more would need to be said before we know the implications of justice as fairness for our present unjust and non-idealized world.

If all this is correct, then the debate between Rawls's justice as fairness and Sen's capability approach can be seen as a paradigmatic example of the dispute between theorists of justice who defend ideal theory versus those who believe that much more attention should be shifted to non-ideal theory and policy implications.[6] In that debate, too, the disputes often boil down to the question: What do we want from a theory of justice?

VIII. Conclusions

The capability approach and justice as fairness are often presented as rivals. Yet, on the basis of the arguments presented in this essay I would like to suggest the following three conclusions. First, it is far from straightforward to compare justice as fairness and the capability approach. While both are profoundly concerned with human freedoms, equality and justice, Rawls and Sen are trying to answer different questions. Rawls wants to investigate the very possibility of unanimous agreement on the principles of justice for a democratic society which is characterized by radical pluralism in visions of the good life. This leads him to engage in an exercise of hypothetical ideal theory, and leads him to place several questions of justice and morality outside the scope of his work. Sen, in contrast, is much more concerned with developing non-ideal theory on justice, with greater *direct* relevance for pressing issues of injustice.

Second, if we want to compare justice as fairness and the capability approach in detail, then each theory needs to be further developed in opposite directions. The capability approach to justice requires more theoretical justification and further development of some of its fundamental parts, such as the selection of the capabilities relevant for the purpose of political justice, and the restrictions, if any,

---

[6] See e.g. the debate in the July 2008 special issue of *Social Theory and Practice* on the relative merits, and the potential and pitfalls of, ideal and non-ideal theorizing on justice.

on the scope of justice. Justice as fairness has to be further developed to show how it would deal with questions of justice in non-ideal circumstances. We would also need to know which principles of "local justice" are compatible with the Rawlsian principles of political justice, and whether spill-over effects from local justice to political justice would prompt a revision of the principles of political justice. It should also be made clear which social primary goods would be included in the index. Since some possible candidates are so similar in nature to capabilities, the question of which of the two approaches best meets the publicity criterion remains open.

Thirdly, rather than regarding both theories as rivals, it is possible to understand the capability approach and justice as fairness as complementary theories. From a capability perspective, objective capabilities are the relevant space in which to legitimize just policies, but the policies themselves will need to be executed in the space of capability inputs. While a capability theory of justice starts by considering people's capabilities, it is highly plausible that the basic structure of society and the distribution of social primary goods will play a major role in a well-elaborated capability theory of justice which meets the publicity requirement. If such a capability theory were developed, I expect that we would see a convergence between Rawls's and Sen's work on justice. Yet in such a capability theory the basic structure and the social primary goods of income and wealth would not be important in their own right, but rather for the instrumental role they play for what really matters to people—their functionings and capabilities.

References

ALKIRE, S. (2002), *Valuing Freedoms: Sen's Capability Approach and Poverty Reduction* (Oxford: Oxford University Press).

ANDERSON, E. (1999), "What is the Point of Equality?", *Ethics*, 109: 287–337.

BARCLAY, L. (2003), "What Kind of Liberal is Martha Nussbaum?", *SATS: Nordic Journal of Philosophy*, 4(2): 5–24.

BRIGHOUSE, H. (2001), "Can Justice as Fairness Accommodate the Disabled?", *Social Theory and Practice*, 27: 537–60.

—— and ROBEYNS, I. (eds) (forthcoming), *Measuring Justice: Primary Goods and Capabilities* (Cambridge: Cambridge University Press).

KITTAY, E. (1999), *Love's Labor: Essays on Women, Equality, and Dependency* (New York: Routledge).

KUKLYS, W. (2005), *Amartya Sen's Capability Approach: Theoretical Insights and Empirical Applications* (Berlin: Springer-Verlag).

LADEN, A. (2003), "Radical Liberals, Reasonable Feminists: Reason, Power and Objectivity in MacKinnon and Rawls", *Journal of Political Philosophy*, 11: 133–52.

Nussbaum, M. (2000) *Women and Human Development* (Cambridge: Cambridge University Press).

——(2003), "Capabilities as Fundamental Entitlements: Sen and Social Justice", *Feminist Economics*, 9(2/3), 33–59.

——(2006), *Frontiers of Justice: Disability, Nationality and Species Membership* (Cambridge, Mass.: Harvard University Press).

Pogge, T. (2002), "Can the Capability Approach be Justified?", *Philosophical Topics*, 30: 167–228.

Rawls, J. (1971), *A Theory of Justice* (Oxford: Oxford University Press).

——(1982), "Social Unity and Primary Goods", in A. Sen and B. Williams (eds), *Utilitarianism and Beyond* (Cambridge: Cambridge University Press), 159–85.

——(1985), "Justice as Fairness: Political not Metaphysical", *Philosophy and Public Affairs*, 14: 223–52.

——(1988), "The Priority of Right and Ideas of the Good", *Philosophy and Public Affairs*, 17: 251–76.

——(1993), *Political Liberalism* (New York: Columbia University Press).

——(1999), *A Theory of Justice*, revd edn (Cambridge, Mass.: Harvard University Press).

——(2001), *Justice as Fairness: A Restatement* (Cambridge, Mass.: Harvard University Press).

Richardson, H. (2006), "Rawlsian Social-Contract Theory and the Severely Disabled", *Journal of Ethics*, 10: 419–62.

Robeyns, I. (2005), "Selecting Capabilities for Quality of Life Measurement", *Social Indicators Research*, 74: 191–215.

——(2006) "The Capability Approach in Practice", *Journal of Political Philosophy*, 17: 351–76.

——(2008) "Ideal Theory in Theory and Practice", *Social Theory and Practice*, 34: 341–62.

Sen, A. (1970), *Collective Choice and Social Welfare* (San Francisco: Holden-Day).

——(1980), "Equality of What?", in S. McMurrin (ed.), *The Tanner Lectures on Human Values* (Salt Lake City: University of Utah Press), 196–220.

——(1981), *Poverty and Famines: An Essay on Entitlement and Deprivation* (Oxford: Oxford University Press).

——(1990), "Justice: Means versus Freedoms", *Philosophy and Public Affairs*, 19: 111–21.

——(1992), *Inequality Re-Examined* (Oxford: Clarendon Press).

——(2004), "Capabilities, Lists, and Public Reason: Continuing the Conversation", *Feminist Economics*, 10: 77–80.

——(2006), "What Do We Want from a Theory of Justice?", *Journal of Philosophy*, 103: 215–38.

Wolff, J., and de-Shalit, A. (2007), *Disadvantage* (Oxford: Oxford University Press).

CHAPTER 22

UNGROUPING INCOME DISTRIBUTIONS

SYNTHESIZING SAMPLES FOR INEQUALITY AND POVERTY ANALYSIS

ANTHONY SHORROCKS

GUANGHUA WAN

I. INTRODUCTION

RESEARCH on inequality and poverty during the past half century has been greatly influenced by the writings of Amartya Sen. Amongst his many and varied contributions, the Radcliffe Lectures on inequality (Sen 1973) and the *Econometrica* article on poverty measurement (Sen 1976) spurred countless readers to attempt to confront distributional questions with empirical evidence. Yet when Sen's publications were written a generation ago, anyone wishing to undertake empirical work faced serious handicaps. Computing hardware and software were rudimentary by current standards. Household microdata were in short supply and rarely accessible to independent researchers. Those interested in inequality, poverty and other distribution-related issues usually had to be content with simple computational procedures applied to summary statistics, grouped frequency tables, and other types of published secondary material.

To compensate for the shortcomings, a variety of ingenious procedures and tools were developed. Many different functional forms were offered as approximations to the empirical income distributions and compared to the alternatives (examples of this genre are provided by Gastwirth 1972; Kakwani and Podder 1973, 1976; Salem and Mount 1974; Kakwani 1976; Singh and Maddala 1976; Kloek and Van Dijk 1978; McDonald and Ransom 1979, 1981; Harrison 1981 and McDonald 1984).[1] Other authors, including Cowell and Mehta (1982), proposed ways of estimating inequality indices from grouped data. Attention was also given to the optimal way of summarizing data in order to preserve distributional information (Davies and Shorrocks 1989).

Nowadays, the quantity, quality and availability of household data sets have rendered this earlier literature largely redundant. Related issues—such as the variability inevitably associated with finite samples—are more likely to be addressed using semi-parametric or non-parametric techniques like kernel density estimation (see DiNardo *et al.* 1996; Deaton 1997; D'Ambrosio 1999). However, the appetite for extracting distributional information from grouped data has not completely vanished. Independent researchers seldom have the capacity to work simultaneously with many microdata sets, and may be obliged to make use of summary information. Micro-information from surveys in the distant past may not have survived, forcing those interested in long-term distributional trends to grapple with published grouped data. In other cases, access to microdata is restricted by concerns about confidentiality or political sensitivity, or because users are charged a high fee.

The continuing need for methods of extracting information from grouped data is well illustrated by the recent flurry of interest in the world distribution of income and its trend over time, as studied by Schultz (1998), Bourguignon and Morrisson (2002), Milanovic (2002, 2005), Sala-i-Martin (2002), Capéau and Decoster (2004), and Dowrick and Akmal (2005), amongst others. While a number of factors contribute to the controversies in this literature—including coverage of countries, the concept used for average income (or expenditure), and the adjustment made to official exchange rates to compensate for purchasing power variations—limitation on access to microdata is perhaps the greatest single source of conflicting results. Milanovic (2002, 2005) utilizes a large number of household surveys, but others have to resort to grouped income distribution data and to adopting simplifying assumptions, conjecturing, for example, that individual countries can be adequately

---

[1] See Bandourian *et al.* (2002) and the references therein for more recent contributions to this topic.

represented by five-person or ten-person distributions whose incomes correspond to quintile or decile shares. Similar concerns apply with even greater force to studies of long-term poverty trends, since the approximation to a five- or ten-person distribution clearly limits the subtlety of the results.

Our own interest in the question of extracting information from grouped data has been prompted by a desire to analyze alternative poverty-trend scenarios for Russia, where income distribution series are only available in grouped form (Shorrocks and Kolenikov 2001).[2] It has been reinforced by exposure to the problems posed by the World Income Inequality Database (WIID), which contains summary observations on 156 countries, most relating to the period 1960–2005.[3] Of the 4,981 observations, 2,945 include information on quintile or decile shares and Gini coefficients. Around 35% of the observations have more details. Comparisons by researchers would be facilitated if all observations had figures for decile shares, and perhaps also for top percentile shares, alternative inequality measures, and poverty rates corresponding to a variety of poverty lines.[4]

Estimates of poverty measures and the Gini inequality index can be obtained from grouped data using the POVCAL software on the World Bank website. In fact, POVCAL was used to generate Gini values for many of the observations inherited by the WIID database from the World Bank. However, POVCAL operates by fitting the general quadratic and beta Lorenz functions to grouped data and then applying the formulae reported in Datt (1998). Unfortunately, as shown later, the general quadratic and beta forms often generate Lorenz curves that dip below the horizontal axis—in other words, the software can generate negative values even when the data refer to consumption rather than income. Furthermore, the quantile shares associated with the fitted functions can differ significantly from the reported values with which the procedure begins.[5]

This paper describes an improved method for calculating distributional indicators such as inequality values and poverty rates from grouped distribution data. An algorithm allows a sample of "income" observations to be reconstructed from any valid set of Lorenz coordinates.[6] This sample may then be used to compute inequality and poverty statistics, by treating the sample observations as if they had

---

[2] Similar hurdles are faced by those interested in inequality trends in China; see, for example, Chotikapanich, Rao and Tang (2007) and Chotikapanich, Griffiths and Rao (2007).

[3] The WIID database is available at <www.wider.unu.edu/wiid/wiid.htm>.

[4] The algorithm described in this chapter has been used recently to generate country wealth samples that allow the global distribution of personal wealth to be estimated: see Davies, Sandstrom et al. (2007, 2008).

[5] The POVCAL software is available at <www.worldbank.org/LSMS/tools/povcal/>. See Minoiu and Reddy (2006) for a detailed critique.

[6] Here and elsewhere in this chapter, the term "income" is used generically. Lorenz curves plot the cumulative income shares against the cumulative population shares when observations are ordered in terms of increasing incomes. Only relative incomes matter for Lorenz curves, so the synthetic sample values can be arbitrarily normalized, for example to ensure that the mean is unity.

been drawn from a household survey with a homogeneous population of equally weighted households.

Two initial restrictions are placed on the synthetic sample, although neither is strictly necessary. First, the observations are constrained to take positive values. This is done to avoid instances in which, say, negative observations are produced for consumption, and also to ensure that values can be computed for all inequality indices in common use. Second, a sample size of 1,000 has been chosen for the synthetic distribution. This number has been selected primarily in order to produce poverty rates accurate to one decimal point for any given poverty line. A smaller sample size, though feasible, is probably unnecessary given the computing power available nowadays. A larger sample would reduce the downward bias in the inequality value due to averaging incomes within each tenth of a percentile; but the scope for improvement in accuracy in this and other respects is likely to be modest, as confirmed later in this paper by experiments with samples of 2,000 observations.

In principle, many different methods can be used to construct the samples, including parametric and non-parametric techniques employed in the past to estimate distributions from grouped data. Three main criteria are used to discriminate between the alternative procedures: the algorithm should be universally applicable, in the sense that it can accommodate any feasible pattern of grouped data; the characteristics of the generated sample should *exactly* match the reported grouped values; and the procedure should perform well in tests that start with an income sample, compute grouped values, and then use the algorithm to reconstruct the ungrouped data. It is also an advantage to have an algorithm that is both speedy and easy to understand.[7]

The criterion of universal applicability appears anodyne, but turns out in practice to be quite stringent when combined with the requirement that the sample values exactly match the reported data. In particular, it is possible to encounter grouped data for which the mean incomes of adjacent groups are identical. Usually this happens because the published data on percentage shares have been rounded to three, or even two, significant figures. If mean incomes are similar for adjacent groups, then the income values in the relevant ranges must be very compressed, perhaps even identical. While this is unlikely to be true in practice, we have taken the view that a feasible pattern of grouped data, however implausible, should be respected, and that the chosen algorithm should be capable of handling problematic situations as well as more common arrangements.

The procedure proposed in this chapter involves two main stages. Stage I fits a parametric distribution to the grouped observations and then generates a sample from the fitted distribution as an initial approximation to the synthetic observations. Stage II of the algorithm takes the raw sample and adjusts the values until

---

[7] Other conditions might be added to this list. For example, it is probably a good idea to have relatively "smooth" data that avoid bunching of values or gaps in the income space.

the sample statistics exactly match the "true" figures. We experimented with several alternative procedures for Stage II, eventually settling on the "stretching" routine described in section II below. For Stage I, any of the standard distributional or functional forms is a potential candidate: the lognormal (LN), general quadratic (GQ), beta, generalized beta (GB) and Singh–Maddala (SM) forms were the candidates chosen for this chapter.

II. The Algorithm

Consider a real interval partitioned into m disjoint income classes which are labeled in increasing order. The grouped distribution data for a population of individuals is captured by $m+1$ Lorenz coordinates (p_k^*, L_k^*), where p_k^* $(k = 1, \ldots, m)$ denotes the aggregate proportion of the population in income classes 1 to k; L_k^* $(k = 1, \ldots, m)$ is the corresponding (cumulative) income share; and $(p_0^*, L_0^*) = (0, 0)$.[8] In practice, these Lorenz coordinates will typically derive from data reported in the form of the quantile shares, for example decile or quintile shares; but they can also originate from frequency distributions which may record additional details, such as the bounds of the income classes. Details of the absolute levels of income are lost in the construction of Lorenz curves, so the overall mean value may be taken to be unity, in which case the mean income of class k is given by

$$\mu_k^* = \frac{L_k^* - L_{k-1}^*}{p_k^* - p_{k-1}^*}, \quad k = 1, \ldots, m. \tag{1}$$

Our aim is to construct a synthetic (and ordered) sample of n equally weighted observations which has a mean value of unity and properties that conform to those of the grouped data. To achieve the required match with the grouped data, the n observations are partitioned into m non-overlapping (and ordered) groups, with group k containing $m_k = n(p_k^* - p_{k-1}^*)$ observations. The value of the ith observation in class k is denoted by x_{ki} $(k = 1, \ldots, m; i = 1, \ldots, m_k)$, and the sample mean of class k is signified by μ_k.

The proposed "ungrouping" algorithm involves two stages. Stage I constructs a rough initial sample with unit mean by generating a set of synthetic values from a parametric form fitted to the grouped data. Suppose, for example, that the underlying distribution is taken to be lognormal and that the sample size is chosen to be 1,000. A value for the standard deviation of log incomes, σ, is obtained by

---

[8] Asterisks are used to distinguish the target (true) values from the (non-asterisked) synthetic sample values, which may not match the target figures.

averaging the $m - 1$ estimates:

$$\sigma_k = \Phi^{-1}(p_k^*) - \Phi^{-1}(L_k^*), \qquad k = 1, \ldots, m - 1, \tag{2}$$

where Φ is the standard normal distribution function (Aitchison and Brown 1957; Kolenikov and Shorrocks 2005: app.). The raw sample may then be generated by the percentile points .05, .15, ..., 99.85, 99.95 corresponding to the fitted lognormal. In addition to the lognormal, a number of other parametric forms were considered as candidates for the initial sample. Results obtained using these alternative specifications are discussed in section III below.

Stage II of the algorithm begins with the initial sample and then adjusts the observations until the sample statistics match the "true" values.[9] Several alternative procedures were considered for Stage II, but many of them failed to converge within a reasonable time period, especially when confronted with unusual data properties, such as adjacent income ranges with similar means. The two-step process eventually chosen is both universally applicable and speedy.

The first step adjusts the sample observations in such a way that each of the class k mean incomes, μ_k, is transformed into the corresponding "true" values, μ_k^*, and appropriate changes are made to the intermediate values. To be precise, consider any interval (μ_k, μ_{k+1}), $(k = 1, \ldots, m-1)$, and convert the initial sample value $x_j \in (\mu_k, \mu_{k+1})$ into the intermediate value $\hat{x}_j$ according to the rule

$$\frac{\hat{x}_j - \mu_k^*}{\mu_{k+1}^* - \mu_k^*} = \frac{x_j - \mu_k}{\mu_{k+1} - \mu_k}, \quad \text{for } k = 1, \ldots, m-1 \quad \text{and} \quad x_j \in (\mu_k, \mu_{k+1}), \tag{3}$$

or equivalently,

$$\hat{x}_j = \mu_k^* + \frac{\mu_{k+1}^* - \mu_k^*}{\mu_{k+1} - \mu_k}(x_j - \mu_k), \quad \text{for } k = 1, \ldots, m-1 \quad \text{and} \quad x_j \in (\mu_k, \mu_{k+1}). \tag{3*}$$

Similar adjustments are made at the bottom and top of the distribution using the rule:

$$\hat{x}_j = \frac{\mu_1^*}{\mu_1} x_j \quad \text{for } x_j < \mu_1; \quad \hat{x}_j = \frac{\mu_m^*}{\mu_m} x_j \quad \text{for } x_j \geq \mu_k. \tag{4}$$

Note that the transformation given by (3) is well defined because the raw sample from Stage I is both distinct and ordered, hence $\mu_{k+1} > \mu_k$. Note also that the transformation defined by (3) and (4) is (weakly) monotonic, so the sample retains its non-decreasing order.

---

[9] Our procedure makes no use of information on the maximum and minimum values within groups, although frequency tables for income distributions often report the interval endpoints. It might be possible to refine our algorithm to exploit this additional information, for example by adjusting the data at the start of Stage II to match the true group endpoints.

The above construction ensures that, within each income group, the true mean lies within the range of sample values; in other words:

$$\min_i \hat{x}_{ki} \leq \mu_k^* \leq \max_i \hat{x}_{ki}, \quad \text{for} \quad k = 1, \ldots, m. \tag{5}$$

The second step keeps the group bounds fixed and compresses the gaps between the sample values and the upper (or lower) bound of the group if the sample mean is below (or above) the true value. Specifically, define the lower bound of each group by

$$c_1 = 0; \quad c_k = \frac{1}{2}\left(\max_i \hat{x}_{k-1,i} + \min_i \hat{x}_{ki}\right), \quad k > 1, \tag{6}$$

and convert the intermediate value $\hat{x}_{ki}$ into the final value $\hat{x}_{ki}^*$ according to the rule

$$x_{ki}^* = c_{k+1} - \frac{c_{k+1} - \mu_k^*}{c_{k+1} - \hat{\mu}_k}(c_{k+1} - \hat{x}_{ki}), \quad \text{if} \quad \mu_k^* > \hat{\mu}_k \quad \text{and} \quad k < m; \tag{7a}$$

$$x_{ki}^* = c_k + \frac{\mu_k^* - c_k}{\hat{\mu}_k - c_k}(\hat{x}_{ki} - c_k), \quad \text{if} \quad \mu_k^* < \hat{\mu}_k \quad \text{or} \quad k = m. \tag{7b}$$

It may be confirmed that this transformation retains the sample ordering both within and across groups, and that the group means compiled for the final sample values, x_{ki}^*, match the true values, μ^*. Within two rounds, therefore, the algorithm produces an ordered sample that exactly replicates the properties of the reported grouped data.

III. EVALUATION

The performance of the "ungrouping" algorithm may be assessed in a variety of ways. One method exploits the additional statistics often attached to grouped data. For example, the values of Gini coefficients (presumably calculated from the original microdata) are sometimes reported alongside published frequency tables. Generating a synthetic income sample from the grouped data enables the Gini index to be estimated and compared to the reported Gini value.

This option was explored in the context of the WIID database using the log-normal as a first approximation. On the whole the results are encouraging, especially when applied to the WIID observations known to be more reliable. In the vast majority of cases, the difference between the "true" Gini value and the "synthetic" estimate was less than .003 (approximately 1%). As expected, this exercise also suggests that the errors associated with our algorithm shrink as the grouping becomes less coarse (and the number of Lorenz coordinates increases).

While this method of assessment has its attractions, a number of problems arise, particularly with regard to reconciling the occasional large discrepancies between the reported Gini figure and the synthetic estimate. It is possible that the published frequency table and Gini value refer to different sets of data for the same country and point of time, or that some of the numbers have been reported incorrectly. Other errors could have been introduced by estimating the Gini values from the grouped data, rather than the original micro-sample. It therefore becomes difficult to evaluate performance without relying heavily on personal judgements concerning the reliability of individual observations.

Another, more stringent, test starts with a suitable micro-sample, constructs a set of grouped data, and then examines the degree to which the "ungrouping" algorithm successfully reconstructs the original data. Information contained in the US Current Population Survey (CPS) for the year 2000 was used for this purpose. A random sample of 1,000 (positive) income observations was drawn from the CPS microdata and various quantile shares computed from the sample. The ungrouping utility was then applied to the grouped data to generate a synthetic sample of 1,000 which could be compared with the original CPS sample. Three patterns of grouped data were considered, representing the most common arrangements found in practice: quintile shares; decile shares; and the intermediate case of quintile shares plus the top and bottom decile shares (indicated by the label "quintile-TB"). To allow for sampling variations, the exercise was repeated first 100 times, then 200 times. To study the influence of sample size, the experiment was later repeated with a sample consisting of 2,000 observations.

Two methods were used to assess the reliability of the synthetic sample. First, the value of each observation in the (ordered) synthetic sample was compared to its counterpart in the true distribution. Second, inequality values calculated from the reconstructed data were compared with their "true" values. On the whole, the first exercise is more comprehensive and insightful, because the synthetic data may contain systematic biases. Our limited experience suggests that the generated sample may underestimate incomes on some segments of the Lorenz curve and exaggerate incomes on other segments. However, estimates of the Gini value and other inequality indices may nevertheless closely approximate their true values, giving a spurious impression of accuracy and reliability.

Five alternative specifications were considered as candidates for the distributional forms used in Stage I: the lognormal (LN), general quadratic (GQ), beta, generalized beta (GB), and Singh–Maddala (SM) functions.[10] The beta distribution

---

[10] Details of the lognormal form are given by Aitchison and Brown (1957); the general quadratic Lorenz curve by Villasenor and Arnold (1989); the beta Lorenz curve by Kakwani (1980); the generalized beta by McDonald (1984); and the Singh–Maddala distribution by Singh and Maddala (1976).

Table 22.1. Percentage of synthetic income samples containing negative observations

Grouping pattern	1,000 observations		2,000 observations	
	beta	GQ	beta	GQ
	100 replications			
Quintile	66	65	79	76
Quintile-TB	92	90	97	96
Decile	88	87	94	93
	200 replications			
Quintile	61	65	78	76
Quintile-TB	93	92	98	97
Decile	90	89	96	94

Note: beta = beta-functional form for Lorenz curve; GQ = general quadratic form for Lorenz curve.
Source: Authors' calculations.

and the general quadratic Lorenz function both proved to have a major flaw which ruled them out of further consideration: most of the synthetic samples generated during Stage I contained one or more negative observations, despite the fact that all income values are positive in the CPS data. With quintile information, both functional forms fail to ensure non-negative values over 60% of the time. The failure rate rises above 90% with the quintile-TB data, and approaches 100% with a sample size of 2,000 (see Table 22.1). This deficiency eliminated the two functions from further consideration.

For each of the three remaining functional forms the synthetic sets of sample observations were compared to their true counterparts. The results recorded in Table 22.2 are obtained by expressing both sets of observations in terms of percentage income shares and then computing the absolute deviations. Thus, for example, if the income share of the poorest (richest) person is 0.01% (4.8%) and the corresponding synthetic value is 0.015% (3.4%), then the absolute deviation is 0.005% (1.4%). In order to identify any distributional pattern of errors, the absolute deviations are summed within each decile.[11]

The six column headings in Table 22.2 refer to the results for the crude (Stage I) samples obtained from the lognormal (LN), Singh–Madalla (SM) and generalized beta (GB) distributions, plus the results (ALN, ASM and AGB, respectively) obtained after the samples are adjusted to match the group details in Stage II of the ungrouping algorithm. The first point to note is that the Stage II adjustment

[11] Because the observations are expressed as income shares, the sum of absolute deviations is preferred to the mean absolute deviation. The value of the latter is reciprocally related to the sample size; in other words, for a fixed gap between the true and synthetic Lorenz curves, the mean absolute deviation will halve when the number of sampling points doubles.

procedure proposed in this chapter usually leads to a significant reduction in the errors. This is seen in Table 22.2 by comparing the deviations for the raw and adjusted samples, holding constant the sample size and grouping assumption. With very few exceptions the adjustment leads to a better match with the true income values, often reducing the average deviation by a factor of two or more. Table 22.2 also hints at an improvement in the match as the sample size increases from 1,000 to 2,000, although the improvement is not uniform, nor much in evidence when the generalized beta distribution is used. Raising the number of sample replications from 100 to 200 appears to have little effect, suggesting that the reported figures are close to their asymptotic values.

Turning to the pattern across deciles, the results—particularly those for the adjusted sample values—show that the errors are heavily concentrated in the top decile and (to a lesser degree) in deciles 1–2 and deciles 8–9.[12] In deciles 3–7, the synthetic income values closely match the true values. The impact of the grouping criterion seems less clear at first. Focusing on the columns corresponding to the unadjusted data, there is little evidence that errors diminish as the grouping pattern becomes less coarse. However, after the sample is adjusted, the absolute deviations decline most of the time as the grouping arrangement changes from quintiles to quintile-TB to deciles.

The final issue concerns the choice of distribution function for the raw data sample. Here the result is a little surprising. The summary of Table 22.2 results reproduced in Table 22.3 demonstrates that before the Stage II adjustment, the lognormal is unambiguously the worst performer and Singh–Maddala performs the best. After the sample is adjusted, the Singh–Maddala form continues to dominate the generalized beta distribution. But the lognormal-based estimates improve so much that they overtake the generalized beta results in each of the 12 scenarios identified in Table 22.3. They also dominate Singh–Maddala in all situations except those corresponding to the coarsest grouping criterion (quintiles alone) and smallest sample size (1,000 observations). More surprisingly, perhaps, the disaggregated results in Table 22.2 show that the adjusted lognormal values provide particularly accurate values in the top decile. This is precisely the region where the lognormal is not expected to perform well; yet the lognormal dominates both of the other candidate distributions in every instance.

It is not clear why the Stage II adjustment leads to such an exceptional improvement in the lognormal-originated estimates. However, our findings support the view that the ungrouping algorithm described above, coupled with an initial lognormal fit, is capable of reproducing sample data from grouped statistics with a high degree of accuracy. Our results also lead to the recommendation that the size of the synthetic sample should be chosen to be as large as possible, since the lognormal

---

[12] The *proportional* deviations may not be greatest in the top decile because the base values are larger.

Table 22.2. Sum of absolute deviations of individual income shares, by decile intervals

Decile	1,000 observations						2,000 observations					
	LN	SM	GB	ALN	ASM	AGB	LN	SM	GB	ALN	ASM	AGB
Quintile pattern, 100 replications												
1	0.63	0.17	0.16	0.28	0.15	0.15	0.64	0.17	0.16	0.28	0.14	0.15
2	0.21	0.09	0.11	0.24	0.13	0.13	0.22	0.08	0.11	0.25	0.13	0.13
3	0.12	0.11	0.13	0.07	0.05	0.05	0.11	0.10	0.12	0.06	0.04	0.04
4	0.41	0.17	0.17	0.08	0.06	0.06	0.40	0.16	0.16	0.07	0.05	0.05
5	0.74	0.22	0.19	0.14	0.09	0.09	0.73	0.20	0.17	0.12	0.07	0.07
6	1.07	0.29	0.21	0.17	0.11	0.11	1.03	0.24	0.17	0.15	0.09	0.09
7	1.17	0.23	0.17	0.15	0.12	0.13	1.13	0.17	0.13	0.13	0.11	0.12
8	0.95	0.27	0.40	0.20	0.15	0.17	0.92	0.23	0.41	0.18	0.13	0.15
9	0.49	0.70	0.98	0.49	0.55	0.84	0.43	0.73	1.02	0.39	0.58	0.89
10	4.14	2.61	3.03	2.18	2.38	2.96	3.88	2.50	3.05	1.81	2.31	3.02
Total	9.92	4.87	5.56	3.99	3.78	4.68	9.47	4.59	5.50	3.44	3.66	4.70
Quintile-TB pattern, 100 replications												
1	0.54	0.12	0.12	0.16	0.11	0.11	0.56	0.12	0.11	0.15	0.10	0.10
2	0.12	0.27	0.30	0.05	0.06	0.06	0.12	0.27	0.30	0.05	0.06	0.06
3	0.22	0.30	0.32	0.05	0.06	0.06	0.21	0.30	0.32	0.04	0.05	0.05
4	0.57	0.36	0.34	0.07	0.06	0.06	0.56	0.35	0.33	0.06	0.05	0.05
5	0.90	0.37	0.31	0.09	0.07	0.07	0.90	0.36	0.30	0.08	0.06	0.06
6	1.23	0.39	0.27	0.11	0.09	0.09	1.20	0.34	0.22	0.10	0.08	0.07
7	1.32	0.24	0.19	0.14	0.10	0.10	1.28	0.18	0.16	0.13	0.08	0.08
8	1.05	0.34	0.54	0.16	0.17	0.18	1.01	0.33	0.57	0.13	0.15	0.16
9	0.52	1.02	1.31	0.25	0.26	0.29	0.47	1.08	1.35	0.18	0.22	0.26
10	5.00	3.09	3.43	1.95	2.66	3.32	4.74	3.04	3.47	1.54	2.71	3.44
Total	11.48	6.50	7.10	3.04	3.64	4.33	11.04	6.38	7.12	2.47	3.56	4.33
Decile pattern, 100 replications												
1	0.58	0.12	0.12	0.16	0.10	0.10	0.59	0.12	0.11	0.15	0.10	0.09
2	0.15	0.22	0.24	0.04	0.04	0.04	0.16	0.22	0.24	0.03	0.03	0.03
3	0.17	0.25	0.24	0.04	0.04	0.04	0.16	0.25	0.24	0.03	0.03	0.03
4	0.50	0.30	0.25	0.05	0.05	0.05	0.49	0.29	0.24	0.05	0.04	0.04
5	0.83	0.32	0.22	0.06	0.06	0.06	0.82	0.31	0.21	0.06	0.05	0.05
6	1.16	0.35	0.21	0.09	0.07	0.07	1.12	0.31	0.15	0.09	0.07	0.06
7	1.25	0.23	0.25	0.10	0.08	0.08	1.21	0.18	0.21	0.08	0.07	0.07
8	1.01	0.33	0.64	0.12	0.11	0.11	0.97	0.32	0.65	0.11	0.08	0.08
9	0.51	0.95	1.31	0.21	0.20	0.22	0.45	0.99	1.34	0.16	0.16	0.18
10	4.61	2.97	3.56	1.93	2.57	3.52	4.35	2.90	3.55	1.53	2.59	3.59
Total	10.75	6.04	7.03	2.81	3.31	4.27	10.31	5.88	6.95	2.28	3.21	4.23

Table 22.2. (*Continued*)

Decile	1,000 observations						2,000 observations					
	LN	SM	GB	ALN	ASM	AGB	LN	SM	GB	ALN	ASM	AGB
	Quintile pattern, 200 replications											
1	0.63	0.17	0.16	0.28	0.14	0.15	0.64	0.17	0.16	0.28	0.14	0.14
2	0.22	0.09	0.11	0.24	0.13	0.13	0.23	0.08	0.10	0.24	0.12	0.13
3	0.12	0.11	0.13	0.07	0.06	0.06	0.11	0.10	0.12	0.06	0.04	0.04
4	0.40	0.16	0.16	0.07	0.06	0.06	0.40	0.15	0.16	0.07	0.05	0.05
5	0.74	0.23	0.20	0.13	0.09	0.09	0.73	0.20	0.18	0.12	0.07	0.07
6	1.07	0.29	0.21	0.16	0.11	0.10	1.03	0.25	0.17	0.15	0.09	0.09
7	1.19	0.23	0.17	0.17	0.12	0.13	1.13	0.17	0.13	0.14	0.11	0.11
8	1.00	0.26	0.37	0.22	0.15	0.17	0.93	0.22	0.40	0.18	0.13	0.15
9	0.52	0.69	0.97	0.52	0.54	0.83	0.43	0.73	1.01	0.40	0.58	0.89
10	4.23	2.58	2.99	2.19	2.33	2.90	3.89	2.52	3.06	1.81	2.33	3.02
Total	10.10	4.81	5.46	4.03	3.72	4.60	9.51	4.59	5.48	3.45	3.67	4.69
	Quintile-TB pattern, 200 replications											
1	0.55	0.11	0.11	0.15	0.10	0.10	0.56	0.11	0.11	0.15	0.10	0.10
2	0.12	0.27	0.29	0.06	0.06	0.06	0.12	0.26	0.29	0.05	0.06	0.06
3	0.22	0.30	0.31	0.05	0.06	0.06	0.21	0.29	0.31	0.04	0.05	0.05
4	0.56	0.35	0.33	0.08	0.07	0.07	0.56	0.34	0.32	0.06	0.05	0.05
5	0.91	0.38	0.32	0.09	0.08	0.08	0.89	0.36	0.30	0.08	0.06	0.07
6	1.23	0.39	0.27	0.12	0.09	0.09	1.20	0.34	0.23	0.10	0.08	0.08
7	1.33	0.26	0.19	0.15	0.11	0.11	1.28	0.19	0.16	0.13	0.09	0.09
8	1.09	0.32	0.50	0.17	0.18	0.19	1.02	0.32	0.55	0.13	0.16	0.17
9	0.55	1.00	1.28	0.25	0.27	0.30	0.48	1.07	1.34	0.19	0.23	0.27
10	5.09	3.07	3.38	1.94	2.60	3.24	4.75	3.05	3.47	1.54	2.71	3.43
Total	11.65	6.43	6.97	3.06	3.61	4.29	11.05	6.34	7.07	2.49	3.58	4.34
	Decile pattern, 200 replications											
1	0.58	0.12	0.11	0.15	0.10	0.09	0.59	0.12	0.11	0.15	0.09	0.09
2	0.15	0.22	0.24	0.04	0.04	0.04	0.16	0.21	0.24	0.03	0.03	0.03
3	0.17	0.25	0.24	0.04	0.04	0.04	0.15	0.24	0.23	0.04	0.03	0.03
4	0.49	0.29	0.24	0.05	0.05	0.05	0.49	0.29	0.23	0.05	0.04	0.04
5	0.84	0.33	0.23	0.07	0.06	0.06	0.82	0.31	0.21	0.06	0.05	0.05
6	1.16	0.35	0.21	0.09	0.07	0.07	1.12	0.31	0.16	0.09	0.06	0.06
7	1.27	0.25	0.24	0.10	0.08	0.08	1.21	0.18	0.21	0.08	0.07	0.07
8	1.05	0.31	0.60	0.13	0.11	0.11	0.98	0.30	0.63	0.11	0.09	0.09
9	0.54	0.93	1.28	0.21	0.20	0.21	0.46	0.98	1.32	0.16	0.16	0.18
10	4.70	2.95	3.51	1.91	2.51	3.43	4.36	2.91	3.54	1.54	2.59	3.57
Total	10.93	5.98	6.90	2.79	3.24	4.19	10.34	5.84	6.88	2.29	3.22	4.22

Note: LN = lognormal, SM = Singh–Maddala, GB = generalized beta; prefix "A" = adjusted data.
Source: Authors' calculations.

Table 22.3. Total absolute deviations of income shares

Number of samples	1,000 observations						2,000 observations					
	LN	SM	GB	ALN	ASM	AGB	LN	SM	GB	ALN	ASM	AGB
						Quintile						
100	9.92	4.87	5.56	3.98	3.78	4.68	9.47	4.59	5.50	3.44	3.66	4.70
200	10.10	4.81	5.46	4.03	3.72	4.60	9.51	4.59	5.48	3.45	3.67	4.69
						Quintile-TB						
100	11.47	6.50	7.10	3.04	3.64	4.33	11.04	6.37	7.12	2.46	3.56	4.33
200	11.65	6.43	6.97	3.06	3.61	4.29	11.05	6.34	7.07	2.48	3.58	4.34
						Decile						
100	10.75	6.04	7.03	2.81	3.31	4.27	10.31	5.88	6.95	2.28	3.21	4.23
200	10.93	5.98	6.90	2.79	3.24	4.19	10.34	5.84	6.88	2.29	3.22	4.22

Note: LN = lognormal, SM = Singh–Maddala, GB = generalized beta; prefix "A" = adjusted data.
Source: Authors' calculations.

is unambiguously best in the runs with 2,000 observations, and increasing the size of the sample improves the data match in all circumstances.

The second method of assessing the performance of the ungrouping algorithm using the CPS involves a comparison between the true inequality values and the estimates generated via the synthetic sample. Four inequality measures were used for this purpose, the Gini coefficient and three members of the entropy family: the mean logarithmic deviation (MLD), the Theil coefficient (T), and the squared coefficient of variation (CV^2). For a sample of n observations x_i ($i = 1, \ldots, n$) with mean μ, these three indices may be written, respectively, as

$$\text{MLD} = \frac{1}{n} \sum_{i=1}^{n} \ln \frac{\mu}{x_i} \tag{8a}$$

$$\text{T} = \frac{1}{n} \sum_{i=1}^{n} \frac{x_i}{\mu} \ln \frac{x_i}{\mu} \tag{8b}$$

$$\text{CV}^2 = \frac{1}{n} \sum_{i=1}^{n} \left\{ \left(\frac{x_i}{\mu} \right)^2 - 1 \right\}. \tag{8c}$$

Tables 22.4–22.7 report the mean absolute percentage error for each of these indices, using both the raw synthetic sample and the adjusted sample.

The results for the Gini coefficient are very encouraging. Table 22.4 shows that the errors for the raw synthetic sample are usually 2–3% (and higher still for the lognormal fit). However, the expected error for the adjusted samples never exceeds 1% and falls below 0.1% for lognormal-generated observations constructed from decile

Table 22.4. Mean absolute percentage error: Gini coefficient

Grouping pattern	Unadjusted data			Adjusted data		
	LN	SM	GB	ALN	ASM	AGB
	1,000 sample observations, 100 replications					
Quintile	4.01	0.91	0.46	0.18	0.48	0.73
Quintile-TB	6.53	3.24	2.31	0.10	0.19	0.28
Decile	5.41	2.48	1.44	0.08	0.22	0.35
	1,000 sample observations, 200 replications					
Quintile	4.07	0.97	0.52	0.20	0.47	0.71
Quintile-TB	6.57	3.29	2.37	0.10	0.19	0.27
Decile	5.47	2.56	1.54	0.08	0.22	0.35
	2,000 sample observations, 100 replications					
Quintile	3.65	0.61	0.33	0.15	0.54	0.78
Quintile-TB	6.17	2.95	2.07	0.11	0.22	0.30
Decile	5.05	2.22	1.01	0.07	0.25	0.37
	2,000 sample observations, 200 replications					
Quintile	3.65	0.62	0.36	0.15	0.55	0.78
Quintile-TB	6.15	2.91	2.06	0.11	0.22	0.30
Decile	5.04	2.20	1.00	0.08	0.25	0.37

Note: LN = lognormal, SM = Singh–Maddala, GB = generalized beta.
Source: Authors' calculations.

share information. This translates into a confidence interval of around ±0.001 for the ungrouping estimates of a typical income Gini value (say, 0.4).

Results for the three entropy indices are less satisfactory. The best that can be achieved with the Theil coefficient is about a 1% error, which is reasonably acceptable (see Table 22.6). But the minimum expected error is 2.5% for the squared CV (Table 22.7), and around 4% for the MLD (Table 22.5).

In some respects, the pattern of results in Tables 22.4–22.7 corroborates the conclusions drawn earlier from Tables 22.2 and 22.3. The Singh–Maddala derived data are better on every count than those obtained using the generalized beta distribution. The lognormal performs poorly before the synthetic sample is adjusted, but improves greatly during Stage II of the algorithm, so much so that it leapfrogs both the Singh–Maddala and generalized beta estimates, unless the mean logarithmic deviation is chosen as the inequality index. As regards the grouping arrangement, the estimates again tend to improve (for the adjusted data at least) as one moves from quintiles to quintile-TB to deciles, echoing the slightly ambiguous results obtained earlier.

The most surprising feature of Tables 22.5–22.7 is the fact that the Stage II adjustment to the synthetic sample does not always improve the accuracy of the estimate of inequality. Indeed, for the Singh–Maddala and generalized beta distributions,

Table 22.5. Mean absolute percentage error: mean logarithmic deviation

Grouping pattern	Unadjusted data			Adjusted data		
	LN	SM	GB	ALN	ASM	AGB
	1,000 sample observations, 100 replications					
Quintile	17.66	10.82	11.24	15.32	11.57	12.01
Quintile-TB	12.90	3.94	4.12	10.36	7.98	8.08
Decile	15.03	5.93	6.91	10.30	8.02	8.10
	1,000 sample observations, 200 replications					
Quintile	17.47	10.58	10.99	15.12	11.35	11.78
Quintile-TB	12.73	3.73	3.92	10.15	7.76	7.86
Decile	14.85	5.64	6.59	10.09	7.79	7.88
	2,000 sample observations, 100 replications					
Quintile	18.23	11.30	11.63	15.35	11.65	12.05
Quintile-TB	13.45	4.20	4.31	10.28	7.96	8.04
Decile	15.59	6.27	7.01	10.22	8.00	8.06
	2,000 sample observations, 200 replications					
Quintile	18.07	11.14	11.46	15.20	11.49	11.90
Quintile-TB	13.34	4.18	4.27	10.17	7.86	7.95
Decile	15.46	6.21	6.92	10.13	7.90	7.97

Note: LN = lognormal, SM = Singh–Maddala, GB = generalized beta.
Source: Authors' calculations.

the adjustment raises the mean absolute percentage error in every case reported for the MLD index in Table 22.5, and in most cases recorded for the Theil coefficient in Table 22.6 and for the squared CV in Table 22.7. In contrast, the Stage II adjustment always improves the accuracy of the lognormal-based estimates, quite dramatically in the case of the Theil coefficient values in Table 22.6.

The post-adjustment deterioration in the predictive accuracy of the Singh–Maddala and generalized beta synthetic samples is unanticipated and not easy to comprehend, since the general tendency for an improvement during Stage II was documented earlier in Table 22.2. To explore the possible explanations, some specific sets of synthetic observations were examined, before and after adjustment. Figure 22.1 illustrates one (inevitably unrepresentative) sample obtained by applying the Singh–Maddala distribution to quintile groups. The graph—which plots the deviation of the synthetic Lorenz curve from the true Lorenz curve—shows the general improvement (and the exact quintile-share match) resulting from the Stage II adjustment. But the ranking of the pre- and post-adjustment samples is less clear in the top-quintile, precisely the place where the greatest inaccuracies occur. In particular, note that the top quintile Lorenz values for the adjusted sample always exceed the true values, but the deviations for the unadjusted sample can be negative

Table 22.6. Mean absolute percentage error: Theil coefficient

Grouping pattern	Unadjusted data			Adjusted data		
	LN	SM	GB	ALN	ASM	AGB
1,000 sample observations, 100 replications						
Quintile	10.19	1.95	3.85	1.42	3.70	5.32
Quintile-TB	16.52	3.53	2.26	0.95	2.66	3.57
Decile	13.69	2.91	4.05	0.95	2.59	3.86
1,000 sample observations, 200 replications						
Quintile	10.48	2.00	3.71	1.52	3.60	5.22
Quintile-TB	16.78	3.83	2.46	0.96	2.60	3.49
Decile	13.96	3.18	4.05	0.96	2.53	3.78
2,000 sample observations, 100 replications						
Quintile	8.78	2.41	4.65	1.15	4.19	5.67
Quintile-TB	15.05	2.55	1.68	0.84	2.99	3.79
Decile	12.24	1.94	3.98	0.84	2.90	4.01
2,000 sample observations, 200 replications						
Quintile	8.78	2.46	4.62	1.15	4.21	5.68
Quintile-TB	14.97	2.59	1.82	0.88	3.00	3.80
Decile	12.20	2.03	4.03	0.88	2.92	4.02

Note: LN = lognormal, SM = Singh–Maddala, GB = generalized beta.
Source: Authors' calculations.

or positive, allowing the possibility that the negative deviations offset the general tendency to underestimate inequality in the top quintile.[13]

Figure 22.2 examines the implications for estimates of the squared coefficient of variation by plotting the partial sum of the expression given in equation (8c), in other words:

$$\text{partial squared CV} = \frac{1}{n} \sum_{i=1}^{k} \left\{ \left(\frac{x_i}{\mu} \right)^2 - 1 \right\}, \quad k = 1, \ldots, n. \tag{9}$$

The pattern is broadly similar to that depicted in Figure 22.1. The Stage II adjustment improves the accuracy of the partial squared CV for most of its range. But it is the errors in the uppermost tail that determine the accuracy of the overall squared CV value, and here the superiority of the post-adjustment sample is not established unequivocally. Indeed, the fact that the Stage II adjustment magnifies the underestimate of the very richest incomes is the most likely explanation why the unadjusted Singh–Maddala sample is a better predictor of the squared CV. For

[13] The inequality bias occurs because the incomes of the super-rich are underestimated, as is evident in the sharp decline in the deviation from the true Lorenz curve at the very top of the distribution.

Table 22.7. Mean absolute percentage error: squared coefficient of variation

Grouping pattern	Unadjusted data			Adjusted data		
	LN	SM	GB	ALN	ASM	AGB
	1,000 sample observations, 100 replications					
Quintile	26.03	6.93	13.14	5.86	9.64	14.53
Quintile-TB	36.89	5.94	11.26	3.92	8.69	11.91
Decile	31.97	6.74	16.17	3.80	8.29	12.72
	1,000 sample observations, 200 replications					
Quintile	26.91	6.71	12.78	6.35	9.40	14.30
Quintile-TB	37.75	5.93	10.85	4.04	8.50	11.69
Decile	32.84	6.65	15.65	3.90	8.09	12.49
	2,000 sample observations, 100 replications					
Quintile	21.61	8.90	15.07	3.68	11.37	15.76
Quintile-TB	31.90	6.51	12.90	2.48	10.03	12.81
Decile	27.24	7.55	17.15	2.48	9.56	13.36
	2,000 sample observations, 200 replications					
Quintile	21.50	9.00	15.06	3.58	11.50	15.85
Quintile-TB	31.67	6.83	12.88	2.53	10.12	12.88
Decile	27.06	7.76	17.05	2.53	9.64	13.42

Note: LN = lognormal, SM = Singh–Maddala, GB = generalized beta.
Source: Authors' calculations.

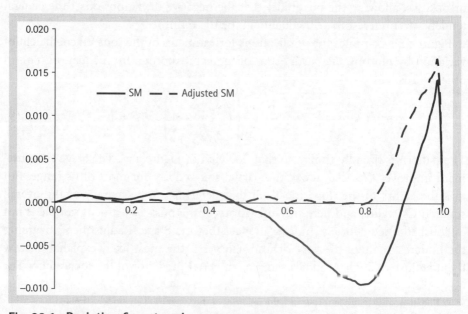

Fig. 22.1. Deviation from true Lorenz curve

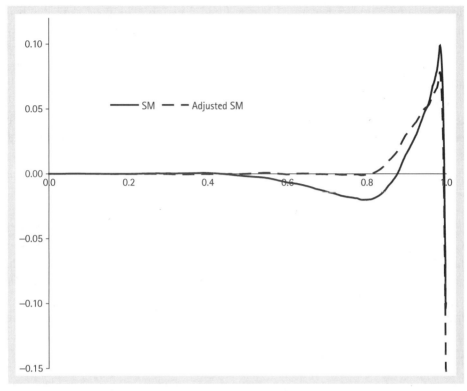

Fig. 22.2. Deviation of partial squared coefficient of variation

lognormal-based samples the adjustment always tends to improve the inequality estimates, so this anomaly does not arise, providing further grounds for favoring lognormal-based samples, despite the well-known deficiencies of the lognormal distribution as a representation of observed income distributions.

IV. SUMMARY AND CONCLUSION

Despite the increasing availability of survey data, analysts of poverty and inequality are often confronted with the need for individual income observations when only grouped data are either accessible or affordable. As a result, there is a continuing demand for algorithms than can generate synthetic samples of observations from grouped information, as demonstrated by the popularity of the POVCAL program offered by the World Bank.

This chapter proposes an alternative method of reconstructing individual income observations from grouped distributional data. It involves two stages: first, fitting a parametric Lorenz curve or distribution function to the grouped data, then adjusting the raw data generated by the fitted function. The procedure has two major virtues: it ensures that the characteristics of the synthetic sample exactly match the reported group values; and it is universally applicable, in the sense of being able to handle any feasible pattern of grouped data. Our method also has the advantages of speed and simplicity.

Using individual income records drawn from the CPS data, our method was tested by comparing the true values of individual observations with their synthetic counterparts. The results clearly demonstrate the superiority of the final adjusted sample, the adjustment leading to a better match with individual incomes in the vast majority of cases. Relative to the raw data, the adjustment often reduces the average deviation by a factor of two or more.

Comparison between the true and generated values of inequality indices provides a second way of assessing our proposed algorithm. In this respect, results for the Gini coefficient are rather encouraging. The expected error never exceeds 1% and falls below 0.1% for lognormal-generated observations constructed from decile share information, which translates into a confidence interval of around ±0.001 for estimates of a typical income Gini value (say, 0.4). Results for a selection of entropy indices are less good, but still satisfactory. Needless to say, the performance of the method improves as the grouping pattern becomes finer, changing from quintiles to quintiles plus the top and bottom deciles, and then to deciles.

As regards the parametric function used to generate the raw sample, the beta and general quadratic Lorenz functions employed in POVCAL and by Datt and Ravallion (1992) are deficient in one major respect: most of the synthetic samples contain one or more negative observations despite the fact that CPS income observations are always positive. Among the remaining candidates, the lognormal form is the clear winner in our test results after the Stage II adjustment has been implemented. Compared to samples derived from the Singh–Maddala or generalized beta distributions, the lognormal-based observations are consistently closer to the true values, and ensure more accurate estimates of most inequality indices.

On the basis of our findings, we conclude that our proposed adjustment procedure, coupled with an initial lognormal fit and a sample size of at least 1,000, is capable of reproducing individual data from grouped statistics with a high degree of accuracy. However, we encourage others to subject our algorithm to further tests, using alternative sources of microdata (for example, the Luxembourg Income Study) and using alternative functional forms to generate the raw sample observations.

References

AITCHINSON, J., and BROWN, J. A. C. (1957), *The Lognormal Distribution with Special Reference to its Use in Economics* (Cambridge: Cambridge University Press).

BANDOURIAN, R., MCDONALD, J. B., and TURVEY, R. S. (2002), *A Comparison of Parametric Models of Income Distribution Across Countries and Over Time*, Luxembourg Income Study Working Paper 305, available at <http://ssrn.com/abstract=s324900>.

BOURGUIGNON, F., and MORRISON, C. (2002), "Inequality among World Citizens: 1820–1992", *American Economic Review*, 92: 727–44.

CAPÉAU, B., and DECOSTER, A. (2004), *The Rise or Fall of World Inequality: A Spurious Controversy?*, UNU-WIDER Discussion Paper 2204/02 (Helsinki: UNU-WIDER).

CHOTIKAPANICH, D., GRIFFITHS, W. E., and RAO, D. S. P. (2007), "Estimating and Combining National Income Distributions Using Limited Data", *Journal of Business and Economics Statistics*, 25: 97–109.

—— RAO, D. S. P., and TANG, K. K. (2007), "Estimating Income Inequality in China Using Grouped Data and the Generalized Beta Distribution", *Review of Income and Wealth*, 53: 127–47.

—— VALENZUELA, R., and RAO, D. S. P. (1997), "Global and Regional Inequality in the Distribution of Income: Estimation with Limited and Incomplete Data", *Empirical Economics*, 22: 533–46.

COWELL, F. A., and MEHTA, F. (1982), "The Estimation and Interpolation of Inequality Measures", *Review of Economic Studies*, 49: 273–90.

D'AMBROSIO, C. (1999), *The Distribution of Wages: A Non-Parametric Decomposition*, Jerome Levy Economics Institute Working Paper 284 (Annandale-on-Hudson, NY: Jerome Levy Economics Institute of Bard College).

DATT, G. (1998), "Computational Tools for Poverty Measurement and Analysis", available at <www.ifpri.org/divs/fcnd/dp/papers/dp50.pdf>.

—— and RAVALLION, M. (1992), "Growth and Redistribution Components of Changes in Poverty Measures: A Decomposition with Application to Brazil and India in the 1980s", *Journal of Development Economics*, 38: 275–95.

DAVIES, J. B., SANDSTROM, S., SHORROCKS, A., and WOLFF, E. (2007), *Estimating the Level and Distribution of Global Household Wealth*, UNU-WIDER Research Paper 2007/77 (Helsinki: UNU-WIDER).

———————— (2008), *The World Distribution of Household Wealth*, UNU-WIDER Discussion Paper 2008/03 (Helsinki: UNU-WIDER).

—— and SHORROCKS, A. F. (1989), "Optimal Grouping of Income and Wealth Data", *Journal of Econometrics*, 42: 97–108.

DEATON, A. (1997), *The Analysis of Household Surveys* (Baltimore: Johns Hopkins University Press).

DINARDO, J., FORTIN, N. M., and LEMIEUX, T. (1996), "Labor Market Institutions and the Distribution of Wages, 1973–1993: A Semiparametric Approach", *Econometrica*, 64: 1001–44.

DOWRICK, S., and AKMAL, M. (2005), "Contradictory Trends in Global Income Inequality: A Tale of Two Biases", *Review of Income and Wealth*, 51: 201–29.

GASTWIRTH, J. L. (1972), "The Estimation of the Lorenz Curve and Gini Index", *Review of Economics and Statistics*, 54: 306–16.

HARRISON, A. (1981), "Earnings by Size: A Tale of Two Distributions", *Review of Economic Studies*, 48: 621–31.

KAKWANI, N. (1976), "On the Estimation of Income Inequality Measures from Grouped Observations", *Review of Economic Studies*, 43: 483–92.

—— (1980), "On a Class of Poverty Measures", *Econometrica*, 48: 437–46.

——and PODDER, N. (1973), "On the Estimation of Lorenz Curves from Grouped Observations", *International Economic Review*, 14: 278–92.

————(1976), "Efficient Estimation of the Lorenz Curve and Associated Inequality Measures from Grouped Observations", *Econometrica*, 44: 137–48.

KLOEK, T., and VAN DIJK, H. K. (1978), "Efficient Estimation of Income Distribution Parameters", *Journal of Econometrics*, 8: 61–74.

KOLENIKOV, S., and SHORROCKS, A. F. (2005), "A Decomposition Analysis of Regional Poverty in Russia", *Review of Development Economics*, 9: 25–46.

McDONALD, J. B. (1984), "Some Generalized Functions for the Size Distribution of Income", *Econometrica*, 52: 647–63.

——and RANSOM, M. J. (1979), "Functional Forms, Estimation Techniques and the Distribution of Income", *Econometrica*, 47: 1513–26.

————(1981), "An Analysis of the Bounds for the Gini Coefficient", *Journal of Econometrics*, 17: 177–88.

MILANOVIC, B. (2002), "True World Income Distribution, 1988 and 1993: First Calculation Based On Household Surveys Alone", *Economic Journal*, 112: 51–92.

——(2005), *Worlds Apart: Measuring International and Global Inequality* (Princeton, NJ: Princeton University Press).

MINOIU, C., and REDDY, S. G. (2006), "The Estimation of Poverty and Inequality from Grouped Data Using Parametric Curve Fitting: An Evaluation of POVCAL", unpubl. MS.

SALA-I-MARTIN, X. (2002), *The World Distribution of Income*, NBER Working Paper 8933 (Cambridge, Mass.: National Bureau of Economic Research).

SALEM, A. B. Z., and MOUNT, T. D. (1974), "A Convenient Descriptive Model of Income Distribution: The Gamma Density", *Econometrica*, 42: 1115–27.

SCHULTZ, T. P. (1998), *Inequality in the Distribution of Personal Income in the World: How it is Changing and Why*, Economic Growth Center Working Paper 784 (New Haven, Conn.: Economic Growth Center, Yale University).

SEN, A. K. (1973), *On Economic Inequality* (Oxford: Clarendon Press).

——(1976), "Poverty: An Ordinal Approach to Measurement", *Econometrica*, 44: 219–31.

SHORROCKS, A. F., and KOLENIKOV, S. (2001), "Poverty Trends in Russia", unpubl. MS.

SINGH, S. K., and MADDALA, G. S. (1976), "A Function for the Size Distribution of Incomes", *Econometrica*, 44: 963–70.

VILLASENOR, J., and ARNOLD, B. C. (1989), "Elliptical Lorenz Curves", *Journal of Econometrics*, 40: 327–38.

....

CHAPTER 23

A PRACTICAL PROPOSAL FOR SIMPLIFYING THE MEASUREMENT OF INCOME POVERTY

....

S. SUBRAMANIAN

In social investigation and measurement, it is undoubtedly more important to be vaguely right than to be precisely wrong.

Amartya Sen (2003: 6)

I. MOTIVATION

....

THIS is a technically very simple chapter prompted by certain practical considerations aimed at simplifying the task of measuring income poverty. It is as well to declare at the outset that the particular route to simplification sought here is not

I am grateful to Kaushik Basu for valuable advice on an earlier version of this chapter. If there are any surviving errors which he has not corrected, I suppose I should take responsibility for them. I am also indebted to R. Dharumaperumal for computational assistance.

devoid of conceptual ambiguities, hence the tentativeness of the proposal outlined. It is noted that extant approaches to poverty measurement are also marked by conceptual and other practical difficulties, and the question which arises is whether the pragmatic gain from simplification is worth the possible loss in conceptual soundness, of one kind, which the simplification may entail. The problem is addressed in a spirit of genuine enquiry, and in the hope that it will provoke the engagement of other concerned scholars in the field.

More specifically, this paper discusses certain serious difficulties with solving the identification problem of conventional poverty measurement. A thoroughgoing fuzzy approach to the measurement of poverty can sidestep the identification problem altogether, and it is demonstrated that a specific vague procedure yields a fuzzy poverty measure which is simply an affine transform of Amartya Sen's well-known measure of aggregate welfare. Similar poverty measures can be derived as vague counterparts of other crisp welfare indicators, including a particularly simple one proposed by Kaushik Basu. The paper poses, and invites an answer to, the question of whether, on a balance of strategic and conceptual considerations, there may be something to be said for measuring poverty (fuzzily) in terms of certain familiar welfare indices.

II. The Problem

As is well known, the task of poverty measurement in income space requires solving two problems—those of identification and aggregation. The first problem is concerned with stipulating a poverty line, which is a level of income intended to separate the poor from the non-poor. Once the poverty line has been specified, the second problem is concerned with using data on the distribution of incomes in order to arrive at a satisfactory real-valued representation of poverty. It will be readily conceded by most practitioners that the specification of a cut-off poverty line income is both (a) intrinsically difficult and (b) instrumentally problematic for the aggregation exercise.

II.1 The Intrinsic Difficulty

To begin with the first issue. In a "relative" view of poverty, it is customary to fix the poverty line as some proportion of a measure of central tendency, such as the mean or median income. For reasons which Sen (1983) has discussed, this can be a very unsatisfactory procedure. As he has pointed out, if the poverty line is fixed at, say, one-half the mean income, then a halving of every person's income would leave the set of identified poor individuals unchanged, a judgement which is hard to accept. This suggests the reasonableness of recognizing an "absolutist core" in the assessment of poverty.

In an "absolute" view of poverty, it is a highly prevalent practice—call this Procedure A—to specify the poverty line in terms of (the income equivalent of) some fixed commodity basket, or in terms of some level of income (such as the World Bank's "dollar a day" requirement) which is corrected only for price changes across space and over time. Such procedures are apparently inspired by the perceived need of having what Sanjay Reddy (2004) has called a "common criterion" to render poverty comparisons meaningful. However, as Reddy persuasively argues, this common criterion is most sensibly specified in the space of *capabilities to function*. Such a procedure—call it Procedure B—is fully compatible with variable commodity baskets and variable "real" incomes, in consonance with Sen's (1983) suggestion that deprivation should be postulated in an absolute sense in the space of functionings but possibly (and for this reason) in a relative sense in the space of commodities, resources and incomes. Reddy (2004: 7) states:

[This] proposal requires identifying a set of elementary income-dependent capabilities which an individual ought to be able to afford in order to be deemed non-poor. Once this set of capabilities is agreed at the global level, the specific resources required to achieve them would be identified in each country. ... The resulting poverty lines will, by construction, refer to a common criterion for identifying the poor and thereby permit meaningful comparison and aggregation of poverty estimates across countries.

I have prescribed something very similar in a time-series context (Subramanian 2005: 63):

[A] coherent approach to the identification problem would probably consist in something like the following. At any period of time t, let $\underline{f}^t \equiv (f_1^t, \ldots, f_K^t)$ be a K-vector of "minimally acceptable levels" for each of K functionings (such as those relating to nutrition, clothing, shelter, health, knowledge, etc.) that are regarded as being essential to human well-being. Let $\underline{c}^t \equiv (c_1^t, \ldots, c_K^t)$ be a corresponding K-vector of associated costs, in time t, that will (at the least) need to be incurred in order to achieve the various minimally acceptable levels of each of the K functionings listed in $\underline{f}^t$. Sensitivity to both perceptions and facts will cause each of $\underline{f}^t$ and $\underline{c}^t$ to be variable functions of time t. Define $z_t \equiv \sum_{k=1}^{K} c_k^t$. Then z_t can be taken to be the (variable) poverty line for time t.

While Procedure B is (at least to some, including the present author) straightforwardly appealing from an abstract point of view, it is likely to be very hard to implement. This has been noted in the paper of mine just cited (Subramanian 2005: 63):

All this is no doubt very simply stated at the conceptual level: but one has serious doubts that this program of identification is at all feasible of execution. For, first, identification of the set of functionings that are "essential for human well-being" is itself no easy task to achieve; the further determination of "minimally acceptable levels" for each of these functionings must be imagined to be an even harder task; and, finally, the empirical job of estimating associated costs is likewise an exercise fraught with non-trivial pragmatic problems.

To this may be added the fact that spatial variations in the ability to convert resources into functionings could call forth a multiplicity of income poverty lines across space: in the context of a country like India, for instance, it is realistic to expect that surely each district should have a poverty line of its own, and with something like 400 districts in the country, this would be a massive burden of administrative effort for the central Planning Commission. Procedure A (or some variant thereof) is simpler (even if not necessarily simple) to implement. What is more, it appears (inexplicably, from the perspective of adherents of Procedure B) to have a very considerable following in terms of its conceptual appeal. For instance, the official Indian poverty time-series, which is based on a Procedure A-type approach to the identification problem, has elicited a fair amount of agreement from the academic community. More recently, however, it has drawn a good deal of flak for allegedly presenting a misleading profile of progressively understated poverty rates over time (see, among others, Mehta and Venkatraman 2000; Patnaik 2004; Ray and Lancaster 2005; and Subramanian 2005).

In performing poverty comparisons, it seems very clear that the common criterion underlying the comparisons should be identified in the space of capabilities to function. This is a major insight of Amartya Sen's, but one which is not distinguished for its widespread observance in empirical work on poverty. Perhaps largely owing to the practical difficulty of translating Sen's insight into the specification of poverty lines in income space, there is a tendency to identify the common criterion in the space of fixed commodity baskets or unvarying income levels. Much effort is then expended in the cause of arriving at income poverty lines with an exactitude that is somewhat at odds with the dubious conceptual basis underlying them: this is a specific instance of getting both social investigation and measurement precisely wrong. In the end, it does not help the cause of poverty measurement if identification is either infeasibly hard or feasible but misleading. The problem is particularly acute when policy formulation, in the matter of such a serious issue as the redress of poverty, is so crucially dependent on getting one's poverty statistics as nearly right as possible.

II.2 The Instrumental Difficulty

The second issue, flagged earlier, has to do with the possibility that the identification problem could pose some instrumental difficulties in terms of its implications for the aggregation exercise. This has been most clearly demonstrated by Kundu and Smith (1983), via an impossibility theorem for poverty indices which suggests that the quest for a real-valued poverty index which is required to satisfy some seemingly innocuous "population monotonicity" properties in conjunction with the "transfer axiom" could terminate in a discovery of non-existence. In diagnosing the source of the difficulty, Kundu and Smith (1983: 431) say:

Turning next to the structural definition of poverty indices themselves, it should be clear that the major restriction in this definition is the completely dichotomous treatment of income levels above and below the poverty line. [One] ... direction for generalizing poverty indices is suggested by the observation above that the notion of a poverty line l is rarely absolute in nature, and hence that the identification of poverty incomes is to some degree uncertain. If one then treats such incomes as defining a "fuzzy set", say L, then one may assign a degree of membership in L (or *poverty degree*), say $l_x \in (0,1)$, to every income level x. ... [I]t is our view that the attempt to specify such a function may well serve to bring into focus the difficult issue of identifying implicit social attitudes toward poverty itself.

If it is acknowledged that the identification problem in poverty measurement is so fraught with conceptual and pragmatic difficulties as to threaten both reliable and coherent measurement, then there might be a case for examining the possibility of measuring poverty without resort to the specification of a poverty line. The Kundu–Smith recommendation of a fuzzy approach to poverty measurement presents itself as a possible (and literal) means to moving in the direction of getting things at least "vaguely right". This approach is explored, in a very elementary way, in the rest of this chapter. It is suggested that particularly simple fuzzy poverty measures can be derived which are closely related to Amartya Sen's (1976b) and Kaushik Basu's (2001, 2006) indices of aggregate welfare. The merits and limitations of this approach are then discussed in a non-dogmatic spirit which invites comment on whether the approach could at all be seen as a constructive proposal.

III. Crisp Welfare as Vague Poverty?

III.1 Preliminary Concepts

Let X_n be the set of all non-negative n-vectors of income $\underline{x} = (x_1, \ldots, x_i, \ldots, x_n)$, where x_i is the income of the ith person in a community of n individuals, n being a member of the set N of non-negative integers. Define the set $X \equiv \cup_{n \in N} X_n$. Let $D \subseteq X$ be the comparison set of income distributions, viz. the set of conceivable income vectors that will be compared in terms of the extent of poverty they reflect. We shall (for reasons which will become apparent at a later stage) find it useful to exclude from D those distributions $\underline{x}$ for which $n(\underline{x})$ is not large enough to permit the approximation of $[n(\underline{x})/2 + 1]/[n(\underline{x})/2]$ to unity. For every $\underline{x} \in D$, let $S(\underline{x})$ be the set of individuals $\{1, \ldots, i, \ldots n(\underline{x})\}$ whose incomes are represented in $\underline{x}$. In everything that follows, D will be taken to be a set of *non-decreasingly ordered vectors of income*: that is, for every $\underline{x} \in D$, the individuals in $S(\underline{x})$ are labeled such that $x_i \leq x_{i+1}$ for all $i \in S(\underline{x}) \backslash \{n(\underline{x})\}$ (ties in income are taken to be broken arbitrarily). For all $\underline{x} \in D$ and for all $i \in S(\underline{x})$, the ith-poorest person's rank order in the vector $\underline{x}$ is defined as $r_i(\underline{x}) \equiv n(\underline{x}) + 1 - i$. We shall also take it that all income levels are finite. Let $\hat{x}$ be the largest income in any of the income distributions contained in D, viz. $\hat{x} \equiv \max_{\underline{x} \in D}\{x_{n(\underline{x})}\}$. For future reference, let x^* be any very large finite income level, $\infty > x^* \gg \hat{x}$: for specificity, one could take x^* to be, say, a thousand times the world's aggregate income. As we shall see later, the precise specification of x^* is of no great moment, and it simply serves the purpose of making the analytical problem under consideration arithmetically tractable. The role of x^* will be made clear in sections III.3–III.5 of this chapter.

III.2 Fuzzy poverty membership functions

We shall here consider certain very rudimentary aspects of fuzzy poverty measurement (for some elements of which the reader is referred to, among others, Shorrocks and Subramanian 1994). Given any income distribution $\underline{x} \in D$ and any individual $i \in S(\underline{x})$, let $m_i(\underline{x})$ signify a *membership function*, which is a function that assigns a real-valued poverty status to person i, with an income of x_i, in the distribution $\underline{x}$. It is useful to draw a distinction between two types of membership function, the first of which may be called *environment-independent*, and the second *environment-sensitive*. An environment-independent membership function is one which, for all distinct $\underline{x}$, $\underline{y} \in D$, pronounces that $m_i(\underline{x}) = m_j(\underline{y})$ whenever there exist $i \in S(\underline{x})$ and $j \in S(\underline{y})$ such that $x_i = y_j$. Such a function assesses a person's poverty status by reference to her *absolute* level of income, and not at all by reference to her income relative to the distribution from which her income is drawn, hence the term "environment-independent". By contrast, for all distinct $\underline{x}$, $\underline{y} \in D$, if there exist $i \in S(\underline{x})$ and $j \in S(\underline{y})$ such that $x_i = y_j$, and it is not necessarily the case that $m_i(\underline{x}) = m_j(\underline{y})$, then such a membership function will be called environment-sensitive. To illustrate: with the income I earn in India, I may belong to the top 10% of the Indian income distribution, while with the same income I may belong to the bottom 30% of the British income distribution; if that is indeed the case, it would be very plausible to assess my poverty status differently in India and Britain, which is the sort of judgement that would be upheld by an environment-sensitive poverty membership function. In everything that follows, we shall restrict attention to the set of environment-sensitive membership functions.

We now impose some more structure on the fuzzy membership function. We shall take poverty status to lie between zero and unity, viz. for all $\underline{x} \in D$ and all $i \in S(\underline{x})$, $m_i(\underline{x}) \in [0,1]$. "Complete poverty" will be associated with zero income: if $x_i = 0$, then this is a necessary condition for $m_i(\underline{x})$ to be unity. This, for obvious reasons, one may call a "normalization" property. For all $\underline{x} \in D$ and all $i, j \in S(\underline{x})$, if $x_j > x_i$, then we shall require, reasonably, that $m_j(\underline{x}) \leq m_i(\underline{x})$. That is, other things being equal, poverty status is taken not to increase with an increase in income. This one may call a "weak monotonicity" property.

As one can immediately see, any number of specific membership functions can satisfy the properties just stated. The choice of a "fuzzy" membership function must remain arbitrary, subject to its satisfying, minimally, the normalization and weak monotonicity properties just discussed. It may be added that, while "arbitrariness" in itself may be unavoidable, this cannot be an excuse for license, or *unreasonable* arbitrariness. To anticipate, the fuzzy membership functions employed in this chapter will certainly turn out to be arbitrary, in the sense of lacking any uniquely and radically rationalizable justification. Even so, it can be asserted that these membership functions are exempt from the charge of unreasonableness. Indeed, they lead, as will be shown, to the derivation of fuzzy poverty indices which bear a strong resemblance to certain welfare-related indicators advanced earlier in the literature. Shorrocks (2005) traces a tendency amongst practitioners to stick with certain formulations and indices to what he calls "inertia" and "network" effects. These effects, and the consensual agreement that implicitly underlies them, may not be a bad excuse for pressing well-worn formulations into service, as long as the formulations are not intrinsically unreasonable, or do not impede the evolution of other reasonable formulations. The issue will not be pursued further here.

A *fuzzy poverty measure* is a function $P: D \rightarrow [0,1]$, which is obtained, for all $\underline{x} \in D$, as a simple arithmetic average of the membership functions of all the individuals whose incomes are represented in $\underline{x}$:

$$P(\underline{x}) = (1/n(\underline{x})) \sum_{i=1}^{n(\underline{x})} m_i(\underline{x}). \tag{1}$$

We shall now consider a set of three "crisp" welfare indices and their relationship to a corresponding set of fuzzy poverty measures.

III.3 The Sen Welfare Index

For any $\underline{x} \in D$, the mean of $\underline{x}$ is denoted by $\mu(\underline{x}) \equiv (1/n(\underline{x})) \sum_{i=1}^{n(\underline{x})} x_i$; and the Gini coefficient of inequality in the interpersonal distribution of incomes is given (see Sen 1973) by

$$G(\underline{x}) = (n(\underline{x}) + 1)/n(\underline{x}) - (2/n^2(\underline{x})\mu(\underline{x})) \sum_{i=1}^{n(\underline{x})} r_i(\underline{x})x_i. \tag{2}$$

Sen's (1976b) index of aggregate welfare is obtained by combining per capita income and the Gini coefficient of inequality in its distribution in a composite measure which, other things equal, rewards an increase in mean income and penalizes an increase in inequality, and is given by

$$W^S(\underline{x}) = \mu(\underline{x})[1 - G(\underline{x})].$$ (3)

We shall return to the Sen welfare index after a brief digression on fuzzy poverty measurement. For all $\underline{x} \in D$ and $i \in S(\underline{x})$, and recalling the income level x^* discussed in section III.1, consider a particular specialization of the environment-sensitive fuzzy poverty membership function given by

$$m_i^S(\underline{x}) = [(x^* - x_i)/x^*][r_i(\underline{x})/n(\underline{x})].$$ (4)

Notice from (4) that if the poorest person (person 1 in the ordered income vector) has an income of zero, then $m_1^S(\underline{x}) = 1$, while for the richest person (person n), $m_n^S(\underline{x}) = (x^* - x_n)/n(\underline{x})x^*$, which tends to zero as x_n tends to x^*. Further, poverty status, as measured by m_i^S, is a declining function of income: m_i^S satisfies both the normalization and the weak monotonicity properties. Given $\underline{x}$, m_i^S, and (1), we can now define a fuzzy poverty measure—call it P^1—as follows:

$$P^1(\underline{x}) \left[= (1/n(\underline{x})) \sum_{i=1}^{n(\underline{x})} m_i^S(\underline{x}) \right] = (1/n(\underline{x})) \sum_{i=1}^{n(\underline{x})} [(x^* - x_i)/x^*][r_i(\underline{x})/n(\underline{x})]$$

$$= [1/n^2(\underline{x})x^*] \left[n(\underline{x})(n(\underline{x}) + 1)x^*/2 - \sum_{i=1}^{n(\underline{x})} r_i(\underline{x})x_i \right].$$

Noting from (2) that $\sum_{i=1}^{n(\underline{x})} r_i(\underline{x})x_i = n(\underline{x})(n(\underline{x}) + 1)\mu(\underline{x})/2 - n^2(\underline{x})\mu(\underline{x})G(\underline{x})/2$, and making the appropriate substitution, we have:

$$P^1(\underline{x}) = [1/n^2(\underline{x})x^*][n(\underline{x})(n(\underline{x}) + 1)x^*/2 - n(\underline{x})(n(\underline{x}) + 1)\mu(\underline{x})/2$$
$$+ n^2(\underline{x})\mu(\underline{x})G(\underline{x})/2].$$

Approximating $(n(\underline{x}) + 1)/n(\underline{x})$ to unity (see the related assumption made in section III.1, and simplifying, we have:

$$P^1(\underline{x}) = 1/2 - (1/2x^*)\mu(\underline{x})[1 - G(\underline{x})].$$

If $\alpha \equiv 1/2$ and $\beta \equiv 1/2x^*$, then, recalling from (3) that $\mu(\underline{x})[1 - G(\underline{x})] = W^S(\underline{x})$, we obtain:

$$P^1(\underline{x}) = \alpha - \beta W^S(\underline{x}).$$ (5)

(5) tells us that the fuzzy poverty measure P^1 is just a negative affine transform of Sen's welfare index W^S.

III.4 The Basu Well-Being Indicator

What might be one goal (among many) of development? Kaushik Basu (2001, 2006) proposes a particularly stark and simple objective of development, that of maximizing what he calls the "quintile income", which is the average income of the poorest 20% of the population. Given an ordered income vector $\underline{x} = (x_1, \ldots, x_i, \ldots, x_n)$, we shall assume that there exists a positive integer t such that the first t individuals constitute the poorest 20% of the population, viz. $t(\underline{x})/n(\underline{x}) = 0.2$. The quintile income is then given by $\mu^Q(\underline{x}) \equiv (1/t(\underline{x})) \sum_{i=1}^{t(\underline{x})} x_i$. Basu's "well-being indicator" W^B is simply the quintile income μ^Q:

$$W^B(\underline{x}) = \mu^Q(\underline{x}). \tag{6}$$

Consider now a fuzzy poverty membership function given by

$$m_i^B(\underline{x}) = [(x^* - x_i)/x^*] \text{ if } i \le t(\underline{x}); \tag{7}$$

$$= 0 \text{ if } i > t(\underline{x}).$$

m_i^B assigns a value of one to person i's poverty status when i belongs to the poorest 20% of the population and has an income of zero; poverty status declines with income in a linear fashion up to the tth individual's income level; and at this income level, poverty status falls discontinuously to zero and remains at zero for all individuals with incomes equal to, or higher than, the tth person's income. If $P^2(\underline{x})$ is the fuzzy poverty index obtained by employing the membership function m_i^B specified in (7) on the right-hand side of (1), then, for all $\underline{x} \in D$,

$$P^2(\underline{x}) \left[= (1/n(\underline{x})) \sum_{i=1}^{n(\underline{x})} m_i^B(\underline{x}) \right] = (1/n(\underline{x})) \sum_{i=1}^{t(\underline{x})} [(x^* - x_i)/x^*]$$

$$= t(\underline{x})/n(\underline{x}) - [t(\underline{x})/n(\underline{x})x^*]\mu^Q(\underline{x}),$$

or, noting that $t(\underline{x})/n(\underline{x}) \equiv 0.2$,

$$P^2(\underline{x}) = 0.2 - (0.2/x^*)\mu^Q(\underline{x}),$$

whence, in view of (6):

$$P^2(\underline{x}) = 0.2 - (0.2/x^*)W^B(\underline{x}). \tag{8}$$

Once more, we note that P^2 is just a negative affine transform of W^B.

III.5 A "Mixed" Welfare Index

In Subramanian (2006), I have proposed a welfare index which is, in effect, a mixture of the concerns reflected by the Sen and Basu welfare indices. Call this the mixed welfare index W^M. The Basu indicator focuses only on the poorest fifth of the population, while, in a similar spirit, the index W^M focuses only on the poorest half of the population; and, like the Sen index, the index W^M explicitly incorporates distributional considerations in assessing welfare. Specifically, W^M is just the Sen index computed for the population with incomes not exceeding the median income. Thus, given an ordered income vector $\underline{x} = (x_1, \ldots, x_i, \ldots, x_n)$, let the income vector of the poorest 50% of the population be denoted by $\underline{x}^M$; let the first p individuals constitute the poorest 50% of the population (that is, $p(\underline{x})/n(\underline{x}) = 0.5$); let $r_i(\underline{x}^M) \equiv p(\underline{x}) + 1 - i$ be the rank order of the ith poorest individual in the vector $\underline{x}^M$; let the average income of the poorest one-half of the population be $\mu^M(\underline{x}) \equiv (1/p(\underline{x})) \sum_{i=1}^{p(\underline{x})} x_i$; and let $G^M(\underline{x}) \equiv (p(\underline{x}) + 1)/p(\underline{x}) - (2/p^2(\underline{x})\mu^M(\underline{x})) \sum_{i=1}^{p(\underline{x})} r_i(\underline{x}^M)x_i$ be the Gini coefficient of inequality in the distribution of incomes among the poorest 50% of the population. Then the mixed welfare index is given by

$$W^M(\underline{x}) = \mu^M(\underline{x})[1 - G^M(\underline{x})]. \tag{9}$$

Next, consider the following fuzzy poverty membership function:

$$m_i^M(\underline{x}) = [(x^* - x_i)/x^*][r_i(\underline{x}^M)/p(\underline{x})]\forall i \leq p(\underline{x}); \tag{10}$$

$$= 0 \forall i > p(\underline{x}).$$

It is very easy to verify that if the membership function m_i^M specified in (10) is employed on the right-hand side of (1), then the resulting fuzzy poverty index— call it P^3—will be given (upon approximating $(p(\underline{x})+1)/p(\underline{x})$ to unity, which is permitted owing to the relevant assumption made in section III.1), for all $\underline{x} \in D$, by:

$$P^3(\underline{x}) = 1/8 - (1/8x^*)[\mu^M(\underline{x})(1 - G^M(\underline{x}))],$$

or, in view of (9):

$$P^3(\underline{x}) = 1/8 - (1/8x^*)W^M(\underline{x}). \tag{11}$$

P^3 is just a negative affine transform of W^M.

III.6 The "Practical Proposal"

Since P^1 is a straightforwardly linear re-cardinalization of W^S, the information on alternative distributions conveyed by P^1 is identical to the information on these distributions conveyed by (the negative of) W^S, so we might as well replace P^1 by $(-)W^S$. Exactly the same point can be made about P^2 vis-à-vis W^B, and about P^3 vis à vis W^M. Poverty reduction targets can then be set in terms of stipulated rates of growth of the welfare indices. This is the sort of approach that is compatible with, and gives concrete content to, the notion of "pro-poor growth", or what the Indian Planning Commission's Draft Approach Paper to the Eleventh Five-Year

Plan calls "inclusive growth". Briefly, there is a well-defined (or at least fuzzy!) sense in which the three welfare indices reviewed above can be interpreted as corresponding poverty measures. If this is the case, then that paves the way for the following proposal: is one free to bypass the identification exercise, and all its attendant difficulties, by measuring poverty in terms of certain easily comprehended welfare indices?

IV. Discussion

Even though $(-)W^S$ can be interpreted as a (fuzzy) poverty measure, there is a sense in which the use of this index as a poverty index could militate against our ordinary intuitions about poverty. This is illustrated by a simple example. Consider some level of income z which we might feel comfortable about thinking of as being in the neighborhood of a conventional "poverty line". Let x and y be two (ordered) income n-vectors given by $\underline{x} = (z, \ldots, z)$ and $\underline{y} = (0, \ldots, 0, 4z, \ldots, 4z)$, such that the first $n/2$ individuals in y receive zero income and the remaining $n/2$ individuals receive an income of $4z$ each (n is assumed to be even). Then it is easy to check that $W^S(\underline{x}) = W^S(\underline{y}) = z$. By the argument of section III, we should conclude that $\underline{x}$ and $\underline{y}$ display the same extent of poverty. But isn't there a sense—given our ordinary notions of "poverty"—in which we would be disposed to judge that y reflects more poverty than x (even though y also reflects more affluence than $\underline{x}$)? How crippling is this objection to the proposal of employing $(-)W^S$ as a poverty measure? The answer—apart from the issue of how often one might actually encounter empirical distributions like x and y—would depend on whether we are prepared to tolerate a similar (though perhaps muted) sort of difficulty in conventional poverty measurement. Specifically, consider Sen's (1976a) poverty index which, for "large" numbers of the poor, can be written as

$$P^S = H[I + (1 - I)G^*],$$

where H is the headcount ratio (or proportion of the population in poverty), I is the income-gap ratio (or proportionate shortfall from the poverty line of the average income of the poor), and G^* is the Gini coefficient of inequality in the distribution of poor incomes. Imagine two ordered n-vectors of income $\underline{u}$ and $\underline{v}$ which have the same number q of poor persons (assumed equal to $n/2$), and given, respectively, by $\underline{u} = (0.1z, \ldots, 0.1z; 2z, \ldots, 2z)$ and $\underline{v} = (0, \ldots, 0, 0.4z, \ldots, 0.4z; 2z, \ldots, 2z)$ such that, in $\underline{v}$, the poorest $q/2$ individuals have an income of zero each and the next poorest $q/2$ individuals have an income of $0.4z$ each (q is also assumed to be even). It can be verified that

$P^S(\underline{u}) = P^S(\underline{v}) = 0.45$. If the example revolving around the vectors $\underline{x}$ and $\underline{y}$ makes us feel uncomfortable about measuring poverty by the index $(-)W^S$, then by the same token, the example revolving around the vectors $\underline{u}$ and $\underline{v}$ should make us feel uncomfortable about measuring poverty by the index P^S. Both entail an uneasy "aggregational" trade-off between the claims of the poor and the less poor, though it can be claimed, with justice, that the trade-off becomes more unsavory when the claims in contention are those of the "poor" and the "affluent". Nevertheless, the difference in degree cannot conceal the similarity in the kind of difficulty under review.

In Subramanian (2006), I have advanced, and withdrawn, the suggestion that $(-)W^M$ could be viewed as a poverty measure. As an example that could offend our intuition, I consider two one-million-ordered income vectors $\underline{x}$ and $\underline{y}$, such that each person in the poorest half of the population has an income of 1,000 rupees in $\underline{x}$, while in $\underline{y}$, each person in the poorest fourth of the population has zero income and each person in the next poorest fourth has an income of a million rupees. Suppose the "conventional" poverty line is set in the region of 100 rupees. Then, it can be verified that $W^M(\underline{x}) = 1,000 < W^M(\underline{y}) = 250,000$, and we would be obliged to conclude that poverty, as measured by $(-)W^M$, is greater in $\underline{x}$ than in $\underline{y}$, even though there is no "absolutely impoverished" person in $\underline{x}$, while there are a quarter of a million wholly destitute individuals in $\underline{y}$. Having said this, it must be noted that even if the identification problem, in terms of specifying an absolute income poverty line, is deemed to have been satisfactorily solved, aggregation can still present problems: in Subramanian (2006), I have indicated that conventional measures of poverty can offend the intuition underlying common-sense moralities in a number of ways—a difficulty that is not confined to the use of an index such as $(-)W^M$ as a poverty measure.

Similarly, examples can be constructed to suggest that the index $(-)W^B$ could go against the grain of "poverty", as that term is conventionally understood. Indeed, Basu (2006: 1365) explicitly cautions against the interpretation of $(-)W^B$ as a measure of poverty:

> The quintile measure should not be confused with a poverty measure (or inverse of a poverty measure) of a society. Hence, the objective of raising the quintile income of a country need not coincide with the objective of lowering poverty. This will certainly be so if we use an absolute measure of poverty (which can become zero and so leave no further target unfulfilled, whereas that can never happen with the target of maximizing quintile income) and may not be true even for most relative poverty measures. The quintile axiom I am recommending is a much more *overall* normative target with which policy makers should be concerned.

At the risk of challenging the author's own authority, one could invite a reconsideration of Basu's view on his quintile measure. (This invitation is based on a reconsideration of my own view in the matter: in Subramanian (2006), I have also rejected the interpretation of $(-)W^M$ as a poverty measure, on the grounds of its being an instance of "Humpty-Dumptyism" in the use of language.) Specifically, and first, conventional poverty measures are themselves not exempt from both practical and conceptual difficulties attending their use; and if simplicity and familiarity are virtues, then there may be something to be said for the employment of indices like $(-)W^S$, $(-)W^B$ and $(-)W^M$ as poverty measures. (The Basu welfare index is particularly attractive for reasons of its pithiness, ready comprehensibility, and directness of focus.) Second, there is a substantive sense in which the measures $(-)W^S$, $(-)W^B$ and $(-)W^M$ *are* concerned with poverty. These indices are descriptions of the welfare (or, more accurately, "illfare") status of the poorer segments of a society, and this arises through a partial or complete discounting of the income achievements of the richer segments of the population. Third, the link with poverty is directly established in equations (5), (8) and (11); and that link surely cannot have been forged *entirely* by brute force! The connection between fuzzy poverty and crisp welfare has been established through the postulation of fuzzy poverty membership functions, which may be arbitrary but are not undisciplined, in the sense that they do satisfy some basic and reasonable restrictions placed on them.

V. An Illustration

A practical application of this chapter's concerns relates to alternative claims that have been made regarding trends in India's poverty. The official statistics on poverty in India—as measured, say, by the headcount ratio—suggest a fairly systematic secular decline over the period from 1977/8 to 2004/5. Poverty comparisons are, of course, crucially dependent on how the identification problem is solved; and the Indian Planning Commission's approach to the identification exercise is instructive. The approach can be briefly described as follows.

The income poverty line was sought to be anchored in a nutritional norm of 2,400 kcals per person per day for rural India (2,100 kcals for urban India) in the following manner. From National Sample Survey data on the distribution of consumption expenditure, and of calorific intake across size-classes of consumption expenditure, it was determined that, in 1973/4, the calorific norms just mentioned were realized at a monthly per capita consumption expenditure level of (approximately) Rs 49 in the country's rural areas, and Rs 57 in its urban areas. These levels of expenditure were taken to be the appropriate rural and urban poverty lines for 1973/4 (at current prices). The commodity baskets corresponding to these poverty lines have since been revalued at ruling prices in order to obtain "updated" poverty lines (at current prices) in subsequent years. Utsa Patnaik (2007) refers to this identification stratagem as an "indirect method" of obtaining poverty estimates, for a reason that is clarified in what follows.

A *consistent* application of the Planning Commission's procedure for identifying the poverty line in 1973/4 would demand that precisely the same procedure ought to be employed in every subsequent year for which poverty is assessed—that is, one ought, in any year, to take the poverty line to be that level of consumption expenditure at which the nutritional norm is realized. In a straightforward way, such an identification exercise might be expected to be compatible with what Patnaik (2007) calls a "direct method" of obtaining poverty estimates. The Planning Commission's "indirect method" fails to allow for the possibility of changes, over time, in preferences, in relative rates of inflation as between food and non-food commodities, and in the non-market availability of certain resources such as firewood for fuel. In consequence, the Commission's poverty lines display a steady "calorie drift" over time: the calorie intake at the officially stipulated poverty lines has progressively fallen short of the nutritional norms to which the lines were originally supposed to be anchored. Table 23.1 provides estimates of the headcount ratio of poverty for those years, between 1977/8 and 2004/5, in which the National Sample Survey Organization conducted its quinquennial surveys on consumption expenditure. Estimates corresponding to the official "indirect method" are available for all these years, and estimates corresponding to the "direct method" have been worked out by Patnaik (2007) for those years in which distributional data on nutritional intake are also available.

As can be seen from Table 23.1, the Planning Commission's approach to the identification problem suggests that the headcount ratio of poverty has been declining over time, while Patnaik's approach suggests a *rising* trend of poverty. Quite apart

Table 23.1. Alternative estimates of poverty in rural India, 1977/1978 to 2004/2005

	1977/8	1983	1987/8	1993/4	1999/2000	2004/5
Official poverty line (current prices, in rupees)	57	90	115	206	328	356
Official headcount ratio of poverty (%)	53.1	45.7	39.1	37.3	27.1	28.3
Poverty line under the "direct" method of identification (current prices, in rupees)	67	120	—	325	565	790
Headcount ratio corresponding to the "direct" method (%)	65.5	70	—	74.5	74.5	87

Notes: 1. The poverty estimates are for those years in which the quinquennial survey on consumer expenditure was conducted by the National Sample Survey Organization.
2. Poverty lines have been rounded off to the nearest integer.
3. The "official" and "direct" methods of identification of the poverty line are explained in the text.
Sources: Data relating to "official" estimates are as issued by the Planning Commission, Government of India. Data relating to estimates under the "direct method" are Utsa Patnaik's calculations, taken from Patnaik (2007: Table 2).

from obtaining any meaningful sense of the magnitude of poverty, one cannot even obtain a sense of the direction of change in poverty from these sorts of conflicting estimates. The poverty line belongs to the domain of normative judgements, while the actual pattern of consumer behavior that might happen to obtain at any point of time belongs to the domain of positive phenomena. The premise underlying both the direct and the indirect approaches to identification is that the one can be *entirely* determined by the other. The premise is a fundamentally questionable one. The indirect method implicitly invokes this premise only for the year 1973/4, and thereby inexplicably confers a unique normative significance on the pattern of consumer expenditure that obtained in that year. The direct method invokes the premise across the board, and if it has any justification at all, it is from the principle that what is sauce for the goose is sauce for the gander: it certainly has polemical value, but little by way of independent rationale. Both methods at bottom are speedy, inadequate, and misleading substitutes for the practically very demanding exercise of identification that would be implied by Sen's view of the matter discussed earlier. This is the view that the poverty line in income space should be derived from a careful accounting of the costs that would have to be incurred in order to

Table 23.2. Measures of central tendency and dispersion in the distribution of consumer expenditure, rural India, 1977/1978 to 2004/2005

	1977/8	1983	1987/8	1993/4	1999/2000	2004/5
μ (current prices, in rupees)	68.89	112.45	158.10	281.40	486.16	564.70
G	0.3423	0.3010	0.3012	0.2863	0.2634	0.2809
μ^Q (current prices, in rupees)	29.14	49.66	72.54	134.62	246.05	280.67
μ^M (current prices, in rupees)	38.68	66.91	95.07	174.35	313.83	354.93
G^M	0.1369	0.1444	0.1322	0.1276	0.1209	0.1173
Price index	100	158	202	361	575	625

Notes: 1. μ stands for mean per capita consumer expenditure; G stands for the Gini coefficient of inequality in the distribution of consumer expenditure; μ^Q stands for mean per capita consumer expenditure of the poorest 20% of the population; μ^M stands for mean per capita consumer expenditure of the poorest 50% of the population; and G^M stands for the Gini coefficient of inequality in the distribution of expenditure amongst the poorest 50% of the population.

2. The price index employed is the Consumer Price Index of Agricultural Labourers (CPIAL). The base year is taken to be 1977/8. The official poverty lines in Table 23.1 are expressed in current prices by updating the 1973/4 poverty line by means of the CPIAL. The price index series in the last row of Table 23.2 has been obtained by setting the poverty line at current prices in 1977/8—Rs 57 (see Table 23.1)—equal to 100.

3. Calculations, based on distributional data from the relevant National Sample Surveys on consumer expenditure, have been done by employing the POVCAL package created by Chen *et al.* (1991).

Sources: Calculations are based on the following Reports of the National Sample Survey Organization: *Report on the Second Quinquennial Survey on Consumer Expenditure*, Report no. 311, 32nd Round, July 1977–June 1978; *Report on the Third Quinquennial Survey on Consumer Expenditure*, Report no. 319, 38th Round, July–December 1983; *Report on the Fourth Quinquennial Survey on Consumer Expenditure*, Report no. 372, 43rd Round, July 1987–June 1988; *Level and Pattern of Consumer Expenditure*, Report no. 402, 50th Round, July 1993–June 1994; *Level and Pattern of Consumer Expenditure*, Report no. 457, 55th Round, July 1999–June 2000; and *Household Consumer Expenditure in India*, Report no. 505, 60th Round, January–June 2004.

avoid a clearly specified set of deprivations in the space of human capabilities. The issue cannot be evaded by resort to the "inevitability of a measure of arbitrariness" in these matters. The direct and indirect approaches to identification are not only arbitrary, they are also unreasonable—in the specific sense that it is hard to derive any meaning from them as a guide to some reasonable conception of poverty.

For those that have some familiarity with the Indian economy (including the familiarity that is bred by simply happening to live in the country), announcements of both massive increases and dramatic declines in income poverty are less than credible. It is relevant to note, in this connection, that the sorts of fuzzy poverty indices discussed in this chapter are clearly less liable to distortions arising from the interpretational license to which conventional poverty measurement seems to be prone. It is instructive to look at the magnitudes and trends of the welfare indices W^S, W^B and W^M (the negative values of which, let us recall, can be interpreted as corresponding fuzzy poverty indices, earlier christened as P^1, P^2 and P^3, respectively). Table 23.2 presents some basic statistics on measures of central tendency and inequality, computed from the quinquennial National Sample Surveys on consumer expenditure, for rural India over the period 1977/8 to 2004/5. Table 23.3, which is based on the data furnished in Table 23.2, provides a brief time-series on the magnitudes of the welfare indices W^S, W^B and W^M.

Table 23.3. Magnitudes and trends of selected welfare indices, rural India, 1977/1978 to 2004/2005.

	1977/8	1983	1987/8	1993/4	1999/2000	2004/5
W^S (1977/8 prices, in rupees)	45.31	49.68	54.69	55.63	62.28	64.97
W^{S*} (1977/8 prices, in rupees)	45.31	54.10	60.89	72.71	86.82	100.65
Ratio of W^{S*} to W^S	1.00	1.09	1.11	1.31	1.39	1.55
W^B (1977/8 prices, in rupees)	29.14	31.43	35.91	37.29	42.79	44.91
W^{B*} (1977/8 prices, in rupees)	29.14	34.79	39.16	46.76	55.84	64.73
Ratio of W^{B*} to W^B	1.00	1.11	1.09	1.25	1.31	1.44
W^M (at 1977/8 prices, in rupees)	31.66	36.23	40.84	42.13	47.98	50.13
W^{M*} (1977/8 prices, in rupees)	31.66	37.80	42.55	50.81	60.66	70.33
Ratio of W^{M*} to W^M	1.00	1.04	1.04	1.21	1.26	1.40

Notes: 1. The welfare indices W^S, W^B and W^M have been explained in the text. The negative values of these indices can be interpreted as the fuzzy poverty indices P^1, P^2 and P^3 respectively, as indicated in the text.

2. W^S, W^B and W^M have been computed, at current prices, from the data provided in Table 23.2; these have then been deflated, employing the price index series presented in the last row of Table 23.2, to obtain their values at 1977/8 prices.

3. The asterisked versions of W^S, W^B and W^M refer to the values these measures would have assumed if their respective 1977/8 levels had grown at an annual compound rate of 3%.

Source: Calculated from information presented in Table 23.2.

The magnitudes of W^S, W^B and W^M are not only absolutely low, but they have also increased over time quite slowly. A modest target rate of growth for these variables would be something like 3% per annum. Table 23.3 reveals that actual performance over time has progressively drifted away from what might have been achieved if the targeted rate of growth had been realized. The picture is one of a modestly plodding climb out of considerable income deprivation. This is no cause for complacency, and even less cause for premature celebrations of India's allegedly dramatic progress on the poverty front. Poverty statistics based on indicators like P^1, P^2 and P^3 will have served their purpose if they afford simple reality checks against extravagant claims of India's ascent to superpower status. It is pertinent to note that such claims are based on—among other things—an essentially unserious engagement with the continuing centrality of poverty in the scheme of things.

VI. Conclusion

The proposal made in this chapter for a simplification of the measurement of income poverty revolves around an approach in which the identification exercise of conventional poverty assessment can be altogether avoided, an exercise which is beset by both conceptual and pragmatic problems. (For an evaluation of the utterly non-trivial magnitude of these problems, the reader is referred to Reddy and Pogge forthcoming). This chapter, effectively, is an invitation to consider the possible merit of applying Occam's razor to the job of "shaving off" the identification problem in poverty measurement. Occam's, like any other razor, must be wielded with care. Therefore, the pragmatic considerations guiding the approach to simplification advanced in this chapter must be carefully weighed against the net loss in conceptual soundness that may result from the effect of the razor's edge. This chapter, in summary, has been concerned to point to the existence of a valid choice problem. How the problem is resolved will presumably depend on the trade-off that is effected between the demands of conceptual rigor and practical implementability.

References

Basu, K. (2001), "On the Goals of Development", in G. M. Meier and J. E. Stiglitz (eds), *Frontiers of Development Economics: The Future in Perspective* (New York: Oxford University Press).

—— (2006), "Globalization, Poverty, and Inequality: What is the Relationship? What Can Be Done?", *World Development*, 34: 1361–73.

CHEN, S., DATT, G., and RAVALLION, M. (1991), *POVCAL: A Programme for Calculating Poverty Measures from Grouped Data* (Washington, DC: World Bank).

KUNDU, A., and SMITH, T. E. (1983), "An Impossibility Theorem on Poverty Indices", *International Economic Review*, 24: 423–35.

MEHTA, J., and VENKATRAMAN, S. (2000), "Poverty Statistics: Bermicide's Feast", *Economic and Political Weekly*, 35: 2377–81.

PATNAIK, U. (2004), "The Republic of Hunger", *Social Scientist*, 32(9–10): 9–35.

—— (2007), "Neoliberalism and Rural Poverty in India", *Economic and Political Weekly*, 48: 3132–50.

RAY, R., and LANCASTER, G. (2005), "On Setting the Poverty Line based on Estimated Nutrient Prices: Condition of Socially Disadvantaged Groups during the Reform Period", *Economic and Political Weekly*, 11: 46–56.

REDDY, S. (2004), "A Capability-Based Approach to Estimating Global Poverty", in *In Focus: Dollar a Day How Much Does It Say?* (New York: United Nations Development Programme).

—— and POGGE, T. (forthcoming), "How *Not* to Count the Poor", in S. Anand and J. Stiglitz (eds), *Measuring Global Poverty* (Oxford: Oxford University Press).

SEN, A. K. (1973), *On Economic Inequality* (Oxford: Clarendon Press).

—— (1976a), "Poverty: An Ordinal Approach to Measurement", *Econometrica*, 44: 219–31.

—— (1976b), "Real National Income", *Review of Economic Studies*, 43: 19–39.

—— (1983), "Poor, Relatively Speaking", *Oxford Economic Papers*, 35: 153–69.

—— (2003), "Development as Capability Expansion", in S. Fukuda-Parr and A. K. Shiva Kumar (eds), *Readings in Human Development* (Delhi: Oxford University Press).

SHORROCKS, A. F. (2005), "Inequality Values and Unequal Shares", in World Institute for Development Economics Research, *WIDER Thinking Ahead: The Future of Development Economics* (Helsinki: United Nations Helsinki), available at <www.wider.unu.edu/conference/conference-2005-5/conference-2005.5.htm>.

—— and SUBRAMANIAN, S. (1994), "Fuzzy Poverty Indices", unpubl. MS, University of Essex.

SUBRAMANIAN, S. (2005), "Unraveling a Conceptual Muddle: India's Poverty Statistics in the Light of Basic Demand Theory", *Economic and Political Weekly*, 40: 57–66.

—— (2006), *Rights, Deprivation, and Disparity: Essays in Concepts and Measurement* (Delhi: Oxford University Press).

PART IV

IDENTITY,
COLLECTIVE
ACTION AND
PUBLIC
ECONOMICS

CHAPTER 24

CONCEPTS AND MEASURES OF AGENCY

SABINA ALKIRE

I. MOTIVATION

In his autobiography, the escaped slave Frederick Douglass wrote of how, on learn-ing to read, "the silver trump of freedom...roused my soul...It was ever present to torment me with a sense of my wretched condition" (Douglass 1845: ch. 7). He also described the journey of conviction. For example, an altercation with his master, Mr Covey, was "the turning-point in my career as a slave. It rekindled the few expiring embers of freedom, and revived within me a sense of my own manhood...I now resolved that, however long I might remain a slave in form, the day had passed forever when I could be a slave in fact" (ch. 10). Douglass then focused his energies on freedom from "the galling chains of slavery" (ch. 5), a freedom he finally acquired, and for which he worked powerfully on others' behalf. For these reasons his writings have been widely drawn upon by those engaged in other struggles.

The importance of action by people such as Douglass to confront situations of serious oppression and deprivation has led many working on poverty reduction to introduce measures of agency, autonomy, empowerment, self-direction and self-determination into poverty analyses. A number of studies draw conceptually

I am grateful to Mridul Eapen for insightful comments on a previous draft of this chapter.

on the human development and capability approach developed by Amartya Sen and others (*inter alia*, Alkire 2005; Alsop and Heinsohn 2005; Alsop *et al.* 2006; Clark 2002, 2003; Gasper and Van Staveren 2003; Ghuman *et al.* 2006; Gibson and Woolcock 2005; Hill 2003; Kabeer 1999; McGillivray 2005; Narayan-Parker 2005; Narayan 2002). Sen argues that agency—a person's ability to act on behalf of what he or she values and has reason to value—is intrinsically valuable and can also be instrumentally effective in reducing poverty. Drèze and Sen describe their approach to analyzing India's development as an approach "which puts human agency (rather than organizations such as markets or governments) at the centre of the stage" (2002: 6).

For a number of reasons, it can be quite useful to measure agency in the context of poverty reduction activities. As some development activities aim to increase people's agency because of its intrinsic value, measures are needed to evaluate whether or not this objective has been realized. Moreover, it is often presumed that when poor people act as agents they reduce their own poverty rather effectively (of course they may do other beautiful or valuable things besides). A more adequate exploration of the instrumental connections between the agency of poor persons and the reduction of their poverty in many different contexts may be useful to identify more effective poverty-reducing interventions. Also, people's agency is deeply informed by their own knowledge and values, and research that identifies people's varied understandings of appropriate agency (for example, appropriate agency for women) may catalyze constructive public discussions on these understandings that shape how people value their own and others' agency. Hence the significance of agency parallels the significance of related capabilities such as participation and democracy, and lies in: "(1) its *intrinsic importance*, (2) its *instrumental contributions*, and (3) its *constructive role* in the creation of values and norms" (Sen 1999: 157). Concrete measures are needed to explore such aspects of agency in many different settings (Alkire 2006).

Agency is inescapably plural in concept and hence in measurement. Considerable interest and new research on agency measurement is emerging; indeed over thirty definitions of empowerment (a related but often differently defined term) have been proposed by those working on measurement issues, and hundreds of indicators are in use or under development for use in the context of poverty reduction and women's empowerment activities.[1]

Given that many authors motivate their discussion of agency with reference to Sen's work, this chapter first briefly reviews Sen's account of agency, drawing attention to the internal pluralism of the concept. I then refract the literature on agency measurement through this account, to articulate four conceptual distinctions which

[1] The definitions of empowerment are presented in Ibrahim and Alkire (2007), which also surveys the current literature and classifies existing indicators. A list of agency and empowerment indicators in use is available on the OPHI website, <www.ophi.org.uk>, under "Missing Dimensions Research". Alsop and Heinsohn (2005) also thoroughly surveyed the indicators then in use.

clarify, and in some cases extend, agency measurement. I also take note of some troubling or missing features in Sen's account. There are many kinds of information and information-gathering processes related to agency; this chapter focuses on quantitative measures of agency arising from surveys conducted at the individual or household level.

The discussion of this chapter is further limited to conceptual considerations in selecting such measures of agency. It must be observed immediately that any final choice of agency indicators will be guided in part by the context and the purpose for which data are being collected. Indicator selection will also depend upon empirical features of the data: whether the indicators prove to be accurate, valid and robust; whether they have explanatory power in analyses, are sensitive to changes over time, are not too highly correlated with other indicators, and can be feasibly applied in the area. This chapter does not discuss these well-known issues, which are presumed to influence the final choice of indicators for any survey or analysis.

II. Agency

The objective of development, Sen argues, is to expand capabilities and to support people's agency. Capabilities are people's real freedoms to enjoy valuable lives—to enjoy beings and doings that they value and have reason to value.[2] Capabilities, like budget sets, convey information on the range of valuable opportunities that a person enjoys. Alongside opportunity freedoms, we may wish to consider process freedoms, which are related to what a person is able to do themselves on behalf of goals they value and are motivated to advance.[3] Sen's capability approach views people, including poor people, as active agents. Agency is an assessment of "what a person can do in line with his or her conception of the good" (Sen 1985b: 206). People who enjoy high levels of agency are engaged in actions that are congruent with their values. When people are not able to exert agency, they may be alienated from their behavior, coerced into a situation, submissive and desirous to please, or simply passive (Ryan and Deci 2004). If development and poverty reduction activities are to promote agency, then "the people have to be seen . . . as being actively involved—given the opportunity—in shaping their own destiny, and not just as passive recipients of the fruits of cunning development programs" (Sen 1999: 53). This requires attention not only to poverty reduction itself but also to the processes by which those outcomes are attained, in particular the extent to which poor people are able to engage actively and freely in the processes.

[2] Nussbaum (1990); Sen (1980, 1985a, 1987, 1992, 1993).
[3] A full discussion of process and opportunity freedoms can be found in Sen (2002: chs 19–21).

Let us review several relevant characteristics of agency in Sen's account. First, and implicit in the above but important for measurement, is the observation that agency will be exercised with respect to *multiple aims*; indeed agency cannot be defined except in relation to goals. For example, agency goals with respect to one's own well-being may be quite diverse, such as the goal of maintaining warm and vibrant family relationships, the goal of finding a more stimulating reading group, and the goal of continuing a new swimming regime.

Second, agency may include *effective power* as well as control. Effective power is the person's or group's "power to achieve chosen results" (Sen 1985b: 208). In situations of effective power, no matter how choices are actually made and executed, power is "exercised in line with what we would have chosen and because of it" (Sen 1985b: 211). Note that at times effective power only pertains to collectivities and groups, not individuals: "Given the interdependences of social living, many liberties are not separately exercisable, and effective power may have to be seen in terms of what all, or nearly all, members of the group would have chosen" (Sen 1985b: 211). *Control* refers instead to the person's ability to make choices and to control procedures directly (whether or not he or she is successful in achieving the desired goal) (Sen 1985b: 208–9).

Third, for many people, capability—as the space in which we consider well-being freedom—is related to agency, for example because whatever goals and commitments people are able to advance, whether through their work or in a personal or voluntary capacity, contributes, in part, to their sense of well-being: "For an integrated person it is likely—possibly even inevitable—that the person's well-being will be influenced by his or her agency role" (Sen 1985b: 187). However, the agency and well-being perspectives remain importantly distinct. Agency does not have to advance one's own well-being at all; it may be *other-regarding*. This distinction is sharply apparent in circumstances in which acting as an agent may reduce other aspects of one's well-being. For example, if a person selflessly does volunteer work late into the evening at a homeless shelter, it may advance his or her agency goals, and simultaneously result in tiredness and anxiety which decrease well-being. Thus agency has *open conditionality* in the sense that it is "not tied to any one type of aim" (Sen 1985b: 203) but advances any goals the person thinks important, whether for themselves, their community, or some other entity or group altogether.

Fourth, agency is, by definition, related to goals that the person *values*. Yet in addition, the identification of agency entails some *assessment* of those goals: "The open conditionality view of agency does not imply... that anything that appeals to [a person] must, for that reason, come into the accounting of his agency freedom... The need for careful assessment of aims, allegiances, objectives, etc., and of the conception of the good, may be important and exacting" (Sen 1985b: 204). This requirement, in essence, imposes upon agency conditions similar to those on capability—namely that agency pertains to the advance of objectives people value *and have reason to value*. I use the foregoing phrase in subsequent discussions to summarize this consideration, and it will prove pivotal in distinguishing autonomy from ability. A standing issue that this distinction raises especially sharply is how to assess agency for very young children (who may, quite defiantly, *not* value going to school) or those who are severely impaired in reasoning, and indeed at what age we should begin to incorporate agency into measures of children's poverty, and with respect to what domains. Sen's conception, which presupposes rational agents, must be extended to address other groups (see Nussbaum 2000).

Fifth, the assessment of a "responsible agent" regarding a situation or state of affairs, and his or her subsequent response to it, will include, if relevant, an assessment of his or her responsibility in bringing about that situation (Sen 1983, 1985b). In Bernard Williams's famous case, Jim, a botanist who finds himself in the central square of a South American town, is presented with the choice of watching a tyrant kill twenty Indian captives to quash a rebellion, or shooting one of them himself and saving the others (Williams 1973). Of this situation Sen writes, "Whereas others have a straightforward reason to rejoice if Jim goes ahead, Jim has no option but to take serious note of his own responsibility in that state and his agency in killing someone himself" (Sen 1985b: 214–15). However, this fifth characteristic seems to pertain not to agency per se, but to the assessment of a state of affairs—which should include one's role (for good or ill) in creating it and hence should convey responsibility. The examples of manslaughter (Jim) and murder (Lady Macbeth, Othello) which Sen uses to illustrate this point rest uneasily alongside the concept of agency as something people value and have reason to value. Murder seems unlikely to be considered an unproblematic exercise of agency, as another's death may not be considered a reasonable goal to value. We will not consider this fifth issue further, as it pertains to the inclusion of one's own causal responsibility in the overall assessment of states of affairs. It does spark the observation that, by defining agency in such a way that it excludes actions that advance cruel or otherwise evil ends, Sen's concept of agency cannot be used to analyze the problems of action-for-ill (oppression, cruelty, theft, etc.).[4]

Sen's account draws our attention to several distinct features of agency:

1. Agency is exercised with respect to multiple goals.
2. Agency includes effective power as well as direct control.
3. Agency may advance one's own well-being or may address other-regarding goals.
4. Recognizing agency entails an assessment of the value of the agency objectives.
5. Agency introduces the need to incorporate the agents' own responsibility for a state of affairs into their evaluation of it.

The first four of these features will be useful in clarifying the distinct kinds of information that agency measures convey or do not convey.

---

[4] A similar point is developed more extensively in Stewart (2005). See also Crocker (1995); Qizilbash (1996, 1998).

III. PROXY MEASURES OF AGENCY

The previous section began with the argument that capability and agency comprise the central individual freedoms that development can and should expand. If we are inquisitive enough to wish to use this approach, and we analyze the information that would be required to implement it we see at once that information on agency, as well as on capabilities, is required (see Sen 1979, 1985b).

The measurement of agency has received considerable attention in the context of the difficult but vital problem of measuring empowerment. A number of recent literature surveys on particular subtopics are available (Alkire 2007; Alsop 2004; Alsop and Heinsohn 2005; Alsop *et al.* 2006; Ibrahim and Alkire 2007; Kabeer 1999, 2001; Malhotra and Schuler 2005; Narayan 2002; Narayan-Parker 2005; Oakley 2001). By far the most commonly used agency measures direct attention to presumed prerequisites of agency. By measuring the presence or absence of these prerequisites one can, it is supposed, identify the agency-poor person. Common proxy measures for agency include literacy, frequency of radio/TV listening, membership in organizations, employment history, food expenditure, health status, and ownership of land or tools.[5] The primary appeal of such measures is their tangibility. Adam Smith described a man as unable to go about without shame if he lacked a linen shirt and leather shoes.[6] Given this definition, any self-respecting analyst of shame would immediately set about to measure the possession of linen and leather (shame being a difficult concept to measure adequately). However, there are a number of problems with using assets as proxy indicators of agency.

First, assets may not translate into agency in the same way for different individuals. This problem is parallel to the issues with resources as a sufficient indicator of functionings, and arises because of human diversity. This diversity may relate to the agents' objectives, or to their personal characteristics. Hence Kabeer calls for far greater caution in presuming connections between assets and agency: "studies which use measures of women's access to land as an indicator of empowerment seldom reflect on the pathways by which such 'access' translates into agency and achievement, let alone seeking to understand these pathways empirically" (Kabeer 1999: 443). As an example, consider two persons who own the same amount of land and the same set of agricultural tools (assets). If we are using an asset-based indicator of agency, their agencies would be judged equal. However, suppose that

---

[5] These examples are taken from kinds of agency indicators identified in Alsop and Heinsohn (2005).

[6] "[I]n the present times, through a greater part of Europe, a creditable day-labourer would be ashamed to appear in public without a linen shirt, the want of which would be supposed to denote that disgraceful degree of poverty which, it is presumed, nobody can well fall into without extreme bad conduct. Custom, in the same manner, has rendered leather shoes a necessary of life in England" (Smith 1776: 351–2, quoted in Sen 1981: 118).

person one wishes to leave agriculture and play the guitar in the city but does not because he can't sell the land. The other has farming in her blood and hopes to live and die on the land with the smell of meadow-grass on the wind. These two are indeed equal when it comes to tool ownership. However, their ability to advance the personal employment-related goals they value and have reason to value is quite different. Again, two people may read newspapers equally often, but have very different levels of political agency; further scrutiny of the intervening processes is required. Thus equality in the space of assets or resources need not imply equality of agency.

Also, an identical expansion of agency may be created by multiple assets or resources, and the link between them may not be predictable except in certain time- and context-specific situations. For example, if, between two waves of a panel survey, a woman's decision-making power within the household increases dramatically, this expansion of agency could be triggered by one or several possible causes, only some of which are related to assets. She might have attended a women's group that trained members in assertiveness and provided social support. A friend or aunt who was quite empowered might have moved nearby, and she might have learned from their example. She might have recently started to listen to a radio program that made her more aware of alternative role-sharing models. Her husband may have fallen ill, or lost interest in home life; or he might have taken a gender-sensitivity training course and changed his habits to suit his newly adopted identity as a feminist. Alternatively, the pair may have worked out for themselves that a change in their roles brought better balance to the household. In this example the same agency expansion could be related to changes in diverse assets in a myriad of ways. It may for that reason be desirable to measure agency and its expansion (in this case, the expansion of decision-making) directly, rather than to extrapolate agency changes from changes in assets.

A related, quite evident, but surprisingly resilient problem is that many so-called agency measures are actually *identical* to measures traditionally used in poverty analysis, such as years of schooling, employment status, land ownership or health status. The interpretation of these measures differs, not the data. For example, in the country studies reported in Alsop and Heinsohn's (2005) masterful review of the literature, literacy and level of income was used to reflect agency in Ethiopia, Nepal and Honduras. Redundancy of agency and poverty indicators preclude meaningful empirical study of the connections between agency and poverty. Hence, because empirical analyses are important for clarifying the instrumental role of expanding agency in poverty reduction, distinctive indicators are required for poverty and agency.

Thus three problems challenge the use of proxy (asset) measures as agency measures. First, the conversion of assets to agency is assumed to occur evenly, which may not be the case (not all who attend assertiveness or gender-sensitivity training become equally assertive or gender-sensitive agents). Second, agency expansions caused by a different trigger (or no external trigger) may be overlooked. Third, it is impossible to explore connections between agency and poverty when the same indicators are used to represent both phenomena.

The remainder of the chapter focuses, then, on more direct measures of agency. These measures may be categorized according to four distinctions:

1. agency as *global* or *multidimensional*;
2. agency as *direct control* or *effective power*;
3. agency as advancing *well-being freedom* or *other commitments*;
4. agency as *autonomy* or *ability*.

At present, most "direct" indicators explore a person's agency with respect to their own well-being, and probe their control (and in some cases its efficacy) in one or more areas that are assumed to matter (ability). In each of the following sections we will review the dominant measures, and draw attention to measures that might probe the less-represented aspects: autonomy, effective power, and commitments to goals beyond well-being. The forceful articulation of the reach and limits of empirical measures of agency may give rise to more incisive and specific analyses that support its expansion.

IV. GLOBAL AND MULTIDIMENSIONAL

Some measures of agency are "global" in the sense that a single indicator, for example parents' education, is interpreted to be a proxy for the individual's agency. Another example of a "global" measure of agency is the "Ladder of Power" questions that are employed, for example, in the *Moving Out of Poverty* study (Narayan and Petesch 2007): "Imagine a 10-step ladder, where at the bottom, on the first step, stand people who are completely powerless and without rights, and on the highest step, the tenth, stand those who have a lot of power and rights. On which step of this ladder are you today? And on which step were you 10 years ago?"

Such questions can give a general sense of a person's agency. At the same time, their interpretation is complicated by the fact that we do not know how respondents defined "power and rights" when they answered the question. Was it in relation to their spouse, their government, their former self, or their boss, or did they think of all of these briefly and take a mental "average" across them? We do not know whether different people (or the same person at different points in time) have the same definition of "power and rights" in mind or whether one respondent was thinking about herself as an employee (perhaps because she had just been rejected for a job), another his citizenship (as an election was coming up), and so on.

A further observation, which emerges regularly in the literature on women's agency, is that the same person's agency, like poverty, may vary across different spheres of life. A person can be fully empowered as a wife and mother, but excluded from the labor force by social conventions; recently empowered to vote by a grassroots political process, but unable to read the ballot.

An understandable assumption might be that although agency levels differ, there are permeable boundaries between kinds of agency—perhaps because there are common "skills" for the exercise of agency in different domains. According to this assumption, if a person becomes more empowered to act as an agent in one sphere—such as by holding office in her women's organization—this will feed over into another sphere—such as her agency within the household. Scrutiny of the evidence, however, has called into question such assumptions, so unless contrary analyses emerge, separate measures for different dimensions of agency should supplement "global" measures.[7] For example, the Demographic and Health Surveys enquire about who makes household decisions with respect to six domains:

1. the money you earn;
2. your husband's/partner's earnings;
3. health care for yourself;
4. major household purchases;
5. purchases for daily household needs;
6. visits to your family or relatives. (ORC Macro 2006: QQ. 820–6)

How are the domains in which agency is (or is not) exercised to be chosen?[8] In practice, the domains that have been selected represent either (a) kinds of goals the person has, or the arenas in which he or she acts (as above), or (b) potentially coercive forces that could impede agency (e.g. spouse, government). For example, in the above case it is presumed that the primary group poised to affect agency is the spouse or family member. The first seems the more basic, although each will be appropriate in different contexts. The first—domains in which agency can be exercised—is in part a value judgement. It identifies domains in which (it is presumed) people have reason to exercise agency—the kinds of agency they "have reason to value". One clear option is to identify, as a minimum, precisely the same dimensions for agency measurement as would be considered for multidimensional poverty analyses. The conceptual motivation for this equivalence is most apparent in the negative: if we do *not* regard agency with respect to employment, for example,

---

[7] This parallels the discussion in the subjective well-being literature regarding the accuracy of a "global" question (how satisfied are you with your life overall?) versus a domain-specific question (how satisfied are you with your children's educational attainment?)—the answers to the latter being arguably more amenable to accurate interpretation (Cummins 1996, 2000).

[8] A compilation of the "domains" that have in fact been used by different surveys is available in the Appendix to Ibrahim and Alkire (2007), which appears on the website <www.ophi.org.uk>. On the choice of dimensions for multidimensional poverty measurement—a similar issue—see Alkire (2008).

to be important (although employment status is a dimension of poverty), we are saying in essence that it is acceptable if one's employment is forcibly allocated by the government or landowner, or imposed by tradition or family decision against one's will.[9] In this case, as in others, the choice of domains may also be informed by empirical characteristics of the data, for example the interconnectedness (and high correlation) of agency in certain sets of domains.

V. Effective Power and Control

Current indicators of agency by and large focus upon agency as "direct control", and rather less clearly on agency as "effective power". For Alsop *et al.*, "Agency is defined as an actor's or group's ability to make purposeful choices—that is, the actor is able to envisage and purposively choose options" (Alsop *et al.* 2006: 11). The person or group's direct action (in this case, choice-making) is the only possible characterizing feature of agency; effective power would not, on this definition, be attributed to agency.

Perhaps the most common direct question regarding agency control is the following, taken from the Demographic and Health Surveys: "Who usually makes decisions about X: you, your husband/partner, you and your husband/partner jointly, or someone else?" (ORC Macro: QQ. 820–6). X is filled in by the six domains mentioned in section IV. In many cases a focus on control is exactly what is required; however, it is worth bearing in mind some limitations of the information arising from such questions.

One limitation of some control measures is that they do not convey whether the lack of control (in this case decision-making) is *favored* by the respondent; people may prefer *not* to be bothered with certain decisions but delegate them to others. Alsop and Heinsohn recommend that, for each decision not made solely or jointly by the respondent, the following counterfactual question be posed: "If you wished to make decisions with respect to X, could you?" (2005: 116, 119). Such a supplemental question potentially generates information as to whether the abstention from decision-making was due to a sensible and mutually agreeable division of labor, or to the coercive imposition of another's view. It thus improves the accuracy of the information on agency expressed as direct control.

Another limitation of control measures is that they do not convey whether the actions are successful in terms of the agency goals. For example, Alsop *et al.*'s

---

[9] I have argued that in the case of basic capabilities, the presence or absence of agency at the individual level may be sufficient to distinguish capabilities from achieved functionings that are imposed, and thus capability measures might be constructed using agency data and achieved functioning data for the same set of dimensions (Alkire 2007).

framework considers the efficacy of agency goals to the extent that this is mediated through the exercise of a choice—that is, the measures clarify not only (1) whether an opportunity to make a choice exists (existence of choice) and (2) whether a person or group actually uses the opportunity to choose (use of choice), but also (3) *whether the choice brings about the desired result* (achievement of choice) (Alsop *et al.* 2006: 17).

Similarly, Narayan and Petesch argue that when outcomes cannot be guaranteed because they result from the interaction of different groups, it is still important to consider whether agency is *likely* to be effective in realizing agency goals (in this case, "escaping poverty"). For them, agency "is about men and women having the means to envision and make choices that *can* lead to their escaping poverty. The term 'can' is stressed because the likelihood or chance of this outcome will be a product of two broad forces: incentives and structures in the wider society...*plus* the assets and capabilities—both individual and collective—that poor and disadvantaged people can marshal in pursuit of their goals" (Narayan and Petesch 2007: 15). In essence, they are requesting attention to something like effective power.

Neither these authors, nor others, would use the term *agency* to refer to effective power. Yet as they acknowledge, it may be useful to consider developing measures of effective power at the individual level (whether or not we call this a kind of agency is a separate matter). However, the measurement of "effective power" is clearly more challenging than that of "direct control" because it is less immediate, and requires an analysis of the situation, some ability to predict others' actions, and some assessment of one's own and others' influence. It will be noted at once that the focus thus far on the efficacy of directly controlled decisions concerns only one kind of effective power. We might also be concerned, as Sen is, with someone's effective power in situations in which he or she is merely one of several actors, or indeed where he or she is not among the actors at all.

In this regard it may be useful to consider the indicators of efficacy developed by Albert Bandura (Alkire 2005; Bandura 1995, 1997, 1998, 2000).[10] Bandura's measures, which arise from his theory of agency, probe people's perceived self-efficacy, "people's belief in their capabilities to mobilize the motivation, cognitive resources, and courses of action needed to exercise control over given events" (Ozer and Bandura 1990: 472). Respondents are asked to rate the strength of their perceived efficacy, or their effective power (in our terms) to achieve a certain state of affairs. The scale ranges from *complete uncertainty* to *complete certitude*. For example, a "practice" question Bandura suggests is, "Can you lift an object weighing x pounds?" (where x = 5, 10, 20, 50, 100, 200, 500 or 1000). What Bandura terms "personal efficacy" corresponds to the assessment that not only does one have direct control in a situation, but that control is likely to achieve the desired outcome. However, like Sen, Bandura recognizes that attention to agency "has centered almost exclusively

---

[10] Bandura (2000) usefully summarizes his efficacy measures.

on the direct exercise of personal agency [understood as direct control]" (Bandura 2000: 75). He introduces two additional measures, which relate more closely to Sen's effective power, namely *proxy agency* and *collective agency*. Regarding proxy agency, he writes:

In many activities...people do not have control over social conditions and institutional practices that affect their lives. Under these circumstances, they seek their well-being and security through the exercise of proxy agency. In this socially mediated mode of agency, people try to get other people who have expertise or wield influence and power to act on their behalf to get the outcomes they desire. People also turn to proxy control because they do not want to saddle themselves with the arduous work needed to develop requisite competencies, and to shoulder the responsibilities and stressors that the exercise of control entails.   (Bandura 2000: 75)

Bandura also develops measures of collective agency, namely agency that pertains to outcomes "achievable only through interdependent efforts" (Bandura 2000: 76). He refers to this as an "emergent group level" property, which may be better or worse than average individual agency levels: "For example, it is not uncommon for groups with members who are talented individually to perform poorly collectively because the members cannot work well together as a unit. Therefore, perceived collective efficacy is not simply the sum of the efficacy beliefs of individual members" (Bandura 2000: 77).

Bandura's measures thus do endeavor to measure people's perceptions of their effective power, and illustrate that the measurement issues, although challenging, are not insuperable. Additional indicators for effective power at the individual level which may be objective should also be identified to supplement perceptual measures.

VI. Advancing Well-Being Freedom and Other-Regarding Commitments

Existing agency measures focus on agency goals that relate to oneself, to one's family or community or others with whom one has sympathy, or to the political unit of which one is a part. That is, the measures focus on agency that has, as a direct or indirect goal, the expansion of one's own well-being freedom. For example, Narayan and Petesch write that "Agency...is about people's ability to act individually or collectively to further *their own interests*" (Narayan and Petesch 2007: 15, emphasis theirs). This is a natural and constructive focus, given that the purpose of many agency studies, such as the *Moving Out of Poverty* study by Narayan and Petesch, is in part to explore the instrumental force of agency and empowerment in reducing poor people's own poverty broadly conceived. Yet in comparison with Sen's description of agency, this view is more restrictive, because it cannot include people's commitments to other-regarding goals, such as saving the rain forests or supporting hip-hop music or caring for orphans. In some evaluative exercises, other-regarding agency may not be relevant. A standing question is whether it should therefore be eliminated from considerations of agency measurement altogether.

Consideration of "other-regarding" agency is complex and likely to require analyses beyond simple measurement. Yet this perspective raises a pivotal issue of responsibility that has not been addressed in agency measures. However delicate an issue it might be, it could be of quite immediate practical interest to analyze the effective power people have that *could* be exercised on behalf of others. People themselves may not grasp their potential effective power, and such oversight may, by default, justify inaction (I feel bad, but what can one person do?). Further, if people do have such power to effect change for others' well-being, they may be encouraged to consider their "imperfect obligation" to use such power on behalf of others (Anand and Sen 2000; Sen 1999, 2000).

Imperfect obligations are "inexactly specified (telling us neither who must particularly take the initiative, nor how far he should go in doing this general duty)" (Sen 2000: 495). This duty is not a strictly legal one, and is not specified with reference to a particular person, nor is the content of the obligation specified. Rather, imperfect obligations are "general—and sometimes loosely specified—duties of others to help a human being who is seen to have certain rights by virtue of his or her humanity" (Sen 2000: 495). In addition, part of some people's own freedom may be expressed by such abilities to act on others' behalf. As Douglass described his work towards other slaves' freedom, "I could do but little; but what I could, I did with a joyful heart" (Douglass 1845: ch. 11). Foster and Handy's account of "external capabilities" (Chapter 19 in this volume) identifies a very similar issue, and the measurement of external capabilities would be likely to parallel measures of effective power on behalf of others. For that reason, it seems appropriate not to exclude this consideration but to wrestle with it to obtain better ways of capturing empirical assessments of other-regarding agency.

VII. Autonomy and Ability

The measures of agency discussed thus far are entirely focused on kinds of agency that people are presumed to value. They do not attempt to investigate issues of people's own opinions and values as to whether or not they value the agency they possess or lack. In other words, they ignore what we will call *autonomy*, and do not probe the positionally objective values that people hold. Perhaps such assessments are deemed too controversial or difficult to accomplish in a way that is at once robust and comparable.

It will prove helpful to distinguish *autonomy* measures from agency measures that focus instead on *ability*. The distinction may seem fussy at first glance, but is arguably of some importance. Agency, as Sen formulates it, can never be captured empirically by a single indicator because the term itself has a twist in the tail: agency is a person's ability to act on behalf of things they *value and have reason to value*. We can identify, empirically, two distinct aspects of agency:

1. *autonomy*: whether people are able to act on behalf of what they themselves *value* (it matters not whether the respondent has reason to value them);
2. *ability*: whether people are able to act on behalf of things that they are assumed to *have reason to value* (whether or not the respondent actually values them).

Autonomy probes the person's own self-understanding of their situation; it reflects their own assessment and valuation of goals and activities. Ability probes the objective powers that a person enjoys and/or uses—such as being able to take a child to the emergency room, being able to seek legal assistance for divorce, being able to make minor purchasing decisions on behalf of the household, being able to vote, being able to go to a nearby town alone. It relates to people's competence, their skills, their knowledge and so on—but unlike autonomy, a study of ability takes no interest in the person's own values and preferences, only in their effective power or control with respect to certain agency goals. Agency indicators used in poverty reduction to date implicitly probe people's ability, such as a woman's ability to make household decisions, or people's perceived efficacy.

In many cases autonomy and ability will coincide. In other words, people will value what they have reason to value *and* will have the skills necessary to use their autonomy, so an autonomy measure will also represent ability and vice versa—and both will represent agency. But in some cases, autonomy and ability may diverge, and such divergences can be quite informative. People may have certain abilities but feel coerced into using them (e.g. the right to vote). The coercion could be of distinct kinds—for example, social pressure or a local militia. If information about ability and autonomy are both gathered, and divergences between them explored, this can be quite a useful tool for understanding agency.

A concrete measure of autonomy has been developed by the psychologists Richard Ryan, Ed Deci, Valery Chirkov, and others working in Self-Determination Theory (SDT).[11] They implement a widely used and well-validated measure of autonomy. The measure is multidimensional, as persons are asked about their autonomy with respect to different domains. Studies to date have found it to be cross-culturally comparable. Furthermore, the measure frames autonomy in

---

[11] Reviews of this literature, and further details on the STD autonomy measure, can be found in Chirkov *et al.* (2003) and Ryan and Deci (2000).

a way that is valued in individualistic and collectivist cultures alike—which is important, as most indicators of agency are correlated with individualism (Chirkov *et al.* 2003).

According to the SDT formulation, a person is autonomous when his or her behavior is experienced as willingly enacted and when he or she fully endorses the actions in which he or she is engaged and/or the values expressed by them. People are therefore most autonomous when they act in accord with their authentic interests or integrated values and desires. SDT contrasts autonomy with *heteronomy*, "in which one's actions are experienced as controlled by forces that are phenomenally alien to the self, or that compel one to behave in specific ways regardless of one's values or interests" (Chirkov *et al.* 2003: 98). Again, this contrast coheres with the concept of agency, in that the opposite of a person with agency is someone who is forced, oppressed or passive.

To determine autonomy, the survey question enquires whether respondents engage in certain practices (related to a set of domains, such as children's education, respondent's employment, household duties, health care, mobility, and participation in groups). Respondents are then asked to rate numerically the strength of each of four possible reasons why one believes or engages in the practice, from a low number, corresponding to *not at all because of this reason*, to a high number, corresponding to *completely because of this reason*. Reason 1, called External Regulation, establishes to what extent the person felt coerced or forced to act (by another person, or by force of circumstances); reason 2, called Introjected Regulation, gauges the extent to which others' opinions and expectations, accompanied by the avoidance of feeling guilt or shame, influenced her choice. Reason 3, called Identified Regulation, appraises whether she herself valued it as an important practice, and reason 4, called Integrated Regulation, whether her thoughts on the matter were integrated with her wider thinking about her own life.

The interpretation of these measures of autonomy is not unproblematic, for they are likely to contain an unpredictable mixture of people's reflected values and their adaptive preferences. For example, wives may feel themselves to be autonomous in relation to their husbands, but others, viewing them from the outside, may question their values. Perhaps their values have been shaped too much by their circumstances; they cannot imagine another way of living which would be more truly autonomous. In recent work in Kerala, this issue arose with respect to the domain of "household duties"—which most women deeply valued as integral to their conception of what it was to be a good and responsible woman. The enumerators and researchers questioned the extent to which women's values had adapted to the local culture of women as mothers and care-givers, the lack of possibilities they had to avoid household work, and the social norms of decency and honor (Alkire, Chirkov *et al.* 2007). Interesting work on both statistical and conceptual analyses of "adaptive preferences" will be needed to facilitate the interpretation of such questions (see Burchardt 2003, 2005; Cookson 2005; Nussbaum 2001; Qizilbash 1997; Ravallion and Lokshin 2001).

VIII. CONCLUSION

Frederick Douglass claimed that "Greatness does not come to any people on flowery beds of ease. We must fight to win the prize. . . . The hardships and dangers involved in the struggle give strength and toughness to the character, and enable it to stand firm in storm as well as sunshine" (Douglass 1881: 515). The development of stronger measures of individual agency may be useful to support the kinds of internal and external freedoms that made Frederick Douglass and others like him agents of change. By refracting the existing measures of agency through four conceptual distinctions, this chapter has encouraged both a broadening of these measures to encompass new features, and a clearer articulation of the strengths, weaknesses and complementaries among such measures.

This chapter has argued that asset proxy measures of agency are at best to be interpreted with considerable care. Direct measures of agency are clearly relevant and helpful, but the dominant measures explore certain features of agency with a great deal of energy, leaving others relatively unexplored and thus ripe for research. Agency measures might be classified according to four categories, each of which has two options, as depicted in Table 24.1. First, agency may be measured with respect to different domains of capability (including consumption, health

Table 24.1. Characteristics of agency measures

	Global (G) or multi-dimensional (M)	Effective power (E) or control (C)	Well-being (W) or other commitment (O)	Ability (Ab) or autonomy (Au)
Dominant (e.g. household decisions)	G, M	C	W	Ab
Autonomy measures (Ryan and Deci)	G, M	E, C	W, O	Au
Efficacy measures (Bandura)	G, M	E	W, O	Ab
Other-regarding analyses	G, M	E, C	O	Ab, Au

actions, work and livelihoods, childbearing, children's education, marriage, politics, and other-regarding activities). Second, the effective exercise of agency may not be individual, and may not necessarily involve direct control by the person or group at all; instead their agency may be exerted as "effective power" by an individual or group. Third, agents may advance their own well-being and that of their family; yet responsible agents also act to advance many other goals to which they are committed, but which do not necessarily expand their own well-being and indeed may decrease it. Fourth, we are fundamentally interested in two questions: (1) are people able to act on behalf of things they *value*?, and (2) are people able to act on behalf of things it is presumed they *have reason to value*? While in practice, these will often be identical, we have observed that any empirical measure will identity only (1) *or* (2), not both. While the development and implementation of adequate measures to advance a fuller account of agency than is now available may seem tedious, it may also be, as Douglass suggested, fundamentally important.

References

ALKIRE, S. (2005), "Subjective Quantitative Studies of Human Agency", *Social Indicators Research*, 74(1): 217–60.

—— (2006), "Measuring Agency: Issues and Possibilities", *Indian Journal of Human Development*, 1(1): 169–78.

—— (2007), "Measuring Freedoms Alongside Well-Being", in I. Gough and J. A. Mcgregor (eds), *Well-Being in Developing Countries: New Approaches and Research Strategies* (Cambridge: Cambridge University Press).

—— (2008), "Choosing Dimensions: The Capability Approach and Multidimensional Poverty", in N. Kakwani and J. Silber (eds), *The Many Dimensions of Poverty* (New York: Palgrave-Macmillan).

ALKIRE, S., CHIRKOV, V., and SILVA LEANDER, S. (2007), "Indicating Agency", unpub. MS, Harvard University and University of Saskatchewan.

ALSOP, R. (2004), *Local Organizations in Nepal: A Study of District and Sub-District Organizations* (Washington, DC: World Bank).

—— BERTELSEN, M., and HOLLAND, J. (2006), *Empowerment in Practice from Analysis to Implementation* (Washington, DC: World Bank).

—— and HEINSOHN, N. (2005), *Measuring Empowerment in Practice: Structuring Analysis and Framing Indicators* (Washington, DC: World Bank)

ANAND, S., and SEN, A. (2000), *Human Development and Human Rights* (New York: Oxford University Press for UNDP).

BANDURA, A. (1995), *Self Efficacy in Changing Societies* (New York: Cambridge University Press).

—— (1997), *Self Efficacy: The Exercise of Control* (New York: Freeman).

BANDURA, A. (1998), "Exercises of Agency in Personal and Social Change", in E. Sanavio (ed.), *Behavior and Cognitive Therapy Today* (Oxford: Elsevier).

—— (2000), "Exercise of Human Agency through Collective Efficacy", *Current Directions in Psychological Science*, 9(3): 75–8.

BURCHARDT, T. (2003), "Identifying Adaptive Preferences using Panel Data: Subjective and Objective Income Trajectories", paper presented at the Third Conference on Capabilties, Pavia.

—— (2005), "Are One Man's Rags Another Man's Riches? Identifying Adaptive Expectations using Panel Data", *Social Indicators Research*, 74(1): 57–102.

CHIRKOV, V., *et al.* (2003), "Differentiating Autonomy from Individualism and Independence: A Self-Determination Theory Perspective on Internalization of Cultural Orientations and Well-Being", *Journal of Personality and Social Psychology*, 84(1): 97–110.

CLARK, D. A. (2002), *Visions of Development: A Study of Human Values* (Cheltenham and Northampton, Mass.: Elgar).

—— (2003), "Concepts and Perceptions of Human Well-Being: Some Evidence from South Africa", *Oxford Development Studies*, 31(2): 173–96.

COOKSON, R. (2005), "QALYs, and the Capability Approach", *Health Economics*, 14: 817–29.

CROCKER, D. A. (1995), "Functioning and Capability: The Foundations of Sen's and Nussbaum's Development Ethic, Part 2", in M. Nussbaum and J. Glover (eds), *Women, Culture and Development: A Study of Human Capabilities* (Oxford: Clarendon Press).

CUMMINS, R. A. (1996), "The Domains of Life Satisfaction: An Attempt to Order Chaos", *Social Indicators Research*, 38(3): 303–32.

—— (2000), "Objective and Subjective Quality of Life: An Interactive Model", *Social Indicators Research*, 52(1): 55–72.

DOUGLASS, F. (1845), *Narrative of the Life of Frederick Douglass, An American Slave* (Boston: Anti-Slavery Office).

—— (1881), *Life and Times of Frederick Douglass: His Early Life as a Slave, His Escape from Bondage, and His Complete History to the Present Time* (Hartford, Conn.: Park Publishing Co.).

DRÈZE, J., and SEN, A. K. (2002), *India, Development and Participation*, 2nd edn (New Delhi and New York: Oxford University Press).

GASPER, D., and VAN STAVEREN, I. (2003), "Development as Freedom—and as What Else?", *Feminist Economics*, 9(2–3): 137–61.

GHUMAN, S. J., LEE, H. J., and SMITH, H. L. (2006), "Measurement of Women's Autonomy According to Women and Their Husbands: Results from Five Asian Countries", *Social Science Research*, 35(1): 1–28.

GIBSON, C., and WOOLCOCK, M. (2005), *Empowerment and Local Level Conflict Mediation in Indonesia: A Comparative Analysis of Concepts, Measures, and Project Efficacy* (Washington, DC.: World Bank).

HILL, M. T. (2003), "Development as Empowerment", *Feminist Economics*, 9(2–3): 117–35.

IBRAHIM, S., and ALKIRE, S. (2007), "Agency and Empowerment: A Proposal for Internationally Comparable Indicators", *Oxford Development Studies*, 35: 379–403.

KABEER, N. (1999), "Resources, Agency, Achievement: Reflections on the Measurement of Women's Empowerment", *Development as Change*, 30(3): 435–64.

—— (2001), "Reflections on the Measurement of Women's Empowerment—Theory and Practice", in A. Sisask (ed.), *Discussing Women's Empowerment: Theory and Practice* (Stockholm: Novum Grafiska AB).

MALHOTRA, A., and SCHULER, S. R. (2005), "Women's Empowerment as A Variable in International Development", in D. Narayan (ed.), *Measuring Empowerment: Cross-Disciplinary Perspectives* (Washington, DC: World Bank).

McGILLIVRAY, M. (2005), "Measuring Non-Economic Well-being Achievement", *Review of Income and Wealth*, 51(2): 337–64.

NARAYAN, D. (2002), *Empowerment and Poverty Reduction* (Washington, DC: World Bank).

——and PETESCH, P. (2007), *Moving Out of Poverty: Cross-Disciplinary Perspectives on Mobility* (Washington, DC: World Bank).

NARAYAN-PARKER, D. (2005), *Measuring Empowerment: Cross-Disciplinary Perspectives* (Washington, DC: World Bank).

NUSSBAUM, M. (1990), "Aristotelian Social Democracy", in R. B. Douglass, G. M. Mara, and H. S. Richardson (eds), *Liberalism and the Good* (New York: Routledge).

——(2000), *Women and Human Development: The Capabilities Approach* (Cambridge: Cambridge University Press).

——(2001), "Adaptive Preferences and Women's Options", *Economics and Philosophy*, 17(1): 67–88.

OAKLEY, P. (2001), *Evaluating Empowerment: Reviewing the Concept and Practice* (Oxford: INTRAC).

ORC MACRO (2006), *Measure DHS Number 2: Model Questionnaire with Commentary for Country with Expanded HIV-AIDS Questions* (Calverton, Md: ORC Macro).

OZER, E. M., and BANDURA, A. (1990), "Mechanisms Governing Empowerment Effects: A Self-Efficacy Analysis", *Journal of Personality and Social Psychology*, 58(3): 472–86.

QIZILBASH, M. (1996), "Capabilities, Well-Being and Human Development: A Survey", *Journal of Development Studies*, 33(2): 143–62.

——(1997), "A Weakness of the Capability Approach with Respect to Gender Justice", *Journal of International Development*, 9(2): 251–62.

——(1998), "The Concept of Well-Being", *Economics and Philosophy*, 14(1): 51–73.

RAVALLION, M., and LOKSHIN, M. (2001), "Identifying Welfare Effects from Subjective Questions", *Economica*, 68 (271): 335–57.

RYAN, R. M., and DECI, E. L. (2000), "Self-Determination Theory and the Facilitation of Intrinsic Motivation, Social Development, and Well-Being", *American Psychologist*, 55(1): 68–78.

————(2004), "Autonomy is No Illusion: Self-Determination Theory and the Empirical Study of Authenticity, Awareness, and Will", in J. Greenberg, S. L. Koole and T. Pyszczynski (eds), *Handbook of Experimental Existential Psychology* (New York: Guilford Press).

SEN, A. K. (1979), "Informational Analysis of Moral Principles", in R. Harrison (ed.), *Rational Action* (Cambridge: Cambridge University Press).

——(1980), "Equality of What?", in S. Mcmurrin (ed.), *The Tanner Lectures on Human Values* (Salt Lake City: University of Utah Press).

——(1981), *Poverty and Famines: An Essay on Entitlement and Deprivation* (Oxford: Clarendon Press; New York: Oxford University Press).

——(1983), "Evaluator Relativity and Consequential Evaluation", *Philosophy and Public Affairs*, 12(2): 113–32.

——(1985a), *Commodities and Capabilities* (Amsterdam: North-Holland; New York: Elsevier Science).

SEN, A. K. (1985b), "Well-Being, Agency and Freedom: The Dewey Lectures 1984", *Journal of Philosophy*, 82(4): 169–221.

—— (1987), "The Standard of Living", in G. Hawthorn (ed.), *The Standard of Living* (Cambridge: Cambridge University Press).

—— (1992), *Inequality Re-Examined* (Oxford: Clarendon Press).

—— (1993), "Capability and Well-Being", in M. Nussbaum and A. Sen (eds), *Quality of Life* (Oxford: Clarendon Press).

—— (1999), *Development as Freedom*, 1st edn (New York: Knopf Press).

—— (2000), "Consequential Evaluation and Practical Reason", *Journal of Philosophy*, 97(9): 477–502.

—— (2002), *Rationality and Freedom* (Cambridge, Mass.: Belknap Press).

SMITH, A. (1776), *An Inquiry Into the Nature and Causes of the Wealth of Nations* (London: W. Strahan and T. Cadell).

STEWART, F. (2005), "Groups and Capabilities", *Journal of Human Development*, 6(2): 185–204.

C H A P T E R   25

··

SEN'S IDENTITIES

··

KWAME ANTHONY APPIAH

> One of the central issues must be how human beings are seen. Should they be categorized in terms of inherited traditions, particularly the inherited religion, of the community in which they happen to be born, taking that unchosen identity to have automatic priority over other affiliations involving politics, profession, class, gender, language, literature, social involvements, and many other connections?
>
> Sen (2006: 150)

AMARTYA Sen's work on the recently much-discussed topic of identity displays his characteristic combination of acuity and humanity, theoretical insight and practical engagement. It also exhibits his preoccupation with developing an understanding of rationality that is normatively more sophisticated and a good deal more richly textured than most economic—and I would add, most philosophical—accounts. His book *Identity and Violence* (Sen 2006), which brings together much of his thinking on these questions, is splendidly cosmopolitan in its range of reference, touching on histories from every continent and over three millennia. And, by and large, the central normative arguments strike me as correct, and the applications of his ideas to particular cases tend to support policies I agree with. So it is, from many points of view, a very fine work.

In the course of the book Sen mentions, at one point, his teacher Joan Robinson's commenting that she thought Indians were "too rude" (Sen 2006: 31). He offers this as a not entirely serious example of an identity stereotype that he knew he could not escape. He has also called himself an "argumentative Indian" (Sen 2005) and it was, I suppose, this argumentativeness that Robinson was responding to. So I expect that he would prefer it if, rather than simply elucidating the many things that I agree with in his analysis, I focus, in that argumentative way, on places where I think the analysis could be strengthened and taken further, as we struggle to make sense of these difficult and important questions. (This is harder for me than for him, I suspect: Ghana and England, where I grew up, are not nearly so happily argumentative!)

I. Identity and Partitioning: A First Proposal

It will help to lay out first, however, the main strands of his analysis. *Identity and Violence* is written for the general reader and it naturally proceeds not by offering technical definitions of terms, but rather by showing them in use, often in examples drawn from history or everyday life. But we can see the account of identity he is presupposing by attending carefully to the way he develops his argument. Here is the first sketch, early on in the first chapter, of the nature of identity:

A person's citizenship, residence, geographic origin, class, politics, profession, employment, food habits, sports interests, taste in music, social commitments, etc., make us members of a variety of groups. Each of these collectivities ... gives her a particular identity.

(Sen 2006: 5)

My particular identity, then, is fixed—or at any rate shaped—by the complete set of these memberships. Now there are, as Sen says, many such "systems of partitioning" the people of the world, "each of which has some—often far-reaching—relevance in our lives" (10). Partitioning, of course, is simply a matter of dividing people into sets. It is, we might say, a purely logical matter. But Sen is clear from the beginning that being a member of a group entails more than simply sharing a property. What else is required?

We could begin by looking at the sorts of examples Sen offers. He is at pains to insist how diverse each person's identities are; we have already seen this in the abstract characterization of the collectivities I have just quoted. And he offers us, early on, some specifics in his own case:

I can be, at the same time, an Asian, an Indian citizen, a Bengali with Bangladeshi ancestry, an American or British resident, an economist, a dabbler in philosophy, an author, a Sanskritist, a strong believer in secularism and democracy, a man, a feminist, a heterosexual, a defender of lesbian and gay rights, with a non-religious lifestyle, from a Hindu background, a non-Brahmin, and a nonbeliever in an afterlife (and also, in case the question is asked, a nonbeliever in a before-life as well).   (19)

Lest we worry about whether this list is complete, he insists that "there are of course a great many other membership categories which, depending on circumstances, can move and engage me" (19).

One difficulty that I want to point to is already evident, I think, in both the variety of ways in which Sen picks out the properties he is interested in and in the diversity of the list of groups to which he says he belongs. It is a simple point, though I hope, by the end, to persuade you that it is an important one: not all of them would ordinarily be thought of as constituting identities. Let us look at the list.

Asian, fine. That's a standard exemplary identity (though which identity the word "Asian" picks out is very different in, say, India, England and New England). But is *Indian citizen* an identity? Normally, I think, we should say that, strictly speaking, being Indian is an identity, but that being an Indian citizen is a legal status and not an identity. There are people of Indian ancestry who are not Indian citizens (many of them in Pakistan and Bangladesh, for example, but also in Britain, North America and the Caribbean). State institutions (inside and outside India) recognize Indian citizens and respond to that status. But in most social life in most places it is not the juridical status but the Indian identity that matters. Furthermore, while citizenship matters to many Indians, their identity as Indians is likely, in their thinking, to be separable from their citizenship, not least because (as Sen points out in a different case) someone who has given up one citizenship for another "may still retain considerable loyalties to her sense of" her original identity (29).

Continuing on down the list, I wonder, too, about at least four others of the groups to which Sen belongs: strong believers in secularism and democracy, defenders of lesbian and gay rights, people with non-religious lifestyles, and non-believers in an afterlife and a before-life. These are, of course, in Sen's most abstract characterization, "partitions", which—being non-empty classes—do indeed have members; but I think Sen belongs to the class of Indians in a different way from the merely logical way in which he belongs to the class of, say, people with non-religious lifestyles. And I think that this distinction in ways of belonging is important for theoretical and for practical reasons.

Now Sen himself insists, as I say, on the distinction between merely having a property in common and sharing an identity. He observes that "classification is cheap, but identity is not" (26). He considers, by way of example, the case of "people who wear size 8 shoes", pointing out rightly that there are possible stories in which this might indeed become a basis for "solidarity and identity". (He sketches one such tale, which involves a Soviet-style bureaucracy that allows size 8 shoes, and only size 8 shoes, to become scarce.) As we'll see in a moment, solidarity presupposes identification, so we don't need to mention the latter explicitly. So we're left with the suggestion that what makes something an identity is the fact that it's a group whose members have solidarity with one another: that partition plus solidarity equals identity.

To make sense of this proposal we need to say a little here about what solidarity involves. Solidarity has, of course, an affective dimension; but let's focus—since the context here is one of identity as a matter of social policy—on the way in which solidarity works in decision and action. By A's acting out of solidarity with his fellow Xes we presumably mean something like this: that A, conceiving of himself as an X, is disposed to seek to assist the flourishing of other Xes *because they are fellow Xes.* He is disposed, for example, to do things for Xes *as Xes*; and to do so *as an X himself.* This double intentionality of solidarity—it involves acting both *as an X* and towards other Xes *as Xes*—would mean that having an identity would require you to conceive of yourself in a certain way, so that you could not have an identity that you did not recognize. This is a schema for acting in solidarity. It is important that Sen is unlikely to allow us to characterize this as a matter of our having a bare preference for our fellow Xes. Solidarity, as he understands it, is responsive to reason: "People see themselves—and have a reason to see themselves," he says, "in many different ways." So acts of solidarity are not *actes gratuits*: they are choices among options, for reasons, under constraints (15).

A proposal of this kind fits with the general tenor of Sen's approach. It is fundamentally methodologically *individualist*, by which I mean, to borrow a formulation of Thomas Pogge's (1992: 48), that it begins from the premise that "the ultimate units of concern are human beings, or persons—rather than, say, family lines, tribes, ethnic, cultural, or religious communities, nations, or states". (I think it is a little unfortunate that the term "individualism", which has, in ordinary usage, a whiff of unsociability about it, should have come to be the technical philosophical label for this position. So it is perhaps worth saying at once that individualism of this sort is the basis for an extensive concern for others.) Throughout the book, when Sen attends to the uses of identity, it is their uses to individual men and women that matter. The strategy here is the classical strategy of welfare economics, ranking social outcomes as a function of the interests of individuals. But Sen is also deeply committed to recognizing the range and complexity of the demands that reason and morality place on those individuals, so that their interests are defined by something far richer than their preferences. The ethical problem of identity as Sen understands it begins with the question of what roles an individual agent's identity is permitted or required to play in her choices. And he believes that in making our way through life—in making decisions—we are entitled to cultural liberty, to the "freedom to preserve or to change our priorities" (113). One of his complaints against many contemporary understandings of identity is indeed that they deny "the role of reasoning and of choice, which follows from our plural identities" (17). This fundamental commitment to individual liberty—a Millian respect for individuality—begins with the thought that it is individuals, not collectivities, that matter, but it adds the further idea that individuals should play the largest role in determining their own fates. This is to go beyond methodological individualism to what we might call "ethical individualism". Sen is theoretically committed to respect for individual agency: to "recognizing and respecting", as he once put it, each person's "ability to form goals, commitments, values, etc." (Sen 1988: 41) (though, it's important to add, he thinks a concern for well-being important, too; and he knows these two concerns may pull us in different directions).

For these reasons, this first proposal—with its focus on individuals responding to one another for reasons—seems consistent with Sen's general approach.

But, unfortunately, I don't think that it's right. Of course, not every partition of human beings—not even every partition whose members care about each other—is a membership group with which people identify. So there's certainly more to identity than mere partitioning. The problem is that that more, as I'll now try to show, isn't solidarity.

II. Beyond Solidarity

It is easy to see that having solidarity is not necessary for identity. There are many paradigm social identities that, far from involving solidarity, actually work against it. It is part of the point of the attitudes that homosexuals are taught to have towards themselves in a homophobic culture that they should regard themselves and each other with contempt. It was a significant social and political achievement to get American homosexuals in the 1960s and 1970s to come to see solidarity with each other as a possibility. Such processes are a characteristic step in the modern politics of recognition. But I don't think we can understand what happens in such cases unless we suppose the members of the group were already more than a mere partition; we must recognize that they had a shared identity before they sought solidarity with each other. Similar things can be said about other groups held in social contempt.

Could the analysis be half right, though? Could solidarity be sufficient for identity, even if it isn't necessary? I think so, but for a reason that makes the claim less illuminating than you might like. For, as we saw, solidarity requires identity; or, to put it another way, solidarity entails identity on its own. So of course partition *plus* solidarity entails identity.

The way that identity showed up in our account of solidarity suggests a way forward. We will understand identity if we understand the double intentionality of solidarity: if we understand what it is to think of yourself as an X and to think of others as Xes too. Being an X is an identity of the relevant kind just in case there is such a thing as thinking of yourself—and thinking of other people—as Xes. In other words, we need to understand what it is to think of someone as an X.

Well, in one sense, we all know what this means. We think of ourselves as all kinds of Xes all the time: Sen's list of his own identities is an instance of a pattern we could all reproduce, *mutatis mutandis*. But can we give a more elaborate explication of what is involved? I think that Sen's account suggests that we can, and that we should do so by focusing precisely on the notion of reason that plays so central a role in his work.

III. IDENTITY AND REASON

Consider one of the many interesting and important things that Sen says about Muslim identity in his book. He points out that some were disappointed when an "important meeting of Muslim scholars in Amman in Jordan" in 2005 declined to treat people as apostates—as no longer being Muslim, that is—so long as they believed in Allah, in Muhammad, and in the other pillars of the faith and did not "deny any necessary article of religion" (Sen 2006: 81). While most of these scholars might also agree that many, perhaps all, acts of terrorism are wrong, they declined to agree, in particular, that a person who carried out such a wrongful act thereby ceased to be a Muslim. This point is important, as Sen argues, in discussions about how to approach terrorists who claim to be acting as Muslims; for reasons internal to the history of Muslim doctrine, we are not going to be able to persuade most Muslims to treat someone as an apostate solely because he is a terrorist.

This doesn't mean they aren't bad people or even bad Muslims. It means that the commonest understanding of Muslim identity, among people who claim it, is one that defines apostasy strictly in terms of turning away from the central articles of doctrine: what's required is denying God, or the Prophet, or the other pillars of the faith, which is something you can do while being otherwise a perfectly good person, and something you can fail to do while being horribly wicked.

Now this debate actually assumes a form that is quite typical in contests over identity. It is about what norms of behavior are required of those who are (to count as) real bearers of the identity. Sen's extensive discussion of Muslim identity reflects his recognition of the ways in which identities are associated with such norms. Thinking of people as Xes is, in large measure, thinking of them not merely as possessing whatever descriptive properties are taken to be constitutive of the class of Xes, but also as governed by norms associated with that identity. I call these "norms of identification" (Appiah 2005: 68). One difference between merely acknowledging that someone is of Polish ancestry and seeing them as having a Polish identity is that the latter requires us to think that there are things they ought or ought not to do *because they are Polish*. These are the Polish norms of identification.

I assume that, generally speaking, we think people ought to do things only when we think they have a sufficient reason do so: but the "ought" doesn't have to be a moral one. Most Americans think that men in this society have sufficient reason not to wear dresses and lipstick in the ordinary course of life; they think that men ought not to do so. But this ought is not a moral one, for most of us. We don't think it would be wicked to do it. We think it would be strange or odd.

Before going on to say more about the account of identity as normative, I want to expand briefly on a point I glossed over just a moment ago. I spoke of descriptive properties taken to be constitutive of a class. The sorts of things I have in mind are such things as this: having grown up in India is one thing that can make you an Indian; *ceteris paribus*, if you were raised in India, Indian is what you are. There are disputes about exactly what other things not being equal make you not an Indian. Sen mentions Cornelia Sorabji—a sari-clad Parsee who came to law school in England from South Asia in the 1880s. There are, no doubt, people who think that her Christianity and her Parsee ancestry undermined her claim to be Indian (Sen 2006: 159). There are people who think that moving to America and renouncing Indian citizenship undermines it, too. Is Sonia Gandhi an Indian? She's an Indian citizen, certainly. But an Indian? This is a topic that can be debated.

The general point is that there are always conditions of a purely descriptive kind that people mostly suppose you must meet in order to have a certain identity. Most of them have the form of these *ceteris paribus* conditions: you're a man if you have male genitals, but only *ceteris paribus*, since there's androgen insensitivity syndrome, which produces people who are chromosomally male but have female external genitalia, and people disagree about how to classify them. You're a Catholic, if you were baptized in a church under the governance of the see of Rome, but only *ceteris paribus*, since you may have converted or lost your faith. People—people in Ireland, for example—disagree about whether "lapsed Catholics" are still Catholics by identity. The *ceteris paribus* character of the descriptive conditions means that there are usually clear cases of people who have the identity, even while there are disputes around cases where something about the circumstances is unusual.

But, as I just argued, there are more than these contested *descriptive* conditions for identity; there are *normative* implications to identity as well, normative implications that go beyond meeting whatever descriptive conditions there are for membership. That, I think, is why being an Indian citizen or a secularist, or a democrat and the rest, don't count as identities of the right kind: there are no distinctive norms associated with these groups that are not simply entailed by the descriptive conditions for their membership. To be a democrat is just to believe in democracy: the only normative constraint that places on you is acting in conformity to the norms of democracy. To turn this into an identity there would have to be further norms of conduct and feeling that went with being a democrat. It is because there is a logical gap between meeting the descriptive conditions and meeting the normative ones that there can be—and often is—a great deal of controversy over what the norms for an identity actually are. Sen himself discusses in eloquent and fascinating detail the history of debates within Islam about how Muslims ought to behave. But there are also norms that are pretty uncontested. Prayer, charity, making the hajj (if you can afford to): all these are uncontroversial demands recognized by Muslims. There are such norms for other kinds of identity, too. Rightly or wrongly, for example, most people not only conform to gender norms in their dress, but they expect others to do so. And the norms not only govern action, they govern feeling: an Indian has a reason to feel shame when the Indian administration does shameful things.

Suppose this is right. Suppose that in order for X to be a serious identity, people have to think there are normative requirements for Xes, ways Xes ought to behave— or, as we might put it, in language that echoes some of Sen's—identity-dependent reasons for action and feeling that Xes should respect because they are Xes. We can immediately see two things that Sen rightly insists on. First, because the descriptive conditions are *ceteris paribus* and contested, we often have a choice as to whether we should think of ourselves as Xes, because we have to decide whether we meet the conditions. And second, even if we meet the conditions uncontroversially—so that our membership strikes us as given, a fact we are faced with—we still have to decide what weight to give the identity, what norms we take it to bring in its wake. As Sen puts it, "Even when the person discovers something important about himself or herself, there are still issues of choice to be faced" (Sen 2006: 39). He is surely right that we have a job to do in deciding what our identities should mean to us, and this requires figuring out what norms of identification we accept and what we are going to ask of our fellow Xes. While respect for human well-being constrains what I can reasonably accept as the normative demands of an identity on myself or on others, there will, in the end, be a wide range of reasonable places to come to, not least because we have to fit our identities together. So, for example, the norms of identification that a person who is gay and Muslim will come to accept will probably require some sort of accommodation of one to the other, but there is unlikely to be a unique best such accommodation. Sen shares the Millian conviction that we ought to offer everyone a large range of freedom in choosing among the reasonable ways of making such accommodations for him- or herself.

In speaking of the norms people accept, we don't commit ourselves to thinking that the norms are valid. What norms people accept is a non-normative question. There is a separate and important set of normative questions about which norms they are right to accept. Sen's discussion—and his theoretical disposition—insists on the fact that all these choices that individuals have to make require reasoning. We may have to reason about whether we are (descriptively) an X. We certainly have to reason about what that means, making up our minds what the fact that I am an X really gives me reason to do (or think or feel). And we have to reason about which of our many identities are relevant in deciding our priorities in a variety of contexts, faced with different options and operating under a variety of constraints. We have also to learn how to balance their competing demands. As Sen writes: "Even when one is inescapably seen—by oneself as well as by others—as French, or Jewish, or Brazilian, or African-American...one still has to decide what exact importance to attach to that identity over the relevance of other categories to which one also belongs" (Sen 2006: 6).

As a result, again like Mill, Sen grasps that the fact that we have to make these decisions for ourselves does not mean we have to make them alone. Indeed, if there is one central normative project in his book, it is to persuade people that they cannot reasonably ignore the diversity of their own identities, not least because in acknowledging that diversity they will be acting in ways that advance their own well-being and, often, the well-being of others. In arguing for this, he is offering other people reasons to think about their own identities in ways they might otherwise not recognize as desirable or even possible. He is thinking with us about our identities, and so he is assuming that it is all right to make these decisions in concert with others. He urges on all of us ways of accommodating that diversity that escape the dangers of "singularism", the view that "despite the plurality of groups to which any person belongs, there is, in every situation, some one group that is naturally the preeminent collectivity for her, and she can have no choice in deciding on the relative importance of her different membership categories" (Sen 2006: 25). In the worst case the singularist thinks that there is one identity that will do for all situations; but even those who recognize that different contexts make different identities relevant are mistaken if they think that, say, politics is a context in which only national identity or religious identity is relevant in deciding what to do. There are thus, on Sen's view, three dimensions that help determine the relevance of an identity: first, there is the *content* of the choice we are facing, what our options are and the constraints under which we are acting; second, there are our other identities; and third, there are our other aims—some imposed on us by morality or reason (aims whose connection with the norms of each identity help determine whether it should be brought into play).

IV. Taming Identity

When one identity leads people into behavior that is immoral—to intolerance, to aggression, to genocide—Sen suggests that one way we can try to escape these dangers is by appeal to "the power of *competing* identities" (Sen 2006: 4). I am not just a Hutu, I am also a Rwandan, a Christian, a human being: and the latter three identities, which unite me with most Tutsis, can give me access to a solidarity that opposes the bellicosity of a Hutu Power identity that makes every Tutsi (and many Hutus) my enemy. This is one reason for insisting on the wrongness of singularism: if I only had one relevant identity, there would be no others to draw on in this way.

But the fact that there is a problem to be met here should remind us of another reason why an account of identity focused on its role in solidarity is to be resisted. The connection between identity and violence is mediated as much as anything else by the fact that people of one identity can be mobilized against people of another, contrasting identity. And that brings into focus a dimension of identity that we might miss if we think of identity, as I have so far, as simply a matter of partitioning plus norms of identification. For that leads us to focus on the role of an identity in the agency of individuals who bear it, attending to how those norms shape what they do. The norms of identification for Xes are norms to which Xes are supposed to conform. But the expectation of conformity here is at least as important as the conformity itself. And the expectation is often the expectation not of other Xes but of people of some contrasting identity. Racial norms of identification for blacks (or whites) are kept in place by the expectations of whites as well as blacks (or blacks as well as whites). And once non-Xes have normative expectations of Xes, they will rely on them in responding to Xes, and that will often have the effect of making deviation from those norms costly; indeed, both Xes and non-Xes are likely to put pressure on Xes to conform, enforcing the norms with the sorts of social sanctions that begin with disapproval and ratchet up from there. More than this, while it isn't a conceptual requirement on identities that there should be distinct norms governing the treatment of Xes by non-Xes, it is often the case that there are. So questions of power and hierarchy arise regularly in the structuring of identities; and these, in turn, raise important moral and political concerns.

All this is consistent with methodological and ethical individualism. But recognizing the ways in which others—whether of our own or of contrasting identities—enforce on us codes of behavior for Xes, by way of expectation, enforcement or other forms of norm-guided behavior towards us, underlines the difficulties that face someone who wants to pursue the ethical individualist goal of shaping her life guided by her own reasons, her own identities and projects, her own ambitions. Part of what Sen is asking for is that all of us should respond with toleration to others as they make their lives by way of identities and understandings of identities that we do not share. He is reminding us that each person's life is, in some fundamental sense, her own.

Sen's treatment of Muslim identity in *Identity and Violence*—it is in many ways the central case in that book—has two major pieces of guidance for us. On the one hand, he invites non-Muslims to recognize the internal heterogeneity of the Muslim world: we are to see both that every Muslim is not just a Muslim and to see that Muslims differ along many, many other dimensions of identity. As a result, responding to Muslims as they really are will never be possible if we apply a stereotypic notion of the Muslim. What makes them Muslim is, from an ethical point of view, minimal enough that we can't infer much from it; and in any case, it is never more than a part of what they are. These possibilities derive from the contested nature of Muslim norms of identification and the existence of norms of identification that are associated with each Muslim's other identities.

On the other hand, there is guidance here too—somewhat less explicitly—for Muslims. For Sen invites them, in effect, to recall the tradition of broad inclusiveness implicit in the view that apostasy occurs only when you deny core Muslim claims. Here again it is the minimal character of shared Muslim identity that he stresses.

The advice to non-Muslims strikes me as helpful and I think the wide readership of his book in Western Europe, North America and South Asia can all profit from remembering these things. But the advice to Muslims strikes me as less obviously helpful. For, while Islamic communities have indeed, as a historical matter, often defined membership in the *ummah* in rather minimal ways, it is also true that there are plenty of contexts, certainly today, in which, for example, Sunni or Shia Muslims each deny that the other are really Muslims at all; and even if they agree that they are all Muslims, they certainly don't agree that they are all Muslims good enough for their presence and their practices to be tolerated. Modern Salafis, in particular, regularly dispute the claim of Sufi or Alawite (or even mainstream Shia) traditions, for example, to be genuinely Islamic.

Now, of course, I believe, with Sen, that it would be better for the world if these Muslim traditions were not divided in these ways, since intolerance of this sort has led to acts of cruelty and to bloodshed. But neither of us is a contemporary Salafi Muslim. And it seems to me that, for a Muslim, the question whether, say, Sufism is genuinely Islamic is a question that requires interpreting the Qur'an, the Sunnah, and whatever other sources of authority you recognize. And someone who is convinced that a conscientious attention to the approved sources entails shunning or even attacking and punishing those who do not conform to the precepts of Islam as he understands them is not likely to find in ethical individualism an independent reason to change his mind. (I need hardly add that the same applies, *mutatis mutandis*, to other religions.) A Salafi Muslim can certainly accept Sen's critique of singularism as an intellectual matter. Muslims mostly accept that there are questions on which the traditions are silent and that on these one is free to make one's own way, trying to decide them by whatever indirect light the traditions shed and by the use of human reason and an understanding of human nature. Since identity is part of human nature, there is, as a result, nothing to stop a Salafi from recognizing the demands of other identities. But he is likely simply to deny Sen's underlying view that religious identity does not fix what one must do in large areas of life. My point is not that Sen has the wrong attitude here; my point is that his defense of his view is unlikely to dissuade the most dangerous of those whom he is criticizing. And, indeed, since he is himself a non-believer, they are likely to see his views as unsurprisingly mistaken on these questions of practical ethics and politics, given that he is wrong on fundamental questions of theology.

It will do no good, in particular, to point to those many places and times where people calling themselves Muslims have practiced toleration. They are likely to take the same view of the Mughal emperor Akbar's toleration, for example, that his grandson Aurangzeb did. Sen writes, "Aurangzeb could deny minority rights and persecute non-Muslims without, for that reason, failing to be a Muslim, in exactly the same way that Akbar did not terminate being a Muslim because of his tolerantly pluralist politics" (Sen 2006: 16). But all that shows is that a dispute about whose practice to follow is a dispute *within* Islam; it does not give Muslims a reason to favor the tolerant side.

Because most Muslims recognize that disagreement about these matters is consistent with being Muslim, the distinction that a Muslim needs is not that between Muslims and non-Muslims but between right and wrong ways for a Muslim to behave. It would be a grave mistake to think that it follows from this that a Muslim must think that the norms of identification for Muslims do not fix whether one should be tolerant. All that it shows is that there are debates among Muslims about what the correct norms of identification for Muslims are, and that, as I say, only makes Muslim identity like most others. It is not that I am against interventions by us infidels in these debates, if anyone is listening. But I don't have a high confidence in their efficacy.

Nevertheless, I don't want to underrate the importance of giving those many Muslims seeking a place for toleration of many kinds—for other Muslims, for non-Muslims, for homosexuals, and so on—Muslim exemplars of the past and present. Friends of toleration, Muslim and otherwise, can surely help each other; they are also more likely to get along with each other because they have a shared faith in toleration. But, in the end, one reason Sen and I disagree with the contemporary propagandists for intolerance in the name of Islam is not just that we are ethical individualists who care about the well-being of all people, but that we think they are wrong about matters of morals and metaphysics. And if, in the name of their mistaken convictions, they plan acts of terror or undermine the rights of women and minorities, then, in the end, we may have to meet them not with reason but with violence. Sen's insight—that violence in the name of identity usually presupposes misunderstandings of identity both descriptive and normative—cannot allow us, alas, to suppose that we can meet that violence simply by trying to correct the misunderstanding. His recognition that the post-11 September war against the Taliban in Afghanistan was justified shows that he understands that sometimes justice requires the sword (Sen 2006: 78–9). So I am not claiming that his theory has no place for this possibility. But the generally hopeful tone of *Identity and Violence* conveys, I think, a greater faith in the power of reason than I am able to share.

V. BEYOND REASON

This worry flows from a wider worry about how we should understand human psychology. A great deal of modern work in a number of fields of experimental psychology suggests that much of what people offer by way of reasons, when asked to account for their behavior, is rationalization. They say they did A as a means to B, but in fact we can show that their behavior has a different cause. Getting the range of rationality right—one of Sen's great projects—is only going to be helpful in predicting, and thus managing, human behavior if people are in fact usually guided by these richer notions of rationality. In the particular case we have been exploring, the way identity leads to violence is not usually by way of a person's reflectively deciding that I, as an X, have a reason all things considered to attack some non-Xes. Sen mentions the appalling treatment of the prisoners at Abu Ghraib as an instance of the pathology of identity. But that sort of mistreatment of prisoners can be produced in a few days, as Philip Zimbardo (2007) showed in experiments with Stanford University students many years ago, among people whose antecedent identities were pretty much the same. It may be easier for someone who behaves in these ways to tell a story about his behavior if his victims are of some obvious contrasting identity, but the identity story almost certainly doesn't explain the behavior. There is a general point here, the general point that is the main burden of modern social psychology: behavior, good and bad, is often best explained by appeal to the situations people find themselves in, rather than to their distinctive thoughts or values (Appiah 2008).

Given these general truths, we should expect (as common sense would also suggest) that once a conflict begins, it isn't usually going to help to point out that you and I, though divided by the identity that has become salient in our context, are in fact also both humans, or lawyers or what not. Sen's thought, which I have already quoted, that we can tame one identity by appeal to others may be true in the study; in the struggles of social life it is usually not much help. His rationalist faith that if we understood that our identities involve choices, we would see that we have choices to make, is attractive; but I am not sure how much help it would be in Sri Lanka or the Middle East or Rwanda to insist upon it. It is surely true that if the world consisted of people who always thought about their own identities in the sort of way Sen does, many of the world's violent identity conflicts wouldn't occur. But even if everyone started out thinking this way, most could probably be drawn back into conflict in the right sort of context. So, for example, many of the extremely tolerant multicultural members of the Bosnian bourgeoisie would have agreed with most of what Sen says in the years before the collapse of the Yugoslav state. But faced with an economic collapse with the consequent everyday struggle for the necessaries of life, they were not all able to resist being drawn pretty quickly into ethno-religious identifications, conceived of in a mostly singularist fashion.

What would have helped wasn't a better understanding of their identities, but rapid intervention to prop up the ailing economy and sustain the basic institutions that guarantee security. They were victims not of mistaken theories of identity but of a situation in which morally misguided behavior was evoked from people who had more or less the same theories of identity as everyone else.

A large part of Sen's theoretical work has consisted in reformulating social analysis—especially economics and rational choice theories of social action—to include a richer understanding of the demands of reason than the one implicit in the classical model of the self-interested utility-maximizer. Much recent economic theory has focused instead on trying to develop modes of analysis that reflect more fully the role that unreason plays. (This has been a slow process, because modern economics has been committed, by professional habit, to thinking that we can see most social patterns as the result of underlying patterns of roughly rational choice.) But however much you extend your understanding of reason in the sorts of ways Sen would like to do—and this is a project whose interest I celebrate—it isn't going to take you the whole way. In adopting the perspective of the individual reasonable person, Sen has to turn his face from the pervasiveness of unreason.

In insisting on this point I am making a criticism that applies to a great deal of work on identity (including, I should say, my own). Sen has helped us in much of his work to expand our understanding of the richness of reason, and in *Identity and Violence* he has taken that project into an important area of social analysis and offered us guidance in dealing with an important social problem. But work of this kind needs to be complemented, I think, by more extensive attention to the ways in which identities are engaged by human situations, not through norms and values and their rational application, but by way of other, less rational psychological processes. I wish I lived in a world that could be healed simply by getting people to adopt Sen's civilizing vision. I fear, alas, that we do not.

REFERENCES

APPIAH, K. A. (2005), *The Ethics of Identity* (Princeton, NJ: Princeton University Press).

—— (2008), *Experiments in Ethics* (Cambridge, Mass.: Harvard University Press).

POGGE, T. W. (1992), "Cosmopolitanism and Sovereignty", *Ethics*, 103: 48–75.

SEN, A. (1988), *On Ethics and Economics* (Oxford: Basil Blackwell).

—— (2005), *The Argumentative Indian: Writings on Indian History, Culture and Identity* (New York: Farrar, Straus and Giroux).

—— (2006), *Identity and Violence* (New York: W. W. Norton).

ZIMBARDO, P. (2007), *The Lucifer Effect: Understanding How Good People Turn Evil* (New York: Random House).

CHAPTER 26

....

WELFARE ECONOMICS AND GIVING FOR DEVELOPMENT

A. B. ATKINSON

I. INTRODUCTION

....

THE economics of welfare is at the heart of economics. We study economics, not so much for its aesthetic qualities or intrinsic interest, as for what it allows us to say about the state of society and about the case for policy choices. The study of such evaluative judgements should be central to the teaching of economics. However, in recent decades welfare economics has been relegated to the sidelines. While economists routinely make policy recommendations, or statements about economic success or failure, they often do so without apparent awareness of the ethical foundations for their conclusions. Economists use national income as a

The first version of this chapter was prepared for the Workshop at the Official Launch of the Oxford Poverty and Human Development Initiative (OPHI), at Queen Elizabeth House on 31 May 2007, and I thank the participants for their comments. The research was supported by ESRC project grant "Giving to Development" (RES-155-25-0061), which forms part of the Non-Governmental Public Action program. The project is being conducted in conjunction with John Micklewright, Cathy Pharoah and Sylke Schnepf. I am most grateful to them for discussion and suggestions, but they are not to be held responsible for the views expressed.

criterion for judging economic performance, or apply cost–benefit analysis, without considering the extent to which these rest on unstated assumptions. It is taken for granted that standard welfare economics provides an evaluative machinery and can answer all questions.

Yet, welfare economics is in need, not just of oxygen, but of a make-over. As Amartya Sen has argued forcefully for many years, the standard formulation imposes severe constraints on the information that is taken into account when making evaluative judgements. As he observes in Sen (1979), public policy is conventionally assessed according to a "social welfare function", where this function is "welfarist" in the sense that social welfare depends only on the well-being of individuals. The adoption of a welfarist social welfare function rules out any information other than individual welfare. There is, for example, no room for direct concern with hunger or homelessness; there is no room for minimum rights. When combined with the further assumption that the social welfare function is non-decreasing in individual levels of welfare (Pareto preference), standard welfare economics allows no place for the egalitarian concerns expressed by Plato or Tawney.

Sen has engaged in a full-frontal assault on the edifice of standard welfare economics. In this chapter, I adopt a different tactic. I take one concrete issue and consider its implications for welfare economics. The issue I have chosen, as indicated by the title, is that of individual giving, specifically for world development. While giving for development is modest in total amount, it is one of the few direct ways in which individuals reveal information relevant to the properties of the social welfare function to be applied to global redistribution. Where individuals themselves express concerns about the distribution of resources, where they are willing to make transfers, how should this be taken into account in the social welfare function? If individuals are non-welfarist in their concerns, should the state continue to adopt a welfarist social welfare function? In section II, I examine individual motives for giving, turning to the specific purpose of development in section III. I then consider in section IV how far these motives are welfarist. In the fifth section, I go on to the implications for the social welfare function. What are the implications, if any, for the social welfare function of individual altruism towards people in poor countries? Finally, in section VI, I address explicitly the geographical dimension, and the fact that the social welfare is a *national* social welfare function, which has to take into account the limited "sphere of control" of national governments.

II. INDIVIDUAL MOTIVES FOR GIVING

Individual transfers have been incorporated into standard welfare economics, via consideration of utility interdependence (as in Arrow 1981). This is usually attributed to a series of contributions in 1969: Hochman and Rodgers (1969), Kolm (1969) and Winter (1969). But utility interdependence has long formed part of welfare economics (see, for example, Graaff 1963: ch. 4), and indeed my starting point is Francis Edgeworth's *Mathematical Psychics* of 1881.[1] For Edgeworth, it was evident that individuals had some degree of concern for others:

between the frozen pole of egoism and the tropical expanse of utilitarianism [there is] the position of one for whom in a calm moment his neighbour's utility compared with his own neither counts for nothing, nor "counts for one", but counts for a fraction.   (1881: 102)

Such a notion arose of course long before Edgeworth. In *The Theory of Moral Sentiments*, published in 1759, Adam Smith had written that "every man feels his own pleasures and his own pains more sensibly than those of other people. The former are original sensations—the latter the reflected or sympathetic images of those sensations" (1976: 359). He goes on to consider the principles "that direct the order in which individuals are recommended to our beneficence" (1976: 372).

Setting the position out formally, if, for person i out of 1 to n, we write individual welfare as u_i, and individual i's objective function as U_i, then the individual is concerned with

$$U_i = u_i + \lambda_i \sum_{j \neq i} u_j / (n - 1), \tag{1}$$

where $0 \leq \lambda_i < 1$. λ_i is the fraction posited by Edgeworth, and it is assumed, for the moment, that a person is equally concerned with all his or her neighbors (I discuss below the Smithian question of the order in which individuals are "recommended to our beneficence"). This formulation is similar to that adopted by Sen (1966) in his analysis of the allocation of labor in a cooperative enterprise where families are not necessarily indifferent to the happiness of others. In (1), person i is assumed to be concerned with his or her own welfare and, to a lesser extent, with the average welfare of others. Or, rewriting equation (1), the person is concerned with a weighted combination of own welfare and the average welfare of society:

$$U_i = u_i[1 - \lambda_i/(n - 1)] + \lambda_i[n/(n - 1)] \sum_j u_j/n. \tag{2}$$

If the individual objective function takes the form described above, what form should the social welfare function take? One key issue is the way in which differences between individuals are treated—the principles of equity—but I put this on one side, assuming that social welfare is the simple sum of individual welfares. I do this to focus on a second key issue—is social welfare a sum of U_i or u_i? This may not matter. As is observed by Sen (1966), where people have the same values of λ, maximization of the utilitarian social welfare function $\sum U_i$ is the same as

[1] I owe this to Collard (1975), who provides a very informative account of Edgeworth's treatment and its relation to more recent literature (which typically neglects Edgeworth).

maximizing $\sum u_i$. But this ceases to be true if people do not treat their fellow citizens symmetrically. And when, as in the next section, we consider giving for development, asymmetry is an essential part of the story.

III. Giving for Development

A person with an objective such as (1) or (2) can be expected to make transfers, where these are feasible, towards others who are regarded as more deserving and whose greater desert outweighs the discount implied by λ_i being less than 1. Motives may however be more circumscribed. The donor may be concerned, not with all his or her neighbors, but with only those who are disadvantaged. The sum in the second term may be limited to those below a poverty line, and those better off may get zero weight. (In the same way, the disadvantaged may not have reciprocal concern for the donors.) The notion of giving "for development" does indeed imply that the objective is restricted in this kind of way.

We could go even further and say that the donor has no specific concern with the individual recipients at all. Rather, as has been discussed in the literature on philanthropy (see the survey by Andreoni 2006), the donor derives a "warm glow" from the act of making the gift. He or she "feels good" about aiding development or about relieving disaster. In the objective function, the second term is then simply a function of the amount of the gift. Such warm-glow-giving behavior can readily be incorporated into standard welfare economics as a consumption externality.

The warm-glow assumption might be sufficient to explain a general disposition to make charitable gifts but does not seem to capture all that lies behind giving for the specific purposes of development (Atkinson 2007). It may explain why people make regular monthly payments to the Charities Aid Foundation (CAF)[2] but not why they send their CAF cheques to Oxfam rather than cancer relief. The main alternative assumption in the literature is that donors are concerned with the end outcome, where this takes on characteristics of a "public good". If we modify the earlier formulation (1) to focus on the set D of disadvantaged, with d members, and we introduce explicitly the gift g_i by person i, then, taking income, y, as the sole argument of the utility function, the objective of person i becomes

$$U_i = u(y_i - g_i) + \lambda_i/d \sum_{j \in D} u[y_j + (g_i + \Sigma^-)/d]. \tag{3}$$

[2] Individuals in the UK can make regular payments into a CAF account (to which is added the Gift Aid tax refund) and then decide, by writing CAF cheques, how the charitable gifts are to be allocated.

The well-being of the recipients depends on their initial income, y_j,[3] and on total transfers divided by the number of recipients. Total transfers is equal to i's transfer plus those made by all other donors, denoted by Σ^-.

This brings us to a second important feature of giving for development: the large number of potential recipients. We are not talking about a small number of neighbors but about millions of potential beneficiaries. We then encounter the problem that, as d becomes large, the marginal contribution of any individual donor tends to zero. Whatever the value of λ_i, there is a value of d large enough to reduce the marginal value of an individual contribution below the cost in terms of reduced personal income.[4] This gives rise to the standard free-riding problem: the individual donor has no personal incentive to contribute.

The warm-glow assumption and the public goods assumption may apply in other contexts, but neither seems to capture adequately the motives for giving for development. We need, in my view, an alternative formulation. The framing of the problem suggested here is that the donor is assumed to be concerned with the impact on the living standards of the recipients; it is not enough simply to put the cheque in the envelope. But the donor does not regard the cheque as being divided among millions of recipients. The donor is assumed to "identify" with the situation of recipients on a one-to-one basis (or one-to-m, where m is a small number). This may be formalized as follows:

$$U_i = u(y_i - g_i) + \lambda_i v[(y_r + g_i)], \qquad (4)$$

where r denotes the representative recipient(s) envisaged by the donor, assumed to receive the whole gift.[5] According to (4), the donor ignores the contributions of other private donors; it is assumed that they are helping other recipients. The donor wishes to make "a real difference" to the people he or she is helping, in contrast to the "spreading out" that would be indicated by measures of diminishing marginal utility.

The "framing" assumption embodied in (4) is no more than a hypothesis, but it is consistent with a number of features of present charitable activity in the development field. Such an assumption is indeed made concrete in aid programs where donors "adopt" families or villages to whom the transfer is channelled. Even where there is no explicit adoption, the information supplied by charities is often designed to help donors to identify with the situation of individual recipients. Moreover, charitable agencies concentrate their activities, rather than spreading their efforts

---

[3] Here I am ignoring any differences in needs arising from differing family size, etc.

[4] The dilution by d would not apply if the objective function were written in terms of the *sum* of the welfares of recipients, but in this case, as d becomes large, so does the second term: the individual's own welfare would become entirely subsidiary. This does not seem a reasonable way to model individual giving behavior.

[5] Issues of leakage (for example, through administrative costs or corruption) are not considered here, but are discussed in Atkinson (2007).

over all potential recipients. Even large charities like Oxfam have projects in a relatively small number of places.

IV. Is Giving Welfarist?

I now assume that the motives for individual giving are those represented by the "framing" formulation (4). Such outcome-oriented giving could be welfarist, in the sense that the function $v[]$ could represent the welfare of the recipients. We would then be returning to a formulation like (1), except that in the second term the average welfare of others would be replaced by the welfare of the representative recipient. Revealed preference however suggests that donors are concerned less with achieved welfare and more with the resources to which a person has access. Donors are moved by the fact that people are living on less than $1 a day, and this is the form of the objective adopted by governments in the Millennium Development Goals (MDGs). An income of $1 may be associated with different levels of welfare for the recipient depending on the circumstances: for example, how many hours of labor are required. The person may have to work long hours, or in unsatisfactory conditions, but these seem typically to be regarded as second-order considerations. Priority is given to ensuring an income of $1 a day, and this is a non-welfarist objective.[6] We can encompass this motive for giving by subtracting a function, $f[]$, of the poverty gap of the representative recipient

$$U_i = u(y_i - g_i) - \lambda_i f[\pi - y_r - g_i], \qquad (5)$$

where π is the poverty line, and people differ in the weight (λ_i) that they attach to reducing poverty. The function $f[]$ is assumed to be increasing and to satisfy $f[0] = 0$; its other properties may be influenced by the considerations discussed in Sen (1976).

Concern with an income poverty measure would represent one form of non-welfarist objective, but it is not the only one possible. The function $v[]$ may contain a range of arguments. As has been stressed by many development economists and by the World Bank, deprivation is multi-dimensional. The Millennium Development Goals refer to the prevention of hunger, to ensuring primary education, to reducing mortality, to limiting the spread of disease, and to the provision of safe drinking water. In evaluating progress towards these goals, we have a multi-dimensional scorecard. But, in order to make decisions, we have to balance one against another.

---

[6] The implications of such a non-welfarist objective for public policy have been examined by Kanbur, Keen and Tuomala (1994); see also Kanbur, Pirttilä and Tuomala (2006).

As a guide to action, an incomplete ordering may not be sufficient. An individual donor has to allocate charitable donations between different uses, such as famine relief, long-term development aid, and safe water.

In balancing these different variables, the donor may be attracted by the notion of "capabilities" introduced by Sen (1980) as an alternative to the welfarist approach. Capabilities refer to the capacity of a person to do certain basic things. Sen uses the example of a bicycle, which provides a person with the capability of transportation over a certain radius (and may, for instance, allow the owner to search for work). It is not the utility generated by ownership of the bicycle that is relevant; indeed, the bicycle may not in fact be used because it is considered undignified. Moreover, it is the set of options that is relevant, which raises the issue, discussed in Sen (1985), of the evaluation of such a set. At the level of the individual donor, however, a choice from such a set must be made. The donor, in entering different capabilities into the function $v[]$, is in effect giving priority to the different dimensions. This remains the case, at one remove, if the gift is made to a non-governmental organization, since the donor is choosing between different charitable agencies.

V. The Social Welfare Function
with Giving

The objective function of the individual donor, person i, has been represented as possessing two elements, $U_i = u_i + \lambda_i v[]$, where u_i is the individual utility and $\lambda_i v[]$ embodies the concern of person i for the disadvantaged. We now wish to form a social welfare function that aggregates the objectives of all citizens, $i = 1, \ldots, n$. Such a national social welfare function is necessary, among other reasons, to evaluate public policy towards individual giving. For example, should there be a deduction against taxable income?[7] A national social welfare function is equally necessary to guide policy towards giving by the state in the form of Official Development Assistance. It should be noted that I focus here on a national social welfare function for a country of donors to recipients who are overseas (and therefore not included in the list of citizens $i = 1, \ldots, n$). There will of course also be donors within the countries in which the recipients live.

How should the two elements enter the social welfare function? Different positions have been taken. The first position is simple: the social welfare function

---

[7] The tax treatment of charitable contributions has been much discussed: see for example Vickrey (1962), Atkinson (1976) and Diamond (2006).

aggregates individual utilities, u_i, and ignores $\lambda_i v[]$ completely. This has obvious appeal in certain situations. If the second element captured *negative* feelings towards others, then we would have little hesitation in ignoring such feelings of jealousy. Sir Dennis Robertson dismissed such elements vigorously. Referring to the possibility that the existence of envy might make it impossible to say that social welfare had increased even if everyone had more of everything, he said that we should "call in the Archbishop of Canterbury to smack people over the head if they are stupid enough to allow the increased happiness … to be eroded by the gnawings of the green-eyed monster" (1954: 678).

But there are also those who argue that we should ignore $\lambda_i v[]$ where the feelings are *positive*. In his recent discussion of warm-glow preferences for giving for public goods, Diamond notes that "the fact that warm glows improve the description of individual behaviour does not necessarily imply that social welfare should be defined including warm glows" (2006: 915). In part, his counter-arguments are specific to the warm-glow formulation, treating it as a concern with process rather than outcome, whereas here I have adopted an outcome interpretation of giving for development. But in terms of outcomes, too, Diamond concludes that "inclusion of warm glow preferences calls for using resources to give people warm glows. Somehow this does not seem like a good use of resources" (2006: 917). In part, this stems from the view that warm glow arises from decreasing the negative feelings associated with social pressure to donate. I agree that this form of interdependence raises interesting wider issues for welfare economics, but there are also those who give independently of social pressures, so this cannot be the whole story. In part, Diamond's argument, drawing on Hammond (1987), is that inclusion of warm-glow motives is double-counting, since enjoyment of the public good by others is already included in the social welfare function. In the present case, however, there is no double-counting, since the recipients are assumed to be in a different country. The only way in which they can enter is via the term $\lambda_i v[]$.

In the case of giving for development, therefore, we cannot, in my view, simply dismiss the concerns expressed by individuals (the term $\lambda_i v[]$). One consequence is that the social welfare function could well become non-welfarist. As argued earlier, donors may well be concerned with income poverty irrespective of other circumstances, such as hours of work. In that case, a social welfare function formed by summing the individual objective functions[8] would be Σu_i minus a function of the representative poverty gap weighted by the average value of λ. If the concerns of donors are multidimensional, or are based on capabilities, the inclusion of the term $\lambda_i v[]$ will modify the social welfare function more radically.

---

[8] I restrict attention to summation, as I do not want to enter the difficulties that arise when we consider the *distribution* of U_i, which would involve comparing the values for people with differing values of λ_i. These difficulties are illustrated by the argument of Dasgupta and Kanbur (2006) that philanthropy may exacerbate inequality.

This brings me to a more fundamental issue. If individuals evaluate the outcome of giving in a non-welfarist manner, should this not affect the way in which we form the social welfare function? If individuals are concerned with development in terms of capabilities, then we have to consider why we are evaluating the performance of our own society in a different way (aggregating individual welfares). One response may be to say that individual giving is a minor part of economic activity (in 2005/6 the average amount given per head in the UK was £2.04 a month (NCVO and CAF 2006: 29)). The tail would be wagging the dog. But as noted earlier, individual giving is one of the few direct ways in which individuals reveal information relevant to the properties of the social welfare function, and this information should not simply be dismissed.

VI. Spheres of Control and Giving by Individuals and by Nations

If the government of a country were to adopt a global cosmopolitan social welfare function, including all world citizens, then the discussion above would need to be modified, but governments do not frame their objectives in this way. In part this is because of the limited sphere of control of national governments. The government of a country can seek to influence the governments of other countries, and their citizens, but it has no direct control. In some respects, the effect is similar to that of political or second-best constraints on social welfare maximization within a country. In his paper on "control areas", Sen described the planner as "part of a political machinery and [as] constrained by a complex structure within which he has to operate" (1972: 486). As I have argued elsewhere (Atkinson 1995), one has to combine welfare economics and political economy.

The notion of sphere of control, however, has wider implications. It not just imposes constraints on the achievement of maximum social welfare, but enters into our conception of social welfare. At the individual level, I have argued, potential donors can be seen as "framing" the issue in a way that makes sense of, on the one hand, their concern for the disadvantaged and, on the other, their capacity to have an impact. They understand that there are millions of potential recipients and that the contribution of one single donor to the resolution of the global problem is of infinitesimal importance, but they also see that their individual contribution can change the life of a representative individual. Suppose that we apply the same reasoning to action by governments. The UK alone cannot resolve the issue of world development. It is not infinitesimal, but it is only some $6^1/_2$ per cent of the population of the countries that currently belong to the OECD Development

Assistance Committee (DAC), which totals some 960 million. It seems reasonable for a country to shoulder its proportionate share, i.e. to represent its concern by the appropriate fraction (in the UK case 6½ per cent) of the total problem. Since the estimated number of people living below the MDG target level of $1 a day is 986 million (World Bank 2007: 65), this would mean—in round terms— each person in a DAC donor country "taking responsibility" for one disadvantaged person.

In this way, we may arrive at a position between, to borrow Edgeworth's phraseology, the frozen pole of national egoism and the tropical expanse of global cosmopolitanism. A country adopting such a position is retreating from the latter in three ways: (a) considering only the disadvantaged, (b) attaching a weight λ less than 1, and (c) considering only a share of the total proportionate to the country's potential contribution. But it would still be a more generous position than the frozen pole.

VII. CONCLUSIONS

This paper has been concerned with the two-way interaction between individual altruism and social welfare, using this interaction to probe the foundations of welfare economics. While giving for development is only a small part of the economy of rich countries, it is one of the few direct ways in which individuals reveal information relevant to the properties of the social welfare function to be applied to global redistribution. I have suggested that, while considerations of warm glow or public goods may apply to other forms of giving, the motives for giving for development are better seen in terms of the impact on a group of representative recipients.

From this, I have drawn the following main conclusions:

- If the motives for giving for development are framed in terms of concern with the situation of representative disadvantaged recipients, then it is quite possible that this concern is non-welfarist in form; the concern may be multidimensional, and may invoke the concept of capabilities.
- These individual concerns for the disadvantaged cannot be totally ignored when formulating the social welfare function.
- If individuals evaluate the outcome of giving in a non-welfarist manner, then these should enter the social welfare function; if individuals are concerned with development in terms of capabilities, then we have to consider why we are evaluating the performance of our own society in a different way.

- The concept of a "representative" recipient for the individual donor has a parallel at the level of the national social welfare function, suggesting how we can derive a formulation that lies between the extremes of national egoism and global cosmopolitanism.

REFERENCES

ANDREONI, J. (2006), "Philanthropy", in L. Gerard-Varet, S. Kolm and J. Ythier (eds), *Handbook for Giving, Reciprocity and Altruism* (Amsterdam: Elsevier).

ARROW, K. J. (1981), "Optimal and Voluntary Income Distribution", in S. Rosefielde (ed.), *Economic Welfare and the Economics of Soviet Socialism* (Cambridge: Cambridge University Press).

ATKINSON, A. B. (1995), *Public Economics in Action* (Oxford: Oxford University Press).

—— (2007), "The Economics of Giving for Overseas Development", unpubl. ESRC project paper.

COLLARD, D. (1975), "Edgeworth's Propositions on Altruism", *Economic Journal*, 85: 355–60.

DASGUPTA, I., and KANBUR, R. (2006), *Should Egalitarians Expropriate Philanthropists?*, Working Paper 2007-03, Ithaca, NY: Cornell University (Department of Applied Economics and Management).

DIAMOND, P. A. (2006), "Optimal Tax Treatment of Private Contributions for Public Goods With and Without Warm Glow Preferences", *Journal of Public Economics*, 90: 897–919.

EDGEWORTH, F. Y. (1881), *Mathematical Psychics* (London: Kegan Paul).

GRAAFF, J. DE V. (1963), *Theoretical Welfare Economics* (Cambridge: Cambridge University Press).

HAMMOND, P. J. (1987), "Altruism", in J. Eatwell, M. Milgate and P. Newman (eds), *The New Palgrave: A Dictionary of Economics* (London: Macmillan).

HOCHMAN, H. M., and RODGERS, J. D. (1969), "Pareto Optimal Redistribution", *American Economic Review*, 59: 542–57.

KANBUR, R., KEEN, M., and TUOMALA, M. (2006), "Optimal Non-Linear Income Taxation for the Alleviation of Income Poverty", *European Economic Review*, 38: 1613–32.

—— PIRTTILÄ, J., and TUOMALA, M. (2006), "Non-Welfarist Optimal Taxation and Behavioural Public Economics", *Journal of Economic Surveys*, 20: 849–68.

KOLM, S.-CH. (1969), "The Optimal Production of Social Justice", in J. Margolis and H. Guitton (eds), *Public Economics* (London: Macmillan).

NCVO and CAF (2006), *UK Giving 2005/06* (London and West Malling: NCVO and CAF).

ROBERTSON, D. H. (1954), "Utility and All What?", *Economic Journal*, 64: 665–78.

SEN, A. K. (1966), "Labour Allocation in A Cooperative Enterprise", *Review of Economic Studies*, 33: 361–71.

—— (1972), "Control Areas and Accounting Prices: An Approach to Economic Evaluation", *Economic Journal*, 82: 486–501.

—— (1976), "Poverty: An Ordinal Approach to Measurement", *Econometrica*, 44: 219–31.

—— (1979), "Personal Utilities and Public Judgements: Or What's Wrong with Welfare Economics", *Economic Journal*, 89: 537–58.

SEN, A. K. (1980), "Equality of What?", in S. McMurrin (ed.), *Tanner Lectures on Human Values*, vol. 1 (Cambridge: Cambridge University Press).

—— (1985), *Commodities and Capabilities* (Amsterdam: North-Holland).

SMITH, A. (1976), *The Theory of Moral Sentiments* (Indianapolis: Liberty Classics; 1st publ. 1759).

WINTER, S. G. (1969), "A Simple Remark on the Second Optimality Theorem of Welfare Economics", *Journal of Economic Theory*, 1: 99–103.

WORLD BANK (2007), *Global Monitoring Report 2007* (Washington, DC: World Bank).

CHAPTER 27

....

JUSTICE, EQUITY AND SHARING THE COST OF A PUBLIC PROJECT

....

RAJAT DEB

INDRANIL K. GHOSH

TAE KUN SEO

I. INTRODUCTION

....

THE two classical principles of taxation are the "benefits principle" and the "ability-to-pay principle". The benefits principle holds that those who benefit from government projects should pay for them in proportion to the benefits received. Strictly interpreted, the ability-to-pay principle tells us that wealthier individuals should pay more for public projects and the differences in payments should not depend on the differences in benefits received by individuals (see Musgrave 1985). The classical

Rajat Deb would like to thank Miriam Steurer and Richard Sturn for their comments, Christian Lager and John Seo for help with computer graphics and Nick Baigent and the University of Graz for providing a stimulating environment during the summer of 1995. The authors would especially like to thank Hideo Konishi for pointing out an error in an earlier version of the chapter, and Hervé Moulin and participants at the Public Choice Society Meetings, 2005 for helpful comments. The usual caveat about any remaining errors still applies.

utilitarian justification for the ability-to-pay principle for the problem of cost-sharing of a public project is based on the assumption that utility is cardinal, with units of utility fully comparable across individuals, who have identical declining marginal utility schedules. Maximizing the sum of utility entails the equating of marginal utilities and hence the wealthier individual having to pay more for the good (see again Musgrave 1985). In this chapter, we remove the classical reasoning for the ability-to-pay principle by assuming that the utility functions of individuals are different and quasi-linear. Now, with quasi-linearity implying constant marginal utilities, and different individuals having different preferences, and with the individual's preference types taken as private information, is it possible to provide a normative justification for the ability-to-pay principle? In this chapter we provide an affirmative answer to this question.

In our simple problem we have a society with two individuals where it has to be decided whether a single unit of an indivisible pure public good is to be produced, and if it is produced, how the cost of the public good should be divided between the individuals. We use alternative theories of justice and equity (utilitarian, Rawlsian, etc.) to choose from a set of strategy-proof mechanisms. We show that these theories may be used not only to provide an alternative normative justification for the ability-to-pay principle but also for some form of "progressive" taxation. The two-person model allows us to use diagrams and simple closed-form solutions for the exposition of these results.

The chapter is organized as follows. In section II, we set up our model and characterize the basic form of the set of strategy-proof cost-sharing rules that we consider in this chapter. We also provide a brief justification for the *ex ante* versions of welfarist and resource-egalitarian theories of justice that we discuss in the chapter. Sections III and IV contain the welfarist and the resource-egalitarian analysis of cost-sharing, respectively. Section V brings out a normative difficulty of applying egalitarian principles when the differences in wealth between individuals is small. Section VI summarizes the main conclusions of the chapter.

II. The Model

We consider a society of two consumers $\{1, 2\}$. The project involves the production of one indivisible unit of a *pure* public good that may be consumed by the two individuals without rivalry. We normalize the cost of the project to be 1. Individuals have preferences representable by a quasi-linear utility function $U^i = \theta^i y + x^i$, $i = 1, 2$, where $y \in \{0, 1\}$ denotes individual i's consumption of the public good.

$y = 0$ indicates that the society does not produce the public good, while $y = 1$ tells us that the public good is produced and is consumed by both individuals. $x^i \in \Re_+$ is individual i's consumption of the private good ("money"). $\theta^i \in [0, 1]$ is agent i's marginal utility from the consumption of the public good. Nature determines the individuals' preference type randomly, with $\theta^i s$ being uniformly and independently distributed between $[0, 1]$. Once determined, θ^i is i's private information. Each individual has an initial endowment $\omega^i \in \Re_{++}$ of the private good. The mechanism designer (in this case the planner or the government) knows the value of ω^i. Without loss of generality we will assume $\omega^2 \geq \omega^1$ and we will refer to 1 as the poorer individual and 2 as the richer individual.

A direct cost sharing mechanism works as follows. Each agent sends a signal s^i to the planner. On the basis of these signals $s = (s^1, s^2)$, the planner determines a recommended allocation $(y(s), p(s))$, where $y \in \{0, 1\}$, $p \in [0, 1]$. If the public good is produced, $p(s)$ is the price paid by individual 1 and $(1 - p(s))$ the price paid by individual 2; if the public good is not produced, then neither of the two individuals pay anything. Thus, individual 1's and 2's utilities are given (respectively) by:

$$U^1 = \theta^1 y(s) + \omega^1 - p(s)y(s) \text{ and}$$
$$U^2 = \theta^2 y(s) + \omega^2 - (1 - p(s))y(s). \tag{1}$$

To avoid corner solutions we will assume $\omega^i \geq 1$.[1] This is sufficient to ensure that both individuals are rich enough for all possible values of p to be feasible and that the necessary non-negativity constraints, $\omega^1 - p(s)y(s) \geq 0$ and $\omega^2 - (1 - p(s))y(s)) \geq 0$, are never binding.[2]

Specializing the existing n-person results to the two-person case, it follows from Serizawa (1996) and Deb and Ohseto (1998) that if we rule out the trivial rule that never provides the public good under any signal profile, then any strategy-proof cost-sharing rule (CSR) that is individually rational and sufficiently "smooth" takes a particularly simple "voluntary" form:

VCSR. Select a p which is independent of the signal s such that $1 \geq p \geq 0$ and $y = 1$ if and only if $s^1 \geq p$ and $s^2 \geq (1 - p)$; otherwise $y = 0$. The two individuals 1 and 2 pay py and $(1 - p)y$, respectively.

Selecting a cost-sharing rule by selecting p corresponds to determining how the burden of the tax necessary for producing the public good should be shared. To formulate different criteria based on alternative theories of distributive justice and to examine the implications of these theories for the determination of the

---

[1] See Deb, Razzolini and Seo (2003) for the general n-person-model analysis of these "corner solutions".

[2] A necessary and sufficient condition in our model can be shown to be $\omega^1 \geq \frac{2}{3}$ and $\omega^2 \geq 1$ (see Deb, Razzolini and Seo 2003).

"optimal" p, we need to interpret these theories using the individuals' wealth and the distribution of preferences. Proponents of different theories of justice base their normative evaluation of situations on what Sen (1992) has called different *focal* variables: utility for Harsanyi, primary goods for Rawls, functioning and capabilities for Sen (1985), rights and entitlements for Nozick (1974), etc. If two individuals are identical in terms of the focal variable of a theory, then that particular theory will recommend identical allocation of cost between the individuals. Thus, charging *different* prices for the public good can only be justified in terms of differences between the individuals with respect to a focal variable. In finding appropriate proxies for the focal variables of the different theories of justice, two important considerations become relevant that have to do with the informational structure of our model.

First, since we follow the tradition in economics of allowing individuals to differ with respect to *only two* variables—wealth and preferences—we can only distinguish between alternative theories of justice when the difference in either wealth or preferences represents a difference in the focal variable of that theory.[3] In this chapter we will consider only those theories of justice that can be put into one of two broad categories:

(a) *Welfarist*: theories for which utility is a good proxy of the focal variable and the principal objective is to maximize some function of utility.
(b) *Resource-egalitarian*: theories that do not depend on utility and for which wealth can represent the focal variable, and where primary importance is attached to considerations of its equitable distribution.[4]

Secondly, in our model, knowledge about the individuals' preferences is uncertain, making both utility and wealth uncertain. If a theory recommends maximizing a function (say, maximizing the product) of a focal variable (say, utility), we must decide whether it is the expected function of the focal variable (the expected product of utilities) or the function of the expected values of the focal variable (the product of expected utilities) that should be maximized. This issue has been discussed thoroughly by Kolm (1998) and he has named these two approaches the *ex post* and *ex ante* approaches to justice, respectively. He argues that the appropriate approach depends on who is responsible for the uncertainty. If the uncertainty is caused by the individuals, the *ex ante* approach is appropriate and the individuals

---

[3] Wealth and/or preferences is inadequate for representing the focal variables of many theories of justice. As a consequence, some dimensionally rich theories like those of Sen and Nozick will not be modeled.

[4] Collapsing the multidimensional focal variables of some theories of justice into just one of the two dimensions—either utility or wealth—will often tone down the difference between the theories and will sometimes fail adequately to model pertinent differences between them. This dichotomization also eliminates from consideration theories such as Nash's bargaining theory, in which *both* utility and initial endowments need to be used to model its objective appropriately (see Nash 1950).

bear the consequences of the uncertainty. Otherwise the *ex post* approach should be used so that the individuals are spared the consequences of the uncertainty. Here, one can certainly argue that the uncertainty about preferences is caused by "rational" individuals' desire to misrepresent preferences to attain a more desirable outcome, in which case the individuals are responsible for the uncertainty. This justifies the *ex ante* approach of this chapter of optimizing on the basis of an objective function viewed as a function of the expected values of the focal variable.[5]

III. WELFARISM AND COST-SHARING

III.1 Welfarist Objectives

Sen's concept of welfarism includes those approaches to justice that use utility (the individual's selfish evaluation of outcomes) as the focal variable. Assuming that the individuals obey the Neumann–Morgenstern axioms, and hence all that matters to any individual is "her" component in the vector of *expected* utilities, leads us to the *ex ante* version of welfarism. Writing about the appropriate functional form of the objective function in the welfarist context, Atkinson and Stiglitz point out: "if distributional values are not sufficiently well formulated to allow us to take a single social welfare function . . . any function (subject to symmetry and quasi concavity) might find support" (1987: 364).

Thus, using E to denote the expectations operator, an *ex ante* version of this Atkinson and Stiglitz type of general welfarist objective can be described by:

$$\text{Max } W(EU^1, EU^2),$$

where the welfarist objective function (henceforth, welfare function), W, satisfies four conditions:

(i) the Pareto criterion (P): if both individuals are strictly better off, then this represents a strict improvement in social welfare.

(ii) Symmetry (S): if the expected utility vector is permuted, the level of welfare does not change.

(iii) Weak Inequality Aversion (WIA): the function W is quasi-concave in expected utilities. (If it is strictly quasi-concave we will say that it satisfies Strict Inequality Aversion (SIA)).

(iv) Continuity (C): W is continuous in expected utilities.

---

[5] In our problem, if one argues that the uncertainty arises because of the planners' "ignorance" and the individuals are not to blame, then the *ex post* approach, such as that used in Ghosh (2002), is appropriate.

(i) needs no explanation and is a value that lies at the heart of the welfarist approach. (ii) ensures that both individuals are treated equally. (iii) is a value judgement that follows the approach in Kolm (1969) and Atkinson (1970) to measuring inequality. As inequality in expected utility levels increases, the same level of social welfare requires a (weakly) larger value of the sum of expected utilities. In our case, with just two individuals, this can be seen by observing that if the expected utilities of the two individuals are measured along the two axes, then along a given social indifference curve, a point further away from the 45° line must necessarily lie on a (weakly) "higher" total iso-expected utility curve. (iv) is a technical condition that will be used to ensure the existence of a solution.

Two particular welfarist theories, representing positions on inequality aversion that are polar opposites, will be of some interest to us:

(a) *Utilitarianism*: $W = EU^1 + EU^2$. This is the *ex ante* version of the welfarism of Bentham and Mill, which has been associated in modern times with Harsanyi (see e.g. Harsanyi 1965). The social indifference curves in expected utility space are linear, with a slope of -1. It satisfies WIA but not SIA. In this case, the distribution of (expected) utility does not matter; all that is relevant is aggregate expected utility.

(b) *Utility egalitarianism*: $W = \text{Min}\{EU^1, EU^2\}$. This is obtained by the application of Rawls's "difference principle" in the expected utility space (see Hammond 1976; Strasnik 1976; Sen 1977). In this case the social indifference curves would be L-shaped. This satisfies SIA. For even the smallest degree of inequality to be acceptable, the expected utility of the worst-off individual has to improve.

III.2 Welfarist Analysis

The first step in applying the welfarist maximization criteria is to identify the feasible set of expected utility vectors under our assumption that preference parameters θ^i are independently and uniformly distributed on $[0, 1]$. From our definition of VCSR, at any price, $p \in [0, 1]$, for the project to be adopted, $\theta^1 \geq p$ and $\theta^2 \geq (1 - p)$. This implies that the probability of the project being adopted is $(1 - p)p$ and that $.5(1 - p)$ and $.5p$ are the expected values of $(\theta^1 - p)$ and $(\theta^2 - (1 - p))$ conditional on the project being accepted. Thus, letting a be the expected utility of individual 1 and b the expected utility of individual 2, the expected-utility possibility frontier S will be given by:

$$S = \{(a, b) : \exists p \in [0, 1] \text{ and } a = .5(1 - p)[(1 - p)p] + \omega^1 \text{ and}$$
$$b = .5p[(1 - p)p)] + \omega^2\}. \tag{2}$$

The Pareto-optimal points of S are described in the following proposition:

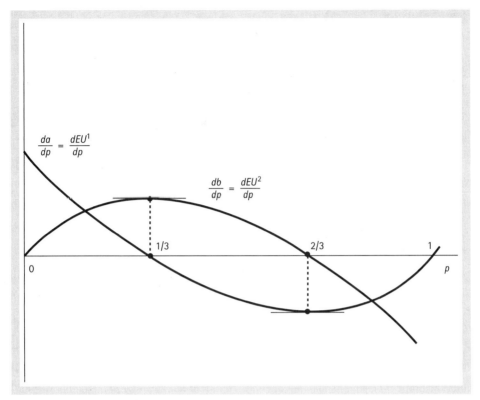

Fig. 27.1. Expected utilities and price

Proposition 1. *The Pareto-optimal points in S can be described as a strictly concave function $b = f(a)$ for $a = .5(1 - p)p(1 - p) + \omega^1$ and $b = .5p(1 - p)p + \omega^2$ generated by values of $p \in [\frac{1}{3}, \frac{2}{3}]$, and f has a slope of -1 at $(a(p), b(p))$ corresponding to $p = .5$.*

Proof. Differentiating b and a with respect to p we have:

$$\frac{db}{dp} = .5p(2 - 3p);$$ (3)

$$\frac{da}{dp} = .5(1 - 4p + 3p^2) = .5(1 - p)(1 - 3p).$$

$\frac{da}{dp}$ and $\frac{db}{dp}$ are illustrated in Figure 27.1. For any point p in $(0, 1)$, for the corresponding a and b to be on the Pareto frontier (i.e. for $\frac{db}{da} < 0$) it has to be the case that $\frac{db}{dp}$ and $\frac{da}{dp}$ have opposite signs. $\frac{db}{dp} > 0$ iff $p < \frac{2}{3}$. The right-hand side of $\frac{da}{dp}$ is quadratic with roots at $\frac{1}{3}$ and 1, and it is negative between these two values and is positive elsewhere. Thus, as shown in Figure 27.1, between 0 and $\frac{1}{3}$ both $\frac{da}{dp}$ and $\frac{db}{dp}$ are positive, between $\frac{2}{3}$ and 1 both are negative, and between $\frac{1}{3}$ and $\frac{2}{3}$ they have opposite signs. Thus, the Pareto frontier corresponds to the values of p between $\frac{1}{3}$

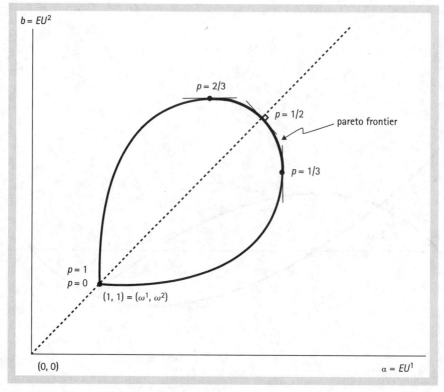

Fig. 27.2. The expected-utility possibilities curve

and $\frac{2}{3}$ and the function $b = f(a)$ is well defined between these two values with its slope given by:

$$\frac{db}{da} = \frac{p(2-3p)}{1-4p+3p^2} \qquad \frac{1}{3} < p < \frac{2}{3}. \tag{4}$$

It is easy to verify that $\frac{db}{da} = -1$ at $p = .5$ and that $\frac{d^2b}{da^2} = 2[\frac{2-6p}{(1-4p+3p^2)^2} + \frac{(4-6p)\frac{db}{da}}{(1-4p+3p^2)^2}] < 0$ for $\frac{2}{3} > p > \frac{1}{3}$. ■

A graph for $b = f(a)$, where $a = .5(1-p)p(1-p) + \omega^1$ and $b = .5p(1-p)\,p + \omega^2$ for $1 \geq p \geq 0$, is shown in Figure 27.2 for $\omega^1 = \omega^2 = 1$.

The economic intuition underlying the graph can be understood by focusing on a decrease in p at $p = .5$. Such a decrease has two effects. First, it decreases the utility of 2 and increases the utility of 1, *if the public project is undertaken*. Secondly, it reduces the probability of the public project being undertaken. Close to $p = .5$, the second effect is small and the expected utility of 1 goes up and that of 2 goes down. As one moves further away from $p = .5$, the second effect dominates, reducing the expected utilities of *both* 1 and 2.

The consequnces of weak inequality aversion can be seen in the following proposition:

Proposition 2. *For a welfare function, W, satisfying C, SP, S, and WIA, there is a unique optimum price, p^W, and at this optimum, $EU^2 \geq EU^1$ and $\frac{1}{3} \leq p^W \leq$ .5 $\leq (1 - p^W) \leq \frac{2}{3}$. If in addition SIA is satisfied and $\omega^2 > \omega^1$, then $\frac{1}{3} \leq p^W < .5 < (1 - p^W) \leq \frac{2}{3}$.*

Proof. By Proposition 1, it is clear that in the expected utility space, with EU^2 being measured on the vertical axis, if $\omega^1 = \omega^2$ the Pareto-restricted portion of the expected-utility possibility curve $b = f(a)$ will have a slope of -1 on the 45° line passing through the origin. (Henceforth, we will refer to this line simply as *the* 45° line). All points on the expected-utility possibility curve with a slope greater (less) than -1 would lie above (below) the 45° line, with the (algebraic) value of the slope decreasing as one moves down along the curve away from the 45° line (see Figure 27.2).

The case of $\omega^2 > \omega^1$ merely consists of changing the origin from being on the 45° line to being above the 45° line, with the point at which the slope of $b = f(a)$ is -1, in this case, being located above the 45° line on the line parallel to it passing through (ω^1, ω^2) (see Figure 27.3, point B).

Now, given our assumption that the welfarist function is symmetric, any social indifference curve will have a slope, if defined, of -1 on the 45° line. Since the

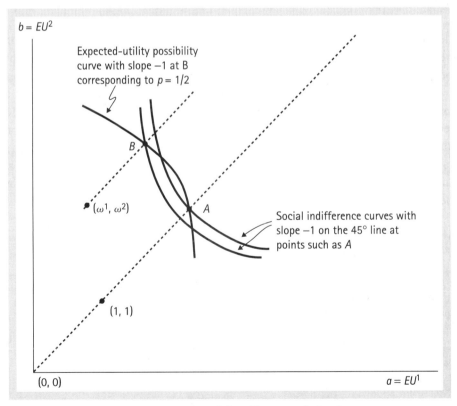

Fig. 27.3. Inequality aversion and social welfare maximization

welfare function is quasi-concave this slope will not increase as one moves further above the $45°$ line along any social indifference curve. In particular, at the point above the $45°$ line where the slope of $b = f(a)$ has a slope of -1 (Figure 27.3, point B), the social indifference curve passing through that point will have a slope (weakly) less than -1. This implies that the maximum will be located on $b = f(a)$ (weakly) below the line parallel to the $45°$ line passing through (ω^1, ω^2) (i.e. below point B in Figure 27.3). This implies $p \le .5$.

To see that at the optimum $EU^2 \ge EU^1$ consider two possible cases: either $b = f(a)$ intersects the $45°$ line or $b = f(a)$ lies entirely above it. In the latter case it is clear that $EU^2 \ge EU^1$ at the optimum. In the former case, using Proposition 1, by strict concavity of $b = f(a)$ for $p \in [\frac{1}{3}, \frac{2}{3}]$, the slope of this curve will be smaller than the slope of the social indifference curve (-1) at the point of intersection of $b = f(a)$ with the $45°$ line (Figure 27.3, point A) and that the maximum will therefore be located on $b = f(a)$ (weakly) above the $45°$ line (i.e. above point A in Figure 27.3). Thus, the former case also implies that at the optimum $EU^2 \ge EU^1$.   ■

How small the optimal p is for a given level of inequality in initial endowments depends, intuitively speaking, on the "degree of inequality aversion". We can think of this as being measured by how quickly the marginal rate of substitution changes as one moves along a social indifference curve away from the $45°$ line. Let us adopt the convention of saying that a particular social welfare function is (weakly) more inequality-averse than a second if for all points in the expected utility space below the $45°$ line, the slope of any social indifference curve of the first function is no less than the slope of the social indifference curve of the second function evaluated at any common intersection point below the $45°$ line.[6] While in general it may not be possible to compare any two arbitrary welfare functions using this criterion, comparisons with the utilitarian and utility-egalitarian welfare functions are always possible and under such comparisons, for all social welfare functions, the utilitarian function is the least inequality-averse and the utility-egalitarian function is the most inequality-averse (see Figure 27.4).

It should be clear to the reader from the proof of Proposition 2 that, for any two arbitrary welfare functions when a comparison of the degree of inequality aversion is possible, the more inequality-averse social welfare function will recommend an

---

[6] The direction of the inequality of the "slopes" would be reversed above the $45°$ line. An equivalent definition would be to say that the first social welfare function is more inequality-averse than the second if and only if both the following conditions hold:

(a) Any social indifference curve of the first social welfare function defines a "not-worse-than set" that is a subset of the "not-worse-than set" of the social indifference curve of the second social welfare function that passes through the same point on the $45°$ line.
(b) No social indifference curve of the first social welfare function intersects a social indifference curve of the second social welfare function at more than two points.

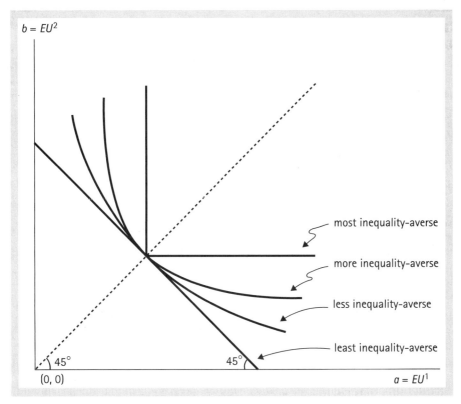

Fig. 27.4. Degrees of inequality aversion

optimal p that is (weakly) smaller. Thus, we have the following:

Proposition 3. *For welfare functions W and $\overline{W}$ satisfying C, SP, S and WIA, if the optimum prices are p^W, $p^{\overline{W}}$ then if $\overline{W}$ is (weakly) more inequality-averse than W, and if p^U and p^{UE} are the optimal utilitarian and utility-egalitarian solutions, then*

$$.5 \geq p^U \geq p^W \geq p^{\overline{W}} \geq p^{UE} \geq \frac{1}{3}.$$

Using Propositions 1 and 2 and recalling that the utilitarian welfare function, $EU^1 + EU^2$, has social indifference curves in the expected utility space with a slope of -1, we get the following:[7]

Proposition 4. *There is a unique utilitarian solution, and the optimal value of p, p^U, is given by $p^U = .5$.*

Now, contrast this with what happens if we maximize the utility egalitarian welfare function $\text{Min}\{EU^1, EU^2\}$.

---

[7] Proposition 4 illustrates the fact that in our model with constant marginal utilities, the classical utilitarian reason for charging different amounts to different individuals has been removed.

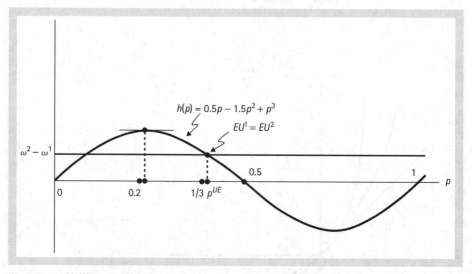

Fig. 27.5. Utility-egalitarian solutions

Using Proposition 1, and defining the Pareto frontier of S, as in Proposition 1, as $b = f(a)$, where $EU^1 = a = .5(1 - p)p(1 - p) + \omega^1$ and $EU^2 = b = .5p(1 - p)$ $p + \omega^2$ for $\frac{2}{3} \geq p \geq \frac{1}{3}$, one can think of two possibilities:

(i) on the curve $b = f(a)$ there exists a point on the 45° line $a = b$;
(ii) for all points (a, b) on the curve $b = f(a)$ we have $b > a$.

For (i), notice that we have:

$$EU^1 - EU^2 = .5p(1 - p)(1 - p) + \omega^1 - .5p(1 - p)p - \omega^2. \qquad (5)$$

Thus, the expected values of the utilities can be equal if and only if:

$$.5p(1 - p)(1 - p) - .5p(1 - p)p = \omega^2 - \omega^1. \qquad (6)$$

Expanding the left-hand side of (6) we get:

$$.5p - 1.5p^2 + p^3. \qquad (7)$$

This is a polynomial with roots at 0, .5 and 1. It is easy to verify that the polynomial itself is positive for $p \in (0, .5)$, negative for $p \in (.5, 1)$, and strictly concave between $(0, .5)$ and convex between $(.5, 1)$. This is illustrated in Figure 27.5.

Equating the slope of the polynomial $.5p - 1.5p^2 + p^3$ to zero, we can see that it reaches a maximum at some value of p, $p^{\min} \approx .21$ and that it attains the maximum value $\Delta\omega^M \approx .048$. Notice, however, that the values of $p < \frac{1}{3}$ are Pareto-inoptimal. Thus, the "Pareto-constrained" maximum that the left-hand side of (6) can attain (say, $\Delta\omega_P^M$) is $\Delta\omega_P^M \approx .037$ at $p = \frac{1}{3}$.

Thus, if $\omega^2 - \omega^1 > \Delta\omega_P^M \approx .037$, (i) cannot be satisfied and the solution in this case would consist of a Pareto-constrained maximization of (5) which we know to

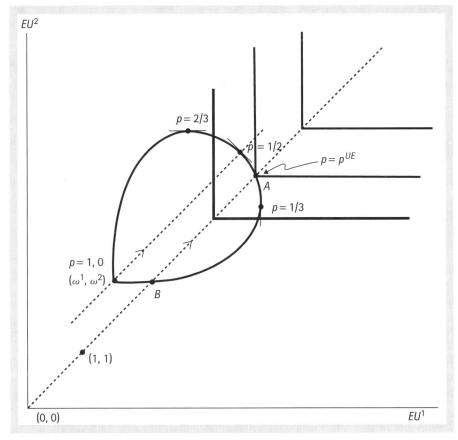

Fig. 27.6. The unconstrained utility–egalitarian solution

be at $p = \frac{1}{3}$. If $\omega^2 - \omega^1 \leq \Delta\omega_P^M \approx .037$ then the optimal price is given by solving equation (6). The two cases are illustrated in Figures 27.6 and 27.7 and the result is summarized as follows:

Proposition 5. *Let g be the inverse of* $.5p - 1.5p^2 + p^3$ *for* $.21 \approx p^{min} \leq p \leq .5$. *There is a unique utility-egalitarian solution,* p^{UE}, *with the optimal value of p given by:*

$$p^{UE} = \begin{cases} g(\omega^2 - \omega^1) \leq \frac{1}{2} & \text{for } \Delta\omega_P^M \approx .037 > (\omega^2 - \omega^1) \\ \frac{1}{3} & \text{for } \Delta\omega_P^M < (\omega^2 - \omega^1) \end{cases}.$$

The function g is strictly monotonically decreasing and strictly concave in $(\omega^2 - \omega^1)$ *for* $\Delta\omega^M \approx .037 > (\omega^2 - \omega^1) \geq 0$.

The fact that g is strictly monotonically decreasing for $\Delta\omega^M \approx .037 > (\omega^2 - \omega^1)$ tells us that the larger the inequality in wealth, the smaller the share of the cost the poorer individual will have to pay. The strict concavity of the function g implies

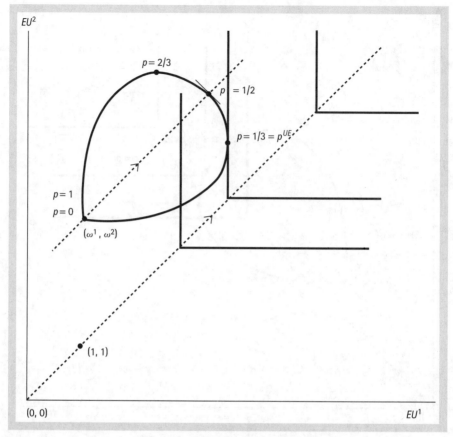

Fig. 27.7. The Pareto-constrained utility-egalitarian solution

that the "marginal tax rate" for individual 2 increases with $\omega^2 - \omega^1$ for $\Delta\omega^M \approx$ .037 > $(\omega^2 - \omega^1)$. Contrast this with the utilitarian social welfare function, which implies a constant "marginal tax rate" of zero.

IV. RESOURCE EGALITARIANISM

IV.1 Egalitarian Objectives

There are theories of justice which specifically exclude utility as a basis for moral judgement. The argument goes that, after all, one's preferences are one's own responsibility (and not society's) and therefore preferences cannot form the basis of a just claim against others. Instead, these theories focus on providing individuals with *equal opportunities* to attain their desired objectives. To describe two versions of these resource-egalitarian theories of justice, we follow the approach associated with Rawls by interpreting the "index of primary goods" within our framework as the measure of resources that individuals have available to them for attaining their goals. Rawls considers both public and private goods in his index of primary goods. If the public good is not produced then the individual's resources consist of his holding of private goods, ω^i; if the public good is produced, then his holdings of goods is the sum of private and public goods: $(\omega^1 - p^1) + 1$ for individual 1 and $(\omega^2 - (1 - p) + 1)$ for individual 2. Thus, Ω^i, the index of primary goods of individual i, is a random variable:

$$\Omega^i = (\omega^i, \omega^i - p^i + 1; (1 - \pi), \pi), \tag{8}$$

where π is the probability of the project being carried out and p^i is the price paid by individual i when the public good is produced.[8]

We will consider two broad types of resource egalitarianism: *intrinsic egalitarianism* and *Rawlsian (derivative) egalitarianism*.

(a) *Intrinsic resource egalitarianism.* This type of resource egalitarian considers equality of resources itself to be the desired objective (see Moulin 1988). This type of objective would also roughly correspond to theories put forward by Foley (1967), Varian (1974) and others who view fairness as "non-envy", and to other theories of justice such as that of Dworkin (1981). Thus, in *ex ante* form, the objective is to minimize the difference in expected holdings of primary goods between the two individuals. This can be represented in our model as:

$$\text{Min}|E\Omega^2 - E\Omega^1|. \tag{9}$$

We adopt the convention that if, for this objective, there are *two* solutions for optimal p and the expected value of Ω is greater for both individuals under one solution than under the other, then the efficient solution which gives both individuals a higher expected Ω will be selected as the solution to the problem.

(b) *Rawlsian resource egalitarianism.* This is egalitarianism derived using Rawls's (1971) difference principle, which has the objective of increasing the holding of primary goods of the individual with the smallest holding of these goods. Thus, in our case, the *ex ante* focal variable is Min $\{E\Omega^1, E\Omega^2\}$ and the social objective can be described by:

$$\text{MaxMin}\,\{E\Omega^1, E\Omega^2\}. \tag{10}$$

---

[8] An alternative definition of resources, focusing only on the holdings of private goods, could be given as: $(\omega^i, \omega^i - p^i; (1 - \pi), \pi)$, where p^i is the price paid by individual i when the public good is produced. This definition gives results which are not significantly different from the ones that we report using our Rawlsian definition, which uses both private and public goods.

IV.2 Resource-Egalitarian Analysis

First, we will argue that the mathematical structure of the "expected-resource possibility" space is similar to that of the expected-utility possibility space of section III. This will enable us to use the geometric analysis in the welfarist case above to establish the results in this case with relative ease.

Recall that since θ^i are uniformly and independently distributed over $[0, 1]$ and since by the VCSR, for the project to be adopted, $\theta^1 \geq p$ and $\theta^2 \geq (1 - p)$, the probability π of the project being adopted is $p(1 - p)$. Thus, using (8), the (expected) "resource possibility curve" $(E\Omega^1(p), E\Omega^2(p))$, $1 \geq p \geq 0$, is given by:

$$E\Omega^1(p) = \omega^1 - p(1 - p)p + p(1 - p); \tag{11}$$

$$E\Omega^2(p) = \omega^2 - p(1 - p)(1 - p) + p(1 - p).$$

Comparing this to the set S describing the expected utility possibility curve (see equation (2)), it is easy to check that at every value of p the two possibility curves have identical algebraic expressions for the slope and that, wherever the slope is defined, it is given by $\frac{p(2-3p)}{1-4p+3p^2}$ (see equation (4)). Just as in the case of the expected-utility possibility curve, the point (ω^1, ω^2) lies on the curve and corresponds to $p = 0$ and $p = 1$. We also know (using Proposition 1) that between 0 and $\frac{1}{3}$ and between $\frac{2}{3}$ and 1 the slope of the curve is positive and that the slope of the curve corresponding to the values of p between $\frac{1}{3}$ and $\frac{2}{3}$ is negative and equal to -1 at $p = .5$. Moreover, the curve is strictly concave at all values of $p > \frac{1}{3}$. In other words, the curve has a shape similar to that of the expected-utility possibility curve in Figure 27.2 (see Figure 27.8).

Just as in the welfarist egalitarian case, there are two possibilities.

(a) If $(\omega^2 - \omega^1)$ is small enough the expected-resource possibility curve will intersect the $45°$ line in the expected resource space at two points. Both of the two intersection points correspond to the intrinsic egalitarian solution obtained by minimizing $|E\Omega^2 - E\Omega^1|$ (Figure 27.8, points A, B). Following the convention that we have adopted, of the two solutions we will take as *the* solution to our problem the "stable" one which gives us higher levels of wealth *and* utility (Figure 27.8, point A): p^{RE}.[9] A closed-form solution may be obtained by observing that $E\Omega^2 = E\Omega^1$ if and only if

$$p - 3p^2 + 2p^3 = \omega^2 - \omega^1. \tag{12}$$

(b) If $(\omega^2 - \omega^1)$ is so large that the entire resource possibility curve lies above the $45°$ line, the solution for p^{RE} is given by the point on the resource possibility curve nearest the $45°$ line (see Figure 27.9).

---

[9] The other solution (Figure 27.8, point B) is "unstable" in the sense of yielding the inegalitarian conclusion that a small perturbation resulting in increased inequality leads to a higher price for the poorer individual.

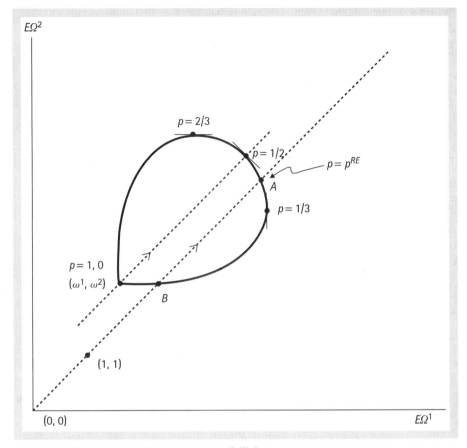

Fig. 27.8. The expected-resource possibilities curve

This solution for p^{RE} is given by the smaller of the two ps at which the slope of the curve is 1. Using equation (4), this gives us:

$$1 - 6p + 6p^2 = 0. \tag{13}$$

Thus, the solution for p^{RE} is $p^{min} = \frac{1}{2} - \frac{1}{6}\sqrt{3} \approx .21$.

Comparing (12) and (7), and using the analysis presented above, we have the following:

Proposition 6. *Let g be the inverse of* $.5p - 1.5p^2 + p^3$ *for* $.21 \approx p^{min} \leq p \leq .5$. *There is a unique resource-egalitarian solution, with the optimal value of p,* p^{RE}, *given by:*

$$p^{RE} = \begin{cases} g(.5(\omega^2 - \omega^1)) \leq \frac{1}{2} \text{ for } 2\Delta\omega^M \approx .096 > (\omega^2 - \omega^1) \\ p^{min} \approx .21 \text{ for } 2\Delta\omega^M < (\omega^2 - \omega^1) \end{cases}.$$

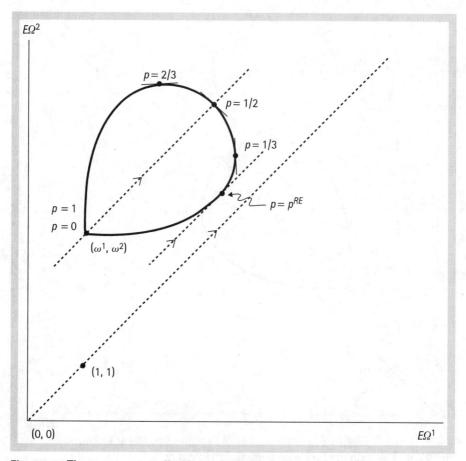

Fig. 27.9. The resource–egalitarian solution

The function g is strictly monotonically decreasing and strictly concave in $(\omega^2 - \omega^1)$ for $2\Delta\omega^M \approx .096 > (\omega^2 - \omega^1) \geq 0$.

Notice that the definition of g in the above proposition is the *same* as that of g in Proposition 5, but its argument is different. Hence, just as in the utility-egalitarian case, for small enough values of $(\omega^2 - \omega^1)$, increases in $(\omega^2 - \omega^1)$ result in increasing taxes for individual 2 and in the increase of his marginal tax rate. However, as compared to the utility-egalitarian case, when we look at the arguments of the g function in the two cases, we can see that p^{RE} is more responsive, with half the wealth differential leading to the same value of optimal p, thus implying a more "progressive" tax structure in the resource-egalitarian case. Moreover, note that unlike our utility egalitarian case, the resource-egalitarian case permits Pareto inefficiency (i.e. $p < \frac{1}{3}$) for large enough inequalities in wealth.[10]

[10] $(\omega^2 - \omega^1) > .074$.

A similar argument can be made for the Rawlsian solution obtained by maximizing $\text{Min}\{E\Omega^2(p), E\Omega^1(p)\}$. It is clear, in this case, that if $(\omega^2 - \omega^1)$ is small enough for the *downward-sloping* portion of the resource possibility curve to intersect the 45° line, the Rawlsian solution, p_R^{RE}, coincides with the the intrinsic-egalitarian solution, p^{RE}. However, once $\omega^2 - \omega^1$ is large enough for $p = \frac{1}{3}$, any further increase in $(\omega^2 - \omega^1)$ will leave the optimal p unchanged. This is because any further reduction in p will cause a decline in both $E\Omega^2$ and $E\Omega^1$ and would therefore no longer be optimal for the Rawlsian objective function (see Figure 27.9). This gives us the following result:

Proposition 7. *Let g be the inverse of $.5p - 1.5p^2 + p^3$ for $.21 \approx p^{\min} \leq p \leq .5$. There is a unique Rawlsian resource-egalitarian solution, with the optimal value of p, p_R^{RE}, given by:*

$$p_R^{RE} = \begin{cases} g(.5(\omega^2 - \omega^1)) \leq \frac{1}{2} \text{ for } 2\Delta\omega_P^M \approx .074 > (\omega^2 - \omega^1) \\ \frac{1}{3} \text{ for } 2\Delta\omega_P^M < (\omega^2 - \omega^1) \end{cases}.$$

The function g is strictly monotonically decreasing and strictly concave in $(\omega^2 - \omega^1)$ for $2\Delta\omega_P^M \approx .074 > (\omega^2 - \omega^1) \geq 0$.

V. Egalitarianism and the Edinburgh Principle

Comparing Proposition 4 with 6 and 7, we can see that both utility egalitarianism and resource egalitarianism provide a justification not only for the ability-to-pay principle but also, for small enough differences in wealth, a normative basis for progressive taxation. Note, however, that both the Rawlsian resource-egalitarianism optimum $(1 - p_R^{RE})$ and the utility-egalitarianism optimum $(1 - p_E^U)$, to remain consistent with versions of the Pareto principle, have $\frac{2}{3}$ as the upper bound for the price that the richer individual can be charged. While giving up the Pareto principle, as is done under intrinsic resource egalitarianism, relaxes this upper bound, it does not remove it altogether. We know that in all three cases, the lower limit on p is binding when the difference in wealth between the two individuals is large enough, but unless a limiting constraint is also imposed when the differences in individual wealth are *small*, all three egalitarian rules may conflict with a compelling normative principle of taxation: the "Edinburgh principle".[11]

---

[11] We are indebted to Richard Sturn for bringing this principle to our attention. As far as we are aware, it was first mentioned by Francis A. Walker in the *Edinburgh Review* in 1833.

The Edinburgh principle (see Walker 1887; Le Breton, Moyes and Trannoy 1996) rules out an extreme form of redistributive taxation in which the redistribution from rich to poor makes the initially richer individual poorer than the initially poorer individual. In our case the Edinburgh principle reduces to

$$\omega^1 - p \le \omega^2 - (1 - p).$$ (14)

To show that this constraint will be violated by the egalitarian approaches if $(\omega^2 - \omega^1)$ is small enough, we will show that this is true for resource egalitarianism. The argument for utility egalitarianism is similar and is omitted.

From Propositions 6 and 7 it is clear that if $.074 > (\omega^2 - \omega^1)$, then $p_R^{RE} = p^{RE}$ and expected wealth is equalized. Equation (11) gives us:

$$E\Omega^1(p) = \omega^1 - p(1 - p)p + p(1 - p) = \omega^2 - p(1 - p)(1 - p)$$

$$+ p(1 - p) = E\Omega^2(p).$$ (15)

Thus we get:

$$(1 - p) - p = \frac{\omega^2 - \omega^1}{p(1 - p)}.$$ (16)

Since $p(1 - p) < 1$, by (16), $(1 - p) - p > \omega^2 - \omega^1$. This violates equation (14), the Edinburgh principle.

VI. Conclusions

After assuming a world of two individuals with (possibly) different (quasi-linear) preferences and different initial endowments, we have looked at the class of dominant-strategy-implementable and individually rational cost-sharing rules for financing a public project. Two groups of alternative norms—welfarist and resource-egalitarian—are considered to furnish a just and equitable basis for cost-sharing. For the welfarist norm, we argue that welfare functions can be partially ordered in terms of their inequality aversion, from the least inequality-averse (utilitarian) to the most (utility egalitarian), with more egalitarian theories recommending a (weakly) lower price for the poor individual. Egalitarian theories not only recommend lower prices for the poorer individual but, at low levels of differences in individual holdings, imply an increasing "marginal tax" rate as the wealth differential increases. For large differences in wealth, the Pareto criterion imposes an upper limit on the price that the richer individual has to pay. Giving up the Pareto criterion while relaxing this upper limit does not remove it altogether. If the project is adopted and the cost shared, all egalitarian theories suffer from a drawback: these theories lead, for small differences in wealth, to a possible violation of the "Edinburgh principle" by leaving the initially rich individual poorer than the individual who is initially poor.

While in a world of quasi-linear utility functions the ability-to-pay principle cannot be derived using the classical reasoning involving identical and declining marginal utility schedules, our model illustrates that such a derivation is possible from principles of justice and equity.

REFERENCE

ATKINSON, A. (1976), "On the Measurement of Inequality", *Journal of Economic Theory*, 2: 244–63.

—— and STIGLITZ, J. (1987), *Lectures in Public Economics* (London: McGraw-Hill).

DEB, R., and OHSETO, S. (1999), "Strategy-Proof and Individual Rational Social Choice Functions for Public Good Economies: A Note", *Economic Theory*, 14: 685–9.

—— RAZZOLLINI, L., and SEO, T. K. (2003), "Strategy-Proof Cost Sharing, Ability to Pay and Free Provision of an Indivisible Public Good", *Mathematical Social Sciences*, 45: 205–27.

DWORKIN, R. (1981), "Equality of Resources", *Philosophy and Public Affairs*, 10: 283–345.

FOLEY, D. K. (1967), "Resource Allocation in the Public Sector", *Yale Economic Essays*, 7: 73–6.

GHOSH, I. (2002), "Distributive Justice and Strategy-Proof Cost Sharing of a Public Good", unpubl. MS, Southern Methodist University.

HAMMOND, P. J. (1976), "Equity, Arrow's Conditions and Rawls' Difference Principle", *Econometrica*, 44: 793–804.

HARSANYI, J. C. (1955), "Cardinal Welfare, Individualistic Ethics and Interpersonal Comparisons of Utility", *Journal of Political Economy*, 63: 309–21.

KOLM, S. (1969), "The Optimal Production of Social Justice", in J. Margolis and H. Guitton (eds), *Public Economics* (London: Macmillan).

—— (1998), "Chance and Justice: Social Policies and the Harsanyi–Vickrey–Rawls Problem", *European Economic Review*, 42: 1393–416.

LE BRETON, M., MOYES, P., and TRANNOY, A. (1996), "Inequality-Reducing Properties of Composite Taxation", *Journal of Economic Theory*, 69: 71–103.

MOULIN, H. (1988), *Axioms of Cooperative Decision Making* (Cambridge: Cambridge University Press).

MUSGRAVE, A. (1985), "A Brief History of Fiscal Doctrine", in A. Aurbach and M. Feldstein (eds), *Handbook of Public Economics* (Amsterdam: North-Holland).

NOZICK, R. (1974), *Anarchy, State and Utopia* (Oxford: Blackwell).

RAWLS, J. (1971), *A Theory of Justice* (Cambridge, Mass.: Harvard University Press).

STRASNICK, S. (1976), "Social Choice Theory and the Derivation of Rawls' Difference Principle", *Journal of Philosophy*, 73: 85–99.

SEN, A. K. (1977), "On Weights and Measures: Informational Constraints in Social Welfare Analysis", *Econometrica*, 45: 1539–72.

—— (1985), *Commodities and Capabilities* (Amsterdam: North-Holland).

—— (1992), *Inequality Reexamined* (Oxford: Clarendon Press).

SERIZAWA, S. (1996), "Strategy-Proof and Individual Rational Social Choice Functions for Public Good Economies", *Economic Theory*, 7: 501–2 (corrigendum in *Economic Theory*, (1997): 379–80).

VARIAN, H. (1974), "Equity, Envy and Efficiency", *Journal of Economic Theory*, 9: 63–91.

WALKER, F. A. (1887), *Political Economy* (New York: Henry Holt).

ISOLATION, ASSURANCE AND RULES

CAN RATIONAL FOLLY SUPPLANT FOOLISH RATIONALITY?

PETER HAMMOND

I. INTRODUCTION

I.1 Isolation versus Assurance

SEN (1967) introduced two simple games to discuss what is an appropriate rate of discount, and what policy measures might help produce an optimal rate of saving or investment in an intertemporal economy. The first game, which he called the "isolation paradox", is a multi-person version of prisoner's dilemma in which each player has two pure strategies, one of which (say D) strictly dominates the other

My intellectual debts to Amartya Sen are accompanied by a friendship deep enough to presume that it will survive not only well into his fourth quarter-century, but also beyond my taking serious liberties with the titles, if not the ideas, of Sen (1967, 1977).

(say C). Moreover, if all players chose their dominated strategy C, the outcome would be unanimously preferred to the outcome when all choose their dominant strategy D. The second game, which he called the "assurance problem", is a significant variant of the first in which C would become a best response just in case all other players choose C; otherwise, D is always better.

I.2 Foolish Rationality?

Of course, both games have a pure-strategy Nash equilibrium where all players choose D. In the isolation paradox, moreover, this is the unique equilibrium. As in prisoner's dilemma, it is the only strategy profile in which all players avoid the strictly dominated strategy C. Indeed, the prisoner's dilemma is a special case of an isolation paradox involving only two players. As in prisoner's dilemma, there is sharp contrast between individual rationality and achieving any sensible collective objective that satisfies the usual Pareto rule. Finally, note that any one player who deviates from equilibrium to play C instead of D is indeed likely to be "isolated".

In the assurance problem, however, there is one other Nash equilibrium in pure strategies, where all play C. This is the best possible outcome that can be reached by a symmetric pure-strategy profile. The "problem", of course, is one of coordination. All of the players would like to be assured that all others will choose C, to which C is the unique best response. But without sufficient confidence that this is what other players will choose, the unique best response reverts to D.

Games rather similar to the isolation paradox also arise in Laffont's (1975) discussion of "Kantian economics", as well as in Harsanyi's discussions of rule utilitarianism (see especially Harsanyi 1977). That is, although there may be a richer strategy space, the pure-strategy rule that is optimal if all follow it is to choose the strategy C, since this is Pareto-superior to the alternative pure-strategy rule where each chooses D.

A utilitarian ethicist should want to transform any isolation paradox into an assurance problem, in the hope of achieving a unanimously preferred outcome. The rest of this chapter discusses various attempts to do this. It will include ways of trying to achieve the optimal symmetric mixed strategy, in case this is better than any pure strategy. Also, the computations turn out to be simpler in the limiting case when the games have infinitely many players, regarded as a random sample of points from a non-atomic probability measure space.

I.3 Outline

After I lay out the game model in section II, section III briefly considers the kind of "warm-glow" effect that Andreoni (1990) introduced to explain some individuals' willingness to donate towards a public good. It also considers additional "rule consequences".

The main idea of the chapter, however, is to consider whether the concept of "quasi-magical" thinking, due to Shafir and Tversky (1992), may represent a useful form of rational folly in this context. This is the subject of section IV, which begins with some remarks on Newcomb's problem and on attempts to motivate cooperative behavior in prisoner's dilemma. The section concludes with a very brief discussion of evidential and causal decision theory, and of the difference between the two.

Next, section V revisits the isolation game, and considers what is needed to reach the optimal proportion of cooperation that is considered in section II.2. Finally, section VI offers a few concluding remarks and suggestions for future research.

II. Two Games with Many Players

II.1 Players, Strategies and Payoffs

The isolation paradox and assurance problem are two games with many features in common. In the limiting versions of both games presented here, there is a large set of many players represented in the usual way by a non-atomic probability space $(N, \mathcal{N}, \lambda)$ of *ex ante* identical agents. This space may as well be the Lebesgue unit interval $[0, 1]$ of the real line $\mathbb{R}$. We will consider only symmetric strategies and correlation devices, so there is no need to bother with labeling the agents.

In both games, each agent has two alternative actions denoted by $a \in A :=$ $\{C, D\}$, where C signifies cooperation and D signifies defection. Alternatively, C can be regarded as conforming to a rule, and D as deviating from it.

Let $\gamma \in [0, 1]$ denote the proportion of agents who cooperate by following the rule in question. Each agent has preferences over lotteries with outcomes in $A \times [0, 1]$ that can be represented by the expected value of a von Neumann–Morgenstern utility function $u(a, \gamma)$. We assume that $u(D, \gamma) > u(C, \gamma)$ for each fixed $\gamma \in [0, 1]$, so strategy D is better than C unless $\gamma = 1$.

For each fixed $a \in A$, assume that the mapping $\gamma \mapsto u(a, \gamma)$ is twice continuously differentiable on $[0, 1]$, with partial derivatives with respect to γ that satisfy $u'(a, \gamma) > 0$ and $u''(a, \gamma) < 0$. Assume too that $u'(D, \gamma) \geq u'(C, \gamma)$, signifying that the (positive) private benefit $u(D, \gamma) - u(C, \gamma)$ of deviating does not decrease as γ increases within the semi-closed interval $[0, 1]$. At $\gamma = 1$, however, $u(C, \gamma)$ may not even be continuous. Using $\lim_{\gamma \uparrow 1}$ to denote a limit as γ tends to 1 from below, we assume that $u(C, 1) \geq \lim_{\gamma \uparrow 1} u(C, \gamma)$. If there is a discontinuity at $\gamma = 1$, therefore, it is due to an upward jump.

II.2 An Optimal Symmetric Strategy Rule

Since all agents have identical preferences, an optimal symmetric mixed-strategy rule is to have each agent play C with probability γ^*, chosen to maximize

$$U(\gamma) := \gamma u(C, \gamma) + (1 - \gamma)u(D, \gamma)$$

with respect to γ. Because

$$U'(\gamma) = u(C, \gamma) - u(D, \gamma) + \gamma u'(C, \gamma) + (1 - \gamma)u'(D, \gamma),$$

it is evident that

$$U''(\gamma) = 2[u'(C, \gamma) - u'(D, \gamma) + \gamma u''(C, \gamma)] + (1 - \gamma)u''(D, \gamma) < 0$$

for all $\gamma \in [0, 1]$, given our earlier assumptions.

In principle, there can be a corner maximum at $\gamma^* = 0$. This holds if

$$0 \geq U'(0) = u(C, 0) - u(D, 0) + u'(D, 0)$$

or $u'(D, 0) \leq u(D, 0) - u(C, 0)$. In the latter case, however, the isolation paradox completely disappears because it is best for everybody to deviate. So we assume from now on that $u'(D, 0) > u(D, 0) - u(C, 0)$.

This leaves two other possible kinds of optimum. First, there is a corner maximum at $\gamma^* = 1$ provided that

$$0 \leq \lim_{\gamma \uparrow 1} U'(\gamma) = \lim_{\gamma \uparrow 1} [u(C, \gamma) - u(D, \gamma) + u'(C, \gamma)]$$

or

$$\lim_{\gamma \uparrow 1} u'(C, \gamma) \geq \lim_{\gamma \uparrow 1} [u(D, \gamma) - u(C, \gamma)] > 0.$$

This is the case when the symmetric optimum is for everybody to follow the pure strategy C. It occurs when, for each $\gamma < 1$, the marginal social gain per head of increasing γ exceeds the marginal private loss per head of having more people cooperate.

An alternative kind of optimum is to have only some people obeying the rule, with others not bothering to do so. For example, it is rarely optimal to have every person vote; only enough are needed so that the (diminishing) marginal benefit of having more vote no longer exceeds the marginal cost, which could be considerable. In the general isolation paradox we are considering, there would then be an interior maximum at the unique $\gamma^* \in (0, 1)$ where $U'(\gamma^*) = 0$. Such an interior optimum γ^* exists if and only if both $u'(D, 0) > u(D, 0) - u(C, 0)$ at $\gamma = 0$, and $u'(C, \gamma) < u(D, \gamma) - u(C, \gamma)$ for all γ close enough to 1. Then the symmetric optimum is for everybody to follow the mixed strategy of choosing C with probability γ^*.

II.3 Distinguishing between Isolation and Assurance

The only difference between the isolation paradox and the assurance problem comes in the relative values of $u(C, 1)$ and $u(D, 1)$. The isolation paradox is a generalized prisoners' dilemma where each player has D as a dominant strategy. In particular, $u(D, \gamma) > u(C, \gamma)$ even when everybody else chooses C and so $\gamma = 1$.

By contrast, in the assurance problem one has $u(D, 1) < u(C, 1)$. Thus, provided that almost every other player chooses C (but only in this case), each player prefers C to D. At $\gamma = 1$, therefore, at least one of the functions $\gamma \mapsto u(C, \gamma)$ and $\gamma \mapsto u(D, \gamma)$ must be discontinuous. For simplicity, we assume that $u(D, \gamma)$ is continuous at $\gamma = 1$, but that $\lim_{\gamma \uparrow 1} u(C, \gamma) < u(C, 1)$.

III. AVOIDING ISOLATION:
MODIFIED PREFERENCES

III.1 Warm-Glow Effects

To transform an isolation paradox into an assurance problem, one can try to modify the players' common preference ordering. As mentioned in section I.3, one way of doing this is to add some sort of "warm-glow" effect. For example, when C is chosen, each player's payoff function could be modified from $u(C, \gamma)$ to $u(C, (1 - \epsilon)\gamma + \epsilon)$, as if the player were placing extra weight on his own cooperation compared with that of all the other players. Then, if $\epsilon \in (0, 1)$ is sufficently large and $\gamma \in [0, 1]$ is sufficiently small, one will have

$$u(C, (1 - \epsilon)\gamma + \epsilon) > u(D, \gamma).$$

So if each player experiences this warm-glow effect strongly enough, then D will no longer dominate C. But the point of this chapter is not to delve into what might work to produce such a warm glow.

III.2 Rule Consequences

A second way of transforming an isolation paradox into an assurance problem is to include a "rule consequence" as an extra argument in each player's utility function. If more players adhere to the rule by choosing C, this somehow reinforces the rule and makes conformity more likely. Also, if there is a succession of opportunities to conform or deviate in a repeated game, players may observe how many have conformed to the rule in past periods, and assign the rule some valuation or reputation accordingly.

Indeed, an obvious way of arriving at an assurance problem is to increase the payoff $u(C, 1)$ from cooperating in the case where the whole population plays C so that it exceeds $u(D, 1)$. Yet in a large population, where an obvious measure of conformity each period is the observed proportion $\gamma \in [0, 1]$ of players who chose C, each individual has a negligible effect on γ, so D may well remain a dominant strategy unless $u(C, \gamma)$ increases discontinuously as $\gamma \uparrow 1$. That is precisely why such a discontinuity at $\gamma = 1$ was allowed.

III.3 Limitations

In any case, all that any such modification achieves is a different payoff function $u(a, \gamma)$ defined on $A \times [0, 1]$. There are two difficulties with this kind of approach. First, though conceivably it might work when $\gamma^* = 1$, it would take a rather sophisticated form of rule consequentialism to achieve an interior optimum $\gamma^* \in (0, 1)$. Indeed, a rigid rule utilitarian may still choose C even when $\gamma^* < 1$. Yet if there are many other players who all choose D, independent of what this rigid player does, the objective of maximizing the average utility of the whole population may not be achieved; the rigid player's gain from bending to play D may well outweigh any (small) negative effect on the other players of having one more person choose D.

Second, consider a Harsanyi (1986) world of "very half-hearted altruists", many of whom may choose C with a probability below γ^*. Then even sophisticated altruists have to estimate the proportions π and $1 - \pi$ of the population who will and will not follow a modified rule. They also need to estimate what proportion $q < \gamma^*$ will play C among the $1 - \pi$ who will not follow a modified rule. Knowing these statistics would enable them to choose their optimal mixed strategy, which consists of playing C with a compensating higher probability $p > \gamma^*$ chosen to satisfy $\pi p + (1 - \pi)q = \gamma^*$, if possible. In fact, the optimum is when

$$p = \min \left\{ 1, q + \frac{1}{\pi}(\gamma^* - q) \right\}.$$

IV. Avoiding Isolation:
Two Forms of Folly

IV.1 Newcomb's Problem

Another way to try converting an isolation paradox into an assurance problem is to alter players' probabilistic beliefs. This possibility is prominently illustrated by Newcomb's problem, to which philosophers in particular have devoted much attention. Indeed, the first published account is due to Robert Nozick (1969; see also Nozick 1993).

The problem postulates an infallible predictor who brings out two boxes. One is transparent, and can be seen to contain $1,000. The second box is opaque; its content when opened will depend on what is predicted about the subject's choice between the following two alternatives:

1. take both boxes, in which case the opaque box will be empty;
2. refuse the transparent box (with its $1,000), in which case the opaque box will contain $1 million.

Note that the predictor has to fill the opaque box, or leave it empty, before the subject's choice. So obviously taking both boxes is a dominant strategy. Yet when the opaque box is found empty, might the subject not regret having tried passing up the $1,000 in the transparent box?

Indeed, consider an alternative version of the paradox. There is no penalty for taking the $1,000 from the transparent box. Before opening the opaque box, however, the subject must decide whether or not to surrender the whole $1,000 as a bet on what the opaque box contains. The subject will get the contents of the opaque box whether the bet is made or not. If the bet is made, however, the predictor will have foreseen this and put $1 million in the opaque box; but if no bet is made, the opaque box will be found empty. Now placing such a bet for $1 million at odds of 1,000 to 1 against seems quite tempting, except to a subject who has an urgent immediate need for the $1,000. Yet the alternative version produces exactly the same monetary outcomes as the original version—either $0 or $1,000 if the opaque box is empty, and either $1 million or $1,001,000 if it is full.

IV.2 Twin Prisoner's Dilemma

Philosophers such as Gibbard and Harper (1978) and Lewis (1979) were quick to realize that the prisoner's dilemma, which is so familiar to game theorists, is closely related to Newcomb's problem. Indeed, suppose two prisoners each have a dominant strategy D of confessing or a cooperative strategy C of staying silent. Suppose however that, before being arrested, both were told that the other could perfectly predict his choice, and would choose C if and only if he predicted that the other player will play C. Then each faces the Newcomb problem, in effect, with tension between the dominant strategy D and, if the prediction claim is believed, the realization that the choice is between (C, C) and (D, D).

Twin prisoner's dilemma is a particularly stark version of this, where the two players are identical twins, who both expect the other twin to choose exactly the same as they do. Indeed, Howard (1988) considers an interesting variant of prisoner's dilemma where the players are two computer programs that are allowed to read each other. Each program could then check whether the other program is an exact copy of itself. Then, of course, it would be rational to cooperate if the two programs really are the same.

IV.3 Magical and Quasi-Magical Thinking

A brief discussion of quasi-magical thinking by an economist can be found in Shiller (1999). He first explains the standard psychological phenomenon of "magical" thinking by referring to the work of the behavioral psychologist B. F. Skinner (1948), who discovered that pigeons that were first starved and then fed a small amount at regular intervals of 15 seconds were prone to develop strange routines, such as turning completely around several times while waiting for food. Skinner explained this as a form of superstition. Having noticed that they were fed every time soon after they followed the routine, the pigeons confused correlation with causation and acted as if they believed that their routine magically caused the food to arrive.

As for "quasi-magical" thinking, and its contrast with magical thinking, Shafir and Tversky (1992: 463) wrote as follows:

Magical thinking refers to the erroneous belief that one can influence an outcome (e.g., the roll of a die) by some symbolic or other indirect act (e.g., imagining a particular number) even though the act has no causal link to the outcome. We introduce the term quasi-magical thinking to describe cases in which people act as if they erroneously believe that their action influences the outcome, even though they do not really hold that belief.

Recently the biologist Masel (2007) has revived this idea. She did so in order to explain observed cooperation in public-good game experiments where offering nothing is a dominant strategy.

IV.4 Evidential versus Causal Decision Theory

Shafir and Tversky (1992: 463) also quote Gibbard and Harper (1978):

a person ... wants to bring about an indication of a desired state of the world, even if it is known that the act that brings about the indication in no way brings about the desired state itself.

That is, in quasi-magical thinking, choosing the act is seen as *evidence* that a desired state of the world will occur, whereas in magical thinking, choosing the act is seen as the *cause* of that desired state. A corresponding distinction between "evidential" and "causal" decision theory has received considerable attention in the philosophical literature (for example, in Hurley 1991, 2005; Joyce and Gibbard 1998; Joyce 1999, 2000, 2007). The point of view taken here, however, is due to Shin (1991), who argues that one can represent Jeffrey's (1983) key notion of ratifiability using counterfactual beliefs, in a way that is more familiar to game theorists—especially following Aumann (1987).

V. RATIONAL FOLLY IN THE ISOLATION GAME

V.1 Universal Cooperation

We now revert to the isolation game considered in section II, where $u(C, \gamma)$ is twice continuously differentiable throughout the closed interval $[0, 1]$. Suppose that, although strategy D dominates C, nevertheless every agent has quasi-magical beliefs implying that the proportion of other agents who will choose C is γ_C if that agent chooses C himself, but only $\gamma_D < \gamma_C$ if he chooses D. Suppose too that $u(C, 1) > u(D, 0)$, so that it is better to have everybody conform than everybody defect. Then, provided that γ_C is close enough to 1 and γ_D is close enough to 0, continuity evidently implies that $u(C, \gamma_C) > u(D, \gamma_D)$. Of course, this is enough to ensure that every agent prefers C to D, so universal cooperation can be sustained.

V.2 Limited Cooperation

Achieving universal cooperation clearly requires that all agents find a reason not to play their dominant strategy D. In our setting, this requires all agents to have quasi-magical beliefs. Suppose, however, that only a proportion $\rho \in (0, 1)$ of randomly selected agents have such beliefs. Also, as customary in Bayesian game theory, suppose this proportion ρ is common knowledge. Then the remaining fraction of the population, $1 - \rho$, will choose their dominant strategy D. Accordingly, even an agent with quasi-magical beliefs will presumably have $\gamma_C \leq \rho$.

Of course, in this case cooperation by at most a proportion ρ of agents can be sustained. Even for this to be possible, however, requires that $u(C, \gamma_C) > u(D, \gamma_D)$, which is impossible unless $u(C, \rho) > u(D, 0)$. Because dominance implies that $u(C, 0) < u(D, 0)$ even when $u(C, 1) > u(D, 0)$, this is possible only if ρ is sufficiently close to 1.

V.3 Optimal Cooperation

In section II.2 it was shown that the optimal proportion γ^* of cooperators might well be in the interior of the interval $[0, 1]$. Only in the very special case when

γ^* coincides with the proportion ρ of agents with quasi-magical beliefs will this optimum be achievable with the kind of pure strategies considered above.

An obvious next step is to consider mixed strategies. But these raise conceptual difficulties when some agents have quasi-magical beliefs. This is because it remains unclear whether the expected proportion γ of cooperators depends upon the pure strategy that results *ex post* from randomization, or upon the mixed strategy that was selected *ex ante*. To avoid this difficulty, we postulate that each agent $i \in N$ receives a personal *disposition signal* $s_i \in A$, suggesting whether they should be disposed to cooperate or not.

In case this signal suggests playing D, we assume that each agent simply chooses what is anyway a dominant strategy. Also, even when the signal suggests playing C, each of the proportion $1 - \rho$ of agents who lack quasi-magical beliefs will still play D. The proportion ρ of agents with quasi-magical beliefs, however, each expect the proportion of cooperators to be $\gamma_C \le \rho$ if they play C, but only γ_D if they play D. So the agents with quasi-magical beliefs who receive the disposition signal C will indeed choose C provided that $u(C, \gamma_C) > u(D, \gamma_D)$. As before, this is impossible unless $u(C, \rho) > u(D, 0)$, which requires ρ to be sufficiently close to 1.

To achieve the optimal proportion γ^* of cooperators, the probability σ that any agent receives the disposition signal C must be selected to satisfy $\rho\sigma = \gamma^*$, where $\sigma \in [0, 1]$. So for γ^* to be achievable, we need $\rho \ge \gamma^*$. In other words, there must be enough quasi-magical thinkers—or enough agents who, for whatever reason, are expected to choose the dominated strategy C instead of the dominant strategy D.

VI. Concluding Remarks

Sen (1967) distinguished between the isolation paradox and assurance games. In the former, each player has a dominant strategy of departing from a rule which, if observed by enough people, would benefit all. In the latter, cooperating is better provided everybody else is cooperating; otherwise, defecting is always better.

This chapter has considered the quasi-magical beliefs that Shafir and Tversky (1992) postulated to explain why experimental subjects might be willing to choose a dominated strategy. It has been shown that such "rational folly" may indeed be able to supplant the kind of "foolish rationality" that excludes dominated strategies in the isolated paradox.

Nevertheless, quasi-magical beliefs involve a form of self-deception that should leave game theorists and economists feeling considerable discomfort. To make such beliefs appear more palatable, it is perhaps worth investigating the evolutionary stability of this kind of behavior, especially in the light of work such as Conley *et al.* (2006) on the role of "memetics".

Meanwhile, however, it is perhaps enough to remind ourselves that many of the issues raised in Sen (1967) and in his later work remain at best incompletely resolved. They still represent challenges that may only be met if philosophers, decision and game theorists, psychologists, and even economists combine all their talents.

REFERENCES

ANDREONI, J. (1990), "Impure Altruism and Donations to Public Goods: A Theory of Warm-Glow Giving", *Economic Journal*, 100: 464–77.

AUMANN, R. J. (1987), "Correlated Equilibrium as an Expression of Bayesian Rationality", *Econometrica*, 55: 1–18.

CONLEY, J. P., TOOSSI, A., and WOODERS, M. (2006), "Memetics and Voting: How Nature May Make Us Public Spirited", *International Journal of Game Theory*, 35: 71–90.

GIBBARD, A., and HARPER, W. L. (1978), "Counterfactuals and Two Kinds of Expected Utility", in C. A. Hooker, J. J. Leach and E. F. McClennen (eds), *Foundations and Applications of Decision Theory*, vol. 1 (Dordrecht: Reidel).

HARSANYI, J. C. (1977), "Rule Utilitarianism and Decision Theory", *Erkenntnis*, 11: 25–53.

—— (1986), "Utilitarian Morality in a World of Very Half-Hearted Altruists", in W. P. Heller, R. M. Starr and D. Starrett (eds), *Essays in Honor of Kenneth J. Arrow*, vol. 1, *Social Choice and Public Decision Making* (New York: Cambridge University Press).

HOWARD J. V. (1988), "Cooperation in the Prisoner's Dilemma", *Theory and Decision*, 24: 203–21.

HURLEY, S. L. (1991), "Newcomb's Problem, Prisoner's Dilemma, and Collective Action", *Synthese*, 86: 173–96.

—— (2005), "Social Heuristics that Make Us Smarter", *Philosophical Psychology*, 18: 585–612.

JEFFREY, R. C. (1983), *The Logic of Decision*, 2nd edn (Chicago: University of Chicago Press).

JOYCE, J. M. (1999), *The Foundations of Causal Decision Theory* (Cambridge & New York: Cambridge University Press).

—— (2000), "Why We Still Need the Logic of Decision", *Philosophy of Science*, 67: S1–S13.

—— (2007), "Are Newcomb Problems Really Decisions?", *Synthese*, 156: 537–62.

—— and GIBBARD, A. (1998), "Causal Decision Theory", in S. Barberà, P. J. Hammond and C. Seidl (eds), *Handbook of Utility Theory*, vol. 1, *Principles* (Dordrecht: Kluwer Academic).

LAFFONT J.-J. (1975), "Macroeconomic Constraints, Economic Efficiency and Ethics: An Introduction to Kantian Economics", *Economica*, 42: 430–7.

LEWIS, D. (1979), "Prisoner's Dilemma is a Newcomb Problem", *Philosophy and Public Affairs*, 8; 235–40.

MASEL, J. (2007), "A Bayesian Model of Quasi-Magical Thinking Can Explain Observed Cooperation in the Public Good Game", *Journal of Economic Behavior and Organization*, 64: 216–31.

NOZICK, R. (1969), "Newcomb's Problem and Two Principles of Choice", in N. Rescher (ed.), *Essays in Honor of Carl G. Hempel* (Dordrecht: D. Reidel).

—— (1993), *The Nature of Rationality* (Princeton, NJ: Princeton University Press).

SEN, A. K. (1967), "Isolation, Assurance and the Social Rate of Discount", *Quarterly Journal of Economics*, 81: 112–24.

—— (1977), "Rational Fools: A Critique of the Behavioral Foundations of Economic Theory", *Philosophy and Public Affairs*, 6: 317–44.

SHAFIR, E., and TVERSKY, A. (1992), "Thinking Through Uncertainty: Nonconsequential Reasoning and Choice", *Cognitive Psychology*, 24: 449–74.

SHILLER, R. F. (1999), "Human Behavior and the Efficiency of the Financial System", in J. B. Taylor and M. Woodford (eds), *Handbook of Macroeconomics*, vol. 1, part 3 (Amsterdam: North-Holland).

SHIN, H. S. (1991), "A Reconstruction of Jeffrey's Notion of Ratifiability in Terms of Counterfactual Beliefs", *Theory and Decision*, 31: 21–47.

SKINNER, B. F. (1948), "Superstition in the Pigeon", *Journal of Experimental Psychology*, 38: 168–72.

CHAPTER 29

.....

SIMPLE FORMULAE FOR OPTIMAL INCOME TAXATION AND THE MEASUREMENT OF INEQUALITY

.....

JOSEPH E. STIGLITZ

I. INTRODUCTION

.....

IT is a pleasure to contribute this essay in honor of Amartya Sen, whose intellectual work has been an inspiration, and whose friendship I have valued, for more than four decades. Amartya's interests, especially in inequality and development,

The author is indebted to Peter Diamond, James Mirrlees, Arjun Jayadev, Ravi Kanbur and the late John Flemming for helpful discussions. This work was supported in part by the National Science Foundation, the MacArthur Foundation, and the Ford Foundation. This chapter is a revised and extended version of an earlier working paper of the same title, IMSSS 215, Stanford University, 1976. The earlier version provides alternative formulae.

have overlapped with mine. At a time when so many developmental economists were advocating Washington Consensus policies—almost completely ignoring the consequences for poverty and inequality—Amartya stood out as a lonely voice, at least within the West. Today many, if not most, of those who pushed these policies have recognized that the policies often have not promoted growth, and even when they have led to growth, not all have benefited. They now recognize the seriousness of the failure to pay attention to the distributive consequences of economic policies.[1]

For this festschrift, however, I want to focus on another area in which Sen has made an important contribution—the measurement of inequality. Some 35 years ago, Michael Rothschild and I asked when one can say that one distribution is "riskier" than another—for any risk-averse individual.[2] The same logic could be applied to income distributions: when can one say that one income distribution is more unequal than another—for any inequality-averse social welfare function? Atkinson noticed that our earlier results had a natural interpretation in terms of the standard Lorenz curve: an income distribution is more unequal than another (such that any inequality-averse Benthamite social welfare function prefers one distribution to the other) if and only if one Lorenz curve lies inside the other.[3] Dasgupta, Sen and Starrett, and Rothschild and I, then extended the analysis to more general inequality-averse social welfare functions.[4]

Sen made two even more important contributions to the policy and conceptual debate. The first was to emphasize that, in assessing the performance of the economy (or more broadly, society), one should look not only at outcomes (the incomes or consumptions that individuals enjoy), but also at the freedom they give for human action, which in turn depends on the capabilities of individuals and the scope they have for participating in the decisions that affect their lives.

[1] For a broader discussion, see J. E. Stiglitz, "The Post Washington Consensus Consensus", in N. Sarra and J. E. Stiglitz (eds), *The Barcelona Consensus* (Oxford: Oxford University Press, 2008).

[2] M. Rothschild and J. E. Stiglitz, "Increasing Risk: I. A Definition", *Journal of Economic Theory*, 2 (1970), 225–43, and M. Rothschild and J. E. Stiglitz, "Increasing Risk: II. Its Economic Consequences", *Journal of Economic Theory*, 5 (1971), 66–84.

[3] A. B. Atkinson, "On the Measurement of Inequality", *Journal of Economic Theory*, 2 (1970), 244–63.

[4] See, for instance, P. Dasgupta, A. Sen, and D. Starrett, "Notes on the Measurement of Inequality", *Journal of Economic Theory*, 6 (1973), 180–7, and M. Rothschild and J. E. Stiglitz, "Some Further Results on the Measurement of Inequality", *Journal of Economic Theory*, 6 (1973), 188–204. Rothschild and I showed that Atkinson's results hold for a much more general class of social welfare functions than he had assumed—they hold for any symmetric, monotone, locally equality-preferring social welfare function (i.e. separability is not required, nor even quasi-concavity). Our analysis also highlighted the problems in measuring inequality which arise when there is more than one commodity and relative prices are not fixed—one of the subjects on which this chapter focuses.

This emphasis on capabilities is congruent with the emphasis of modern political discourse on "opportunity".[5] If all individuals had the same opportunities, including education and access to basic necessities of life (e.g. health care or food, so that, for instance, they do not suffer the lifelong consequences of lack of medical care or malnutrition), inequalities in income or consumption would not be of great concern; in such circumstances, inequalities would simply reflect the fact that some individuals work harder and others do not.[6] The inequalities that are so marked in our societies are, however, only partly the result of differences in preferences; they reflect differences in opportunity sets and in "luck"—that is, even when individuals *on average* have the same opportunity set, even when individuals work just as hard, some win one of life's many lotteries and wind up wealthy, and others lose. Parsing out the relative importance of these different sources of inequality is not easy; but there are obviously fundamental differences in the appropriate policy responses.[7]

The difficulties of ranking opportunity sets (when one opportunity set is "more equal" than another) are even greater than those we discussed earlier in ranking probability distributions of income. When focusing on just two commodities, it is easy to assess whether one individual's opportunity set is better than another's (see Figure 29.1): if it lies outside the other, it clearly is better. But even if one individual's opportunity set lies outside the other, the extent to which it does so depends on the axis (vertical or horizontal) on which we make our measurements.

However, the situation changes if budget constraints cross. Then some individuals might prefer one budget constraint, others the other. The point becomes particularly relevant when we think about the two goods as "consumption" and "leisure", for all individuals have the same endowment of leisure, though not necessarily the ability to use it well (see Figure 29.2).

One aspect whose importance can shift greatly over time is the provision of public goods. To the extent that public goods are truly public goods and are equally enjoyed by all individuals, societies where a greater fraction of GDP is spent on public goods will, in a fundamental sense, be more egalitarian; focusing on the

---

[5] It should be clear, however, that the focus on economic opportunity sets touches on only one aspect of Sen's broader conception, which includes participation rights and opportunities, seen as more than just instrumental in ensuring equality (or fairness) in outcomes.

[6] There are, of course, deeper concerns: do those individuals who "choose" not to work really have the freedom to make those choices, given their upbringing, their inherited psychological make-up, etc.?

[7] One of my own earliest papers was concerned with trying to understand the dynamics of inequality, the forces which give rise to its persistence. See J. E. Stiglitz, "Distribution of Income and Wealth among Individuals", *Econometrica*, 37 (1969), 382–97. Interestingly, it appears that many conservatives think that most inequality arises from differences in choices; "liberals" emphasize the importance of luck. See Matthew Miller, *The Two-Percent Solution: Fixing America's Problems in a Way that Conservatives and Liberals Can Love* (New York: Public Affairs Books, 2003). Many successful individuals obviously attribute their success to their hard work and their insight (itself a result of self-determined investments in, say, education) rather than "luck", including the luck of being born with good brain power or parents who provide one with a good education.

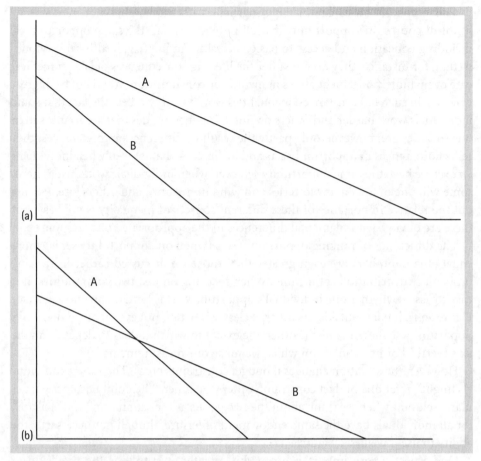

Fig. 29.1. Ranking opportunity sets
(a) Opportunity set A is better than opportunity set B: all individuals (regardless of their preferences) would prefer A over B.
(b) When the budget constraints cross, one cannot rank the opportunity sets: some individuals would prefer A to B; others would prefer B to A.

inequality of *private consumption* may, accordingly, misrepresent the degree of inequality in society.[8]

This highlights the fact that there are many dimensions to an individual's well-being or that of society. One of Sen's most important practical contributions was the role he played in the construction of the Human Development Indicator (HDI),

---

[8] Of course, many goods provided by the public sector are really publicly provided private goods (in the terminology of Atkinson and Stiglitz), and there needs to be an independent assessment of how these are distributed within a society. But even pure public goods can be goods that are more valued by the poor or by the rich, and therefore, in a fundamental sense, either reduce or increase the overall degree of inequality in society.

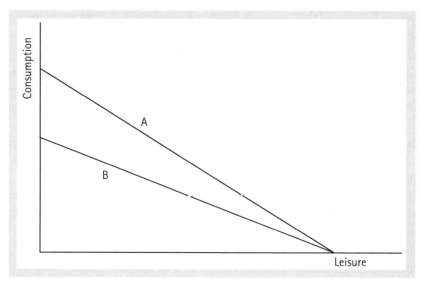

Fig. 29.2. Measuring inequality with different wages when all individuals have the same endowment of leisure

a centerpiece of the annual *Human Development Report* published by the UN Development Programme (UNDP). The HDI provides a metric of societal well-being that goes beyond GDP per capita and includes, for instance, measures of health and education. It is a metric which has made an enormous positive contribution to the policy debate by drawing attention to aspects of society which would receive inadequate attention were GDP the main metric of success. What you measure is what you strive for. By noting that some societies that may rank towards the top on GDP per capita (like the US) score much more poorly in the HDI (more poorly, in particular, than all of the Scandinavian countries), it at least raises questions about the appropriate direction of policy.[9]

One of the dimensions of societal well-being that is not captured at all in measures of *average* GDP per capita is how access to goods is distributed among those in society. Atkinson went on from his analysis of the question of when one society has a "better" distribution of income than another to construct a simple and powerful measure of inequality: how much a society would be willing to give up in order to eliminate inequality.[10] The amount was simply related to society's inequality

[9] There are broader objections to the use of GDP. It does not, for instance, take into account resource depletion or environmental degradation; it looks at the output produced within a country, not the well-being of the citizens of the country, etc. See, for instance, J. E. Stiglitz, *Making Globalization Work* (New York: W. W. Norton, 2006).

[10] Corneo and Fong find, on the basis of survey data, that on average, individuals would be willing to sacrifice 20% of income to eliminate inequality. See G. Corneo and C. Fong, "What's the Monetary Value of Justice?", *Journal of Public Economics*, forthcoming.

aversion (a measure of the concavity of the social welfare function, analogous to the Arrow–Pratt measure of risk aversion) and the magnitude of the inequality itself.

Just as Rothschild and Stiglitz's work highlighted that often one could not rank two distributions (one might be preferred by some risk-averse individual, and another by another risk-averse individual), so too Atkinson's work highlighted that whenever two Lorenz curves cross, some inequality-averse individual would prefer one distribution, another the other. And just as Rothschild and I highlighted that standard measures of risk (like variance) may be misleading, Atkinson's work highlighted that standard measures of inequality (like the Gini coefficient) may be misleading. These limitations in ranking were not the result of an incompleteness in the theory; they called attention to the fact that one could "improve" the distribution of income at one place (such as reducing poverty) and, at the same time, make it worse (transferring income from the middle class to the rich.)

This measure (often referred to as the Atkinson–Dalton measure, because of its earlier use by Hugh Dalton[11]) may, however, not be the best measure of inequality, for several reasons.[12] There are two that I do not take up in this chapter. The first is that the Atkinson–Dalton measure is a static measure, a glimpse of inequality at one point in time. If there is individual variability of income over time, and individuals can smooth their consumption, then this overstates the degree of inequality of "well-being" (or consumption). If there is an increase in year-to-year income variability, it may seem as if there is an increase in inequality, but this may in reality be of little consequence. On the other hand, if capital markets are imperfect (as they are), so that individuals cannot effectively smooth consumption over time, and if there are imperfect insurance markets (as there are), so that individuals cannot insure against this variability, then the increased year-to-year variability will have adverse welfare consequences, though it is still the case that looking at income inequality (or even consumption inequality) at a certain point in time exaggerates the degree of lifetime inequality. Year-to-year variability gives rise to insecurity, which can be very costly to risk-averse individuals. Indeed, much of the political debate in recent years has focused on how to reduce various forms of insecurity.[13]

The second issue I do not discuss here is related, but in some sense has even more profound social consequences: the Atkinson–Dalton measure is not a measure of social mobility and therefore does not capture the dynamics of equality of

---

[11] H. Dalton, "The Measurement of the Inequality of Incomes", *Economic Journal*, 30(119) (1920), 348–61.

[12] Sen himself provided a critique of the Atkinson measure in *Inequality Re-Examined* (Cambridge, Mass.: Harvard University Press, 1992), 97–9.

[13] That is, how to reduce various forms of insecurity without adverse incentive effects. The UN has promoted a "Human Security" agenda, in which Amartya Sen has played an important role. See the final report of the UN Commission on Human Security, chaired by Sadako Ogato and Amartya Sen, *Human Security Now: Protecting and Empowering People* (New York: United Nations, 2003). The World Bank's *World Development Report, 2000* (Washington, DC: World Bank, 2001) emphasized the importance of insecurity among the poor.

opportunity, that is, to what extent the life chances of someone born at the bottom of the income distribution differ from someone born at the top. A society's social mobility is characterized by a mobility matrix, which describes, for instance, the probability distribution (measured by the decile of the population) of a person born in a particular decile. If the probability distributions of each decile were the same, there would be true equality of opportunity. One concern is that there is some evidence that opportunities for upward mobility in the US may be decreasing.[14] Just as we can ask when one income distribution is more egalitarian than another, we can ask when one mobility matrix is more egalitarian than another (i.e. preferred by a society with an inequality-averse social welfare function). The difficulties noted by Rothschild, Stiglitz and Atkinson in ranking income distributions (or probability distributions) are compounded in ranking mobility matrices.[15]

However, there are several limitations to the Atkinson–Dalton measure which this chapter does address. The Atkinson–Dalton measure illustrates the percentage of national income which society would be willing to sacrifice if all inequality were eliminated. It is, in other words, a measure of the total cost of inequality. We wish to develop a *marginal* measure of inequality, i.e. a measure of how much society is willing to sacrifice to reduce inequality a given amount.

As in most aspects of economic analysis, it is marginal valuations, not total valuations, which are crucial to resource allocation. The question which is often of relevance is how society should trade off distribution and efficiency. That there is a trade-off between "distribution" and "efficiency" has long been recognized, for instance, in the literature on income taxation. More progressive tax structures have greater disincentive effects but, in principle at least, result in more egalitarian income distributions.

It has sometimes been suggested that some countries have gone too far in their attempts to obtain more egalitarian income distribution: that the cost in loss of efficiency and disincentives is too great relative to the benefits of attaining a "better"

[14] See, in particular, C. I. Lee and G. Solon, "Trends in Intergenerational Income Mobility", unpubl. manuscript, University of Michigan (2004); D. I. Levine and B. Mazumder, "Choosing the Right Parents: Changes in the Intergenerational Transmission of Inequality between 1980 and the Early 1990s", Federal Reserve Bank of Chicago Working Paper 2002-08, June 2002; B. Mazumder, "Earnings Mobility in the US: A New Look at Intergenerational Inequality", Federal Reserve Bank of Chicago Working Paper 2001-18, March 2001; S. Bowles and H. Gintis, "The Inheritance of Inequality", *Journal of Economic Perspectives*, 16(3) (Summer 2002), 3–30; L. Chadwick and G. Solon, "Intergenerational Income Mobility among Daughters", *American Economic Review*, 92 (2002), 335–44; A. Fertig, "Trends in Intergenerational Mobility", Center for Research on Child Wellbeing Working Paper 01-23, 2001; T. Hertz, "Understanding Mobility in America", Center for American Progress and American University Working Paper, April 2006; Daniel P. McMurrer and Isabel V. Sawhill, *Getting Ahead: Economic and Social Mobility in America* (Washington, DC: Urban Institute Press, 2007).

[15] See, for instance, R. Kanbur and J. E. Stiglitz, "Mobility and Inequality: A Utilitarian Analysis", University of Cambridge Economic Theory Discussion Paper 57, May 1982, and R. Kanbur and J. E. Stiglitz, "Intergenerational Mobility and Dynastic Inequality", Princeton University Economic Research Program Research Memorandum 324, April 1986.

income distribution, at least at the margin. Such a statement involves judgements of two sorts:

(a) empirical judgements concerning the order of magnitude of the "costs", the disincentive effects, and benefits, i.e. the change in the income distribution; and

(b) value judgements concerning one's attitudes towards inequality.

The Atkinson–Dalton measure addresses (b). But no one proposes eliminating all inequality—the Atkinson–Dalton measure tells us how much we would be willing to give up to achieve this, but such a number is not relevant for policy. Rather, the question is posed *at the margin*: what is the marginal cost of more progressivity, and what is the marginal benefit? There are standard ways of calculating the marginal costs, the increments in the dead-weight loss. But it would be useful to have a measure of the marginal benefit from reducing inequality; we need, in short, a *marginal measure* of inequality. This is what I provide here.

Since the marginal value of a reduction in inequality may, in some sense, exceed the total value, previous measures have understated the social cost of inequality, or perhaps more accurately, the social gain from reducing it. That is, intuitively, if, in the process of transferring money from the rich to the poor, one loses a proportion of the resources being transferred, and if society has a great deal of inequality, one might be willing to pay a great deal to reduce inequality a little bit, but the socially acceptable proportion of resources that could be lost would get smaller as the degree of inequality is reduced.

There is a second problem with these measures of inequality: they assume implicitly either that the supply of labor is inelastic or that the only source of inequality is in inherited income. In other words, differences in income arising out of differences in ability when labor is elastically supplied—and the consequent differences in leisure consumed—are not appropriately taken into account.

The first objective of this essay, then, is to construct a new measure of inequality, a measure which focuses, on the one hand, on the value of marginal reductions in equality (rather than its total elimination), and on the other hand, on differences in abilities to earn. While focusing on the evaluation of marginal changes in inequality suggests that the Atkinson–Dalton measure understates the costs of inequality, my analysis of the consequences of wage inequality with an elastic labor supply suggests that the conventional measures overstate the cost of inequality.

There is a second objective of this essay: to relate the optimal tax structure to some simple observable parameters and to my newly developed measure of inequality. My results provide a simple formula for determining the optimal tax rate.

The analysis proceeds within the utilitarian framework for analyzing the desirability of redistribution and the design of tax structures, a tradition dating back at least to Edgeworth and Bentham.[16] Whether this is an appropriate framework for analyzing these questions is an issue we discuss briefly in the concluding section of the chapter, which will bring us back to issues to which Sen has made fundamental contributions.

II. On the Cost of Inequality and the Benefits of Redistribution: A New Measure of Inequality

Social attitudes about the importance of inequality have varied greatly. At times, there has been a general consensus that economic growth, while not eliminating poverty itself, will increase the standard of living of the poor far more than would be possible under any redistributive scheme; this led to the belief that attention should be directed at growth rather than inequality. More recently, however, there has been a widespread feeling that some of the worst manifestations of poverty are a result of the *relative* position of the poor, and, if that is the case, growth which does not eliminate the degree of inequality will not alleviate the problems of poverty.[17]

What do statements such as "Inequality is a significant problem in the US" mean? We can measure the degree of inequality, say, by statistical measures such as the coefficient of variation. But how can we decide what is a large number and what is a small number? One way of attacking the problem is a suggestion originally put forward by Dalton, and developed by Kolm, Atkinson and others. Assume you did not know where in the income distribution you were going to be. One could calculate the expected utility of income, $Eu(Y)$. If individuals are risk-averse, the expected utility is lower than that which individuals would have received if the same total income were distributed equally, i.e.

$$Eu(Y) < u(E(Y)) \quad \text{if } u'' < 0. \tag{2.1}$$

---

[16] See F. Y. Edgeworth, "The Pure Theory of Taxation", *Economic Journal*, 7(28) (December 1897), 550–71, resuscitated in the "New Public Finance Literature" of Mirrlees, Diamond and Mirrlees, Stiglitz and Dasgupta, Atkinson and Stiglitz, Feldstein, and others.

[17] See, in particular, M. Ravallion, "Inequality is Bad for the Poor", in J. Micklewright and S. Jenkins (eds), *Inequality and Poverty Re-Examined*, (Oxford: Oxford University Press, 2007); M. Ravallion, "Economic Growth and Poverty Reduction: Do Poor Countries Need to Worry about Inequality?", in *2020 Focus Brief on the World's Poor and Hungry People* (Washington, DC: IFPRI, 2007); and C. Citro and R. Michael (eds), *Measuring Poverty: A New Approach* (Washington, DC: National Academies Press, 1995).

Thus, to eliminate inequality, one would be willing to give up a fraction of total income, $\hat{\mu}$, where

$$E u(Y) = u((1 - \hat{\mu})E Y).$$ (2.2)

Thus, the measure of inequality is given by

$$\hat{\mu} = 1 - \frac{u^{-1}[E u(Y)]}{E Y}.$$ (2.3)

As an approximation, it is easy to show that

$$\hat{\mu} \approx \frac{R s_Y^2}{2},$$ (2.4)

where

$$R = -\frac{u'' Y}{u'}$$ (2.5)

is the elasticity of marginal utility (sometimes referred to as the measure of inequality aversion), and

$$s_Y = \frac{\sqrt{E(Y - \overline{Y})^2}}{\overline{Y}}$$ (2.6)

is the coefficient of variation.[18]

Thus, for example, if $R = 1$, and the coefficient of variation of income is .5, then one is willing to sacrifice approximately 12.5% of national income to eliminate inequality, a seemingly large figure (though still only equal to a few years' growth).

This provides a measure of the total gains to eliminating all inequality and is thus a measure of the total degree of inequality. But for many problems, a marginal notion is more useful. Assume we could take 1% of all incomes and redistribute a fraction of the amount collected equally to all individuals. The marginal measure of inequality is defined as the fraction which just leaves social welfare unaffected:

$$E u'(Y)(\overline{Y} - Y) = \hat{m} \overline{Y} E u'$$ (2.7)

or

$$\hat{m} = \frac{E u'(\overline{Y} - Y)}{\overline{Y} E u'}.$$ (2.8)

---

[18] For the lognormal distribution with a logarithmic utility function, we can calculate $\hat{\mu}$ precisely:

$$\hat{\mu} = 1 - \frac{1}{(1 + s_Y^2)^{\frac{1}{2}}}.$$

If, for instance, $s_Y = .5$, then $\hat{\mu} = .11$.

The LHS of (2.7) is the gain from the redistribution. $E u'(Y)$ is the loss in expected utility in subtracting a dollar from each individual. $\hat{m}$ can be rewritten in a slightly different way:

$$\hat{m} = \frac{-E[u' - \overline{u}'][Y - \overline{Y}]}{\overline{Y}\overline{u}'},$$

where $\overline{u}' \equiv E u'$.

$\hat{m}$ is just the normalized covariance between the marginal utility of income and income. $\hat{m}$ is generally greater than $\hat{\mu}$, reflecting diminishing marginal returns to redistribution.

Although $\hat{m}$ and $\hat{\mu}$ are defined differently, for small variance $\hat{m} \approx 2\hat{\mu}$:

$$\hat{m} \approx \frac{u'(\overline{Y})E(\overline{Y} - Y) - u''(\overline{Y})E(Y - \overline{Y})^2}{\overline{Y}u'(\overline{Y})} \approx R s_Y^2 = 2\hat{\mu}. \qquad (2.8')$$

This means, for instance, that if $R = 1$ and $s_Y = .5$, a redistribution scheme which took 1% of each person's income away and redistributed just over three-quarters of that amount back again, but this time equally to everyone, would increase social welfare.[19]

Of course, while all complete reductions of inequality are the same, every reduction of inequality is marginal in its own way. The amount society would be willing to pay to move a little bit of income from the very top to the very bottom is obviously much larger than it would be willing to pay to move a little bit of income from someone just above the median to someone just below the median. The particular marginal measure we have used is tailor-made for analyzing the optimal *linear* income tax. For greater progressivity in that context entails taking away a fraction of each individual's income, and returning the proceeds as a uniform lump sum (demi-grant) to each individual. We know that there is a distortion as a result of the higher marginal tax rate—a dead-weight loss. Our marginal measure is designed to answer the question: how large can this dead-weight loss be (as a fraction of the revenue raised) before it is no longer worthwhile (at the margin) to raise the tax rate still further?

II.1 Measures of Inequality with Wage Differences

I have just developed a marginal measure of inequality; like the earlier Atkinson–Dalton measure, however, I ignored leisure. But individuals enjoy leisure, just as

[19] For the lognormal distribution with a logarithmic utility function,

$$\hat{m} = \frac{\overline{Y}E\frac{1}{Y} - 1}{\overline{Y}E\frac{1}{Y}} = \frac{e^{\sigma^2} - 1}{e^{\sigma^2}} = \frac{s_Y^2}{1 - s_Y^2}.$$

Thus, if $s_Y = .5$, $m = 1/3$.

they enjoy goods; and individuals differ in their consumption of leisure, just as they differ in their consumption of goods.

The measurement of inequality when individuals "consume" goods and leisure poses a classical index-number problem. The natural question is, can we develop measures of inequality analogous to Atkinson's total measure and our marginal measure which take leisure into account? What relationship would such a new measure have to the older measures?[20]

Intuitively, it would seem that ignoring leisure leads the Atkinson measure to overstate the significance of inequality. This may be seen in several ways. Clearly, if all individuals had the same ability (received the same wage) but differed with respect to their preferences for goods and leisure, the conventional measures of inequality, focusing just on difference in consumption of goods, would provide a gross overestimate of the significance of inequality in "welfare". If hours of leisure have increased generally, and particularly if they have increased more for low-wage workers than for high-wage workers, then the conventional measure may overstate the increase in inequality over time.

When the source of inequality is a difference in wages, the endowments of leisure are still the same. Hence, if we formulated a simple index of welfare consisting of a weighted average of leisure and consumption,

$$W = \delta(1 - \ell) + (1 - \delta)C,$$

where the time available is normalized at unity, ℓ is the percentage of time spent working, and C is consumption, then it is clear that if ℓ is, say, constant (zero elasticity of labor supply), then the coefficient of variation of W, s_W, is less than that of C, s_C:

$$s_W = \frac{(1 - \delta)\overline{C}}{\delta(1 - \overline{\ell}) + (1 - \delta)\overline{C}} s_C,$$

where $\overline{C}$ and $\overline{\ell}$ are the mean values of labor and consumption.

But even this exaggerates the magnitude of inequality. Inequality in wages affects the ability to transform leisure into consumption commodities. The more willing that individuals are to substitute leisure for consumption goods (i.e. the greater the elasticity of substitution) the less the "cost" of inequality. Moreover, if the elasticity

---

[20] We could also ask when one distribution of goods-cum-leisure will be more equal than another. This is a question which Kolm has addressed in "The Optimal Production of Social Justice", in J. Margolis and H. Guitton (eds), *Public Economics* (London: Macmillan, 1968). It is clear that looking at the distribution of each good (leisure) separately is not appropriate. If there were two goods (x_1, x_2), then in A, the distribution of x_1 could be more unequal (in the sense of Rothschild and Stiglitz in "Some Further Results on the Measurement of Inequality") than in B, and the distribution of x_2 could be more unequal than in B. But if utility, $u = x_1 + x_2$, it is clear that u may be more equally distributed. If everyone has the same tastes, the utility function provides the natural basis for aggregation.

of labor supply is positive, inequality in incomes will be greater than inequality in wages.[21]

The problem is highlighted in the case of a high elasticity of substitution, for which it is immediately apparent that a mean-preserving increase in the inequality of abilities[22] (which preserves the mean level of ability) actually *raises* expected utility (social welfare).[23] Consider what happens with an infinite elasticity of substitution. Assume originally that all individuals have the same productivity (= "unity") and that the marginal rate of substitution between leisure and consumption goods is unity. Then assume that one-half the population has a productivity of $1 + \Delta w$ and one-half the population has a productivity of $1 - \Delta w$. Obviously those who have a lowered productivity simply consume "leisure" and are no worse off than before, but those who have a higher productivity are better off. Thus the cost of "productivity" inequality would appear to be negative.[24] As Figure 29.3 makes clear, the result is more general: the gain in utility when wages (productivity) are increased more than offsets the losses when they are decreased symmetrically.

For the remainder of this chapter I focus on inequalities arising from differences in ability. This is a very important assumption that has become conventional within the optimal income tax literature. Yet ironically, its implications for the measurement-of-inequality literature do not seem to have been explored. All workers are assumed to be perfect substitutes for one another; i.e. they differ only in the number of "efficiency units of labor" which they embody. I choose my units so that an individual of "unit" efficiency receives a wage of unity. Hence, the before-tax income of somebody of efficiency w is

$$Y = wL, \tag{2.9}$$

[21] This sounds like a proposition which could easily be verified. Unfortunately, this is not the case, for what we mean by the "wage" rate is the payment for a standard unit of effort for one hour. Although differences in wages per hour are easy to observe, differences in effort are difficult, if not impossible, to observe and quantify.

[22] For a discussion of the concept of a mean-preserving increase in inequality, see Rothschild and Stiglitz, "Some Further Results on the Measurement of Inequality".

[23] There have been numerous extensions to our understanding mean-preserving changes in distributions, notably in the literature on income polarization. These (like the writings on the role of relative deprivation cited earlier) highlight that there may be mean-preserving changes in distributions which raise inequality but which also increase, or decrease, polarization, or increase, or decrease, relative deprivation. These important dimensions of changes in income distribution are not captured in the standard utilitarian model, or in measures that are derived from that model. See, for instance, J. Y. Duclos, J. Esteban, and D. Ray, "Polarization: Concepts, Measurement, Estimation", *Econometrica*, 72 (2004), 1737–72; and J. Esteban and D. Ray, "On the Measurement of Polarization", *Econometrica*, 62 (1994), 819–51.

[24] It should be clear by now that the problem of ability inequality is much like the problem of price uncertainty, just as the problem of income inequality is much like the problem of income uncertainty. See, for instance, J. E. Stiglitz, "Portfolio Allocation with Many Risky Assets", in G. P. Szego and K. Shell (eds), *Mathematical Methods in Investment and Finance* (Amsterdam: North-Holland, 1972), and Rothschild and Stiglitz, "Further Results in the Measurement of Inequality".

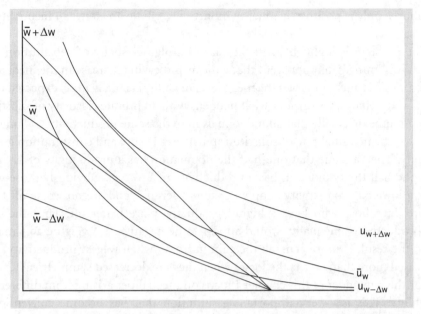

Fig. 29.3. Increasing variability in wages may lead to an increase in welfare: the loss in welfare from a reduction in the wage is much smaller than the increase in welfare from a symmetric increase in the wage.

where L is the amount of labor supplied. We again define the total measure of social loss to be that amount of consumption goods one would be willing to give up to obtain complete equality. To do this we let $U(C, L)$ be the level of utility as a function of consumption and work, and $U_1 > 0$ and $U_2 < 0$. We then define the indirect utility function

$$V(w, I) = \max U(C, L) \tag{2.10}$$

$$s.t. \quad C = wL + I,$$

giving the maximum level of utility attainable as a function of the wage rate and "exogenous" income, I. Then our new "total" measure of inequality, μ, is given by

$$EV(w, 0) = V(1, -\mu Y),$$

where we have normalized $Ew = 1$. I show (in Appendix A) that

$$\mu \approx \frac{V_{11}}{2V_2} s_w^2 = \frac{s_w^2}{2(1 + n_L)^2} \left(R - n_L - \frac{\partial L}{\partial I} \right), \tag{2.11}$$

where

$$n_L = \frac{d \ln L}{d \ln w}, \text{ the supply elasticity of labor,}$$

$$R = \frac{-V_{22}C}{V_2} \left(= \frac{-u'C}{u'} \quad \text{if the utility function is additive} \right),$$

the elasticity of marginal utility of income, where s_w is the coefficient of variation of abilities (wages), and where, in the conventional notation,

$$V_1 = \frac{\partial V}{\partial W}, \quad V_2 = \frac{\partial V}{\partial I}.$$

Note that if $n_L = 0$ and $\partial L/\partial I = 0$, then (2.11) is identical to (2.4), as we would have expected; otherwise, the measures differ. And as I noted intuitively earlier, if R is small (low measure of income-inequality aversion) but the labor supply is highly elastic, μ may be negative; wage variability increases expected utility.

More generally, the percentage of income that one would be willing to forgo to eliminate wage inequality is a function not only of R and the coefficient of variation of income, s_Y^2, but also of the wage elasticity of labor and the income elasticity of labor. The greater the wage elasticity, the greater the magnitude of the overestimate of the degree of inequality yielded by the Atkinson measure.

In the Appendices, two special cases are presented:

(a) additive utility function

$$\mu \approx \frac{s_Y^2}{2(1+n_L)^2} \left[R - n_L \left(\frac{1-2R}{1-R} \right) \right], \quad R \neq 1 \qquad (2.12')$$

$$\mu \approx \frac{s_Y^2}{2} \left(1 - \frac{\partial L}{\partial I} \right), \quad R = 1$$

and

(b) homothetic indifference curves

$$\mu \approx \frac{s_Y^2}{2(1+n_L)^2} [R + (1-L) - n_L], \qquad (2.12'')$$

where L is to be interpreted here as the fraction of the time available that is worked.

If, in addition, we assume a constant elasticity utility function, we obtain

$$\mu \approx \frac{s_w^2}{2}[R + (1-L)(2-\sigma)] = \frac{s_Y^2[R + (1-L)(2-\sigma)]}{2[1 + (\sigma-1)(1-L)]^2}, \qquad (2.12''')$$

where σ is the elasticity of substitution.

In Table 29.1 I provide some estimates of μ and $\hat{\mu}$ for different values of the parameters. Notice that the measure may differ considerably from the Atkinson measure, even for small values of n_L. Indeed, as I suggested earlier, if n_L is large and R small, $\hat{\mu}$ may be negative.

More generally, in a command economy (where the government assigns everyone a level of consumption and work) expected utility is always higher if abilities are unequally distributed than if all individuals have the same productivity, equal to

Table 29.1. Social losses from inequality (per cent), $s_Y = .4$

	$R = 1, n_L = 0, \overline{u}n_L = \frac{1}{2}$	$R = \frac{3}{2}, n_L = \frac{1}{4}, \overline{u}n_L = \frac{1}{2}$
Atkinson measure	8	12
No tax: relative to zero inequality	4	5.1
Optimal linear income tax rate	32	48
Gains from optimal linear tax	2.6	5.8
Egalitarian lump-sum tax: relative to zero inequality	−4	−2.6

the mean productivity in the situation with inequality. That is, each individual could work the same amount in the situation with inequality as without it, and then net output would be the same, so each individual could receive the same consumption goods. However, this will not in general be optimal for the economy with inequality, so that the attainable level of expected utility must be higher. Indeed, *everyone* can be made better off. Whether they are or not depends on what kinds of redistribution taxes are introduced. If we allow lump-sum taxes but insist on everyone remaining at the same level of utility, the social gain from inequality in abilities is approximately equal to

$$\frac{1}{2} \left(\frac{\partial L}{\partial w} \right)_{\overline{u}} s_w^2$$

(see Appendix C).

With the linear income tax, there may be either a social gain or social loss, although for reasonable values of the relevant parameters the gain or loss appears to be small. To see this, we must first analyze the optimal linear income tax, to which I turn in section III.

Before that, however, we must define the analog to m, our marginal measure of inequality, for the case where there is an elastic labor supply. Two such measures will prove useful in the subsequent discussion. The first is

$$m_C \equiv \frac{EU_C(\overline{C} - C)}{ECEU_C} = \frac{E(U_C - \overline{U}_C)(\overline{C} - C)}{\overline{C}\,\overline{U}_C}, \tag{2.13}$$

the normalized covariance of consumption with marginal utility. If we had an additive (Benthamite) social welfare function and took 1% of consumption away from everyone and redistributed it equally to everyone, m_C tells us the fraction of consumption we could lose in the process and still be better off.

If there is an additive utility function,

$$m_C \approx R s_C^2. \tag{2.14}$$

A natural extension of this measure is to the case where the social welfare function is of the form (where $f(w)$ is the density distribution of abilities):

$$\int W(U(C, L)) f(w) dw,$$

in which case we obtain, instead of (2.13),

$$m_C = \frac{EW'U_C(\overline{C} - C)}{ECEW'U_C}. \tag{2.13'}$$

We define analogously

$$m_Y \equiv \frac{EW'U_C(\overline{Y} - Y)}{EYEW'U_C}. \tag{2.15}$$

For some purposes, however, these are not good measures: when we take income away from individuals or give it to them, individuals adjust their effort supply, and this affects tax revenue and the amount we can redistribute. Thus, the net social gain from giving an individual a dollar is not $W'U_C$, the social marginal utility of income, but $W'U_C + \lambda \tau w \, (dL/dI)$, where λ is the shadow price on government revenue and τ is the (marginal) tax rate. If we define

$$\beta \equiv \frac{W'U_C}{\lambda} + \tau w \frac{\partial L}{\partial I}$$

as the marginal social utility of income to an individual of wage w, then we can define

$$m_\beta \equiv \frac{-E(\beta - \overline{\beta})(Y - \overline{Y})}{\overline{\beta} \, \overline{Y}}. \tag{2.16}$$

III. Optimal Linear Income Tax

In this section, I shall derive several simple alternative expressions for the optimal linear income tax rate, in terms of our measure of inequality and certain characteristics of individuals' behavior (in particular, the elasticity of supply of labor). It should be observed that although I shall write down expressions in which the tax rate appears explicitly on the left-hand side of an equation, it often appears implicitly on the right-hand side. For instance, the elasticity of supply of labor will in general not be constant. The alternative expressions may be useful in deriving the optimal tax rate, depending on what assumptions are made about what parameters in the system are constant (e.g. whether the compensated or the uncompensated demand curves have constant elasticity).[25]

A linear income tax rate is characterized by an equation of the form

$$T = \tau Y - I, \tag{3.1}$$

where T is total tax payment, τ is the marginal tax rate, assumed to be constant, Y is before-tax income, and I is the value of the tax credit. The essential characteristic of the linear income tax is said to be progressive if $I > 0$, i.e.

$$\frac{T}{Y} = \tau - \frac{I}{Y} \tag{3.2}$$

is an increasing function of income. It is regressive if $I < 0$.

Mirrlees shows some examples in which the optimal tax structure is approximately linear.[26] If this conclusion is correct more generally, then focusing on linear income taxes may not be too restrictive.

The national income identity takes on the form

$$\int w L_w f(w) dw = (1 - \tau) \int w L_w f(w) dw + I + G, \tag{3.3}$$

where $f(w)$ is the density function of the population by ability, G is per capita expenditure on government services, and L_w is the labor supplied by an individual of wage w.[27] Alternatively this can be written as

$$\tau = \frac{I + G}{\int w L_w f(w) dw}. \tag{3.4}$$

For given government revenue $(I + G)$ there are in general at least two values of τ satisfying (3.4). That is, government revenue is not a monotonic function of τ; at $\tau = 0$, government revenue equals zero, and at $\tau = 1$, revenue equals zero.[28] With

[25] Saez calculates optimal tax formulas based on compensated and uncompensated elasticities of earnings with respect to taxes: E. Saez, "Using Elasticities to Derive Optimal Income Tax Rates", *Review of Economic Studies*, 68 (2001), 205–29. Other recent theoretical explorations of the issue of optimal taxation include P. Diamond, "Optimal Income Taxation: An Example with a U-Shaped Pattern for the Optimal Marginal Rates", *American Economic Review*, 88 (1998), 83–95; R. Kanbur and M. Tuomala, "Inherent Inequality and the Optimal Graduation of Marginal Tax Rates", *Scandinavian Journal of Economics*, 96 (1994), 275–82; and R. Kanbur, M. Keen and M. Tuomala, "Optimal Non-Linear Income Taxation for the Alleviation of Income Poverty", *European Economic Review*, 38 (1994), 1613–32.

[26] J. A. Mirrlees, "An Exploration in the Theory of Optimum Income Taxation", *Review of Economic Studies*, 38 (1971), 175–208.

[27] We are thus assuming that all individuals of a given ability are identical. Alternatively, we could interpret L_w as the average labor supplied by individuals of wage level w.

[28] This obvious result, which I noted in the early 1970s, was popularized under President Reagan, in the 1980s, by Arthur Laffer, and came to be called the Laffer curve. It provided the basis of supply side economics, featuring in arguments that lowering taxes could lead to more revenues and increased welfare.

multiple solutions, it is clear that the relevant solution is the one with the lowest value of τ.

For simplicity, I assume as I did in section II that all individuals have the same utility function and that the utility from public goods is separable from that of private goods, i.e. $U^* = U(C, L) + H(G)$. For this part of the analysis, I assume G is fixed.

Individuals maximize utility,

$$U = U(C, L), \; U_1 > 0, \; U_2 < 0, \tag{3.5}$$

where C = consumption, subject to the budget constraint:

$$C = I + (1 - \tau)wL \tag{3.6}$$

$$= \tau\overline{Y} - G + (1 - \tau)Y,$$

where $Y = wL$, so

$$\overline{Y} = \int wL_w f(w)dw.$$

The maximized value of this, expressed as a function of after-tax wage and I, is, as I mentioned before, the indirect utility function, $V(w(1 - \tau), I)$.

The government has a social welfare function of the form

$$\int W(U_w) f(w)dw \quad \text{with} \quad W' > 0, W'' \leq 0.^{29} \tag{3.7}$$

The problem of the optimum income tax may be formulated as

$$\max \int W(V(w(1 - \tau), I)) f(w)dw,$$

subject to the constraint (3.3). Thus, letting λ be the Lagrange multiplier associated with (3.3), we obtain

$$E W' V_I = \lambda E \left(1 - \tau w \frac{\partial L}{\partial I} \right) \tag{3.8a}$$

or

$$E\beta = 1$$

and

$$E W' V_w w = \lambda E \left[wL - \tau w^2 \frac{\partial L}{\partial w} \right] \tag{3.8b}$$

---

[29] The government's social welfare maximization problem is actually slightly different. It is to maximize $E\{W(U^*)\}$, which differs from (3.7) only because of the valuation of the public good. So long as G is fixed, the problems are identical. However, when G changes, one must be careful in interpreting the results. If $W''' = 0$, then the analysis proceeds unchanged; but if $W'' < 0$, an increase in G affects the covariance (in the notation below, m_β).

or

$$\tau = \frac{-E(\beta - \overline{\beta})(Y - \overline{Y})}{\overline{Y}\,\overline{\beta}} \times \frac{1}{_u\overline{n}_L} = \frac{m_\beta}{_u\overline{n}_L},$$ (3.9)

where

$$_u\overline{n}_L = \frac{E\,Y_u n_L}{\overline{Y}} = \text{weighted average compensated labor supply elasticity.}$$

(3.9) is the key result of the paper, providing a remarkably simple formula for the optimal linear income tax. It relates the optimal tax rate to the normalized covariance between income and the marginal social utility of income—what I identified earlier as our marginal measure of inequality—and the weighted mean value of the compensated supply elasticity of labor. The greater the marginal measure of inequality, the greater the tax rate, and the smaller the elasticity of supply—the less the loss in welfare from the income tax—the greater the tax rate. This is just as one might expect, although the simplicity of the expression may be seen as somewhat surprising. The optimal tax rate is equal to the marginal measure of inequality divided by the (average) compensated supply elasticity of labor.

In some special cases, (3.9) might be a useful expression for obtaining some idea of the magnitude of the optimal tax rate. Assume, for instance, that we have an additive utility function with constant marginal utility of labor. Then, by taking an approximation to m_β, we obtain

$$\tau \approx (1 + \overline{\eta}_L)s_w^2/_u\overline{\eta}_L,$$

where $\overline{\eta}_L$ is the weighted average (uncompensated) elasticity of labor supply ($\equiv E\,Y\eta_L/E\,Y$). The tax rate is proportional to the coefficient of variation of wages and the ratio of (1 plus the uncompensated wage elasticity) to the compensated wage elasticity. Of course, for small variance, the weighted average elasticities are equal to the elasticities evaluated at $\{\tau = 1,\ w = 1\}$. If we assume further that $u(C) = \ln C$, we can show that

$$\tau \approx s_w^2$$

For instance, if $s = .4$, the optimal tax rate is .16.

Note that in the case of an additive (Benthamite) social welfare function (and with government expenditures having no effect on labor supply or the marginal social utility of income), the tax rate does not depend at all on government expenditures; but this is obviously a limiting and special case.[30]

---

[30] In a more general analysis, there are several effects going on. Assume that, at one extreme, public goods were a perfect substitute for private goods, i.e. the utility function was of the form $U(C + G, L)$. Then an increase in G is equivalent to increasing the endowment of I by the same amount. More generally, a change in the supply of a public good can affect the marginal rate of substitution between private goods and leisure. (In the case of the separable utility function on which we focus, this effect is absent.)

Although (3.9) provides a simple and intuitively appealing formula, it suffers from the tax rate being explicitly involved in the definition of m_β. An alternative formula is derived directly from (3.8b):

$$-E\tau w^2 \frac{\partial L}{\partial w} = \frac{E\,W'V_I wL}{\lambda} - \overline{Y}$$

$$= \frac{E\,W'V_I wL}{E\,W'V_I}\left(1 - \tau E w \frac{\partial L}{\partial I}\right) - \overline{Y},$$

so

$$\tau = -\frac{E\,W'V_I(Y-\overline{Y})}{E\,W'V_I\overline{Y}}\left[\frac{1}{\overline{n}_L - \frac{E\,W'V_I Y}{E\,W'V_I E\,Y}E\frac{dY}{dI}}\right]$$

$$= m_Y\left[\frac{1}{\overline{n}_L - (1-m_Y)\frac{d\overline{Y}}{dI}}\right]. \tag{3.10}$$

(3.10) stresses one further aspect of the determination of the optimal tax rate; if total income is reduced as a result of the lump-sum payment (because of income effects), the optimal tax will be lower. The importance of this term depends on the degree of inequality; with a very high degree of inequality, this term is insignificant.

Notice that in (3.10) it is the uncompensated elasticity which is used. However, if the aggregate labor supply equation approximately satisfies the Slutsky equation, we can write

$$_u\overline{n}_L \approx \overline{n}_L - \frac{d\overline{Y}}{dI};$$

then (3.10) becomes

$$\tau \approx m_Y\left[\frac{1}{_u\overline{n}_L + m_Y\frac{d\overline{Y}}{dI}}\right]. \tag{3.10'}$$

A third expression for the optimal tax formula is in terms of the marginal measure of inequality of C. Using (2.13), we obtain directly from (3.10)

$$\tau(1-\tau)[\overline{n}_L - \frac{d\overline{Y}}{dI}] + \tau m_C\frac{d\overline{Y}}{dI}(1-g) = m_C(1-g), \tag{3.11}$$

where g is the proportion of optimal income spent on government expenditures. This is a quadratic equation in τ which can be solved in a straightforward manner. If τ is small, the solution can be approximated by

$$\tau \approx \frac{m_C(1-g)}{\overline{n}_L - \frac{d\overline{Y}}{dI} + m_C(1-g)}. \tag{3.12}$$

A fourth expression relates the optimal tax rate to m_y, when $G=0$:[31, 32]

$$\tau = m_y/d\ln \overline{Y}/d\tau \qquad (3.13)$$

$$\approx m_y/{}_u\eta_L \qquad (3.14)$$

The optimal tax rate just depends on the marginal measure of income inequality divided by the percentage change in national income as a result of a change in the tax rate, which in turn depends on the *total* wage elasticity. As the tax rate increases, the lump sum payment increases, further reducing labor supply. The similarity between equation (3.9) and equation (3.14) follows directly from the fact that when inequality is small, the tax rate is small, and m_β and m_y are approximately the same.

The expressions derived so far have been either general expressions, valid for any utility function[33] and valid regardless of the magnitude of the degree of inequality, or valid so long as inequality is small and government expenditure is zero.

The expressions derived thus far have been general expressions, valid for any utility function and valid regardless of the magnitude of the degree of inequality, so long as inequality is small and government expenditure is zero. There are two approaches that one might take at this point. First, one could specify a particular utility function and distribution of abilities and then compute precisely the optimal tax rate (depending on the social welfare function posited, and the level of government expenditures). Alternatively, we can use the approximations derived earlier to obtain approximate numerical magnitudes for the optimal tax rate and to ascertain

---

[31]   (3.14) can be derived directly from our maximization problem: substituting (3.6) into (3.7), we obtain

$$\max_\tau \int W(U((1-\tau)wL + \tau(\overline{Y} - G), L))f(w)dw$$

or

$$-\int W'U_1(Y - \overline{Y})f(w)dw + \left(\tau\frac{d\overline{Y}}{d\tau} - G\right)\int W'U_1 f(w)dw = O.$$

[32]   Note, that

$$\frac{d\ln\overline{Y}}{d\ln\tau} = \frac{\partial\ln\overline{Y}}{\partial\ln I}\frac{d\ln I}{d\ln\tau} + \frac{\partial\ln\overline{Y}}{\partial\ln\tau};$$

and the national income identity,

$$\frac{dI}{d\tau} = \tau\frac{d\overline{Y}}{d\tau} + \overline{Y},$$

so

$$\frac{d\ln\overline{Y}}{d\ln\tau}\left(1 - \tau\frac{d\overline{Y}}{dI}\right) = \tau\frac{\partial\overline{Y}}{\partial I} + \frac{\tau}{Y}\frac{\partial\overline{Y}}{\partial\tau}.$$

[33]   With the exception of (3.12′).

what parameters are likely to be important in determining the optimal tax rate. This is the approach taken here.[34]

For deriving our approximations, the most convenient expression to use is (3.10). We then obtain, for small variance, with an additive utility function and assuming no government expenditure,

$$\frac{\tau}{1 - \tau} \approx \frac{R s_Y^2}{u \overline{n}_L}. \tag{3.15}$$

With government expenditures we obtain

$$\frac{\tau}{1 - \tau} = \frac{R s_Y^2}{u \overline{n}_L (1 - g)}. \tag{3.16}$$

(3.15) displays several of the properties which we would expect of an optimal tax rate: the greater the degree of equality or equality aversion, and the smaller the magnitude of the compensated price elasticity, the higher the tax rate. What this expression also makes clear is that the optimal tax rate will be extremely sensitive to estimates of the compensated price elasticity and the magnitude of inequality aversion (R).

Estimates of the compensated supply elasticity vary greatly, although the estimates are almost all small. Ashenfelter and Heckman, for instance, estimate the compensated supply elasticity as .12, so that if $R = 1$, $s_Y = .4$, and $g = 0$, we obtain as our optimal tax rate 4/7. On the other hand, if we assume that the compensated price elasticity is approximately one-half, then the optimal tax rate is .4, while if the compensated price elasticity is unity, the optimal tax rate is 2/7. Higher degrees of inequality aversion will clearly result in much higher tax rates, making our approximations less valid.[35]

---

[34] Further expressions, in terms of the consumption elasticities, may be derived in a straightforward manner. Since, however, numerical estimates tend to be expressed in labor supply elasticities, I have chosen to express our formulae in those terms.

[35] There are several reasons for believing that conventional cross-section estimates of the supply elasticity of labor may not provide an accurate estimate of the magnitude of the elasticity. First, if real wages consist of a pecuniary and non-pecuniary component,

$$w^* = w + \epsilon,$$

with ϵ uncorrelated with w, then very high wages will on the average represent a lower real wage, and low wages will represent a higher real wage. Thus, for reasons analogous to those analyzed by Friedman in his *A Theory of the Consumption Function* (Princeton: Princeton University Press, 1957), the estimated elasticity of the supply of labor will be biased downwards.

One of the reasons that real wages and measured wages will differ, besides non-pecuniary characteristics of the job, is that some jobs have more training associated with them. Evidence of the potential importance of this effect is provided by the differences in supply elasticities calculated for older workers.

Secondly, if there are some jobs which systematically have long working weeks (doctors) and others which have short working weeks (differences in training costs would explain why such differences are to be expected) then, if the jobs were otherwise identical, on average those individuals with a smaller

IV. How Much Good Does the Optimal Linear Income Tax Do?

In section II of this chapter, I derived an estimate of the social loss from ability inequality. How much is this reduced by the optimal linear income tax? Obviously, there is a gain in inequality at a cost of dead-weight loss from the tax. As a first approximation, the dead-weight loss is just equal to

$$\frac{\overline{Y}\tau^2}{2} {}_u\overline{n}_L,$$

where ${}_u\overline{n}_L$ is the compensated price elasticity. The gain from the reduction in equality is equal to

$$\tau \overline{Y} m_Y \approx R s_Y^2 (1 - \tau)\tau \overline{Y}.$$

Thus the net gain is (if $g = 0$)

$$\approx \tau^2 \overline{Y} \left\{ \frac{1 - \tau}{\tau} R s_Y^2 - \frac{{}_u\overline{n}_L}{2} \right\}$$

$$\approx \frac{\tau^2 \overline{Y}}{2} {}_u\overline{n}_L$$

$$\approx \frac{R^2 s_Y^4}{2 {}_u\overline{n}_L},$$

e.g. if $s_Y = .4$, ${}_u\overline{n}_L = .5$ and $R = 1$, then the net social gain from imposing the optimal linear income tax (at a rate of 32%) is only 2.5% of net national product. Obviously, higher values of inequality aversion increase the net gains.

V. Concluding Comments

It is always difficult to think rationally about a subject with all the political and moral overtones of inequality. Is there "too much inequality", as many economists and the popular press often suggest? What can one mean by such a statement? This chapter has re-examined these issues, within a framework that has long been put

aversion to work would choose the jobs with longer working weeks. Thus, the differences in the wages between the two jobs are less than the difference in wages that would be required to induce an individual with a low-hour job to work a long week.

forward as providing a justification for progressivity. Two results of the analysis may, at one level, seem particularly disturbing:

(a) the "cost" of inequality may be much smaller when the sources of inequality are differences in ability rather than some exogenously provided wealth endowment; and

(b) the net social gain from an optimal linear income tax may be relatively small.[36]

These propositions will undoubtedly be the subject of debate; using other values of some of the parameters may yield different results.

But more than that, this analysis calls into question the usefulness of the standard optimal income tax framework for thinking about these essential questions. That framework has emphasized differences in wages (abilities) as giving rise to inequalities. But to the extent that inequality is the result of other factors—"luck", the good fortune of a farmer having a good crop, of a real estate investor buying a plot of land next to where a road is constructed years later, of an entrepreneur coming up with the right product at the right time, or of an investor betting on the right stock—then the trade-offs on which I have focused are not the key determinants of the optimal income tax. Analyses based on these determinants of inequality would suggest far higher optimal income tax rates within a utilitarian framework.

Sen's work, however, leads us to the conclusion that the conventional presumptions about the importance of inequality and the desirability of progressivity in taxes probably should be justified on grounds other than the individualistic utilitarian framework used by Edgeworth, Lerner, Samuelson and others. We should focus our attention not so much on the distribution of income itself, but on the processes by which it is generated; our concern should be more with equality of opportunity than with equality of incomes; we should look at opportunities to participate in political processes as well, because the distribution of goods (economic power) has consequences for the distribution of political power, with further consequences for the outcomes of these political processes; and, finally, what is at stake is both the nature of society itself and the ability of individuals to live meaningful lives, living up fully to their potentials.

---

[36] A third set of results, on the relationship between the degree of progressivity and the level of government expenditures, is highly dependent on assumptions of separability between government expenditures on the one hand, and consumption and leisure on the other. How the result is altered under more general assumptions is a subject of ongoing enquiry.

As for net social gains from optimal income tax, matters may even be worse. I have shown that the optimal income tax, within a utilitarian framework with two classes (skilled and unskilled workers), entails negative marginal tax rates at the top (J. E. Stiglitz, "Pareto Efficient Taxation and Expenditure Policies, with Applications to the Taxation of Capital, Public Investment, and Externalities", paper presented at a conference in honor of Agnar Sandmo, Bergen, Norway, 1998).

APPENDIX A. CALCULATION OF SOCIAL LOSS FROM INEQUALITY OF WAGES: NO REDISTRIBUTION

The measure of social loss is defined by

$$EV(w, 0) = V(1, -\mu \overline{Y}). \tag{A1}$$

Taking a Taylor series expansion, we obtain

$$V(w, 0) \approx V(1, 0) + V_1(w - 1) + \frac{V_{11}}{2}(w - 1)^2, \tag{A2}$$

$$EV(w, 0) \approx V(1, 0) + \frac{s_w^2}{2} V_{11} \tag{A3}$$

and

$$V(1, -\mu \overline{Y}) \approx V(1, 0) - \mu Y V_2(1, 0). \tag{A4}$$

Thus,

$$\mu \approx -\frac{V_{11}}{2V_2} \frac{s_w^2}{\overline{Y}}. \tag{A5}$$

Our problem is to interpret V_{11}. Recall that

$$V_1 = LV_2, \tag{A6}$$

$$V_{12} = V_2 \frac{\partial L}{\partial I} + LV_{22}, \quad \text{and} \tag{A7}$$

$$V_{11} = L V_{21} + V_2 \frac{\partial L}{\partial w} = V_2 \left(\frac{\partial L}{\partial w} + L \frac{\partial L}{\partial I} \right) + L^2 V_{22}.$$

Defining

$$R = -\frac{V_{22}C}{V_2}, \quad n_L = \frac{\partial \ln L}{\partial \ln w}$$

we obtain

$$\mu \approx \frac{1}{2} \left(R - \frac{dL}{dI} - n_L \right) s_w^2. \tag{A8}$$

Thus, since the coefficient of variation is

$$s_Y^2 = \frac{E(wL - EwL)^2}{(EwL)^2} = s_w^2 (1 + n_L)^2,$$

we obtain

$$\mu \approx \frac{s_Y^2}{2} \frac{\left(R - n_L - \frac{dL}{dI} \right)}{(1 + n_L)^2}. \tag{A9}$$

If the individual has homothetic indifference curves between leisure goods and consumption and if we normalize the length of the day at unity, then (if $w = 1$),

$$-\left(\frac{dL}{dI}\right)_{I=0} = 1 - L.$$

If there is a constant elasticity-of-substitution utility function of the form

$$[\delta C^{-\rho} + (1 - \delta)(1 - L)^{-\rho}]^{-\frac{1}{\rho}},$$

with $1/(1 + \rho) = \sigma$, the elasticity of substitution, then

$$\left[\frac{1-L}{I+wL}\right]^{1+\rho} = \frac{1-\delta}{\delta w}.$$

Straightforward differentiation of the above expression leads, when $I = 0$, to

$$n_L = -\frac{\rho}{1+\rho}(1 - L) = (\sigma - 1)(1 - L).$$

Substituting this into (A8) we obtain (2.12'''').
  If there is an additive utility function,

$$U = u(C) - Z(L),$$

$$u'w = Z',$$

$$\left(\frac{\partial L}{\partial w}\right)_{I=0} = -\frac{u''w + u''w}{u''w^2 - Z''}, \quad \text{and}$$

$$\frac{dL}{dI} = -\frac{u''}{u''w^2 - Z''}.$$

Hence

$$\left(\frac{\partial L}{\partial w} + L\frac{dL}{dI}\right)_{\substack{w=1 \\ I=0}} = -\frac{u'}{u''w^2 - Z''}(1 - 2R)$$

$$= \left(\frac{\partial L}{\partial w}\right)\left(\frac{1-2R}{1-R}\right) \quad \text{if } R \neq 1.$$

APPENDIX B. CALCULATION OF SOCIAL LOSS FROM INEQUALITY: LINEAR INCOME TAX, ADDITIVE UTILITY FUNCTION

The measure of social loss is

$$EV((1 - \tau)w, I) = V(1, -\hat{\mu}\overline{Y}) \tag{B1}$$

where $\hat{\mu}$ is the fraction of national income that could be given away (required to be added) were there no variable in w (i.e. if $W^* = E_w = 1$) or

$$\max E u((1 - \tau)wL + \tau \overline{Y}) - Z(L) = \max U(L(1 - \hat{\mu})) - Z(L), \qquad (B2)$$

where $Z(L)$ is the disutility of labor. The left-hand side can be approximated by

$$E V(w, 0) + \tau \left(\frac{dEV}{d\tau} \right)_{\tau=0} + \frac{\tau^2}{2} \left(\frac{d^2 EV}{d\tau^2} \right)_{\tau=0}.$$

At $\tau = 0$,

$$\frac{dEV}{d\tau} = EU'(\overline{Y} - wL) + EU'\tau\frac{d\overline{Y}}{d\tau}$$

$$\approx -U'' \left(\frac{dY}{dw}(1 - \tau) \right) \frac{dY}{dw} s_w^2$$

$$= [R(1 + n_L)^2 s_w^2]U'\overline{Y}(1 - \tau) \quad \text{and}$$

$$\tau^2 \left(\frac{d^2 EV}{d\tau^2} \right)_{\tau=0} \approx \tau^2 \frac{d\overline{Y}}{d\tau}U' \approx -U'\tau^2 {}_u n_L \overline{Y}.$$

Thus

$$\hat{\mu} = \hat{\mu} + \left(R(1 + n_L)^2 s_w^2 \tau - \frac{\tau^2 U''L}{2} \right).$$

APPENDIX C. CALCULATION OF SOCIAL LOSS (GAIN): EQUAL UTILITY

This appendix calculates the social loss (gain) from inequality on the assumption that the government can provide lump sum taxes/subsidies as a function of w to equalize utility

We let the lump-sum subsidy (tax) $I(w)$ be such that

$$\frac{dV(w, I(w))}{dw} = V_1 + V_2 I' = 0 \qquad (C1)$$

and

$$EI(w) = 0. \qquad (C2)$$

Thus, using the standard result that $V_w = Lv_L$,

$$I' = -L, \qquad (C3)$$

We define the social loss (gain) as $I(1)$ since

$$EV(w, I(w)) = V(1, I(1)).$$

From (C2)

$$I(1) + \frac{I''}{2}s_w^2 \approx 0,$$

so

$$I(1) \approx -\frac{I''}{2}s_w^2$$

While from (c.3)

$$I'' = -\left(\frac{\partial L}{\partial w}\right)_{\bar{u}}.$$

Hence, the social "gain" is approximately

$$\frac{1}{2}\left(\frac{\partial L}{\partial w}\right)_{\bar{u}}s_w^2.$$

APPENDIX D. QUADRATIC UTILITY FUNCTION, WITH CONSTANT MARGINAL DISUTILITY OF LABOR

First,

$$U = -\frac{b(\hat{c} - c)^2}{2} - L.$$

Then

$$b(1 - \tau)w(\hat{c} - c) = 1.$$

Hence

$$c = \hat{c} - \frac{1}{b(1 - \tau)w} = I + (1 - \tau)wL,$$

$$L = \frac{\hat{c} - I}{(1 - \tau)w} - \frac{1}{b((1 - \tau)w)^2},$$

$$Y = wL = \frac{\hat{c} - I}{1 - \tau} - \frac{1}{b(1 - \tau)^2 w}, \quad \text{and}$$

$$\overline{Y} = \frac{\hat{c} - I}{1 - \tau} - \frac{1}{b(1 - \tau)^2}\int \frac{1}{w}f(w)dw,$$

assuming that the distribution is sufficiently concentrated that everyone works. (The modifications in the general case are straightforward but tedious.) Hence the national income identity can be written:

$$\tau\overline{Y} = \frac{\tau(\hat{c} - I)}{1 - \tau} - \frac{\tau A}{(1 - \tau)^2} = I + G,$$

or

$$I = \tau\left(\hat{c} - \frac{A}{1-\tau}\right) - G(1-\tau),$$

where

$$A = \int \frac{1}{bw} f(w)dw.$$

The maximization problem thus becomes

$$\max -\frac{1}{2b(1-\tau)^2} E\frac{1}{w^2} - EL.$$

Since

$$L = \frac{\hat{c}}{(1-\tau)w} - \frac{\tau}{(1-\tau)w}\left(\hat{c} - \frac{A}{1-\tau}\right) - \frac{1}{b((1-\tau)w)^2} + \frac{G}{w},$$

it follows that

$$\overline{L} = bA(\hat{c} + G) + \frac{A^2\tau b}{(1-\tau)^2} - \frac{bB}{(1-\tau)^2},$$

where

$$B = \frac{1}{b^2}\int\left(\frac{1}{w}\right)^2 f(w)dw.$$

Thus optimality requires

$$\max -A(G + \hat{c}) - \frac{\tau A^2}{(1-\tau)^2} + \frac{1}{2}\frac{B}{(1-\tau)^2},$$

that is,

$$-\tau A^2 + \frac{1}{2}B - \frac{(1-\tau)A^2}{2} = 0$$

or

$$\tau = \frac{1}{A^2} - 1.$$

Observe that

$$\frac{d\tau}{dG} = 0,$$

so

$$\frac{dI}{dG} = -1.$$

An increase in government expenditure reduces the progressivity of the tax.

APPENDIX E. COBB–DOUGLAS UTILITY FUNCTION

First,

$$U = \frac{\ln C}{b} + \ln(\hat{L} - L).$$

Then

$$\frac{(1-\tau)w}{bC} = \frac{1}{\hat{L} - L}$$

or

$$L = \hat{L} - \frac{bI}{(1-\tau)w} - bL$$

$$= \frac{\hat{L}}{1+b} - \frac{Ib}{(1+b)(1-\tau)w},$$

$$\overline{Y} = \frac{\hat{L}}{1+b} - \frac{Ib}{(1+b)(1-\tau)}$$

(where we have used the fact that $Ew = 1$). Thus

$$\tau\overline{Y} = \frac{\tau\hat{L}}{1+b} - \frac{\tau Ib}{(1+b)(1-\tau)} = I + G$$

or

$$\frac{\tau\hat{L}}{1+b} = G + I\left(1 + \frac{\tau b}{(1+b)(1-\tau)}\right)$$

or

$$I = \frac{(\tau\hat{L} - G(1+b))}{(1+b-\tau)}(1-\tau).$$

Also

$$C = \frac{1}{1+b}(w\hat{L}(1-\tau) + I)$$

$$= \frac{(1-\tau)}{(1+b)(1+b-\tau)} \times [\hat{L}(w(1+b-\tau)+\tau) - G(1+b)].$$

Our problem is thus to maximize

$$\phi(\tau, G) \equiv E \ln[\hat{L}(w(1+b-\tau)+\tau) - G(1+b)] - \ln(1+b-\tau)$$

$$+ \frac{1}{1+b}\ln(1-\tau)\frac{d\tau}{dG} = -\frac{\phi_{\tau G}}{\phi_{GG}} > 0,$$

since

$$\phi_G = -E\frac{1+b}{\hat{L}(w(1+b-\tau)+\tau)-G(1+b)} \quad \text{and}$$

$$\phi_{G\tau} = E\frac{(1+b)\hat{L}(1-w)}{[\hat{L}(w(1+b-\tau)+\tau)-G(1+b)]^2} > 0.$$

When $G = \tau\hat{L}/(1+b)$, $I = 0$. We can solve for the value of τ for which $\phi_\tau = 0$, when $G = 0$:

$$\phi_\tau = E\frac{1-w}{w(1+b-\tau)} + \frac{1}{1+b-\tau} - \frac{1}{(1+b)(1-\tau)} = 0$$

or

$$\frac{\tau}{1-\tau} = \frac{1+b}{b}\left(E\frac{1}{w}-1\right).$$

If there is a lognormal distribution, and if individuals in the absence of taxation would have spent approximately half of the available time working (so $b = 1$), then

$$\frac{\tau}{1-\tau} = 2s_w^2.$$

If $s_w = .4$, $\tau \approx .24$.

INDEX OF NAMES

Index of Subjects